INVESTMENT PLANNING

Your unique textbook registration number is below. Please register your new textbook at www.money-education.com for access to our Student Practice Portal, updated errata, Money Tips, and other valuable resources.

IBCR03922478

INVESTMENT PLANNING

CONCEPTS AND STRATEGIES

James F. Dalton
James M. Forjan

3rd Edition

MONEY
EDUCATION
™

2920 Kingman Street
Suite #116
Metairie, LA 70002
888-295-6023

Printed in the U.S.A.

ISBN-13: 978-1-946711-11-3

About the Authors

James F. Dalton, MBA, MS, CPA, CFA®, CFP®

- Chief Academic Officer, CeriFi (2020 - Present)
- Chief Executive Officer, Money Education (2011 - Present)
- Former adjunct professor at George Mason University (2014 - 2017)
- Former adjunct professor at Georgetown University (2002 - 2014)
- Former Executive Vice President, Assessment Technologies Institute LLC
- Former Senior Vice President, Kaplan Professional
- Former President, Dalton Publications LLC
- Former Senior Manager of KPMG, LLP, concentrating in personal financial planning, investment planning, and litigation consulting
- MBA from Loyola University New Orleans
- Master of Accounting in Taxation from the University of New Orleans
- BS in accounting from Florida State University in Tallahassee, Florida
- Member of the CFP Board of Standards July 1996, Comprehensive CFP® Exam Pass Score Committee
- Member of the *Journal of Financial Planning* Editorial Review Board
- Author of *Money Education's Quick Sheets*
- Co-Author of *Fundamentals of Financial Planning* (1st - 7th Editions)
- Co-author of *Retirement Planning and Employee Benefits* (1st - 17th Editions)
- Co-author of *Investment Planning* (1st - 3rd Editions)
- Co-author of *Cases in Financial Planning: Analysis and Presentation* (1st - 4th Editions)
- Contributing Author of *Insurance Planning* (1st - 7th Editions)
- Contributing Author of *Estate Planning* (1st - 13th Editions)
- Author of Kaplan Schweser's Personal Financial Planning Understanding Your Financial Calculator
- Author of Kaplan Schweser's Understanding Your Financial Calculator for the CFA® Exam
- Co-author of BISYS CFA® Study Notes Volumes I and II
- Co-author of Kaplan Schweser's Personal Financial Planning Cases and Applications
- Co-author of the Kaplan Schweser Review for the CFP® Certification Examination, Volumes I–VIII and Kaplan Schweser's Financial Planning Flashcards

James M. Forjan, PhD, CFA®

- Associate Professor of Finance, York College of Pennsylvania
- PhD, University of North Texas (1993), Major: Finance
- M.S, Pennsylvania State University (1985), Major: Finance
- B.S, Pennsylvania State University (1984), Major: Accounting
- Education and Instructional Support for CFP® and CFA® Providers, including Dalton Review and Analyst Prep
- Author of academic articles published in *Review of Financial Economics*
- Co-Author of Academic Articles published in *The Financial Review, The Journal of Finance and Economics, Managerial Finance, Studies in Economics and Finance, Journal of Applied Business Research*
- Co-author of *Investment Planning* (1st - 3rd Editions)

About the Contributing Authors

Michael A. Dalton, Ph.D., JD, CPA, CLU, ChFC, CFP®

- Former Chair of the Board of Dalton Publications, L.L.C.
- Associate professor of Accounting and Taxation at Loyola University in New Orleans, Louisiana (retired)
- Adjunct professor at George Mason University (2014 - 2017) and Georgetown University (2002 - 2014)
- Ph.D. in Accounting from Georgia State University
- J.D. from Louisiana State University in Baton Rouge, Louisiana
- MBA and BBA in Management and Accounting from Georgia State University
- Former board member of the CFP Board's Board of Examiners, Board of Standards, and Board of Governors
- Former member (and chair) of the CFP Board's Board of Examiners
- Author of *Dalton Review for the CFP® Certification Examination: Volume I – Outlines and Study Guides, Volume II – Problems and Solutions, Volume III - Case Exam Book, Mock Exams A-1 and A-2* (1st - 8th Editions)
- Author of Money Education's *Retirement Planning and Employee Benefits* (1st - 17th Editions), *Estate Planning* (1st - 13th Editions), *Fundamentals of Financial Planning* (1st - 7th Editions), and *Insurance Planning* (1st - 7th Editions)
- Co-author of Money Education's *Income Tax Planning* (1st - 15th Editions) and *Cases in Financial Planning: Analysis and Presentation* (1st - 4th Editions)

Thomas P. Langdon, JD, LL.M., CFP®, CFA®

- Professor of Business Law, Gabelli School of Business, Roger Williams University, Bristol, RI
- Principal, Langdon & Langdon Financial Services, LLC (Connecticut-based tax planning & preparation firm)
- Former Member (and Chair) of the CFP Board's Board of Examiners
- Master of Laws (LL.M.) in Taxation from Villanova University School of Law
- Juris Doctor, from Western New England College School of Law
- Master of Science in Financial Services from The American College
- Master of Business Administration from The University of Connecticut
- Bachelor of Science in Finance from The University of Connecticut, Storrs, CT.
- Associate Editor of the *Journal of Financial Services Professionals*
- Co-author of Money Education's *Estate Planning* (1st - 13th editions), *Income Tax Planning* (1st - 15th editions), and *Insurance Planning* (1st - 7th editions)
- Faculty member for National Tax Institute

Sherri Donaldson, CFP®, ChFC®, MSFS, CASL®, CAP®, EA

- Editing Princess for Money Education
- Former Author/Editor/Lead instructor, Keir Educational Resources
- Former Assistant Vice President, Senior Training Specialist, M&T Securities
- Former Associate Financial Consultant, M&T Securities
- Former Financial Sales Specialist, Nationwide Financial
- Former Financial Services Representative, Nationwide Retirement Solutions
- MSFS from The American College Bryn Mawr, PA
- BS in business, concentration in financial services, Pennsylvania State University
- Member of the Financial Planning Association
- Co-Author/Editor of Keir *General Financial Planning Principles* textbook
- Co-Author/Editor of Keir *Risk Management and Insurance Planning* textbook
- Co-Author/Editor of Keir *Introduction to Financial Planning* textbook
- Co-Author/Editor of Keir *Retirement Savings and Income Planning* textbook
- Co-Author/Editor of Keir *Tax Planning* textbook
- Co-Author/Editor of Keir *Estate Planning* textbook
- Co-Author/Editor Keir *Investments Planning* textbook
- Contributing author of *Fundamentals of Financial Planning* (6th - 7th Editions)
- Contributing author of *Insurance Planning* (6th - 7th Editions)
- Contributing author of *Investment Planning* (1st - 3rd Editions)
- Contributing author of *Income Tax Planning* (12th - 15th Editions)
- Contributing author of *Retirement Planning and Employee Benefits* (15th - 17th Editions)
- Contributing Author of Estate Planning (12th - 13th Editions)
- Contributing author of *Cases in Financial Planning: Analysis and Presentation* (4th Edition)
- Editor Keir *Financial Plan Development* and *Practical Applications for Your Financial Calculator* textbooks
- Co-Author/Editor Keir CFP® exam review books (*Core Knowledge Book 1* and *2*, *Essential Keys* book, *Case Studies* book), practice exams, flashcards, MP3 scripts, Key Concept Infograhics, and Quick Concept videos

Acknowledgments & Special Thanks

We are most appreciative for the tremendous support and encouragement we have received throughout this project. We are extremely grateful to the faculty members and program directors of CFP Board-Registered programs who provided valuable comments during the development stages of this text. We are fortunate to have dedicated, careful readers at many institutions who were willing to share their needs, expectations, and time with us.

We owe a special thanks to the following reviewers for their constructive feedback throughout this very challenging first edition. Their thorough editing, detailed calculation reviews, helpful suggestions for additional content, and other valuable comments, improved this text. To each of these individuals we extend our deepest gratitude and appreciation.

Dr. Russ Blahetka is the founder of Vestnomics Wealth Management, LLC. He started his financial planning career in 2002 with Waddell & Reed where he served as a Financial Advisor and District Manager. He also provided compliance guidance in an office of 30 advisors. When not working with his clients to help them achieve their goals, Dr. Blahetka is an instructor at the UC Santa Cruz Extension where he teaches in the CFP® and CPA programs.

Dr. James Coleman has over 15 years teaching experience, including undergraduate, graduate, and Executive MBA programs at Troy University, Mercer University, and Dalton State College. In addition, as Vice President of Market Results, a financial planning training and consulting firm, he has helped hundreds of candidates pass the Certified Financial Planner™ exam over the last decade. Prior to his academic career, Jim spent over a decade in public accounting and corporate management, concluding with the position of Managing Director of Public Relations at Federal Express, where he was responsible for the company's global public and investor relations activities. His degrees include a MS and Ph.D. from University of Alabama as well as BBA in accountancy from University of Mississippi.

Donna Dalton is the reason this title finally became a reality after many years. Her leadership and motivation was undaunted by failure. Donna organized and directed the entire project and worked diligently with the authors and reviewers. First editions are particularly challenging and this book would definitely not have been possible without her extraordinary dedication, skill, and knowledge. Donna has a Masters in Business Administration and a Bachelor in Business Administration from Loyola University in New Orleans.

Dr. David W. Durr has over 25 years teaching experience primarily in the areas of investments, financial planning, portfolio management, corporate finance and risk management. Durr holds the Arthur J. Bauernfeind Endowed Chair in Investment Management at Murray State University. Dr. Durr earned a Ph.D. in finance from the University of North Texas, a Master of Business Administration degree from Stephen F. Austin State University and a Bachelor of Business Administration from the University of Texas at Austin. Dr. Durr holds the Certified Financial Planner (CFP®) designation and the Chartered Financial Analyst (CFA) designation. Each year he teaches financial planning classes and review courses throughout the U.S.

Harvey Hutchinson is a member of the Money Education team. He is an instructor for Emory University's paralegal program, teaching courses in estate planning, contract law, bankruptcy law, and business organizations; furthermore, he was an instructor for Emory University's CFP® program. He is an adjunct professor with Thomas Jefferson School of Law, teaching courses in wealth management, banking law, tax law, and consumer compliance. Harvey earned three business degrees (B.S.B.A. (Finance), M.B.A., and M.Acc.) and two law degrees (J.D. and LL.M. (Taxation)). He is a licensed attorney holding the following designations: AEP, CTFA, and CFP®.

Kate Kearns made a significant contribution to this textbook by her thoughtful and meticulous editing of all chapters. Ms. Kearns is a poet by training and an editor by trade at her agency, Black Squirrel Workshop. She works with authors of both novels and non-fiction to strengthen their written works while preserving their authentic voices. Kate earned a Masters of Fine Arts Degree in Creative Writing from Lesley University and a Bachelor of Arts Degree Sarah Lawrence College.

Robin Meyer is a valuable member of our Money Education team. She worked diligently throughout this project with the authors and reviewers, and performed numerous reviews and revisions. Robin provided many valuable improvements to both the textbook and instructor materials and this book would not have been possible without her extraordinary dedication, skill, and knowledge. Robin is the joy in our office as she always works tirelessly with a great work ethic and an enormous sense of humor. We are always grateful for her contributions to our products as well as our office happiness.

Kathy Oakley is a CPA and CFP® Certificant. She is a consultant to (and former academic program director of) Rice University's CFP® Certification Education program. She has taught courses in the General Principles of Financial Planning, Income Tax Planning and Case Analysis. She is a co-author of Money Education's Cases in Financial Planning: Analysis and Presentation (1st - 4th Editions). Mrs. Oakley served on the CFP Board's Council on Education from 2013 - 2017.

Mary Titus is a graduate student at Tulane University in New Orleans pursuing a Master of Business Administration and Master of Health Administration. She earned a Bachelor of Science from the University of Alabama with a double major in Biology and Psychology. Mary is pursuing a career in healthcare doing strategic planning and working in the revenue cycle.

Jenny Lehman is a PhD student and part-time instructor in the Personal Financial Planning program at Texas Tech University. She earned her MPA/JD from University of North Carolina Chapel Hill and bachelor's degree Summa Cum Laude from Texas Christian University. Ms. Lehman is an economist, policy analyst, attorney and educator with 15 years of government (federal, state and local), non-profit, legal and academic experience.

We have received so much help from so many people, it is possible that we have inadvertently overlooked thanking someone. If so, it is our shortcoming, and we apologize in advance. Please let us know if you are that someone, and we will make it right in our next printing.

PREFACE

Investment Planning is written for graduate and upperdivision undergraduate level students interested in acquiring an understanding of investment planning from a professional financial planning viewpoint. The text is intended to be used in an Investment Planning course as part of an overall curriculum in financial planning or finance. The text is also intended to serve as a reference for practicing professional advisors.

This textbook was also designed to meet the educational requirements for an Investments Course in a CFP Board-Registered Program. Therefore, one of our goals is to assure CFP Board-Registered Program Directors, instructors, students, and financial planners that we have addressed every relevant topic covered by the CFP Board Exam Topic List and the most recent model curriculum syllabus for this course. The book will be updated, as needed, to keep current with any changes in the law, exam topic list, or model curriculum.

Special Features

A variety of tools and presentation methods are used throughout this text to assist the reader in the learning process. Some of the features in this text that are designed to enhance your understanding and learning process include:

- **Learning Objectives** – At the beginning of each chapter is a list of learning objectives to help you focus your studying of the material. These learning objectives will provide a preview of the important topics covered in the chapter.

- **Key Concepts** – At the beginning of each subsection are key concepts, or study objectives, each stated as a question. To be successful in this course, you should be able to answer these questions. So as you read, guide your learning by looking for the answers. When you find the answers, highlight or underline them. It is important that you actually highlight/underline and not just make a mental note, as the action of stopping and writing reinforces your learning. Watch for this symbol:

Key Concepts

- **Quick Quizzes** – Following each subsection you will find a Quick Quiz, which checks and reinforces what you read. Circle the answer to each question and then check your answers against the correct answers supplied at the bottom of the quiz. If you missed any questions, flip back to the relevant section and review the material. Watch for this symbol:

Quick Quiz 1.1

- **Examples** – Examples are used frequently to illustrate the concepts being discussed and to help the reader understand and apply the concepts presented.

- **Exhibits** – The written text is enhanced and simplified by using exhibits where appropriate to promote learning and application. Exhibits are identified with the following symbol:

- **Cases** – Several chapters contain real world case summaries to help the reader appreciate the application of particular topics being discussed in the chapter.

- **End of Chapter Questions –** Each chapter contains a series of discussion questions and a sample of multiple-choice problems that highlight major topics covered in the chapter. The questions test retention and understanding of important chapter material and can be used for review and classroom discussion. Additional problems are available at money-education.com by accessing the Student Practice Portal.

- **Quick Quiz Explanations –** Each chapter concludes with the answers to the Quick Quizzes contained in that chapter, as well as explanation to the "false" statements in each Quick Quiz.

- **Glossary –** Key terms appear in **boldfaced type** throughout the text to assist in the identification of important concepts and terminology. A compilation of the key terms identified throughout the text is located at the end of the book.

Student Practice Portal
available by registering your textbook at money-education.com

TABLE OF CONTENTS

Chapter 4 | Portfolio Theory

Chapter 5 | Investment Decisions and Attribution Analysis

Chapter 6 | Market Efficiency & Behavioral Finance

Chapter 7 | Fixed-Income Securities

Chapter 8 | Fixed-Income Securities - Analysis

Chapter 10 | Equity Securities - Analysis

Chapter 13 | Investment Company - Analysis

Appendices

1

INTRODUCTION TO INVESTMENTS

INTRODUCTION TO INVESTING

Every individual makes investments during their lives, from saving for homes and cars to planning for future education and retirement needs. The idea behind investing is not a new one that developed with stock and bond markets. Investment in the future can be traced back at least to the ancient Egyptians, who built large silos to preserve grains, fish, butter, wild birds, and milk. Of course, the consumption of all this great food was reserved for the leaders and not for the lower classes. Today, everyone has the opportunity to save for their future.

Investing is the engine that drives the possibility of success and is part of planning for the uncertainty that all individuals face. For many, however, investing is not easy to accomplish or even to understand. The current 'instant gratification' society is the antithesis of the principles of investing. Investing requires time, patience, and sacrifice, which many are unwilling to do. The first step in the investment process is the education of individuals. Almost everyone invests time, energy, effort, capital, and/or work with the hope of achieving something better in the future, and that type of planning should extend to investments. The process of investing should begin at the earliest of ages. For example, many parents talk to their unborn children. Recent research suggests that certain types of music played to the unborn and to infants can increase their IQs.[1] Many grandparents provide financial gifts in the form of savings bonds or stock certificates to their newborn grandchildren. These activities plant the seeds of savings and investment.

Parents spend time and energy helping their children learn to eat, to crawl, to draw, to talk, and to learn a million other things as part of their development into adulthood. The time parents spend is assuredly an investment. Like any other investments, parents hope for a return. Actually, they hope for a highly positive return. They hope that their children will become well-educated, become contributing members of society, make wise decisions, become professionals in their fields, and perhaps even change the world. Of course, many parents hope that part of their return on the investment made in their children is the possibility that they will need to be taken care of by their children during their golden years.

As children weave their way through high school and college, they make investments on a daily basis. They invest time to study, to participate in extracurricular activities, to work part-time jobs, and to plan for their futures. They fundamentally believe that this time is well spent and will pay off at some point in their lives. They believe that the time they spend studying, learning, working, and pursuing recreational activities will help secure a better position in society and that will lead to a better life. [2]

As children spend time studying or working, they are learning about opportunity costs and risk. The choice to not spend the time with their friends or to engage in entertainment, community service, sleep, sports, reading for pleasure, or other activities are clear investment decisions. On the other hand, the risk of failure to study or work has consequences of its own. Why do they decide to study? The answer to this question is simply that they believe it is worth it. They believe that the time spent studying will help them obtain good grades and will ultimately lead to long-term success and happiness. There may be a few steps left out in that process, but ultimately, it is accurate.

1. The Baby Einstein Company was acquired by The Walt Disney Company in 2001. It was subsequently sold to Kids II, Inc. in 2013. The founders invested $18,000 to start the company and it had estimated revenue in the hundreds of millions.
2. In his autobiography, *I Love Capitalism*, Ken Langone tells the story of how he was an average student but loved working, even as a child. Langone describes how he delivered Christmas wreaths, worked in a butcher shop and a supermarket, and as a construction worker. These experiences of investing in his future paved the way for his highly successful career as an entrepreneur, co-founder, and owner of The Home Depot.

Consider the following graph of rates of earnings and employment based on levels of educational attainment.

Exhibit 1.1 | Median Annual Earnings Based on Years of Education

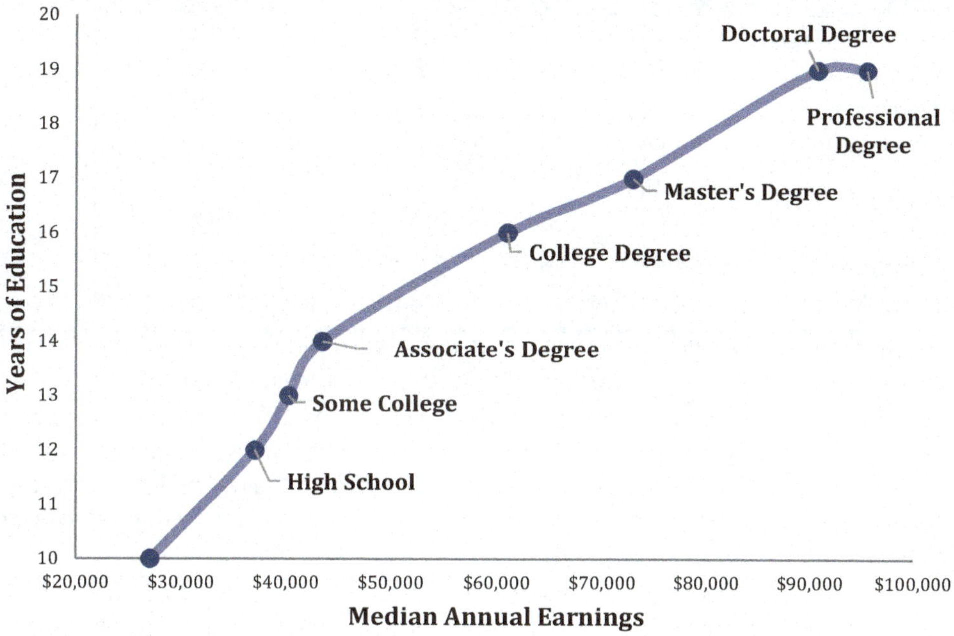

Exhibit 1.2 | Unemployment Rates and Earnings by Educational Attainment, 2017

Educational Attainment	Unemployment Rate (%)	Median Annual Earnings	Approx. Years of Education	Change in Earnings per Year of Education after High School
Professional Degree	1.5%	$95,472	19	$8,350
Doctoral Degree	1.5%	$90,636	19	$7,659
Master's Degree	2.2%	$72,852	17	$7,166
Bachelor's Degree	2.5%	$60,996	16	$5,993
Associates Degree	3.4%	$43,472	14	$3,224
Some College, No Degree	4.0%	$40,248	13	$3,224
High School Diploma	4.6%	$37,024	12	
Less than a HS Diploma	6.5%	$27,040	10	

Note: Data are for persons age 25 and over. Earnings are for full-time wage and salary workers.
Source: Current Population Survey, U.S. Department of Labor, U.S. Bureau of Labor Statistics

Doctoral or professional degree. Completion of a doctoral degree (Ph.D.) usually requires at least three years of full-time academic work beyond a bachelor's degree. Completion of a professional degree usually requires at least three years of full-time academic study beyond a bachelor's degree. Examples of occupations for which a doctoral or professional degree is the typical form of entry-level education include lawyers, physicists, and dentists.

Master's degree. Completion of this degree usually requires one or two years of full-time academic study beyond a bachelor's degree. Examples of occupations in this category include statisticians, physician assistants, and educational, guidance, school, and vocational counselors.

Bachelor's degree. Completion of this degree generally requires at least four years, but not more than five years, of full-time academic study beyond high school. Examples of occupations in this category include budget analysts, dietitians and nutritionists, and civil engineers.

Associate's degree. Completion of this degree usually requires at least two years but not more than four years of full-time academic study beyond high school. Examples of occupations in this category include mechanical drafters, respiratory therapists, and dental hygienists.

Postsecondary nondegree award. These programs lead to a certificate or other award, but not a degree. The certificate is awarded by the educational institution and is the result of completing formal postsecondary schooling. Certification, issued by a professional organization or certifying body, is not included here. Some postsecondary nondegree award programs last only a few weeks, while others may last one to two years. Examples of occupations in this category include nursing assistants, emergency medical technicians (EMTs) and paramedics, and hairstylists.

Clearly, there is a strong correlation between education and earning potential. The average earnings of a college graduate are 65 percent higher than the earnings for a high school graduate and 126 percent higher than for someone who fails to complete high school. In addition to compensation, there is a clear relationship between more education and lower unemployment levels. The more educated suffer less unemployment than the less educated. The lower unemployment for the higher educated is at least partially due to the flexibility in terms of the types of jobs that could be filled. Despite this clear and convincing evidence of the correlation between formal education, income and employment, there are those who are enormously successful without formal education and those who are complete failures that had solid educations. Consider the following examples of three individuals who clearly excelled even in the absence of receiving an advanced formal education.

Example 1.1

Bill Gates, the former CEO and co-founder of Microsoft, is one such person. At an early age, he had a passion for computers and dropped out of Harvard to pursue his passion. It is this passion that catapulted him to enormous success and a net worth that consistently ranks him as one of the wealthiest people on Earth.

Example 1.2

Another successful individual, who did not even complete high school and has since gone on to build an empire of hundreds of companies that span across the world, in addition to owning two islands in the Caribbean, is Richard Branson. He is the founder of Virgin Airlines and the first individual to make a self-funded space trip in a rocket built by his company Virgin Galactic during the summer of 2021. Branson is among the wealthiest men in the world with an estimated net worth of $4.5 billion in 2021.

Example 1.3

New Orleans native, Al Copeland, never finished high school and at one point lived in the St. Thomas housing project.[3] Copeland created Popeyes Chicken & Biscuits fast food restaurant, acquired Church's Chicken and established numerous restaurants in New Orleans. Although he ended up losing the Popeyes and Church's restaurants in bankruptcy, he retained rights to the spices used by Popeyes, which continue to be manufactured by his company Diversified Foods. He passed away in 2008 after a battle with a rare form of cancer.[4]

The three entrepreneurs above are examples of individuals attaining great success without higher levels of education. However, they each invested tremendous time and effort in growing their knowledge, skills, and businesses, which ultimately paid off for all of them. To pursue their passions, they had to sacrifice time, energy, money and countless other things.

Would these entrepreneurs have been happier doing other things? No one can answer that question, but life is certainly a trade off of choices. Although, "money can't buy happiness," money is a critical part of our society. Most individuals are taught at an early age that if they work hard, they will have the opportunity to earn and acquire "stuff" and take trips and do "stuff."

In each of the above examples, there was a sacrifice, whether through time or effort, in pursuit of a return or goal. This return might be monetary or otherwise, but it was undoubtedly uncertain when the sacrifice was taking place. In other words, there is no way that Bill Gates could have predicted that the first software he wrote would lead to a company worth billions of dollars. Even if he thought it might be worth billions of dollars, there are many more examples of entrepreneurs who have gone bankrupt in the pursuit of their dreams.

3. The St. Thomas housing project became one of the country's most dangerous housing developments by the late 1980s.
4. It should be noted that Copeland's red beans and rice are one of the best (if not the best) versions of the dish found.

Investing has these same characteristics, namely the characteristics of sacrifice of both time and money, and the pursuit of a return. The first part of the success equation is sacrifice. While most of what has been discussed above has focused on the sacrifice of time and effort, the same concept applies to an investment in a financial asset or a real asset. For someone to make an investment in a financial asset, such as a share of stock or a bond, they first have to sacrifice current consumption and save.

Individuals have choices in how they spend accumulated or acquired money and wealth, whether through inheritance, lottery winnings or more traditional legal means, such as work. If people choose to spend money on consumables, then the money is not available to be saved or invested. Therefore, the first step in making an investment is not spending the money (or time in the previous examples) that can be used to make the investment.

Generally, the purpose of investing is to generate a return that is consistent with risk tolerance. Individuals forego consumption for the expected earnings on investments. It is important to note that the expected earnings may be different than the actual earnings that are received. This concept is discussed in greater detail under the topic of risk. For example, Jordan might invest $100 in a single share of stock that might appreciate to $120. Jordan gave up spending the $100 to purchase a share of stock that increased in value by $20. There is certainty in terms of the sacrifice of current consumption. However, the returns are uncertain, as Jordan's investment could have been worth much more than $120 or much less. The link between the level of sacrifice and expected return forms the foundation of many investment decisions.

How to Save More

1. **Credit card debt** - Never accumulate credit card debt. Always pay off your credit card balance every month. Credit card debt is referred to as "bad debt" and is financially dangerous. It carries very high interest rates.
2. **Spend less than you make** - It sounds simple and it is. It is a matter of being disciplined enough to not spend what you do not have.
3. **Implement the 4-week rule** - Don't buy anything unless you have waited four weeks. This technique minimizes impulse buys and helps bring logic to spending decisions. Often, the desire for the purchase will have waned. You might also get off the email lists of your favorite companies. This step reduces temptation.
4. **Fund your 401(k) plan** - Save in your 401(k) plan as much as you can - often, there is a company match that is free money. In addition, it is more difficult to get to the money, which means there is less temptation. Finally, retirement plans, such as 401(k) plans are protected from creditors.
5. **Pay yourself first** - Young people should be saving at least 10% to 15% of their compensation. These savings at a young age can compound over decades to accumulate to millions. Paying yourself first means setting up a system whereby funds from your paycheck automatically go to your 401(k) plan, brokerage account, and/or savings account. Warren Buffett is famous for saying, "Do not save what is left after spending but spend what is left after saving."
6. **Automate savings** - There are various apps that help individuals save money. When it is automatic, saving is accomplished without additional effort.
7. **Save your raise** - Congratulations, you just got a raise! Why not save the entire after-tax amount? This increase can go directly into your 401(k) plan or into a savings or brokerage account.
8. **Bad money habits** - Eliminate at least some bad money habits - these might include daily high-priced coffees or lunches or monthly subscriptions (cable, Netflix, gym, or software). Some of these can be eliminated. The savings that result can be accumulated and invested.
9. **Pack your lunch** - Pack your lunch, fatten your wallet and reduce your waistline - bringing your lunch to work can often be a healthier option as well as saving you more than $1,000 per year.

The matrix below shows the value of annual savings. To accumulate $1 million, an individual would have to save annual amounts at various interest rates. For example, a 20-year-old saving $4,000 annually at four percent would take until the age of 82 to generate a total future value of $1 million. However, a 25-year-old saving $6,000 in her IRA earning ten percent per year would accumulate $1 million before they were 60 years old.

Exhibit 1.3 | Want to be a Millionaire? Here is How Long it Will Take (in Years)

	Compound Annual Return								
Annual Savings	4%	5%	6%	7%	8%	9%	10%	11%	12%
$4,000	61.14	53.34	47.58	43.12	39.56	36.63	34.18	32.10	30.30
$6,000	51.93	45.78	41.15	37.53	34.60	32.17	30.13	28.38	26.86
$10,000	41.04	36.72	33.40	30.73	28.55	26.72	25.16	23.81	22.63
$15,000	33.13	30.05	27.62	25.64	23.98	22.58	21.37	20.32	19.39
$20,000	28.01	25.68	23.79	22.23	20.91	19.78	18.80	17.94	17.17

Even more fascinating is the fact that the 25-year old would only have 'sacrificed' $180,000 to accumulate the $1 million desired retirement value. The difference of $820,000 is from investment returns. This objective is attainable, but requires sacrifice, time, and discipline.

GOALS OF INVESTING

The purpose of investing is to generate a return that is consistent with risk tolerance. That description, however, is perhaps too broad and simplistic. Typically, goals of investors fall within one or more of these categories:

1. Preservation of capital
2. Income generation
3. Growth in value

It is common to think that all three of the goals are important and they are all equally desired. However, it is important to identify the most important goal for each individual. For example, a young person with a small amount of money might be primarily interested in the growth of their funds. In contrast, a recently retired couple may want to generate income and some growth for retirement, but they are primarily concerned about preservation of capital. They cannot afford to replace the capital if it is lost.

Preservation of Capital - This objective is focused on protecting the capital that is invested. Therefore, any investment considered must be evaluated with regard to the risk that the capital may decrease in value. For example, an investment in most equity securities, which can increase or decrease in value, is not consistent with a goal of preservation of capital. This goal might be appropriate if the investor is retired or has a short time horizon for the investment.

Income Generation - This objective is primarily focused on producing income from the investment. This income can be from interest payments from fixed-income securities (bonds), dividend payments from stocks, or rents from real estate.

Growth - This objective is to invest in securities that have more potential growth than other types of securities. However, often these securities are also the ones that have more volatility than other securities.

Whether the primary goal is to preserve capital or provide growth, an essential consideration is the amount of risk that is being undertaken when pursuing an investment goal. The topic of risk is discussed thoroughly in Chapter 3 and other parts of the text.

Regardless of the socioeconomic position or type of entity, whether corporate, pension, government or other, almost all individual investors and entities desire wealth, and when it is acquired, must manage this wealth. The next section identifies several of these investors.

Investors and Their Goals

This section discusses the common goals of several types of investors. Individuals are discussed along with a few types of institutional investors. However, this section is not an exhaustive discussion of all of the goals or of all of the types of investors.

Individuals

Individuals have an almost unlimited number of wants and desires in life, whether it is the purchase of a car, the purchase of a house, or the desire for financial security during retirement. Most individuals' goals can be segmented into short-term, intermediate-term or long-term. Depending on the length of the time horizon, the returns (income and capital appreciation) generated by the investment will vary.

Compound interest is the most powerful force in the universe.

Short-term goals might include purchasing a car, saving for a down payment for a house, or even the purchase of a 150-inch flat screen TV on which to watch the New Orleans Saints.

Intermediate goals are a bit longer in duration and might include saving for the purchase of a second residence such as a beach home or paying for a child's college education.

Longer-term goals include saving for retirement, which could last from a few years to more than 30 years. Retirement might require the accumulation of literally millions of dollars to support one's lifestyle for that many years. For example, a person living off of $100,000 per year, might need close to $2 million.[5] This amount is a simple estimate and is based on many assumptions, but the actual return on the savings can make an enormous difference in the amount ultimately accumulated. Consider that if an individual were to save $12,000 every year for 30 years and the savings earned ten percent annually, the balance at the end of the 30 years would be $1.97 million. If, however, the rate of return were eight percent, the accumulated balance would be $1.36 million. In either case, the total amount saved is $360,000, which is far less than the final amount accumulated.

5. A good rule of thumb is that a retiree needs to accumulate assets for retirement of between 16 and 20 times their compensation prior to retirement.

As illustrated in the retirement example above, goals of individuals often include the accumulation of wealth. However, individuals who have accumulated wealth, such as a person who has saved her entire life for retirement or a person who has won the lottery or inherited a fortune, small or otherwise, may have the goal of first preserving the wealth and secondly, growing the wealth.

Pension Funds

Pension funds are designed to accumulate assets over time and make distributions to retirees, generally for life. These pension funds are generally established by businesses and governments to provide retirement benefits to employees and their beneficiaries. Since the business is a going concern, meaning that it is expected to continue indefinitely, it will undoubtedly continue to hire new workers as older workers retire. Because of this continuing cycle, the pension fund does not have a specific target date at which the funds are needed. Rather, the funds will be needed indefinitely. As such, the funds should be invested with the goal of providing the necessary payments to retirees while maximizing the long-term growth of the assets in the fund.

Endowments and Foundations

Wealthy individuals often provide capital for the establishment of foundations as part of their philanthropic goals. Many universities, hospitals, and museums have endowment funds that are established to provide funds to the beneficiaries of the institution. For example, the endowment fund for Harvard University had a value at the end of fiscal year 2017 slightly in excess of $44 billion.[6] In the Annual Report for the Harvard Endowment Fund, the new CEO for Harvard Management Company (HMC) provides the following context for the management of the endowment fund:

> Since arriving at HMC, I have focused my priorities upon positioning the endowment for better future performance. As investors are well aware, performance can only be meaningfully evaluated over a full market cycle, including inevitable ups and downs. One or even three-year performance is not informative. Our focus at HMC will reflect a longer-term view.
>
> Our primary focus has now shifted to having the Generalist investment team gain a collective understanding of the entire portfolio. As we do so, we will gain proficiency in our new processes and continue to develop the analytics which support them. At the same time, we will make portfolio moves accordingly.

Because the investment horizon is indefinite, the fund can invest in assets that have an extremely long-term horizon.

PBGC - The Pension Benefit Guarantee Corporation

The PBGC is a quasi government entity that insures pension benefits for millions of Americans. PBGC was created by the Employee Retirement Income Security Act of 1974 to encourage the growth of defined benefit pension plans, provide timely and uninterrupted payment of pension benefits, and keep pension insurance premiums at a minimum. It only insures defined benefit pension plans that promise to pay a specified monthly benefit at retirement, commonly based on salary and years on the job. The PBGC guarantees payment, up to the legal limit, of pension benefits earned by nearly 40 million American workers and retirees.

6. Source: Final Harvard University Financial Report 2017

The PBGC pays benefits to nearly 840,000 participants in 4,845 failed single-employer plans, as well as providing benefits to multiemployer plans. During fiscal year 2017, the PBGC paid over $5.8 billion in retirement benefits to over 900,000 retirees, while only collecting $6.7 billion in insurance premiums. It has total assets of $108 billion and total liabilities of $184 billion for a net deficiency of $76 billion.[7]

The PBGC goals are:

1. preserving plans and protecting pensioners,
2. paying timely and accurate benefits, and
3. maintaining high standards of stewardship and accountability.[8]

Without the achievement of the first goal of preserving assets, the PBGC would not be in a position to pay benefits.

Life Insurance Companies

Life insurance is an important tool for families to insure against premature death, especially for a person who has family members depending on their annual earnings. Imagine the financial situation a family would find itself in if the primary worker of the family (mom or dad) unexpectedly died. Would the family have enough money to continue to pay current bills, such as the mortgage, food, and other expenses? Would there be enough to send the children to college? Life insurance can provide the funds to mitigate against such a situation.

Life insurance is sold with a face amount, such as $1 million. A policy is purchased with periodic premium payments that may last for a specific term, such as 20 years, or for life. The insurance company must collect the insurance premiums and manage the assets to be in a financial position to pay the face value of the policy in the event that a premature death occurs.

Banks

Most everyone is familiar with savings and checking accounts at a bank. Individuals make deposits at the bank, which are available and often earn interest. The bank induces people to make deposits for access to the funds as well as the interest. The bank turns around and loans the money, in the form of short-term loans, construction loans, home mortgage loans, and other loans. The bank has to balance the funds it has on hand and the inflows form the various loans in its portfolio with the likelihood of a need for the cash by the depositors.

Each of the investors above, whether individual or institution, has a different set of circumstances and a different set of objectives that influence how their funds are invested. They may also have different needs regarding income generated from the portfolio versus long-term growth. These objectives can be addressed in the creation of a portfolio.

How Investors Build Portfolios

A portfolio is a combination of investments that is designed to achieve specific goals for the investor. As mentioned above, investors have unique goals, whether they are long-term growth or preservation of capital, or a combination of goals. These goals are considered when creating a portfolio. In addition to these goals, or in refinement thereof, investors need to consider return objectives, time horizon, liquidity needs, tax situation, unique circumstances and any legal or regulatory considerations in building a portfolio.

7. It should be noted that PBGC premiums have increased significantly in the past few years, which has helped with generating revenue for the PBGC.
8. PBGC 2017 Annual Report.

Return objectives - An investor's return requirement is the return necessary to meet their financial goals.

Time horizon - An investor's time horizon dictates their ability to handle fluctuations in portfolio asset values. Shorter time horizons generally require more liquid and less risky investments. Longer time horizons, such as those of a young person saving for retirement or an endowment, permit investments that are less liquid and riskier, but have higher potential for growth over longer periods of time.

Liquidity needs - Investors who have spending commitments are constrained by the need to keep enough liquid assets on hand to meet those commitments. Generally, cash is considered the most liquid asset, followed by assets that can be converted into cash quickly and without loss of principal, such as certificates of deposit, Treasury bills, and other short-term debt instruments. Investors know whether they have liquidity needs. For example, a 25-year-old saving for retirement does not need the money if the purpose of the funds is for retirement. However, an endowment fund that pays out 4 percent of the assets in the fund actually needs a small level of liquidity to satisfy the annual payout. Someone who has just retired will typically want to hold enough liquid assets to satisfy at least one year of expenses, if not two years.

Tax situation - The investor needs to consider the taxability of the assets being invested. Individual taxpayers generally have taxable accounts, such as savings accounts or brokerage accounts and tax-deferred accounts, such as IRAs or retirement plans (401(k) plan). Charities and other tax exempt entities are not subject to income tax, which allows these entities to invest in more income producing investments without being concerned about the income tax implications. Similarly, IRA assets can be invested without being too concerned about the income that is generated within the account, since the account is not subject to income tax. However, income, such as interest and dividends, is taxable if earned in a brokerage account. Therefore, anyone putting together a portfolio must consider the tax implications as well as the investment implications.

Unique circumstances - Unique circumstances are conditions that are unique to the investor and will impact the investments in a portfolio. For example, an increasing number of investors use the environmental, social and governance (ESG) record of a company as a screen before considering investment.

In addition to the issues mentioned above, an investor must also consider their own tolerance for risk. Risk is discussed in great detail in this text. However, for now, risk can be considered as uncertainty of future outcomes or volatility in asset values. There are two aspects to risk from an investor's point of view: the ability to take risk and the willingness to take risk. Some of the factors discussed above impact an investor's ability to take on risk. However, an investor's experience with risky assets (such as stocks, bonds, or derivatives) affects the willingness to take on risk.

One additional challenge facing all investors is the tendency to allow behavioral issues to influence investment decision making. Investors make mistakes regularly, and these mistakes can drive prices away from their fundamental values, but they can also distort the investor's portfolio. The irony is that when investors allow behavioral issues to affect their decisions, they believe they are making the 'right' decision when in fact they are not. For example, an investor who invests in a portfolio with a value of $100,000 might feel 'anchored' to that number. If the portfolio falls to $90,000, the investor might hold onto the assets in the portfolio until it returns to at least the original investment value, even if those assets are no longer appropriate. This anchoring mistake is a cognitive error that will affect the ability of the portfolio to deliver the investor's goals.

Investors make both cognitive errors and have emotional biases that limit the positive outcomes of the portfolio. Behavioral issues are discussed extensively in Chapter 6.

In building a portfolio, each of the above factors, including the willingness and the ability to take risk, are considered in the design and creation of the portfolio. Professional investment advisers often assist investors with these decisions and create a document called an investment policy statement that includes all of these factors. An investment policy statement is designed to be a guide to implement the investment portfolio.[9]

Habits of Successful Investors

The list below is a summary of many important investment lessons that many successful investors use. However, this list is not all-inclusive, nor does it exclude success for those who do not follow the list.

- Invest long-term. That means you that if you need the money soon, it can't be invested long-term. Long-term is typically 10 years or more.
- Save early and be consistent. As the millionaire example illustrates, compound earnings are extremely powerful in the accumulation of assets over time.
- Diversify your investments. Many fortunes have been lost by being concentrated in a single asset or a few assets. As Peter L. Bernstein said, "We simply do not know what the future holds." No one can consistently predict the investment winners and losers.
- Do not attempt to time the market by investing when the market is believed to be down and selling when the market is believed to be high. This approach usually does not work out well for the average investor.
- Fees and costs are a drag. Paying too much for investment management erodes the power of compound returns significantly over time.
- Take advantage of free returns in 401(k) plans. Many 401(k) plans offer employer matching contributions that are available to employees who save in the 401(k) plan. These matching contributions are effectively free money and boost retirement savings.
- Understand that humans are full of emotions and biases, which impact how investors actually manage their money.
- Understand that stock prices and values are volatile, but over time, stocks tend to deliver higher returns than fixed-income securities.
- Understand that a good company is not always a good investment. As Warren Buffet said, "It's far better to buy a wonderful company at a fair price than a fair company at a wonderful price."
- Value is driven by cash flow. There will always be those who speculate on companies and investments that show promise but do not generate positive cash flow. As many of the chapters in this text illustrate, value is based on cash flow.

9. This text purposely spells adviser with an "e" rather than an "o" because the laws that govern this type of investment professional spell the title this way. See finra.org for more information.

HOW THE TEXT IS DESIGNED

This text is structured so that a solid foundation in the material is provided in the first six chapters. The next ten chapters provide a thorough discussion of various asset classes, including fixed-income securities, equity securities, investment companies, derivatives, and alternative investments. The last two chapters cover the tax implications of investment transactions and how to develop policy statements that can be used to implement an investment plan.

Chapter	Topic
2	Provides an overview of securities laws, markets, and an introduction to the basic asset classes.
3	Provides a thorough discussion of investment returns and investment risks, including a couple of comprehensive examples.
4	Provides a discussion of portfolio theory and asset allocation.
5	Discusses performance measures and attribution.
6	Contrasts the concepts of the efficient market hypothesis and observations of human behavior found in behavioral finance.
7	Provides a thorough discussion of fixed-income securities.
8	Discusses the analysis of fixed-income securities, including valuation, duration, convexity, and immunization.
9	Provides an introduction into equity securities.
10	Discusses fundamental and technical analysis as it relates to equity securities.
11	Discusses the techniques used to value equity securities.
12	Provides an introduction to investment companies, including mutual funds, exchange-traded funds, unit investment trusts, and closed-end funds.
13	Discusses concepts of managing portfolios of mutual funds.
14	Explains the fundamentals of derivatives, futures contracts, forward contracts, and swap contracts.
15	Continues the discussion of derivatives with a focus on option contracts.
16	Completes the discussion of investment vehicles with an emphasis on alternative asset classes.
17	Explores the practical issues surrounding the taxation of investments.
18	Offers a practical application of developing investment policy statements, which are used as the basis for executing investment plans.

Investment returns and personal growth both come with sacrifice and generally require a great deal of time. A great many examples and illustrations are included in the text to help make complex material in the chapters as easy to comprehend as possible.[10] Good luck with your investments now and in the future.

10.Einstein said, "The definition of genius is taking the complex and making it simple."

2

MARKET STRUCTURE, ASSET CLASSES, AND SECURITIES LAW

LEARNING OBJECTIVES

1. Identify the five types of market structures.
2. Recognize the importance of primary and secondary markets.
3. Distinguish between and among assets classes.*
4. Identify the risk levels of investing in each asset class.
5. Report the ways in which money market securities provide liquidity in capital markets.
6. Understand the various types of bond issues, including the purpose of the issue and the source of repayment.*
7. Compare mortgage-backed securities with collateralized mortgage obligations.*
8. Differentiate between the various types of equity securities.*
9. Differentiate between the various types of risks in the equity markets.
10. Understand the value of adding alternative investments to a portfolio.
11. Distinguish between the various types of alternative investments.
12. Understand the value and application of securities laws.*
13. Recognize the importance of the financial history of the United States, particularly the time period between WWI and WWII.
14. Examine the pieces of legislation passed by the United States Congress after the stock market crash of 1929.
15. Understand the importance and function of the Securities and Exchange Commission.*
16. Defend the existence of independent organizations.
17. Define an investment adviser.*

** Ties to CFP Board Student-Centered Learning Objectives.*

MARKET STRUCTURE

There are five types of capital markets: Money markets, fixed income markets, equity markets, alternative markets, and currency markets. Each has its own characteristics and purposes. These markets gather buyers and sellers of tradeable assets, assign a value to each asset, and allocate resources to their presumably most efficient use.

There are generally two types of microeconomic agents: those with capital and those who need it. The most basic function of a market structure is to provide an opportunity for these two agents to interact and trade. The only way to generate trade is for both parties to be willing and able participants and for each to believe they are benefiting from the transaction. The suppliers of capital expect risk-adjusted compensation, whilst those demanding the capital expect to earn a positive spread from investing or using it. The following example is an illustration of how each party involved in capital markets behaves and benefits.

Example 2.1

The state of Alaska issues a twenty-year municipal bond designed to provide financial support for Kodiak Island. The island, home to 3,500 bears, is also one of the top fishing ports in the United States. Alaska intends to use the proceeds of the bond issue to increase commerce to the island and to protect its bear population. The bond offers an interest rate of 5% with a minimum investment of $1,000, and Alaska hopes to raise $25 million for the project. In addition to comparing the interest rate to their own unique required return, potential investors will evaluate the ability of Alaska to repay the entire amount. In addition to offering bondholders an annual interest payment, municipal bonds also have some tax advantages, making them attractive to a range of investors.

In this case, a successful bond issue will provide Alaska with the necessary capital to increase economic activity on one of its islands as well as providing compensation to the bondholders. All participants in the bond issue will be satisfied if the funds are raised relatively quickly and invested wisely and if Alaska makes timely and complete payments to the bondholders.

Primary Versus Secondary Markets

The two biggest capital markets are the primary and secondary markets, both of which are critical to the success of the free enterprise system. Initial sales of securities are made in the primary market while resales of securities are conducted in the secondary market.

The primary market for equity and fixed income securities is the means to raise capital for businesses and governments, both national and local. Borrowers typically rely on the investment banking community acting as intermediaries to locate willing lenders. Companies offer the right to sell securities to the intermediaries in exchange for cash.

The agreement between the two parties is either a best efforts or **firm commitment**. In a best-efforts case, the investment banker agrees to sell the securities by working really hard to attract investors. If the bank sells all the securities, it is considered to be a successful effort. If not, then the unsold shares are returned to the issuer. In firm commitments, which constitutes the majority of primary market offerings, the bank agrees to a firm price to purchase the securities and then holds the right to sell those securities to the public. Under the firm commitment, the investment bank assumes the price risk, but under the best efforts, the issuer does.

The importance of the primary market for businesses cannot be understated. The ability to access capital quickly is a necessary condition for firms to be able to achieve their goals. For example, a business that needs to expand operations to meet increased consumer demand must be able to raise new funds quickly or it risks losing market share to its competition.

The primary market is essentially a place where capital is provided by investors in exchange for a repayment promise from the borrower. The issuers of bonds promise to pay interest and principal while the issuers of stock promise to pay dividends but only if the firm is successful and the board of directors approves the dividend payment. The promise made to bondholders is a contractual obligation while the promise to shareholders is not. One of the distinguishing characteristics of owning stock is the limited liability enjoyed by shareholders.

A secondary market involves the purchase and sale of securities that have already passed through the primary market. Secondary markets are the financial counterpart to markets for used consumer products, such as automobiles. They are 'used' in the sense that the capital for the issuer has already been raised and the issuer has no real trading function in the market. Buyers and sellers are essentially trading the promises made by the issuing entity.

Example 2.2

When the state of Alaska issues a bond to benefit Kodiak Island, it will access the capital markets through the primary market. Alaska will most likely use the services of an investment banking firm to help raise the capital. The investors who purchase the bonds from the banker provide the capital in the primary market. Those bondholders can hold on to the bonds until they mature or they can sell them at market value in the secondary market.

The most famous of all secondary markets is the New York Stock Exchange (NYSE), which was created as part of the Buttonwood Agreement in 1792 but officially began trading bank stocks and government bonds in 1817 as the New York Stock and Exchange Board. Over the years, the NYSE has been at the center of the US and global economies, helping corporations raise cash and providing a trading forum for investors in their pursuit of wealth. According to the NYSE website:

> *"The New York Stock Exchange has been the premier exchange of choice for innovators, visionaries, and leaders for over 225 years. As the #1 global listing exchange and at the heart of capital markets, the NYSE's unique market model, unmatched network, brand visibility, and core services help companies access capital and navigate global markets."*

Of course, there are other secondary markets. In 1971, the National Association of Securities Dealers Automated Quotation system (Nasdaq) market was founded by the National Association of Security Dealers. In stark contrast to the physical trading system of the NYSE, Nasdaq's automated quotation system was an over-the-counter design in which dealers could trade among themselves without having to be in one location. Initially, all trading was executed over a computer bulletin board system and over telephone lines. As technology advanced over the years, trading has evolved into automated trading systems that link the global dealer markets.

According to its web page, the Nasdaq market is a global leader in financial innovation:

> *"We began primarily as a U.S.-based equities exchange. Today, Nasdaq is recognized around the globe as a diversified worldwide financial technology, trading and information services provider to the capital markets, with more than 3,500 colleagues serving businesses and investors from over 50 offices in 26 countries across six continents – and in every capital market.*
>
> *Nasdaq is built strategically around four complimentary business segments – Tech, Trade, Intel, and List – that guide our clients as they pursue opportunities to create, or maximize, value in the world's capital markets."*

In summary, primary and secondary capital markets combine to form the pulse of the free enterprise system. In essence, primary markets represent the source of free enterprise and the secondary markets provide nourishment to keep the economy expanding.

TYPES OF MARKETS

The **money market** is a collection of short-term investors at either the wholesale or retail levels. In the wholesale market, large sums of capital are traded among financial institutions, governments, and large corporations. Time periods for the loans are less than one year and many of them occur overnight. Liquidity is high, returns are relatively low and during periods of economic expansion, risk is generally thought of as being almost non-existent. During stressful times, however, such as the financial crisis of 2008, substantial losses are common. Many of the funds traded in the wholesale markets trickle down to the retail level, in which individual investors and consumers participate. Interest rates in the money market are key determinants of other longer term interest rates that impact economic growth.

Key Concepts

1. Explain the difference between primary and secondary markets.
2. Discuss the differences in the investment horizons among the different types of markets.

The **fixed income market** is a long-term debt market in which government and firms borrow large amounts of capital in return for promises to make interest and principal payments to lenders. Time periods are typically 30 years but can be almost any maturity date that exceeds one year. One interesting minor trend that began at the turn of the 21st century is the issuance of 100-year bonds. Firms such as Disney and Coca-Cola and the national governments of Mexico and Austria issued bonds with century long maturity dates. There are two basic kinds of risk in the fixed income market: **interest rate risk** and **default risk**. The risk in the fixed income market depends on these two risks in addition to general economic risks and the return on these securities has a very wide range.

The **equity market** is a large market of ownership. Corporations trade ownership shares to institutional and individual investors in return for capital. Shareholders expect to receive some combination of dividend payments and capital gains. The time period is infinite as firms operate as going concerns while the risk level is significant. Shareholders only receive dividend payments after all other creditors have been paid. Returns can be substantial and most investors have some exposure to equity markets.

The **alternative investment market** is a collection of opportunities that do not fit into one of the traditional financial markets. Assets traded in these markets include derivatives, collectibles, private equity, real assets, hedge funds, and commodities. Alternative investments have a wide range of time horizons, and varying risk levels that are often increased by a lack of liquidity and reliable performance data.

Quick Quiz 2.1

1. Primary and secondary markets are an important link in the establishment of a sound economy.
   a. True
   b. False
2. A firm that issues a fixed income security promises its investors that it will make regular dividend payments.
   a. True
   b. False
3. A hedge fund that invests in stocks, bonds, derivative securities, and diamonds can be characterized as an alternative investment.
   a. True
   b. False

True, False, True.

Some investment professionals consider the currency market a fifth type of market, which is the largest market of all, trading approximately $5 trillion per day in 2019. Because of the global nature of investments, others view the currency market as more of a subset of the other market types. It is an over-the-counter market in which the price of buying or selling one currency using another is quoted as the exchange rate. Governments, businesses, and individuals demand foreign currency units when importing goods or services while those same entities are able to supply the market with currencies. Risk in the currency market depends mainly on economic and political stability of each country.

ASSET CLASSES

Asset classes are usually characterized as groups of securities with similar liquidity, marketability, return expectations, and risk levels. These securities are traded in the five markets described above.

Cash and Money Market Securities

This category of asset class is the most liquid and marketable. These types of securities are generally short-term in nature, with maturities of one-year or less, and are easily convertible into cash quickly and without a significant loss in value. In addition, money market securities are not subject to many risks.

Key Concepts

1. Discuss the main reason that Treasury bills are considered as money market securities.
2. Describe the similarities and differences between commercial paper and Treasury bills.

Treasury Bills

Treasury bills (T-bills) are short-term securities issued by the U.S. Treasury Department to help finance the national budget deficit. T-bills make no explicit interest payments but rather are sold at a discount to face value. Investors can purchase T-bills directly with face values for as little as $100 or as much as $5 million. As of 2020, the Treasury Department regularly issues 4, 8, 13, 26, and 52-week T-bills.

T-bill prices are quoted as a percentage of face value. $100,000 face value of a T-bill quoted at 99.125, for example, could be purchased for $99,125. An investor who holds this security until maturity would receive the face value of $100,000 and hence make a gain of $875.

Example 2.3

Tom Green purchases T-bills with a par value of $100,000 at a price of 97.608. Green expects to hold the securities until they mature in 52 weeks.

When Green buys the bills, he pays $97,608 and will receive $100,000 when the bill matures in 52 weeks. Green receives no interest payments during the time period but will generate an implicit interest income at maturity as the difference between the purchase price and its par value or $2,392. This translates into a return of 2.45%, which is known as the yield to maturity on the security.[1]

The returns on T-bills are functions of inflation rates, US monetary policy, maturity dates, and general US economic conditions that impact investor risk tolerance.

1. $2,392 ÷ $97,608 = 2.45%

Commercial Paper

Commercial paper consists of a private sector company's issue of short-term, unsecured promissory notes that are generally used as part of the firm's working capital or cash management strategies. This type of debt is issued in denominations of $100,000 or more and serves as a substitute for short-term bank financing. It is issued with maturities of 270 days or less (costly registration procedures are required for securities over 270 days) and often backed by lines of credit from banks. Generally, maturities are much shorter than 270 days, the majority mature in 45 to 90 days.

In comparison to Treasury bills, these instruments have a slightly higher default risk, and are slightly less liquid. Therefore, commercial paper has slightly higher yields than T-bills of similar term structures.

Commercial paper is generally, but not always, very safe because it is issued by companies with high credit ratings. During the 2008 financial crisis, however, there were actually some defaults. In September of 2008, a large money market mutual fund announced it had suffered large losses on its Lehman Brothers commercial paper investment, marking one of the first times that a money market fund reported its net asset value at less than $1.00. This ultimately led the Federal Reserve to provide stability to the commercial paper market in the form of a Commercial Paper Funding Facility.[2]

> **Quick Quiz 2.2**
>
> 1. Commercial paper is issued with maturities of 270 days or less to avoid costly registration requirements.
>   a. True
>   b. False
> 2. A guarantee of payment by a bank during an international transaction becomes a banker's acceptance when sold in a secondary market.
>   a. True
>   b. False
> 3. A traditional CD is typically a deposit of at least $100,000.
>   a. True
>   b. False
>
> True, True, False.

Example 2.4

Claudia buys 45-day commercial paper issued by a large U.S. retail firm at a market price quoted as 99.25 on a face value of $500,000. Claudia will pay $496,250 for the paper today and receive $500,000 on the maturity date. The yield on this security can be computed as 6%. Claudia will earn an annualized 6% return if she buys at the current price and holds the paper until it matures in 45 days.

Certificates of Deposit (CDs)

Negotiable **certificates of deposit**, also known as Jumbo CDs, are deposits of $100,000 or more placed with commercial banks at a specific stated rate of interest. These short-term securities can be bought and sold in the open market. They usually yield slightly higher returns than T-bills because they have more default risk and less marketability.

2. The Federal Reserve Board (October 7, 2008) announced the creation of the Commercial Paper Funding Facility (CPFF), a facility that will complement the Federal Reserve's existing credit facilities to help provide liquidity to term funding markets. The CPFF will provide a liquidity backstop to U.S. issuers of commercial paper through a special purpose vehicle (SPV) that will purchase three-month unsecured and asset-backed commercial paper directly from eligible issuers. By eliminating much of the risk that eligible issuers will not be able to repay investors by rolling over their maturing commercial paper obligations, this facility should encourage investors to once again engage in term lending in the commercial paper market. Added investor demand should lower commercial paper rates from their current elevated levels and foster issuance of longer-term commercial paper. An improved commercial paper market will enhance the ability of financial intermediaries to accommodate the credit needs of businesses and households.

Traditional CDs can have much smaller denominations, as low as $500, and are sold by many banks. This type of certificate, however, is not negotiable and thus not traded on the open market.

Repurchase Agreements

Securities dealers use **repurchase agreements** (known as repos) to finance large inventories of marketable securities from one to a few days. The issuer or seller agrees to repurchase the underlying security at a specific price and specific date. The repurchase price is higher than the selling price, creating the required return for the holder participating in the repo. There are three types of repos in the market: deliverable, tri-party, and held in custody. The most common is the tri-party repo, which uses a third party as an intermediary between the two primary parties to the agreement.

Bankers' Acceptances

Bankers' acceptances are securities that act as a line of credit issued from a bank. Usually, the bank acts as an intermediary between a U.S. company and a foreign company. Companies that are too small to issue commercial paper will use bankers' acceptances to fund short-term debt needs. These securities usually have slightly higher interest rates than commercial paper.

Example 2.5

A Norwegian food distributor orders $100,000 worth of cucumbers from a Michigan farmer. The two parties have never transacted with each other before, so the farmer requires a financial institution to guarantee payment before shipping. The food distributor requests and receives a promise of payment of $100,000 to the farmer within ten business days. The farmer, satisfied with the credit rating of the bank, ships the cucumbers to Norway.

The farmer has a few choices, two of which are to:

- Wait for 10 days to receive payment from the bank.
- Sell the guarantee in the open market at a discount to receive the funds before the payment date.

The bank guarantee becomes a banker's acceptance when the farmer sells it in the secondary market. The acceptance can then be sold multiple times until it matures.

Short-Term Municipal Obligations

States, counties, parishes, cities, towns, and boroughs are politically incorporated bodies other than the Federal Government and its agencies that also have the authority to issue bonds. These municipalities issue debt instruments ranging in term from 30 days to 30 years. The shorter-term maturities are considered money market instruments.

Although many of these money market securities are available to individual investors, most obtain exposure to this asset class by investing in money market mutual funds.

Fixed-Income Securities

Bonds

Bonds are referred to as fixed income securities because they typically make regular interest payments and then one final lump sum principal payment. Bonds are issued by governments, government-related entities, financial institutions, and large corporations. Bonds are purchased by individuals and institutions mainly for their regular income but also for potential capital gains.

> **Key Concepts**
>
> 1. Identify the sources of repayment for different types of municipal bonds. Explain why municipal bonds are not considered to be default risk-free.
> 2. Explain the difference between time to maturity of a bond and its duration.

Bonds provide investors with an excellent alternative to other types of securities and can be used for the purpose of diversifying portfolios or providing income to individuals who need a stream of cash flows. Although bonds generally have lower returns than equity investments, they are generally less risky than equities and provide higher returns than bank certificates of deposit, savings accounts, and other lending alternatives.

The key features of a bond include:

- Coupon rate
- Yield to maturity
- Length of term, or maturity

The coupon rate is applied to the face value of the bond and tells the investor the amount of interest that will be received on every coupon date. For example, a $1,000 face value bond with a five percent annual coupon will pay interest of $50 ($1,000 x 5%) annually. The yield to maturity is a measure of the return an investor is getting by investing in the bond, and therefore also the cost to the issuer of issuing the bond. It takes into account the difference between the proceeds raised by the bond issue (the price paid by the investor) and the face value, as well as the coupon payments. The maturity of the bond is the period of time it must continue to make coupon payments, and at the maturity date the issuer must repay the face value of the bond.

Typically bonds with longer maturities have higher yields, but expectations of future interest and inflation rates may cause yields on longer maturity bonds to fall. Maturity also affects the volatility of the bond, specifically how much the price changes in response to changes in interest rates. This interest rate risk is measured by duration, and longer maturity bonds typically have higher durations, meaning they are more sensitive to changes in interest rates. The calculation of duration is covered in detail in the fixed income chapter.

U.S. Treasury Notes and Bonds

The United States Treasury borrows money to fund government functions and has done so since its independence from Great Britain. The Department of Finance was created in 1781 to help pay for the Revolutionary War. The total debt amounted to $43 million in 1783 and Congress was given the authority to collect taxes to help pay the debt. Tax revenues were insufficient to completely retire the debt, so the government began issuing bonds. By 1789, the Treasury Department was fully established as one of the founding fathers, Alexander Hamilton, assumed the position of Secretary of the Treasury. Over the next 150 years, the Treasury Department's responsibilities and power expanded until the Great Depression during the 1930s, when its influence exploded.

When the Treasury Department borrows in the short-term, it does it through Treasury bills. When borrowing in the long term, however, it issues notes and bonds. The only real difference between the two is the maturity date. T-notes typically are issued for two, three, five, seven and ten years while bonds are 30-year securities. Treasury notes and bonds are coupon securities that pay interest on a semiannual basis and are universally considered to be the safest securities in the world. In fact, most finance academics and professionals agree that Treasury securities are default risk-free, which means that investors are effectively guaranteed to receive interest payments and have their principal returned.

Inflation-Indexed Treasury Notes and Bonds

In 1997, the Treasury began issuing notes and bonds that are indexed with the consumer price index. Treasury inflation protected securities (TIPS) with terms of five, ten, and thirty years and can be purchased for a minimum of $100 through **Treasury direct**. These securities have the same basic characteristics as non-inflation-adjusted Treasury notes and bonds, except for the inflation-adjustment feature. The principal is adjusted for inflation and the coupon rate is fixed.

One of the primary risks to which fixed-income securities are subject is change in interest rates, both from devaluation in principal and from loss of purchasing power. The indexed Treasuries provide protection from both of these risks making them an attractive security for those investors concerned about rising inflation and devaluation due to loss of purchasing power.

Quick Quiz 2.3

1. TIPS are hedges against inflation.
   a. True
   b. False
2. Water bonds are repaid by user fees.
   a. True
   b. False
3. The interest received by investors from a municipal bond is always taxed at the state level.
   a. True
   b. False

True, True, False.

Example 2.6

Lucas Financial is an institutional investor who purchases $500,000 worth of five-year Treasury notes that protect against inflation. The coupon rate on the note is 4.4%. Changes in the consumer price index determine the semi-annual coupon payments.

In six months, the CPI increases by 2.1%, which will result in a higher principal base.

The new principal can be computed as: $500,000 × 1.021 = $510,500

The higher principal base causes the coupon payments to increase as well. The adjusted semi-annual coupon payment is now: $510,500 × {0.044 ÷ 2} = $11,231

Thus, TIPS have the ability to adjust to changing inflationary conditions.

Municipal Bonds

Municipalities, which include states, counties, parishes, cities, and towns, issue debt instruments to finance their budget deficits or to finance public projects. The unique characteristic of municipal bonds is their income tax treatment. The interest from municipal bonds is not subject to federal income tax, and residents in the state that issued the bond are also typically not subject to state income tax. Residents from other states, however, are likely to suffer tax at the state level. Although the yields on municipals are generally lower than that of Treasuries, their special tax treatment makes them the choice for higher income investors because of their higher after-tax yields. Two common types of municipal bonds are general obligation bonds and revenue bonds.

General obligation bonds are issued for general purposes to serve the general public of the municipality. Common uses for bond proceeds include finance road construction, parks development, and public safety projects and investors are repaid through the taxing authority of the municipality.

Revenue bonds on the other hand are issued for specific projects such as the ones shown in **Exhibit 2.1** and are repaid by the revenue generated by each project.

Key Concepts

1. Identify three benefits that corporations enjoy when issuing bonds.
2. Describe the characteristics and risks of mortgage backed securities (MBS).

Muni bonds are discussed in additional detail in Chapter 7.

Exhibit 2.1 includes examples of the various types of revenue bonds.

Exhibit 2.1 | Types of Revenue Bonds

Name	Purpose	Repaid
Airport bonds	Construction of airports	Lease payments paid by tenants, landing and fuel fees paid by airlines
Industrial development bonds	Construction of stadiums and manufacturing facilities	Lease payments by tenants, fees and concession stand revenue
Hospital bonds	Construction and renovation of medical facilities	Payments made by patients and health insurance
Housing bonds	Construction of residential housing units	Mortgage payments made by homeowners
Water bonds	Finance water and sewage projects	Fees paid by users
Toll road bonds	Construction of toll roads, bridges, and tunnels	Tolls and gasoline tax revenues

Although relatively safe, municipal bonds are often insured by third party insurance companies to further reduce credit risk. Insured bonds have lower risk and therefore lower returns than bonds without backing by an insurance company.

Corporate Bonds

Corporations issue bonds primarily to finance the investment in wealth-increasing projects, but sometimes use the proceeds for dividends or share repurchases or to engage in merger activity. The benefits of using debt include no dilution of equity ownership, receiving an interest deduction, and obtaining a lower cost of capital.[3] There is a trade-off, however, as excessive amounts of debt can strain the financial health of the company by using precious resources for debt service. Using debt finance instead of issuing new equity increases the leverage of a company and can positively impact its return on equity. However, additional interest payments increase the risk of financial distress and can lead to an increase in share price volatility.

3. The TCJA 2017 limited the ability of companies to deduct interest for years after 2018. While the details are beyond the scope of this text, the new law limits larger companies ability to deduct interest expenses.

The corporate bond market is very broad and is typically classified by the type of issuer. The five broad categories of corporate bonds are banks and finance companies, industrials, public utilities, transportations, and international. Each of these categories can be further subdivided. For example, transportation can be divided into airlines, railroads, and trucking. These subcategory classifications can assist investors in analyzing and comparing various debt issues.

Mortgage-Backed Securities

Although relatively new, the market for **mortgage-backed securities** has seen tremendous growth since its inception in the 1970s. Mortgage-backed securities are ownership claims on a pool of mortgages. The originating mortgage lender sells loans to investors in the secondary market. These investors pool mortgages together and sell interests in the pool to other investors. This process of transforming mortgages into securities that can be sold to the public is known as securitization.

Mortgage-backed securities (MBSs) are often referred to as "pass-through" securities because the monthly mortgage payments are passed along to the holders of the MBSs, less a small servicing fee. These monthly mortgage payments consist of scheduled interest and principal payments, as well as unscheduled principal prepayments. These unscheduled principal prepayments result from borrowers making additional principal payments on their loans or from paying off loans, such as in the case of refinancing.

Because MBSs are supported by the underlying mortgages and the mortgage payments, many of which are backed by the government and all of which are secured by real property, they tend to have low credit risk. MBSs, however, are subject to other risks. Like other fixed-income obligations, these securities are subject to the fluctuation in interest rates. As interest rates increase, the value of the MBS decreases, and as interest rates decrease, the value of the MBS increases.

Quick Quiz 2.4

1. Mortgage-backed securities have relatively low credit risk but high prepayment risk.
   a. True
   b. False

2. A municipal bond issued to construct a toll road between two large cities would be classified as a general obligation bond.
   a. True
   b. False

True, False.

Since MBSs pass through mortgage payments on a monthly basis, the investor must reinvest these cash flows into some other investment. This reinvestment rate risk impacts MBSs in the same manner as other fixed-income securities that have cash flows occurring during the life of the security.

Unlike other fixed-income obligations, however, MBSs are subject to prepayment risk, which is the risk that homeowners will pay off their loans before the scheduled loan maturity date. Since the value of these securities is based on the schedule of cash flows, any mortgage prepayments will impact the return an investor receives on a mortgage-backed security. In addition to creating uncertainty as to the timing of the cash flows, these prepayments create a situation in which the investor must reinvest the additional principal payments most likely at a lower interest rate.

Ratings Agencies

Rating agencies are responsible for assisting investors in evaluating the default risk of fixed-income securities. Bond rating agencies analyze the financial information of thousands of companies attempting to determine a credit rating for the various debt issues in the market. The two largest and most popular rating agencies are Standard & Poor's and Moody's, but there are others including Fitch, Duf and Phelps, and Dun and Bradstreet. These agencies use similar research methodology and produce similar ratings levels. In some cases, however, there may be a slight difference in assigned default risk by two or more agencies, which results in what is known as **split rating**. Two credit rating systems are listed in **Exhibit 2.2**

Exhibit 2.2 | Bond Ratings

Grade	Moody's	Standard & Poor's	Explanation
Investment	Aaa	AAA	The safest bonds with the highest probability of meeting the interest and principal obligations, but not quite default risk-free.
Investment	Aa	AA	One notch below the safest bonds with a small degree of default risk.
Investment	A	A	Short-term obligations remain very safe but payments over the longer term might not be sustainable in the event of a slowdown in the economy.
Investment	Baa	BBB	The highest default risk within the investment grade, still safe but these issues are more sensitive to changes in economic conditions.
Junk	Ba	BB	Probability of payments depends on changes in economic conditions, the first level of speculative grade.
Junk	B	B	Payments depend highly on economic conditions.
Junk	Caa	CCC	Extremely sensitive to deteriorating economic conditions.
Junk	Ca	CC	Very high level of default risk with probability of default increasing dramatically.
Junk	C	C	Nearing default, interest payments are highly uncertain and may be in arrears.
Junk	D	D	In default, no interest or principal payments are being made, nor will be over the short term

Investment grade bonds have a high probability of timely payment of both interest and repayment of principal, while non-investment grade bonds are those where a significant risk exists to either interest or principal payments or both.

Equities

A company can raise capital by issuing equity shares that represent ownership in the company. Owners of equity shares, also known as common shares, own a share of the company's net assets and have the right to vote on matters such as the appointment of board members. Publicly listed companies can offer these shares to the general investing public. The advantage of issuing equity rather than debt is that the company is not obligated to make interest and principal repayments, and hence there is no risk of defaulting on equity as there is with debt. However, in the long run equity holders will expect a higher return than debt holders via dividends and capital gains. If the company does not earn enough profit to make dividend payments, the share price is likely to fall and raising further capital may become difficult or impossible.

A firm that generates positive net income has two choices: It can distribute the earnings to shareholders in the form of cash dividends or by repurchasing some of its outstanding shares. It can reinvest back into the company in the form of new projects or improvements to existing product lines. This process becomes more complex for global firms who generate cash flows in multiple currencies. Multinational firms are exposed to the additional risks of exchange rate fluctuations and political differences.

Key Concepts

1. Explain choices a firm has when considering the distribution of earnings to shareholders.
2. Describe the differences between systematic risk and unsystematic risk.

From a theoretical standpoint, the company should reinvest the additional income if it is able to earn returns that are higher than shareholders require for taking on the risk of owning the shares. If this is not the case, then companies should pay the additional cash to the shareholders in the form of dividends. It is also important to note that shareholders will very likely face tax consequences on dividend receipt.

The risk of investing in equity depends to a certain extent on the sector the company operates in. A common measure of risk is the volatility of a company's share price, and certain sectors display much more volatility than others. Utility companies, for example, tend to show less volatility than the market in general, as their customers must still purchase their services regardless of economic conditions. Biotech companies on the other hand tend to be more volatile, as investors pull out of these more speculative investments when the economy starts to falter. The upside of taking on riskier investments is the expectation that they will deliver higher returns when the market rises. Lower risk equities tend to deliver lower returns.

Quick Quiz 2.5

1. The stock price reaction to a firm operating in the banking industry announcing its CEO has been fired for contractual violations is an example of systematic risk.
   a. True
   b. False
2. Exchange rate risk adds extra volatility to the portfolios of global equity investors.
   a. True
   b. False

False, True.

The risk of investing in equity securities has two general components: Systematic risk and unsystematic risk. **Systematic risk** is the variability in returns due to changes in economic factors, such as inflation, changes in GDP, and the political environment. **Unsystematic risk**, on the other hand, is the variability in returns due to changes in firm specific factors, such as dividend payments, free cash flow, and executive leadership. When these macro or micro factors change, so do equity values.

Systematic risk is most commonly measured by the **beta** of the stock, which generally has a range of between 0 and 2. The average beta in the equity market is 1.0, which means stocks with betas that exceed 1.0 have higher systematic risk than the market, whilst stocks with betas that are less than 1.0 have lower systematic risk than the market. For example, utility firms tend to have low betas and technology firms tend to have high betas.

Alternative Investments

Any security or investment opportunity that does not fall into one of the traditional asset classes is most likely characterized as an alternative investment. These include but are not limited to the vast range of derivative securities, venture capital, private equity, commodities, collectibles, hedge funds, and real assets such as buildings, farms, and gold mines. The popularity of these investments among all types of investors surged in the 1990s and have become an integral component of well-diversified portfolios.

Key Concepts

1. Discuss the reason that the purchase of Hollywood memorabilia is considered to be part of the alternative investments class.
2. Discuss the limitations of the portfolio construction process for hedge fund managers.

Derivatives are contractual securities which participants use for hedging, speculating, and arbitrage strategies. A derivative security is one whose value depends on or is reliant upon the value of an underlying security. Derivatives can have maturity dates that range from a few days to multi-year periods. The derivative market is unique in that it can have super high-risk levels for speculators but can have low or even zero risk for hedgers and arbitragers. Examples include futures contracts, option contracts, and swap contracts.

Example 2.7

Gold Coast Mining Inc (GCM) is the leading firm in the gold mining industry and owns and operates assets globally. It is exposed to commodity price risk because the price of gold fluctuates widely over time. In order to manage this risk, GCM can use a gold futures contract to lock in its future selling price of gold, enabling it to better predict its operating cash flows.

Suppose the spot price of gold is $1,000 per troy ounce, the three month gold futures contract price is $950 per troy ounce, and suppose GCM expects to mine 50,000 troy ounces during the next three months in its US properties. GCM could simply mine its gold and sell it at future spot prices. The risk is that the price of gold falls and perhaps falls precipitously. A drop in spot prices over the net three months of just 10% would cost GCM $5 million in revenues. Alternatively, GCM could sell 50,000 troy ounces of three month gold futures contracts at $950 per troy ounce. This would commit GCM to delivering the gold in three months and receiving $47.5 million in revenue (at the futures price of $950 per troy ounce). Whether the spot price is above or below $950 in three months is unknown, but using a futures contract GCM can remove that uncertainty and hence eliminate price risk. This is a case of using the futures market to create a perfect hedge, thereby eliminating commodity price risk.

Hedge funds are somewhat of a misnomer in that hedging is only a small part of hedge fund strategies. Hedge funds are collections of investments that can include almost any financial opportunity. Hedge fund managers invest in derivatives, private equity, stocks, bonds, and any asset they believe will appreciate in value. For these reasons, the hedge fund universe is much less restrictive than the industry for equity mutual funds.

Alternative securities are characterized by low correlation coefficients with most other securities including equities, fixed income, and other types of alternatives like commodities. As such, they provide the investor with a high degree of diversification. There is the potential for significant returns but they come at the cost of extra risk and lack of liquidity.

SECURITIES LAWS

Global financial markets are currently monitored, regulated, and maintained by myriad government bodies and private organizations. The goal of oversight is to promote transparency, integrity, and accuracy in financial reporting and decision making. Financial markets operate with a high degree of efficiency and are structured to satisfy a host of market participants. Such was not always the case.

Significant government influence over capital markets began in earnest after the epic stock market crash in 1929, in which the Dow Jones Industrial Average lost $30 billion. In fact, the market lost nearly 90 percent from the high in 1929 to the low in 1932. Total market capitalization in 1929 was around $125 billion. In 2021, total market capitalization is around $40 trillion. It is almost inconceivable what a 90 percent loss in market cap would look like in current markets.

Quick Quiz 2.6

1. Speculators use the derivatives market to reduce their risk positions.
   a. True
   b. False
2. The correlation coefficient between the return on a stamp collection and the return on Amazon stock is likely to approach 1.0.
   a. True
   b. False

False, False.

To understand the history of financial regulation in the United States, it is helpful to revisit the causes of the crash and the subsequent recession during the 1930s. The completion of the transcontinental railway system by 1890 and the emergence of large U.S. corporations producing steel and oil led to vast economic growth throughout the country. The surge was led by Henry Ford, who applied Frederick Taylor's Scientific Management to the production of automobiles, which resulted in more efficient ways to manage labor and the workplace environment. Ford was so successful that his company was able to reduce the price of a Ford car from $850 in 1908 to $300 by 1924. The Ford Motor Company was joined by Standard Oil and U.S. Steel as corporate innovators in productivity. Henry Ford, John Rockefeller, and JP Morgan were the pioneers of leadership who directly influenced the prosperity the entire country enjoyed during the 1920s. Couple the emergence of these influential men with advances in technology in the production of airplanes, appliances, phonographs, and radios, and the recipe for the Roaring 20s was in place.

The **Roaring 20s** were characterized by consistent economic growth and the expansion of the middle class. Advertising became a science and many of the working class owned cars, appliances, and radios, and began spending their money on leisure activities. It was not until both the Ford Motor Company and large department stores began offering extended credit plans that the economy truly soared. Married couples were familiar with mortgage loans, but now they had access to installment loans. By the mid 20s, many homes had a car, a washing machine, a vacuum cleaner, a radio, and a refrigerator. The availability of credit surely increased the demand for these products and increased the consumer's appetite for leverage.

Key Concepts

1. List the important pieces of legislation following the stock market crash in 1929 and state their purposes.
2. Identify the commonalities in the mission statements from the various professional investment organizations.

In its 200 plus years of existence, the U.S. stock markets have been subject to serious fraud and price manipulation. In most cases, however, the corruption occurred between and among wealthy individual investors. This changed dramatically after WWI, when many Americans began investing in stocks. During the 1920s, wealthy investors began to form 'stock pools,' in which they would control large amounts of shares. These individuals would use their influence in the banking world to drive up the price of the stock. Press stories would magically appear suggesting the stock was considerably undervalued, resulting in even more upward pressure on prices. Coupled with the use of leverage and up to 90 percent margin buying, the manipulation resulted in substantial gains for the individuals. When prices rose, the individuals would sell their positions and realize a profit. This was insider trading, and there was little government oversight to prevent it. This activity continued until the market collapse in 1929.

The Dow Jones Industrial Average was less than 100 in 1920 and rose to almost 400 by mid-1929, with much of those gains coming from the two-year period before the crash in October 1929. The Dow increased in value during 1928 by approximately 49 percent, but those positive returns plus the others during the 1920s were given back in the next five years and the Dow bottomed out at under 100 in 1934.

The carnage of the crash can be seen in the **Exhibit 2.3**. While the absolute value of the daily negative returns may not seem epic at first glance, the losses were magnified because of the massive 90 percent margin accounts. The losses were catastrophic enough to contribute to a decade of economic recessions.

Exhibit 2.3 | 1929 Crash

Date	Return
Black Thursday October 24, 1929	-11%
Black Monday October 28, 1929	-13%
Black Tuesday October 29, 1929	-12%

Government Legislation

Government officials were quick to blame the greedy Wall Street bankers for the crash and the ten-year depression that followed, and some of that blame is warranted. There were, however, a host of contributing factors that led to the crash, and the government was determined to avoid another one. Some historians argue that the Federal Reserve's low interest rate policy during the 20s followed by an increase in interest rates after the crash contributed significantly to the decade's recession. In the years after the crash, however, the U.S. Congress crafted new laws that were intended to curb bubbles before they could occur.

Exhibit 2.4 is a summary of the major securities laws passed by Congress since the crash of 1929.

Exhibit 2.4 | Major Securities Laws

Major Legislation	Year	Purpose
Securities Act	1933	Regulates the offering and sale of securities to ensure more transparency in financial statements
Banking Act	1933	Separates commercial from investment banking (Glass Steagall Act)
Securities Exchange Act	1934	Governs secondary market trading (established the Securities and Exchange Commission)
Trust Indenture Act	1939	Requires the appointment of a suitable trustee for security issue
Investment Company Act	1940	Forms the backbone of financial regulation and established the foundation for mutual funds and hedge funds.
Investment Advisers Act	1940	Regulates investment advisers. Requires registration with the SEC for firms or any individual advisers with assets under management exceeding $110 million
Financial Services Modernization Act (Gramm–Leach–Bliley Act)	1999	Repealed part of Glass-Steagall Act of 1933 and removes barriers among securities firms, financial institutions, and insurance companies
Sarbanes Oxley Act	2002	Establishes expanded financial regulations in response to the major accounting scandals of late 1990s
Dodd Frank Act	2010	Establishes new government agencies to reduce volatility in financial markets in response to the Great Recession

Securities and Exchange Commission

The formal goal of the SEC as shown in many of its publications is as follows:

> *"The mission of the U.S. Securities and Exchange Commission is to protect investors, maintain fair, orderly, and efficient markets, and facilitate capital formation"*

Common crimes prosecuted by the SEC include insider trading, spreading false information, accounting fraud, market manipulation, collusion, and breach of fiduciary obligations.Investment Advisers Act of 1940.

The Investment Advisers Act of 1940 is particularly important for investor protection. The law was a direct result of the manipulation and corruption that was an important factor in the stock market bubble and crash during the late 1920s.

Following are portions of the Act taken from a March 2013 publication of the SEC entitled "Regulation of Investment Advisers by the U.S. Securities and Exchange Commission.'

Definition of Investment Adviser

Section 202(a)(11) of the Act defines an investment adviser as any person or firm that:

- *For compensation, is engaged in the business of, providing advice to others or issuing reports or analyses regarding securities.*
- *A person must satisfy all three elements to fall within the definition of "investment adviser."*

There are several exclusions from the investment adviser definition available to persons who presumably (or at least arguably) satisfy all three elements of the definition. A person eligible for one of the exclusions is not subject to any provisions of the Act. The following are exclusions from the definition of an investment adviser:

- Banks and bank holding companies
- Lawyers, accountants, engineers, and teachers whose performance of such services is solely incidental to the practice of their profession
- Brokers and dealers whose performance of such services is solely incidental to the conduct of their business as a broker or dealer and who receives no special compensation
- Publishers of any bona fide newspaper, news magazine, or financial publication of general and regular circulation
- Government security advisers
- Credit ratings agencies
- Family offices
- Government and political subdivisions
- Non-U.S. advisers

Any adviser with assets under management of $110 million or more must register with the Securities and Exchange Commission. Those advisers with less than $110 million are either encouraged or required to register with their respective states and often times are required to register in multiple states.

High Profile Cases

Martha Stewart was indicted in 2003 for her role in selling approximately 4,000 shares of ImClone stock. The charges included making false statements, conspiracy, and obstruction of justice. Stewart sold her shares on December 27, 2001 for $58.43 per share. The following day, the Food and Drug Administration announced it would not review a promising cancer drug made by ImClone. The stock fell to $45.39 on its way to below $10 by mid-2002.

The trade saved Stewart about $50,000 at the end of December and about $200,000 six months later. The interesting note is that ImClone's price regained its near $60 share price by early 2004, by which time the value of her investment would have returned to the pre-trade level.

Stewart was found guilty on four counts and was sentenced to five months in a federal prison and served her time from October 2004 to March 2005.

Bernie Madoff was an established money manager who convinced thousands of investors to provide capital to his firm. He was indicted in 2008 for fraud, money laundering, perjury, and theft. Madoff promised superior returns to his investors and was able to continually raise money for perhaps five decades. He generated a stable return for his clients that ranged from 10 percent to 20 percent. He would take a portion of the new funds raised to pay off old investors and take a portion to spend on 'undisclosed commissions' for his firm. This worked for so long mostly because his investors trusted him, and he was able to convince many of them to stay fully invested to participate in future superior returns. This changed dramatically in 2008 when a few investors requested about $7 billion in redemptions because of the financial crisis. Very quickly, it was discovered that Madoff had only about $300 million and was finally arrested.

In 2009, Madoff pled guilty to 11 felonies and was sentenced to 150 years in prison.

Independent Organizations

There are many organizations whose goal is to promote integrity within the financial services industry. The organizations tend to operate independently and often times have requirements for memberships, such as passing an exam and verifying experience in the field. These organizations also tend to offer professional certifications, such as the Certified Financial Planner Mark or the Chartered Financial Analyst designation. As part of its membership, these organizations require their members to act professionally and ethically in order to advance the brand. Several examples are described below:

1. **Chartered Financial Analyst Institute**
   Mission Statement: "To lead the investment profession globally by promoting the highest standards of ethics, education, and professional excellence for the ultimate benefit of society."
2. **Global Association of Risk Professionals**
   Mission Statement: "To be the leading professional association for risk managers, dedicated to the advancement of the risk profession through education, research, and the promotion of best practices globally."
3. **Chartered Alternative Investment Analyst Association**
   Mission Statement: "As the leader in alternative investment education, CAIA Association seeks to act as the catalyst for the best and most current knowledge and practices in the industry."
4. **Certified Financial Planner Board of Standards, Inc.**
   Mission statement: The mission of Certified Financial Planner Board of Standards, Inc. (CFP Board) is to benefit the public by granting the CFP® certification and upholding it as the recognized standard of excellence for competent and ethical personal financial planning.

Quick Quiz 2.7

1. The cause of the depression during the 1930s includes margin trading, artificially low interest rates, and rapid economic expansion.
   a. True
   b. False
2. Any financial adviser who manages in excess of $50 million in assets must register with the Securities and Exchange Commission.
   a. True
   b. False

True, False.

DISCUSSION QUESTIONS

SOLUTIONS to the discussion questions can be found exclusively within the chapter. Once you have completed an initial reading of the chapter, go back and highlight the answers to these questions.

1. Explain the factors that contributed to the Great Depression in the 1930s.
2. Discuss the importance of the 1933-1934 legislation that was designed to create more stability in financial markets.
3. Identify the characteristics of financial advisers.
4. Explain Treasury Direct and discuss the reasons for its popularity among investors.
5. Identify a common goal outlined by each of the professional organizations as stated in their respective mission statements.
6. Discuss differences between primary and secondary markets.
7. Explain the auction process used for the issuance of treasury securities.
8. Identify the different types of alternative investments.
9. Discuss how commercial paper is similar to and different from a corporate bond issue.
10. Describe the differences between the two main types of municipal bonds.
11. Define mortgage-backed securities.
12. Discuss the necessity for bond ratings in the fixed-income market.
13. Explain the attraction of investing in alternative investments.
14. Describe the difference between systematic and unsystematic risks and provide examples of each.

MULTIPLE-CHOICE PROBLEMS

A sample of multiple choice problems is provided below. Additional multiple choice problems are available at money-education.com by accessing the Student Practice Portal.

1. A wealthy investor purchases a money market mutual fund to manage the liquidity of her portfolio. The least likely security that would be included in the fund is:
    a. U.S. Treasury note.
    b. Commercial paper.
    c. 180-day certificate of deposit.
    d. Banker's acceptance.

2. A long-term investor who searches for protection against rising consumer prices would most likely purchase a:
    a. U.S. Treasury bond.
    b. Mortgage-backed security.
    c. U.S. Treasury inflation protection security.
    d. Equity shares in a financial institution.

3. An investor buys $100,000 in par value of TIPS with a coupon rate of 8%. Inflation during the first six months is 2.4%. The first semi-annual coupon payment is closest to:
    a. $2,000.
    b. $2,048.
    c. $4,096.
    d. $8,192.

4. The most likely reason a business would issue commercial paper is to:
    a. Manage working capital.
    b. Finance a budget deficit.
    c. Invest in long-term projects.
    d. Refinance a long-term bond issue.

5. A Canadian apple farmer buys fertilizer from a U.S. based firm located near the Canadian border. The apple farmer receives a guarantee of payment from a Canadian bank and sells the guarantee in the secondary market. The risk of the banker's acceptance depends most likely on the:
    a. Apple farmer.
    b. U.S. fertilizer firm.
    c. Canadian bank.
    d. Apple market.

QUICK QUIZ EXPLANATIONS

Quick Quiz 2.1

1. True.
2. False. Firms that issue equity shares make dividend payments.
3. True.

Quick Quiz 2.2

1. True.
2. True.
3. False. That describes a negotiable CD or a jumbo CD.

Quick Quiz 2.3

1. True.
2. True.
3. False. Interest received by investors who live in a particular state is exempt from income tax on that state's income.

Quick Quiz 2.4

1. True.
2. False. This would be classified as a revenue bond.

Quick Quiz 2.5

1. False. Stock price reaction to information that is specific to each firm is unsystematic risk.
2. True.

Quick Quiz 2.6

1. False. Speculators typically make directional bets in the derivative markets, making these investments high risk.
2. False. Correlations between traditional investments like stocks and collectibles is close to zero.

Quick Quiz 2.7

1. True.
2. False. Financial advisers who manage assets in excess of $110 million must register with the SEC.

3
RISK & RETURN

LEARNING OBJECTIVES

1. Understand the relationship between risk and return for various investments.
2. Calculate total return.*
3. Identify, measure, and interpret investment returns including after-tax, holding period return, effective annual rate, annual percentage rate, time- and dollar-weighted returns, geometric and arithmetic returns.
4. Calculate weighted average return and real rate of return.*
5. Calculate and interpret statistical measures such as mean, standard deviation, z-statistic, correlation, and R^2, and interpret the meaning of skewness and kurtosis.
6. Understand what beta is and how it is used as a measure of portfolio risk.*
7. Know the difference between beta and standard deviation.*
8. Identify, measure, and differentiate between types of investment risks including systematic risk, unsystematic risk, interest rate risk, liquidity risk, default and credit risk, inflation risk, operating and financial risk, reinvestment rate risk, exchange rate risk, and country (political) risk in a client's portfolio.
9. Understand correlation, the coefficient of variation, coefficient of determination, and covariance.*
10. Understand and be able to calculate semi-variance and Value at Risk.*
11. Explain the impact of low-probability economic events on clients' welfare.*
12. Differentiate between the various types of risks in the equity markets.*

**Ties to CFP Board Student-Centered Learning Objectives.*

INTRODUCTION

The decision to consume or invest is an age-old issue for individuals. Many consumers decide to forego current consumption in favor of saving for personal financial goals, such as retirement or financing education for their dependents. The savings-consumption decision can be simply reduced to a marginal cost, marginal benefit analysis. The returns to the savings component must exceed the sacrifice made. The complicating factor is the uncertainty of those returns. This uncertainty leads to risk.

Key Concepts

1. Understand how to calculate each type of return.
2. Understand the concepts and limitations of each type of return.
3. Understand that several returns are based on the same underlying concept but may be different only due to the numbers used.

Risk can be defined and interpreted in many different ways. One way is to simply suggest that risk is the possibility of an adverse result. Another way is to define risk as the variability in outcomes. Financial risk managers sometimes define risk as the probability of a loss. Yet another way is to describe risk as a chance of loss. The link between uncertainty and risk should be obvious. Essentially, risk implies the outcome of the savings component is unknown. A famous quote that was popularized during the Great Depression of the 1930s summarizes this link, "You pays your money and you takes your chances." [1]

1. Said repeatedly by James' grandmother. She grew up in the depression and is 100 years old as of the writing of this chapter in 2018. She lived long enough to know that there are few guarantees in life and that even if you spend your money there are no guarantees it will work out the way you want.

There are many ways to calculate the return from an investment, as well as a number of methods to evaluate or consider the riskiness of an investment. Regardless of the approach taken in evaluating risk and return, the relationship should remain fairly constant: as the risk of making an investment increases, so should the potential return.

Example 3.1

An investor decides to forego current consumption and invest in a financial security to help pay for a wedding present for her son. The investor must choose between two securities according to the following table:

	Initial Price	Expected Return
Security 1	$20	10%
Security 2	$20	10%

At first glance, it might seem the investor should be indifferent between the two securities. An extra piece of information not shown in the table is that the investor believes the second security is much riskier than the first. Consequently, the investor will be attracted to Security 1 and will very likely avoid Security 2. If enough other investors have similar risk estimates, the price of Security 1 will increase while the price of Security 2 will decrease. Of course, the expected return for Security 1 will fall while the expected return for Security 2 will rise as a result of the differences in risk. As such, observing prices and forming return expectations does not represent a complete decision-making information set.

METHODS OF MEASURING RETURN

The two sources of return from an investment are the yield and the capital gain.

Yield + Capital Gain = Total Investment Return

Yield is generally defined as the ratio of cash payments to the current price of the investment. Payments to investors include interest, dividends, and other cash distributions. Investors must choose between spending the cash, reinvesting it back into the original investment, or finding a new one.

Example 3.2

Lily purchases 100 shares of Capitol Construction (CC) equity shares for $20 per share. The board at CC recently announced its upcoming quarterly dividend will be $0.25 per share and expects to pay $1.00 per share annually. Lily's dividend yield is 5% ($1.00/ $20.00).

A **capital gain** is the change in value of an investment from one period to the next. Investors typically expect an increase in the value of their investments, which results in a capital gain. The value of investments, however, can fall, so some investors will realize a capital loss. Investors can select the timing of their capital gains or losses as they will only be realized when the investment is sold.

Example 3.3

Marshall purchased 10 shares of Lincoln Industries (LI) equity shares exactly one year ago for $100 per share. During the past year, the economy has grown and LI has substantially improved its profitability and its cash flows. The current price for LI is $136 per share. If Marshall decides to sell his shares today, he would generate a 36% capital gain ($136/$100 -1).

If Marshall received a dividend of $5 per share from LI in the last few days, he would have earned a 5.0% dividend yield ($5/100).

Marshall's total return for the year would be 41% by summing the dividend yield and the capital gain. Note that an investor who bought the stock at the current price of $136 would earn a dividend yield of 3.7% if the dividend payment remained constant ($5/ $136).

There are many ways to accurately depict the total return on an investment. The key is to understand how the various approaches handle the timing of cash flows and the dollar amounts invested. Some approaches even consider additional variables ignored in the previous discussions. For example, after-tax returns depend on the investor's tax bracket and real returns are computed net of inflation. **Exhibit 3.1** summarizes a fairly comprehensive list of possible return measures.

Exhibit 3.1 | Summary of Return Measures

- Holding Period Return
- Arithmetic Mean Return
- Geometric Mean Return
- Internal Rate of Return:
  - Dollar-Weighted
  - Time-Weighted
- Annualized Return
- Weighted Average Return
- After-Tax Returns
- Real Returns
- Effective Annual Rate of Return

Holding Period Return

Perhaps the most straightforward method of calculating investment returns is the **Holding Period Return (HPR)**, which measures the total return over the entire period of investment. The Holding Period Return (HPR) is the ending value of the investment minus the beginning value of the investment, plus or minus any cash flows, divided by the beginning value of the investment.

$$\text{HPR} = \frac{\text{Ending Value - Beginning Value +/- Cash Flows}}{\text{Beginning Value}}$$

Example 3.4

Barney purchased equity shares of Canine Foods (CF) exactly one year ago for $60 per share. During the past year, CF paid Barney $3 in dividends. Barney sells his CF shares today for $72. The holding period return is computed as follows:

$$\text{HPR} = \frac{\$72 - \$60 + \$3}{\$60} = 25\%$$

Although simple to calculate, the HPR is difficult to interpret without knowing the investment's holding period. An HPR of 25 percent for Barney in the previous example is impressive given his holding period of one year. But an HPR of 25 percent for a 50-year holding period would be less impressive. This limits how useful the HPR is when comparing investment returns.

Annualized Holding Period Returns

To make return calculations more comparable, it is common to state them on an annual basis.

Example 3.5

Ralph Kitchens purchased equity shares in Flower Industries (FI) and earned a six-month holding period return of 5.2%. If Kitchens holds the shares for another six months and the holding period return is repeated, he will have generated an annual holding period return of 10.67%, computed as:

$$(1.052)^2 - 1 = 0.1067$$

Note that this annualized return is greater than twice the semi-annual return.

Example 3.6

Robyn's grandmother gave her a financial security that was worth $500 on the day she was born. The security increased in value to $1,500 by the time Robyn turned 21. This is a 200% holding period return, but the holding period is 21 years. On an annual basis, however, Robyn earned:

$$\text{Annualized Return} = (\$1{,}500/\$500)^{1/21} - 1 = 5.37\%$$

Average Return

The problem with computing a meaningful return for an investment is compounded when evaluating performance over multiple periods. To handle this challenge, most practitioners compute the average return over the specified time period. The arithmetic and geometric returns are two common ways to measure performance. Unlike the standard holding period return, these two approaches explicitly address the time component of returns, but do so in very different ways.

The **arithmetic return** is the simple average calculated using the following formula:

$$AR = \frac{\sum_{t=1}^{n} HPR_t}{n}$$

Example 3.7

Consider four years of total returns for Funds A and B. Calculate the arithmetic return for each fund.

	Return Fund A	Return Fund B
Year 1	45%	10%
Year 2	(10%)	10%
Year 3	(25%)	10%
Year 4	30%	10%

Fund A	Fund B
$\frac{45 + (10) + (25) + 30}{4} = 10\%$	$\frac{10 + 10 + 10 + 10}{4} = 10\%$

Notice that the consistency of the returns or variability of the returns has no effect on their average, or arithmetic means. Most investors prefer to lock in a steady rate of return (as seen in Fund B) to one that fluctuates dramatically from year to year (Fund A) if they expect both to earn about the same return over time.

The following calculation helps to demonstrate why, generally speaking, the geometric mean is the preferred approach for evaluating investment returns over a period of time. The following formula is for the calculation of the geometric return:

$$GR = [(1 + R_1)(1 + R_2)...(1 + R_n)]^{1/n} - 1$$

R_n = holding period return for period n
n = the number of periods

The geometric return for the two example funds discussed above are calculated as follows:

Fund A: $[(1.45)(0.9)(0.75)(1.3)]^{1/4} - 1 = 0.062$

Fund B: $[(1.1)(1.1)(1.1)(1.1)]^{1/4} - 1 = 0.10$

The **geometric mean** formula calculates the average return over time assuming all earnings remain invested. In other words, the geometric mean calculates the compound annual return, not the simple average return.[2] The geometric mean is equivalent to the internal rate of return (IRR) for a set of cash flows. An important assumption of this model is that all cash flows that occur during the term of the investment are reinvested at the geometric rate of return. This assumption is the same for IRR, which is discussed later in this chapter.

The more volatile Fund A has a lower geometric (or compound) return than Fund B, even though it has the same arithmetic average return. Note that when the annual returns do not vary from year to year, the geometric mean is equal to the arithmetic mean, as demonstrated by the returns for Fund B. Other than when returns are the same every year, the arithmetic return is always greater than the geometric return.

Quick Quiz 3.1

1. The holding period return is not as accurate a measure of return as the IRR.
   a. True
   b. False
2. The internal rate of return and the geometric return are equivalent.
   a. True
   b. False

False, True.

The example above highlights several important points:

- The greater the volatility of investment returns, the lower the compound return over time as compared with the arithmetic average return. This concept explains why variability of returns is an essential factor in almost all investment valuation methods.
- The maximum geometric mean return is the arithmetic mean, which only occurs when there is zero variability, as with Fund B.

Example 3.8

Sondra invested in a volatile mutual fund exactly two years ago. She doubled her investment during the first year (+100%) but lost one-half of the investment during the second year (-50%). A quick arithmetic mean calculation shows that Sondra averaged a 25% return over that two-year period.

On further examination, however, Sondra is very likely not satisfied with the change in the value of her investment. Suppose that Sondra originally invested \$10,000, which then increased in value to \$20,000 after one year (+100%). During the following year, Sondra lost one-half of the investment, which returned her value to the original \$10,000 (-50%).

The arithmetic return is accurately computed as 25% {(100% - 50%)÷2}, but clearly Sondra's wealth did not increase by 25%. In fact, her value did not change over the two-year period.

To reflect the explicit change in wealth, the geometric return should be computed, which turns out to be 0%.

$$(2.0 \times 0.50)^{1/2} - 1 = 0\%$$

While the arithmetic return equals 25%, the geometric return is a much more accurate 0%, entirely because the arithmetic return ignores the compounding effect, making the

2. A compound annual return is equal to the internal rate of return for a set of cash flows. For example, assume Cliff invests \$100 and has total funds of \$121 at the end of the second year. His compound return equals 10%: $\$100 \times 1.10^2 = \$121$. However, just because his annual compound return equals 10% does not mean that he earned 10% each year. He might have earned 0% in year 1 and 21% in year 2.

geometric return much a much more reasonable measure of performance. Note the arithmetic return becomes much less accurate as the level of volatility in the investment increases.

Example 3.9

Theo purchased a ten-year zero-coupon bond for \$610 and held it until it matured (\$1,000). The performance of this investment can be measured three ways:

The ten-year Holding Period Return is 63.9%, computed as (\$1,000 - \$610)÷\$610.

The Arithmetic Return is 6.39%, computed as 63.9%÷10.

The Geometric Return is 5.07%, computed as $(1.639)^{0.10} - 1$.

Note the arithmetic return is simply the average annual holding period return. The geometric return can also be computed using the TVM calculation:

PV	-610
N	10
PMT	0
FV	1,000
i	5.067%

Exhibit 3.2 | Rules to Remember

- The geometric mean is always less than the arithmetic mean, except when the returns for each period are equal, in which case the geometric and arithmetic means are equal.
- The difference between the arithmetic mean and the geometric mean increases with the amount of variation in the returns.
- The geometric mean is the same as the IRR or annual compound return, as illustrated in the example above.

Internal Rate of Return

The **internal rate of return (IRR)** is the earnings rate of a series of cash inflows and outflows over a period of time assuming all earnings are reinvested. The IRR is one of the most common measures of return. It is calculated as the discount rate that equates the present value of an investment's future cash flows to the cost of making the investment today. In other words, it is the discount rate that results in a net present value (NPV) of zero. Consider the basic present value model:

$$CF_0 = \frac{CF_1}{(1 + IRR)^1} + \frac{CF_2}{(1 + IRR)^2} + \ldots + \frac{CF_n}{(1 + IRR)^n}$$

CF_0 = the initial cost of the investment
CF_n = the cash flow that occurs at period n
IRR = the discount rate that makes the equation hold

Example 3.10

Vanessa has purchased an investment security from a well-known insurance company for $5,000. The security is tailored to fit Vanessa's future cash flow needs and provide her with a minimal rate of return of 8.0%. She will receive annual end-of-year payments according to the following schedule:

Year 1	Year 2	Year 3	Year 4	Year 5
$750	$1,000	$1,240	$1,500	$2,000

The internal rate of return on this investment security is 8.0%, which can be computed using the following cash flows in a financial calculator:

CF_0	-5,000
CF_1	750
CF_2	1,000
CF_3	1,240
CF_4	1,500
CF_5	2,000
Solve for IRR	7.999%

When each of the security's future cash flows is discounted at the IRR of 8.0%, their present value is $5,000. This is equal to the initial investment Vanessa made, hence the NPV of the investment is zero.

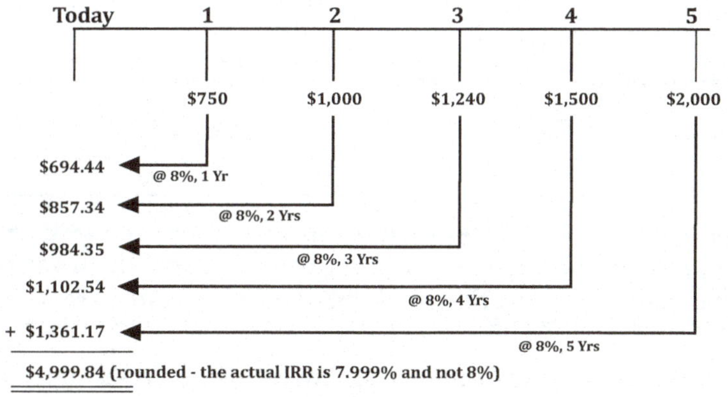

An important assumption of the IRR model is that all cash flows are reinvested at the IRR. While this assumption is not an unreasonable one, it is still limiting in that investors are assumed to have equally profitable investment opportunities when future cash flows are realized. In addition, those profitable opportunities are assumed to have similar risk levels.

Example 3.11

Walter purchases a five-year bond that pays a 10% annual coupon. He pays par value of the bond as its yield to maturity is also 10%. To test the IRR assumption that cash flows are reinvested at the internal rate of return, compute the terminal value of the bond. One mathematical note is that the yield on the bond is actually an internal rate of return. Therefore, the terminal value of the bond will simply be the future value of the reinvested coupons plus the par value received at maturity. The following table shows the terminal value assuming various reinvestment rates according to the following steps:

Step 1: Compute terminal value at 10% reinvestment rate assumption.

PV	=	0
PMT	=	100
N	=	5
i	=	10
FV	=	610.51

Step 2: Add the par value of the bond to obtain terminal value.

$610.51 + $1,000 = $1,610.51

Step 3: Solve for IRR using cash flow buttons.

CF_0	=	-1,000
CF_1	=	0
N_j	=	4
CF_2	=	1,610.51
IRR	=	10%

Reinvestment Assumption	10%	20%	0%
Future Value of Coupons	$610.51	$744.16	$500.00
Terminal Value	$1,610.51	$1,744.16	$1,500.00
IRR	10.00%	11.77%	8.45%

The IRR method of performance evaluation is an excellent one if the investor can reinvest the cash flows at the internal rate of return. If not, then other tools are more helpful.

The IRR can be used to analyze the performance of investments. It is most appropriate when an investment manager has full discretion over the portfolio, as it takes into account the timing of cash inflows and withdrawals. Because of its focus on cashflows, it is also known as the **dollar-weighted return**, or money-weighted return.

The **time-weighted return**, on the other hand uses only the returns generated by the investment, and ignores the timing of the investor's cash flows. It is calculated as the geometric mean of the holding period return for each time-period and hence is based on the investment's capital gain (or loss) and cash distributions (for example dividends or coupon payments) for each period. It is a more appropriate measure of return when the investor has discretion over the timing of cash flows, as it measures the return generated per dollar invested in the fund and is unaffected by the timing of investments and withdrawals.

Example 3.12

Assume that Skylar makes the following investments in Fly Cheap Airlines stock.

Date	Share Price	Transaction
01/01/Year 1	$12	Purchases 100 shares.
01/01/Year 2	$11	Receives a dividend of $1 per share and buys another 100 shares immediately after receiving the dividend.
12/31/Year 2	$20	Sells all 200 shares.

The cash flows associated with this investment are:

Period	Cash Flows	Calculations	Use Uneven Cash Flow Keys:
0	($1,200)	A cash outflow of $12 times 100 shares.	CF_0 = -1,200 CF_1 = -1,000 CF_2 = 4,000 Solve for IRR = 45.6%
1	($1,000)	A cash inflow of $100 from the dividend minus the $1,100 outflow from purchasing the additional shares.	
2	$4,000	A cash inflow of $20 times 200 shares sold.	

The dollar-weighted return (IRR) is 45.6%.[3] Note that this represents the *return to the investor* since it takes into consideration all of the transactions initiated by Skylar, the investor. To distinguish the *return of the security* from those driven by the investor's timing decisions, we use the time-weighted return, and the relevant cash flows are:

Period	Price/ Dividends	Calculations
0	Price $12	The initial price of the investment is $12. The number of shares purchased is irrelevant for the time-weighted return.
1	Price $11 Dividend $1	The share price fell to $11 over the period, but also paid a $1 dividend.
2	Price $20	The share price rose from $11 to $20 during the 2nd period.

Skylar held the investment for two periods. The time-weighted return in the geometric mean of the holding period return for each period.

The holding period return for period 1 = ($11- $12 + $1) ÷ $12 = 0.0%

The holding period return for period 2 = ($20 -$11 + $0) ÷ $11= 81.8%

The time-weighted return = $(1.00 \times 1.818)^{1/2} - 1 = 34.8\%$

Note that in this example the dollar-weighted return is higher than the time-weighted return. This is because Skylar had more dollars invested in the period two than period one. As the dollar-weighted return takes this into account, it will be weighted towards that

3. The IRR in this problem is solved using the uneven cash flow keys on a financial calculator. This topic is discussed in detail in Money Education's *Fundamentals of Financial Planning* text book Chapter 7: Time Value of Money.

period, which happened to have a higher return. The time-weighted return, however, ignores how much she invested and is just a geometric average of the two HPRs. If the holding period for period two had been lower than that for period one, the dollar-weighted return would have been dragged down below the time-weighted return.

Effective Annual Rate of Return

Interest rates are typically stated annually, regardless of the frequency with which payments are made. Nominal rates are annualized simply, meaning they ignore the impact of compounding. A security that paid interest of two percent every quarter, for example, would have a nominal rate of eight percent (simply four x 2%). The effective annual rate, however, takes the impact of compounding into account. When compounding occurs more frequently than annually, the effective annual rate of interest is higher than the nominal rate. The more frequent the compounding, the higher the effective rate. For example, a nominal rate of eight percent compounded quarterly results in an effective annual rate of 8.24 percent, and compounded monthly results in an effective annual rate of 8.30 percent.

The effective annual rate can be calculated using the formula:

$$\mathbf{EAR} = \left(\mathbf{1} + \frac{\mathbf{i}}{\mathbf{n}}\right)^{\mathbf{n}} - \mathbf{1}$$

i = nominal rate
n = number of compounding periods

Example 3.13

Finn invests in a bank CD with a nominal yield of 7% compounded weekly. Finn's effective annual rate of return is:

$$\text{EAR} = \left(1 + \frac{0.07}{52}\right)^{52} - 1 = 0.0725 = 7.25\%$$

Alternatively, the effective annual rate can be calculated using a financial calculator by determining the FV of $1 invested.

Step 1: Determine the future value of $1 invested:

PV	=	-1
PMT	=	0
N	=	52
i	=	7/52
FV	=	1.0725

Step 2: Solve for i:

PV	=	-1
PMT	=	0
N	=	1
FV	=	1.0725
i	=	7.25

Bond Equivalent Yield (BEY)

BEY is a method of determining the yield for a bond sold at a discount based on the current price and the remaining days until maturity. The formula for BEY is as follows:

$$\text{BEY} = \frac{\text{Par Value} - \text{Price}}{\text{Price}} \times \frac{365}{d}$$

Par value = the face value of the bond, generally $1,000
Price = the price of the bond in the market or the price paid for the bond
365 = the number of days in a year
d = the number of days until maturity

Example 3.14

Assume Lydia buys a bond with 192 days until maturity for $950. The BEY equals 10% as follows:

$$\text{BEY} = \frac{\$1{,}000 - \$950}{\$950} \times \frac{365}{192} = 10\%$$

The BEY is often used to compare yields for bonds with different maturities.

Investors should also be aware that T-bill bid and ask quotes are calculated using a 360-day convention. Thus, most financial reporting sources also provide the *bond equivalent yield* for T-bills, converting the quoted yield to one using a 365-day year for comparability purposes.

Weighted-Average Return

Investors generally hold well-diversified portfolios, which makes the weighted average return on the entire portfolio quite useful. The equation is shown as:

$$R_w = \sum_{i=1}^{N} R_i W_i$$

R_w = weighted average return
R_i = return for investment i
W_i = weight for investment i as a percentage of the portfolio
N = number of investments

Quick Quiz 3.2

1. Assume an investor has 80% invested in Stock A and 20% invested in Stock B. If the returns for Stocks A and B are 7% and 4%, respectively, then the weighted average return equals 6.4%.
   a. True
   b. False
2. The arithmetic return will generally be greater than the geometric return.
   a. True
   b. False
3. The nominal return is net of inflation.
   a. True
   b. False

True, True, False.

The overall weighted average return is computed by:

1. summing the market value of the investments,
2. multiplying the percent return of each security by the individual market value to obtain the individual dollar returns, which are then added together, and
3. dividing the total dollar return by the total market value.

Example 3.15

Assume Marie has $3,000 invested in Apple, $3,000 invested in Google, and $4,000 invested in Amazon. Apple, Google and Amazon have earned returns of 20%, 25%, and 50%, respectively, this past year. Below is how the weighted average return is calculated.

Security	Market Value	Security Return	Dollar Return
Apple	$3,000	20%	$600
Google	$3,000	25%	$750
Amazon	$4,000	50%	$2,000
Total	$10,000		$3,350
Weighted Average Return = 33.5% ($3,350 / $10,000)			

As an alternative approach, which provides the same result, the portfolio weightings can be multiplied by the security returns, as follows:

Security	Portfolio Weighting	Security Return	Weighted Return
Apple	30%	20%	6.0
Google	30%	25%	7.5
Amazon	40%	50%	20.0
Weighted Average Return	100%		33.5%

This same methodology can be used to calculate the weighted average beta of a portfolio, as well as the weighted average duration for a portfolio of bonds (as long as the individual durations are known).[4] Duration is discussed more thoroughly in Chapter 8.

After-Tax Return

Investors in high marginal income tax brackets should evaluate investments based on their after-tax returns to determine whether any of the investment options have some sort of tax advantage or penalty. The income from municipal bonds, for instance, is exempt from federal income tax and may be exempt from state income tax if the bond is issued by the state of the investor's residence. As a result, the income is worth more on an after-tax basis when compared with investments yielding fully taxable income. Any capital gain on the sale of municipal bonds, however, is subject to federal income tax (and state tax if applicable). The simplest method of adjusting taxable returns for varying tax effects is to calculate the after-tax rate of return:

$$\text{After-Tax Return} = \text{Realized Taxable Return} \times (1 - \text{Marginal Income Tax Rate})$$

Realized taxable return = the return from the investment without considering income tax
Marginal income tax rate = the tax rate percentage applied to incremental taxable income

4. It should be noted that the standard deviation of a portfolio is not equal to the weighted average of the standard deviations of the components of the portfolio, unless the correlation between components is equal to 1.0. This concept is discussed later in the chapter.

Example 3.16

Hank compares a corporate bond with a municipal bond. The corporate offers a yield to maturity of 5% while the muni has a yield of just 4%. At first glance, it appears the corporate offers a superior investment. Hank, however, pays taxes at a marginal rate of 30% and will receive tax benefits from the muni bond, but not from the corporate. In fact, the after-tax return of the corporate will be only 3.5% or [5% x (1 - 30%)], making it less attractive than the muni.

The equation can be rearranged or solved for the tax rate that equates two bonds subject to different tax treatment. Consider the following example.

Example 3.17

Jesse is considering a corporate bond yielding 8.0% and a municipal bond yielding 5.6%. The tax rate at which Jesse would be indifferent between the two bonds is 30%, as follows:

$$8.0\% \times (1 - \text{Tax rate}) = 5.6\%$$
$$1 - \text{Tax rate} = 70\%$$
$$\text{Tax rate} = 30\%$$

If Jesse's marginal rate is less than 30%, then he would be better off from an after-tax perspective with the corporate bond. If his tax rate is in excess of 30%, then he would be better off with the municipal bond. This topic is further discussed in Chapter 8 (Fixed Income Securities - Analysis).

Real Return

Ben Franklin said, "In this world nothing can be said to be certain, except death and taxes." His quote should be updated to include inflation. The rate of inflation may vary from year to year, but most professionals typically use a long-term average of two to three percent for investment planning forecasts. Inflation of two or three percent per annum makes a considerable difference over long periods of time when attempting to accumulate wealth for a specific reason, such as retirement needs or the purchase of a retirement home. The long-term inflation rate in the US over the last century is approximately three percent, but soared to over eight percent in 2022.

Based on the "Rule of 72" and an inflation rate of three percent, the cost of goods and services doubles approximately every 24 years.[5] That means that if a gallon of milk costs $6 at age 50, it will cost approximately $12 at age 74.

Therefore, when attempting to estimate the future purchasing power (investment returns net of inflation) for an investment, the inflation-adjusted, or **real rate of return** formula is appropriate:

$$\textbf{Real Rate of Return} = \left[\frac{1 + R_n}{1 + i} - 1\right]$$

R_n = nominal rate of return

i = inflation

5. The rule of 72 is a method of estimating the number of years required for an investment to double in value at a given annual rate of return. The rule states that 72 is divided by the rate of return (expressed as a percentage) with the result equaling the number of years required for the investment to double. Annual inflation of 4% should result in the cost of goods to double in 18 years according to the rule of 72 (72 ÷ 4% = 18).

It should be noted that simply subtracting the inflation rate from the nominal rate does not provide the correct answer, and it also slightly underestimates the effect of inflation. Over a long period of time, this error will dramatically overstate the future value of savings. The inflation adjusted return is always slightly less than subtracting the inflation rate from the nominal rate.

Example 3.18

Jane's retirement fund is expected to earn a nominal rate of 9%, and the inflation rate is estimated at 3%, so the real rate of return is:

$$\text{Real Rate of Return} = \frac{(1 + 0.09)}{(1 + 0.03)} - 1 = 0.058252 \text{ or } 5.8252\%$$

Example 3.19

Carmela, who is 30 years old, just started a retirement plan and is saving $12,000 a year. She might be surprised to learn that the savings will accumulate to over $2 million at age 65 assuming a 9% return (see column A). If she were earning $100,000 a year right now, then she would be even more impressed to learn that the fund might generate well over $250,000 a year for about 30 years during retirement. She might be thinking "Wow, that is a huge raise! I can go buy that boat I've been wanting."

Below are the calculations based on nominal dollars and real dollars. Notice that in terms of nominal dollars, her savings accumulates to more than $2.5 million, while in real dollars it is just under $1.3 million, assuming inflation of 3%.

	(A) Nominal Dollars	(B) Real Dollars
PV	-	-
PMT	$12,000	$12,000
N	35	35
i	9.0000%	5.8252%
FV (Savings at 65)	($2,588,529.06)	($1,288,485.77)
PV	($2,588,529.06)	($1,288,485.77)
N	30	30
i	9.00%	5.8252%
FV	-	-
PMT (Annuity)	$251,957.97	$91,863.43

The future value is equivalent to an annuity of $251,957.97 in nominal dollars, but only $91,863 in real dollars. It should be obvious that inflation has an enormous effect on the real value of Carmela's future savings. The real return of 5.8252% is calculated as [(1.09 ÷ 1.03)-1].

Example 3.20

Willow just purchased an investment for $1,000 that will earn 10% for the next ten years. Inflation is expected to be 3% over the same time period. The future value of the investment equals $2,593.74 [$1,000 x $(1.10)^{10}$].

However, after inflation, the value of the investment in ten years will only be $1,929.99. This amount is found using the inflation adjusted discount rate of 6.79612%. [(1.10 ÷ 1.03)-1]

To prove this, we can inflate the $1,000 by 3% for ten years, which equals $1,343.92. This amount represents 34.39% more in ten years than compared with today. Thus, if we divide $2,593.74 by 1.3439, it results in $1,929.99.

Real rates of return are used in calculations designed to determine savings necessary for funding retirement or children's education. Real returns are also found in other calculations that require the incorporation of two different types of rates, such as an earnings rate and an inflation rate.

METHODS OF ASSESSING RISK

As mentioned earlier, investors expect to be rewarded for accepting higher levels of risk through higher investment returns. Some very conservative investors may seek to avoid all risks by putting their money in an extremely safe investment such as government-backed, short-term T-bills or FDIC insured bank CDs. However, this strategy absolutely does not eliminate all risks. While it is true that this approach protects the investor from the dramatic volatility of the stock market, the portfolio is still subject to purchasing power risk. The simple truth is that investors cannot avoid all risks. Investors must choose the risks to which they are willing to be subjected.

Key Concepts

1. Understand that risk is unavoidable.
2. Differentiate between systematic and unsystematic risks.
3. Understand the various types of risks to which an investment might be subject.

So, the question isn't, "How can I avoid risk?" Instead, investors should ask, "How can I structure my portfolio to balance the types of risk to which I am exposed for the best long-term result?" Only after investors understand that risk is never completely avoidable can they begin the process of focusing on the categories and degrees of risk that they are most comfortable accepting.

Broadly speaking, there are two categories of risk. **Systematic risks** are driven by macroeconomic factors that affect nearly all investments. Investors generally cannot avoid these types of risks by diversifying their portfolios. **Unsystematic risks** affect some individual types of investments while not necessarily affecting others. Typically, the effects of unsystematic risks can be eliminated through proper diversification strategies. The following exhibit shows examples of both systematic and unsystematic risks.

Exhibit 3.3 | Systematic and Unsystematic Risks

Systematic Risks	Unsystematic Risks
Market Risk Interest Rate Risk Purchasing Power Risk Exchange Rate Risk Reinvestment Rate Risk	Accounting Risk Business Risk Country (Political) Risk Default (Credit) Risk Executive Risk Financial Risk Government Risk

The combination of systematic and unsystematic risk is called **total risk** or **portfolio risk** and can be reduced through diversification. Diversification is accomplished by adding additional securities to a portfolio, which reduces unsystematic risk. As the number of securities increases, total risk approximates systematic risk as unsystematic risk is eliminated. However, no amount of diversification can reduce or eliminate systematic risk.

Exhibit 3.4 | Total Risk

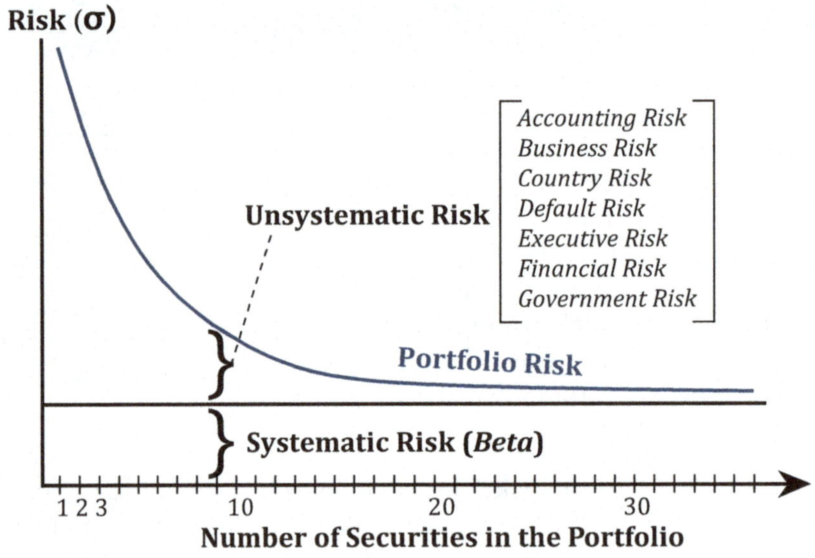

The chart above illustrates the concept that the amount of unsystematic risk can be greatly reduced with the addition of a relatively small number of securities (randomly selected). Investors do not have to buy the entire market to reduce most of the diversifiable risk.

Total risk, which includes both systematic risk and unsystematic risk, is measured by **standard deviation**. Portfolios that are sufficiently diversified consist predominantly of systematic risk. With these portfolios, risk can be measured using beta. Standard deviation and beta will be discussed later in this chapter.

Types of Systematic Risks

Market Risk

Market risk represents the tendency for changes in the market to influence the prices of equities. When the market is increasing, most stocks increase in value. Conversely, stocks tend to fall with declines in the market. Often, a move in the market is prefaced by some change in the economic environment.

The equity market is quite volatile, and its value may change significantly within short periods of time. This may occur without any direct cause. When the change occurs, especially on the downside, equities tend to decline in value.

When the market changes direction, it does so rapidly, and the changes are often significant. These ups and downs in the market cause the value of investor's portfolios to change dramatically within short periods of time. While the annual compound rate of return for the S&P 500 over a 50-year period is approximately 10 percent per year, there have been decades with a compound rate of return in excess of 20 percent and decades with relatively no return. This risk is not related to the quality of the companies within the market, but rather the overall market at the time.

During the late 1990s, most stock investments, even many of those involving poorly managed companies, performed quite well. As John F. Kennedy said in 1963, "a rising tide lifts all boats."

In the early 2000s, the opposite was true, even for well-managed firms. However, well-managed firms suffer less than poorly managed firms when markets are unfavorable. Consider Warren Buffet's famous saying, "You only find out who is swimming naked when the tide goes out." In other words, when the market goes down, those who have been poorly managing firms are exposed.

The concept of market risk also applies to other financial investments, such as bonds and real estate, but of course, the markets differ from the equity markets. Consider the housing crisis that occurred in 2008 discussed in Case Study 3.1. The housing crisis was not a random event, but rather a series of policies and decisions, combined with unreasonable expectations that resulted in massive global losses.

Interest Rate Risk

The variability in asset prices due to changes in interest rates or yields defines interest rate risk and includes changes in inflation and changes in default risk levels and includes changes to both inflation and the yield to maturity in the bond market.

Interest rate risk is one of the major risks affecting fixed-income securities and bond portfolios. As interest rates increase, it decreases the value of fixed-income securities. The reason for this decline is that the cash flows of the bond or bond portfolio are generally fixed and these cash flows have to be discounted at a higher rate. This process results in a lower current value for the bond. An alternative way of thinking is that newer bonds are issued with higher rates of interest than older bonds and are thus more valuable.

Equity securities also are impacted by changes in interest rates. When interest rates increase, there is negative pressure on the value of common stocks, and when interest rates decrease, stocks tend to increase in value. There are three primary reasons for this relationship: increased borrowing costs, attractiveness of alternative investments, and the valuation of securities.

Most companies use debt as a means of financing capital expansion and acquisition of assets. The cost of debt is interest payments. When interest rates increase, the cost of future borrowing increases. This increased borrowing cost can cause earnings to decline. When earnings decrease, the value of the company is reduced. Therefore, changes in interest rates have a direct impact on the cost of borrowing and on the earnings of a firm.

Valuing securities involves discounting future cash flows to today. As interest rates increase, the discount rate used to value a security must also increase. Because an increase in the discount rate results in a lower valuation, stocks generally decline when interest rates increase.

Example 3.21

Paulie just purchased a 30-year, zero-coupon bond yielding 7%. He paid $126.93 for the bond. The price assumes semi-annual compounding. To illustrate the impact of changes in interest rates, assume that yields for this type of bond move from 7% to 6% or 8%:

Yields = 6%		Yields = 8%	
FV	= 1,000	FV	= 1,000
N*	= 60	N*	= 60*
i*	= 3%	i*	= 4%
PMT	= 0	PMT	= 0
PV	= (169.73)	PV	= (95.06)

** For semi-annual bonds, the term (N) is doubled and the YTM (i) is divided by 2.*

If yields for these types of bonds increase to 8%, then the value of the bond will decrease by more than 25% from $126.93 to $95.06. If yields for these types of bonds decrease to 6%, then the value of the bond will increase to $169.73, which represents an increase of more than 33%.

The extreme volatility in this example is attributable to the long maturity and lack of coupon payments for this bond. These concepts are discussed in more depth under the topic of duration.

CASE STUDY 3.1

"From 1978 to 2007, the amount of debt held by the financial sector soared from $3 trillion to $36 trillion, more than doubling as a share of gross domestic product. The very nature of many Wall Street firms changed—from relatively staid private partnerships to publicly traded corporations taking greater and more diverse kinds of risks. By 2005, the 10 largest U.S. commercial banks held 55% of the industry's assets, more than double the level held in 1990. On the eve of the crisis in 2006, financial sector profits constituted 27% of all corporate profits in the United States, up from 15% in 1980. Understanding this transformation has been critical to the Commission's analysis (of the housing crisis)."[1]

The housing crisis that began in 2008 led to a financial crisis in the United States and a recession that had not fully recovered by the end of 2014. Numerous causes contributed to this crisis, including government policy, regulator failure, Federal Reserve policy, leverage ratios of Freddie Mac and Fannie Mae, lack of standards by financial institutions and other reasons.

However, one of the overarching contributors to this debacle was the government's misguided housing policy combined with unchecked greed and reckless policies of financial institutions. This backdrop allowed irresponsible borrowers to obtain money that could never be paid back.

The fact that high-risk mortgages formed almost half of all U.S. mortgages by the middle of 2007 was not a chance event, nor did it just happen that banks and other mortgage originators decided on their own to offer easy credit terms to potential homebuyers beginning in the 1990s.

In 1992, Congress enacted Title XIII of the Housing and Community Development Act of 1992 (the GSE Act), legislation intended to give low-and-moderate-income borrowers better access to mortgage credit through Fannie Mae and Freddie Mac. This effort, probably stimulated by a desire to increase home ownership, ultimately became a set of regulations that required Fannie and Freddie to reduce the mortgage underwriting standards they used when acquiring loans from originators. The focus on loans for "low-and-moderate-income persons" gradually resulted in a deterioration of lending standards.

HUD (The U.S. Department of Housing and Urban Development) actually established and administered what was in effect a mortgage quota system in which a certain percentage of all Fannie and Freddie mortgage purchases had to be loans to low-and-moderate-income (LMI) borrowers-defined as persons with income at or below the median income in a particular area or to borrowers living in certain low-income communities. The LMI goal was initially 30%, but it increased over the years and by 2008 was 56%. Over this same time, underwriting standards declined to provide more access to mortgages for the LMI borrowers.

The government's efforts to increase home ownership through the LMI goals succeeded. Home ownership rates in the U.S. increased from approximately 64% in 1994 (where it had been for 30 years) to over 69% in 2004. Almost everyone in and out of government was pleased with the achievement of this long-term housing policy goal, until the true costs became clear when the housing bubble collapsed in 2007.

1. The Financial Crisis Inquiry Commission's report entitled, CONCLUSIONS OF THE FINANCIAL CRISIS INQUIRY COMMISSION, February 25, 2011.

CASE STUDY 3.1 (CONTINUED)

Much of the crisis centered around subprime mortgages, which are loans that are made to people who are more likely to have difficulty paying back the borrowed money due to their financial situations. These loans generally have higher interest rates and less favorable terms compared to conventional loans in order to account for the increase in risk. These subprime mortgages were then sold as mortgage-backed securities.

Combined with the riskiness of the subprime mortgage market was the level of risk undertaken by individual homeowners as well as financial institutions. For example, it was common for people to purchase homes with very little equity and with monthly payments that resulted in extremely high housing ratios - certainly much higher than the 28% and 36% ratios banks regularly use when making loans to home buyers.

As most know, Bear Stearns went bankrupt as a result of the subprime mortgage crisis and due to its leverage. At the end of 2007, Bear Stearns had $11.8 billion in equity and $383.6 billion in liabilities and was borrowing as much as $70 billion in the overnight market. As with any leveraged asset, small changes in the value of the asset have a significant impact on the value of the firm. As the value of the assets dropped, Bear Stearns became insolvent.

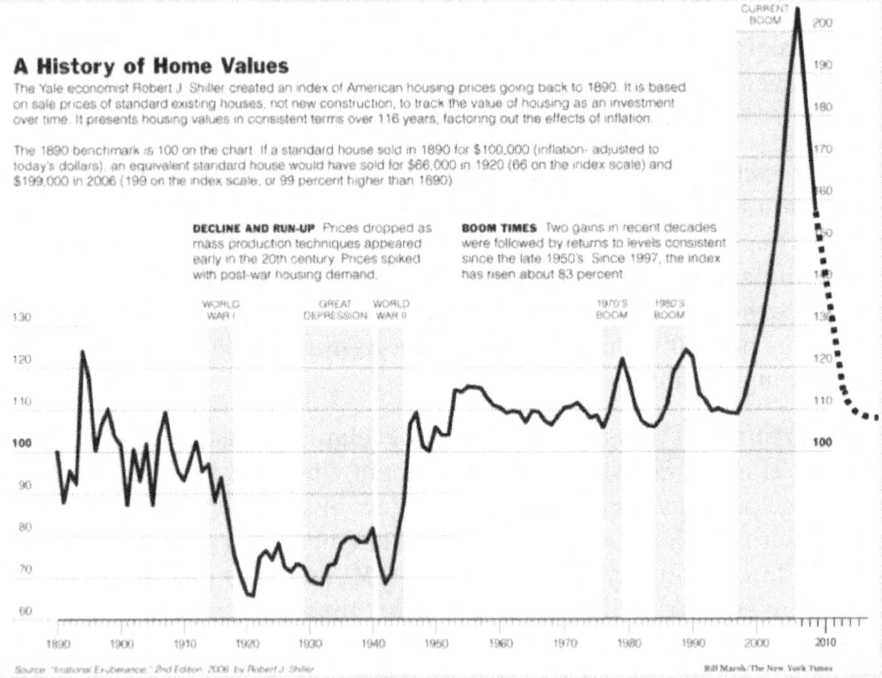

Lenders created mortgage products that were, for a lack of a better term, ludicrous. For example, Fannie Mae actually approved what was referred to as a "Ninja" product. Ninja stands for no income, no job, and no assets. Assuming the value of the property increases, this might have worked out, but it did not.

Because of this housing bubble, property values plummeted, the equity market plummeted precipitously, and many Americans suffered tremendous financial losses. While there were devastating losses throughout America, the equity markets eventually rebounded to set new records in 2016 through 2019.

Purchasing Power Risk

The variability in asset values due to changes in inflation defines purchasing power risk.

As inflation rises, the value of an investment's purchasing power declines. Bonds and other fixed investments have the greatest level of purchasing power risk because the ending valuation is a fixed amount. The exception is for bonds that are inflation-adjusted, such as TIPS (Treasury Inflation-Protected Securities). Investments such as real estate have a tendency to offer some level of protection through more rapid appreciation during times of higher inflation.

As discussed earlier in the chapter, with inflation of three percent, the cost of goods and services doubles approximately every 24 years. If an investor needs $30,000 to cover her expenses at age 50, then she will need $60,000 at age 74. She is subject to this risk regardless of the investment choices or other choices she makes.

Exchange Rate Risk

The uncertainty of returns in foreign investments due to changes in the value of a foreign currency relative to the valuation of the investor's domestic currency is referred to as **exchange rate risk**. A foreign investment is not only subject to the inherent risk of the investment, but also the risk that the foreign currency will weaken relative to the domestic currency, decreasing the gains (or increasing the losses) from the investment.

International equity managers attempt to avoid such drastic results from the change in currency rates by hedging against currency fluctuations. Forward or futures contracts may be used as hedging devices against currency risk. However, academic studies have shown that over long periods of time, hedged and unhedged portfolios perform similarly.

An investment in a foreign country may perform well in the local currency, but if the dollar strengthens compared to that currency, the investment's return may be significantly reduced. Although it is arguable that investments within one country are not subject to exchange rate risk, it is hard to construct a well-diversified portfolio in the U.S. and still avoid indirect exchange rate risk. Few of the companies in the S&P 500, for example, earn all of their income within the United States.

Can the risk of adverse currency movements be reasonably predicted? Certainly not with precision, but most analysts use some variation of a 'market basket' of goods priced in various currencies to attempt to identify unusually over-and under-valued currencies. The Economist magazine uses only one item in its market basket: McDonald's Big Mac.[6]

A more direct illustration involves purchasing the stock of a foreign corporation, or perhaps an international mutual fund. In either case, changes in the exchange rate among the world's currencies can affect the investor's total return.

6. Source: http://www.economist.com/content/big-mac-index

Example 3.22

Vito invests USD 50,000 in Vodafone, a UK corporation trading at £20 on the London stock exchange. If the conversion rate for pounds to dollars were £1 to USD 1.80, Vito's U.S. dollars would equal £27,778 (USD 50,000 / 1.8), and he would be able to purchase 1,389 shares. Vodafone does well, and the share price rises to £25. If Vito sells the stock for £34,725 and converts the pounds into dollars after the dollar has strengthened to £1 to USD 1.50, he will receive USD 52,087.50 (£34,725 * 1.5).

$$\textbf{Total Return} = (1 + \textbf{NR}) \times \frac{\textbf{EOP Value of Foreign Currency}}{\textbf{BOP Value of Foreign Currency}} - 1$$

NR = Nominal return
EOP = End of period value of foreign currency in U.S. dollars
BOP = Beginning of period value of foreign currency in U.S. dollars

$$\text{Nominal Return} = \frac{£25 - £20}{£20} = 0.25 = 25\%$$

$$\text{Total Return} = 1.25 \times \frac{\$1.50}{\$1.80} - 1 = 4.2\%$$

Thus, his total gain is only 4.2%: the net result of a 25% gain on the investment as Vodafone rose from £20 to £25, offset by a loss of 16.67% ($1.80 - $1.50 / $1.80) from the change in the currency.

CASE STUDY 3.2

The "Big Mac index was invented by The Economist in 1986 as a lighthearted guide to whether currencies are at their 'correct' level. It is based on the theory of purchasing-power parity (PPP), the notion that in the long run, exchange rates should move towards the rate that would equalize the prices of an identical basket of goods and services (in this case, a burger) in any two countries."[1] While this is not a perfect "crystal ball" into the over and undervaluation of currencies, it does provide a useful tool to understand how currencies can influence the value or price of goods and assets.

1. http://www.economist.com/content/big-mac-index

Example 3.23

Adriana invests USD 50,000 in a Japan-based energy company. At an exchange rate of ¥120/USD, Adriana's international investment would be ¥6,000,000. She wants to sell her position and convert back to U.S. dollars. Consider Scenarios A and B.

Scenario A: After one year, the energy company's shares are worth ¥8,450,000, but the exchange rate has changed to ¥130/USD.

> The capital gain in the Japanese market is approximately 41%:
> (8,450,000/6,000,000) – 1 = 0.4083.
> Adriana's U.S. dollar capital gain is only 30%:
> 8,450,000/¥130/USD = USD 65,000
> (65,000/50,000) – 1 = 0.30 = 30%

Scenario B: After one year, the energy company's shares are worth ¥8,450,000, but the exchange rate has changed to ¥110/USD.

> The capital gain in the Japanese market remains 41%: (8,450,000/6,000,000) – 1 = 0.4083.
>
> Adriana's U.S. dollar capital gain is now 54%:
>
> ¥8,450,000/¥110/USD = USD 76,818
>
> (76,818/50,000) – 1 = 0.536

In the first case, the Japanese yen has depreciated. This U.S. dollar appreciation hurts the U.S. investor because the foreign currency is exchanged for fewer U.S. dollars. In the second case, the Japanese yen has appreciated. This U.S. dollar depreciation magnifies the Japanese capital gain. The change in the Japanese yen caused the USD capital gain to increase from 30% to 54%.

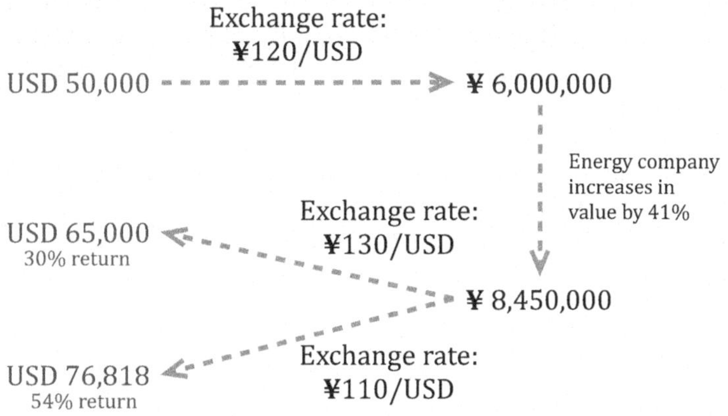

The formula from the previous example can be used for these two scenarios. However, the exchange rate is not in dollars. The easy way to resolve this is to take the reciprocal of EOP/BOP, which is the same as using (1+NR) x BOP/EOP. For example, the return for Scenario A = (¥8,450/¥6,000) x (¥120/¥130) - 1 = 0.30 = 30%.

As more companies compete globally, there is more exchange risk exposure than in the past. Exchange rate risk is a form of systematic risk, so it cannot be completely eliminated through diversification. However, exposure to exchange rate risk can be mitigated by investing in more foreign countries, as opposed to fewer foreign countries.

Reinvestment Rate Risk

The variability in the terminal value of an asset due to changes in the rate of return on reinvestment opportunities defines reinvestment rate risk.

In the discussion of the internal rate of return earlier in the chapter, we noted that the calculation assumes that any interim cash flows will be reinvested at the same rate as provided by the investment. The risk that the investor is unable to reinvest cash flows at the IRR is **reinvestment rate risk**.

The same situation applies to a dividend paying stock: will the investor be able to earn the same return on the dividends received as he expects for the stock? The answer is 'yes' if the company offers a dividend reinvestment plan or DRIP, but otherwise it may be unlikely. Investors in growth stocks paying no dividends, and investors owning zero-coupon bonds need not be concerned with reinvestment rate risk since they do not receive any periodic cash flows from those investments. Investment companies, such as mutual funds, automatically reinvest distributions, which can help to minimize reinvestment rate risk for investors.

Types of Unsystematic Risks

Unlike the broad pervasive types of risk discussed above, unsystematic risks tend to affect specific industries, companies or countries. This is why unsystematic risks are sometimes referred to as unique or firm-specific risks. What may be a calamity for the auto industry-a rapid rise in interest rates-may provide increased earnings for the banking industry. Fortunately, investors can substantially reduce or eliminate the consequences of unsystematic risk through the process of portfolio diversification.

Example 3.24

Rose Oil Company's operating cash flows depend heavily on the price of oil. If the price of oil is relatively high, such as it was in 2008 when it peaked around $145 per barrel, Rose will greatly benefit. If the price of oil falls substantially to a price that is less than the cost of extraction, it will greatly suffer.

National Trucking Company, however, has the opposite exposure from Rose Oil. When the price of oil is high, National Trucking experiences a decline in operating cash flows unless it can pass along the entire cost of oil to its customers. When the price of oil is low, National Trucking benefits greatly.

Example 3.25

Assume an investor owns only one company's stock, perhaps a small growth stock, with an enviable track record of rapidly rising profits and steady sales growth, founded by a highly-regarded CEO. On days the overall market rises, we would expect this stock to rise. When the market declines, we would expect this stock to decline. So clearly, some part of the investment's variability is driven by the market - the systematic risk. All financial investments are subject to this systematic type of risk.

Assume the market rose five percent one day, but the CEO sold all her stock and resigned shortly before the SEC announced an investigation into the company's accounting practices. The stock would in all likelihood decline substantially, despite the overall market rise. This rapid decline in stock price resulting from an SEC investigation is an example of the unique or unsystematic risk associated with individual investments. This form of risk can be mitigated through a program of portfolio diversification.

If the investor in the above example had put half her money in just one additional stock, it easily could have reduced the loss by 50 percent. As **Exhibit 3.4** implies, by adding additional randomly chosen companies, the total portfolio risk is greatly reduced.

Note that, as in **Exhibit 3.4**, the total portfolio risk is measured by standard deviation (σ), which captures the total variability of the investments. **Beta** (β), on the other hand, measures only the variation related to the systematic risk (see bottom of **Exhibit 3.4**). For that reason, beta is not generally recommended as an appropriate measure of investment risk unless the investment will become part of a well-diversified portfolio. These common measures of risk (standard deviation and beta) and their calculations are discussed in the next section of this chapter.

There are numerous kinds of risks that fall into the unsystematic category, but most fit within the following areas: accounting risk, business risk, country risk, default risk, executive risk, financial risk, and government risk.

Accounting Risk

Accountants prepare financial statements to provide information about a business to its managers and shareholders. These financial statements should be prepared according to standards that ensure that they adequately reflect the firm's income and financial position. However, in some cases accounting standards may be interpreted in more than one way. Since these financial statements may incorporate thousands or millions of transactions and may require the application of complicated accounting standards, they are subject to error. For these reasons, accounting statements may be partially misleading. Finally, financial statements may include fraud, which may also be misleading, depending on the size and scope of the fraud. **Accounting risk** is the risk that financial statements do not accurately reflect the financial condition of a business due to fraud or error.

Many equity analysts use the financial statements as a starting point when calculating the value of a company. For example, when using a free cash flow valuation model, the financial statements can be used to calculate free cash flow (essentially the cash flow available for distribution to shareholders) and its predicted growth. When financial statements do not accurately reflect the firm's financial results, it results in an improper valuation of the company. Once these accounting errors are discovered and reported to the shareholders, the value of the stock adjusts rapidly to reflect the new information. Generally, inaccurate accounting statements overstate the income or financial position of a company and, when discovered, result in a rapid decline in the value of the stock. Consider the cases of WorldCom and Waste Management as examples.

CASE STUDY 3.3

WORLDCOM

The Securities and Exchange Commission (SEC) accused WorldCom of fraudulently overstating its income before income taxes and minority interests by approximately $3.055 billion in 2001 and $797 million during the first quarter of 2002.

Starting at least in 2001, WorldCom engaged in an improper accounting scheme intended to manipulate its earnings to keep them in line with Wall Street's expectations, and to support WorldCom's stock price. One of WorldCom's major operating expenses was its so-called "line costs." In general, "line costs" represent fees WorldCom paid to third-party telecommunication network providers for the right to access the third parties' networks.

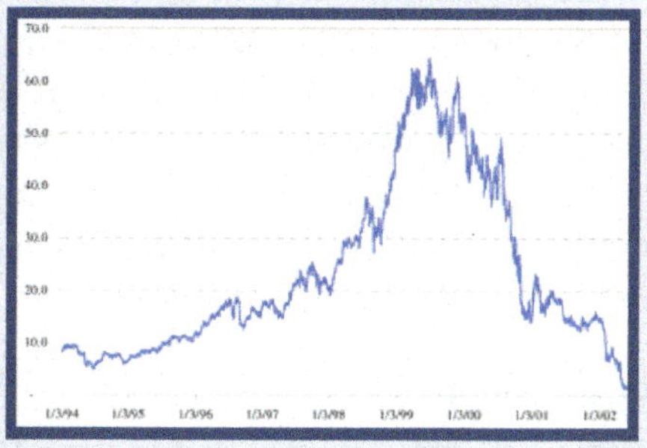

Under GAAP, these fees must be expensed and may not be capitalized. Nevertheless, beginning at least as early as the first quarter of 2001, WorldCom's senior management improperly directed the transfer of line costs to WorldCom's capital accounts, rather than expense them, in amounts sufficient to keep WorldCom's earnings in line with the analysts' earnings expectations. In doing so, WorldCom materially understated its expenses and materially overstated its earnings, thereby defrauding investors.

CASE STUDY 3.4

WASTE MANAGEMENT

In March 2002, the SEC said this was "one of the most egregious accounting frauds" they had ever seen. In the Waste Management fraud case, the defendants, who were company executives, fraudulently manipulated the company's financial results to meet predetermined earnings targets between 1992 and 1997.

The company's revenues were not growing fast enough to meet these targets, so defendants improperly eliminated and deferred current period expenses to inflate earnings. They employed a multitude of improper accounting practices to achieve this objective. Among other things, the defendants delayed or even avoided depreciation expenses on their garbage trucks by both assigning unsupported and inflated salvage values and extending their useful lives.

Depreciation is an accounting concept that allows for the purchase price of an asset to be expensed over the asset's useful life. For example, a piece of equipment might be depreciated over five years. However, if the equipment has a salvage value, then it would reduce the amount that would be expensed over the period. For example, a truck that cost $60,000 and had a useful life of 5 years would result in a (straight line) depreciation charge of $12,000 per year (60,000/5). However, if the life was extended to 10 years, and a salvage value of $20,000 applied, the annual expense would be only $4,000 per year (as the salvage value is deducted from the cost before calculating depreciation expense).

The defendants' scheme eventually unraveled. In mid-July 1997, a new CEO ordered a review of the company's accounting practices. That review ultimately led to the restatement of the company's financial statements for 1992 through the third quarter of 1997. When the company filed its restated financial statements in February 1998, the company acknowledged that it had misstated its pre-tax earnings by approximately $1.7 billion. At the time, the restatement was the largest in corporate history.

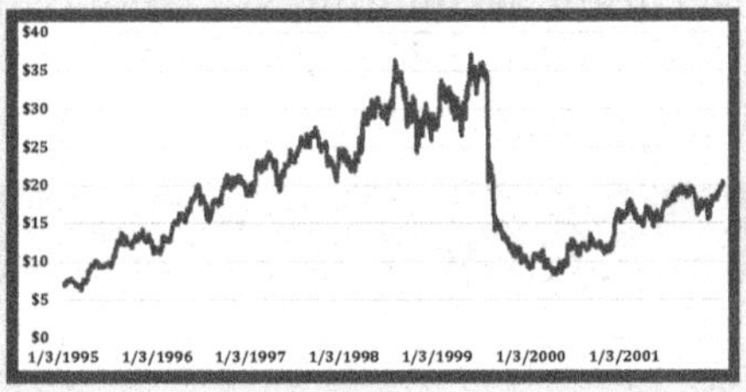

These two case studies illustrate accounting risk, in addition to other risks. As a result of fraudulent corporate reporting cases similar to these, on July 30, 2002, President Bush signed into law the Sarbanes-Oxley Act, which he characterized as "the most far reaching reform of American business practices since the time of Franklin Delano Roosevelt." The Act mandated a number of reforms to enhance corporate responsibility, enhance financial disclosures and combat corporate and accounting fraud, and created the "Public Company Accounting Oversight Board," also known as the PCAOB, to oversee the activities of the auditing profession.

Business Risk

Business risk is the riskiness of a specific business, which includes the speculative nature of the business, the management of the business, and the philosophy of the business. Different types of businesses have different levels of risk. Business risk can also be thought of as the uncertainty of operating income.

All businesses are subject to a variety of risks. Some businesses are naturally riskier than others. For example, biomedical research tends to be more speculative than consumer products. Owners, employees and customers of businesses often believe that their companies can never go out of business. However, all businesses face risks that are known as well as unknown. As a result, they must adapt or perish. Below are a few examples of famous companies that are surprisingly out of business today.

Example 3.26
Arthur Anderson (1913 – 2002)

This firm was one of the "Big Five" accounting firms in the world with a prestigious reputation. In 2002, the firm voluntarily surrendered its licenses to practice as CPAs after being found guilty of criminal charges in the Enron scandal. As a result of the criminal conviction, 85,000 jobs were lost. Paradoxically, the Supreme Court overturned Anderson's criminal charges in 2005. However, by that time, the damage to the firm's reputation was too much for the company to survive. Most of its assets were sold to competing accounting firms.

Example 3.27
Standard Oil (1870-1911)

Standard Oil was established by John D. Rockefeller in 1870 and was the dominant oil company in the world until 1911. At that time, the Supreme Court ruled it was an illegal monopoly and ordered it to be dissolved and split into 34 companies. The breakup of Standard Oil turned into what is now Chevron, Exxon Mobil and ConocoPhillips.

Example 3.28
Woolworth's (1879 – 1997)

Woolworth's became the model for five-and-dime stores throughout the U.S. and grew to be one of the largest retail chains in the U.S. It continued its growth by acquisition and expansion, buying such specialty shops as Kinney Shoes, Champs Sports, and Foot Locker. However, rapid expansion proved to be the company's undoing. By 1997 all Woolworth's shops had closed, and in 2001, the company changed its name to Foot Locker.

Example 3.29
Blockbuster (1985 – 2011)

At its peak, Blockbuster operated 9,000 stores and had 60,000 employees. Blockbuster was the largest home movie and video game rental service. However, it lost tremendous revenue and market share from rivals Netflix and Redbox. The company did not adapt quickly enough to changing technology and customer demands. Interestingly enough, it had the opportunity to purchase Netflix in 2000 for $50 million. It would later attempt to change strategy by competing with Netflix. DISH Network purchased it at auction in 2011. As of 2014, all corporate stores had closed, but there were remaining franchise locations continuing to operate.

There are many other very famous companies that have gone out of business, including MCI WorldCom, Pan Am Airlines, Eastern Airlines, and Enron.

Government-regulated monopolies, such as utility companies, are normally regarded as fairly low-risk industries since the rates they are allowed to charge customers are designed to provide a relatively steady return on assets. That remains a reasonable expectation as long as the regulatory atmosphere does not change rapidly. Highly cyclical businesses, such as auto manufacturing and housing, entail greater risk that the expected cash flows will not materialize in the quantity or time frame originally anticipated. Because the nature of these risks revolve around the types of plant and equipment needed to operate in the industry chosen, they are sometimes referred to as being related to the asset side of the balance sheet. In other words, business risk deals with the nature of the assets and industry in which the business operates.

Financial Risk

A firm is exposed to **financial risk** when it uses debt to finance its operations. The more debt a firm takes on, i.e., the higher its leverage, the more cash flow it must commit to servicing that debt. This fixed commitment increases the variability of returns to shareholders, and hence the likelihood of the firm being unable to meet those commitments resulting in financial distress, and in a worst-case scenario, bankruptcy.

Immediately following the 9/11 terrorist attacks, the airline industry suffered tremendous losses. However, Delta and American Airlines weathered the immediate difficulties better than some other large airlines, in part because they had lower debt-to equity ratios. As financial risk is a direct result of the firm's capital structure, it is related to the liability side of the balance sheet.

Example 3.30

ALLEQ Inc., and LEVG Inc., both produced Earnings Before Interest and Tax (EBIT) in the previous year of $120 million and paid tax at a rate of 20%. ALLEQ has no debt on its balance sheet, while LEVG has $500 million in debt with an associated interest cost of $40 million per year.

In the current year, both firms experienced a drop in EBIT of 20%. Their net income figures for the previous and current year are as follows:

	ALLEQ		LEVG	
	Previous Year	**Current Year**	**Previous Year**	**Current Year**
	$m	$m	$m	$m
EBIT	120.0	96.0	120.0	96.0
Interest	-	-	(40.0)	(40.0)
Profit Before Tax	120.0	96.0	80.0	56.0
Tax Payable (20%)	(24.0)	(19.2)	(16.0)	(11.2)
Net Income	96.0	76.8	64.0	44.8

The 20% drop in EBIT resulted in a 20% drop in Net Income for ALLEQ (from $96m to $76.8m). However, due to the financial risk resulting from LEVG's debt, it experienced a 30% drop in Net Income (from $64.0m to $44.8m) given the same drop in EBIT. The dramatically larger fall is due to the interest cost of $40 million which LEVG must still meet.

The reason a firm might choose to take on financial risk is that debt is cheaper than equity, and financing assets through debt rather than equity increases return on equity (ROE), a key profitability measure used by investors analyzing a firm's performance.

Example 3.31

ALLEQ Inc., and LEVG Inc., both earned EBIT in the previous year of $120 million, but ALLEQ has no debt on its balance sheet, while LEVG has $500 million in debt with a total interest cost of $40 million per year. Both firms pay tax at 20%.

ALLEQ has total equity of $900 million whilst LEVG has total equity of $400 million.

	ALLEQ	LEVG
	$m	$m
Equity	900.0	400.0
Debt	-	500.0
Total Capital	900.0	900.0
EBIT	120.0	120.0
Interest	-	(40.0)
Profit Before Tax	120.0	80.0
Tax Payable (20%)	(24.0)	(16.0)
Net Income	96.0	64.0
Return on Capital Employed (ROCE)	13.3%	13.3%
Return on Equity (ROE)	10.7%	16.0%

Both firms had the same EBIT for the year, and the same amount of total capital. As a result, they both had the same return on total capital employed (EBIT/Total Capital) of 13.3% (120/900). However, as debt makes up the majority of LEVG's total capital, it's return on equity is significantly higher than that of the all equity financed ALLEQ, at 16.0% compared to only 10.7%.

LEVG has achieved a higher ROE by taking on the financial risk associated with increased leverage. Note that ALLEQ could choose to do the same by replacing some of its equity with debt. For this reason, it is generally believed that firms should use at least some debt in their capital structure. During economic expansions, as demonstrated above, leverage can dramatically improve ROE. However, during recessions the debt service payments can become a serious drain on profitability and potentially lead to a firm's failure.

Default (Credit) Risk

At the extreme, high levels of financial risk can result in the company's inability to meet current debt and interest obligations, causing creditors to foreclose on any pledged assets. If the value of the assets is less than the debt owed, the creditors suffer default risk. Note that only *creditors* of the company encounter default risk. The common stockholders generally have no legal expectation of fixed payments, and therefore, the company cannot default even if bankruptcy occurs.

Investors in U.S. Government securities are free of default risk since they are backed by the full faith and credit of the federal government, and the U.S. government has never defaulted on its debt obligations. Most investors rely upon the major rating agencies (Moody's and Standard & Poor's) to assess the probability of default by corporations and municipalities. See Chapter 7 for a more detailed discussion of default risk as it relates to debt securities.

Country, Political, and Regulatory Risk

All investments are subject to the political and economic conditions of the country in which the issuer operates. The U.S. is considered to have one of the lowest country risks because its government and economic systems are relatively stable. This characteristic explains why investors move funds into U.S. investments during global crises.

In 2015, Venezuela's socialist government took over control of Dia Dia, a supermarket chain, which was founded in 2005 by José Vicente Aguerrevere and Lucia Brower. Despite the fact that Dia Dia was privately owned, the government seized the business and its assets.[7] Clearly, this type of political climate causes investors to look to other countries with less country risk.

Executive Risk

Businesses tend to be run by individuals with substantial amounts of confidence. Some of them have agendas and egos. Generally, these do not create problems as the economic incentives of business managers are aligned with those of the shareholders of companies. However, sometimes the economic incentives, as well as shareholder pressure and expectations, provide the foundation for executives to manipulate earnings or engage in fraud that robs shareholders of wealth.

In other cases, executives simply make poor decisions. Consider the case of Blockbuster's opportunity to purchase Netflix. There was no element of fraud in that case. It was simply a decision that turned out to be the beginning of the end for Blockbuster.

The unsystematic risks discussed in this section can be summarized as:
A – Accounting risk (misstatements and/or inaccuracies in accounting information)
B – Business risk (risks unique to a specific business or industry)
C – Country risk (risks unique to a specific country or region)
D – Default risk (likelihood of not repaying debt)
E – Executive risk (risk that an executive will make decisions that negatively impact a business)
F – Financial risk (the amount of leverage within the business capital structure)

It is important to understand that these unsystematic risks can be largely eliminated through diversification. In other words, the exposure to any one unsystematic risk should be relatively low if the portfolio includes a sufficient number of securities.

Quick Quiz 3.3

1. Systematic risks can be eliminated through diversification.
   a. True
   b. False
2. A company that has debt as part of its capital structure will have magnified returns and losses due to financial leverage.
   a. True
   b. False
3. Default risk applies equally to equities and fixed-income securities.
   a. True
   b. False

False, True, False.

7. http://www.reuters.com/article/us-venezuela-supermarket-idUSKBN0LN1NV20150219

Liquidity and Marketability

As the old adage goes, it is easier to get in to trouble than to get out of trouble. In many ways, the same can be said of investments. It is often easier to buy than it is to sell. The concepts of liquidity and marketability are extremely important when choosing appropriate investments. **Marketability** is an investor's ability to easily find a market to sell an investment. **Liquidity** is the ability to quickly sell an asset at its fair market price. Consider the example of real estate. It may be fairly easy to buy a home. However, to sell the home, it may take significantly more time to sell the house depending on the market for real estate. In addition, the owner may have to suffer a price concession to get the house sold. Real estate is marketable, as there is a ready market for real estate. However, it is not liquid. Real estate tends to be marketable, especially in desirable geographic locations. Real estate, however, may or may not be highly liquid. For example, some properties remain on the market for years because a willing buyer cannot be found. Other pieces of property, however, may sell within a few hours. It is important for risk managers to assess both the marketability and liquidity of an investment. In contrast, there is a ready market for Treasury bills with a significant daily volume of trades or transactions. Treasury bills are both marketable and liquid. Cash is thought of as the most liquid asset.

> **Quick Quiz 3.4**
>
> 1. Poor decisions by a CEO are an example of executive risk.
>   a. True
>   b. False
> 2. Purchasing power risk is a systematic risk.
>   a. True
>   b. False
>
> True, True.

Example 3.32

A private equity fund has a minimum investment requirement of $5 million. The managers of the fund use the capital to invest in small privately held companies. The funds are specifically dedicated to create growth opportunities for each company. The fund also has a lock up period for investors of 180 days.

The combination of a substantial minimum investment, a six-month lock up period, and the investment in private firms reduces the marketability and liquidity of this private equity fund.

METHODS OF MEASURING RISK

Many investors do not distinguish between risk and uncertainty, but there are subtle and crucial differences. In the traditional sense, risk is typically characterized as an event or outcome that has a measurable probability. For example, given a set of historical prices, an investor can estimate the probability of a specific loss. Uncertainty, on the other hand, occurs when the probability of an event cannot be defined or reasonably estimated. Examples of uncertainty include the inability to determine which financial institutions will avoid bankruptcy after an accounting scandal within the industry.

Risk in the investments world is frequently defined as the variability in returns. Managing risk involves three steps:

1. Identify an investment objective, such as savings for retirement or purchasing a vacation house.
2. Determine if there is a risk-free or low risk option to achieve the objective.
3. Identify which portfolio of risky securities will provide enough compensation to achieve the goal.

Ultimately, the investor will select a portfolio that has a level of variability that is comfortable. Investors use risk measures such as standard deviation and beta to estimate future variability in their portfolios.

Managing uncertainty is much less scientific, and relies heavily on behavioral defenses against potential losses. For example, an entrepreneur with only one product line will very likely be exposed to a great deal of uncertainty surrounding cash flows over the next period, with the uncertainty being a function of market and economic conditions as well as the quality of the product. The entrepreneur will make decisions under this level of uncertainty by making judgments based on experience, intuition, and gut feelings. In many cases, investors manage uncertainty by minimizing their maximum level of regret.

Key Concepts

1. Understand standard deviation and beta, two common methods used to measure risk.
2. Explain how standard deviation can be used to determine the probability that an investment will generate a negative return.
3. Explain the limitations in using beta by understanding how beta is determined.
4. Understand correlation, R^2, covariance and semi-variance.

Standard Deviation (σ)

Standard deviation is a measure of dispersion, a measure of the distance between data points and their mean, and a measure of risk. For example, the standard deviation of stock returns for a bio tech company is likely to be relatively high, an indication that the dispersion of returns is likely to be substantial. One obvious conclusion would be that the risk of investing in this firm is also relatively high. On the other hand, the standard deviation of a public utility company is likely to be relatively low, indicating minimal dispersion and relatively stable returns.

More specifically, standard deviation is a measure of total risk or total variability. The two components of standard deviation are systematic risk and unsystematic risk. The implication is that standard deviation is a function of both economic variables and variables that are unique to each firm. When combined with other statistical tools, standard deviation can be helpful in estimating probabilities of investment outcomes.

Standard deviations can be computed over population data or sample data. The following steps are necessary for the calculation of standard deviation:

1. Compute the mean of the data set.
2. Subtract the mean from each possible outcome and square the difference.
3. Sum the squared differences.
4. Divide the sum by the total number of observations (for population SD) or the total number of observations less 1 (for the sample SD).
5. Take the square root of the result.

The formula is written as follows:

Population Standard Deviation of Historical Returns

$$\sigma_r = \sqrt{\frac{\sum_{t=1}^{n} (r_t - \bar{\mu})^2}{n}}$$

r_t = historical returns
$\bar{\mu}$ = arithmetic mean of historical returns
n = number of returns used
σ_r = standard deviation

The above formula is the formula for the standard deviation of a population. In other words, it includes all outcomes. However, statisticians modify the formula when dealing with samples of data used to estimate the standard deviation of the population. The formula for the standard deviation of a sample is as follows:

Sample Standard Deviation of Historical Returns

$$s = \sqrt{\frac{\sum_{t=1}^{n} (r_t - \bar{r})^2}{n-1}}$$

r_t = historical returns
$\bar{r}$ = sample mean of historical returns
n = number of returns used
s = sample standard deviation

Notice that the only difference between the two formulas is that the denominator is reduced by one when determining the standard deviation of the sample of outcomes. Generally, with investments, the standard deviation of a sample of returns is used and not the standard deviation of the population.

Example 3.33

Assume that CJD Investments had annual returns of 10%, 15% and 20% over the last three years. Below is the calculation of the standard deviation of returns.

A	B	C	D
	Return	**Difference from Mean**	**Difference Squared**
Year1	10%	(5%)	25
Year 2	15%	0%	0
Year 3	20%	5%	25
Arithmetic Mean Return	**15%**	**Total**	**50**
		(n-1 years):	2
		Sample Variance (s^2):	25
		Sample Standard Deviation(s):	**5%**

As this very simple example illustrates, the calculation for determining standard deviation is fairly straightforward.

- First, from (Column B), calculate the arithmetic mean return.
- Second (Column C), calculate the difference between each year's actual return and the arithmetic mean.
- Next (Column D), square the differences and divide the sum by the number of years minus one to determine the variance (discussed in the following section).
- Finally, take the square root of the variance to determine the standard deviation.

Example 3.34

Ronda, CFP, is evaluating the performance of the hedge fund, CDJ Investments. Ronda collected return data and computes the standard deviation of CDJ summarized in the following table (the average return is 17%).

	Annual Holding Period Return	Difference from Mean	Difference Squared
Year 1	22%	5%	25%
Year 2	34%	17%	289%
Year 2	(16%)	-33%	1,089%
Year 4	28%	11%	121%
Arithmetic Mean Return	**17%**	**Total**	**1,524**
		Divide by (n-1) years:	3
		Sample variance (s^2):	508
		Standard Deviation (s):	**22.54%**

Using the 4 years of data collected by Schultz, the sample standard deviation of returns is 22.54%. This means that, on average, the fund return is 22.54% from its mean of 17%.

All financial calculators provide a shortcut for this calculation, which makes it a bit more efficient. Check the calculator manual for instructions on using the 'Σ+' and 'S' keys.[8]

While understanding the calculation is important, being able to interpret the standard deviation is more important. The following exhibit helps to explain the relationship between standard deviation and probabilities of outcomes.

Exhibit 3.5 | Normal Distribution

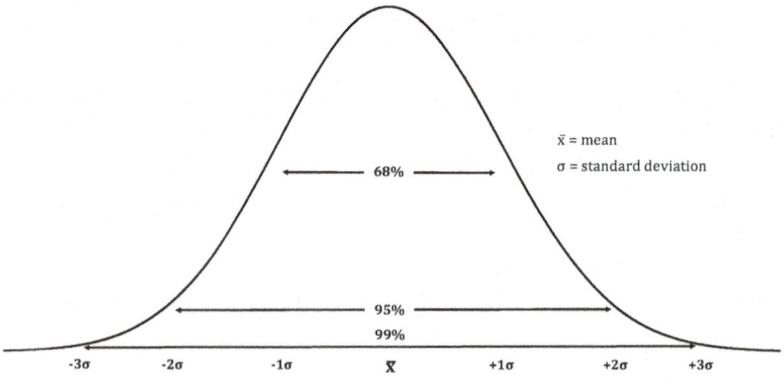

Normal Distribution: 68-95-99

Approximately 68% of returns fall within ±1σ of the mean

Approximately 95% of returns fall within ±2σ of the mean

Approximately 99% of returns fall within ±3σ of the mean

8. These keys can be found on the HP12C calculator. Other financial calculators have the same functionality, but key notations may be different.

The curve in **Exhibit 3.5** shows the bell-shaped curve of a normal distribution. The vertical axis represents the probability of observing an outcome and the horizontal axis represents the possible outcomes. The curve peaks at the mean of the distribution, as the mean is the most likely outcome to be observed. Observing values further and further away from the mean becomes less and less likely, hence the curve slopes down towards the tails. The likelihood of seeing observations far out in the tails becomes extremely low, but never quite hits zero.

The most useful property of the normal distribution is that the percentage of observations within a given number of standard deviations of the mean is known. For example: Approximately 68% of outcomes fall within one standard deviation (both above and below) of the mean.

- Approximately 95% of outcomes fall within two standard deviations (both above and below) of the mean.
- Approximately 99% of outcomes fall within three standard deviations (both above and below) of the mean.

Example 3.35

Assume the return for Meyer, Inc. is normally distributed with a mean of 18% and a standard deviation of 6%. The area under the bell curve represents 100% of all outcomes. However, we can also make the following statements:

1. 68% of the outcomes fall between 12% and 24%	The mean of 18% + 6% = 24% The mean of 18% - 6% = 12%
2. 95% of the outcomes fall between 6% and 30%	The mean of 18% + 12% = 30% The mean of 18% - 12% = 6%
3. 99% of the outcomes fall between 0% and 36%	The mean of 18% + 18% = 36% The mean of 18% - 18% = 0%

These assumptions allows investors to estimate possible outcomes. For example:

- The probability of a negative return equals 0.5%.
- The probability of a return greater than 36% is 0.5%.
- The probability of a return less than 12% is 16%.

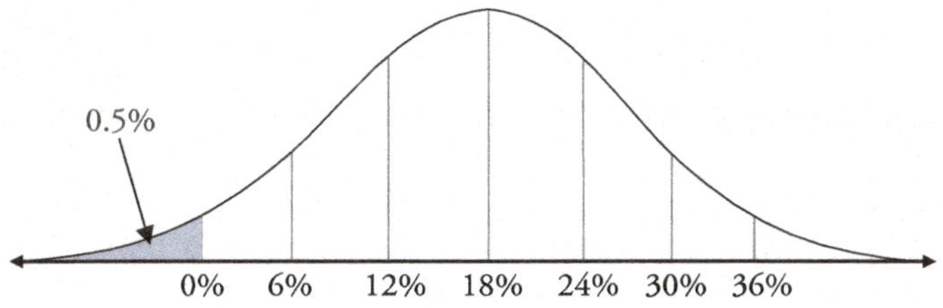

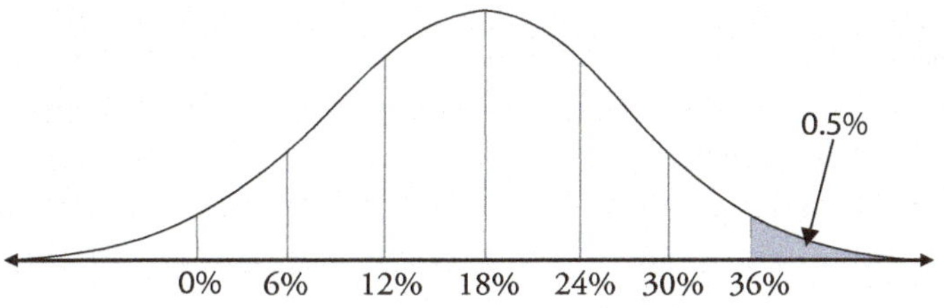

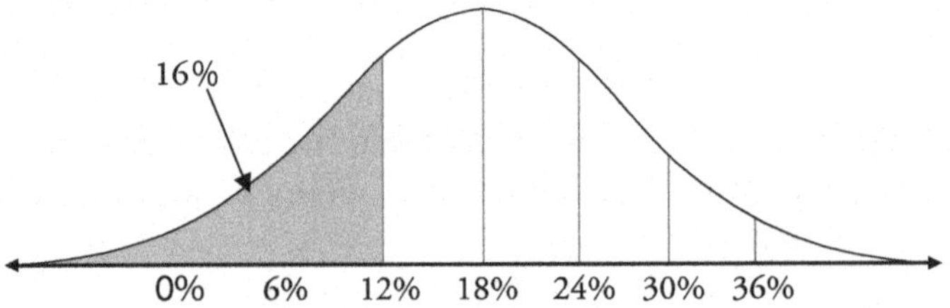

Example 3.36

Assuming an investment's returns are normally distributed with a mean of 25% and a standard deviation of 5%, what is the probability this investment will earn *less than 15%*?

The area in between two σs above and below the mean represents 95%. Thus, the area to the left of the second standard deviation below the mean is half of the remaining 5%, or 2.5%. There is also a 2.5% probability this investment will earn greater than 35% (the area to the right of two σs above the mean).

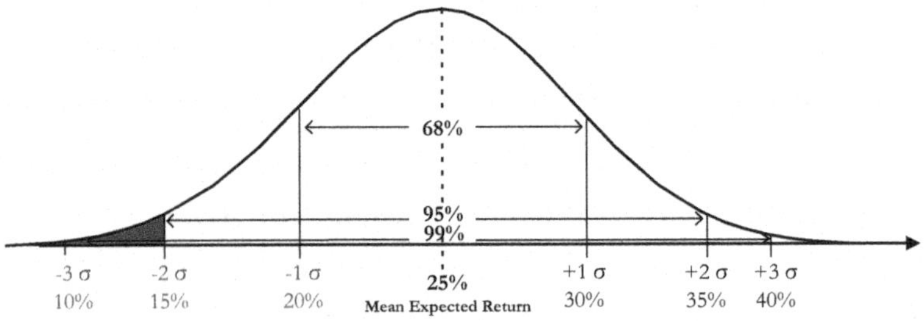

Exhibit 3.6 | What Does the Distribution of Large Caps Look Like?

Large U.S. stocks over an extended time frame have earned an average return of about 10%, with a standard deviation of approximately 20%.

Thus, using the method illustrated above, there is a 68% probability that in any given year returns from this type of investment might be as low as -10% or as high as +30%.

At a 95% probability, the range of equity returns expands from -30% to +50%.

Since small cap stocks have a higher standard deviation, the range of returns expands even further, which should make sense for a riskier investment category.

In the process of calculating standard deviation, another measure of variability was calculated. This other measure is called variance. The interpretation of the variance is not as meaningful as the standard deviation, and it is used much less often as a result. The **variance** is simply the standard deviation squared, and investments with high variances tend to be riskier than those with lower variances.

Skewness and Kurtosis

The discussion of standard deviation focused on normal distributions. However, not all data sets are normally distributed around the mean. Some data sets may be skewed to the right or left or have more or less kurtosis than other data sets.

Skewness is a measure of the lack of symmetry for a data set. A distribution is symmetric if it appears the same to the left and right of the center point.

Consider the following graphs of the distribution of heights of three groups of people. The first chart is positively skewed, the second chart is symmetric, and the third is negatively skewed. With a normal distribution, the mean, median, and mode are generally equal. However, that is not the case with distributions that are skewed. A positively skewed distribution has a mean greater than the median, which is greater than the mode.[9]

Exhibit 3.7 | Skewness

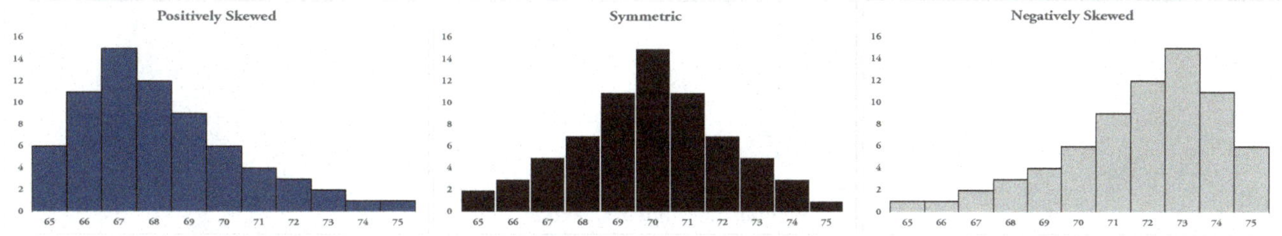

The following exhibit illustrates the relationship between the mean, median, and mode for positively and negatively skewed distributions.

Exhibit 3.8 | Skewness and Measures of Central Tendency

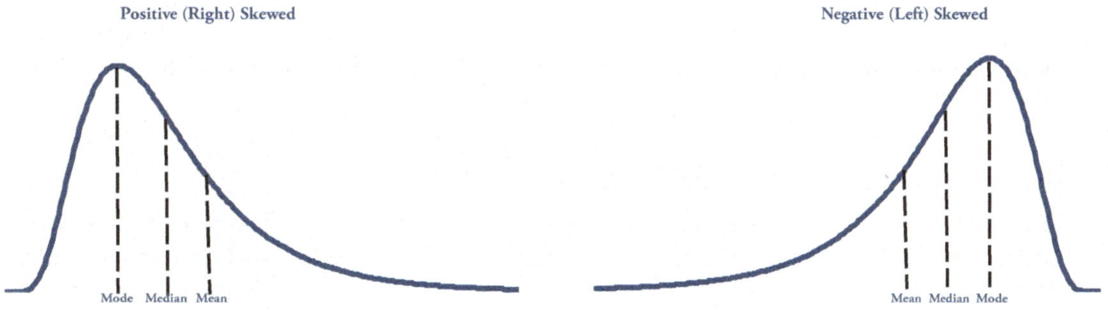

9. The mean is the arithmetic average, the median is the number that is in the middle if all of the numbers are listed in order from smallest to largest, and the mode is the number that is repeated most often.

Kurtosis is a measure of whether the data are heavy-tailed or light-tailed relative to a normal distribution. Distributions with high kurtosis tend to have heavy tails, or outliers. Data sets with low kurtosis tend to have light tails, or lack of outliers. A uniform distribution is the extreme case, one in which the probability for all outcomes are the same. A distribution that is more peaked (more kurtosis) than normal is **leptokurtic**, while a distribution that is less peaked (less kurtosis) is **platykurtic**.

Exhibit 3.9 | Kurtosis

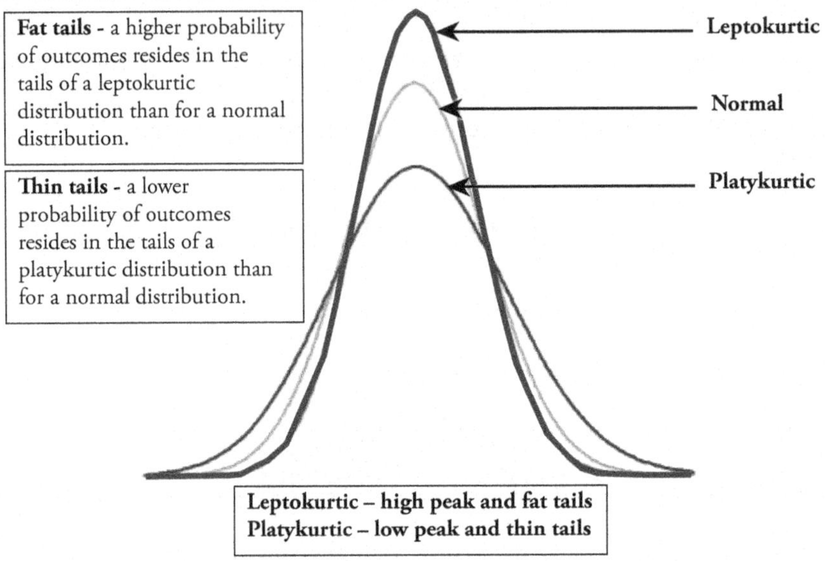

Treasury securities have returns with low kurtosis, compared with returns from small cap equities, which vary significantly more than returns from Treasuries.

Normal distributions of outcomes are helpful because we understand the probabilities of certain outcomes, such as 50 percent of outcomes will be above the mean or that 95 percent of all outcomes will fall within two standard deviations. However, not all distributions are normally distributed. As a result, the same conclusions cannot be drawn in the same way from a skewed distribution or one that is leptokurtic or platykurtic.

Low-Probability, High-Impact Economic Events

For centuries it was believed that all swans were white. However, in the 17th century it was discovered that black swans do exist, thus revealing that shortcomings in knowledge and imagination often lead to flawed conclusions and decisions. Low probability, high impact economic events are sometimes referred to as "black swan" events. They are events that might cause investment returns to fall into the "tails" (the 0.5% probability range) of our normal distribution graphic, such as unidentified market bubbles, war, extreme natural disasters, or pandemic biological disasters.

Retroactive studies of black swan events imply that many catastrophic economic events should have been predictable but were not predicted due to design flaws in the models. Rational investors make decisions based on available information and personal perspective, often omitting the possibility of these low-probability high-impact events. Other investors may consider the possibility of such an event, but ultimately determine that the likelihood is so low that it is unreasonably costly to protect against it. These random and unexpected events, however, can have a devastating impact on clients' financial plans. Examples of black swan events include:

- the 2008 financial crisis,
- the 2003 SARS outbreak,
- the events of September 11, 2011,
- the severe drought in East Africa in 2011, and
- the COVID pandemic that began in 2019.

These events are difficult to predict, challenging to manage, and sometimes impossible to overcome.

Clients with long-term time horizons are likely to experience one or more black swan events at some point during their lives, which will have a significant impact on their investment portfolio. While portfolio diversification can help to reduce the impact of these events to a certain extent, investment managers may also set measurable parameters for unexpected and unusually extreme market volatility that trigger temporary portfolio adjustments or initiate the use of hedging strategies to mitigate the downside effects of these occurrences, while being cautious to avoid overreaction. Communication with clients is critical in that regard.

Studies of low probability, high impact events indicate that people have a tendency to deal with them poorly, whether the event is a natural disaster, war, premature death, living to age 100+, or a market bubble. Many people have a tendency to be overconfident or feel that these things will never be a problem for them, then overreact when such an event does occur, and seek protection from the possibility that the event will occur again. Often, though, within a few years the recency of the event has diminished, and protection no longer seems worth the cost. In cases where these psychological biases are causing clients to make irrational and potentially costly decisions, it is up to the investment adviser to serve as the voice of reason and remind clients to continue following sound investment and financial planning principles. These principles include maintaining adequate insurance coverages, maintaining appropriate levels of emergency funds (highly liquid investments), diversifying investment portfolios, using hedging strategies to protect investment portfolios, and maintaining a long-term outlook. A review of the Investment Policy Statement (Chapter 18) is often helpful for reminding clients of the long-term goals and objectives for the portfolio.

Quick Quiz 3.5

1. Beta and standard deviation are interchangeable under all conditions.
   a. True
   b. False
2. Assume a portfolio has a mean of 10% and a standard deviation of 5%. The probability that the portfolio has a negative return is 2.5%.
   a. True
   b. False
3. Systematic risk can be reduced as the number of randomly selected securities increases for a portfolio.
   a. True
   b. False
4. An S&P 500 index fund and the S&P 500 index should have an R^2 equal to 100%.
   a. True
   b. False

False, True, False, True.

Value at Risk

Risk management tools have traditionally included such volatility and sensitivity measures as standard deviation, beta, duration, convexity, and delta. One drawback to using these measures is that they tend to measure total volatility, which includes asset returns that are both positive and negative. Many investors, however, are highly concerned about potential losses, especially over relative short terms. The sensitivity to large losses became acute after the October 1987 stock market crash, in which The DJIA lost 23 percent in one day and the S&P 500 Index lost 33 percent of its value over the three-month period surrounding the crash. Traditional measures of risk were not too helpful during the fall of 1987. It was during the aftermath of the 1987 crash that bankers developed a newer measure known as Value at Risk. It is interesting to note that some banks were more prepared for the 2008 financial crisis than others perhaps because they used Value at Risk as part of their risk management tool box.

Value at Risk is a risk management tool that quantifies the level of risk during a specific time period. It measures the potential loss in terms of either a percentage loss or in terms of dollars. For example, the 90 percent three-month Value at Risk of a fixed-income portfolio might be $250,000. This means the portfolio manager can be 90 percent confident that over the next three months, the portfolio will not lose more than $250,000. Value at Risk has much more practical appeal than traditional risk measures. This fixed-income portfolio might have a standard deviation of 9.2 percent and a $250,000 loss might be consistent with that level of volatility. A statement on standard deviation, however, does not say anything about potential losses. Value at Risk fills that gap in portfolio management and has become a valuable tool for all portfolio managers.

Three common ways to compute Value at Risk include the historical method, the variance-covariance method, and the Monte Carlo method. These methods are discussed below.

The historical method simply examines historical returns over a specified period and establishes a boundary for a significant loss. This method does not require much knowledge about the statistical distribution of returns or that of the market. It simply examines the security price changes over the specified period. Consider the following example.

Example 3.37

Consider a fixed-income mutual fund that was opened 100 weeks ago. The fund currently has $75 million in assets. The fund manager collects weekly return data since inception and computes an average return of 0.0011. The manager then notes that the five worst weeks of performance can be summarized:

Week 12	-0.00071
Week 17	-0.00112
Week 51	-0.00068
Week 62	-0.00049
Week 86	-0.00093

The least negative return during the worst five weeks is -0.00049. Since there are 100 weeks of data points, the performance of the fund for 95 of those weeks exceeded the least negative return. The fund manager can reasonably state that with 95% confidence, the fund will not lose more than -0.00049 during any week in the future. Since the fund's market value is $75 million, the dollar Value at Risk is $36,750.

The main reason the historical method is commonly used is that it is relatively easy and makes no assumptions about the underlying distribution of returns. The problem is that it relies on the notion that history over a specified period will repeat itself over that same future period. In addition, there are really no limits established on the magnitude of the losses. For example, the Value at Risk might be $36,750 in the bond fund example, but this method does not suggest anything about identifying maximum losses. All that can be concluded is that historically, only five percent of losses have been worse than 0.048 percent.

Many researchers use the Variance-Covariance method to overcome some of the disadvantages of using the historical method. It assumes that distribution of returns is normal, which means it can be fully described by its mean, variance, and covariances. The steps include computing all of the covariances between and among the individual components of the portfolio and then using normal distribution properties to estimate significant losses for a given confidence level.

Example 3.38

Khabib is a 30-year-old small business owner with a $1 million portfolio that consists of collectibles, investment grade bonds, and large cap stocks. Khabib understands how to measure volatility but wants to know more about risk management and the possibility of incurring large losses. Khabib computes an annual Value at Risk measure given the following annual data:

Asset	Return	Standard Deviation	Allocation
Collectibles	11%	15%	30%
IG Bonds	6%	8%	50%
Large Cap Stocks	8%	12%	20%

Correlation Matrix

Asset	Collectibles	IG Bonds	Large Cap Stocks
Collectibles	1.00	0.38	0.21
IG Bonds	0.38	1.00	0.82
Large Cap Stocks	0.21	0.82	1.00

The return on the portfolio is the weighted average return:

$$R_p = (0.3 \text{ x } 11\%) + (0.5 \text{ x } 6\%) + (0.2 \text{ x } 8\%) = 7.9\%$$

The variance of the three-asset portfolio is:[10]

$VAR_p = (0.3)^2 \text{ x } (0.15)^2$	Collectibles
$+(0.5)^2 \text{ x } (0.08)^2$	IG Bonds
$+(0.2)^2 \text{ x} (0.12)^2$	Large Cap Stocks
$+2(0.3) \text{ x } (0.5) \text{ x } (0.15) \text{ x } (0.08) \text{ x } (0.38)$	Collectibles & IG Bonds
$+2(0.3) \text{ x } (0.2) \text{ x } (0.15) \text{ x } (0.12) \text{ x } (0.21)$	Collectibles & Large Cap Stocks
$+2(0.5) \text{ x } (0.2) \text{ x } (0.08) \text{ x } (0.12) \text{ x } (0.82)$	IG Bonds and Large Cap Stocks

$$= \mathbf{0.007597}$$

$$\sigma_p = \mathbf{8.716\%}$$

10.The variance of a multi-asset portfolio is calculated in a similar manner as the variance or standard deviation of a two-asset portfolio, however, there are more terms in the equation.

Khabib can use these statistics to calculate a Value at Risk figure. For example, if Khabib wants to calculate a 5% annual Value at Risk figure, his first step is to identify the z-score (see **Exhibit 3.10**) that has 5% of observations below it. Using a set of z-tables (or NORM.S.INV in excel) the relevant z-score is -1.645.

Given Khabib's portfolio has a standard deviation of 8.716%, its return will therefore be 14.34% or more below the mean (8.716% x -1.645) 5% of the time. As the mean return is 7.9%, Khabib's portfolio will lose no more than 6.44% (7.9% - 14.34%) 95% of the time. Give the portfolio value of $1 million, this equates to a loss of $64,400. Hence, the 5% annual Value at Risk is $64,400.

Take the difference between 7.9% and 14.34% to obtain 6.44%. The yearly Value at Risk is $1 million × 0.0644 = $64,400. There is a 95% probability that the value of the portfolio will not fall by more than $64,400 during the next year.

Exhibit 3.10 | What is a Z-Score?

A **z-score** is a standard score that can be calculated for any raw observation from a data set. It measures the distance of an observation from the mean of its data set in terms of standard deviations.

$$z = \frac{\textbf{Observed Value} - \textbf{Mean}}{\textbf{Standard Deviation}}$$

The mean itself has a z-score of zero, as it is zero standard deviations from the mean. A data point that is one standard deviation below the mean has a z-score of minus one. Given the properties of a normal distribution, z-scores can be used to calculate the probability of observing data points above or below that z-score. As stated in exhibit 3.5, 68% of observations are within one standard deviation of the mean. That means 32% of observations are more than one standard deviation from the mean, and as the distribution is symmetrical, 16% must be more than one standard deviation below the mean, and 16% more than one standard deviation above it. It can therefore be concluded that 16% of observations are below the observation with a z-score of -1.0. Using the same logic, approximately 2.5% of observations are below an observation with a z-score of -2 (more precisely -1.96). The percentage of observations below any z-score can be derived using software (function 'NORM.S.INV' in Excel, for example) or by looking it up in a set of z-tables.

The main disadvantages of using the variance-covariance method are the reliance on normally distributed asset returns and the possibility of prohibitive costs in collecting so many variances and covariances. The attraction is that it is easy to compute once the data is collected.

The final method for determining Value at Risk is through a Monte Carlo simulation. This process involves estimating the range of variables that influence the returns in a portfolio, generating random numbers assigned to each of the variables, simulating many returns as each of the variables change by small amounts, computing portfolio returns over each iteration, identifying the bottom percentile of returns, and finally computing the Value at Risk based on total portfolio value.

The problem with a Monte Carlo simulation is that it can become highly complex. In the Khabib example, possible variables that might influence portfolio returns include:

- Collectibles: Depth and liquidity of market, theft, insurance, and commissions
- Investment Grade Bonds: Inflation, default risk, duration, convexity, and covenants
- Large Cap Equities: Beta, price to book ratios, growth rates, profitability, and leverage

Understanding and using Value at Risk can add significant knowledge to an investor's ability to quantify and manage risk. It should be utilized as part of a complete risk management system so investors appreciate all the risks associated with their portfolios.

Beta (β)

Beta is commonly used to measure the risk of a portfolio or security relative to the market or a benchmark. It measures systematic risk and provides an indication of the volatility as compared to the market or index. While standard deviation measures total risk, beta only measures systematic risk. The market is defined as having a beta of 1.0. Portfolios (or securities) with a beta greater than 1.0 are more volatile than the market, while portfolios with a beta less than 1.0 are less volatile than the market. A portfolio with a beta of 1.5 is considered to be 50 percent more volatile than the market. Similarly, a portfolio with a beta of 0.7 is considered to be 30 percent less volatile than the market.

Example 3.39

Meisha is considering two stocks to add to her portfolio: RBT and TRTL. RBT has a beta of 1.5, while TRTL has a beta of 0.5. If the market increased 10% next year, then RBT should increase by 15% and TRTL should increase by 5%. However, if the market decreased by 6% next year, then RBT should decrease by 9%, while TRTL should only decrease by 3%. Beta provides insight into the volatility of each security relative to the market.

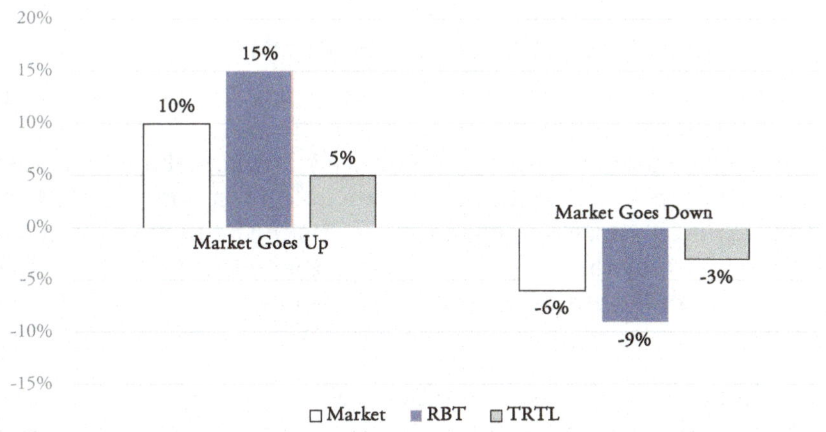

Example 3.40

A well-diversified portfolio includes the following three equity securities:

- JL Industries has a high beta, operates in an industry that currently has a higher than average growth rate, and its stock price is very sensitive to changes in the broad stock market index.
- TF Companies has a beta that is historically close to 1.0, operates in the financial services industry, and its profit margins are highly sensitive to changes in its borrowing costs.
- Pennsylvania Global Inc has a beta that is greater than 1.0, operates in the North American energy market, and a large percentage of its revenues are dominated in Mexican pesos.

Identify the most likely stock market reactions and the type of risk that influences prices under the following conditions:

- The U.S. stock market suffers broad losses.
- The U.S. Federal Reserve lowers its target for interest rates.
- The U.S. dollar appreciates against the Canadian dollar and the Mexican peso.

JL: Stock price will most likely fall more than the average company because its beta is greater than 1.0. This is market risk.

TF: Stock price will most likely fall as the spread between its rate on deposits and loans becomes narrower. This is interest rate risk.

PG: Stock price will most likely fall because the appreciating dollar will lower the repatriated currency values. This is exchange rate risk.

How can Beta (β) be Used with Individual Securities?

It is well-known that unsystematic risk can be managed through diversification. Investments in a minimal number of securities can substantially reduce unsystematic risk. Many investors seek to virtually eliminate unsystematic risk by holding stocks with relatively low correlations. It still remains, however, that a single security is exposed to a significant amount of unsystematic risk. If beta only measures systematic risk, then how is it an appropriate measure of risk? The presumption is that if beta is used with an individual security, it is for the purpose of adding that security to a portfolio which is already diversified. If that is not the intended purpose, then beta does not provide a full view of the total risk for a particular security.

Since beta measures systematic risk, it is a suitable measure of risk for fully diversified portfolios. Diversified portfolios have minimal unsystematic risk, which means that beta is capturing the majority of the risk of the portfolio. However, when the diversification of the portfolio is low, and the portfolio has a substantial amount of unsystematic risk, beta does not capture all of the volatility or risk within the portfolio. Beta is more appropriate for portfolios and mutual funds that are well-diversified and, therefore, highly correlated to the market.

The formula for beta (β) is as follows: $\beta_i = \frac{Cov_{im}}{\sigma_m^2} = \frac{\sigma_i R_{im}}{\sigma_m}$

β_i = beta of asset i

Cov_{im} = covariance between asset i and the market

R_{im} = correlation between asset i and the market

σ_i = standard deviation of asset i

σ_m = standard deviation of the market

σ_m^2 = variance of the market

Beta is calculated using regression analysis. **Regression analysis** is a statistical method for estimating the relationship among variables. For example, the relationship between the changes in price or value of a security or a portfolio can be compared to the changes in price or value of a market index. Regression attempts to find the "best fit" line that represents a set of data, such as the value of a security compared with the value of the market. Out of the regression analysis also comes the correlation between the variables. The correlation coefficient, which is generally denoted with the letter "R," explains the strength and direction of the relationship between two variables. If the strength of the relationship is low, as indicated by the correlation coefficient, then beta is less reliable. Beta is more reliable when the strength of the relationship is strong.

Another aspect of beta is that it could be negative. A positive beta means that the security and the market move in the same direction. A negative beta means that the security and the market move in opposite directions. This type of movement occurs when the correlation between the variables is negative, which is discussed below.

Correlation

Correlation indicates strength and direction of a relationship. It answers the question: how do you determine the level of diversification within a portfolio? The statistics used to provide the answer are the **correlation coefficient (R)** and the **coefficient of determination (R^2)**, commonly referred to as R-squared. Referring back to the formula for beta, notice that the first part is the relative total variability, or a ratio of the standard deviation of the portfolio return compared to the standard deviation of the overall market return. This ratio is then multiplied by the second part: the correlation between the portfolio return and the market return.

Exhibit 3.11 | The Correlation Coefficient

R = +1.00	Perfect positive relationship.
R = +0.50	Positive relationship between two variables.
R = 0.00	No relationship between two variables. The two variables move independently.
R = -0.50	Negative relationship between two variables.
R = -1.00	Perfect negative relationship.

The correlation coefficient, *R*, explains the relationship between two variables. It ranges from +1.0 (perfectly positively correlated) to -1.0 (perfectly negatively correlated). For example, as the temperature rises in the summer, the air conditioning system consumes more electricity. Thus, the temperature and the electrical consumption are positively correlated during the summer because they move in the same direction. However, as the temperature drops in the winter your heating system uses more natural gas, so temperature and natural gas consumption are negatively correlated because they move in opposite directions.

Exhibit 3.12 | Natural Gas Correlation

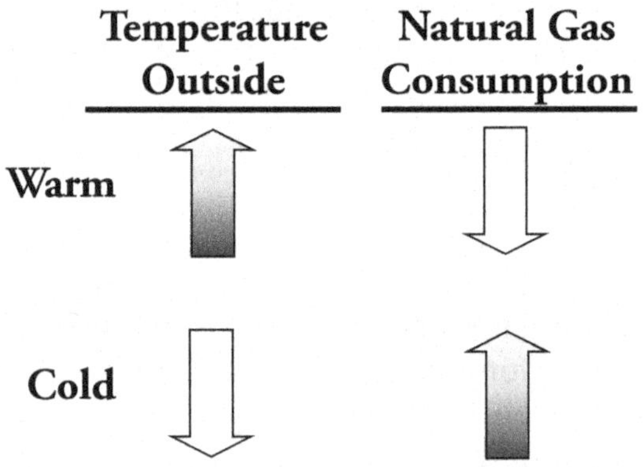

Consider the left chart in **Exhibit 3.13** labeled A. The correlation between Variable A and Variable B is positive and perfect (R should equal 1.0). With the center graph (labeled D), the correlation is zero, which occurs when the variables are unrelated. In the chart labeled G, the two variables are perfectly negatively correlated. This negative correlation occurs when one variable goes up while the other variable goes in the opposite direction.

Exhibit 3.13 | Graphical Representation of Correlation Coefficient

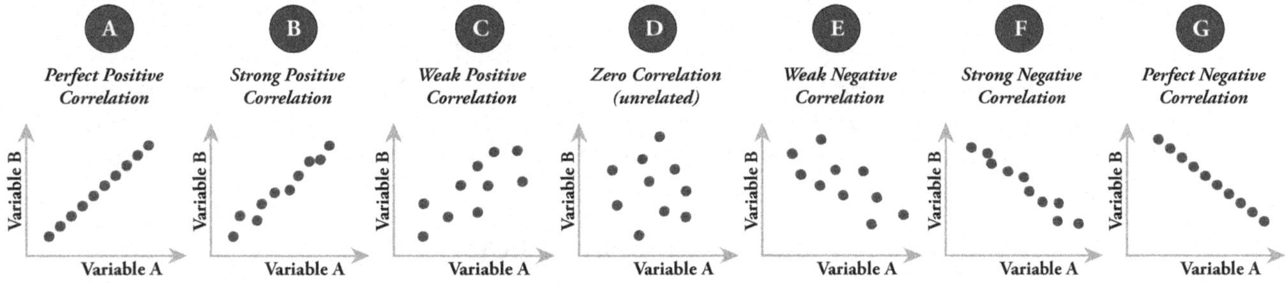

As mentioned, regression analysis is the mathematical process of determining the line that best fits the graph of two (or more) variables. In the exhibit above, it is easy to draw the line that best fits the dots in charts A and G. It is fairly easy to draw an accurate line for charts B and F. On the other hand, it is fairly difficult for a line to represent the relationships in charts C, D, and E. However, a software package can easily run a regression analysis on any set of data and produce a line of best fit. When the returns on a stock are regressed against the returns on a benchmark index, the slope of that line is the stock's beta. The package will also calculate the correlation coefficient, which will be low or zero for relationships like those shown in charts C, D and E.

Exhibit 3.14 provides an example of the movement of two stocks (Stock A and Stock B) over time with varying correlation coefficients.

Exhibit 3.14 | Range of Correlation Between Two Investments

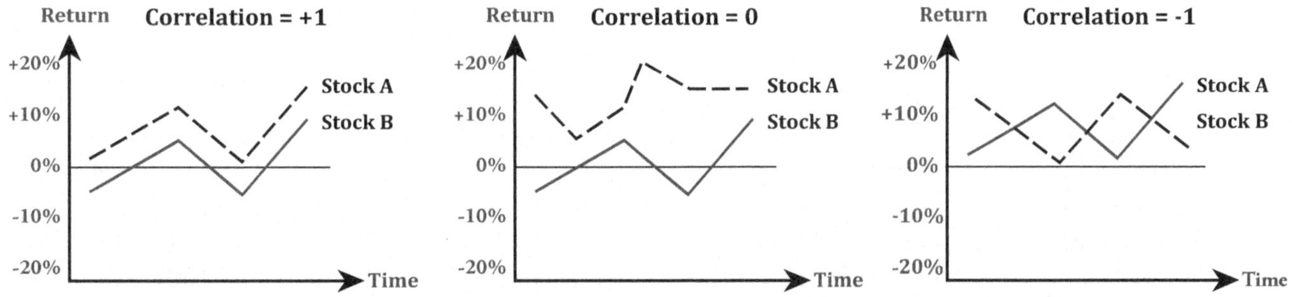

In the left chart, the returns of the two stocks move up or down at nearly the same rate and time, and are therefore highly positively correlated. In the right chart, the returns of the two stocks move in opposite directions, and are thus highly negatively correlated. In the middle chart, there is no apparent relationship between the returns of the two stocks, and they are described as uncorrelated ($R = 0.0$).

Normally, a well-diversified investment portfolio would be expected to be highly correlated with some indicator of the overall market, such as the S&P 500 Index. Correlation, however, does not provide a complete diversification analysis. To determine the magnitude of diversification contained in a portfolio, the fund's return variation as a percentage of the total market's return variation is used. This statistic is referred to as r squared and is simply the correlation coefficient squared.

The **coefficient of determination**, which is represented as r^2 or R^2, ranges from 0 to 100 percent and is defined as the percent change in the dependent variable that is explained by changes in the independent variable. An R^2 of 1.0 or 100 percent means that 100 percent of the change in one variable is explained by changes in the other variable. An example of this is an index fund. Consider an S&P 500 index fund. It should have an R^2 of 100 percent, because 100 percent of the change in the fund should be attributable to changes in the market. Effectively, 100 percent of the risk is systematic risk. Assume that a mutual fund had an R^2 of 0.5. In this case, it means that 50 percent of the change in the mutual fund is explained by changes in the market.

Exhibit 3.15 | Total Risk

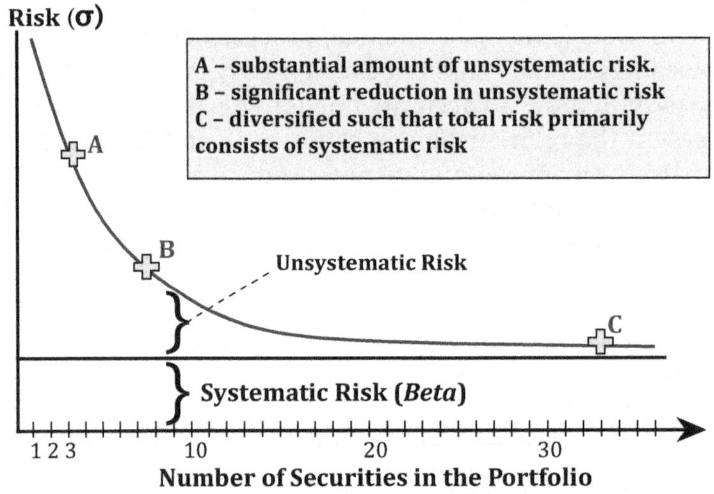

Example 3.41

Dominick invests in an equity portfolio with only a few securities. Dominick completes a correlation analysis and a regression analysis comparing his portfolio with a broad market index. The correlation coefficient is 0.4 while the coefficient of determination is 0.16. Dominick concludes that while his portfolio is positively related to the index, the relationship is not very strong. In addition, only 16% of the variability in his portfolio can be attributed to changes in the index. With 84% of the variability in his portfolio originating from changes in factors that are unique to the few securities in the portfolio, Dominick concludes his portfolio is not highly diversified.

Example 3.42

After realizing his portfolio is not very diversified, Dominick invests in a handful of additional stocks. The correlation coefficient and coefficient of determination are now 0.7 and 0.49, respectively. Dominick concludes that his portfolio has a much stronger positive relationship with the index and that his level of unsystematic risk has fallen to 51%.

Dominick is likely to remain unsatisfied with the level of diversification of his portfolio, so he will continue to add securities until his r squared approaches 90% to 100%.

Many investors will achieve complete diversification by simply buying a passive index mutual fund. Other investors, however, who hope to beat the market portfolio, will be comfortable with r squared less than 90%, perhaps even significantly so.

The reliability of beta is impacted by R^2, which measures the percentage of systematic and unsystematic risk. Because beta only measures systematic risk, it is less reliable when R^2 is low. A low R^2 indicates a higher level of unsystematic risk.

Example 3.43

Rosa is evaluating the Random Y Fund. The chart depicts the values for the fund and the S&P 500. She is told that the black line is the line of best fit and that the beta for the fund is 1.0. Should Rosa have faith that the fund has a beta of 1.0? What do you think the correlation is for the fund and the S&P 500? The answer to these two questions is that Rosa should not have faith as the correlation is very low, if not zero. As a result, the R^2 is very low and beta is unreliable.

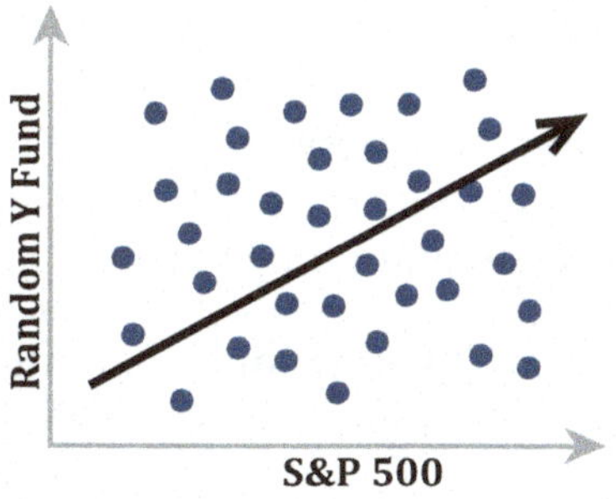

In other words, the slope of the line (Beta = 1.0) cannot be relied on.

Covariance

Covariance is another measure of the relationship between two variables. Although not as intuitive as the correlation coefficient, it does at least indicate whether variables are positively or negatively related. Variables with a positive covariance have a positive correlation (and hence tend to move in the same direction), and those with a negative covariance have a negative correlation (and hence tend to move in opposite directions).

However, unlike the correlation coefficient, the covariance is not constrained by -1 and +1, and may take any value (from negative to positive infinity). As such it is more difficult to interpret.

The covariance and correlation coefficient are related by the following formula:

$$\textbf{Covariance} = \sigma_A \sigma_B R_{AB}$$

σ_A = standard deviation of asset A
σ_B = standard deviation of asset B
R_{AB} = correlation between assets A and B

Example 3.44

Philip evaluates the strength of the relationship between two equity securities. One security has a standard deviation of 40% while the other security has a standard deviation of 12%. The correlation coefficient between the two securities is 0.20. Philip estimates the covariance is:

$$Cov_{AB} = \sigma_A \sigma_B R_{AB}$$

$$COV = (0.40)\ (0.12)\ (0.20)$$

$$COV = 0.0096$$

Covariance is used in the calculation of beta, as well as in the calculation of the standard deviation of a multi-asset portfolio, which is discussed in Chapter 4.

Semivariance

Investors dislike negative volatility, but they love positive volatility. The problem with standard deviation is that large positive returns impact the size of standard deviation as much as large negative returns. However, the positive returns are welcome, while the negative returns are not. **Semivariance** is based on this notion, and only takes into consideration volatility below the mean return. There have been attempts to mainstream this concept, but it is still not commonly used.

Semivariance can be measured using returns below the mean. Alternatively, it could be measured using returns below a target return. As an example, semivariance might be calculated is as follows:

$$\textbf{Semivariance} = \frac{\sum_{\text{for all } x_i \leq \bar{x}} (x_1 - \bar{x})}{n - 1}$$

$\bar{x}$ = mean factor
R_i = the return for period i that is below the mean
n = the number of observations that are below the mean

Example 3.45

Consider two investments, Zig and Zag. The returns for Zig and Zag over the last six years are as follows:

Year	Zig	Zag
1	-7%	15%
2	18%	-13%
3	10%	8%
4	4%	12%
5	-11%	20%
6	21%	-7%

As part of the evaluation of the performance of Zig and Zag, the mean and standard deviation of both investments are computed and shown in the table below:

	Zig	Zag
Arithmetic Mean	5.833%	5.833%
Geometric Mean	5.154%	5.137%
Standard Deviation	13.014%	13.014%

Zig and Zag have the exact same average return and the exact same standard deviation. However, it turns out that Zig may be better than Zag. How is that possible? The semivariance is greater for Zag. The chart below calculates semivariance for Zig and Zag. In each case, the difference is calculated for those returns that are below the mean. Each difference is then squared, summed and divided by the sample size minus 1, in this case 5. Note that the total sample size minus 1 is used, regardless of how many observations were below the mean. Some analysts prefer to divide by the sample size (in this case 6), which is also acceptable. Being consistent in the method when comparing data sets is the most important consideration.

Year	Zig	Mean	Difference	Difference Squared
1	-7%	5.83%	-12.833%	164.69
2	18%	5.83%		
3	10%	5.83%		
4	4%	5.83%	-1.833%	3.36
5	-11%	5.83%	-16.833%	283.35
6	21%	5.83%		
			Sum	451.40
			Semivariance	**90.28**

Year	Zag	Mean	Difference	Difference Squared
1	15%	5.83%		
2	-13%	5.83%	-18.83%	354.68
3	8%	5.83%		
4	12%	5.83%		
5	20%	5.83%		
6	-7%	5.83%	-12.83%	164.69
			Sum	519.37
			Semivariance	**103.87**

As depicted in the chart above, Zig has a lower semivariance as compared to Zag. As a result, most investors would prefer Zig over Zag.

It should also be noted that Zig has a slightly higher geometric rate of return as compared to Zag. The geometric return is 5.15% for Zig, while it is only 5.14% for Zag. This example should help illustrate the importance of not simply relying on one method of determining returns or measures of risk.

Coefficient of Variation (CV)

While measures of return and measures of risk are useful in isolation, investors also benefit from statistics that measure a security's return relative to its level of risk. The simplest of these measures is the **coefficient of variation (CV)**. Quite simply, the CV measures the amount of risk per unit of return. Take a minute to compare the following two investment choices:

	Fund A	Fund B
Mean Return	20%	9%
Standard Deviation	25%	10%

If an investor is 26 years old with a high tolerance for risk and is saving for retirement, Fund A appears to be a good choice because it is likely to experience greater growth given enough time to ride out the highly probable bad years. If an investor is a recent retiree, concerned mainly with conservation of principal, they might be more comfortable with Fund B, even though it does not offer the attractive potential returns of Fund A.

What about an investor who is 45 years old, moderately tolerant of risk, and attempting to simultaneously save for retirement and their young children's college education? One potential answer is to diversify and split the investment between the two funds, with the retirement monies going to Fund A and the education monies invested in B.

The CV offers a method of directly comparing the return and risk characteristics of these two very different investment choices. The CV is easy to calculate since it is simply the standard deviation divided by the average return.

$$CV = \frac{\text{Standard Deviation } (\sigma)}{\text{Average Return } (\bar{x})}$$

Fund A's CV (25/20) is 1.25, while Fund B's (10/9) is 1.11. Therefore, assuming both funds were appropriate to an investor's circumstances, Fund B, the more conservative fund, would require less risk per unit of return earned. Although this ratio is a rough indicator of the relative risk-adjusted return of the two choices, it is not the only method of determining a risk-adjusted return, and it has certain deficiencies.

Exhibit 3.16 | The Four "Cs"

1. **Coefficient of Variation:** Standard deviation divided by expected return (total risk per unit of return).
2. **Correlation Coefficient:** Ranges from −1.0 to + 1.0. Maximum risk reduction occurs at perfect negative correlation (−1.0). No risk reduction occurs at perfect positive correlation (+1.0).
3. **Covariance:** A measure of how much two assets move together.
4. **Coefficient of Determination**: Known as R^2 this statistic provides the percentage variation in portfolio returns that is explained by the variation in the benchmark returns.

For instance, the CV fails to take into account that some of the return of both investments is available to the investor without *any* risk (the money could be placed into 90-day T-bills with essentially no return risk). How does this fact affect the comparison? The answer is one of the topics addressed by Modern Portfolio Theory (MPT), which is covered in Chapter 4. In addition, three MPT-based measures of risk-adjusted returns or portfolio performance are covered in Chapter 5: the Sharpe Ratio, the Treynor Ratio, and Jensen's Alpha. These performance measures are generally considered to be superior measures of risk-adjusted return because, unlike the CV, they do adjust for the risk-free rate of return.

COMPREHENSIVE EXAMPLES

Below are three examples that provide an understanding of how to apply much of what is discussed in the chapter so far, along with a basic discussion of regression analysis and the outputs from regression analysis.

New York Yankees

There are many sets of data that are obviously related. For example, the more a student studies, the better grades he or she should achieve. Another example is that the weight of a taller person should generally be greater than that of a shorter person, all other factors being equal.

To illustrate how these types of relationships might be measured, the following example uses the heights and weights from the 2015 New York Yankees 40-man roster (NYYs), as follows:

	Height	Weight (pounds)
High	6'8"	300
Low	5'10"	150
Average	6'2"	215
Standard Deviations	2.4"	24.9

The chart below reflects the plotted height (x-axis) and weight (y-axis) of the NYYs team members.

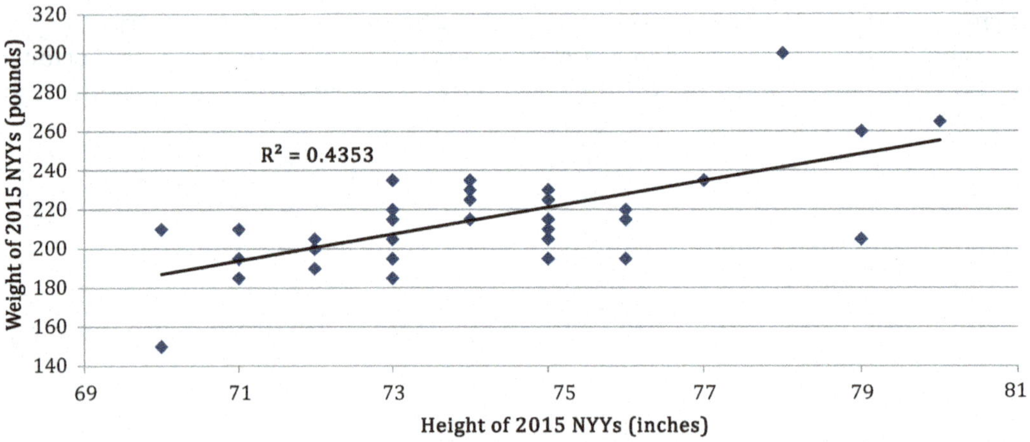

Despite what someone might think about the height and weight of major league baseball players, the relationship between height and weight is not terribly strong among these athletes. The line in the graph above attempts to represent this relationship between height and weight using regression. However, the line is not a perfect fit with the data. Some of the data points are above the line and some are below the line.

The coefficient of determination in this example is approximately 43 percent. With an R^2 of 0.43, it means that about 43 percent of the change in one variable is explained by changes in the other variable. In this case, it means that 43 percent of the weight of a player is attributable to the height of the player. Implicit in this analysis is that the other 57 percent is attributable to other factors, such as body makeup, muscle mass, or bone structure.

Another important factor that results from regression analysis is beta, which is the slope of the regression line. A slope of 1.0 means that both variables move equally and in the same direction. For the NYY data, beta turns out to be 6.8, which means that each incremental inch in height should be accompanied by an additional 6.8 pounds. However, since R^2 is only 43 percent, that means that the relationship between the variables is moderate, at best.

Assuming the height and weight of these players was normally distributed, the likelihood that a player would have a height or weight within a certain range could be determined.

	Height		Weight (pounds)	
Within 1 standard deviation - 68%	6'0"	6'5"	190	240
Within 2 standard deviations - 95%	5'9"	6'7"	165	265
Within 3 standard deviations - 99%	5'7"	6'9"	140	290

The NYY 40-man roster consists of 18 players who are not pitchers. Interestingly enough, excluding the pitchers from the data set results in an increase of the R^2 from 0.43 to 0.63. This change implies that there is a stronger relationship between height and weight for non-pitchers compared to pitchers. When the data for just the pitchers is analyzed, the R^2 equals 0.32.

Apple Stock

This example applies many of the concepts in this chapter to actual stock data for Apple Inc. (Ticker AAPL) from 1/1/2013 through 12/31/2015. The exhibit includes four charts. The two charts on the top depict the price of AAPL and the S&P 500 on a daily basis. The two charts on the bottom reflect the relative price of AAPL and the S&P 500 on a weekly basis (left) and a monthly basis (right). Based on the charts alone, there are several observations that can be made:

The daily price change for AAPL is greater than for the S&P 500. This volatility results in larger swings in value for an investment in AAPL as compared with an equal investment in the S&P 500. This volatility can be measured using standard deviation.

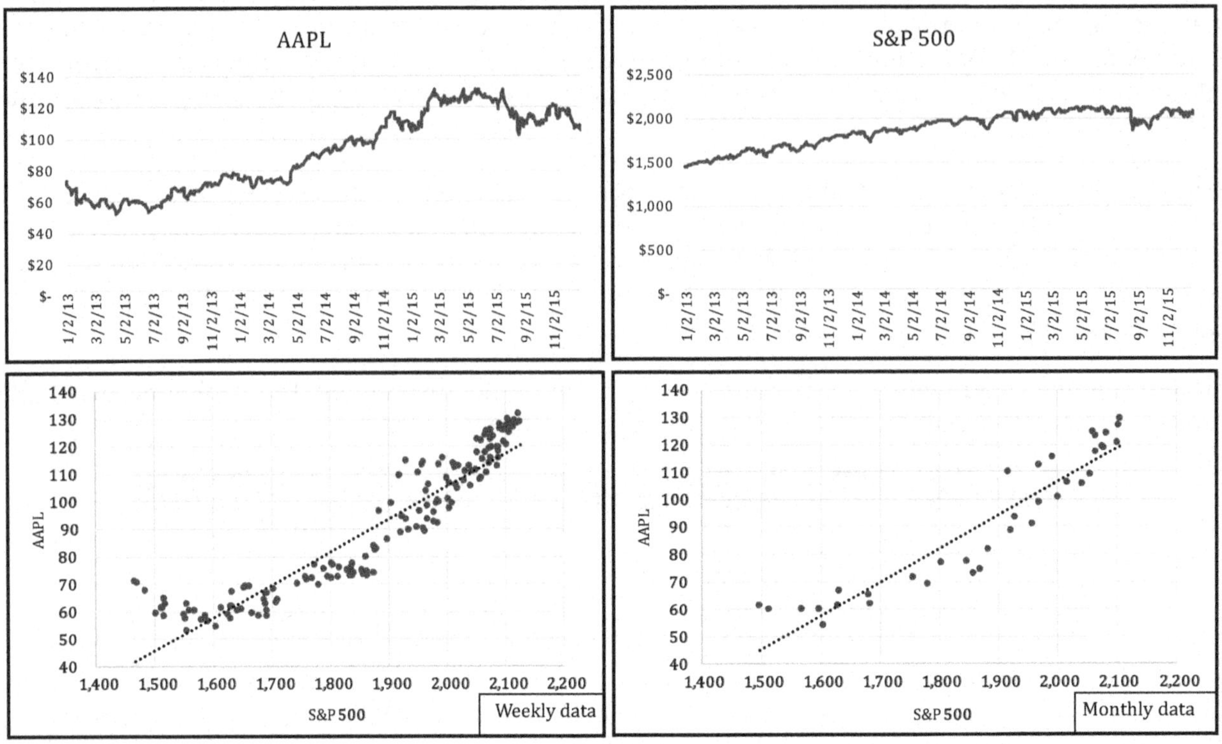

The black dashed lines in the two bottom charts are the trend or regression lines. These lines are fairly representative of the data. However, they are not perfect. Calculating R^2 provides an indication of the strength of the regression line.

Using the monthly data, we calculated the R^2 as 88 percent and the beta as 1.33. The trend line in the graph is the line that best represents the data. Since the R^2 is 88 percent, it means that 88 percent of the change in AAPL is attributable to changes in the market. R^2 also implies that 12 percent of the change in AAPL is attributable to other factors (unsystematic risks). With a beta of 1.33, AAPL is approximately 33 percent more volatile than the market.

The results of these calculations change if a different time period (such as five years instead of three years) is selected or if weekly data is used in lieu of monthly data. We recalculated beta and R^2 using weekly data over the same time period. This recalculation resulted in an R^2 of 87 percent and a beta of 1.02. These results are significantly different from what we originally calculated using monthly data. It is important to understand that these variables will change based on how they are calculated.

In addition to beta, we calculated the standard deviation of the volatility of the S&P 500 and AAPL over this time period on a daily, weekly, monthly, and annual basis. The results are below:

Standard Deviation	S&P 500	Apple Inc. (AAPL)
Daily	0.80%	1.62%
Weekly	1.60%	3.66%
Monthly	3.03%	6.64%
Yearly	13.58%	23.28%

Notice that the standard deviation for AAPL is more than twice that of the S&P 500 for daily, weekly, and monthly calculations. However, it is only 70 percent greater when calculated on an annual basis. This result should not be surprising as it illustrates the difference between systematic and total risk. Recall that the S&P 500 Index is a well-diversified portfolio that contains only systematic risk, while Apple stock is exposed to both systematic and unsystematic risk.

While R^2 is fairly high at 88 percent, calculated on a monthly basis, beta still does not provide the same insight into the total variability that is captured with standard deviation.

We calculated the average return over the three years, as well as the geometric return over the same period.

Annual Return[1]	S&P 500	Apple Inc. (AAPL)
Average Return (mean)	12.4%	14.1%
Geometric Mean	11.8%	12.6%

1. Dividend distributions were not included in the calculations, which would have changed the numbers slightly but would not have changed the point of the discussion.

Several observations can be made from the chart above in combination with the earlier information. AAPL's volatility has resulted in the average return being overstated relative to the geometric return. AAPL outperformed the S&P 500 over the three-year period by 0.8 percent, which is a significant increase. However, one of the important questions for investors is whether the incremental return is worth the incremental risk and volatility. In this example, there is a small increase in return, but a large increase in the volatility.

It should be noted that this example is comparing a single stock to an index. This type of analysis is also performed on portfolios in comparison to an index.

Jack's Portfolio

Jack has been investing his own money and wants to compare the returns for his portfolio with the returns from the S&P 500. Below are the returns over the last ten years. In addition, Jack has calculated several types of returns and measures of risk, which are also included below.

Year	S&P 500	Jack's Fund
1	5%	13%
2	-6%	6%
3	6%	13%
4	5%	-4%
5	7%	11%
6	3%	-15%
7	7%	20%
8	10%	2%
9	8%	15%
10	4%	14%

Risk, Return & Performance Measures	S&P 500	Jack's Fund
Arithmetic Mean	4.90%	7.50%
Geometric Mean	4.82%	7.00%
Ten-Year Holding Period Return	60.05%	96.73%
Standard Deviation	4.33%	10.53%
Variance	0.19%	1.11%
Covariance		0.00097
Beta	1.00000	0.51806
R-Squared	1.00000	0.04540
Correlation	1.00000	0.21307
Sharpe*	0.66975	0.52232
Treynor*	0.02900	0.10616

** Sharpe and Treynor are discussed in Chapter 5. They were calculated using a risk-free rate of 2%.*

Observations:

1. The arithmetic mean is higher for Jack than for the S&P 500.
2. The geometric mean is also higher for Jack than for the S&P 500.
3. The standard deviation for Jack is more than double the market.
4. Beta for Jack is 0.51806, which implies it is 48% less volatile than the market.
5. Based on R-squared, only 4.5% of the change in Jack's portfolio is attributable to the S&P 500.
6. Beta is not reliable for Jack's Fund based on R-squared.
7. Sharpe and Treynor provide different rankings in terms of risk adjusted return.

SUMMARY

Summary of key points:

- Risk is the uncertainty of future outcomes or the possibility of an adverse result.
- Risk and expected return are directly related: the greater the risk, the higher the expected return.
- Short-term T-bills are generally regarded as the closest available choice to a risk-free investment because they are backed by the full faith and credit of the U.S. government.
- The two sources of return from an investment are the yield (the amount of cash the investment generates) and the appreciation (the change in the investment's value): yield + appreciation = total return.
- There are numerous approaches to calculate return, including: holding period return, arithmetic mean return, geometric mean return, internal rate of return, dollar-weighted return, time-weighted return, annualized return, weighted average return, after-tax returns, real returns, and effective annual returns.
- Holding period return (HPR) measures the total return over the entire period of investment.
- The arithmetic mean is calculated by summing the annual holding period returns and dividing the sum by the number of years.
- The geometric mean measures the compound annual return over time, assuming all cash flows are reinvested at the geometric rate of return.
- The greater the volatility of investment returns, the lower the geometric return over time as compared with the arithmetic average return. The arithmetic average tends to overstate the average return, especially when both positive and negative returns are experienced.
- The internal rate of return (IRR) is the earnings rate of a series of cash inflows and outflows over a period of time assuming all earnings are reinvested. It equates discounted future cash flows to the net present value of an asset.
- The dollar-weighted return is the IRR of all of the cash flows an investor controls. It is used to determine the investor's combined result of the timing and dollar volume of the transactions during the period, as well as the performance of the investment security. It is also appropriate for gauging the performance of an investment manager with full discretion over an investor's account.
- The time-weighted return is a geometric mean of holding period returns. It ignores the dollar volume and timing of investor cash flows in and out of an investment. Thus, this method is more appropriate for assessing the performance of a fund manager or a security.
- The weighted average return is used to calculate the return on a portfolio.
- An investor's after-tax return is equal to: realized taxable return x (1 – marginal income tax rate).
- The real return (inflation-adjusted return) adjusts the nominal return to reflect the impact of inflation. Real rates of return are used in retirement funding, education funding and other calculations that require the incorporation of two different types of rates, such as an earnings rate and an inflation rate.

- All investments (including holding cash) are exposed to some type of risk.
- No amount of diversification can reduce or eliminate systematic risk.
- Total risk, which includes both systematic risk (risk attributable to macroeconomic factors that affect all investments) and unsystematic risk (risk that is individual to the specific firm, industry, or country), is measured by standard deviation.
- Beta can be used as a measure of risk for portfolios that are sufficiently diversified to eliminate unsystematic risk.
- An inverse relationship exists between changes in interest rates and prices of fixed-income securities. Most stocks also have an inverse relationship to interest rate changes.
- Investors in growth stocks paying no dividends, and investors owning zero-coupon bonds need not be concerned with reinvestment rate risk since they do not receive any periodic cash flows from those investments.
- Investors can virtually eliminate unsystematic risk through the process of portfolio diversification.
- Marketability is an investor's ability to easily find a market to sell their investment.
- Liquidity is the ability to sell an investment quickly at a competitive price without any loss of principal or any price concessions.
- Standard deviation measures variability of returns in relation to the mean return. A larger standard deviation implies greater uncertainty of outcomes.
- With a normal distribution, approximately 68% of the outcomes fall within ± 1 standard deviation from the mean, approximately 95% of the outcomes fall within ± 2 standard deviations from the mean, and approximately 99% of the outcomes fall within ± 3 standard deviations from the mean.
- Beta is used to measure the volatility of a portfolio as compared to the market. Beta measures systematic risk only.
- The market is defined as having a beta of 1.0. Portfolios (or securities) with a beta greater than 1.0 are more volatile than the market, while portfolios with a beta less than 1.0 are less volatile than the market.
- The correlation coefficient, *R*, explains the relationship between two variables. It ranges from +1.0 (perfectly positively correlated) to -1.0 (perfectly negatively correlated).
- The coefficient of determination, which is represented as r^2 or R^2, measures the percentage of the change in the portfolio that is explained by the change in the market.
- The R^2 value represents the amount of systematic risk in the portfolio. The amount of unsystematic risk is equal to $1 - R^2$.
- The coefficient of variation measures the amount of risk per unit of return.
- Value at Risk is a risk management tool that quantifies (in terms of a percentage loss or in terms of dollars) the level of risk during a specific time period.

DISCUSSION QUESTIONS

SOLUTIONS to the discussion questions can be found exclusively within the chapter. Once you have completed an initial reading of the chapter, go back and highlight the answers to these questions.

1. Discuss the components of total return.
2. Explain the basic premise of holding period return (HPR) and its biggest limitation.
3. Compare arithmetic and geometric returns.
4. What is the internal rate of return (IRR) and how is it related to net present value (NPV)?
5. Contrast dollar-weighted and time-weighted returns.
6. Explain an annualized return.
7. Define weighted return.
8. List five common systematic risks.
9. Explain how adding securities to a concentrated portfolio can reduce unsystematic risk.
10. Explain how financial risk impacts return on equity (ROE).
11. Compare standard deviation and beta.
12. Explain correlation and the coefficient of determination.

MULTIPLE-CHOICE PROBLEMS

A sample of multiple choice problems is provided below. Additional multiple choice problems are available at money-education.com by accessing the Student Practice Portal.

1. The geometric mean of a set of holding period returns for a security is used to calculate:
    1. The time weighted return.
    2. The dollar weighted return.
    3. The IRR.
        a. 1 only.
        b. 1 and 3.
        c. 2 and 3.
        d. 1, 2 and 3.

2. Which of the following is the most accurate definition of risk?
    a. The return expected by investors over a long-term holding period.
    b. A prior periodic return.
    c. The uncertainty of future returns.
    d. The market premium, defined as the difference between the market and the return on a riskless asset, such as a T-bill.

3. Which of the following statements concerning risk and return is not correct?
    a. Market risk includes a wide range of factors, including business cycles, changes in interest rates, global conflicts, as well as changes in consumer preferences.
    b. Total return = yield + price change.
    c. Exchange rate risk is the risk that currency fluctuations will cause an adverse effect on the return from an investment.
    d. Liquidity risk is a more significant risk for securities such as Treasury bills.

4. Which of the following is a systematic risk?
    a. Country risk.
    b. Exchange rate risk.
    c. Executive risk.
    d. Business risk.

5. Assume that an American's investment in the stock of a French company yielded a nominal rate of return of 18% in the past 12 months. Assume also that the Euro was worth $0.20 at the start of the period and $0.25 at the end of the period. In this case, the true rate of return for the investor was:
    a. -5.6%.
    b. 11.3%.
    c. 22.5%.
    d. 47.5%.

QUICK QUIZ EXPLANATIONS

Quick Quiz 3.1

1. False. Both calculations are accurate, they are just based on different data.
2. True.

Quick Quiz 3.2

1. True.
2. True.
3. False. The nominal return is not net of inflation, rather, it is the gross return.

Quick Quiz 3.3

1. False. Systematic risks cannot be eliminated through diversification; however, unsystematic risks can be eliminated through diversification.
2. True.
3. False. Default risk only applies to fixed-income securities.

Quick Quiz 3.4

1. True.
2. True.

Quick Quiz 3.5

1. False. The significance of beta is dependent on the value of R^2 - the lower the R^2, the less significant the beta.
2. True.
3. False. It should be unsystematic risk, as diversification does not reduce systematic risk.
4. True.

4

PORTFOLIO THEORY

LEARNING OBJECTIVES

1. Understand that the optimal portfolio is one designed to achieve a targeted rate of return while minimizing risk.*
2. Realize that combining different sets of assets allows for the creation of a portfolio that maximizes return for a given level of risk.*
3. Understand that there are optimal risk-return trade-off portfolios.*
4. Understand that portfolios can be constructed to meet time horizon objectives.*
5. Describe how portfolios should be constructed to meet risk tolerance objectives.*
6. Realize that, as a general rule, short-term assets should be used to meet short-term time horizon objectives.*
7. Know that there is an efficient frontier for portfolio returns.*
8. Understand that modern portfolio theory (MPT) combines the efficient frontier with a risk-free rate along with a portfolio risk measure (either beta or standard deviation).*
9. Distinguish between the capital asset pricing model and the arbitrage pricing theory.
10. Explain the three approaches to asset allocation: strategic, tactical and mean variance optimization.*
11. Identify the pros and cons of, and apply advanced analytic techniques such as forecasting, simulation, sensitivity analysis and stochastic modeling.*
12. Develop and communicate to a client a portfolio rebalancing strategy.*
13. Explain and apply investment strategies such as buy-and-hold, immunization, core and satellite, passive (indexed) and active management techniques such as tactical allocation, market timing, and sector rotation.*

**Ties to CFP Certification Learning Objectives*

INTRODUCTION

While knowledge of the various investment options open to investors is instructive, investors are best served when they hold a portfolio of assets designed to achieve a targeted rate of return while minimizing risk. All assets, including fixed-income investments, subject the investor to risk. Investors who combine sets of assets with different risk characteristics into a portfolio of investments have the best chance of meeting their return objectives whilst keeping their risk exposure at an acceptable level. This approach to portfolio construction is the hallmark of good portfolio management. This chapter discusses many of the concepts introduced in prior chapters to demonstrate how portfolios can be constructed to achieve an optimal risk-return tradeoff. Specifically, this chapter discusses the historical basis for modern portfolio theory as well as the practical steps for implementing an asset allocation decision, which is generally accepted as the driving force behind long-term investment returns.

HISTORICAL RETURNS AND RISK

Before constructing portfolios, investors will consider their goals and objectives, the relevant time frame for the investment, their risk tolerance, the various appropriate asset classes, and the risk of each potential investment.

Individuals invest for many different reasons. Some investors hope to accumulate specific amounts of capital over intermediate time periods for typical family expenses, including major consumer purchases and down payments for homes. Other investors have longer-term funding goals, such as paying for their children's college education costs or funding retirement. Still others have very long-term wealth accumulation objectives to create capital that can be transferred during their lifetime or at death to family members. In practice, most people have more than one objective, so it is important to understand how various investments may be used, taking into consideration their risk and return characteristics.

Example 4.1

Twyla, a recent college graduate, would like to save $50,000 within the next 3 to 5 years that can be used as a down payment for her first home. While in college, Twyla took several investment and financial planning classes, and understands that she should also start saving for her retirement that is 40 to 45 years away. The types of investments that would be appropriate for Twyla to employ in funding her goal of accumulating enough for a down payment on a home in 3 to 5 years, and the investments that would be appropriate for her to fund her retirement are likely to be very different. Twyla should consider relatively safe, liquid assets to accumulate the down payment on the home due to the short term nature of this objective, but can employ assets that pose more risk (with commensurate higher expected returns) to fund her retirement objectives. As this example illustrates, Twyla's goals determine her investment time horizons, which, in turn, determine the type of investments that are most suitable for achieving those goals.

Key Concepts

1. Efficient portfolios are formed by considering both expected return and risk.
2. All financial assets subject the investor to some degree of risk.
3. Investors manage risk by combining risky assets into portfolios while hoping to achieve targeted rates of return.
4. Shorter term investments typically have lower total risk and lower expected returns than longer term investments.
5. Investments should be chosen to match the investor's time horizon, risk tolerance, and other unique conditions.

Risk tolerance is also important to consider when evaluating the suitability of investments. Risk tolerance refers to the investor's ability and willingness to accept variability in returns over the holding period of an asset, a concept that will be discussed in more detail later in this chapter.

The concept of investment risk is developed in other chapters of this text. Recall, however, that investment risk is associated with the variability of returns expected to be received on an investment. The higher the variability of return, the higher the risk. A rational, risk-averse investor expects to be compensated for the level of risk exposure and expects to receive a higher return when that exposure increases. While the expected return on riskier investments is high when compared to lower-risk investments, investors cannot simply use expected returns to determine the suitability of investments. When an investor has a relatively short-term need for funds, a riskier investment, such as a stock portfolio, might offer a higher expected return, but also might experience an adverse price movement at the time the investor needs the funds, forcing the investor to sell the investment at a loss.

Once the investor's time horizon is determined, investments suitable for achieving the investor's goals can be selected. Investments are available in many forms, including short term money market securities, fixed income and equity securities, plus derivatives and alternative investments. As the expected return on an investment increases, the risk (or potential variability of return) on the investment also increases. As a rule of thumb, short-term goals should be funded with low-risk investments to minimize the possibility of adverse price movements when cash is needed to fund investor goals. Likewise, long-term goals can be funded with higher-risk investments. Even though the price variability (risk) of longer-term investments may be greater, the longer time horizon for the need of funds permits the investor to mitigate that risk by holding onto the investment through downward price cycles to achieve the higher expected return associated with accepting that higher risk. Selecting investments that match the investor's time horizon is an important part of the portfolio management process.

Exhibit 4.1 | S&P 500 Historical Rolling Average Returns

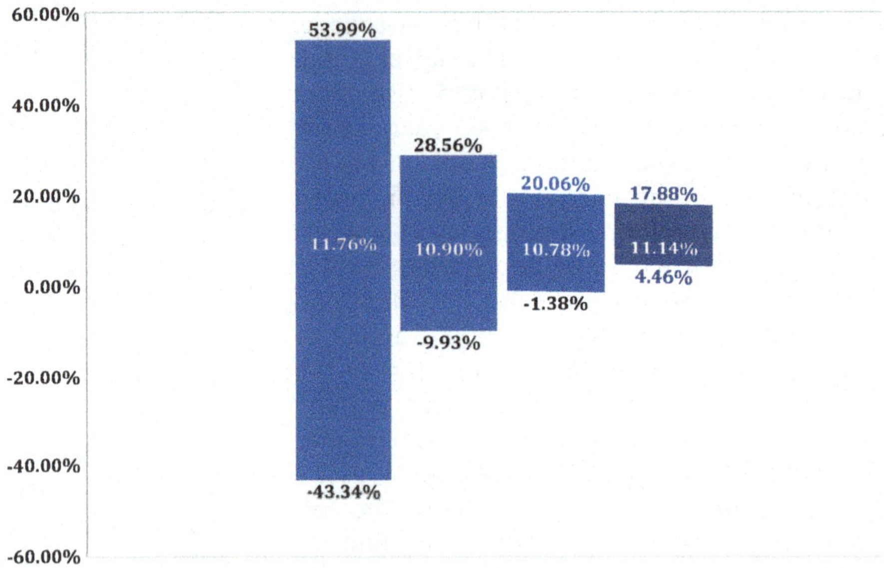

S&P 500 Historical Rolling Averages from 1930-2020

Exhibit 4.1 illustrates the volatility that the S&P 500, which is used as a proxy for the "stock market," can experience in a one-year period. The chart also illustrates the high, low and average geometric returns over one, five, ten, and twenty year periods. For example, the highest 10-year return equals 20.06 percent.

Even though the average S&P 500 return for a one-year period is 11.76 percent, the returns from 1930 to 2020 range from positive 54 percent to a negative 43 percent. Therefore, an investor cannot logically expect any specific return when they invest in the S&P 500 for a period of one year. Thus, the stock market is not appropriate for investors with short time horizons.

As the time period over which the returns are measured increases, the range of returns narrows. As indicated in **Exhibit 4.1**, over the last 90 years, the lowest 20-year annualized return equals 4.46 percent. Therefore, as investors' time horizons are longer, there is less chance of having a cumulative negative return - based on historical returns. This data lends to the notion that investors with short-term time horizons should invest conservatively (fixed-income securities), while investors with longer-term time horizons can accept higher levels of risk (equities).

DIVERSIFICATION

A simple method of minimizing risk in a portfolio of assets is to employ the concept of diversification. Diversification, which was introduced in Chapter 3 (Risk and Return) of this text, involves including a number of different investments in a portfolio to mitigate the risk presented by any one investment. Each additional security that is added to a portfolio has the potential to reduce the overall risk of the portfolio without necessarily sacrificing potential portfolio return. As the number of securities added to a portfolio increases, however, the impact of adding the last security to the portfolio is to increase portfolio diversification, but at a decreasing rate.

Key Concepts

1. Diversification reduces total portfolio risk.
2. The degree of diversification depends on the relationship between and among investment returns.
3. The correlation coefficient measures the magnitude and direction of a relationship between two variables.
4. Correlations range from perfectly negative correlation (-1.0) to perfectly positive correlation (+1.0).
5. Efficient diversification is typically found by combining assets with low or negative correlation coefficients.

The effect of diversification on risk depends on the correlation coefficient between and among all the securities contained in the portfolio. If correlations are high, then portfolio risk will remain relatively high as there are few diversification benefits. If correlations are low or even negative, then portfolio risk can be greatly reduced.

Recall that correlation, which is discussed in an earlier chapter, is a statistical is a statistical measure of the strength and direction of the relationship between two variables. Financial assets that move in opposite directions to each other are said to be negatively correlated; when one asset increases/decreases in value, the other asset decreases/increases in value. The degree to which two assets are correlated with each other is measured by the correlation coefficient, which ranges from +1 to -1. Two assets that always move in the same direction and at the same rate are perfectly, positively correlated, and would have a correlation coefficient of +1. Two assets that always move in opposite directions and at the same rate are perfectly, negatively correlated, and would have a correlation coefficient of -1. Two assets that have no relationship with each other are said to be uncorrelated, and would have a correlation coefficient of zero.

It is possible to reduce portfolio risk by adding two assets that are positively correlated. Assume, for example, that an investor has a one asset portfolio, and the investment has a high level of risk. Adding another asset that is positively correlated with the existing asset, but has lower risk, will reduce the overall portfolio risk, but since the assets tend to move in the same direction (they are positively correlated but less than +1), the investor will still be subject to variability in portfolio return since both assets tend to move in the same direction.

To achieve the full benefit of diversification, investors should include in their investment portfolio assets that are negatively correlated with each other. By adding negatively correlated assets to the portfolio, the variability of portfolio return (risk) will be minimized while preserving the opportunity to achieve an expected portfolio return.

Example 4.2

Johnny currently has one stock in his portfolio - Rainy Day Industries, Inc., which produces umbrellas and foul weather gear. In years when the weather is good, Rainy Day Industries, Inc. does not sell a lot of umbrellas, and has relatively low returns on investment. In years when the weather is foul, Rainy Day Industries, Inc. has strong sales and high returns on investment. Johnny is currently considering an investment in UV Protection, Inc., which is the leading producer of sunscreen in the United States. The expected return on an investment in UV Protection, LLC is the same as the expected return on an investment in Rainy Day Industries, LLC, but UV Protection, LLC has high returns when the weather is good, and low returns when the weather is foul - a trend that is negatively correlated with the performance of Rainy Day Industries, LLC. By adding UV Protection, Inc. to his portfolio, Johnny could diversify the portfolio by reducing the variability of his portfolio returns (risk) while preserving the portfolio expected return (both companies had the same expected return on investment). When the weather is bad and UV Protection, Inc. is doing poorly, those poor results will be offset by the better performance of Rainy Day Industries, Inc, and when the weather is good and UV Protection, Inc. is providing strong returns, those strong returns will offset the poor returns earned by Rainy Day Industries, Inc.

Quick Quiz 4.1

1. The correlation coefficient ranges from 0 to 1.0.
   a. True
   b. False
2. Investments should be matched with time horizon.
   a. True
   b. False
3. The addition of negatively correlated risky assets can reduce the risk in a portfolio.
   a. True
   b. False

False, True, True.

PORTFOLIO RISK AND RETURN

The risk and expected return trade-off is the critical building block for creating investment portfolios. Successful portfolio managers are those that can evaluate the risk and expected return components of both individual securities and groups of securities. Effective portfolio managers attempt to earn the highest level of return for each given level of risk.

Calculating the expected return on a portfolio is a relatively easy process, and can be accomplished by weighting the portfolio holdings by the expected returns on an asset. A thorough analysis of the approach to calculating a weighted average portfolio return was covered in Chapter 3, but a brief review of that approach is warranted here.

Example 4.3

Jocelyn holds a portfolio of two assets:

Equity Security	Weight	Expected Return
Bridge Manufacturing, Inc.	40%	8%
Outland Tech Co.	60%	6%

Expected Return = 0.40(0.08) + 0.60(0.06) = 0.068%

Jocelyn can reasonably expect to earn 6.8% from this portfolio, but this information is incomplete. Jocelyn also should evaluate the riskiness of the portfolio.

A common measure of the total risk of an investment is the variation in its returns. As shown in **Exhibit 4.1**, the average annual total return for the S&P 500 index for the 80-years up to 2020 was 11.76 percent, but it varied between a high of 52.56 percent and a low of -43.84 percent. It is possible that an investor expecting a gain of around 12 percent could have lost nearly half of their investment, or gained more than 50 percent.

By contrast, U.S. T-bonds over the same period averaged approximately five percent, a significantly lower return. But the variation in returns, with a high of 33 percent and a low of -11 percent was also much lower. The benefit of accepting a lower expected return, was exposure to a lower level of risk.

The most commonly used statistical measure of total risk is the standard deviation of an investment's returns. The standard deviation measures the variation in data around the mean or expected value. A large standard deviation means there is a large variation and in the case of investment returns, more risk. Investments with smaller standard deviations have less variation in their returns and hence lower risk.

Key Concepts

1. The expected return on a portfolio is the weighted average of the expected returns of the individual securities in the portfolio.
2. Unsystematic risk can be managed through the process of diversification.
3. Standard deviation is a measure of the total risk of a security's variability in returns.
4. Using a mean-variance framework, investors can construct an efficient frontier. The optimal portfolio will lie on this frontier.
5. MPT (modern portfolio theory) adds two components to the efficient frontier: a risk-free rate and beta as a risk measure.

Exhibit 4.2 | Variation of Return Around the Mean

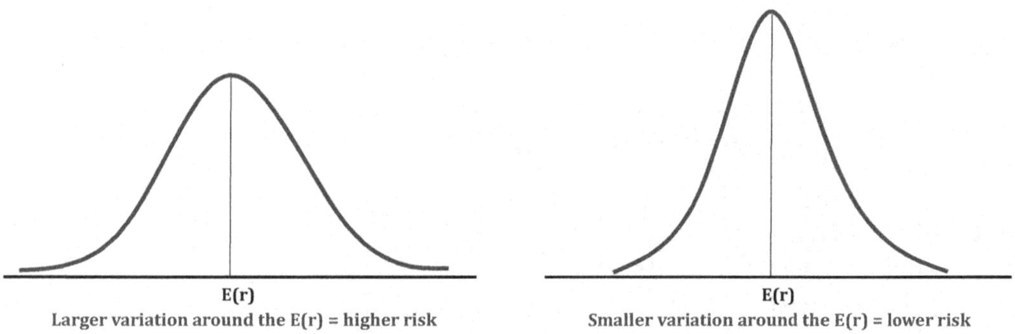

The standard deviation of an asset is equal to the square root of the variance in the asset's returns. The variance in the returns of a given asset is calculated by taking the sum of the squared differences between the actual returns on an asset and its expected return, and dividing that result by the number of observations minus one. Unlike the case with calculating portfolio expected return, which is determined by taking a weighted average of the returns of the assets making up the portfolio, a portfolio standard deviation cannot be determined by a simple weighted average. When calculating a portfolio standard deviation, then the correlations between the assets must be considered.

For example, if an investor holds a portfolio consisting of two assets, only in the unique case where those two assets are perfectly positively correlated will its standard deviation equal the weighted average of the two assets' standard deviations.

When the correlation between the two assets is less than +1, combining them will result in some diversification of risk, and the portfolio's standard deviation will be lower than the weighted average standard deviation.

Portfolio Risk (Two Asset Portfolio)

As discussed above, the standard deviation for a portfolio of securities is greatly influenced by the correlation between the securities within the portfolio. Naturally, the portfolio standard deviation is also affected by the weightings of each security and the standard deviation of each security within the portfolio. While the standard deviation for a portfolio can be calculated with any number of securities, the math becomes more complicated as the number of securities increases. Therefore, only the calculation of the standard deviation for a two-asset portfolio is presented. The formula for calculating the standard deviation of a two-asset portfolio is below:

$$\sigma_p = \sqrt{(w_A)^2(\sigma_A)^2 + (w_B)^2(\sigma_B)^2 + (2)(w_A)(w_B)(COV_{AB})}$$

The above formula has covariance as one of its input variables. The below formula uses correlation as one of the inputs.

$$\sigma_p = \sqrt{(w_A)^2(\sigma_A)^2 + (w_B)^2(\sigma_B)^2 + (2)(w_A)(w_B)(\sigma_A)(\sigma_B)(R_{AB})}$$

w_A = weight of Asset A
σ_A = the standard deviation of Asset A
w_B = weight of Asset B
σ_B = the standard deviation of Asset B
COV_{AB} = covariance between Asset A and Asset B [$COV_{AB} = (\sigma_A)(\sigma_B)(R_{AB})$]
R_{AB} = correlation between Asset A and Asset B

Example 4.4

Ronnie has $100,000 invested in his portfolio, which consists of two mutual funds – Fund A and Fund B.

	Amount	Standard Deviation	Weighting
Fund A	$60,000	15%	60%
Fund B	$40,000	8%	40%

Below are the calculations for the standard deviation of Ronnie's portfolio assuming the correlation between Fund A and Fund B equals +1, 0, and -1.

If correlation equals 1:

$$\sigma_p = \sqrt{(0.60)^2(0.15)^2 + (0.40)^2(0.08)^2 + (2)(0.60)(0.40)(0.15)(0.08)(1)}$$
$$\sigma_p = \sqrt{0.00810 + 0.00102 + 0.00576}$$
$$\sigma_p = 12.20\%$$

If correlation equals 0:

$$\sigma_p = \sqrt{(0.60)^2(0.15)^2 + (0.40)^2(0.08)^2 + (2)(0.60)(0.40)(0.15)(0.08)(0)}$$
$$\sigma_p = \sqrt{0.00810 + 0.00102}$$
$$\sigma_p = 9.55\%$$

If correlation equals -1:

$$\sigma_p = \sqrt{(0.60)^2(0.15)^2 + (0.40)^2(0.08)^2 + (2)(0.60)(0.40)(0.15)(0.08)(-1)}$$
$$\sigma_p = \sqrt{0.00810 + 0.00102 - 0.00576}$$
$$\sigma_p = 5.80\%$$

Summary Chart	
R	σ_p
R =+1	12.20%
R = 0	9.55%
R = -1	5.80%

Notice that when the correlation coefficient is +1, the standard deviation of the portfolio is equal to the weighted standard deviation; however, as the correlation coefficient decreases, the portfolio becomes less volatile (and less risky), as measured by standard deviation. Diversification benefits begin when correlation is something less than 1. As soon as assets do not move in the same exact direction and strength (correlation is less than 1), the standard deviation of the portfolio is reduced. The greatest diversification benefits occur when the correlation is equal to negative 1.

From a practical application perspective, not many portfolios only have two assets. Portfolios have many securities, and even though the above formula could be extended to accommodate a multi-asset portfolio, it would be mathematically cumbersome without the aid of computer software. Instead, tools are available to professionals, such as Morningstar Principia, that will calculate the standard deviation, beta, and other characteristics of a multi-asset portfolio.

Example 4.5

Consider two securities, A and B. Security A has an average return of 11%, while security B has an average return of 6%. Security A has a standard deviation of 20%, while security B has standard deviation of 10%. The chart below illustrates the standard deviation of a portfolio consisting of 50% security A and 50% security B at varying correlations that range from +1.00 to -1.00. As the correlation decreases, so does the portfolio standard deviation. The weighted return remains the same at 8.5%.

Security A	Security B	Weighted Return	Correlation	σ
50%	50%	8.50%	1.00	15.00%
50%	50%	8.50%	0.80	14.32%
50%	50%	8.50%	0.60	13.60%
50%	50%	8.50%	0.40	12.85%
50%	50%	8.50%	0.20	12.04%
50%	50%	8.50%	0.00	11.18%
50%	50%	8.50%	-0.20	10.25%
50%	50%	8.50%	-0.40	9.22%
50%	50%	8.50%	-0.60	8.06%
50%	50%	8.50%	-0.80	6.71%
50%	50%	8.50%	-1.00	5.00%

Example 4.6

Moira considers two securities, A and B. Security A has an average return of 11%, while Security B has an average return of 6%. Security A has a standard deviation of 20%, while Security B has a standard deviation of 10%. Assume that the correlation between A and B is zero. Assume that Moira bought Security B. She could expect an average return of 6% and a standard deviation of 10%. The variability and expected return for Security A is higher. If Moira were to invest a portion of her funds in Security A, then a reasonable expectation is that the expected return and the risk should increase. The chart below illustrates the expected return and the standard deviation when varying percentages of Moira's investment is allocated between A and B.

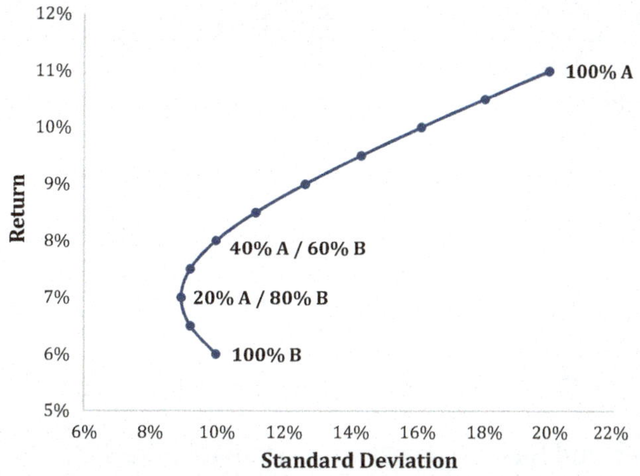

Security A	Security B	Return	σ
100%	0%	11.00%	20.00%
90%	10%	10.50%	18.03%
80%	20%	10.00%	16.12%
70%	30%	9.50%	14.32%
60%	40%	9.00%	12.65%
50%	50%	8.50%	11.18%
40%	60%	8.00%	10.00%
30%	70%	7.50%	9.22%
20%	80%	7.00%	8.94%
10%	90%	6.50%	9.22%
0%	100%	6.00%	10.00%

Notice that if Moira were to invest 80% in B and 20% in A, her return would increase from 6.00% to 7.00%, while her risk would decrease to 8.94% from 10%. By making this change, she is able to increase her return and decrease her portfolio risk. If she were to invest 60% in B and 40% in A, her return would increase from 6.00% to 8.00%, while her risk would remain the same. Clearly, the 60/40 portfolio is a more efficient portfolio than the 100% invested in B. The phrase, "more efficient," means a higher return for the given level of risk.

MODERN PORTFOLIO THEORY

In 1952 Harry Markowitz founded Modern Portfolio Theory, a portfolio selection model based on the assumption that rational, risk-averse investors use a mean-variance framework to choose their optimal efficient portfolio. Markowitz's mean-variance framework assumes that investors make choices based solely on expected returns, as measured by an investment's mean return, and risk, as measured by the variance of those returns.

In addition to the assumption that investors use a mean-variance framework, the theory also requires the following key assumptions:

1. There are no transaction fees or taxes.
2. Perfect competition exists amongst all market participants (such that no single investor can influence prices).
3. All investors have free and instant access to all available market information.

Under these assumptions an investor can construct an **efficient frontier** from all possible combinations of investable risky assets using each asset's mean, variance, and covariance with other assets.

The efficient frontier consists all of combinations of assets that result in an efficient portfolio and can be combined with an investor's utility function, or indifference curves, to identify that investor's optimal portfolio.

To create the efficient frontier, all possible investment portfolios are constructed and the expected return and risk for each portfolio is calculated. If all of these portfolios are plotted on a graph, the universe of potential portfolio options emerges.

Exhibit 4.3 | The Efficient Frontier

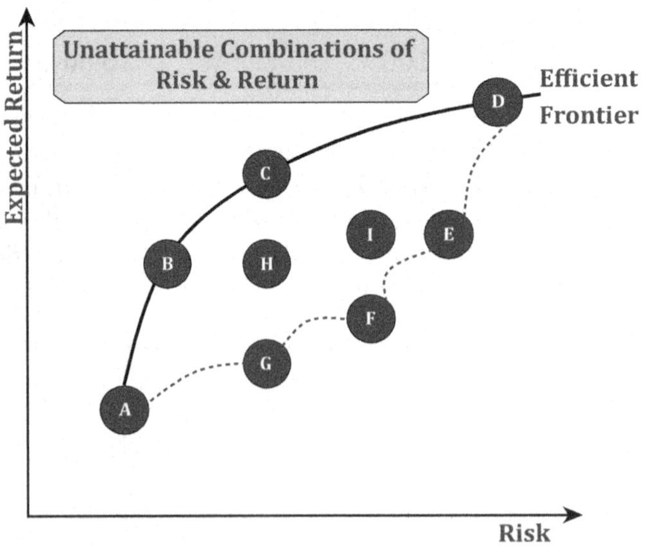

In **Exhibit 4.3**, the area A-B-C-D-E-F-G represents all possible portfolios that can be constructed, plotted in accordance with their expected return and risk characteristics. Each of the points A-B-C-D-E-F-G, as well as points H and I, represent one of the many possible investment portfolios that could be created by an investor. The boundary A-B-C-D in the graph above shows all of the possible portfolios providing the highest return (measured on the Y axis) for a given level of risk (measured on the x axis), and is known as the efficient frontier. Any risk return combinations above the efficient frontier are referred to as unattainable. Any points below the efficient frontier (portfolios E, F, G, H and I) are inefficient. An inefficient portfolio is one in which there is an alternative portfolio with a higher expected return and the same risk or one with the same expected return and less risk.

Since investors seek to receive the maximum expected return for a given level of risk, they prefer some portfolios over others. For example, if you compare portfolio C to portfolios H and G in the graph above, a rational investor would always choose portfolio C. All three portfolios present the same level of risk to the investor, but portfolio C has a higher expected return than portfolios H or G. Likewise, a rational investor comparing portfolio B to portfolio H would always prefer portfolio B, since both portfolios provide the same expected return, but portfolio B provides that return while posing less risk to the investor than portfolio H. While there are a large number of portfolios that could be constructed, a rational investor would only select those portfolios that provide the highest expected return for a given level of risk.

While the efficient frontier identifies all of the portfolios that provide the highest return for a given level of risk, there are still a lot of portfolios for an investor to choose from. Which one should the investor select? The answer depends upon the investor's utility, or **indifference curve**. The indifference curve indicates those portfolios an investor would be indifferent to holding. Several factors go into determining the utility function, including the investor's risk tolerance, goals and objectives, and time horizon. Unlike the efficient frontier, which is concave, an investor's indifference curve is convex. An indifference curve moving up and to the left indicates a higher utility than a curve plotted lower and to the right. The optimal portfolio for a given investor, point X on the graph below, is the point where the investor's highest indifference curve is tangent to the efficient frontier. By investing in this portfolio, the investor will be able to obtain the highest expected return possible for the amount of risk the investor is willing to undertake.

Exhibit 4.4 | Optimal Portfolio

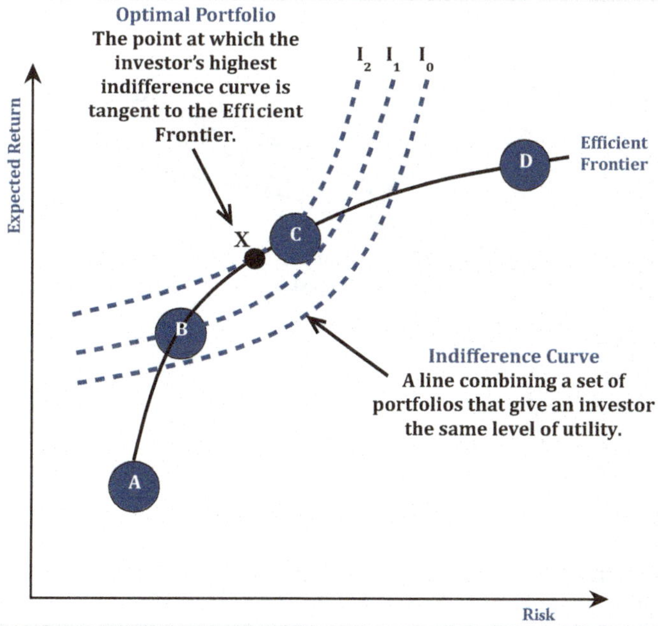

One problem with using this approach to portfolio management is that the efficient frontier, coupled with investor indifference curves, is theoretical and is, therefore, difficult to apply in a practical way. Modern Portfolio Theory takes the theoretical constructs established by the efficient frontier strategy and moves them to a more practical setting.

THE CAPITAL MARKET LINE

The Markowitz efficient frontier allows investors to choose their optimal portfolio based on all investable risky assets. However, this frontier can be improved upon by adding in a risk-free asset. An asset's total risk is measured by its standard deviation. By definition, the risk-free asset will have no risk, and hence its standard deviation will be zero. On a risk return diagram showing the efficient frontier, the risk-free asset will therefore sit on the vertical (return) axis. Typically, a government security such as a treasury bill is used as a proxy for the risk-free asset.

With the addition of this risk-free asset, investors can now choose to split their investment between a risky portfolio and that risk-free asset. As the risk-free asset has a standard deviation of zero, it is uncorrelated with any risky assets. Any combination of a risky portfolio and the risk-free asset therefore lies on a straight line as shown in **Exhibit 4.5**.

This line is the steepest one that can be drawn connecting the risk-free asset and a risky portfolio and is hence the most efficient. Note that a steeper line is not attainable, and shallower lines would cut through the Markowitz efficient frontier and hence include inefficient portfolios.

The line shown in **Exhibit 4.5** is specific to the case where all investors have homogenous, that is identical, expectations. In this case they will all construct the same Markowitz efficient frontier, and choose to lie on the same straight line, known as the **Capital Market Line (CML)**.

Exhibit 4.5 | Capital Market Line

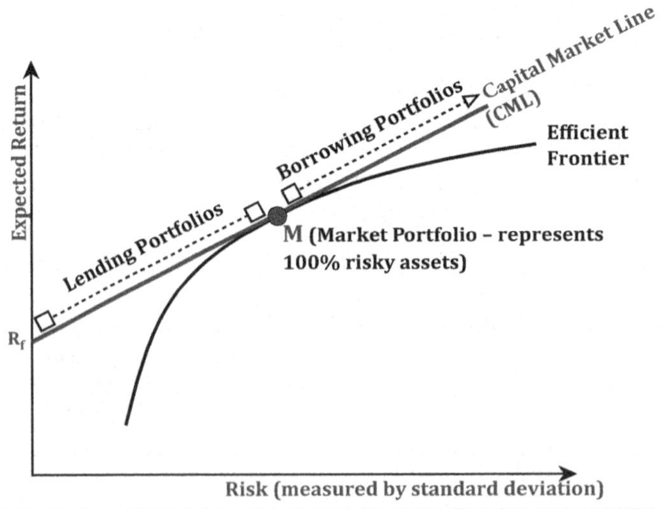

The point of tangency where the CML and efficient frontier meet is referred to as the market portfolio, which is a portfolio of all risky assets. In **Exhibit 4.5** the point of tangency, M, represents the market portfolio.

Recall that the efficient frontier represents all possible investment portfolios of risky assets. To the left of point M, an investor uses a portion of their investable assets to purchase a portfolio on the efficient frontier reserving the rest of the portfolio for investment at the risk-free rate of return. In essence, the investor is lending money to the government at the risk-free rate, therefore portfolios to the left of portfolio M are often referred to as **lending portfolios**.

If an investor were to put all of their assets into the market portfolio, the investor would be at the point of tangency between the CML and the efficient frontier, or at point M on the graph.

Points to the right of Portfolio M on the CML are referred to as **borrowing portfolios**. Investors with higher required returns and a higher risk tolerance can use margin accounts or other types of leverage to form borrowing portfolios. One major assumption of the Markowitz efficient frontier and the CML is that investors can borrow at the risk-free rate.

The equation for the CML is:

$$r_p = r_f + \sigma_p\left(\frac{r_m - r_f}{\sigma_m}\right)$$

Where:

r_p = required portfolio rate of return
r_f = risk-free rate of return
r_m = return on the market
σ_m = standard deviation of the market
σ_p = standard deviation of the portfolio

Portfolios to the left of point M on the CML would consist of both T-bills and the Index fund. These portfolios would not be leveraged, and would, effectively, be lending money to the government at the risk-free rate (referred to a Lending Portfolios, above). If an investor places 100 percent of their assets in the Market portfolio but did not engage in any borrowing (a non-leveraged investment portfolio), the investor would be at point M on the CML. Portfolios to the right of point M on the CML would be fully invested in the market portfolio, and the investor would be borrowing at the risk-free rate to leverage their portfolio (the borrowing portfolio mentioned above).

Notice the term at the end if the CML equation: $(r_m - r_f)/\sigma_m$. It equals the risk premium (the extra reward for investing in the market portfolio instead of the risk-free asset), divided by the standard deviation of the market. This term is referred to as a Sharpe ratio and is discussed more thoroughly in Chapter 5. The Sharpe ratio measures return above the risk-free rate per unit of risk and effectively acts as the slope of the CML line. If the risk premium goes up and the risk-free rate does not change, then the slope of the CML will increase. If the risk premium goes down and the risk-free rate does not change, then the slope of the CML will decrease.

Note that the CML uses the same measure of risk used in determining the efficient frontier - standard deviation. The CML gives an investor a broad perspective of the risk-return relationship, but a more versatile measure is needed to deal with specific portfolios and individual securities.

Capital Asset Pricing Model

To add that needed versatility, the CML equation can be adjusted by substituting beta for the ratio of market and security standard deviations. The resulting equation is the CAPM formula and can be illustrated with the **Security Market Line (SML)**. The SML, illustrated in **Exhibit 4.6** shows the relationship between the level of systematic risk and the expected return on an individual security. It is quite simply a picture of the capital asset pricing model. The convention is to show the equation for individual securities, but it can be easily extended to consider portfolios of securities as well. The equation for the capital asset pricing model is shown below:

$$r_i = r_f + \beta_i(r_m - r_f)$$

Where:

r_i = expected return on an individual security
r_f = risk-free rate of return
β_i = beta, the level of systematic risk of the individual security
r_m = return on the market

The CAPM relies on a set of strict assumptions regarding the market and investor behavior, including the assumption that:

1. All investors are rational and have uniform expectations concerning the risk-return relationships of available investment alternatives.
2. Investors can borrow and lend at the risk-free rate of return.
3. Taxes are zero and there are no transaction costs for investors.

While these assumptions do not perfectly reflect the reality facing investors, the assumptions simplify the analysis providing some context for investors faced with making investment decisions. The term $(r_m - r_f)$ is again referred to as the **risk premium**, which is the incremental return provided by a market portfolio over the risk-free rate of return. The risk premium provides an inducement for investors to purchase risky assets by providing compensation for the additional risk they undertake. Another way of describing this is that the risk premium is the additional expected return over the risk-free rate of return that an investor will require to induce them to invest in an asset that exposes them to risk. This implies that the return on the market includes both the risk-free rate of return plus an appropriate risk premium to compensate the investor for undertaking additional risk.

Exhibit 4.6 | Security Market Line

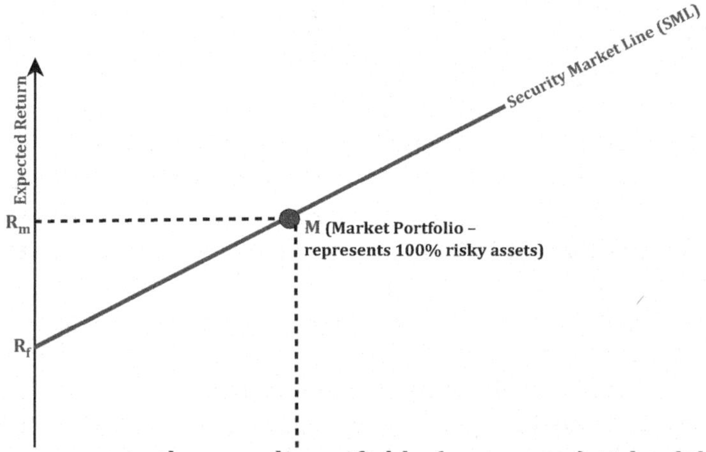

As used in the SML, beta represents the non-diversifiable (systematic) risk of the portfolio, and can be calculated by taking the weighted average of the betas of individual assets in the portfolio. To determine the beta of an individual asset, the individual asset's return is compared to the return of the market as a whole. The beta of the market portfolio is defined as 1.0, since the covariance between the market return and itself equals the market portfolio's variance. An asset that experiences price changes less dramatic than the market would have a beta of less than one, and an asset that experiences price changes more dramatic than the market would have a beta of more than one. Beta, therefore, provides a measure of the riskiness of an asset measured by the variability of its price movement as compared to the price movement of the market. Betas of less than one imply that the security is less risky than the market, while betas of more than one imply that the asset is more risky than the market. The following examples illustrate the use of the CAPM.

Example 4.7

Ryan recently purchased 100 shares in an S&P 500 Index Fund. The S&P 500 Index fund holds a portfolio of assets in the same proportions as the underlying market (the S&P 500). Consequently, the beta of the S&P 500 Fund will be 1.0, since its price variability will be equal to the price variability of the market as a whole. Assuming that the risk-free rate is 4% and the return on the market is 11%, Ryan's required return on his S&P 500 investment can be calculated using the CAPM (SML) formula:

$$r_p = r_f + \beta(r_m - r_f)$$

Required Return on Portfolio = 4% + 1(11%-4%) = 11%

When purchasing a market index fund, Ryan should expect to receive the return on the market, in this case, 11%. Note that the 11% return on the market consists of the risk-free rate of return (in this case 4%) plus the risk premium of 7% representing the total return on the market less the risk-free rate. Since Ryan invested in the market, his beta was 1 and he received the risk-free rate of return plus the required risk premium to induce him to invest in the risky asset.

Example 4.8

In addition to his S&P 500 Index Fund purchase, Ryan also purchases 100 shares of a Technology Fund with a beta of 2. The Technology Fund's beta of 2 indicates that it is a high-risk fund - an investor should expect the return (positive or negative) on the Technology fund to be almost twice the return (positive or negative) on the market. Of course, a beta of 2 does not imply that the Technology Fund's return should be 2 times the market return, since the risk-free rate must be taken into account when calculating expected return in the CAPM equation. Assuming that the risk-free rate is 4% and the expected return on the market is 11%, Ryan's required return on the technology fund would be:

$$r_p = r_f + \beta\,(r_m - r_f)$$

Required Return on Portfolio = 4% + 2(11%-4%) = 18%

The technology fund clearly has twice the systematic risk as the market index fund, but will not have twice the expected return. Instead, it will earn twice the market risk premium plus the risk-free rate of interest.

As both of the above examples illustrate, an investor receives an incremental return for taking additional risk that is measured by the risk premium on the market multiplied by the investment's beta (the risk of the investment relative to the market as a whole). An investor can receive the risk-free rate without subjecting himself to any risk. When investing in a risky asset, the asset's beta will impact the return associated with the risk premium, but not the risk-free rate, since the risk-free rate can be obtained without undertaking any risk.

When managing investment portfolios, it is important to estimate expected returns when constructing the portfolio as well as measure actual performance of the portfolio experienced by the investor. Measures of portfolio performance based on modern portfolio theory concepts will be discussed at length in Chapter 5.

Quick Quiz 4.2

1. Systematic risk can be eliminated using diversification.
   a. True
   b. False
2. Standard deviation measures the variability of expected and actual returns.
   a. True
   b. False
3. A portfolio with a beta of 1.4 is expected to return 12.4% when the market risk premium is 6% and the risk-free rate is 4%.
   a. True
   b. False

False, True, True.

Arbitrage Pricing Theory (APT)

The CAPM is a one-factor model and places substantial pressure on the beta of an individual security to capture all the relevant systematic risk. The Arbitrage Pricing Model, developed in 1976 by Stephen Ross, is viewed as an alternative to the CAPM and is a multi-factor model. Ross believed that a security's expected return was a linear function of macroeconomic variables.

While the CAPM assumes that markets are efficient, the **arbitrage pricing theory (APT)** allows for the possibility that securities can be mis-priced. This makes the APT attractive to analysts who hope to find overvalued or undervalued securities. The drawback to using the APT is that Ross never defined which economic variables are important nor the number which are relevant. It is up to the wealth manager to determine the inputs and to determine which systematic risk factors remain. Many academic and professional studies show that unexpected changes in inflation, gross domestic product, changes in currency and commodity values, and yield spreads are important APT variables that can be used to estimate the return on individual securities.

The APT model follows the general form:

$$r_j = a_j + \lambda_{j1} f_1 + \lambda_{j2} f_2 + ... + \lambda_{jn} f_n + \varepsilon_j$$

Where r_j is the return on security j;
a_j is a constant term for security j;
f_n is a systematic factor;
λ_{jn} is the sensitivity of the jth security to the nth factor;
ε_j is a shock return for security j and has an expected value of zero.

To describe the relationship between security returns and factor sensitivities, the APT takes the following form:

$$E(r_j)= r_f + \lambda_{j1} RP_1 + \lambda_{j2} RP_2 + ... + \lambda_{jn} RP_n$$

Where RP is the risk premium for factor n and r_f is the risk-free rate of interest.

Example 4.9

Carl Towns uses the arbitrage pricing model to estimate the expected return on Bob's Baking Company (BBC), a US based firm that specializes in chocolate donuts. Naturally, BBC's profits are sensitive to commodity input prices as well as other relevant economic conditions. Towns decides that BBC's returns are functions of an index of sugar, cocoa, corn, wheat, and dairy prices, changes in gross domestic product (GDP), and changes in consumer sentiment. After collecting data on each variable, Towns produces the following output:

Economic Variable	Sensitivity	Risk Premium
Commodity Index	1.27	4.2%
GDP	0.89	3.3%
Consumer Sentiment	0.59	2.6%

Towns also observes the risk-free rate of interest is 2.9%.
The expected return on BBC is computed as:

$$E(r_{BBC}) = 0.029 + (1.27)(0.042) + (0.89)(0.033) + (0.59)(0.026) = 0.127$$

RISK TOLERANCE

While Modern Portfolio Theory provides a tool for investors in constructing appropriate investment portfolios, determining which portfolio is most appropriate for a particular investor is often a function of the investor's risk tolerance.

Risk tolerance is a measure of an investor's ability and willingness to expose themselves to risk (price fluctuation in investments) in order to seek higher investment returns. There is a direct relationship between risk and return: to obtain higher expected returns on a portfolio, an investor must be willing to accept additional risk. As risk increases, the price variability of an investment also increases, meaning that the investor may experience larger losses in down market cycles.

Some investors like the prospect of higher returns in rising markets and jump on the market bandwagon as markets are rising, but panic and sell those investments when the markets begin to decline. When this occurs, the investor often does the opposite of what he or she should do when purchasing and selling investments - buy low and sell high. When an investor is in a portfolio that is riskier than their risk tolerance permits, the investor may act on impulse and sell those investments when markets decline, triggering a permanent loss of capital. Risk tolerance, in many ways, is a measure of the investor's ability to stick with investments experiencing downward price variability in the market cycle in an effort to obtain higher, long-run returns.

There are several factors that must be considered when determining an investor's risk tolerance. These factors include loss aversion and risk aversion; available liquidity, savings, and insurance programs; time horizon; goals; phase in the life cycle; and psychographics.[1]

Key Concepts

1. Risk tolerance is the ability and willingness to take on portfolio risk.
2. Loss aversion and risk aversion are factors that influence risk tolerance.
3. Time horizon and investor goals influence risk tolerance.
4. Position in the life cycle can influence risk tolerance.

The perspective of an investor concerning the price variability of investments is important to consider when determining an appropriate level of risk tolerance. Researchers have demonstrated that individuals tend to strongly prefer avoiding losses as compared to acquiring gains - a concept known as loss aversion. Loss aversion asserts that the pain associated with loss is often more acute than the joy associated with gain. In the stock market decline of 2008-2009 that began the Great Recession, many investors decided that they had experienced too many losses and sold their equity investments just before the markets began to recover. This behavior is an example of loss aversion. Individuals with high loss aversion should consider more conservative investment portfolios, since a down market cycle with declining investment prices may cause them to sell their investments at an inopportune time.

While loss aversion is associated with actions taken by investors to avoid losses, risk aversion is the tendency of investors, when exposed to uncertainty, or risk, to take steps to reduce that uncertainty. A rational investor would, for example, properly diversify their portfolio to limit or eliminate their exposure to unsystematic risk. Applying the efficient frontier concept introduced by Markowitz, if given a choice of two portfolios with the same expected return, a rational investor should choose the portfolio that exposes them to the least amount of risk. An investor should always attempt to undertake the least amount of risk necessary to achieve their target expected return. Generally speaking, as an investor's risk aversion increases, the expected return on their ideal portfolio decreases, since the investor is willing to trade off higher potential returns for the safety of a less risky portfolio.

An investor's risk tolerance may also be a function of their financial health. Financial planners recommend that individuals maintain emergency funds and have proper risk management plans in place to guard against the bad consequences associated with an unfortunate occurrence. Investors who have

1. Demographics and psychographics both provide information on consumers. Demographics include age, income, gender, and marital status. Psychographics include information on hobbies, activity, interest, opinions, attitudes, values and behavior. They are both used to categorize consumers.

adequate emergency funds and have appropriate risk management plans in place permit themselves to have a higher risk tolerance with their investment portfolios, since an unexpected event at an inopportune time will not require them to liquidate their portfolio to cover those expenses when asset values decline. The increased ability (capacity) to take on risk may lead to an increased willingness (propensity) to take on risk.

Example 4.10

Thelma and Louise have identical income, and identical investment portfolios. In addition to her investment portfolio, Thelma also has an emergency fund equal to five months of her non discretionary expenditures and has purchased adequate disability, health, life, liability, and long-term care insurance. Louise felt current consumption was more important than insurance planning, so she has only one month of expenditures set aside as an emergency fund, and has some health insurance, but no other insurance coverages.

Over the past six months, the market has been in a steep decline as the economy sank into recession, and both Thelma and Louise have been laid off from their jobs. As a result of the layoff, Louise needs to access some cash to cover her living expenses, such as her mortgage, food, and family costs. After one month of being unemployed, Louise starts to sell off investments to cover these expenses at a time when the prices of those investments are low. Thelma, on the other hand, can draw from her emergency fund and hold onto the investments for a longer period of time, permitting the market to recover.

Since Thelma has adequate liquid savings to carry her through this temporary period of unemployment without having to liquidate her portfolio, Thelma's investment portfolio can stay intact while Louise has to sell assets and realize losses. All else equal, Thelma's risk tolerance will likely be higher than Louise's, since Thelma has staying power in her portfolio during a market downturn when compared to Louise.

Time horizon and investor goals can also impact an individual's investment risk tolerance. If funds used for investment are needed in the near future, the likelihood of having to sell those investments in a market downturn is higher than if the investment portfolio satisfies a longer-term goal.

Example 4.11

Desiree is saving for a down payment on her first home. She expects to purchase the home within three years. Since Desiree's need for the funds is relatively short-term, she will not want to take on excessive risk in the portfolio used to accumulate the down payment. If, for example, she purchased the market portfolio, and 30 months after the purchase the market goes down as the economy enters into a recession, Desiree will have to sell her investment at a loss when she goes to buy her house, requiring her to make up the difference from other sources. Instead, Desiree should purchase a safe investment, such as T-bills, or a bond issued by the U.S. government, or a bond with a three-year maturity issued by a stable company to ensure that the funds will be available when she needs them.

Example 4.12

Julio is 30 years old and is making regular contributions to his 401(k) plan at work. He expects to retire in 40 years at age 70. Consequently, Julio has a long time horizon - in this case 40 years - before he begins to need the money. All else equal, Julio's risk tolerance on his retirement portfolio will be higher than Desiree's risk tolerance in the example above, since Julio can go through several business cycles without appreciably increasing the likelihood that he will need to liquidate the portfolio to cover his retirement expenses. If, for example, the market declines in 30 months due to a recessionary cycle, Julio can stay invested throughout the period to market recovery since he will not need the money for another 37½ years, while Desiree, in the above example, would have to sell and incur losses since she would have an immediate need for the money.

An investor's position in the life cycle can also impact risk tolerance. As individuals move from one phase of the life cycle to another, their financial planning goals and investment objectives may change over time, thereby impacting their risk tolerance.

Exhibit 4.7 | Life Cycle

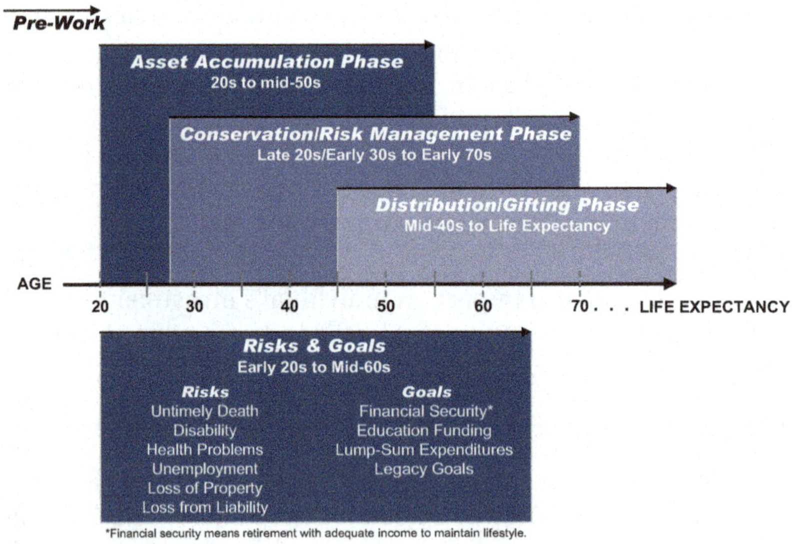

During the early working years of the life cycle, an individual, typically age 25-44, has recently completed their education and is establishing a career. During this phase, debt management (paying off student loans and credit card debt) is often important, as well as establishing an emergency fund and adequate risk management plan. The purpose of an emergency fund is to have liquid assets available in the event of a sudden or unexpected need for cash, implying that the investor should have a relatively low risk tolerance for the assets purchased in the emergency fund. Individuals in this phase of life often have children, and one of the common financial objectives of parents is to fund the children's college education. When children are born, there is a long-term investment horizon (18 years) for education funding, but as the children increase in age, the investment horizon decreases. Many individuals establish college savings funds during this period of the life cycle, which, on average, could be described as funds requiring an intermediate-term investment horizon. During the early working years, an individual should also begin saving for retirement - an activity with a very long time horizon, which could be as much as 40-45 years. When assessing the client's risk tolerance for retirement assets, the long-term investment horizon implies that, all else equal, the investor could take on more risk to achieve a greater return since the need for those funds, and therefore the liquidation of the investments, is a long time in the future.

During the pre-retirement years of the life cycle, an individual, typically aged 45-65, faces new financial challenges, such as paying for the college education of children, continuing to save for retirement, and engaging in risk management planning for longer-term objectives (such as long-term care and legacy planning). As the individual progresses through this phase, it may be wise to reduce the risk of the education funding and retirement portfolio, since the need for those funds to pay for tuition expenses and provide retirement income is approaching. As the time horizon of the investment decreases, all else equal, the risk tolerance of the client will also decrease.

During retirement years, typically age 65 until death, there is still a need for growth in an investment portfolio to provide retirement income, but there is also an immediate need to liquidate retirement assets to fund that income. Often, advisers recommend that a certain portion of a retirement portfolio at this point should consist of relatively liquid investments (enough, perhaps, to fund five years of expenditures), while the rest of the portfolio is structured for moderate growth. This approach provides inflation protection for the portfolio while satisfying the investor's immediate need for retirement income so that market downturns do not induce the investor to sell growth assets at an inopportune time. Some, but not all, investors in their retirement years also engage in legacy planning, which involves the transfer of assets from a senior generation to a younger generation. Even at an advanced age, individuals concerned with legacy planning often have a long-term time horizon, since they are not only considering their life cycle, but rather the life cycle of the extended family. While conventional wisdom often suggests that a person's risk tolerance should decline when in retirement, and their asset portfolios should be conservatively invested, that wisdom does not serve an investor well when legacy planning is one of their major objectives.

Since the individual's place in the life cycle has an impact on the time horizon necessary to fund their various financial goals, life cycle position is an important factor to consider when assessing an individual's risk tolerance.

An investor's psychographics, or their personality, values, opinions, attitudes, interests, and lifestyles, can also impact their risk tolerance. Some individuals are naturally more risk averse than others, and, indeed, some are risk-seeking. An investor who spends their free time sky-diving, scuba diving and engaging in other physically risky activity is likely to have a higher innate risk tolerance than an investor who shuns these activities because of the risk they impose. Understanding the investor's interests, values, and lifestyle often gives clues about their financial risk tolerance. For example, an investor who routinely saves a large portion of their income each year to provide a cushion against the uncertainty of receiving income in the future is likely to be less risk tolerant than an individual who spends all of their income, and then borrows some more to leverage current spending, since that individual believes their income will steadily increase in the future and, consequently, they can save and invest later. Assisting an investor in understanding their risk tolerance and how it should impact their investment choices involves both art and science.

There are numerous risk tolerance questionnaires available that can assist investors in estimating and understanding, their risk tolerance. These questionnaires provide a guideline for the investor, and in some cases may suggest the appropriate amount of risk that can be undertaken in an investment portfolio. Remember, however, that the risk tolerance outcomes are guides, not absolute measures. Investor risk tolerance can change over their life cycle, and may be impacted by other factors, such as the psychographic characteristics of the investor, their goals and objectives, and the time horizon for the use of investment funds, as discussed above.

Stochastic modeling is used to forecast probable outcomes based on one or more random variables. Monte Carlo is a form of stochastic modeling that can be used to assist investors in understanding the risk that they undertake. A Monte Carlo simulation takes an investment portfolio and models several hundred or several thousand possible random outcomes based, in part, on historical data regarding investment returns and assigning those returns in a random order with each iteration. The outcomes of all of these trials can be used to determine the statistical probability that the portfolio will achieve its stated objective. For example, if an investor runs a retirement portfolio through a Monte Carlo model, and the model predicts a 70 percent likelihood of success (meaning that the investor will have their desired retirement income throughout the entire period of their retirement), and the investor is uncomfortable with that result, that might be an indication that the investor is more risk averse and should consider saving more and investing in a more conservative portfolio to achieve a higher probability of success. Monte Carlo simulations do not predict actual results, but provide a measure of the probability of success given the underlying investments in the portfolio and the uncertainty likely to be encountered in the market.

> **Quick Quiz 4.3**
>
> 1. A risk tolerance assessment measures both ability and willingness.
>   a. True
>   b. False
> 2. Loss aversion and risk aversion are effectively the same.
>   a. True
>   b. False
> 3. Time horizon plays a critical role in portfolio construction.
>   a. True
>   b. False
>
> True, False, True.

Another measure that can be used to quantify the level of financial risk in an investment portfolio over a specific period of time is value at risk, or VAR, as discussed in Chapter 3. VAR assists an investor in determining an occurrence ratio of potential losses in their investment portfolio. Unlike a Monte Carlo simulation, which calculates the probability of success in achieving a particular investment objective, VAR calculates the likely magnitude of the price change in a portfolio over a specific period of time, such as a day, a week, or a month. If an investor is uncomfortable with the potential loss predicted by VAR, that might be an indication that they should have a more conservatively structured portfolio, since their risk tolerance is likely to be lower.

Risk Tolerance and Asset Allocation

Investing is challenging as certainty resides only in past and not in future investment performance. However, it is generally accepted that asset allocation is the largest contributor to investment performance over time and two key components in determining a proper asset allocation are risk tolerance and time horizon.

As part of the investment planning process, a financial planner evaluates a client's goals in terms of both dollar value and time. The client's goals are assessed together with risk tolerance in designing the appropriate asset allocation and investment strategies.

Financial planners employ tools to assess the client's willingness to accept investment risk, thus helping to determine the client's risk tolerance as part of the investment planning process. The Global Portfolio Allocation Scoring System (PASS) is such a tool.[2] PASS considers both time horizon and risk tolerance in determining an appropriate asset allocation. Step one is to have the client answer the following questions, which have scores ranging from 5 to 1. Once the questions are answered, each of the point values is summed and the score is used as part of the asset allocation process.

Exhibit 4.8 | The Global Portfolio Allocation Scoring System (PASS)

Global Portfolio Allocation Scoring System (PASS) for Individual Investors						
Questions		Strongly Agree	Agree	Neutral	Disagree	Strongly Disagree
1	Earning a high long-term total return that will allow my capital to grow faster than the inflation rate is one of my most important investment objectives.	5	4	3	2	1
2	I would like an investment that provides me with an opportunity to defer taxation of capital gains to future years.	5	4	3	2	1
3	I do not require a high level of current income from my investments.	5	4	3	2	1
4	I am willing to tolerate some sharp down swings in the return on my investments in order to seek a potentially higher return than would normally be expected from more stable investments.	5	4	3	2	1
5	I am willing to risk a short-term loss in return for a potentially higher long-run rate of return.	5	4	3	2	1
6	I am financially able to accept a low level of liquidity in my investment portfolio.	5	4	3	2	1

2. Dr. William Droms, CFA, the Powers Professor of Finance in the McDonough School of Business at Georgetown University and a principal with Droms Strauss Advisors, Inc. has granted Money Education permission to use his Global Portfolio Allocation Scoring System (PASS) in this text. More information can be found at http://www.droms-strauss.com, as well as the complete article from the Journal of Financial Planning.

The next step is to determine the time horizon of the investment goal and then to use the PASS score to determine the appropriate asset allocation. The higher the score, the more tolerance for risk the client has shown and the more aggressive the portfolio's asset allocation can be.

PASS defines short-term as three years or less, intermediate-term as three to seven years and long-term as more than seven years. With the PASS score and the time horizon, the asset allocation can be determined. There are other models that can be used to assess risk tolerance and determine an appropriate asset allocation. However, Dr. Drom's PASS is a valid model and his article in the Journal of Financial Planning can be used as an additional reference on the subject.

Exhibit 4.9 below depicts the recommended asset allocation for investors. The recommended asset allocation is based on the sum of the points for the PASS questionnaire and the investor's time horizon. For example, an investor who scored 27 and has a long-term horizon would have an allocation as represented in the farthest right column of the chart below.

Cash and fixed income	6%
International bond funds	4%
Domestic equity funds	55%
International equity funds	15%
Real estate funds	20%
Total	**100%**

Exhibit 4.9 | PASS Asset Allocation Recommendations

	Short-Term Horizon				Intermediate-Term Horizon				Long-Term Horizon			
	RT1 Target	RT2 Target	RT3 Target	RT4 Target	RT1 Target	RT2 Target	RT3 Target	RT4 Target	RT1 Target	RT2 Target	RT3 Target	RT4 Target
PASS Score	6 - 12	13 - 18	19 - 24	25 - 30	6 - 12	13 - 18	19 - 24	25 - 30	6 - 12	13 - 18	19 - 24	25 - 30
Cash and Money Market Fund	40%	30%	20%	10%	5%	5%	5%	5%	5%	5%	3%	2%
Treasury Bonds/ Bond Funds	40%	30%	30%	20%	60%	35%	20%	10%	30%	20%	12%	0%
Corporate Bonds/ Bond Funds	20%	30%	30%	40%	15%	15%	15%	10%	15%	10%	10%	4%
Subtotal	**100%**	**90%**	**80%**	**70%**	**80%**	**55%**	**40%**	**25%**	**50%**	**35%**	**25%**	**6%**
International Bond Funds	0%	0%	0%	0%	0%	5%	5%	5%	0%	5%	5%	4%
Subtotal	**0%**	**0%**	**0%**	**0%**	**0%**	**5%**	**5%**	**5%**	**0%**	**5%**	**5%**	**4%**
Index Fund	0%	10%	10%	10%	10%	15%	20%	20%	20%	20%	20%	25%
Large Cap Value Funds/Stocks	0%	0%	5%	5%	5%	5%	10%	10%	10%	10%	5%	5%
Large Cap Growth Funds/Stocks	0%	0%	0%	0%	5%	5%	5%	10%	15%	10%	10%	5%
Mid/Small Growth Funds/Stocks	0%	0%	0%	0%	0%	0%	5%	5%	0%	0%	5%	10%
Mid/Small Value Funds/Stocks	0%	0%	0%	5%	0%	5%	5%	5%	0%	5%	5%	10%
Subtotal	**0%**	**10%**	**15%**	**20%**	**20%**	**30%**	**45%**	**50%**	**45%**	**45%**	**45%**	**55%**
International Stock Funds	0%	0%	0%	5%	0%	5%	5%	10%	0%	5%	10%	15%
Subtotal	**0%**	**0%**	**0%**	**5%**	**0%**	**5%**	**5%**	**10%**	**0%**	**5%**	**10%**	**15%**
Real Estate Funds	0%	0%	5%	5%	0%	5%	5%	10%	5%	10%	15%	20%
Subtotal	**0%**	**0%**	**5%**	**5%**	**0%**	**5%**	**5%**	**10%**	**5%**	**10%**	**15%**	**20%**
Total	**100%**	**100%**	**100%**	**100%**	**100%**	**100%**	**100%**	**100%**	**100%**	**100%**	**100%**	**100%**

Exhibit 4.10 is designed to narrow the number of asset classes and simplify the application of the PASS system. The assumed return and standard deviation for each asset class can be used in conjunction with the recommended asset allocations in **Exhibit 4.9** to create a condensed allocation matrix. In addition, the expected return and expected risk can be calculated for each recommended asset allocation.

Exhibit 4.10 | Assumed Asset Class Returns and Risk

	Expected Rates of Return	Standard Deviation of Returns
Cash and Money Market Fund	2.5%	2.0%
Treasury Bonds / Bond Fund	4.0%	4.0%
Corporate Bonds / Bond Fund	6.0%	5.0%
International Bond Funds	7.0%	6.0%
Index Funds	9.0%	14.0%
Large Cap Funds / Stocks	10.0%	16.0%
Mid / Small Funds / Stocks	12.0%	18.0%
International Stock Funds	13.0%	22.0%
Real Estate Funds	8.0%	12.0%

These asset classes are used in Money Education's *Cases in Financial Planning: Analysis and Presentation* textbook. In practice, some of these asset classes might be excluded while other asset classes might be included. In addition, expected returns and variability will change over time.

The following chart reflects the condensed asset classes and weightings with the corresponding expected return and estimated standard deviation for each portfolio.

Exhibit 4.11 | Condensed PASS Allocations[3]

	Short-Term Horizon				Intermediate-Term Horizon				Long-Term Horizon			
	RT1 Target	RT2 Target	RT3 Target	RT4 Target	RT1 Target	RT2 Target	RT3 Target	RT4 Target	RT1 Target	RT2 Target	RT3 Target	RT4 Target
PASS Score	6 - 12	13 - 18	19 - 24	25 - 30	6 - 12	13 - 18	19 - 24	25 - 30	6 - 12	13 - 18	19 - 24	25 - 30
Cash and Money Market Fund	40%	30%	20%	10%	5%	5%	5%	5%	5%	5%	3%	2%
Treasury Bonds/ Bond Funds	40%	30%	30%	20%	60%	35%	20%	10%	30%	20%	12%	0%
Corporate Bonds/ Bond Funds	20%	30%	30%	40%	15%	15%	15%	10%	15%	10%	10%	4%
International Bond Funds	0%	0%	0%	0%	0%	5%	5%	5%	0%	5%	5%	4%
Index Fund	0%	10%	10%	10%	10%	15%	20%	20%	20%	20%	20%	25%
Large Cap Funds/Stocks	0%	0%	5%	5%	10%	10%	15%	20%	25%	20%	15%	10%
Mid/Small Funds/Stocks	0%	0%	0%	5%	0%	5%	10%	10%	0%	5%	10%	20%
International Stock Funds	0%	0%	0%	5%	0%	5%	5%	10%	0%	5%	10%	15%
Real Estate Funds	0%	0%	5%	5%	0%	5%	5%	10%	5%	10%	15%	20%
Total	**100%**	**100%**	**100%**	**100%**	**100%**	**100%**	**100%**	**100%**	**100%**	**100%**	**100%**	**100%**
Expected Return	3.80%	4.65%	5.30%	6.50%	5.33%	6.78%	7.73%	8.58%	6.93%	7.73%	8.51%	9.77%
Expected Standard Deviation (est)	2.79%	3.85%	4.84%	6.40%	5.13%	7.26%	8.73%	10.25%	7.75%	8.94%	10.12%	12.20%

The information in the chart above can be used to support the required returns in a comprehensive case. In practice, this analysis will often be conducted using a software package that incorporates mean variance optimization. However, the above approach is effective for comprehensive case studies.

3. The standard deviation for each portfolio has been estimated. To calculate it as accurately as possible, a correlation matrix would be required.

Example 4.13

Samantha answers the PASS with the following answers for each of the six questions: strongly agree, agree, agree, neutral, agree, strongly agree. Based on the scoring for each answer, her total score is 25 (5 + 4 + 4 + 3 + 4 + 5). Assuming that she is positioning her portfolio for retirement, a long-term goal, then she would be considering the long-term portfolio RT4, with an expected return of approximately 9.77%. She would allocate her portfolio as indicated in the above chart based on the right-most column. Based on PASS score, her portfolio consists of 70% equity, 20% real estate, and 10% cash and fixed income.

Example 4.14

Darius is interested in buying a house in five years. He wants to invest his savings and make contributions to the fund so that he can accumulate a sizeable down payment by the time he buys the house. His answers to the PASS total 14 (4 + 3 + 3 + 2 + 2). Clearly, Darius is more risk averse than Samantha and has a shorter time horizon. As a result, his allocation should have far less equity exposure and be more conservative. Based on his time horizon and answers to the questionnaire, his recommended allocation is RT2 under Intermediate-Term Horizon. This allocation consists of 35% equities, 5% real estate, with the remaining 60% in cash and fixed-income investments.

Example 4.13 and **Example 4.14** with Samantha and Darius illustrate the process of using the PASS tool. However, like any other tool, it is not perfect. It cannot predict the future. Given the recommended allocation for Darius, he could suffer a significant loss or decline in the value of his equity positions. Going back to **Exhibit 4.1**, the lowest five-year rolling return was close to a negative ten percent. Given that, Darius might choose to run the risk or to be a bit more conservative than what is recommended by the PASS.

In practice, investment advisers will have their own opinions about expected returns, expected volatilities and expected correlations based on an understanding of the economy and the business cycle. These assumptions, along with the assessment of the investor's risk tolerance, the goals of the investor, and the investor's time horizon will all impact the ultimate asset allocation. Once all of these assumptions and factors are considered, the client ultimately has to make the decision about how to allocate the funds being invested. After a thorough analysis and much discussion, an advisor may recommend an asset allocation of 40 percent fixed income securities and 60 percent equity securities. However, the client may choose to follow the advice or modify the recommendation such that the allocation is more or less conservative.

TIME DIVERSIFICATION

As discussed earlier in this text, the risk of an investment, as measured by its standard deviation, tends to decrease as the holding period of the investment increases. The reason for this is that the longer time period permits the portfolio to weather several business cycles and thereby minimizes the likelihood that an investment purchased at the height of one business cycle will have to be sold at the trough of that same cycle (See **Exhibit 4.1**).

While, in concept, this conclusion is a sound one, it is important to recall that the further one attempts to forecast into the future, the greater the likelihood that forecast will be wrong. Investors may use forecasting to evaluate individual stocks (for example, reviewing earning expectations) or to evaluate economic trends (which impact various assets held within the portfolio). If the forecast is wrong and was spread across many periods, the error is compounded and can significantly distort the results. Furthermore, as the length of the projection period increases, the uncertainty about the accuracy of the forecast grows. Sensitivity analysis may be applied in conjunction with forecasting to provide the portfolio manager with an understanding of how the portfolio may change under various what-if scenarios, such as interest rate changes, tax law changes, and inflation rate changes. These projections may include a best-case, worst-case, and most likely case scenario.

Investors should also be aware that while risk appears to diminish over long holding periods, the probability of significant variability in returns in any one year or years does not change. There is always the possibility that an asset held over a long time frame will have to be sold at an inopportune time, resulting in a lower than expected return on the asset, even though the expected risk of that occurrence decreased as the holding period increased.

Furthermore, investors need to remember that assuming the future will resemble the past implies, statistically, that a longer time frame results in a higher probability of achieving an outcome approaching the mean return for the period, but there is no protection from volatility that occurs during the last years of the time horizon. For example, an individual investing for retirement (which is typically considered a long-term investment horizon goal) may feel more comfortable purchasing riskier assets due to the perceived reduction in that risk due to the long holding period, but if the market experiences a significant downturn right before retirement, assets may need to be liquidated at a low price to fund the current year retirement cashflow for the investor. In this instance, since the time horizon grows shorter as retirement approaches, it may be prudent to reduce the risk exposure of the portfolio to avoid such unpleasant surprises, keeping in mind, of course, that a person retiring at age 65 has a life expectancy of about 20 years, which still requires some allocation to growth-oriented investments. This is why some advisers recommend that several years of retirement income be invested in relatively liquid investments to cover immediate cashflow needs, while the rest of the portfolio can be invested for the long term to achieve the desired level of growth. In practice, following this approach is akin to having an "emergency fund" to cover immediate retirement needs while still permitting investment for growth in the rest of the portfolio.

Building Portfolios of Mutual Funds, ETFs, and Separately Managed Portfolios

While MPT provides the tools for investors to create and manage their own investment portfolios, constructing and managing those investment portfolios requires time and skill. Instead of conducting the research necessary to purchase individual stocks and securities to fund a well-diversified portfolio, many individuals delegate that task to investment managers by investing in mutual funds and ETFs, and focus on the **strategic asset allocation** of their overall portfolio.

There are thousands of mutual funds and ETFs available to investors today. Some are designed to mirror specified markets and are referred to as index funds. Others are actively managed funds where the fund managers (hopefully) employ a superior ability to pick the best stocks to purchase in a **tactical asset allocation** to outperform the market. Mutual fund and ETF managers are often highly trained individuals who possess the skills and knowledge necessary to choose the best assets to include in their portfolios.

An individual investor may, based on the factors discussed in this chapter, establish a target strategic asset allocation for their portfolio. Once this is established, instead of investigating individual stocks and securities to purchase in the portfolio, the investor can leave the stock/security selection to the experts and instead purchase mutual funds or ETFs that match the asset classifications specified in the asset allocation. This simplifies the investment process for individual investors, letting them focus on those activities that provide the most value for them.

Example 4.15

Bruno has determined that the strategic asset allocation for his investment portfolio should be 20% in fixed income and 80% in stocks. Bruno would like his portfolio to reside on the efficient frontier to maximize his portfolio return while minimizing exposure to risk. One option is to invest 20% of his portfolio in Treasury bills and use the remaining 80% to purchase all of the stocks in the S&P 500 fund in proportion to their market capitalization. By doing this, Bruno's portfolio is consistent with the capital market line by holding only the risk-free asset and the market itself.

An alternative approach for Bruno, and one that would be much less time consuming, would be to use 80 percent of his portfolio to purchase an S&P 500 Index fund, or SPDR, and use the remaining 20 percent to purchase either T-bills or a bond fund. In this case, Bruno leaves the management and complexity to the experts, and simply establishes a strategic asset allocation that he will seek to keep in balance through periodic rebalancing.

Since Bruno has access to several different types of mutual funds and ETFs, he does not need to limit his strategic asset allocation to the risk-free asset and the market as a whole. Bruno can further segment his equity investments into different risk categories, which, when combined, have the potential to minimize his risk (by choosing asset classes that are negatively correlated with each other) while maximizing his return.

There is some oversight that needs to be exercised when an investor takes this approach to investing, especially when the investor purchases actively managed mutual funds or ETFs to satisfy their asset allocation needs. Over time, as fund managers change and the size of the fund increases or decreases, the mutual fund or ETF may experience style drift. Style drift occurs when the mutual fund's portfolio begins to diverge from its stated investment style or objective. When this occurs, it may be necessary to rebalance the portfolio to match the stated asset allocation.

Example 4.16

When Bruno established his strategic asset allocation for his retirement portfolio, he had a target investment percentage of 15% in mid cap stocks. Bruno purchased a reputable actively managed mid-cap mutual fund, called the Middle Growth Fund, to satisfy that portion of his asset allocation. Over time, the Middle Growth Fund has experienced a fair amount of success, and caught the attention of many other investors. As money poured into the Middle-Growth Fund, and as the asset value grew, the style of the fund started to resemble a large cap growth fund instead of a mid cap growth fund. As a result, Bruno would need to re-balance his portfolio to bring his investments back in line with his strategic asset allocation.

Regardless of the approach taken in establishing investment portfolios, constant vigilance is a necessity, since an investor will need to guard against style drift when investing in mutual funds and ETFs and make sure that the portfolio's asset allocation is maintained. The reward of that vigilance is a well-managed portfolio that will maximize the potential investment return for the investor while minimizing the investor's exposure to risk.

SUMMARY

Summary of key points:

- Portfolio construction is based on the investor's goals, objectives, time horizon, and risk tolerance, with additional consideration for types of available investments and their risk characteristics.
- Portfolios should be designed to achieve a targeted rate of return while minimizing risk.
- As the expected return on an investment increases, the risk (or potential variability of return) on the investment also increases.
- Short-term goals should be funded with low-risk investments to minimize the possibility of adverse price movements when cash is needed to fund investor goals, while long-term goals can be funded with higher-risk investments.
- The risk of an investment, as measured by its standard deviation, tends to decrease as the holding period of the investment increases. Risk is not eliminated with longer holding periods because there is still no protection from volatility that occurs during the last years of the time horizon.
- Diversification is a simple method that is used to reduce portfolio risk by adding investments with low or negative correlations to the portfolio.
- A high standard deviation implies that there is a higher variability of returns, and therefore more risk, associated with an investment when compared to an asset with a low standard deviation.
- An efficient portfolio is one with the highest return for a given amount of risk, or the lowest risk for a given amount of expected return.
- The optimal portfolio for a client is the point of tangency between the investor's highest indifference curve and the efficient frontier.
- Modern Portfolio Theory assumes that investors are rational, that investors can borrow and lend at the risk-free rate, and that there are no taxes or transaction costs.
- The Capital Market Line (CML) consists of all possible combinations of the risk-free asset and the market portfolio.
- The point of tangency where the CML and efficient frontier meet is referred to as the market portfolio (M), which is a portfolio of all risky assets. Portfolios to the left of point M are lending portfolios, and portfolios to the right of point M are borrowing portfolios.
- The market risk premium is equal to the return of the market minus the risk-free rate of return. It is the additional return above the risk-free rate that is required to induce the investor to accept exposure to the risk of the market.

- The Security Market Line (SML) shows the relationship between the level of systematic risk, as measured by beta, and the expected return on an individual security. It is quite simply a picture of the capital asset pricing model (CAPM).
- The Capital Asset Pricing Model (CAPM) is a single-factor model for pricing assets based on their level of systematic risk, as measured by beta.
- Arbitrage pricing theory (APT) is a multi-factor asset-pricing model that is designed to overcome some of the limitations, such as unrealistic assumptions about investor rationality, in the CAPM.
- Risk tolerance is a measure of an investor's ability and willingness to expose themselves to risk (price fluctuation in investments) in order to seek higher investment returns.
- Factors affecting an investor's risk tolerance include loss aversion and risk aversion; available liquidity, savings, and insurance programs; time horizon; goals; phase in the life cycle; and psychographics.
- Monte Carlo simulation measures the probability of success in achieving a particular investment objective by running hundreds or thousands of iterations of random potential combinations of investment returns.
- Asset allocation is the largest contributor to investment performance over time, and the two key components in determining a proper asset allocation are risk tolerance and time horizon.
- Strategic asset allocation addresses the risk-return tradeoff of the investments in a portfolio by developing an appropriate diversification strategy across a broad set of asset classes to minimize the probability of substantial losses in one investment category significantly impacting the performance of the portfolio as a whole.
- Tactical asset allocation seeks to outperform the market over shorter periods of time by placing investment dollars in those asset classes that the investor expects will outperform market returns over the period.
- Mean-variance optimization (MVO) models are software packages that calculate an efficient frontier based upon user supplied estimates of the returns, standard deviations, and correlations among sets of investment vehicles, then seeks to maximize the expected return of a portfolio based on a selected level of risk.
- Style drift occurs when an actively managed mutual fund's portfolio begins to diverge from its stated investment style or objective. When mutual funds have been selected to match an investor's desired asset allocation and style drift occurs, it may be necessary to rebalance the portfolio to match the stated asset allocation.

DISCUSSION QUESTIONS

SOLUTIONS to the discussion questions can be found exclusively within the chapter. Once you have completed an initial reading of the chapter, go back and highlight the answers to these questions.

1. Compare the volatility of equity returns over short, medium and long time horizons.

2. Explain how to determine portfolio return and risk.

3. Differentiate between efficient and inefficient portfolios.

4. Describe the optimal portfolio for an investor.

5. Discuss the CAPM (Capital Asset Pricing Model).

6. Explain the concept of risk tolerance.

7. Differentiate between strategic and tactical asset allocation.

8. Explain the difference between the Security Market Line and the Capital Market Line.

9. Describe the importance of the lending and borrowing portfolios for investors who are trying to locate their personal optimal portfolio.

10. Explain how the Arbitrage Pricing Theory (APT) adds value to investor's understanding of asset pricing.

MULTIPLE-CHOICE PROBLEMS

A sample of multiple choice problems is provided below. Additional multiple choice problems are available at money-education.com by accessing the Student Practice Portal.

1. What type of risk is present in a portfolio with a beta of 1.5?
    a. Systematic risk only.
    b. Unsystematic risk only.
    c. Systematic and unsystematic risk.
    d. Cannot determine from the question.

2. Which tools can help to determine an optimal investment portfolio?
    1. Mean-variance optimization model.
    2. Risk tolerance questionnaire.
    3. Tactical asset allocation.

    a. 1 only.
    b. 2 only.
    c. 1 and 2.
    d. All of the above.

3. The highest annual range of returns for the S&P 500 has occurred for which of the following?
    a. 1-year rolling returns.
    b. 5-year rolling returns.
    c. 10-year rolling returns.
    d. 20-year rolling returns.

4. Which of the following is a graphical representation of expected return and beta?
    a. APT.
    b. CML.
    c. SML.
    d. Efficient frontier.

5. Jocko was just told that the expected return for Echo stock was 20%, based on the CAPM. Assuming that the market return and the risk-free rate are 12% and 4%, respectively, what is the beta for Echo?
    a. 1.0.
    b. 1.5.
    c. 2.0.
    d. 2.5.

QUICK QUIZ EXPLANATIONS

Quick Quiz 4.1

1. False. The correlation coefficient ranges from +1 to -1.
2. True.
3. True.

Quick Quiz 4.2

1. False. Systematic risk cannot be eliminated through diversification. Only unsystematic risk can be managed using diversification.
2. True.
3. True.

Quick Quiz 4.3

1. True.
2. False. Loss aversion is associated with actions to avoid losses, risk aversion is to avoid uncertainty.
3. True.

5

INVESTMENT DECISIONS AND ATTRIBUTION ANALYSIS

LEARNING OBJECTIVES

1. Define attribution analysis.
2. Contrast security selection with asset allocation decisions.
3. Describe the importance of a benchmark portfolio.*
4. Identify the characteristics of an appropriate benchmark portfolio.*
5. Recommend specific indexes as components of a benchmark portfolio.*
6. Determine whether a portfolio manager has outperformed their benchmark.*
7. Compare the Treynor ratio, the Sharpe ratio, and Jensen's alpha as measures of portfolio performance.*
8. Compute Treynor, Sharpe, and Jensen's alpha for a mutual fund.*
9. Demonstrate the asset allocation decision.*
10. Define rebalancing strategies, including buy and hold, constant weighting, and dynamic allocation.*
11. Summarize how changes to asset allocation and selection affect portfolio returns.
12. Define asset selection methods, including discounted cash flow, relative value, technical analysis, and passive investing.
13. Compute the intrinsic value of a security using a simple discounted cash flow method.*
14. Compare relative value multiples when comparing securities.*
15. Define multiples, including price to earnings, price to book value, price to sales, price to cash flow, and enterprise value to EBITDA.*
16. Discuss the Fama decomposition.
17. Compute the return to diversification and net selectivity in the Fama decomposition.
18. Discuss attribution analysis as described by BHB.*
19. Compute return attribution on a security by dividing performance into selection and attribution.*
20. Contrast the components of a bond attribution analysis, including trading, policy, rate anticipation, and analysis effects.
21. Draw the bond market line.

**Ties to CFP Certification Learning Objectives*

INTRODUCTION

Financial analysts typically begin the process of evaluating the performance of a portfolio by computing the various types of returns shown in Chapter 3. Popular measures of performance include time and dollar weighted returns as well as holding period returns, which provide an important first step in determining the historical quality of a financial asset. Returns, however, do not provide the complete story about an asset's performance.

Subsequent steps include adjusting the performance measures for risk in the manner also described in Chapter 3. To measure the variability in returns, financial analysts compute standard deviations and betas. Both the return and risk measures are used as inputs to compute the Sharpe ratio and Jensen's alpha. Even still, the story on performance remains incomplete.

To finalize the discussion on portfolio performance, an attribution analysis must be executed. The first two steps answer the relevant question of how a portfolio has performed. **Attribution analysis** provides the reasons behind that performance. Eugene Fama was the first academic researcher to develop a formal attribution analysis model. Fama is best known for his work on the efficient markets hypothesis, and he was awarded the Nobel Prize in economic science for his lifetime contributions to the understanding of asset pricing. Some of his lesser known work includes a 1972 paper on the decomposition of investment performance into its basic component parts. It was Fama who developed the notion that managed portfolios should be compared against naively selected portfolios that are composed of similar securities with similar risk levels. It is interesting to note that Fama's work in the early 70s did not receive the attention it deserved and has typically taken a backseat to other types of attribution analysis. Those other types, however, have their roots in what is known as the Fama decomposition.

In 1986, three professional investment advisers, Gary Brinson, Randolph Hood, and Gilbert Beebower (BHB) developed a formal and more easily applied attribution model. They authored a paper on the determinants of portfolio performance for equity securities. Other researchers have added to their work and improved the understanding of performance.

Any discussion of attribution analysis, whether authored by Fama or BHB, begins with a discussion of the creation and the importance of a **benchmark portfolio**.

BENCHMARK PORTFOLIOS

Evaluating the performance of a portfolio without comparing that performance to similarly constructed portfolios ignores the systematic risk influence that affect all portfolios. It is necessary, therefore, to compare each portfolio against a relevant benchmark.

Example 5.1

Consider a client with a 10% return objective. A financial adviser creates a policy statement for that client, identifies relevant financial securities that fit the risk return profile for this client, and drafts an optimal asset allocation using specialized optimization techniques. After one year, the financial adviser's recommendations produce a return of 10%.

Question: Is this client satisfied with the performance of the portfolio?

Answer: It might initially appear that the client should be satisfied because the return objective is met. A more in-depth review of performance, however, should measure the return against a relevant benchmark or index. Suppose that a benchmark portfolio, which contains securities that have identical risk characteristics as the client's portfolio, produces a 15% return during the period. The relative performance of the client's portfolio is inferior. Few, if any, clients, would be satisfied with a portfolio that underperformed the benchmark by 5%.

Historically, most investors have settled on popular indexes, such as the Standard and Poor's 500 Index or the Wilshire 5000 Index, as benchmarks against which to compare their portfolio performance.

These are important indexes and are appropriate for many clients, including passive investors. Popular indexes have been important to investors for over a century. For example, the Dow Averages were first published in 1885, and the S&P Index was created in 1923, with 233 companies. A wave of passive investing began in the mid 1970s with the introduction of the Vanguard 500 Index Fund. Other investment firms joined the process and created their own index funds. According to Morningstar, the total investment in US passive equity index funds exceeded $4 trillion by the end of 2019 and for those investors, the related index serves as the appropriate benchmark to evaluate performance.

Key Concepts

1. Define a benchmark portfolio.
2. Describe conditions under which a benchmark portfolio is appropriate for a specific equity portfolio.

Example 5.2

Consider an investor who owns the Atlantic 500 Index Fund. The Atlantic fund generated a 9% return during the previous year. The related Standard & Poor's 500 index generated a 9.1% return over that same time period. One might be initially tempted to conclude that Atlantic underperformed by 10 basis points, and that is probably true, but those 10 basis points can most likely be attributed to the expense ratio for the Atlantic fund. Passive investors will typically generate a return equal to the performance of the related index minus expenses.

For other investors, comparing performance to a popular index is inappropriate. Those investors or financial advisers who inappropriately use an index as a benchmark are really just taking shortcuts as described in the Behavioral Finance section of Chapter 6.

Forming an appropriate benchmark is critical for effective portfolio management. Sometimes referred to as a **normal portfolio**, a benchmark is a customized portfolio that contains the securities in the universe the manager typically holds, and is weighted as the manager would typically weight the portfolio.

Any deviation from the normal portfolio by an investment adviser will result in a difference in performance between the two portfolios.

If performance differences are identified, attribution analysis can then be used to identify the sources of the those differences, and whether it is reasonable to expect them to be replicated. Consider the following example which compares two active managers.

Example 5.3

Darnell spends significant time and resources performing macro-economic analyses, industry analyses, and security analyses. Darnell forms his portfolio only after careful consideration of all relevant factors, including using a proprietary software allocation model tailored to fit the risk and return objectives outlined in the portfolio's prospectus. Darnell's portfolio generally consists of large cap firms. Darnell generated a return of 10% over the previous period.

Penelope spends significant time and resources watching Hollywood movies. Whenever she sees a product placement in one of the scenes, she buys shares in that company. If she sees an identical product in two movies within a month's time, she doubles the allocation to that company. Penelope's portfolio consists almost entirely of large cap firms. Penelope generated a return of 11% over the previous period.

Assume both money managers outperformed their respective benchmarks by exactly 50 basis points. Which one is the better manager?

It seems reasonable to think that using fundamental analysis would make Darnell more likely to repeat his outperformance than Penelope. In the absence of perfect knowledge about the two manager's decision making tools, an attribution analysis can begin to shed insight on which manager has superior skills.

Forming a Benchmark Portfolio

The process of forming a benchmark or normal portfolio can be fairly straightforward or extremely complicated. Under certain circumstances, it is appropriate to use an index or combination of indexes as the benchmark, as long as many of the securities held in the portfolio are contained in the index. A more complex way is to locate securities that have high correlations with the securities in the portfolio. Either way, the formation of the benchmark portfolio is critical in determining relative performance.

Example 5.4

Zack Pickler owns a well-diversified portfolio consisting of twenty-five large cap stocks and twenty-five small cap stocks.

Ellen Woods owns a well-diversified portfolio consisting of ten large cap stocks, twenty international mid cap stocks (Germany, Spain, and UK), ten emerging market stocks, and ten micro U.S. stocks.

Identify an appropriate benchmark for each.

Pickler: One-half of the S&P 500 Index and one-half of the S&P Small Cap 600. This is an easy one. Investors should structure the benchmark weights to be similar to those in the portfolio.

Woods: Some combination of the S&P 500 Index (20%), the MSCI Emerging Market Index (40%), Dow Jones Micro Cap Index (20%), and the Stoxx Europe 500 (20%). This one is slightly more challenging, as the investor must search for indexes that have high correlations with the underlying stocks. Once again, the weights should be similar to the invested portfolio weights.

A more challenging but still appropriate benchmark selection for both Woods and Pickler would include 40 stocks that operate in the same industry as the companies in the portfolio. The allocations in the benchmark should be similar to those in the portfolio. The benchmark should be monitored for changes in variances and covariances.

Quick Quiz 5.1

1. A portfolio with 100 equity securities and 100 fixed-income securities will most likely have a benchmark that contains identical stocks and bonds.
   a. True
   b. False
2. A portfolio manager who generates a return in excess of the benchmark portfolio has outperformed.
   a. True
   b. False
3. An appropriate benchmark is one that contains securities with high positive correlations to those securities in the portfolio.
   a. True
   b. False

False, True, True.

PERFORMANCE MEASURES

Before the development of modern portfolio theory in the 1960s, investors generally measured performance by using one yardstick, the return on an investment. Investors at that time were aware of risk but had no formal way of measuring it. Consequently, investors made decisions based on incomplete information.

Key Concepts

1. Define the three types of ratios of portfolio performance evaluation.
2. Discuss systematic and total risk in the context of portfolio performance evaluation.

For example, the stock market generated substantial returns virtually every year during the 1920s with a high return of 45 perfect in 1928. The subsequent 1929 crash and depression produced substantial negative returns for several years and hit the bottom in 1932 with a loss of about 50 percent. Investors had few risk management tools at their disposal to help them manage the volatility from 1920 through the beginning of World War II. Of course, the Great Depression significantly eliminated much of the wealth that was generated during the roaring 20s, and most investors were concerned about survival rather than risk management.

At about this time in history, using inflation adjusted returns as a measure of performance became popular.

For example, the Dow Jones Industrial Average surged about 50 percent after the Battle of Midway to the end of WW II but inflation was almost 10 percent during 1941 and 1942. Clearly, investor returns were being affected by the rate of price changes in the economy.

Using inflation adjusted returns was not a satisfactory way to handle volatility, but the concept led to the idea that portfolio returns should be compared to some other performance measure.

When Harry Markowitz applied standard deviation to the development of the efficient frontier in 1952, other researchers were able to create relative and absolute measures of performance.

A three-year period in the mid 1960s saw the development of three performance measures that are still used by financial advisers today.

Quick Quiz 5.2

1. A financial adviser compares two funds and computes a Sharpe ratio of 0.62 and 0.69. The adviser would identify the fund with the higher ratio as the one that outperformed.
   a. True
   b. False
2. A Jensen's alpha of 0.03 indicates the mutual fund outperformed the relevant equity index on a risk-adjusted basis.
   a. True
   b. False

True, True.

The first was introduced by Jack Treynor, a mathematician who is credited as one of the four original authors of the capital asset pricing model. Treynor worked at the famed management consulting firm Arthur D. Little but studied for one year at MIT where he met Franco Modigliani and Merton Miller and shared research with William Sharpe and Fisher Black. After returning to the consulting world, he developed a practical application of his work, which is known as the **Treynor Ratio**. This ratio is the first performance ratio and uses systematic risk to measure risk adjusted returns.

A year later, William Sharpe published a similar ratio, called the **Sharpe ratio**. He used standard deviation as the measure of total risk instead of the beta used by Treynor.

The following year, Michael Jensen developed what has become known as **Jensen's alpha**. Jensen was interested in evaluating fund managers to determine if they could regularly outperform. He used similar metrics as Sharpe and Treynor, but he added market data to the model. As such, Jensen's alpha is an absolute measure of performance and is widely interpreted as a measure of excess return. Financial advisers often speak of positive or negative alphas as barometers of managerial value added. **Alpha** is the difference between the actual return on a portfolio and its expected return as outlined by the capital asset pricing model.

Exhibit 5.1 summarizes the formulas and important concepts of the three measures of performance.

Exhibit 5.1 | Performance Measures

	Treynor Ratio	Sharpe Ratio	Jensen's Alpha
Equation	$T_p = \frac{r_p - r_f}{\beta_p}$	$S_p = \frac{r_p - r_f}{\sigma_p}$	$\alpha_p = r_p - [r_f + \beta_p(r_m - r_f)]$
Risk Statistic	Beta	Standard Deviation	Beta
Risk Type	Systematic	Total	Systematic
Performance Measure	Relative	Relative	Absolute

Example 5.5

Grayson is a financial adviser comparing two mutual funds. Grayson collects the following information:

	Polar Bear Fund	Grizzly Bear Fund
Return on Fund	16.1%	14.8%
Beta	1.11	1.05
Standard Deviation	18.6%	16.4%
Risk-Free Rate	3.1%	3.1%
Return on Market Index	12.9%	12.9%

The three performance ratios are computed as follows:

	Treynor Ratio	Sharpe Ratio	Jensen's Alpha
Polar Bear	$\frac{0.161 - 0.031}{1.11} = 0.117$	$\frac{0.161 - 0.031}{0.186} = 0.699$	$0.161 - [0.031 + 1.11(0.129 - 0.031)] = 0.021$
Grizzly Bear	$\frac{0.148 - 0.031}{1.05} = 0.111$	$\frac{0.148 - 0.031}{0.164} = 0.713$	$0.148 - [0.031 + 1.05(0.129 - 0.031)] = 0.014$

Interpretation:
Grayson will notice that a comparison of the two mutual funds using the traditional relative measures of performance produces mixed results. Polar Bear Fund has a higher Treynor ratio but a lower Sharpe ratio than Grizzly Bear Fund. If Grayson uses just those two measures, he will have to decide which risk statistic is more appropriate, beta or standard deviation. Grayson might have clients with completely diversified portfolios, which makes Polar Bear superior, but for other clients with different risk preferences, Grizzly Bear might be appropriate.

Jensen's alpha provides a possible tie-breaker. Both funds have positive alphas, indicating they perform above the market index. Polar Bear, however, has the higher alpha, indicating superior performance.

Based on the entire analysis, Grayson is most likely to identify the Polar Bear Fund as the better of the two funds.

THE ASSET ALLOCATION DECISION

Key Concepts

1. Explain how allocation decisions affect portfolio risk and returns.
2. Summarize a tactical asset allocation strategy.
3. Discuss three costs of rebalancing a portfolio.

Asset allocation is an investment decision in which portfolio weights are assigned to reflect the investor's risk profile. These weights are typically produced by optimization software in which inputs to the model include expected returns, volatility, market expectations, and some measure of risk tolerance. The original Harry Markowitz 1952 PhD dissertation is the typical reference research upon which most of the current models are based. The weights can be adjusted over time to increase or reduce exposure to a particular security or asset class.

If an investor owns \$50 in equities and \$50 in fixed-income securities, then the asset allocation is 50 percent debt and 50 percent equity. Over time, the prices of the securities in the portfolio change, causing the weights to deviate from their original values. Investors then face the portfolio rebalance decision. If equity values rise to \$75 while debt values rise to \$60, the new weights become 55 percent equity and 45 percent debt. Advisers should determine beforehand which changes are significant enough to justify rebalance trades.

Asset Allocation Strategies

Buy and Hold Strategy

Some investors are comfortable allowing rising and falling markets to change their original allocations. A **buy and hold strategy** is one in which the investor does nothing to rebalance the portfolio weights. This implies that over an extended period of time, the current allocation could potentially be much different than the original weights in the allocation. The major problem with this approach is that the portfolio can have significantly different return and risk profiles than when originally constructed.

Most investors are compelled to rebalance the portfolio weights over time at least to reduce the volatility of the portfolio. Most investors believe the benefits of rebalancing outweigh the costs, which include:

- transaction costs, including commission, bid ask spreads, and liquidity problems;
- resources to determine rebalancing method; and
- resources to execute rebalancing trades.

Constant Weighting Allocation

Investors initially decide on a strategic allocation model, in which the target weights for the portfolio are typically allowed to fluctuate within a narrow tolerance range. When that tolerance range is exceeded, the securities in the portfolio are either underweighted or overweighted. Some trades will be necessary to return the portfolio to its original strategic weights.

Example 5.6

Consider an investor who owns two mutual funds, one an equity fund and one a fixed-income fund:

Mutual Fund	Shares	Net Asset Value	Total Value	Allocation
Ash Equity	200	$10	$2,000	20%
Smoke Treasury	200	$40	$8,000	80%

The strategic asset allocation is 20% Ash and 80% Smoke in the portfolio with an initial market value of $10,000.

Suppose that Ash changes to $12 and Smoke changes to $38. The portfolio now looks like:

Mutual Fund	Shares	Net Asset Value	Total Value	Allocation
Ash Equity	200	$12	$2,400	24%
Smoke Treasury	200	$38	$7,600	76%

The portfolio still has as a market value of $10,000, but the weights have changed from 20%/80% to 24%/76%. To maintain the constant weighting allocation, 33 shares of Ash should be sold and 11 shares of Smoke should be purchased.

Mutual Fund	Shares	Net Asset Value	Total Value	Allocation
Ash Equity	167	$12	$2,004	20%
Smoke Treasury	211	$38	$8,018	80%

The portfolio weights are now returned to their original strategic levels (with some rounding errors). This rebalancing method tends to buy securities when the price falls and sell when price rises. One major issue is for the investor to decide how much of a price change warrants a rebalancing. Some investment professionals suggest changes of 5% or 10% are sufficient to significantly affect portfolio volatility, while others wait until changes of 25% occur.

Tactical Asset Allocation

Strategic asset allocation is long term by nature, but many investors like to have some flexibility to take advantage of mispricings over the short term. Some investors even expect to time the market. A **tactical asset allocation** strategy is one in which deviations from the long-term allocations are pursued over the short term to increase returns by taking advantage of current market conditions that favor one asset class over another.

In the example of Ash and Smoke, a tactical decision is to change the allocations to 15 percent and 85 percent when the investor believes one fund's shares are overvalued and one fund's shares are undervalued because treasuries are expected to outperform equities. The underweighting of one fund reduces the downside risk while the overweighting of the other fund increases the upside return.

A key to successful tactical strategy is to have the skill to be able to not only determine when an asset will outperform, but also when that performance will return to its normal levels.

Dynamic Asset Allocation

Dynamic allocation is a strategy in which the portfolio weights are constantly being adjusted to reflect changing market conditions and changing asset values. Dynamic allocation is an active strategy where macroeconomic variables determine which asset class should be overweighted. For example, when equity securities are rising because of economic growth, the dynamic weights to equity should be increased. Money managers use mathematical models to determine the new weighting schemes, but the decision to overweight one asset class is typically done the old fashioned way: by performing complete economic analyses.

> **Quick Quiz 5.3**
>
> 1. An investor who believes a security is undervalued should increase allocation to that security as part of a tactical asset allocation strategy.
>   a. True
>   b. False
> 2. A portfolio that beats its benchmark because of asset allocation decisions is most likely due to the manager's skill.
>   a. True
>   b. False
>
> True, True.

The decisions to rebalance typically follow either a calendar based or rules based model. A calendar-based model is one in which the weights are adjusted every predetermined calendar period, usually annually, but could be monthly, quarterly or even every decade. The big risk of using this type of method is there is no accounting for market condition changes. A rules-based model is one in which the weights are only adjusted if certain characteristics have changed. For example, a rebalance is required if prices move by 10 percent or if volatility changes by 20 percent. Dynamic trades can be executed after other predetermined changes, such as tax policy or correlations.

ASSET SELECTION DECISION

Asset selection is the stage of the investments process in which the investor decides which financial securities are to be included in the portfolio. Each security identified should possess risk and return characteristics that are consistent with client or investor preferences. Many investors choose to populate their portfolios with mutual funds, although some investors, particularly institutions, select individual stocks and bonds.

To help with the selection of individual assets, investors use a range of valuation techniques to try and identify assets that may be mispriced. The most common valuation techniques include:

1. Discounted cash flows
2. Relative valuation with multipliers
3. Technical analysis
4. Indexing

Discounted Cash Flows

Discounted cash flow models estimate the intrinsic value of an asset by calculating the present value of all future cash flows the asset is expected to generate. For an option-free bond, this is a simple, this is a simple process of discounting the coupon and principal payments to arrive at an intrinsic value. For bonds with embedded options, the payments are contingent on interest rate paths or price movements, but the intrinsic value can still be computed using sophisticated mathematics. For equity securities, there is a range of different cash flow measures that may be used including free cash flow, operating cash flow and dividend payments.

Key Concepts

1. Understand the importance of asset selection.
2. Summarize four ways to identify undervalued securities.
3. Distinguish differences between intrinsic and relative valuation models.

To compute present value, the analyst needs to estimate the future payment streams as well as estimate the appropriate discount rate. The appropriate discount rate to use is the rate of return an investor would require in order to invest in the asset.

Example 5.7

The Michaels Distribution Company (MDC) expects to generate \$220 million in operating cash flows during the next year of operations. MDC experienced a slowdown in growth because of problems with a few of its warehouses and trucks. It has resolved those issues, but the competition has taken enough market share to reduce its long-term growth rate to 3.3%. Using a well-established pricing model, MDC's required rate of return is now 9.4%.

Assuming MDC operates over an extended period of time, the intrinsic value of the company can be computed as follows:

$$\text{Total Market Value} = \frac{\text{Operating Cash Flow}_1}{(\text{Required Return on Equity} - \text{Sustainable Growth Rate})}$$

$$\text{Total Market Value} = \frac{\$220{,}000{,}000}{(0.094 - 0.033)} = \$3{,}606{,}557{,}377$$

MDC has 340 million outstanding shares, so its intrinsic value per share can be computed as follows:

$$\text{Intrinsic Value} = \frac{\$3{,}606{,}557{,}377}{340{,}000{,}000\ \text{Shares}} = \$10.61\ \text{per share}$$

If the intrinsic value is greater than the market price of the security, then the security is undervalued. The money manager will buy this security with the expectations that the price will rise when all other market participants realize it is undervalued. If the stock is overvalued, money managers can either short the shares or use derivative securities to hedge against a falling stock price.

This model is simply an application of the Gordon Growth stock pricing model and makes the limiting assumption that operating cash flows increase at a constant rate over an infinite time period. Nevertheless, the model is extremely useful in estimating reasonable market values.

Relative Valuation

Relative valuation techniques compare the fundamentals of similar companies with the aim of identifying which are relatively undervalued. Price-multiples, such as the Price Earnings (PE) ratio, are commonly used for relative valuation.

The first step in the process is to identify a peer group of similar assets. Relative valuation is based on the law of one price, the idea that assets with the same payoffs should also have the same price. Once a group of similar assets have been identified, their price multiples are calculated and compared.

In the case of the PE ratio, this involves dividing the company's expected earnings by its current price. For example, a company with a share price of $5.00 and expected earnings per share of $1.00 would have a PE ratio of 5x. The share price is five times earnings. If a similar asset has a PE ratio of 4x, an investor may conclude that it is relatively undervalued and represents the better investment.

The drawback to the relative valuation method is that in reality very few investments are identical. Although peer groups can be constructed that contain similar assets, for example firms from the same country and industry, each asset is likely to have different characteristics. In the illustration above, for example, the PE ratio of 5x for the first company may be entirely justified by a much higher predicted growth rate. In addition, many fundamental characteristics used in multipliers, such as earnings, are not directly comparable if they have been calculated using different accounting standards or policies.

Investors must therefore use their skill and judgment to assess whether or not a price multiple genuinely reflects an over or undervaluation. **Exhibit 5.2** shows the most common multipliers that may be used and how they should be analyzed by investors.

Exhibit 5.2 | Popular Multiple Valuation Metrics

Multiple	Definition (Formula)	Analysis (Rationale)
Price to Earnings (PE)	$\frac{\text{Stock Price}}{\text{Estimated Earnings}}$	• Firms with higher PE ratios are considered to be more 'expensive' • Advisers must ensure a buy decision is worth the high ratio
Price to Book (PB)	$\frac{\text{Stock Price}}{\text{Book Value of Equity}}$	• Low ratio is signal of potential undervaluation • Book values are more stable than earnings • Advisers must be careful of accounting differences among firms
Price to Sales (PS)	$\frac{\text{Stock Price}}{\text{Total Revenues}}$	• Revenue figures are very difficult to manipulate • Advisers must be careful not to ignore the firm's efficiency as high PS ratios do not always result in high earnings
Price to Cash Flow (PCF)	$\frac{\text{Stock Price}}{\text{Operating Cash Flow}}$	• Cash flows are a much better indicator of a firm's strengths than earnings • Analysis is industry specific • High ratios indicate the firm's shares are 'expensive'
Enterprise to Earnings (EE)	$\frac{\text{Enterprise Value}}{\text{Earnings Before Interest Taxes, and Depreciation}}$	• EV is Market Value of Equity + Market Value of Debt – Cash • EE ratio is not influenced by changes to capital structure • Ignores capital expenditures

Example 5.8

Bernice is a financial adviser searching for one stock to add to one of her institutional client's portfolios. Bernice has narrowed her choices to three firms in the same industry, each with acceptable risk levels for the client. Bernice uses relative valuation to estimate the following multiples for each firm.

Multiple	Firm 1	Firm 2	Firm 3
PE	15.4	21.5	16.4
PB	3.1	2.7	3.9
PS	2.8	3.4	3.3
PCF	15.7	16.9	15.8
EE	11.2	7.6	10.1

Bernice has an interesting choice. In evaluating the three firms, the immediate conclusion might be to avoid Firm 2 because it has the highest PE and PCF ratios. On closer inspection, however, the high ratios seem to be justified as it is complimented with favorable PB and EE ratios, indicating the firm is relatively inexpensive when debt levels and book values are considered.

Advisers must be aware that each ratio can have different applications for different industries. For example, the **enterprise value ratio** is important for industries characterized by firms with high use of leverage, while the ratio is less important for tech firms with little leverage. Price to Sales is more useful for newer firms with a lack of history of established earnings.

The big challenge in using multiples is to find acceptable peer groups. In the Bernice example, she simply compared multiples of three firms in the same industry before making her decision. In reality, advisers must select from firms in various industries across sizes, capital structures, and even countries. It is much more complex than the Bernice example. Being a good adviser, Bernice would have likely established an industry peer group based on their prospects for growth and return on invested capital.

Relative value analysis is as much an art as it is a science. Historical perspective as well as intuition regarding which multiples are more relevant for each situation are both required to successfully and consistently identify undervalued securities.

Technical Analysis

Technical analysis is the use of historical pricing and volume data to make asset selection decisions.

Both the discounted cash flow and relative valuation methods are part of fundamental analysis, in which the investment adviser uses basic economics and financial principles to value a financial asset. Technical analysts, however, believe that market sentiment and past price and volume data can be used to give more accurate predictions of future asset prices.

For example, when the demand for a security increases, technicians observe the price of the asset rises. Since changes in the supply of shares of stock occur infrequently, technicians determine if the increase in demand is significant enough that a rising price pattern will occur. If the pattern meets predetermined criteria, the technical analyst makes a buy recommendation and maintains it until something in the sentiment of the market causes a reversal in prices.

Technicians believe that patterns exist and that history does repeat itself. Technical analysis relies on the market not being completely efficient. Inefficiencies might occur because of trading restrictions, government regulations, or the existence of behavioral investors who drive prices away from their fundamental values.

Quick Quiz 5.4

1. Identifying undervalued stocks is a key component of asset selection models.
   a. True
   b. False
2. An analyst using a discounted cash flow technique is using relative valuation model.
   a. True
   b. False
3. Indexing is popular because it conforms to modern portfolio theory.
   a. True
   b. False

True, False, True.

Indexing

Passive investors do not believe that advisers can add any value to the investment decision process. Passive investors simply select mutual funds or exchange traded funds that match a specific index. For example, the Vanguard 500 Index Fund and the Schwab Total Stock Market Index Fund are two very popular funds for passive investors.

Indexing necessarily results in performance that closely matches general stock market returns. Passive investing is appropriate for those investors who have average risk tolerance. Like all investments, passive investors must be sensitive to the expense ratios charged by the passive vehicle managers.

Many passive investors choose a portfolio of different index funds.

SUMMARY EXAMPLE

James Taft uses relative value analysis to select the following equity portfolio:

	Allocation	Return
Washington Agriculture	0.33	0.08
Lincoln Energy	0.18	0.14
Hancock Industries	0.21	0.11
Adams Manufacturing	0.28	0.03

The Taft portfolio has a return of:

$$\text{Return on Portfolio} = (0.33 \times 0.08) + (0.18 \times 0.14) + (0.21 \times 0.11) + (0.28 \times 0.03) = 0.0831$$

When selecting a benchmark, Taft could easily select four different stocks with similar risk and size characteristics, or he could select exchange traded funds or indexes that mirrored the risk and size profile of the four stocks. In this case, however, Taft uses the same four stocks but equally weights them as his benchmark portfolio. This will illustrate the importance of asset allocation. As such, the benchmark return is:

$$\text{Portfolio Benchmark Return} = (0.25 \times 0.08) + (0.25 \times 0.14) + (0.25 \times 0.11) + (0.25 \times 0.03) = 0.09$$

The Taft portfolio has less return than the normal, equally-weighted portfolio simply because of differences in asset allocation. Taft underweighted Lincoln and Hancock and overweighted Washington and Adams, causing an **underperformance** of 69 basis points. This example illustrates the importance of asset allocation decisions.

Taft's Discounted Cash Flow Analysis

Taft continues to evaluate his portfolio and uses discounted cash flow analysis to estimate intrinsic values for each of the companies. Taft decides to change the weights to reflect his new analysis according to the following table (assume no changes to returns for each stock):

	Allocation	Return
Washington Agriculture	0.14	0.08
Lincoln Energy	0.36	0.14
Hancock Industries	0.31	0.11
Adams Manufacturing	0.19	0.03

Changing the allocation to the weights in the table will produce a return of:

$$\text{Return on Portfolio} = (0.14 \times 0.08) + (0.36 \times 0.14) + (0.31 \times 0.11) + (0.19 \times 0.03) = 0.1014$$

Taft is now overweighting Lincoln and Hancock while underweighting Washington and Adams, and the portfolio outperforms the benchmark by 114 basis points.

Taft's Technical Analysis

Taft uses technical analysis to find other securities that he feels are undervalued. Suppose he substitutes Quincy Manufacturing for Adams Manufacturing, as outlined in the following exhibit:

	Allocation	Return
Washington Agriculture	0.33	0.08
Lincoln Energy	0.18	0.14
Hancock Industries	0.21	0.11
Quincy Manufacturing	0.28	0.09

Quincy enjoys a 600 basis point advantage over Adams, which increases the portfolio return to:

$$\text{Return on Portfolio} = (0.33 \times 0.08) + (0.18 \times 0.14) + (0.21 \times 0.11) + (0.28 \times 0.09) = 0.0999$$

Taft Summary

The original four stocks underperformed the benchmark. Small changes in asset allocations and substituting a superior stock improved the performance of the portfolio. It should be clear that if asset allocation changes and security selection changes were applied to a well-diversified portfolio of 40 or 50 equity securities, changes in portfolio returns could be quite dramatic. The allocation and selection decisions are critical to portfolio performance.

For this reason, attribution analysis is a critical component of portfolio management.

ATTRIBUTION ANALYSIS AND FAMA DECOMPOSITION

In his 1972 paper, published in the Journal of Finance, Eugene Fama acknowledged the previous work done by Sharpe, Treynor, and Jensen. Portfolio performance, as outlined by those three accomplished researchers, was based on risk and return. Fama points out that the return component used as an input in previous measures could be divided into its critical components. Fama wondered if manager performance was due to luck or unique skill sets developed by the managers. In particular, Fama was interested in measuring if the performance was due to the manager's skill in finding efficient allocations of securities or if the performance was due to the manager skill in finding undervalued securities. To accomplish either, Fama knew active managers would have to expose their clients to total risk.

Key Concepts

1. Discuss reasons the risk-free rate is the starting point for Fama decomposition.
2. Explain Fama decomposition in terms of market timing skills.
3. Explain how the lack of diversification in a portfolio is captured by the Fama Decomposition.

The **Fama decomposition model** begins with the idea that the total return on portfolio can be broken into four component pieces:

1. The risk-free rate of return
2. The expected return demanded by the client
3. The extra return provided by the manager due to market timing skills
4. The extra return provided by the manager due to security selection skills

Example 5.9

An endowment fund hires Edward York, CFA, to manage its portfolio. The endowment fund has a target beta of 1.11, but allows York to deviate from that level as part of a tactical strategy. York identifies a diversified portfolio that has an actual beta of 1.23. Additional critical data is shown in the table below:

Risk-free rate of interest	3.4%
Market risk premium	7.1%
Market portfolio volatility	18%

After one year, the portfolio has generated a return of 15.1% with a standard deviation of 23%.

The first step in the Fama Decomposition is to gather some preliminary data and make some preliminary calculations:

York was given a strategic beta of 1.11 but tactically chose to invest in a portfolio with a beta of 1.23. Given a market risk premium of 7.1%, the difference in expected return for the client and York's portfolio can be calculated as follows:

Client's Return	1.11 × 7.1 = 7.881%
York's Return	1.23 × 7.1 = 8.733%

Therefore, York exceeded the client's return by 0.852% (8.733 – 7.881).

Fama suggests that York's return could reasonably be expected to be:

Risk-Free Rate	3.400%
Client's Return	7.881%
York's Extra Return for Higher Beta Portfolio	0.852%
Total Expected Return for York's Portfolio	12.133%

The actual return on York's portfolio is 15.1%. Fama attempts to explain the difference between the actual return and the expected return associated with York's portfolio.

Fama believes that York outperformed by 2.967% (15.1 – 12.133). Fama refers to this outperformance as the return for selectivity, which attributes the extra performance to York's ability to find undervalued securities.

Fama decomposes selectivity into two components: Return for lack of diversification and net selectivity. **Net selectivity** is defined as the difference between the actual return on the portfolio and the return that should have been earned based on total risk. The equation for this return is similar to the capital market line equation:

Return = Risk-Free Rate + Market Risk Premium × (SD_p/SD_m)

Return = 3.4 + 7.1 × (0.23/0.18) = 12.472%

Net selectivity is: 15.1 – 12.472 = 2.628%

Quick Quiz 5.5

1. The Fama decomposition uses both systematic and unsystematic risk measures.
   a. True
   b. False
2. If the manager beta is equal to the investor's beta, the return for security selection in the Fama decomposition will be zero.
   a. True
   b. False
3. Net selectivity in Fama decomposition can be attributed to asset allocation.
   a. True
   b. False

True, True, False.

The return that accounts for the lack of diversification is simply the difference between total selectivity and net selectivity.

Risk-Free Rate	3.400%
Strategic Return of Portfolio	7.881%
Tactical Outperformance (market timing)	0.852%
Net Selectivity	2.628%
Return for Lack of Diversification	0.339%
Total Portfolio Return	15.100%

BRINSON, HOOD, AND BEEBOWER (BHB) MODEL

Key Concepts

1. Explain BHB decomposition in terms of market timing skills.
2. Explain BHB decomposition in terms of asset selection skills.
3. Discuss the difference between Fama and BHB in regard to attribution of performance.

The **Brinson, Hood, and Beebower (BHB) model** was introduced to investors in 1986 and is considered by many to be the pioneering work in attribution analysis. This is clearly inaccurate, as the Fama decomposition preceded it by 14 years. Nevertheless, the BHB model is an extremely important contribution to the understanding of the sources of performance. BHB investigated the performance of pension plan returns and found that asset allocation decisions were the most significant driver of portfolio variability. In fact, BHB found that over 90 percent of the pension plan's return variability is explained by asset allocation. This piece of research ignited a wave of academic papers, most of them finding at least minimal support for BHB findings and many of them confirming the results of the original study.

Most academics and practitioners agree that the BHB study focused the attention of the investment community on the importance of having a sound strategic asset allocation model.

BHB intended to evaluate the effectiveness of active management. Much like Fama, BHB wanted to verify that a portfolio manager's alpha was due to skill rather than luck.

Example 5.10

A manager who outperforms its benchmark by 3% can arrive at that result by many different avenues. Using the BHB technique, consider three possible portfolios in which the manager outperforms by 3% (300 basis points).

	Selection	Allocation	Total
Possible Portfolio 1	150 BP	150 BP	300 BP
Possible Portfolio 2	400 BP	-100 BP	300 BP
Possible Portfolio 3	-200 BP	500 BP	300 BP

The contribution of BHB is to distinguish between allocation and selection skills.

Investors hope to identify managers than can consistently do both.

Example 5.11

Hugo is a single 40-year-old investor with above average risk tolerance and a preference for small cap stocks. Hugo and his financial adviser, Potts, meet to discuss an appropriate investment strategy for the coming year and beyond. After a series of interviews, Potts and Hugo agree that a 8.75% return over the next year will satisfy Hugo's income needs while considering his investment constraints.

Potts decides that Hugo can achieve his goals if exposed to three basic asset classes: a money market fund, a fixed-income fund, and a small cap fund. Potts recommends the Clements Money Market Fund, the Weber Investment Grade Bond Fund, and the Ferguson 5000 Small Cap Fund.

Quick Quiz 5.6

1. A portfolio manager who outperforms in asset allocation will necessarily outperform in asset selection.
   a. True
   b. False
2. A portfolio manager who outperforms in asset allocation by 100 basis points and who underperforms in security selection by 120 basis points will have beaten the benchmark.
   a. True
   b. False

False, False.

Potts creates a benchmark portfolio in order to compare against Hugo's portfolio. Potts identifies three indexes that have the same characteristics as his client's portfolio, one from each asset class, and forms the benchmark in the following way:

	Benchmark Weights	Benchmark Return
National Money Market Index	5%	1%
National High Quality Bond Index	35%	6%
National Small Cap Index	60%	9%

The benchmark return:

$$\text{BM Return} = (0.05 \times 0.01) + (0.35 \times 0.06) + (0.60 \times 0.09) = 0.0755$$

After meeting with Hugo, Potts recommends an allocation consisting of 3% Clements, 47% Weber, and 50% Ferguson. One year later, the portfolio has the following performance:

	Potts Recommended Weights	Actual Hugo Portfolio Return
Clements Money Market Fund	3%	1%
Weber Investment Grade Bond Fund	47%	7%
Ferguson 5000 Small Cap Fund	50%	11%

$$\text{Hugo Actual Return} = (0.03 \times 0.01) + (0.47 \times 0.07) + (0.50 \times 0.11) = 0.0882$$

To compare performance against the benchmark:

Excess Return = Hugo Return - Benchmark Return = 0.0882 - 0.0755 = 0.0127

Potts' recommended portfolio outperformed the benchmark by 127 basis points. It is now crucial to determine the source of that out-performance, and an attribution analysis will provide those necessary details.

The following table illustrates the part of the out-performance due to asset allocation decisions made by Potts:

Asset Class	Hugo Weights	BM Weights	Active Weight (AW)	BM Return (BM)	Contribution (AW x BM)
Cash	0.03	0.05	-0.02	0.01	-0.02
Bonds	0.47	0.35	+0.12	0.06	0.72
Equity	0.50	0.60	-0.10	0.09	-0.90

The Contribution column is the product of the Active Weight column and the BM Return column. Summing the Contribution column yields -0.20.

Potts underperformed the benchmark by 20 basis points in his asset allocation decisions. Potts overweighted bonds but under-weighted equity, and the net result was 20 basis points less in return.

The following table illustrates the part of the out-performance due to security selection decisions made by Potts:

Asset Class	Hugo Performance	BM Performance	Active Performance (AP)	Hugo Weights (FW)	Contribution (AP x FW)
Cash	0.01	0.01	0.00	0.03	0.00
Bonds	0.07	0.06	+0.01	0.47	0.47
Equity	0.11	0.09	+0.02	0.50	1.00

The Contribution column is the product of the Active Performance column and the Hugo Weights column. Summing the Contribution column yields +1.47 percent.

Potts outperformed the benchmark by 147 basis points in his security selection decisions, as both Weber and Ferguson outperformed their index components.

The final attribution analysis illustrates that the under-performance in asset allocation of 20 basis points was offset by out-performance of 147 basis points, as shown in the following matrix.

Asset Allocation	-20 basis points
Security Selection	+147 basis points
Total Performance	+127 basis points

FIXED-INCOME ATTRIBUTION ANALYSIS

Fixed-income portfolio management and analysis was originally dominated by concerns surrounding income, default risk, and liquidity. Up until the 1970s, most bondholders invested in fixed-income securities based on the semiannual coupon payments received, the security of each coupon and principal payment, and whether or not the bond could be sold at a fair price before maturity. There was little, if any, active bond portfolio management and therefore no need for fixed-income attribution analysis. The dominant investors in the bond market were insurance companies and commercial banks. The dominant issuer in the bond market was the federal government. As such, investors with structured liabilities invested in bonds that were best suited to meet those future obligations.

Key Concepts

1. Explain the relative difficulty in performing an attribution analysis on fixed-income securities.
2. Discuss the difference between the management effect and the policy effect.
3. Categorize the performance of a fixed-income security.

In the current bond market, both investors and issuers have become much more complex in their needs as have the characteristics of the bonds being issued. Although fixed rate bonds are the most commonly issued bonds today, both governments and corporations issue new securities with embedded options, contingent payments, floating rate structures, and a variety of underlying collateral. These complexities and the active management that has accompanied a rise in the demand for financial services make attribution analysis relevant for fixed-income securities.

Attribution models, as applied to active equity portfolio management, must be modified before they are relevant to fixed-income portfolio management analysis. Income remains an important determinant of performance for fixed-income portfolio managers, but yield curve movements, including shifts, twists and butterflies, are even more important. Consequently, the duration and convexity of a bond portfolio are critical components of fixed-income attribution analysis. Think of duration and convexity as measures of interest rate risk, which is the sensitivity of bond prices to changes in yields. These are two critical concepts that will be further investigated in Chapter 8 on fixed income analysis.

Attribution analysis for fixed-income securities is quite different than it is for equity securities, although there are commonalities. Both equity and fixed-income managers search for undervalued securities and both make allocation decisions. For fixed-income managers, the added complexity of interest rate exposure makes those decisions more difficult. For example, an equity manager might substitute a higher beta stock for a lower beta stock as part of a tactical selection strategy in the hopes of a market surge. A fixed-income manager, however, might substitute a bond with a higher duration for one with a lower duration expecting interest rates to fall. Yields seldom change uniformly, with yield curve shifts, curves, and twists affecting the ultimate total return on the bond. In addition, fixed-income portfolio managers must consider the influence that unexpected changes in inflation, default risk, and spreads have on total returns.

These extra components of interest rate risk make attribution analysis more challenging for fixed-income securities.

Equity securities are relatively simple, while bonds are not. Equity managers invest in publicly held companies, but fixed-income managers add government issuers, quasi government issuers, as well as structured securities that can be quite complex. In addition, fixed-income managers can weight their portfolios by price or duration while managing reinvestment risk.

To perform a reasonable attribution analysis for bonds requires consideration for the entire spectrum of interest rate movements as well as the additional complexities of investing in bonds.

The components of fixed-income attribution analysis are:

- Policy Effect
- Rate Anticipation Effect
- Analysis Effect
- Trading Effect

The **policy effect** measures the return impact of the difference between the duration of the benchmark and the duration of the portfolio. This is a basic policy decision that reflects the general difference in interest rate risk between the two. Higher portfolio duration suggests higher portfolio return in periods of falling rates.

The **rate anticipation effect** measures the return impact of the difference between the strategic duration of the portfolio and tactical deviations from it. Managers can add value by shortening duration when rates rise and lengthening duration when they fall. Changing portfolio duration in this manner is a strategy of minimizing capital losses while maximizing capital gains.

The **analysis effect** measures the ability of the manager to locate undervalued securities. This can be due to many factors, but primarily measures a portfolio manager's ability to find securities that outperform securities with similar default risk.

The **trading effect** measures the return impact of short-term changes in portfolio composition. The final three effects are frequently referred to as the management effect. The rate anticipation, analysis, and trading effects measure the active skills of the portfolio manager.

Quick Quiz 5.7

1. Duration is a measure of the price sensitivity of a bond to changes in its yield to maturity.
   a. True
   b. False
2. A portfolio manager who increases the allocation to high duration bonds outperforms when interest rates fall.
   a. True
   b. False
3. Successful active fixed-income managers have a positive management effect in the attribution analysis.
   a. True
   b. False

True, True, True.

This type of analysis relies on the **bond market line** and a linear relationship between the duration and the rate of return on the portfolio. Analysts must be careful when using attribution analysis as it does not differentiate between and among bonds with different levels of default risk.

Example 5.12

Consider a bond portfolio with a strategic duration of 7.8 years and an expected return according to the bond market line of 7.5%. The bond market line is similar to the capital and security markets lines for equity securities.

The Pacific Bond Index has a duration of 7.0 years and has an expected return of 6.75%.

The manager currently has the portfolio duration at 9.1 years, which translates into an expected return of 8.75% on the bond market line. Finally, a buy and hold strategy results in a return of 9%.

The total return on the portfolio is 10.5%. The measurement of each effect is shown below:

Policy Effect	7.8 years - 7.0 years = 0.8 years 0.075 - 0.0675 = 0.0075
Interest Rate Anticipation Effect	0.0875 - 0.075 = 0.0125
Analysis Effect	0.09 - 0.0875 = 0.0025
Trading Effect	0.105 - 0.0875 = 0.0175 0.0175 - 0.0025 = 0.0150

The index return is 6.75%, while the portfolio return is 10.5%. The difference is 375 basis points, and the table below shows each effect:

Policy Effect: 75 Basis Points
Rate Anticipation Effect: 125 Basis Points
Analysis Effect: 25 Basis Points
Trading Effect: 150 Basis Points

Interpretation:

- The policy decision to hold bonds with longer durations increased total return by 75 basis points. Note that this policy decision only pays off during a falling interest rate environment over the long run.

- The manager also makes duration bets over the shorter term, and this is the interest rate anticipation effect. The manager increased return by 125 basis points by profiting from changes in duration during the period.

- The ability to invest in securities that are undervalued at least over the short term is the analysis effect. The manager increases total return by 25 basis points.

- The trading increase on total return can be derived from two components: either short term selection ability due to reasons other than rate movements, or efficient access to bond markets.

Exhibit 5.3 | Bond Attribution

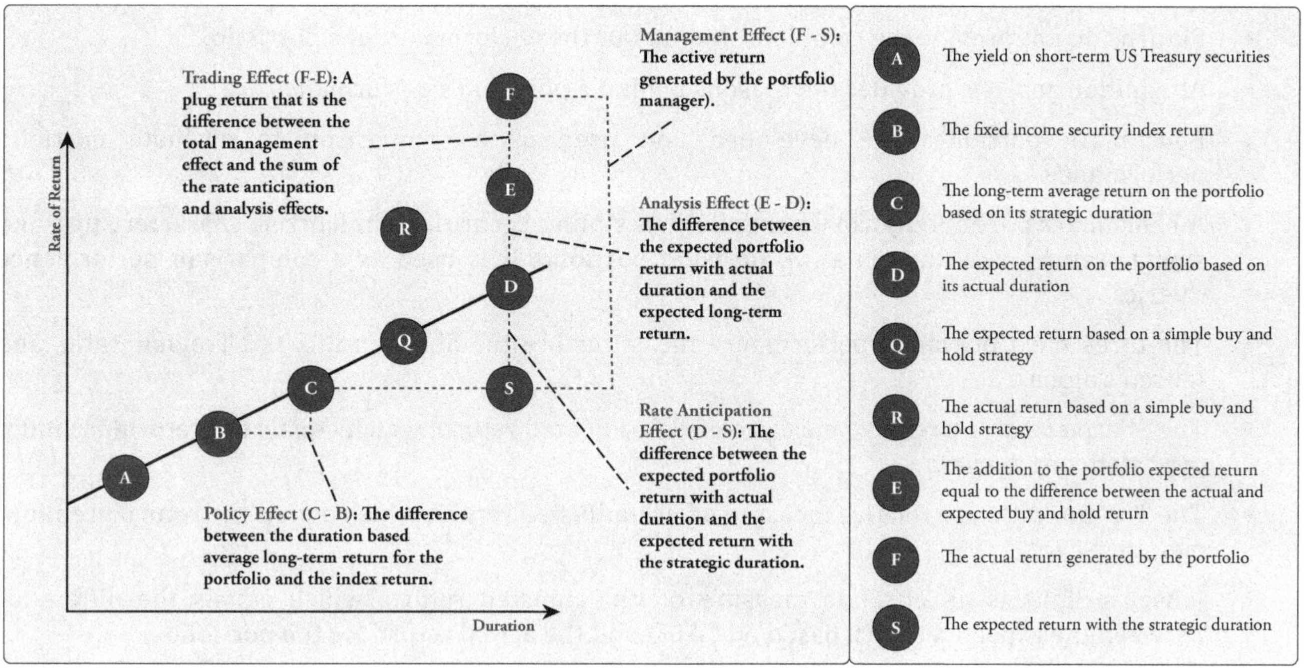

SUMMARY

Summary of key points:

- Returns do not provide the complete story about the performance of a portfolio.
- Attribution analysis provides the reasons behind a portfolio's performance.
- Benchmark portfolios are developed and used as a comparison to evaluate portfolio performance.
- A benchmark portfolio (normal portfolio) has similar securities, similar risk characteristics, and similar return expectations as an invested portfolio. It is used as a comparison performance metric.
- The three most prevalent performance measures are the Sharpe ratio, the Treynor ratio, and Jensen's alpha.
- The Sharpe ratio is a relative measure of risk-adjusted return, which equals the return premium over standard deviation.
- The Treynor ratio is a relative measure of risk-adjusted return, which equals the return premium over beta.
- Jensen's alpha is an absolute measure of risk-adjusted return, which equals the difference between the expected return based on CAPM and the actual return for the portfolio.
- A buy and hold strategy will generally result in a far different asset allocation over time.
- A constant weighting allocation is one in which allocations to asset classes are maintained on a percentage basis through rebalancing.
- Tactical asset allocation is one in which deviations from the long-term allocations are pursued over the short term to increase returns by taking advantage of current market conditions that favor one asset class over another.
- Dynamic allocation is a strategy in which the portfolio weights are constantly being adjusted to reflect changing market conditions and changing asset values.
- The four asset selection methods are discounted cash flows, relative valuations, technical analysis, and indexing.
- The Fama decomposition breaks total return into four components: risk-free rate of return, the expected return demanded from the client, the extra return from market timing, and the extra return from security selection.
- The contribution of the BHB model, which came after Fama's work, is to distinguish between allocation and selection skills.
- Attribution analysis for fixed-income securities is quite different than it is for equity securities, although there are commonalities. The components of fixed-income attribution analysis are policy effect, rate anticipation effect, analysis effect and trading effect.

DISCUSSION QUESTIONS

SOLUTIONS to the discussion questions can be found exclusively within the chapter. Once you have completed an initial reading of the chapter, go back and highlight the answers to these questions.

1. Define a benchmark portfolio and discuss its importance in portfolio evaluation.
2. Distinguish between popular indexes that are used properly and improperly as benchmark portfolios.
3. Describe the asset allocation process.
4. Discuss the buy and hold strategy.
5. Discuss the constant weighting strategy.
6. Discuss the dynamic allocation strategy.
7. Evaluate the appropriate implementation of a tactical asset allocation strategy.
8. Assess the following investments scenario from a rebalancing perspective: an investor owns an equally-weighted portfolio of treasury bonds, investment grade bonds, and large cap equity securities. Over the subsequent six-month period, the treasury bonds fall by 2%, investment grade bonds fall by 6%, and equity securities rise by 12%.
9. Explain the asset selection decision.
10. Summarize the discounted cash flow technique.
11. Summarize relative valuation.
12. Discuss specific relative valuation multiples.
13. Summarize technical analysis.
14. Summarize indexing.
15. Distinguish between fundamental analysis and technical analysis.
16. Explain the Fama decomposition.
17. Discuss the important distinction between total risk and systematic risk in the Fama decomposition.
18. Demonstrate how portfolio managers are evaluated on market timing skills in the Fama decomposition.
19. Discuss the contributions of BHB as researchers in attribution analysis.

20. Distinguish between asset allocation skills and asset selection skills in the BHB model.

21. Contrast attribution analysis of equity securities as described in the BHB model with the analysis of fixed-income securities.

22. Explain the policy effect of fixed-income attribution analysis.

23. Explain the interest rate anticipation effect of fixed-income attribution analysis.

24. Explain the analysis effect of fixed-income attribution analysis.

25. Explain the trading effect of fixed-income attribution analysis.

MULTIPLE-CHOICE PROBLEMS

A sample of multiple choice problems is provided below. Additional multiple choice problems are available at money-education.com by accessing the Student Practice Portal.

1. Eugene Fama is known for each of the following except:
    a. Research on fixed-income attribution analysis.
    b. Decomposition of portfolio manager's performance.
    c. Development of the efficient markets hypothesis.
    d. Winner of the Nobel Prize in economic sciences.

2. An investor owns a well-diversified portfolio that contains the equity securities of large U.S. corporations. The beta of the portfolio is 1.0. The most appropriate benchmark for this portfolio is:
    a. S&P Small Cap 600.
    b. Wilshire 5000.
    c. Dow Jones Industrial Average.
    d. S&P 500 Index.

3. A financial analyst computes the present value of a firm's operating cash flows to calculate an intrinsic value of the shares. The analyst is most likely using:
    a. A discounted cash flow technique.
    b. Relative valuation methodology.
    c. Indexing.
    d. Technical analysis.

4. A financial analyst computes the price-to-sales ratio as a comparison to determine which company is most expensive. The analyst is most likely using:
    a. A discounted cash flow technique.
    b. Relative valuation methodology.
    c. Indexing.
    d. Technical analysis.

5. An investor who purchases a variety of mutual funds that mimic the performance of the S&P 500 Index, the Russell 2000, and the NASDAQ Composite is most likely pursuing a strategy of:
    a. Discounting cash flows.
    b. Indexing.
    c. Technical analysis.
    d. Relative valuation.

QUICK QUIZ EXPLANATIONS

Quick Quiz 5.1

1. False. Acceptable benchmarks include similar risk securities weighted in a similar way to the portfolio. Benchmarks typically contain many of the securities in the portfolio only if similar risk securities are unavailable or if there are significant differences in liquidity or firm specific characteristics.
2. True.
3. True.

Quick Quiz 5.2

1. True.
2. True.

Quick Quiz 5.3

1. True.
2. True.

Quick Quiz 5.4

1. True.
2. False. Relative valuation models include using ratios such as the Price-Earnings ratio to find undervalued securities. The discounted cash flow technique computes the intrinsic value of a firm and is not a relative valuation model.
3. True.

Quick Quiz 5.5

1. True.
2. True.
3. False. Net selectivity measures the manager's security selection skills.

Quick Quiz 5.6

1. False. Asset selection and asset allocation skills are not necessarily complimentary.
2. False. Performance in allocation and selection skills are linear and can be summed. A fund manager who underperforms in security selection more than asset allocation will underperform its benchmark.

Quick Quiz 5.7

1. True.
2. True.
3. True.

6

MARKET EFFICIENCY & BEHAVIORAL FINANCE

LEARNING OBJECTIVES

1. Appreciate the history of asset bubbles.
2. Understand the fundamental causes of asset bubbles.
3. Compare the basic premises of traditional financial theory of investor decision making to that of behavioral finance.*
4. Identify the components of an efficient market.*
5. Understand the manner in which the traditional finance explanation of efficient markets does not hold if investors exhibit behavioral traits.*
6. Explain how bounded rationality impacts investment decisions.*
7. Understand heuristic-driven biases that impact investors' decision making.*
8. Explain the importance of framing.*
9. Discuss prospect theory and how it relates to the decisions made under modern portfolio theory.*
10. Identify cognitive errors made by investors and the consequences of making those errors.*
11. Identify emotional biases made by investors and the consequences of exhibiting those biases.*

**Ties to CFP Certification Learning Objectives*

BRIEF HISTORY OF FINANCIAL DECISION MAKING

One of the beauties of economics is that it explains decision making in its simplest form, dating to the original financial decisions made by Earth's first men and women faced with uncertain futures. Those decisions include the choice between planting seeds or eating them. It was a classic marginal cost and marginal benefit tradeoff that could only be made when the early investors made forecasts about future states of nature. They understood that more saving today meant more consuming in the future. Their decisions were based on a primitive form of risk management with the ultimate penalty of starvation.

Historical investors most likely thought of themselves as being skilled decision makers, perhaps even rational ones, even if only in the sense that they invested in projects that had positive expected outcomes.

Key Concepts

1. Explain how tulip bulbs became overvalued and led to a mania in 17th century Holland.
2. Identify the fathers of modern portfolio theory and their specific contributions to our understanding of risk and return.
3. Discuss the three levels of stock market efficiency.

While today's investors are not often faced with the specter of starvation, they are faced with a myriad of challenges, including a failure to meet their financial goals.

Investors have always been aware of risk but often lacked the knowledge or technology to measure it. They tended to think in terms of extreme outcomes. For example, the merchants who provided capital and the farmers who provided livestock and grains to supply the explorations to the new world five hundred years ago expected positive returns, but they were aware of the high probability the ships would never return with gold, jewelry, and other riches. Those 15th and 16th century early investors may have thought they were being entirely rational, but surely they made investing mistakes because they had incomplete information and because they were incapable of measuring uncertainty. The mistakes made, especially by the merchants, almost certainly had emotional components and were subject to cognitive errors.

Investors throughout history have discounted unfavorable outcomes, shown overconfidence, suffered from biased expectations, and most likely were subject to framing issues. Financing early sea explorations was the original lottery game, and the investors who provided funds for those trips most likely exhibited similar behavioral biases that can be observed in financial markets today.

Irrational decisions made by the consuming public can be revealed by comparing the chances of winning a lottery payout with the actual payout of a lottery win.

Example 6.1

The state of Pennsylvania offers a daily Pick Four lottery in which gamblers select four numbers ranging from 0000 to 9999. It should be obvious that the chance of winning is one in ten thousand, but the payoff for picking the winning number is only $5,000 for a $1 ticket. The expected value of the gamble is $0.50 while the cost of the gamble is $1.00. Clearly, only an irrational investor would play the Pennsylvania Pick Four, but thousands do every day.[1]

Investors in expeditions that set out to discover the new world suffered from similar behavioral issues. The risks of investment were not identified, quantified or managed as investors lacked modern risk management tools. Therefore, their poor decision making (quantitatively and behaviorally) was not entirely their fault. The bad news, of course, was these investors and many who followed them regularly lost 100 percent or more of their initial investment.[2]

Emotions and cognitive errors continued to be components of investing even after financial markets were formalized during the 1600s and 1700s. In one well known example, emotions and brain malfunctioning hit the tulip bulb market in the early 17th century.

Example 6.2

Tulip flowers were first grown and traded thousands of years ago but became a symbol of wealth and prosperity in Turkey in the 16th century. The government outlawed the cultivation and sale of tulips outside of the country's capital, and tulips came to be viewed by all as being the flower of choice among the sultans. The Turkish people even held Tulip Festivals, which further glamorized the flower. Such was the attitude of western Europe when tulips were exported to Holland.

The tulip flower became a hobby for the wealthy in Holland who quickly took advantage of its popularity by selling not just the blooming flowers, but their bulbs as well. The popularity of the bulbs spread to the lower classes as many became tempted by the possibility of quick profit. By the early 1600s, a type of mania occurred in that the trading for bulbs entered a new type of market. Most bulbs were sold during the spring and summer months, but by 1633, they were being sold in terms of weight while they were still under the ground. An early form of a note would be issued with the weight of the bulb before it was planted and the expected timing of the harvest clearly shown on the note,

1. The formal equation for expected value is: Expected Value = $\Sigma\ p_i \times x_i$
   Where p is the probability of an event occurring and x is the payoff for that event.
   Expected Value = $5,000 × (1 ÷ 10,000) = $0.50
2. How can investors lose more than 100%? This type of outcome can occur with margin accounts, real estate investments, and other investments that involve debt financing and borrowed money.

signed by both parties. Although not formalized in any sophisticated way, tulip bulb trading became a futures market. With settlement not being completed until the bulbs were delivered, months after the date of the signed contract, there was rampant speculation. Speculation drove prices upward and an **asset bubble** was formed.[3]

In modern futures markets, almost all trades are cash settled, but in the 1630s, it was common to use barter as a currency. Individuals pledged livestock, homes, farming equipment, and almost anything else of value to enter one of these tulip bulb contracts. The bubble burst in the spring of 1637 as traders became doubtful that prices would rise even further and that all the notes could be honored. Prices fell dramatically and many investors (speculators) lost their fortunes, livestock, and homes.

History is littered with investment manias. Examples of bubbles include the UK railroad industry in the 1840s, the Japanese stock market in the early 1980s, the U.S. stock market in 1929 and 1987, dot.com stocks in the late 1990s, and in the housing market in 2008. There is little doubt that emotions and cognitive errors played huge roles in both the formation and subsequent collapse of all of these asset bubbles.

Markets became powerful forces during the 1800s and the evolution of the modern day publicly held corporation allowed investors to participate as equity owners. It was not until the 1950s, however, that investors learned how to explicitly quantify the risk levels of financial securities.

MODERN DAY FINANCE & MODERN PORTFOLIO THEORY (MPT)

In 1952 Harry Markowitz outlined how standard deviation could be used to measure an asset's risk. Using investable assets' expected returns, standard deviations and covariances with other assets, he then demonstrated how efficient portfolios that minimized risk for a given level of return could be identified. This formed the basis of his **modern portfolio theory**, which is still used by investors making asset allocation decisions today. The idea that standard deviation is a good measure of total risk quickly spread throughout the economics world and was one of the original catalysts in creating the discipline of finance.

Soon after Markowitz, William Sharpe (1964) followed by arguing that a significant component of total risk could be diversified over a large number of securities, depending on their covariances. Sharpe identified systematic and unsystematic risks and showed that **systematic risk** was the only relevant risk after diversification and therefore the only risk worth pricing. This led to the development of the **capital asset pricing model** and the importance of a firm's **beta** (ß) to its expected return. Some years later, Stephen Ross (1976) developed the arbitrage pricing model to introduce other relevant factors to the stock pricing model.

Eugene Fama (1970) followed Markowitz and Sharpe by describing efficiency levels in capital markets. Fama based the idea that capital markets reflect all relevant information on the ability of investors to identify which information is relevant and which is not.

3. Asset bubbles occur when investors bid up the price of a security (or asset) well beyond its intrinsic value.

Exhibit 6.1 | Modern Portfolio Theory Assumptions

- Financial securities can be fully described by their means and standard deviations.
- Financial security returns are random variables.
- Investors are rational and risk averse.
- Investors make decisions that maximize their end of period expected wealth (utility).
- Financial markets have no trading costs (taxes, fees, bid-ask spreads, etc).
- Investors are price takers and their trades have no impact on prices.
- Investors form homogeneous expectations about risk and expected returns because they have identical information sets.
- Investors can borrow and lend at the risk-free rate of interest.

The theory suggests that all investors are risk-averse and rational and that they follow these rules:

1. Make decisions that maximize expected utility.
2. Forecast in the absence of any biases.
3. Identify decision points using rational expectations.

Modern portfolio theory requires all investors to be expected utility maximizers, which means they focus on final wealth. These utility maximizers can only be rational if they:

1. are *complete* in their consideration of all possible investment choices;
2. exhibit a *transitive* nature in their investment choices (if A is preferred to B and B is preferred to C, then A is preferred to C);
3. are *independent* in evaluating new investments that become available; and
4. maintain continuous *indifference* curves along their efficient frontiers.

Example 6.3

Suppose an investor selects 25 equity securities to be included in the construction of a diversified portfolio. This decision can only maximize expected utility if the investor:

- Evaluates the entire population of equity securities available (*complete*).
- Eliminates specific equity securities because they have either more risk or lower expected return than any in the portfolio (*transitive*).
- Analyzes new equity issues (perhaps an IPO) as part of the current diversified portfolio and without any biases (*independent*).
- Maintains a positive and convex slope of their preference between risk and expected return resulting in continuous indifference curves. Tangent indifferent curves with the efficient frontier result in optimal portfolios (*indifference*).

Modern portfolio theory relies on the ability of every investor to be perfect decision making agents, perfect in the sense that they never make a mistake. MPT does not preclude investors from losing money, it just prevents them from investing in assets in which the expected returns are inconsistent with risk levels.

Quick Quiz 6.1

1. Individuals have a centuries long history of being able to accurately compute risk levels of investments.
   a. True
   b. False
2. Standard deviation and beta were identified as reasonable measures of risk of investments during the 1950s and 1960s.
   a. True
   b. False
3. Modern portfolio theory relies on the notion that investors make expected utility maximization decisions that are unbiased.
   a. True
   b. False

False, True, True.

The Efficient Market Hypothesis

In his theory of efficient markets, Fama identified three information sets that are reflected in asset prices. He also suggests that changes in relevant information will be immediately and completely reflected in changing asset prices. Fama divided markets into three levels or degrees of informational efficiency:

1. **Weak Form Efficiency:** Market prices are functions of historical prices and volume data.
2. **Semi-Strong Form Efficiency:** Market prices are functions of publicly available information (which includes the first data set).
3. **Strong Form Efficiency:** Market prices are functions of all relevant information (which includes private information plus both the first and the second data sets).

Exhibit 6.2 | Efficient Market Assumptions

- Financial markets are informationally efficient (prices reflect relevant information).
- Investors form rational expectations regarding future price movements.
- Security prices follow a random walk, suggesting that price changes are random and therefore unpredictable.
- Changes in relevant information (which are random) will instantaneously be reflected in an asset's price.
- Price changes are unbiased and virtually impossible to predict.
- There are large numbers of financial market participants who maximize profits as they process new and relevant information.
- Three levels of market efficiency are weak form, semi-strong form, and strong form.

Weak Form Market

In a weak form market, asset prices reflect only historical pricing and volume information. The key implication for weak form efficiency is that investors cannot use this information set to generate a return that exceeds its risk adjusted expected value (known as an excess return). Consider an investor who forms her portfolio using historical prices only and buys shares of stock in companies who experience a stock price decline in excess of $1 per share for three consecutive days. If this portfolio can always outperform a relevant benchmark, then the market cannot be described as being weak form efficient because prices do not even reflect price patterns. If a market is at least weak form efficient, then technical analysis does not result in out-performance. [4]

Semi-Strong Form Market

In a semi-strong market, asset prices reflect all publicly available information. Examples for equity markets would include both firm-specific information as well as economic information. Examples of information unique to each firm include dividends, executive leadership skills, operating cash flows, the firm's weighted average cost of capital, and merger activity. Examples of economic information include changes in gross domestic product, inflation rates, relative currency values, energy prices, and global uncertainty. The implication is that investors cannot use publicly available information to generate an excess return because that information is already reflected in security prices. Consider an investor who forms her portfolio using publicly available information and buys shares of stock in any company that announces a stock dividend. If this portfolio can always outperform a relevant benchmark, then the market cannot be described as being semi-strong form efficient because prices do not reflect relevant public information. If a market is semi-strong form efficient, then fundamental analysis will not result in out-performance.[5]

Strong Form Market

In a strong form market, asset prices reflect all relevant information, including private information. Examples in equity markets include dividend decisions discussed at a board of director's meeting before it becomes public knowledge, and private merger negotiations between two large firms in the same industry. The implication is that investors cannot use private information to generate an excess return. Consider an investor who forms her portfolio using private information and buys shares of stock in any company that becomes a takeover target before the acquiring firm announces its intentions. If this portfolio can always outperform a relevant benchmark, then the market cannot be described as strong form efficient because prices do not reflect private information. If a market is strong form efficient, then neither **technical analysis**, **fundamental analysis**, nor the use of private information result in out-performance because all investors have identical information sets.

The majority of academic studies show that having access to private information in fact produces superior performance. Historical examples include the case of Albert Wiggin who was the president of Chase National Bank during the 1920s. In September of 1929, Wiggin began shorting his company's stock because he had access to client account information and the degree of leverage being used. Recall in those days it was standard practice to borrow 50 percent and even up to 90 percent of the stock's value for margin accounts. Wiggin knew this bubble could not continue, so he shorted Chase shares, which resulted in a $4 million profit. Even more surprising is that these trades were legal. In some twist of irony, Wiggin was part of an investments commission that provided funds to stabilize the market after the crash in October of 1929, and his legal short trades were not discovered until 1932. In short, Wiggin benefited from the use of inside information, which means the market could not have been strong form efficient in 1929.

It should be clear that investors, including corporate leaders who have access to inside information, enjoy a substantial trading advantage over those who do not.

4. Technical analysis is the use of historical data, including prices and trends, to make predictions about the future price of securities. See Chapter 10.
5. Fundamental analysis is the use of publicly held relevant information, including the use of financial statements and government data, to make predictions about the future price of securities.

Current academic and professional research indicates that there is very little evidence in favor of the market being strong form efficient, but significant research shows the market to be at least semi-strong form efficient. This research typically falls under the category of event studies in which stock prices are shown to react quickly to new information releases.

Market Anomalies

There is a growing body of evidence that suggests that the market may not be even semi-strong form efficient. This research began in the early 1980s with the creation of a daily stock price data set. Researchers were able to identify specific outliers to the semi-strong market in the form of what has become known as **market anomalies**. Consider the following:

- **January Effect:** It has been shown that a strategy of buying stocks in late December and selling them in early January generated excess returns. The January Effect has been reasonably explained by suggesting investors sell losers at the end of December to take and report capital losses on the current year's tax returns. Those same investors then enter the market in early January to rebalance their portfolios, thus providing a bump in January returns that cannot be observed in any other month.
- **Dogs of the Dow:** Another well-known market anomaly is the Dogs of the Dow. Investing in the highest dividend-yielding stocks contained in the Dow Jones Industrial Average outperforms the entire Dow Index. These stocks tended to be the lowest priced stocks in the index.
- **Low Price to Book Value:** There is a significant amount of research showing low price to book value stocks outperform over very large samples. The problem with this anomaly is that small changes in the definition of book value dramatically alter the performance levels. Some time periods show significant out-performance for book value of total assets while others show it for book value of tangible assets.
- **Neglected Firm Effect:** Neglected firms and small firms outperform. These firms tend to have a limited number of analysts following them, they tend to be out of the spotlight, and they tend to have fewer outstanding shares than larger firms. This combination produces firms that can produce relatively higher returns as they become larger.

Quick Quiz 6.2

1. An efficient market is one in which financial asset prices react immediately to changes in relevant information.
   a. True
   b. False
2. A semi-strong form market contains prices that reflect private information.
   a. True
   b. False
3. Technical analysis is useful in generating abnormal returns if the market is semi-strong form efficient.
   a. True
   b. False

True, False, False.

Other anomalies include small cap firms generating superior risk-adjusted returns than large cap stocks, stock returns being a function of Super Bowl winners, reversals, which are winning stocks that tend to drop in price over time and losing stocks that tend to rise, and growth stocks being overpriced. Proponents of the **efficient market hypothesis** frequently stated that although anomalies might exist, they are not sufficiently persistent or of enough magnitude to have any value to investors.

The debate regarding the efficient markets hypothesis continues today with research focusing on the behavioral aspects of investing. This research has gained much traction.

BEHAVIORAL FINANCE

Behavioral finance has been investigated by many who focus not on the outcomes of decisions made by perfectly informed investors, but on the decision making process itself, and its links to political science, sociology, and psychology.

Behavioral scientists have shown that investors are influenced by emotions when making decisions under uncertainty, that investors are influenced by group dynamics, and that investors are not immune to collective decision making even when those decisions are highly personal. These characteristics are decidedly different from those required by modern portfolio theory.

Behavioral issues apply equally to individual investors, money managers, and corporate executives.

Key Concepts

1. Discuss the differences between rational investors and behavioral investors.
2. Describe how modern portfolio theory is different from behavioral finance.
3. Explain how framing can influence decisions faced by investors and consumers.
4. Explain prospect theory.

Exhibit 6.3 | Comparison of Rational Behavior and Behavioral Finance

Rational Investors	Behavioral Investors
• Securities are valued rationally • Investors possess perfect complete information • Investors act in their own self-interest and never make mistakes • Investors seek to maximize expected utility • Arbitrage opportunities are not available • New information priced according to Bayes' Rule • Investors are risk averse	• Securities are valued heuristically • Investors process incomplete information • Investors act in their own self-interest, but make cognitive errors and have emotional biases • Investors seek to minimize regret • Arbitrage available because of bounded rationality • New information not immediately and completely priced • Investors are loss averse (Prospect Theory)

Markets that are efficient provide no opportunities for the rational investor to beat the market. This is mostly because prices reflect all relevant information but also because markets are assumed to be devoid of emotions. Video from the stock market crash of 1987 casts significant doubts on traders and investors not being emotional, especially during stressful markets.

Exhibit 6.4 | Black Monday: October 19, 1987

The Philadelphia Inquirer

Dow Dives 508.32 Points In Panic on Wall Street

Navy blasts Iran oil site in retaliation

Billions lost in trading

There is a large body of academic research suggesting that even in the presence of behavioral investors, it is difficult to beat the market. In one well-cited study, Professor Kenneth French shows that active investors lose about 0.67 percent of the value of their portfolios annually in their attempts to outperform passive investment strategies.

Behavioral investors are not perfect creatures like their rational counterparts. A behavioral market is by definition one that is imperfect, influenced by traders who make cognitive mistakes during the portfolio construction process.

Daniel Kahneman and Amos Tversky, together with Richard Thaler are generally considered to be the founding fathers of behavioral finance. Their work has been advanced by numerous researchers who have uncovered evidence that financial decision makers are not the perfect machines suggested by the founders of modern portfolio theory. In fact, there is a mountain of evidence suggesting that investors are subject to a variety of behavioral biases

Exhibit 6.5 | Behavioral Finance Assumptions

- Decision makers are not perfectly rational agents and they exhibit bounded rationality.
- Investors are easily influenced by their peers.
- Investors view gains and losses differently from each other and their decisions are characterized by prospect theory.
- Investors make information processing errors that result in over reaction and under reaction to information changes.
- Investors make processing errors.
- Investors are emotional.

Framing

Much of behavioral finance can be explained though the concept of **framing**. Investment decisions can be influenced by the manner in which the decision is framed. In one classic academic research example, consumers were much more inclined to purchase beef at the grocery store if it was labeled 75 percent lean instead of 25 percent fat. The way the decision is framed by the grocery store influenced whether or not the consumer purchased the beef. 75 percent lean beef sounds much more appetizing than 25 percent fat, which explains how important framing is to marketers and others attempting to influence consumer decision making. Similar cases exist in the investments world.

Consider an investor who has already decided to add a balanced mutual fund to their portfolio. They narrow their choices down to two funds that are heavily invested in large cap stocks. Both funds have a current net asset value of $30, but one fund manager predicts the fund will have a net asset value (NAV) of $36 while the other predicts a 20 percent annual return. Based on this information alone, the investor should be indifferent between the two funds, but some investors purchase the 20 percent return fund while others prefer the $36 prediction. The frame determines the outcome. This is simply because all humans do not perceive outcomes in the same manner, which is quite a difference from the requirements for the rational investor from modern portfolio theory.

It has also been shown that investors tend to act irrationally when faced with decisions that might result in a loss.

Example 6.4

Using a discounted cash flow model Clyde Smith estimated the intrinsic value of Tomotty, Inc. shares to be $29.50, and immediately purchased 5,000 shares at $28.00 each. However, Tomotty recently lost a long-term government contract which analysts agree will reduce its long-term growth prospects significantly, and the share price subsequently dropped to $27.20.

After taking into account the new consensus growth rate, Smith's discounted cash flow model now estimates a value of $25.50. As a result, Smith decides to place a limit order to sell all of his holding once the price recovers to his purchase price of $28.00.

Smith is demonstrating a common behavioral trait known as loss aversion. Smith's fundamental analysis now values Tomotty at $25.50. His rational decision should therefore be to sell at the current price of $27.20. However, he is clearly loss averse as instead he intends to hold onto the position in the hope that the price recovers to $28.00 and he can exit the position without realizing a loss.

Behavioral investors are guilty of attaching great importance to the individual components of a portfolio, rather than viewing the portfolio in its entirety. This phenomenon is known as narrow framing and is harmful to overall portfolio performance. It leads to a lack of diversification and an overreaction to firm-specific events. It also leads to other behavioral mistakes that compromise performance.

One area of behavioral finance that has gained widespread acceptance is the ability of the framing effect to explain at least partially the existence of the **equity premium puzzle**. It has been observed that returns to equity securities have been superior to returns on government bonds for at least the past century. The first reaction to this observation is to simply note that equity securities are much riskier than government fixed-income securities, so naturally they should experience higher returns. The magnitude of the difference between the two returns, however, cannot be fully explained by risk differentials. Some researchers suggest the difference can only exist if there are ridiculously high levels of investor risk aversion, levels that are so high they are not consistent with modern portfolio theory or any of its assumptions.

Framing and **myopic loss aversion** sheds some light on the equity premium puzzle. Investors are so concentrated on avoiding short-term losses that they require high long-term returns to compensate them for their aversion to loss. The 'extra' return demanded by behavioral investors might be enough to explain the equity premium puzzle.

Behavioral Finance and Prospect Theory

While modern portfolio theory relies on investors following a utility maximization objective function, behavioral theory, on the other hand, allows investors to value gains and losses rather than final wealth. This is much closer to reality and is the general idea behind **prospect theory**. Investors are risk averse when choosing among alternatives that will produce a gain but risk seeking when choosing among alternatives that will produce a loss.

Prospect theory suggests that individuals are faulty in their estimation of probabilities and the associated outcomes. Investors overweight small chance outcomes just to avoid a loss.

In research that contributed to a Nobel Memorial Prize in Economic Sciences, Tversky and Kahneman discuss the impact of framing on decision making.[6] Below is a summary of one of the research studies they conducted on framing. In this questionnaire, they presented a problem with alternative solutions. Students picked between the two alternative solutions.

Problem	Alternatives	152 Total Respondents Choice for A & B
Problem 1: Imagine that the U.S. is preparing for the outbreak of a flu-like pandemic that is expected to result in 600 deaths. Two alternative programs to combat the disease have been proposed. Assume that the exact scientific estimate of the consequences of the programs are as follows:	If **Program A** is adopted, 200 people will be saved.	72%
	If **Program B** is adopted, there is 1/3 probability that 600 people will be saved, and 2/3 probability that no people will be saved.	28%

Problem	Alternatives	155 Total Respondents Choice for C & D
Problem 2: Imagine that the U.S. is preparing for the outbreak of a flu-like pandemic that is expected to result in 600 deaths. Two alternative programs to combat the disease have been proposed. Assume that the exact scientific estimate of the consequences of the programs are as follows:	If **Program C** is adopted 400 people will die.	22%
	If **Program D** is adopted there is 1/3 probability that nobody will die, and 2/3 probability that 600 people will die.	78%

The outcome of each of the four alternative programs is the same. However, the framing of the alternatives clearly influences the choice by the respondents. In Problem 1, most of the respondents chose the risk-averse program over the riskier option. In Problem 2, most respondents chose the riskier option than the certainty of 400 deaths.

Tversky and Kahneman point out that there is a common pattern about choices. Those that involve gains are often risk-averse, while those involving losses are often risk seeking.

6. The Framing of Decisions and the Psychology of Choice, Amos Tversky; Daniel Kahneman, Science, New Series, Vol. 211, No. 4481. (Jan. 30, 1981), pp. 453-458.

Example 6.5

According to the 2021-22 American Pet Products Association (APPA) survey, 54% of U.S. households have a dog. Most of those pets visit a veterinarian at least once per year to receive shots and for minor illnesses. Some visits, however, are more serious, such as cancer diagnosis, joint replacement, kidney disease, and Lyme disease. Treatments for major issues is extremely expensive with cancer treatments often times exceeding thousands of dollars.

Because most dog owners want to avoid the large potential losses of these expensive treatments, many seek to transfer risk to an insurance company. Pet insurance is not inexpensive, but dog owners willingly pay for it because they attach a much higher probability of a health event for their dog than is statistically reasonable.

The behavior described in the above example can be explained by prospect theory.

Prospects are potential investment opportunities that are viewed identically by rational investors in terms of variances and covariances, but that can be and are viewed differently by behavioral investors depending on the manner in which they are framed.

When children are playing limbo at the roller skating rink, they do not take precise measurements of the height of the stick before lowering their heads to skate under it. They use short-cut decision making because their instincts about the general height level help them be successful in navigating the stick. Prospect theory allows investors to take similar short cuts, which are sometimes referred to as **heuristics**. Behavioral investors do not compute the entire probability distribution of possible outcomes of an investment in a specific equity security. They might estimate the future gains or losses depending on certain economic conditions, but they do not spend the energy to discover all possible outcomes under multiple economic scenarios.

Quick Quiz 6.3

1. Investors can be highly sensitive to the manner in which an investment decision is framed.
   a. True
   b. False
2. Behavioral finance principles offer a reasonable explanation for the persistence of the equity premium puzzle.
   a. True
   b. False
3. Prospect theory suggests that investors process information about investment decisions completely and perfectly.
   a. True
   b. False

True, True, False.

Investors, much like roller skaters, use low-energy shortcuts or heuristics by relying on just one or a few frames when making decisions even if there is a multitude of possible outcomes. This can lead to some very poor investment decisions. It makes perfect sense to allow for roller skaters to take short cuts because they do not have to be precise in their estimation of the height of the stick, but taking investment planning short cuts is likely to result in incomplete and inefficient portfolio management decisions.

Prospect theory is linked to the concept of **bounded rationality**. Behavioral scientists have found that investors reduce complex decisions into scenarios that are more reasonable to comprehend. Rational investors make optimal decisions, but behavioral investors are more human and make decisions that are an approximation of the rational investor's optimal decision. Behavioral investors collect lots of information, but not complete information. They process it as best they can. Thus, they are bounded in their ability to be fully rational. They still, however, make decisions that are satisfactory to themselves.

Prospect investors tend to underreact to low probability events, even if the event would result in significant loss of wealth. Prospect theory at least partially explains why individuals continue to build houses in hazardous areas even after floods, volcanoes or hurricanes have destroyed properties. In the investments world, prospect theory explains why many individuals take more risk than they should by not diversifying completely, by using too much leverage, and by ignoring or significantly discounting the possibility of severe market corrections.

The prospect theory suggests that investing agents are influenced by emotional and cognitive factors and that they follow these rules:

- Make decisions that minimize feelings of regret, which makes them loss-averse.
- Forecast in the presence of a variety of biases.
- Identify decision points using naive expectations.

Behavioral Finance and Cognitive Errors

Cognitive errors are made when investors inaccurately process new information about asset prices. Behavioral investors violate the assumptions of modern portfolio theory by either reacting slowly to new information or valuing the information incompletely or incorrectly.

Key Concepts

1. Explain cognitive errors made by investors and why these errors are never made by rational investors.
2. List each cognitive error and create an example of each.

Common Cognitive Errors

Some of the more common cognitive errors include representativeness, anchoring, cognitive dissonance, gambler's fallacy, and mental accounting.

Representativeness is an assessment by investors of new information or decisions based on superficial traits rather than fundamental analysis. For example, investors have been shown to bid up the price of a firm's equity after a name change. Nothing about the company has changed, not its cash flows, leadership, or capital structure. A change in company name should not affect equity prices, but investors superficially believe that a name change impacts profitability. Another example includes investors who have lost money in certain securities and then avoid investing in similar assets for fear of repeating those losses.

The consequence of representative decision making is a likely buy or sell decision that ignores the fundamentals behind the company in favor of simple heuristics. It can also lead to heavy portfolio turnover as new information dominates the cognitive function of the decision.

Anchoring is the use of immaterial information in making investment decisions. For example, investors have been shown to make buy or sell decisions based on an anchored price, such as a round number like $100 or the original purchase price of the shares.

The consequences of making anchored decisions include missed investment opportunities because the investor holds onto current shares too long or waits too long until a possible investment drops in price.

Cognitive dissonance is the process of ignoring or discounting any new information that is not consistent with the fundamental view the investor has of the company. For example, an investor might hold onto shares in a high dividend-paying firm even though recent reports show significant drops in profitability and cash flows. This investor ignores the underlying changes in the likelihood of the firm being able to maintain its high dividend history or discounts that information enough to maintain the equity position even though it might be prudent to sell.

The consequence of having dissonance influence decision making is the inability to fairly evaluate securities.

Gambler's fallacy is the mistaken notion that the onset of an outcome either increases or decreases the probability of that outcome occurring again. The name is derived from the classic gambler who wins the first time playing a specific casino game and then expects to win more often than other gamblers. The opposite part of the gambler's fallacy is that an investor is likely to attach a very low probability to a negative event after it occurs.

The consequences of this cognitive error include the inability to quantify risk accurately. This leads to misallocation of investor's resources, inefficient portfolios, and a portfolio constructed to provide short-term results.

Mental accounting occurs when investors make decisions based on individual mental categories, which can be unique to each investor. The following example illustrates how this cognitive bias impacts decision making: compare two scenarios, one in which a consumer purchases a retail gift card in the amount of $25. Upon arriving at the store, the consumer realizes she has lost the card. The second scenario involves this same consumer who does not purchase a gift card but plans on spending $25 in cash at the store. The consumer arrives at the retail store and realizes she has lost $25. Will she react identically to each scenario? Mental accounting suggests the answer is no, but clearly she is out $25 in each scenario, so she should feel equally upset. The reality is that she will be much more upset with herself if she loses the cash.

Quick Quiz 6.4

1. Cognitive errors are made when investors react slowly or incompletely to new information.
   a. True
   b. False
2. Investors who tend to ignore relevant new information when making buy/sell decisions are guilty of mental accounting.
   a. True
   b. False
3. Investors who own large allocations of the firm in which they are employed are practicing the behavioral issue of illusion of control.
   a. True
   b. False

True, False, True.

Another component to the mental accounting decision making is the assignment of certain activities to different accounts. For example, some parents specifically open December holiday gift accounts after the new year. They make deposits throughout the year specially earmarked for the purchase of gifts for their children by year's end. They tend to treat these "mental" accounts as separate entities, most likely with different risk and return characteristics.

Consequences of mental accounting include significant opportunity costs and lack of diversification. There are also likely to be mismatches between risk and return objectives as the investor is likely to have a different risk tolerance for each mental account.

Other Cognitive Errors

Other cognitive errors include illusion of control, hindsight bias, and confirmation bias. **Illusion of control** is when investors expect a different outcome than others because they believe they can exert some form of control over the outcome when in fact they cannot. One clear example of the illusion is the investor who trades heavily believing, especially in shares of familiar companies, he can time the market better than anyone else. **Hindsight bias** is when investors conveniently forget bad outcomes and remember good ones. This leads to the repeat of historical trading errors and an inaccurate judgment on the portfolio winners. **Confirmation bias** is when investors search for news articles or opinions that confirm their own personal viewpoint while avoiding disagreeing positions.[7]

Behavioral Finance and Emotional Biases

Emotional biases occur when the investor's emotions and personality drive the decision making process. Investing and investment results can provide a positive emotional effect or a negative one. Modern portfolio theory assumes investors are rational, and almost robotic in their ability to make decisions without any emotional attachment. Behavioral investors, however, are human, and are mostly incapable of separating emotions from decisions.

> ***Key Concepts***
>
> 1. Explain the emotional biases of investors and why these biases never appear in rational decision making.
> 2. List each emotional bias and create an example of each.

One of the main results of observing emotional investors is that positive and negative results are not symmetric. The pleasure of generating a positive outcome is not nearly as great as the pain suffered from a negative outcome. The world of professional sports is filled with examples, including Tom Brady reacting to the Super Bowl XLII loss that it was the worst moment of his career. The 18 wins during that regular season and playoffs paled in comparison to that final loss.

Loss Aversion

Loss aversion is an emotional trait that is very different than the risk aversion exhibited by the rational investor. Behavioral investors arrange their portfolios to avoid losses rather than structuring them to generate gains because the pain of loss is so great. Recall that the Pennsylvania Pick Four lottery tickets are only worth $0.50 a piece based on the expected payoff. Most people would be unwilling to sell the ticket after they bought it because the possibility of the pain of selling it for a few dollars and losing "thousands" is too great.

The consequence of loss aversion is a tendency to trade excessively by selling winners much too early and then being forced to buy other securities that will likely not have the appropriate risk and return components unique to the investor. This frequently occurs during the short term, making the long-term portfolio performance even more inefficient. Loss averse investors also hold onto losing securities much too long in the hopes that they increase in value enough to become winners. The cognitive error of anchoring compounds the poor decision making of the loss averse investor.

7. Many people make this error in their personal lives (e.g., politics, diet, parenting, etc.).

Regret Aversion

Similar to loss aversion is **regret aversion**, in which investors fear making poor decisions. Picking losers is a signal of bad judgment and investors hope to avoid being labeled as such. Regret aversion is a clear case of allowing fear of potential embarrassment to dictate financial decisions.

Consequences of a portfolio formed by loss averse investors is typically one that lacks complete diversification because high risk stocks are not included. Investors associate high risk with a high probability of loss, which makes risky securities unattractive.

Quick Quiz 6.5

1. Individuals have difficulty ignoring their emotions when making financial decisions.
   a. True
   b. False
2. Investors who are loss averse tend to retain ownership of outperforming stocks.
   a. True
   b. False
3. Optimism in investment decisions leads to overconfidence, self control issues, and ignoring downside risk.
   a. True
   b. False

True, False, True.

Overconfidence Bias

Overconfidence is a significant behavioral emotional bias where investors overestimate their ability to identify mispriced securities. In addition, they tend to overestimate the reliability of their research on a specific security. The **overconfidence bias** is not confined to errors made by individual investors during security selection. It applies mostly to the difference between what an investor thinks she knows and the reality of the information. As such, overconfidence is more pronounced in experts, although anyone making financial decisions can be guilty of the overconfidence bias at some point in their lives.

Like many other biases, overconfidence leads to an undiversified portfolio but it also leads to portfolios characterized by excessive risk and discounted expected returns as overconfident investors tend to expect too much return while being able to minimize risk. They believe in their unique ability to find securities with little risk and high expected returns.

Other Emotional Biases

Self-control bias is when investors are unable to limit their trading activity while losing clear sight of their long-term goals. **Clustering illusion** is the tendency to believe that short-term trends will repeat over subsequent short terms. **Irrational escalation** is the belief that a price run up in a security warrants additional capital even though there is contradictory evidence that the original investment decision was incorrect. The **optimism bias** occurs when an investor fails to consider downside risk even while focusing on the entire range of positive outcomes.

Exhibit 6.6 | Summary of Behavioral Consequences

Imperfect Diversification	Missed Opportunities
• Representativeness	• Anchoring
• Gambler's Fallacy	• Cognitive Dissonance
• Illusion of Control	• Mental Accounting
• Loss Aversion	• Hindsight Bias
• Overconfidence	• Lack of Self-Control
• Optimism Bias	• Clustering Illusion

Note: Although many behavioral mistakes have multiple consequences, those listed are the primary consequence.

MONEY MANAGERS AND BEHAVIORAL ISSUES

Most cognitive issues and emotional biases discussed previously occur in the optics of the individual investor. Money managers, however, are not immune to exhibiting similar biases.

One of the primary biases shown by money managers is suffering from the **herd mentality**. Managers often receive scrutiny from their clients when an investment trend is taking place. Clients encourage money managers to pursue strategies being employed by other managers, even if the strategy is simply a fad. Consequently, herding frequently occurs as managers mimic behavior instead of pursuing the goals of the fund as outlined by the prospectus or policy statement. One costly example of herding occurred in the 1990s with the Internet bubble.

Exhibit 6.7 | Internet Bubble

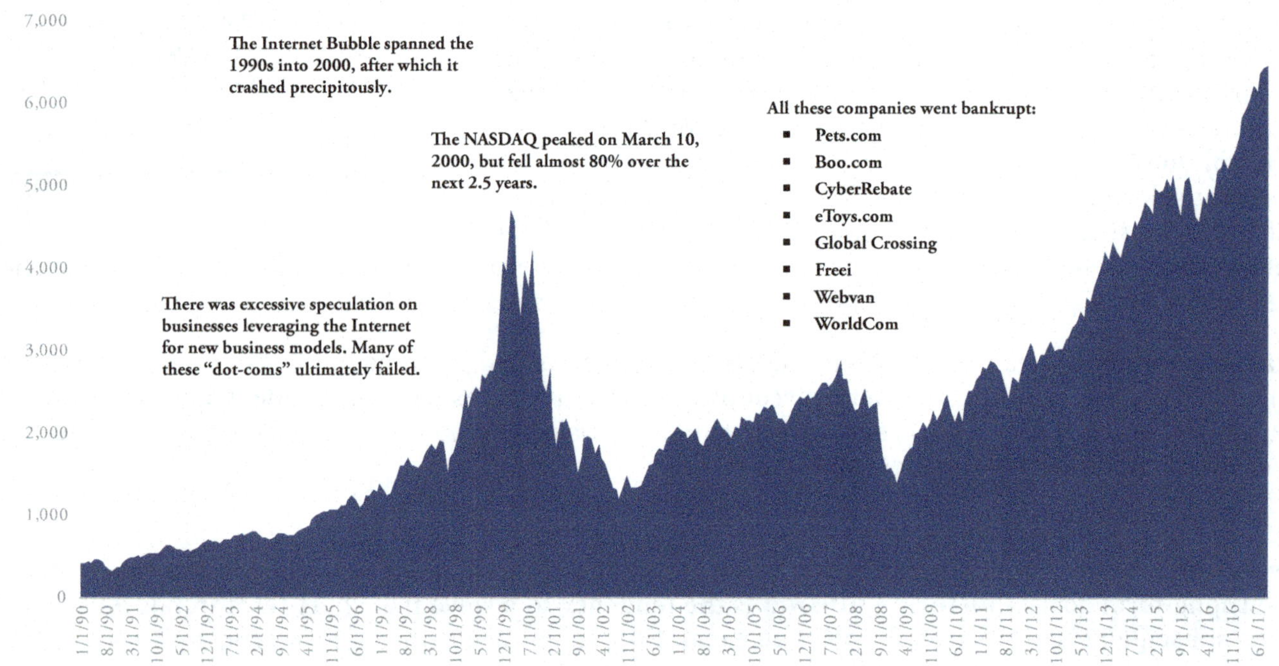

Investment managers also suffer from confirmation biases. Managers make asset selection picks regularly but tend to place more emphasis on research that confirms their purchase decision and discount any research that suggests the stock is overvalued.

They also appear to be overconfident, especially in their estimates of future price ranges for a stock and their estimates of profitability of these companies. In addition, there is ample evidence that managers over advertise their skills by claiming to be the only ones pursuing specific strategies.

CONCLUDING REMARKS REGARDING A BLEND OF TRADITIONAL AND BEHAVIORAL FINANCE

The existence of asset bubbles which have occurred in recent history and over the past several centuries provides enough evidence to contradict the severe assumptions maintained by modern portfolio theory and the efficient markets hypothesis. The implication is that markets today are not perfectly efficient, that there are pockets of inefficiencies, and that skilled investors might have an advantage when trading with less informed investors. Prices tend to drift away from their efficient market pricing equilibrium levels. There are scores of analysts, however, attempting to take advantage of their computing or processing skills, which tends to push prices back to their fair values. Not many are successful, as it has been shown by many studies that few are able to beat the market consistently.

The portfolio construction issues in a world filled with individuals subject to behavioral biases pose a considerable problem for investors and financial advisers. Recall that Harry Markowitz identified the efficient frontier in which all investors would find their optimal portfolios. Daniel Kahneman and Amos Tversky, however, show that individuals exhibit signs of loss aversion, which is clearly in opposition to modern portfolio theory.

The learning outcome, therefore, is to find a balance between the two theories. The first step for investors is to find their optimal portfolios outlined by Markowitz and available through many software packages. The second step is to determine if any cognitive or emotional biases exist in enough capacity to warrant a change to asset selection or allocation. The second step can only be successful if both investors and advisers become educated about the presence of the biases and the consequences of allowing them to go unchecked. The third step includes careful monitoring of both portfolio performance and any biased behavior as a continuing education to ensure investors can reach their financial goals. Successful investment strategies must include both traditional and behavioral elements.

SUMMARY

Summary of key points:

- Investors throughout history have tended to discount unfavorable outcomes, were overconfident and suffered from biased expectations, and most likely were subject to framing issues.
- Irrational decisions made by the consuming public can be revealed by comparing the chances of winning a lottery payout with the actual payout of a lottery win.
- History is littered with investment manias. Examples of bubbles include the UK railroad industry in the 1840s, the Japanese stock market in the early 1980s, the U.S. stock market in 1929 and 1987, dot-com stocks in the late 1990s, and in the housing market in 2008. There is little doubt that emotions and cognitive errors played huge roles in both the rise and subsequent fall of asset prices.
- Modern portfolio theory (MPT) relies on both efficiencies in financial markets and the ability of rational investors to make perfect decisions. In essence, MPT assumes behavioral biases do not exist.
- The three forms of the efficient market hypothesis (EMH) are the weak form, semi-strong form, and the strong form.

- Most academic studies show that private information certainly produces superior investment performance.
- Various anomalies support the notion that the market is not entirely efficient. Examples of these anomalies include the January Effect, Dogs of the Dow, and the Neglected Firm Effect.
- Behavioral scientists have shown that investors are influenced by emotions when making decisions under uncertainty, that investors are influenced by group dynamics, and that investors are not immune to collective decision making even when those decisions are highly personal. These characteristics are decidedly different from those required by modern portfolio theory.
- Framing refers to how something is presented, and much of behavioral finance can be explained through framing.
- Prospect theory suggests that individuals are faulty in their estimation of probabilities and the associated outcomes. Investors overweight small chance outcomes just to avoid a loss.
- Behavioral scientists have found that investors reduce complex decisions into scenarios that are more reasonable to comprehend. Rational investors make optimal decisions, but behavioral investors are more human and make decisions that are an approximation of the rational investor's optimal decision.
- Cognitive errors are made when investors inaccurately process new information about asset prices. Examples of cognitive errors include representativeness, anchoring, cognitive dissonance, gambler's fallacy, and mental accounting.
- Loss aversion is an emotional trait that is very different than the risk aversion exhibited by the rational investor. Behavioral investors arrange their portfolios to avoid losses rather than structuring them to generate gains because the pain of loss is so great.
- Regret aversion is a clear case of allowing fear of potential embarrassment to dictate financial decisions.
- Overconfidence is a significant behavioral emotional bias whereby investors overestimate their ability to identify mispriced securities.
- Investment managers often suffer from herd mentality and confirmation bias.

DISCUSSION QUESTIONS

SOLUTIONS to the discussion questions can be found exclusively within the chapter. Once you have completed an initial reading of the chapter, go back and highlight the answers to these questions.

1. Identify and explain historical examples of decision making under uncertainty and the errors made by historical investors.

2. Discuss the development of modern portfolio theory and explain the fundamental principles on which it is based.

3. Discuss the efficient market hypothesis and identify the three levels of market efficiency.

4. Explain the difference among weak form, semi-strong form, and strong form market efficiency.

5. Identify and discuss well-known stock market anomalies.

6. Define behavioral finance and compare it to traditional finance.

7. List important behavioral finance assumptions.

8. Discuss the concept of framing and how it explains the equity premium puzzle.

9. Explain prospect theory and how behavioral decision makers estimate the probability of future events.

10. Explain how behavioral investors process information in the context of bounded rationality.

11. Define cognitive errors.

12. List common cognitive errors.

13. Discuss how representativeness can lead to poorly managed portfolios.

14. Define anchoring and discuss anchoring in the context of the Dow Jones Industrial Average surpassing 10,000, 20,000, and 30,000 levels.

15. Provide an example of mental accounting and discuss the consequences of this cognitive error.

16. Provide examples of both confirmation and hindsight biases.

17. Discuss how cognitive errors are violations of modern portfolio theory.

18. Summarize the reason loss aversion is regularly exhibited by some investors.

19. Contrast loss aversion with regret aversion.

20. Discuss why investors tend to be overconfident.
21. Review self-control and optimism biases and explain why each mishandles risk assessment.
22. Discuss how emotional biases are violations of modern portfolio theory.
23. Describe how money managers exhibit behavioral investing characteristics.
24. Explain how lesser known emotional biases, such as clustering illusion and irrational escalation, affect portfolio performance.
25. Explain the existence of asset bubbles in the context of behavioral finance.

MULTIPLE-CHOICE PROBLEMS

A sample of multiple choice problems is provided below. Additional multiple choice problems are available at money-education.com by accessing the Student Practice Portal.

1. Modern portfolio theory was originally advanced by:
    a. Harry Markowitz and the identification of standard deviation as a measure of risk.
    b. William Sharpe and the capital asset pricing model.
    c. Eugene Fama and the efficient markets hypothesis.
    d. Stephen Ross and the arbitrage pricing theory.

2. The behavioral finance aspect that most likely offers a unique and reasonable explanation for the persistence of the equity premium puzzle is:
    a. Emotional bias.
    b. Bounded rationality.
    c. Myopic loss aversion.
    d. Heuristic security valuation.

3. A large firm announces it has hired a design company to change its corporate logo. The new logo will be shown publicly for the first time the following day. Shareholders react by bidding up the shares by 10% over the relevant benchmark. No other information about this firm is released. The shareholder reaction can best be described as:
    a. Anchoring.
    b. Representativeness.
    c. Cognitive dissonance.
    d. Mental accounting.

4. Reese sits on four boards of directors of publicly held companies, each operating in a different industry. She has an ethical clause in each of her board contracts but ignores them by trading on information she learns during board meetings. Reese generates an average return on these trades that is well above any relevant benchmark. If Reese's strategy was repeatable by all investors over the long term, this would violate which form of the efficient market hypothesis?
    a. Inefficient.
    b. Weak form efficient.
    c. Semi-strong form efficient.
    d. Strong form efficient.

5. Perhaps the biggest behavior mistake made by both individual investors and money managers during the dot com bubble was:
    a. Loss aversion.
    b. Mental accounting.
    c. Assuming market efficiency.
    d. Herd mentality.

QUICK QUIZ EXPLANATIONS

Quick Quiz 6.1

1. False. Even with today's investment tools, it remains difficult to quantify risk. For those investors faced with great uncertainty over the past 500 years, the task of measuring risk levels was extremely difficult. They did not have the ability to collect data, to process information, or to link expected returns with risk levels. They did, however, use simple metrics to help them make decisions in the face of uncertainty.
2. True.
3. True.

Quick Quiz 6.2

1. True.
2. False. Strong form capital markets reflect all relevant information, including private information. A semi-strong form market has prices that reflect all relevant publicly available information.
3. False. Technical analysis is the use of historical price or volume data to make asset selection decisions. Technicians can only be successful in generating abnormal returns if the market is inefficient.

Quick Quiz 6.3

1. True.
2. True.
3. False. Prospect theory suggests that investors take short cuts, sometimes referred to as heuristics, to make decisions. These short cuts, then, make it impossible for investors to completely and perfectly process information.

Quick Quiz 6.4

1. True.
2. False. Ignoring new information that is relevant to an asset's price is a form of cognitive error that leads to poor decision making. Mental accounting is the separating of accounts that leads to incomplete diversification and poor asset allocations.
3. True.

Quick Quiz 6.5

1. True.
2. False. Loss averse investors tend to sell winning stocks too quickly to confirm their superior skills and to hold onto losing stocks too long to avoid be labeled as a poor stock selector.
3. True.

7
FIXED-INCOME SECURITIES

LEARNING OBJECTIVES

1. Explain the various types of fixed-income securities.*
2. Understand that fixed-income securities are often used in combination with equity securities to create a well-diversified investment portfolio.*
3. Recognize that term (maturity) is a key element of a bond and may range from short term to 100 years.
4. Understand characteristics of fixed-income securities, including whether they pay or accrue interest, are secured or unsecured, are callable or convertible.*
5. Differentiate between the taxation of corporate and municipal bonds.*
6. Explain how STRIPS are created from Treasury securities.*
7. Illustrate how mortgage-backed securities (MBS) are created and explain how cash flows from MBS are paid to investors.*
8. Recognize the standard credit rating system for S&P and Moody's.

**Ties to CFP Certification Learning Objectives*

INTRODUCTION

Fixed-income securities are credit instruments that have fixed maturity dates. Short-term fixed income securities, or money market instruments, can be generally defined as those with maturities of up to one year. Many short-term fixed income securities do not pay intermediate interest; instead, they are purchased at a discount and mature for their face value or pay face value plus interest at maturity. Most long-term fixed-income securities, however, pay interest during the life of the security and make a final face value payment at maturity. Issuers of long-term fixed-income securities promise lenders that they will make regular interest payments followed by a principal payment. Examples of money market securities include commercial paper, bankers' acceptances, and certificates of deposit. Examples of long-term securities include corporate and government bonds, mortgage backed securities, and collateralized debt obligations.

Key Concepts

1. There are many types of fixed-income securities that can be used in portfolio construction.
2. T-bills, commercial paper, money market accounts, CDs, and bankers' acceptances are considered short term fixed-income securities.

Fixed income securities are often used in combination with equity securities in a well-diversified portfolio to reduce overall risk, whilst still allow the portfolio to meet its return objectives. They are useful in this role due to their less than perfect positive correlation with equities.

Although the risk of fixed income securities is on average lower than that for equities, they do expose a portfolio to interest rate risk and credit risk. Interest rate risk results from the sensitivity of fixed income security prices to changes in interest rates. As rates rise, fixed income prices generally fall. Credit risk is the risk that the issuer's financial position deteriorates to the point where they cannot make the interest and principal payments that were promised. These risks are discussed in detail in Chapter 8. Used properly in portfolio construction, however, fixed-income instruments give investors the opportunity to mitigate portfolio risk and provide cash flows to take advantage of future investment opportunities or, in the case of asset-liability management, to maximize portfolio profit by eliminating exposure to reinvestment rate risk.

There are many types of bond issuers, including both domestic and foreign governments and companies. The majority of bonds, however, are issued by the U.S. federal government, its agencies, municipalities and U.S. corporations. The bonds of each of the issuers may be issued in public or private markets and generally have different investment characteristics. The differences in bond characteristics impact the perceived value of the bond, and as a result, impact the required return.

One of the key features of a bond is the length of its term, or maturity. The **maturity** of the bond is the period of time through which the issuer has control over the bond proceeds and the period of time it must continue to pay **coupon or interest payments**. The maturity of a bond also impacts the yield that is received by the investor. Generally, the yield received by an investor is higher for longer maturity bonds. However, this depends on the shape of the **yield curve**. The maturity of a bond also impacts the volatility of the bond value and can impact other types of risks associated with the bond.

Although most bonds are issued with maturities ranging from one to thirty years, bonds are sometimes issued with maturities as long as 100 years. In addition, some issuers include a feature in the bond agreement that allows the issuer to call the bond from the holder prior to the maturity date. This call feature allows the issuer to redeem the bond issue prior to its scheduled maturity, which may be beneficial to the issuer if interest rates have declined. In such a case, the bond issuer may call the bonds from the holder and then issue new bonds at a lower coupon rate, thereby reducing the cost of its debt (this is called refunding). Call features will be discussed later in this chapter.

This chapter provides an overview of the characteristics of fixed-income securities. Analysis of fixed income securities will be covered in Chapter 8.

TYPES OF FIXED-INCOME SECURITIES

Fixed-income securities include a wide variety of instruments that range in terms of risk, maturity and structure. As of the end of the second quarter, 2018, there were more than $41.8 trillion in outstanding fixed-income securities in the United States. This figure does not include securities issued outside of the United States. As the chart below depicts, the largest fixed-income markets are the U.S. Treasury and the mortgage related bond markets, representing more than 50 percent and more than $24 trillion in outstanding loan amounts.

Exhibit 7.1 | Outstanding U.S. Bond Market Debt

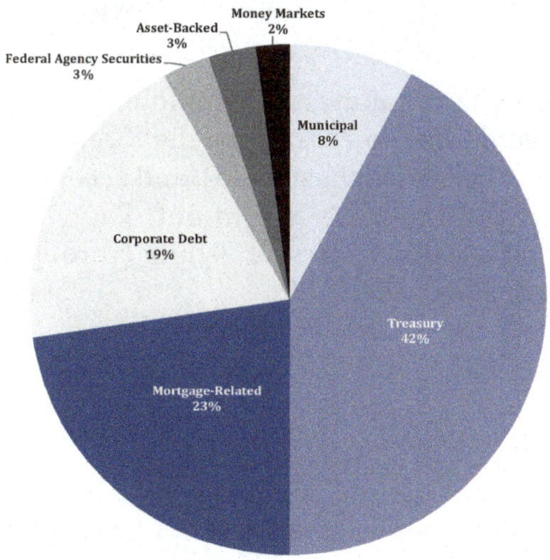

Source: sifma.org

MONEY MARKET AND SHORT-TERM DEBT SECURITIES

Fixed-income securities can range in maturity from a few days to 100 years. As a result, they are often segmented into short-term debt securities with a maturity of up to one year and long-term debt securities with a maturity greater than one year. Short-term debt securities, often referred to as money market securities, include Treasury bills, commercial paper, money market deposit accounts, certificates of deposit, bankers acceptances, repurchase agreements, federal funds, short-term municipal debt obligations, and Eurodollar deposits. Because these securities pay no explicit interest, they will sell at a discount from their face value.

Treasury Bills (T-Bills)

Treasury bills (T-bills) are short-term U.S. Government debt instruments issued in denominations of $100 that are auctioned on a weekly basis. The maturity dates for T-bills are typically four weeks, 13 weeks, 26 weeks, or 52 weeks.[1] Due to their short-term nature and the creditworthiness of their issuer, the U.S. Government, T-bills are viewed as default-risk-free instruments, and as such the current rate on T-bills is a proxy for the risk-free rate of return.

T-bills are issued at a discount, and mature at their par, or face, value.

Example 7.1

Adele buys a $1,000 T-bill at a price per $100 of $99.986111. She would pay $999.86 ($1,000 x 0.99986111 = $999.86111). When the bill matures, she would be paid its face value, $1,000. Her interest is the face value minus the purchase price ($1,000 - $999.86 = $0.14).

The weekly auction for T-bills is conducted on a competitive and noncompetitive bid basis. Regardless of the type of bidding process used, all bidders purchasing T-bills at the auction receive the yield of the highest accepted competitive bid, which is referred to as the **stop-out yield**. The discount rate, price, and investment yield are determined in each auction. Bidding is in terms of the discount rate, which is calculated as:

$$\textbf{Discount Rate} = \frac{\textbf{Par} - \textbf{Price}}{\textbf{Par}} \times \frac{\textbf{360}}{\textbf{Days to Maturity}}$$

In the competitive bid process, purchasers indicate the amount they would like to purchase (in $1,000 increments) and the yield they would like to receive on the T-bills. The Treasury orders the bids from highest price (lowest yield) to lowest price (highest yield), and accepts bids in this order until the amount the government needs is reached and the issue is sold out. The yield on the last bid accepted in this process is the stop-out yield, that all-purchasers of T-bills (through both the competitive and non-competitive bid process) auction receive.

1. The 52 week T-bills are only auctioned every four weeks, instead of on a weekly basis. https://www.treasurydirect.gov/instit/auctfund/work/auctime/auctime.htm

Example 7.2

Jade places a non-competitive bid for $100,000 (par value) for T-bills. Because she is a non-competitive bidder, her bid will be filled. The interest rate that she and all the other non-competitive and competitive bidders receive is the same and is the stop-out yield.

Exhibit 7.2 | Treasury Auction Results

TREASURY NEWS

Department of the Treasury • Bureau of the Fiscal Service

For Immediate Release
June 18, 2019

CONTACT: Treasury Auctions
202-504-3550

TREASURY AUCTION RESULTS

Term and Type of Security	364-Day Bill
CUSIP Number	912796SV2
High Rate [1]	1.985%
Allotted at High	73.55%
Price	97.992944
Investment Rate [2]	2.049%
Median Rate [3]	1.950%
Low Rate [4]	1.920%
Issue Date	June 20, 2019
Maturity Date	June 18, 2020

	Tendered	Accepted
Competitive	$74,428,840,000	$25,538,215,000
Noncompetitive	$460,116,700	$460,116,700
FIMA (Noncompetitive)	$1,700,000	$1,700,000
Subtotal [5]	**$74,890,656,700**	**$26,000,031,700[6]**
SOMA	$0	$0
Total	**$74,890,656,700**	**$26,000,031,700**

	Tendered	Accepted
Primary Dealer [7]	$62,105,000,000	$13,545,825,000
Direct Bidder [8]	$495,000,000	$411,775,000
Indirect Bidder [9]	$11,828,840,000	$11,580,615,000
Total Competitive	**$74,428,840,000**	**$25,538,215,000**

[1] All tenders at lower rates were accepted in full.

[2] Equivalent coupon-issue yield.

[3] 50% of the amount of accepted competitive tenders was tendered at or below that rate.

[4] 5% of the amount of accepted competitive tenders was tendered at or below that rate.

[5] Bid-to-Cover Ratio: $74,890,656,700/$26,000,031,700 = 2.88

[6] Awards to TreasuryDirect = $212,931,700.

[7] Primary dealers as submitters bidding for their own house accounts.

[8] Non-Primary dealer submitters bidding for their own house accounts.

[9] Customers placing competitive bids through a direct submitter, including Foreign and International Monetary Authorities p
Bank of New York.

All noncompetitive bidders are guaranteed to receive the dollar amount of their bid, up to $5 million per auction. In **Exhibit 7.2**, the auction amount is $26 billion. The noncompetitive bids are subtracted from the total auction amount to determine the amount available to competitive bidders. In this case, there are about $462 million of noncompetitive bids leaving about $25.538 billion.

Taxation of T-Bills

Unlike most government bonds issued at a discount with maturities in excess of one year, T-bills are not subject to the original issue discount (OID) rules.[2] Calculating the interest income for purchasers of T-bills who hold them to maturity is relatively simple: upon maturity the amount paid for the T-bill is subtracted from the maturity value, or par value, of the instrument ($100). This difference represents the holder's interest income, which is subject to income tax at the taxpayer's marginal ordinary income tax rate. One benefit of holding T-bills is that state and local governments are not permitted to tax the interest income earned on these bonds. The only tax the holder has to pay is the federal income tax.

If a T-bill is sold prior to maturity, a capital gain or loss may result if interest rates have changed since the date of purchase. Since, by their nature, T-bills are short-term instruments (they have maturities of less than one year), any gain or loss is treated as a short-term capital gain or loss and is subject to ordinary income tax rates.

Commercial Paper

Corporations regularly raise short-term funds by issuing commercial paper. When a need to raise short-term funds arises, corporations can seek short-term financing from banking institutions or public markets. Many large, stable corporations find that seeking short-term financing in the public markets is less expensive than undertaking short-term bank financing. **Short-term debt instruments** issued in the public markets by corporations are referred to as **commercial paper**. The companies that issue commercial paper are often large, financially stable companies that have solid credit ratings. While T-bills are considered riskless securities due to the government's taxing power, commercial paper does carry some default risk, albeit a very small amount. Due to the increased risk taken on by the investor in commercial paper, yields often slightly exceed those on T-bills.

Commercial paper is generally issued in denominations of $100,000 or more and typically has a maturity of 270 days or less. Usually, however, commercial paper maturities are set at six months or less. As added protection for investors, commercial paper is often backed by lines of credit from banks to reduce default risk, a particularly important issue in economic environments where the issuance of new commercial paper for refunding at maturity is not possible.

Taxation of Commercial Paper

Interest received on commercial paper is considered to be ordinary income in the year it is received. If commercial paper is sold before its maturity date, the investor realizes a short-term capital gain or loss if prevailing interest rates have changed since the date of purchase. Short-term capital gains and losses are subject to tax at ordinary income tax rates.

Unlike T-bills, interest income on commercial paper is subject to state and local income tax as well as federal income tax.

2. The OID rules require that the annual amortized discount be included in taxable income.

Money Market Deposit Accounts

Money market deposit accounts (MMDAs) permit investors to earn interest on funds that are not currently deployed in other investment opportunities. MMDAs typically pay an interest rate that is based on a short-term variable interest rate and are typically issued by banks (in which case FDIC insurance is available) or mutual fund companies. MMDAs are accounts, not securities, and as such are non-negotiable and non-transferable. They often limit the number of withdrawals that can be made per month, and may set a minimum dollar amount for each withdrawal.

Taxation of MMDAs

Interest earned on MMDAs is considered ordinary income and is subject to federal, state, and local income tax in the year in which it is earned.

Certificates of Deposit (CDs)

Certificates of deposit (CDs) are used by small and large investors to obtain rates of return that are higher than traditional deposit accounts (money markets). The yield for a bank CD is higher than for the bank's savings account but the funds in the CD are committed for a set term, such as two years.

Certificates of deposit come in two forms: non-negotiable and negotiable (Jumbo CDs).

Non-negotiable CDs are used for short-term deposits of at least $500. Due to their short-term nature and the small amount, non-negotiable CDs often have low default risk and are highly liquid. Non-negotiable CDs are not marketable but can often be cashed in prior to maturity by forgoing receipt of interest payments, which the banks refer to as an early withdrawal penalty. If a non-negotiable CD is issued by a bank, it receives deposit protection from the FDIC, which further reduces the default risk undertaken by the investor. Individuals and businesses use non-negotiable CDs for short-term deployment of cash not currently needed.

Negotiable, or Jumbo CDs, are short-term deposits of $100,000 or more. Like non-negotiable CDs, negotiable CDs have very low default risk and are highly liquid. Unlike non-negotiable CDs, negotiable CDs can be purchased and sold in the secondary market, permitting the holder to cash out without incurring an early withdrawal penalty. The sale of a negotiable CD could, of course, generate a capital gain or loss for the investor if the amount received in the sale does not equal the amount paid for the CD plus the accumulated interest earned as of the date of the sale. Negotiable CDs issued by federally insured banks also receive FDIC protection up to the specified deposit limit ($250,000 per depositor per institution in 2019). Very large Jumbo CDs are not fully covered by FDIC insurance, but default risk remains low since they are typically issued by fiscally sound banks. Troubled banks may have difficulty attracting customers for Jumbo CDs due to the increase default risk they present. Due to their high minimum investment amount, negotiable CDs are typically used by large institutional investors.

Quick Quiz 7.1

1. The U.S. fixed-income market is less than $100 billion.
   a. True
   b. False
2. Treasury bills are pure discount bonds that make periodic interest payments.
   a. True
   b. False
3. Both competitive and noncompetitive bidders receive the yield known as the stop-out yield.
   a. True
   b. False
4. The taxation of commercial paper, certificates of deposit, and money market deposit accounts is identical.
   a. True
   b. False

False, False, True, False.

Taxation of CDs

Interest income is subject to federal and state income tax at ordinary income tax rates in the year the interest is earned. CDs, whether negotiable or not, that have terms of more than one year, or cross a tax year, are subject to the Original Issue Discount rules that require interest earned during the tax period be subjected to tax in that tax period regardless of whether or not the owner of the CD has withdrawn or received the interest income.

If the holder of a non-negotiable CD withdraws funds prior to maturity and is subject to an early withdrawal penalty, that early withdrawal penalty is deductible as an adjustment to gross income. The deduction, in this case, offsets the interest income that the holder received so that the actual amount of income subject to income tax reflects the amount the holder actually received in excess of the basis in the CD.

As mentioned earlier, when negotiable or Jumbo CDs are sold in the market, the seller may realize a capital gain equal to the difference between the sale price of the CD and the original purchase price plus accumulated interest earned on the CD.

Additional money market securities include banker's acceptances, repurchase agreements, short-term debt obligations, and Eurodollar deposits, each of which is discussed in detail in Chapter 2.

COMMON FEATURES OF BONDS & BOND TERMINOLOGY

Coupon Rate

Bonds are debt securities that pay interest, on a periodic basis, typically semi-annually or annually. The **coupon rate** is the rate of interest paid on the face value (par value) of the bond.

Example 7.3

Sand Enterprises (SE) is a glass producer that specializes in the manufacture of bottles for soft drink companies. SE issues a fixed rate bond that is expected to raise $2 billion to finance an expansion to South America. Like most bond issues, SE will issue the bond in increments of $1,000 to appeal to global investors. The bond matures in 30 years and offers an annual coupon rate of 8%. Investors who purchase the SE bond can expect to receive $80 every year for the next 30 years and then a final principal payment of $1,000.

The term "coupon" is a reference to the old method investors used to collect the periodic interest payments on the bond. In the days when bearer bonds were common, there would be coupons attached to the bond certificate that the investor could clip and present to a bank at a specific date to collect the scheduled interest payment. In modern times, this time consuming process is no longer used as bonds are registered, typically with the issuing organization, and interest payments are made directly to the bond's owner of record.

Yield to Maturity

When comparing bonds for potential purchase, an investor often considers the bond's **yield to maturity (YTM)**. The yield to maturity is the bondholder's required rate of return, and is calculated as, the internal rate of return on the cash flows received by the bondholder. This measure assumes that the investor can reinvest cash flows from the bond at the same rate as the IRR. If the coupon payments received are reinvested at a rate higher or lower than the calculated YTM, the actual return the investor receives will be higher or lower than the calculated YTM.

Example 7.4

Empress Holdings (EH) issues a 10 year bond with a coupon rate of 6% and a promise to make interest payments annually on June 30. Any bondholder who buys the EH bond on the issue date and receives ten coupon payments and can reinvest those payments at 6% will have generated a realized return on the bond of 6%.

Secured and Unsecured Bonds

Bonds can be issued on either a secured or an unsecured basis.

Secured bonds are backed by some form of collateral, which gives the investor the ability to recover some or all of the invested capital in the event the bond issuer defaults. A common example of a secured bond is a GNMA (Government National Mortgage Association or Ginnie Mae), which is a mortgage bond secured by real property owned by the borrower. Banks that issue mortgages typically sell those mortgages, which are then pooled together in a fund against which bonds are issued to investors. As mortgage payments are made, interest payments are transferred to the bondholders, and if the borrowers default on their mortgage, the real estate pledged as collateral for the loan is used to pay back the investors.

Unsecured bonds, sometimes referred to as **debenture bonds**, do not have any collateral backing the issuer's promise to make interest and principal payments. Purchasers of unsecured bonds rely on the creditworthiness of the issuer and the issuer's promise to make payments as scheduled. Sometimes, unforeseen circumstances arise making it difficult or impossible for the issuer to make all payments as promised. With no collateral to back up the payment promise, unsecured bonds have a higher risk of default than secured bonds. To compensate the investor for the additional risk undertaken when the investor purchases an unsecured bond, the rate of interest paid on unsecured bonds is typically higher than that paid on secured bonds issued by comparable borrowers.

Key Concepts

1. Bonds usually pay interest semi annually or annually.
2. Yield to maturity is the same as internal rate of return (IRR).
3. Bonds can be issued secured or unsecured.
4. Unsecured bonds are debenture bonds.
5. Bonds may be issued that are callable, convertible, or zero coupon.

Bonds with Embedded Options

Not all bonds are structured to provide interest payments for a fixed period of time. Depending upon the expectation of future interest rate changes, or a desire to encourage bondholders to take an equity position in the issuer, bonds often include special features (embedded options) to permit these types of adjustments. Commonly issued bonds with embedded options include callable bonds, puttable bonds, and convertible bonds.

When a bond issuer anticipates that interest rates may be lower in the future, it may include a **call provision** in the bond. A call provision permits the issuer to repurchase the bond from the investor prior to the stated maturity of the bond. Typically, a callable bond is retired at the time a new bond issue is floated in the market, allowing the issuer to reduce the carrying cost of debt by paying a lower interest rate on the newly issued bonds. While this feature is favorable to the issuer, the purchaser is assuming reinvestment rate risk: if the issuer calls the bond when interest rates have fallen, the investor then has to reinvest the bond proceeds at lower rates of return, thereby reducing the overall rate of return they would receive as compared to a non-callable bond, which guarantees a given rate of interest until the maturity date of the bond. Since a call feature is favorable to the issuer and requires the investor to assume more risk, the issuer of a callable bond has to pay a higher rate of interest to compensate the investor for undertaking that risk when compared to a similar, but non-callable bond. In addition to a higher rate of interest, issuers of callable bonds typically pay bond holders a premium over par value when the bond is called. From the investor's perspective, the increase over par value is a **call premium**. However, from the bond issuer's perspective, it is considered a **call penalty**.

A **puttable bond** is a bond that contains a put option that allows the owner of the bond to sell the bond back to the issuer at a predetermined price prior to the stated maturity of the bond. While not as common as callable bonds, puttable bonds provide an advantage to bondholders in that the put option provides price protection in a climate of rising interest rates or an increase in the default risk of a bond issue. Naturally, this type of feature is beneficial to the bondholder and therefore increases the price of the bond. Since puttable bonds are less risky, they have lower YTMs than other similar bonds without such a feature.

Some bonds permit the purchaser to convert the bond, which is a form of debt financing, into an equity position in the issuer. Bonds with this feature are referred to as **convertible bonds**. Convertible bonds may be attractive to investors who enjoy the benefit of receiving fixed payments from traditional bonds, but also prefer the option to participate in capital gains if the company performs well. Since convertible bonds permit conversion of the bond for a specified number of common shares in the company, or for a specified price, the holder of the bond can compare the market price of the company's stock in the future against the conversion price for the bond. If the market price is higher than the conversion price, the bondholder can convert the bond into an equity stake in the company and possibly earn a higher return than he or she would have received had the bond not been converted. All else equal, this option provides a benefit to the bondholder, so the interest rate paid on a convertible bond is lower than the interest rate paid on a similar, non-convertible bond.

Exceptions to Common Bond Designs

While most bonds pay a specified interest rate on an annual or semi-annual basis until maturity of the bond, there are two common exceptions to this bond design: zero-coupon bonds and serial bonds.

A **zero-coupon bond** does not make any regular interest or **coupon payments**. Instead, all of the interest paid on a zero-coupon bond is paid at the maturity date along with the return of the principal. Instead of being issued at face value, zero-coupon bonds are issued at a discount to face value and pay the face value of the bond to the investor upon maturity of the bond. The discount that applies is a function of prevailing interest rates at the time the bond is issued; the higher the interest rate, the larger the discount, all else equal. One attractive feature of zero-coupon bonds is that the investor does not incur any reinvestment rate risk. Since coupon payments are not received during the term of the bond, the investor is not exposed to the risk that the coupon may have to be invested at a rate lower than the yield to maturity, thereby lowering the investor's overall return on the bond. When an investor purchases a zero-coupon bond, the yield to maturity on the bond equals the investor's return assuming the bond is held to maturity.

In the United States, individual taxpayers are considered to be cash-basis taxpayers, which means that they pay income tax on income received. In the case of a zero-coupon bond, interest is not received until maturity of the bond, so under the normal tax rules that apply to cash-basis taxpayers, all of the income tax could be deferred until maturity. Unfortunately for those wishing to defer income tax liability, a special rule applies - the doctrine of constructive receipt - which requires cash basis taxpayers to report the income on an accrual basis. The doctrine of constructive receipt invokes the original issue discount (OID) rules under the Internal Revenue Code, which requires that holders of zero-coupon bonds pay income tax on interest income as it is earned, rather than when it is received. Due to this tax treatment, investors who are tax sensitive will prefer to hold zero-coupon bonds in tax qualified accounts, such as IRAs, to avoid being taxed until distributions are made from the account.

Example 7.5

In early January, Xavier purchases a thirty-year zero coupon bond at a price of $95.06. The yield to maturity on the bond is 8%. At the end of the year, the price of the bond is $95.28, but Xavier will report $7.60 of taxable income for the year. This amount is calculated by applying the 8% yield to the $95.06 price (0.08 x 95.06).

In some instances, bond issuers prefer to make periodic repayments of principal as well as interest. A **serial bond** has multiple maturity dates, and permits the issuer to partially retire the bond issue at dates specified in the bond. Serial bonds may be advantageous to issuers, particularly when interest rates are expected to decline, since at least part of the higher obligation issue can be retired, and, if necessary, refinanced at a lower rate. This type of bond, of course, exposes the bond investor to additional reinvestment-rate risk. If rates rise, however, the bond investor benefits from the serial principal payments, since those amounts can then be reinvested at a higher rate of return.

Serial bonds are often used by issuers who would like to match both the interest and principal payments of the bond to the expected cashflows to be received from the project being financed. This approach to cash-flow management may reduce default risk for the lender, and by matching projected revenues and expenses, also provide financial management benefits for the issuer.

Sometimes, the issuer of a traditional (non-serial) bond would like to reserve part of the principal payment each year so that, at maturity, there is not as large a cash outflow from the issuer as would have been. When a bond issuer sets aside a portion of the principal of the bond each year for repayment of investors at maturity, often they do so through the use of a sinking fund. If investors are concerned that the issuer of a bond may have difficulty repaying the principal amount upon maturity of the bond issue, one way to induce investors to purchase that bond

Quick Quiz 7.2

1. The coupon rate on a bond determines the dollar amount of interest paid to the bondholder.
   a. True
   b. False
2. Yield to maturity is equal to the internal rate of return.
   a. True
   b. False
3. Yield to maturity assumes that the reinvestment rate is equal to the IRR.
   a. True
   b. False
4. A bond secured by a manufacturing facility is known as a debenture.
   a. True
   b. False
5. When a zero-coupon bond is held to maturity, the original YTM calculated equals the return to the investor.
   a. True
   b. False

True, True, True, False, True.

(in addition, of course, to offering a higher interest rate on the bond to compensate the investor for additional risk they are undertaking) is to create a sinking fund required by the bond indenture, managed by an independent trustee, so that investors have a greater sense of confidence that the principal will be repaid at maturity.

Accrued Interest

Accrued interest is interest that has accumulated since the last coupon payment. Generally, investors do not purchase a bond exactly on its coupon payment date. Rather, they purchase bonds between coupon payments. For the seller of a bond, they have earned the interest from the coupon payment date up to the date of sale of the bond. The interest during this period is referred to as accrued interest.

The buyer must compensate the seller for the interest earned from the last coupon payment date to the date the bond is sold (settlement date). The buyer of the bond pays the market price (ask price) plus the accrued interest up to, but not including, the settlement date.

Exhibit 7.3 | Accrued Interest on Bonds

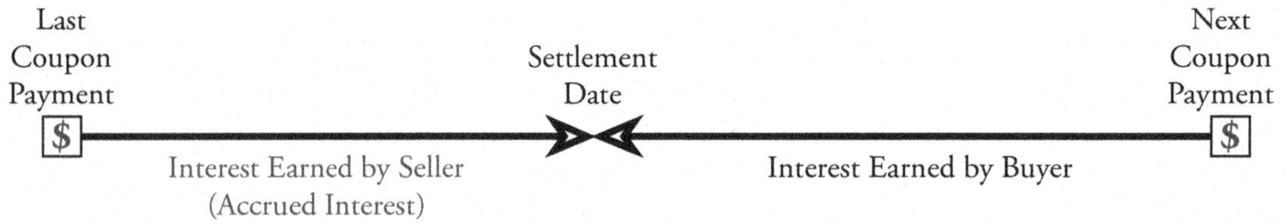

The formula for accrued interest is as follows:

$$\textbf{Accrued Interest} = \textbf{Semi-Annual Coupon Payment} \times \left(\frac{\textbf{Days Since Last Coupon Payment}}{\textbf{Days in Coupon Period}}\right)$$

Essentially, the accrued interest equals the coupon payment multiplied by the ratio of time that has elapsed from the last coupon payment divided by the time between coupon payments. Interest for corporate and municipal bonds is calculated using a 360-day year. Interest for government bonds is calculated using a 365-day year.

Example 7.6

A $1,000 par value bond has four semi-annual coupon payments remaining until the bond matures. The semi-annual interest payments are $30.00 and the annual coupon rate is 6 percent. Assume that there are 180 days in the coupon period and that there are 60 days between the settlement date and the next coupon payment date. The accrued interest equals $20 as follows: $30 x [120 days / 180 days]. Therefore, the price of the bond is increased by the $20 of accrued interest.

When the value of a bond is determined by calculating the present value of all future cash flows, accrued interest is included in the price. This price is often referred to as the **full price**, or **dirty price**. The buyer pays the seller the full price. The full price less the accrued interest equals the quoted price of the bond, which is referred to as the **clean price**. The clean price, plus any commissions paid on the transaction, represents the buyers cost basis for tax purposes. With regard to the first coupon payment, the taxpayer will only be taxed on the portion that is earned from the time the bond is purchased until the first coupon payment.

Bond Price Quotes

Corporate and municipal bonds are typically priced as a percentage of par value ($1,000), with three decimal places. Consider the following examples:

- A Microsoft bond quote of 99.688 equates to 99.688% of par value, which equals $996.88.
- A Johnson & Johnson bond quote of 100.832 equates to 100.832% of par value, which equals $1,008.32.

When investors buy bonds in the secondary market, they pay the ask price (the price the bond is being sold for) plus accrued interest plus a commission, which is a fee paid to the broker selling the bond.

Exhibit 7.4 | Treasury Note and Bond Quotes

Issue	Coup	Maturity	Bid	Ask	YTM
United States Treasury Note	2.00%	11/15/2026	94.12	94.16	2.629%

Treasury note and bond prices are quoted in dollars and fractions of a dollar. By market convention, the normal fraction used for Treasury security prices is 1/32. In the chart above, the decimal point separates the full dollar portion of the price from the 32nds of a dollar, which are to the right of the decimal. Thus the bid quote of 94.12 means $94 plus 12/32 of a dollar, or $94.375, for each $100 face value of the note. The ask price above is 94.16, which equates to $94 plus 16/32, or $94.50 per $100 face value.

Ask prices are always higher than bid prices for notes and bonds. The ask price is the price to buy the bond and the bid is the price to sell the bond.

Treasury note and bond quotes often have a change column and a yield column. The change indicates the change in the price of the bond. The yield indicates the YTM for the bond.

In some cases, active issues may be quoted in 64ths instead of 32nds. However, the traditional quotes are in 32nds.

U.S. GOVERNMENT BONDS AND AGENCY SECURITIES

The United States government issues a variety of debt instruments to finance its expenditures. In financing short-term cash needs, the government issues T-bills, which were discussed earlier in this chapter. Now we turn to longer-term debt financing issued by the government.

Exhibit 7.5 | U.S. Federal Debt Held by the Public

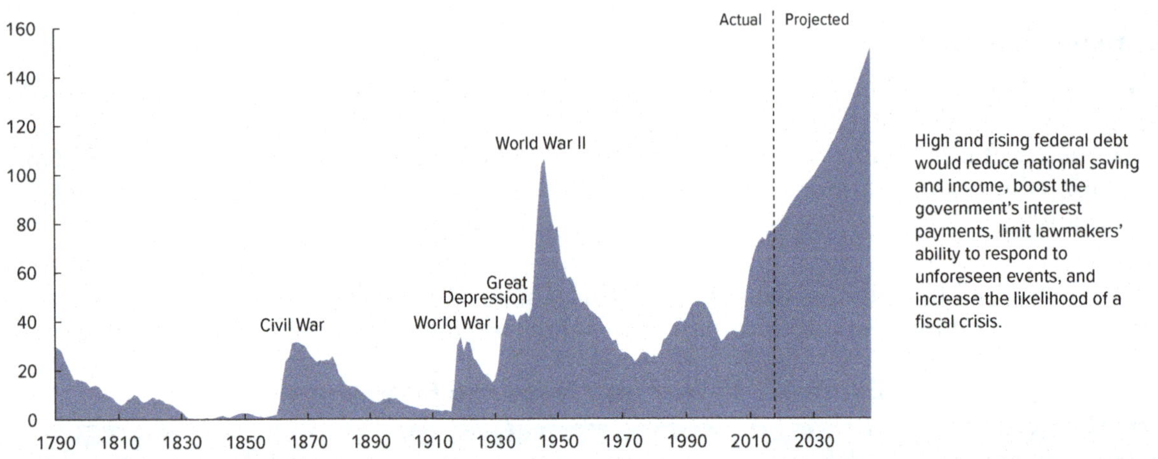

Source: Congressional Budget Office.

Treasury Notes and Bonds

U.S. Treasury notes are currently issued for maturities of 2, 3, 5, 7, and 10 years. Treasury bonds are issued for a term of up to 30 years. Both Treasury notes and bonds make coupon payments semi-annually and are issued in increments of $100.

The price and interest rate of Treasury notes and bonds are determined at auction. The price may be greater than, less than, or equal to the par value. Investors may hold the notes and bonds to maturity, or may sell them prior to maturity. Newly created notes and bonds are issued electronically. Some investors may hold older notes and bonds issued on paper certificates, which can be converted to electronic instruments at the option of the investor.

Investors can purchase Treasury notes and bonds in a manner similar to the process used to purchase T-bills. Bids for notes and bonds can be placed on a competitive or non-competitive basis. Investors who wish to purchase the instruments using the non-competitive bid process receive the yield determined at auction. All those participating in the non-competitive bid process are guaranteed to receive a note or bond for the term they specify, and for the full amount they would like to invest. Non-competitive bids may be made through a bank, a broker, or directly with the Treasury using the website

Key Concepts

1. Treasury notes are from 2-10 years, Treasury bonds are for up to 30 years.
2. Treasury notes and bonds can be stripped to be more attractive to niche investors.
3. Treasury Inflation Protected Securities (TIPS) are adjusted for inflation semi-annually.
4. Mortgage-backed securities may be guaranteed by the government.

TreasuryDirect. Investors who participate in the competitive bidding process submit a yield that they are willing to accept, and the treasury either (1) accepts the bid in the full amount requested if the bid is less than the yield determined at auction; (2) accepts the bid for a portion of the amount requested if the bid is equal to the high yield determined at auction; or (3) rejects the bid if the yield specified is higher than the yield set at auction. Competitive bids may not be placed through the Treasury's website, TreasuryDirect, and must be placed directly with a bank or broker. In a single auction for Treasury notes or bonds, an investor may purchase up to $5 million in notes through the non-competitive bidding process, or up to 35 percent of the initial offering amount in the competitive bidding process.

Interest income from Treasury bonds and notes, and capital gains or losses realized upon sale of bonds and notes, receive the same income tax treatment as T-bills. Interest income is subject to federal income tax when earned (due to the imposition of the original issue discount, or OID rules), but is not subject to state or local tax. Capital gains and losses realized upon sale of notes or bonds are taxed as either long or short-term capital gains for federal income tax purposes, and are often taxed by state and local governments as well.

The appropriateness of Treasury notes and bonds in a given investor's portfolio is a function of the investor's objectives and risk tolerance. Treasury bonds and notes are typically considered to be default risk-free because the U.S. Treasury Department has the ability to issue new debt to pay for maturing debt. As such, Treasury notes and bonds are often viewed as attractive investments for investors with high risk aversion. To date, the U.S. government has never missed a bond payment, but this does not mean that an investor deploying capital into a government bond portfolio has avoided all potential investment risks. Other risks, such as purchasing power (inflation) risk, reinvestment risk, and interest rate risk remain. If an investor is looking for an instrument that will provide a specified income without the risks associated with equity investing, however, Treasury notes and bonds may be appropriate investments. Treasury notes and bonds can also be used as collateral for a loan, and are marketable securities, which gives the investor access to their capital when needed.

Quick Quiz 7.3

1. Treasury notes are issued for up to 30 years.
   a. True
   b. False
2. Treasury notes and bonds may be issued at a discount or a premium to par value.
   a. True
   b. False
3. Treasury STRIPS are considered by investors as zero-coupon bonds.
   a. True
   b. False

False, True, True.

Treasury STRIPS

Sometimes, investors have different time-horizon needs for their fixed-income investing. Treasury notes and bonds have fixed maturity periods of 2, 3, 5, 7, 10 and 30 years, which could be problematic for investors who would like to purchase a bond and hold it for some different period of time. There are two ways investors can address this concern: (1) they can purchase a Treasury bond or note that was issued in prior years whose maturity date matches their desired investment horizon, if one is available; or (2) they can purchase Treasury STRIPS. **STRIPS** is the acronym for Separate Trading of Registered Interest and Principal of Securities. STRIPS let investors hold and trade the individual interest and principal components of eligible Treasury notes, bonds, and TIPS (Treasury Inflation-Protected Securities) as separate securities.

The process of turning a note or bond into a Treasury STRIP involves creating a series of zero-coupon bonds sold to investors, where each cashflow received on the original note or bond represents a maturity date on the underlying Treasury STRIPS.

Example 7.7

A Treasury note with a 7-year maturity has 14 semi-annual coupon dates and one principal repayment date upon issuance. To add flexibility for investors who would like to purchase a bond with a different maturity horizon, a financial institution may strip the note into 14 or 15 separate securities - one for each semi-annual coupon payment (for a total of 14), and one for the principal payment upon maturity, although many combine the final coupon and principal payment into one security. Investors now have the choice of purchasing a Treasury STRIPS with a maturity equal to 6-months, 1-year, 1 1/2 years, 2 years, 2 1/2 years, 3 years, 3 1/2 years, 4 years, 4 1/2 years, 5 years, 5 1/2 years, 6 years, 6 1/2 years, or 7 years. By stripping the coupon payments into separate securities, more choice is afforded to investors.

Exhibit 7.6 | STRIPS Cash Flows: 20 Ten-Year Treasury Bonds (10% Semi-Annual Coupon)

Years	0.50	1.00	1.50	2.00	2.50	3.00	3.50	4.00	4.50	5.00	5.50	6.00	6.50	7.00	7.50	8.00	8.50	9.00	9.50	10.00
Bond 1	$ 50	$ 50	$ 50	$ 50	$ 50	$ 50	$ 50	$ 50	$ 50	$ 50	$ 50	$ 50	$ 50	$ 50	$ 50	$ 50	$ 50	$ 50	$ 50	$ 1,050
Bond 2	$ 50	$ 50	$ 50	$ 50	$ 50	$ 50	$ 50	$ 50	$ 50	$ 50	$ 50	$ 50	$ 50	$ 50	$ 50	$ 50	$ 50	$ 50	$ 50	$ 1,050
Bond 3	$ 50	$ 50	$ 50	$ 50	$ 50	$ 50	$ 50	$ 50	$ 50	$ 50	$ 50	$ 50	$ 50	$ 50	$ 50	$ 50	$ 50	$ 50	$ 50	$ 1,050
Bond 4	$ 50	$ 50	$ 50	$ 50	$ 50	$ 50	$ 50	$ 50	$ 50	$ 50	$ 50	$ 50	$ 50	$ 50	$ 50	$ 50	$ 50	$ 50	$ 50	$ 1,050
Bond 5	$ 50	$ 50	$ 50	$ 50	$ 50	$ 50	$ 50	$ 50	$ 50	$ 50	$ 50	$ 50	$ 50	$ 50	$ 50	$ 50	$ 50	$ 50	$ 50	$ 1,050
Bond 6	$ 50	$ 50	$ 50	$ 50	$ 50	$ 50	$ 50	$ 50	$ 50	$ 50	$ 50	$ 50	$ 50	$ 50	$ 50	$ 50	$ 50	$ 50	$ 50	$ 1,050
Bond 7	$ 50	$ 50	$ 50	$ 50	$ 50	$ 50	$ 50	$ 50	$ 50	$ 50	$ 50	$ 50	$ 50	$ 50	$ 50	$ 50	$ 50	$ 50	$ 50	$ 1,050
Bond 8	$ 50	$ 50	$ 50	$ 50	$ 50	$ 50	$ 50	$ 50	$ 50	$ 50	$ 50	$ 50	$ 50	$ 50	$ 50	$ 50	$ 50	$ 50	$ 50	$ 1,050
Bond 9	$ 50	$ 50	$ 50	$ 50	$ 50	$ 50	$ 50	$ 50	$ 50	$ 50	$ 50	$ 50	$ 50	$ 50	$ 50	$ 50	$ 50	$ 50	$ 50	$ 1,050
Bond 10	$ 50	$ 50	$ 50	$ 50	$ 50	$ 50	$ 50	$ 50	$ 50	$ 50	$ 50	$ 50	$ 50	$ 50	$ 50	$ 50	$ 50	$ 50	$ 50	$ 1,050
Bond 11	$ 50	$ 50	$ 50	$ 50	$ 50	$ 50	$ 50	$ 50	$ 50	$ 50	$ 50	$ 50	$ 50	$ 50	$ 50	$ 50	$ 50	$ 50	$ 50	$ 1,050
Bond 12	$ 50	$ 50	$ 50	$ 50	$ 50	$ 50	$ 50	$ 50	$ 50	$ 50	$ 50	$ 50	$ 50	$ 50	$ 50	$ 50	$ 50	$ 50	$ 50	$ 1,050
Bond 13	$ 50	$ 50	$ 50	$ 50	$ 50	$ 50	$ 50	$ 50	$ 50	$ 50	$ 50	$ 50	$ 50	$ 50	$ 50	$ 50	$ 50	$ 50	$ 50	$ 1,050
Bond 14	$ 50	$ 50	$ 50	$ 50	$ 50	$ 50	$ 50	$ 50	$ 50	$ 50	$ 50	$ 50	$ 50	$ 50	$ 50	$ 50	$ 50	$ 50	$ 50	$ 1,050
Bond 15	$ 50	$ 50	$ 50	$ 50	$ 50	$ 50	$ 50	$ 50	$ 50	$ 50	$ 50	$ 50	$ 50	$ 50	$ 50	$ 50	$ 50	$ 50	$ 50	$ 1,050
Bond 16	$ 50	$ 50	$ 50	$ 50	$ 50	$ 50	$ 50	$ 50	$ 50	$ 50	$ 50	$ 50	$ 50	$ 50	$ 50	$ 50	$ 50	$ 50	$ 50	$ 1,050
Bond 17	$ 50	$ 50	$ 50	$ 50	$ 50	$ 50	$ 50	$ 50	$ 50	$ 50	$ 50	$ 50	$ 50	$ 50	$ 50	$ 50	$ 50	$ 50	$ 50	$ 1,050
Bond 18	$ 50	$ 50	$ 50	$ 50	$ 50	$ 50	$ 50	$ 50	$ 50	$ 50	$ 50	$ 50	$ 50	$ 50	$ 50	$ 50	$ 50	$ 50	$ 50	$ 1,050
Bond 19	$ 50	$ 50	$ 50	$ 50	$ 50	$ 50	$ 50	$ 50	$ 50	$ 50	$ 50	$ 50	$ 50	$ 50	$ 50	$ 50	$ 50	$ 50	$ 50	$ 1,050
Bond 20	$ 50	$ 50	$ 50	$ 50	$ 50	$ 50	$ 50	$ 50	$ 50	$ 50	$ 50	$ 50	$ 50	$ 50	$ 50	$ 50	$ 50	$ 50	$ 50	$ 1,050
Total	$1,000	$1,000	$1,000	$1,000	$1,000	$1,000	$1,000	$1,000	$1,000	$1,000	$1,000	$1,000	$1,000	$1,000	$1,000	$1,000	$1,000	$1,000	$1,000	$21,000

3 Year STRIP — 5 Year STRIP — 7.5 Year STRIP — 21 Ten Year STRIPs

The interest income earned on the purchase of Treasury STRIPS is subject to federal income tax when earned under the original issue discount (OID) rules.

Treasury Inflation Protected Securities (TIPS)

When purchasing fixed income securities, investors face purchasing power risk, which occurs during periods of rising consumer prices. Inflation reduces the purchasing power of the dollars received by an investor from a security. If inflation is high enough, it is possible the purchasing power of the dollars the investor has at maturity is lower than that of the cash paid at the date of purchase. For example, if an investor paid $80 for a zero-coupon bond three years ago, and collected $100 at maturity, an investor would be worse off in real terms if a basket of goods costing $80 three years ago now costs $110 (due purely to inflation). In these situations the investor gets a lower utility from the dollars at maturity than she would have received by spending the $80 on goods instead of buying the bond.

In an effort to protect investors from this utility loss, and, indirectly, encourage them to continue to invest in Treasury bonds and notes, the Treasury began to issue **Treasury Inflation-Protected Securities**, or **TIPS** in January 1997. TIPS pay interest at a fixed rate. The principal amount of the bond is adjusted by changes in the Consumer Price Index every six months, and the fixed rate of return paid on the instrument is applied to the inflation adjusted principal amount. As inflation increases, for example, the interest paid on the note increases, and if deflation occurs, the interest paid on the note decreases. When a TIPS matures, the investor is paid the greater of the inflation adjusted principal amount or the original principal investment.

TIPS are issued with maturities of 5, 10, and 30 years, are sold in increments of $100 (with the minimum purchase being $100), and are issued electronically. An investor purchasing a TIPS may hold the security until maturity, or sell it prior to maturity.

Like all T-bills, Treasury notes, and Treasury bonds, TIPS may be purchased using the competitive or non-competitive bidding process as earlier described.

Treasury Floating Rate Notes (FRNs)

Treasury Floating Rate Notes (FRNs) have a two-year maturity, are offered for a minimum purchase price of $100, and pay a varying amount of interest quarterly until maturity. The rate of interest rises and falls each week based on the discount rates in auctions of 13-week Treasury bills, plus a spread. The FRNs can be held until maturity or can be sold prior to maturity. Like other Treasury notes, interest income is taxed at the federal level, but is not taxed at the state or local level. Investors may find these FRNs attractive when short-term interest rates are expected to rise rapidly. In addition to the potential for an increasing interest rate, the price of floating rate securities tends to remain relatively stable versus the price of fixed-rate securities, which go down when interest rates go up.

U.S. Savings Bonds

In addition to the issuance of T-bills, Treasury notes, and Treasury bonds, which are typically purchased by institutions and large investors, the U.S. Government issues savings bonds to permit smaller investors to acquire an interest in government debt instruments and, in some cases, achieve favorable tax benefits.

The government currently issues two types of savings bonds to investors: Series EE bonds and Series I bonds. Some individuals may be holding other types of government savings bonds that still pay interest, but are no longer issued; these instruments are classified as Series E, Series H, and Series HH bonds.

Series EE and Series I bonds are purchased electronically for any amount of $25 or more to the penny. They are issued at face value, and earn interest monthly that is compounded semi-annually for up to 30 years. The maximum amount that can be purchased under any social security number each calendar year is $10,000 per series. An investor may purchase up to $5,000 (out of the $10,000 maximum) in Series I bonds with their income tax refund. All other purchases of both Series EE and I bonds are issued electronically. The bonds can be redeemed at any time after 12 months, but a penalty of three months of interest is charged if the bonds are redeemed within five years of issuance.

Interest earned on U.S. Savings bonds is subject to federal income tax, but is not subject to state or local income taxes. One advantage of Series EE and Series I savings bonds over other treasury debt securities is that the income tax on interest earned on savings bonds does not have to be paid until the bond matures or is redeemed. The original issue discount (OID) rules do not apply to Series EE and Series I savings bonds. Investors who wish to do so, however, may make an election to include the accrued interest in their tax return as it is earned instead of deferring the entire tax liability on the interest earnings until maturity or redemption. The ability to choose the timing of tax payments on Series EE and Series I savings bonds is an attractive feature for some investors.

In some circumstances, the interest earned on savings bonds that are redeemed to pay for higher education expenses is exempt from federal income tax. Specifically, the following must be met to be able to exclude the interest earned on savings bonds:

- A savings bond is redeemed to pay for qualified higher education expenses of a taxpayer or the taxpayer's spouse or dependents or to make deposits to a qualified tuition program (Section 529 plan) or Coverdell Education Savings Account,
- The bond was issued after December 31, 1989 to an individual who was at least 24 years old at the time of issuance,
- The taxpayer's modified adjusted gross income falls below a specified threshold, and
- If married, the taxpayer does not file as married filing separately.

If these conditions are met, then the interest income received is not subject to federal income tax.

Series EE bonds issued from May 1997 through April 2005 earn variable rates based on 90 percent of the six-month average of 5-year Treasury security yields. Series EE bonds issued after April 2005 earn a fixed rate of interest. The interest rate paid on Series I bonds includes a fixed percentage specified upon issuance of the bond plus an inflation rate that is calculated twice a year based on the CPI-U measure. The CPI-U measure is the consumer price index for all urban consumers, excluding those living in rural areas, and covers approximately 80 percent of the U.S. population. Since Series I bonds include an inflation-based interest adjustment, the purchase of a Series I bond assists the investor in reducing purchasing-power risk, while the purchase of a newly issued Series EE bond leaves the purchaser subject to purchasing-power risk.

Prior to September, 2004, investors could purchase Series H or Series HH bonds with the redemption proceeds of Series E or Series EE bonds. Purchase of Series H or HH bonds allowed investors to defer federal income tax on the redeemed Series E or EE bonds until the maturity date of the Series H or HH bonds. Series H bonds were issued until December 1979, and had maturities of up to 30 years. All Series H bonds have stopped earning interest. Series HH bonds were issued from January, 1980 to August 2004, and had maturities of up to 20 years. The last HH bonds that were issued will mature in 2024. Unlike Series E and EE bonds, Series H and HH bonds paid interest semi-annually, which is fully subject to federal income tax (but not state and local income tax) in the year received.

All Series E bonds, which were the predecessors of the current Series EE bonds have stopped earning interest, but investors can still cash them in. The Treasury stopped issuing series E bonds after May, 1980.

Exhibit 7.7 | Summary of U.S. Savings Bonds

	Series EE	Series HH	Series I
Denominations	$25, $50, $75, $100, $200, $500, $1,000, $5,000, $10,000	$500, $1,000, $5,000, $10,000	$50, $75, $100, $200, $500, $1,000, $5,000, $10,000
Purchased	With cash	By exchanging E or EE bonds	With cash
Issued at	100% of face value	100% face value	100% face value
Maturity	30 years	20 years	30 years
Interest Rate	Fixed rate after 2005	1.5% fixed rate	Combination of fixed and variable rates
Interest	Accrues	Paid semi-annually	Accrues
Taxation of Interest	Deferred	Taxable annually	Deferred
Interest Can be Completely Excluded for Qualified Higher Education Costs	Yes	No	Yes

U.S. Government Agency and Sponsored Securities

In addition to T-bills, Treasury notes, Treasury bonds, and savings bonds, which are issued to finance government spending, the U.S. Government issues or sponsors debt instruments backed by collateral to support important public policy goals.

Key Concepts

1. The government promotes public policy using debt instruments.
2. In some cases, the tool used to promote public policy is the tax law.
3. In other cases, the tool to promote public policy is guarantees, which eliminate default risk.

Assisting citizens in achieving the American dream of home ownership has long been a policy objective of the government, and is accomplished in many ways. For example, the government makes home ownership less expensive by subsidizing the cost of ownership though various income tax benefits, such as the personal income tax deduction for home mortgage interest and real estate taxes on a principal residence. The government also encourages investors to provide capital to facilitate home purchases by permitting banks to pool the mortgages they generate and sell that pool of mortgage loans to investors. When banks sell existing mortgages to investors, they free-up capital that can be used to make more loans. Furthermore, the government encourages investors to purchase these securities by guaranteeing a return of the investor's principal, thereby eliminating default risk for the investor. GNMA (the Government National Mortgage Association, or "Ginnie Mae") directly issues **mortgage-backed securities** with government guarantees to investors.

The U.S. Government also provides guarantees for investors in other non-U.S. government issued securities that encourage investors to provide capital for home purchases, which are referred to as U.S. Government sponsored securities. These include bonds issued by FNMA (the Federal National Mortgage Association, or "Fannie Mae"), FHLMC (the Federal Home Loan Mortgage Corporation, or "Freddie Mac"), FFCB (Federal Farm Credit Bureau), FHLB (Federal Home Loan Bank), and TVA (Tennessee Valley Authority). Although these agencies are government sponsored, their bond issues do not receive the same tax treatment as Treasury notes and bonds. The income from agency issues is taxed at all three levels: federal, state, and local.

Mortgage-backed securities pass through the monthly mortgage payments made by the borrowers to the purchasers of the securities, less a servicing fee that is paid to the issuer of the security. Unlike most fixed-income investments, which pay interest for a period of time followed by a balloon payment of principal at maturity of the instrument, mortgage-backed securities amortize the loan and make both principal and interest payments each month to investors. If underlying mortgages are paid off early (due to borrower refinancing, for example), those payments are also passed through to the investors in the mortgage-backed security. While the government has taken away the investor's risk of default by providing a guarantee of payment, due to the possibility of pre-payments, the investor is subject to prepayment risk. **Pre-payment risk** is a special form of interest rate risk, and has to be considered by investors before purchasing a mortgage backed security. Mortgage prepayments are much higher when interest rates decline, allowing borrowers to refinance their mortgages at a lower rate. Refinancing at a lower rate is a good thing for the borrower, but perhaps not such a good thing for the investor, who now has to reinvest those prepayments at lower rates of interest.

Quick Quiz 7.4

1. Government backed mortgage securities eliminate default risk.
   a. True
   b. False
2. Collateralized mortgage obligations are issued by the federal government.
   a. True
   b. False
3. Mortgage-backed securities pay both principal and interest to investors regularly.
   a. True
   b. False
4. Investors in mortgage-backed securities face serious prepayment risk in a declining interest rate environment.
   a. True
   b. False

True, False, True, True.

MUNICIPAL BONDS

Municipal bonds are debt instruments issued by state and local authorities, or territories of the United States (such as Puerto Rico and the District of Columbia). Like the federal government, state and local authorities may need access to capital markets to finance long-term projects and spending initiatives.

Municipal bonds are issued in two primary forms. **General Obligation Bonds** are backed by the taxing authority of the government issuing the bond, which is sometimes referred to as the "full faith and credit" of the issuer. State and local governments that issue general obligation bonds make interest and principal payments to the bondholders out of periodic tax revenues collected by the government. **Revenue Bonds** are backed by a particular project (such as a toll bridge, airport, or stadium project), and are repaid from the revenue generated from the project that is financed. Revenue bonds expose investors to more risk than general obligation bonds since the full faith and credit of the government is not backing the bond. To compensate the investor for the additional risk, revenue bonds typically provide a higher yield than general obligations bonds.

Exhibit 7.8 | Las Vegas Monorail Case Study

In 2000, the Nevada Department of Business and Industry sold nearly $650 million in bonds in a deal underwritten by Salomon Smith Barney and Bank of America Securities to fund the development of a nearly four-mile monorail stretching from the MGM Grand to the Sahara Hotel & Casino by the newly formed Las Vegas Monorail Company (LVMC). These bonds were issued as revenue bonds intended to be repaid from ridership fees and advertising revenue. With significantly lower ridership and revenue, the LVMC was unable to service the debt. To make matters worse, AMBAC, which insured part of the bond issue ended up filing for bankruptcy.

On June 8, 2010, Moody's made the following announcement: "Moody's has withdrawn the underlying and insured ratings on the Nevada Department of Business and Industry Las Vegas Monorail Project's (Monorail Project) 1st Tier Series 2000 Revenue Bonds. The ratings withdrawal follows the downgrade of AMBAC as the bond insurer."

Municipal bonds also have two primary classifications for income tax purposes. **Public purpose municipal bonds** are used to finance classic government projects, such as the construction of schools, police stations, fire stations, roads and bridges. **Private activity (purpose) municipal bonds** are bonds issued by a state or local government to finance projects that have some component of private or business use. In particular, if more than 10 percent of the proceeds are for private business use, to secure an interest in property to be used for private business use, or are derived from payments for property used for private business use, the bond is considered a private activity bond. Typical examples of private activity bonds are bonds used to finance sports stadiums, toll bridges, or airports. Many, but not all private activity bonds are issued as revenue bonds.

Key Concepts

1. Interest on municipal bonds is free of federal income tax.
2. There are two common types of municipal bonds: general obligation bonds and revenue bonds.
3. Private activity bond interest is subject to alternative minimum tax (AMT).

Interest received on municipal bonds is generally exempt from federal income tax. In additional to regular federal income tax, high-income taxpayers may be subject to an additional 3.8 percent Medicare surtax on investment income called the Net Investment Income Tax (NIIT, discussed in Chapter 17); however, interest income from municipal bonds avoids both the income tax and the NIIT. Typically, the interest income is also exempt from income taxation in the state that issued the bond, but investors who reside in other states may have to pay income taxes to their state on the interest income from the bond.

Example 7.8

Frank and Marie are residents of Connecticut who purchase newly issued New York State municipal bonds. The proceeds of the bonds were used to finance the construction of a new elementary school in New York City. Frank and Marie will not have to pay income tax on the interest income to the federal government or to New York State, but will have to pay Connecticut income tax on the interest income they receive.

Example 7.9

Continuing with the facts above, assume that Frank and Marie moved from Connecticut to New York just before they purchased the bonds. Since they are now residents of New York, and New York issued the bonds, Frank and Marie will not have to pay any federal or state income tax on the interest generated on the bonds.

One major exception to the exclusion of municipal bond interest income from tax occurs when a taxpayer is subject to the Alternative Minimum Tax (AMT). The AMT was designed to ensure that all taxpayers with certain levels of taxable income pay a minimum level of income tax. The AMT was enacted into law to prevent high income taxpayers from engaging in tax-planning activities that would exempt all of their income from tax, such as placing all of their investment funds in municipal bonds. The interest on private purpose municipal bonds is subject to federal income tax when a taxpayer is subject to the Alternative Minimum Tax.

Since the interest income on municipal bonds is not subject to federal income tax, an adjustment has to be made to the bond yield when comparing it to alternative taxable investments. Municipal bonds may yield a lower amount than a taxable bond on a pre-tax basis, but from the investor's perspective, it is the after-tax yield that counts. The adjustment to equate the yield on tax-exempt municipal bonds and taxable bonds is made by calculating the Tax Equivalent Yield (TEY). The TEY calculation takes into consideration the marginal tax rate of the investor so that bond investments can be compared on an equivalent basis.

Quick Quiz 7.5

1. General obligation bonds expose investors to more risk than revenue bonds.
   a. True
   b. False
2. There is no federal income tax on municipal bond interest, nor are sales of municipal bonds subject to capital gains tax.
   a. True
   b. False
3. The tax equivalent yield is established as the tax exempt yield divided by 1 minus the marginal tax rate.
   a. True
   b. False

False, False, True.

$$\text{Tax Equivalent Yield (TEY)} = \frac{\text{Tax-Exempt Yield}}{1\text{-(marginal tax rate)}}$$

The marginal tax rate is the tax rate payable on the next dollar of income an investor receives. This depends on several factors including the investor's tax bracket and the interaction between state and federal taxes. Before deductions available at the federal level for state taxes paid, the marginal tax rate can be simple calculated by adding together the state and federal tax rates. For example, an investor who pays federal tax at 22 percent and state tax at five percent would have a marginal tax rate of 27 percent.

Example 7.10

Belle is considering the purchase of two bonds, one that is a municipal income-tax exempt bond, and one that is a corporate bond fully subject to income tax. Belle is in the 22% federal marginal income tax bracket and her state tax rate is 5%, giving him a marginal tax rate of 27%. The municipal bond she is considering has a yield of 4% and is issued by a municipality in the state in which Belle resides. The Tax Equivalent Yield (TEY) for a taxable bond, given these facts, would be 4%/(1-0.27) = 5.48%. Consequently, if the taxable corporate bond that Belle is considering yields less than 5.48%, Belle will earn more on a post-tax basis by purchasing the municipal bond. If the taxable bond that Belle is considering yields more than 5.48%, and assuming that Belle's marginal income tax rate remains the same, Belle would earn more on a post-tax basis by purchasing the taxable bond.

Example 7.11

Dylan is considering the purchase of two bonds, one that is a municipal income-tax exempt bond, and one that is a corporate bond fully subject to income tax. Dylan is in the 35% federal marginal income tax bracket, is subject to the federal 3.8% Net Investment Income Tax, and his state tax rate is 5%. The municipal bond Dylan is considering has a yield of 4% and is issued by a municipality in the state in which Dylan resides. If Dylan purchases the municipal bond, he will not have to pay federal income tax, the 3.8% NIIT, or state income tax; therefore, he will save a total of 43.8% (35% + 3.8% + 5% = 43.8%) in taxes. The Tax Equivalent Yield (TEY) for a taxable bond, given these facts, would be 4%/(1-0.438) = 7.12%. Consequently, if the taxable corporate bond that Dylan is considering yields less than 7.12%, Dylan will earn more on a post-tax basis by purchasing the municipal bond. If the taxable bond that Dylan is considering yields more than 7.12%, and assuming that Dylan's marginal income tax rate remains the same, Dylan would earn more on a post-tax basis by purchasing the taxable bond.

High-income investors, like Dylan, who are subject to the extra 3.8% Net Investment Income Tax (NIIT) are likely to find municipal bonds to be very attractive due to the additional tax savings.

While states and municipalities have the ability to impose taxes to meet bond servicing requirements, some states and municipalities find it difficult to issue bonds at favorable rates due to concerns about potential default. This concern has been highlighted in recent years with several instances of default or potential default on bonds issued by some governments in California, Puerto Rico, and Detroit. Municipalities can purchase municipal bond insurance, which protects investors against default thereby reducing the credit risk of the bond issue. Several organizations issue municipal bond insurance, including The American Municipal Bond Assurance Corporation (AMBAC Financial Group), the Municipal Bond Insurance Association and Municipal Bond Investment Assurance Corp (MBIA), and the Financial Guarantee Insurance Corporation (FGIC).[3]

3. AMBAC filed for bankruptcy protection in 2010 after suffering huge losses from risky mortgages. It emerged from bankruptcy in 2013.

CORPORATE BONDS

Corporations, like government agencies, often need to source cash to finance their operations. As discussed earlier, short-term cash needs may be satisfied by issuing commercial paper, but sometimes corporations need financing for longer periods of time. Corporations can access capital markets in two primary ways: through the issuance of equity (stock) and the issuance of debt (bonds).

Key Concepts

1. Corporate bonds may be secured or unsecured (debenture).
2. Corporate bonds are rated as to default risk by a number of rating agencies.
3. Corporate bonds may be callable or convertible.

When a corporation believes it can earn more on its investments than it has to pay in debt service, a corporation may wish to raise capital in the form of debt financing through the issuance of bonds. This is particularly true in low interest rate environments. Stock investors leverage their returns when corporations issue bonds that carry an interest rate lower than the earnings rate on the project being financed. While bond investors receive a lower return than equity investors in this circumstance, as bondholders they have a more secure investment, which may appeal to investors with lower risk tolerances.

Example 7.12

Pitt Enterprises (PI) uncovers a wealth increasing project and decides to issue $100 million in 20-year bonds at par value to finance the project. PI can raise the capital by offering a 4% coupon rate on the bonds, which means the bondholders expect to receive $4 million in interest payments annually.

PI estimates the internal rate of return for the project is 10%, which translates into a 20-year annual operating cash flow of $11.74 million.

Therefore, the cash flows exceed the debt service payments by a factor of almost 3.0, making this a relatively safe investment.

PI might choose to use a sinking fund to retiree the principal amount of the bond, making the bond even less risky.

Another advantage of issuing bonds as opposed to stock is that when a corporation issues a bond, the corporation is permitted to deduct the interest payments it makes on the bond on the corporation's income tax return. Dividend payments to shareholders are not deductible. Since the interest payments on bonds are tax deductible, this lowers the cost of issuing debt from the corporation's perspective.

The details of a corporate bond issue are outlined in the bond **indenture**, which is the legal and binding document specifying the rights accorded to the bondholders and the duties of the issuing company. The indenture includes terms for repayment of principal and interest, whether or not the owners or corporation have a right to redeem the bonds early or convert some of the bond issue into equity in the corporation, and the total amount of the bond issue. Sometimes, the bond issue is backed by collateral, which provides more security for the bondholders in the event the corporation defaults on its obligations. If a bond issue is not backed by collateral, it is referred to as a **debenture**.

Since bondholders receive a fixed coupon payment and do not share in the residual profits of the corporation, bonds are considered senior securities of the corporation, and in the event of a corporate dissolution and liquidation, the claims of bondholders are satisfied prior to the claims of stockholders. Having preference over stockholders in corporate liquidations provides more security for bondholders that the principal amount of their investment will be repaid. This additional security may be attractive to investors with relatively low risk tolerances who would like to earn yields greater than those offered by government bonds.

A maxim of investment planning is that higher degrees of risk require higher returns to attract investors to provide capital for a given project. Different corporations present different levels of risk to investors in the form of credit risk. The ability of the company to make interest and principal payments, and the financial strength of the company are factors that investors must consider. Bonds issued by strong, financially healthy corporations carry lower interest rates than bonds issued by weak, financially unstable companies. When a company has a high probability of making interest and principal payments, the bonds it issues are considered **investment grade bonds**. If a company issuing a bond has a high risk of default, the bonds are considered **non-investment grade bonds**. Non-investment grade bonds are sometimes referred to as High-Yield bonds, or Junk bonds. Non-investment grade bonds must pay higher rates of interest to bondholders to compensate them for the additional risk they are accepting.

Quick Quiz 7.6

1. Corporate bonds are rated as to riskiness.
   a. True
   b. False
2. Corporate bond interest expense is deductible to the issuing corporation for federal income taxes.
   a. True
   b. False
3. An indenture is the legal document specifying the rights of bond holders and the duties of the issuer corporation.
   a. True
   b. False

True, True, True.

COLLATERALIZED MORTGAGE OBLIGATIONS (CMOs)

Collateralized Mortgage Obligations (CMOs) are bonds created by private investment firms that are backed, or collateralized, by a pool of underlying mortgages. CMO's are similar to the mortgage backed securities issued and guaranteed by the federal agencies that were discussed earlier in this chapter.

Like government issued or government sponsored mortgage-backed securities, CMOs backed by residential mortgages reduce credit risk for the investor since the bond is secured by the real estate underlying the pool of mortgage loans in the CMO. For those CMO's backed by mortgages issued by government sponsored entity, credit risk is effectively zero. Investors in these CMOs are still subject to risk, however, in the form of interest-rate risk, reinvestment rate risk, and **prepayment risk**.

- Interest rate risk is the risk that interest rates will change, thereby affecting the price of the security.
- Reinvestment rate risk is the risk that interest payments received under the CMO will have to be reinvested at a lower rate if interest rates decline over the holding period of the bond.

Key Concepts

1. Collateralized mortgage obligations (CMOs) are bonds created by private firms and collateralized by a pool of underlying mortgages.
2. An investment pool of CMOs may be split into tranches to attract various investors.

- Prepayment risk is a special type of reinvestment rate risk that applies to mortgage-backed securities and CMOs. Specifically, prepayment risk is the risk that mortgage holders will prepay their mortgage when rates decline, which will be passed through to CMO investors, who will then have to reinvest those cashflows at a rate lower than the rate they were earning on the CMO.

Exhibit 7.9 | Mortgage Securitization

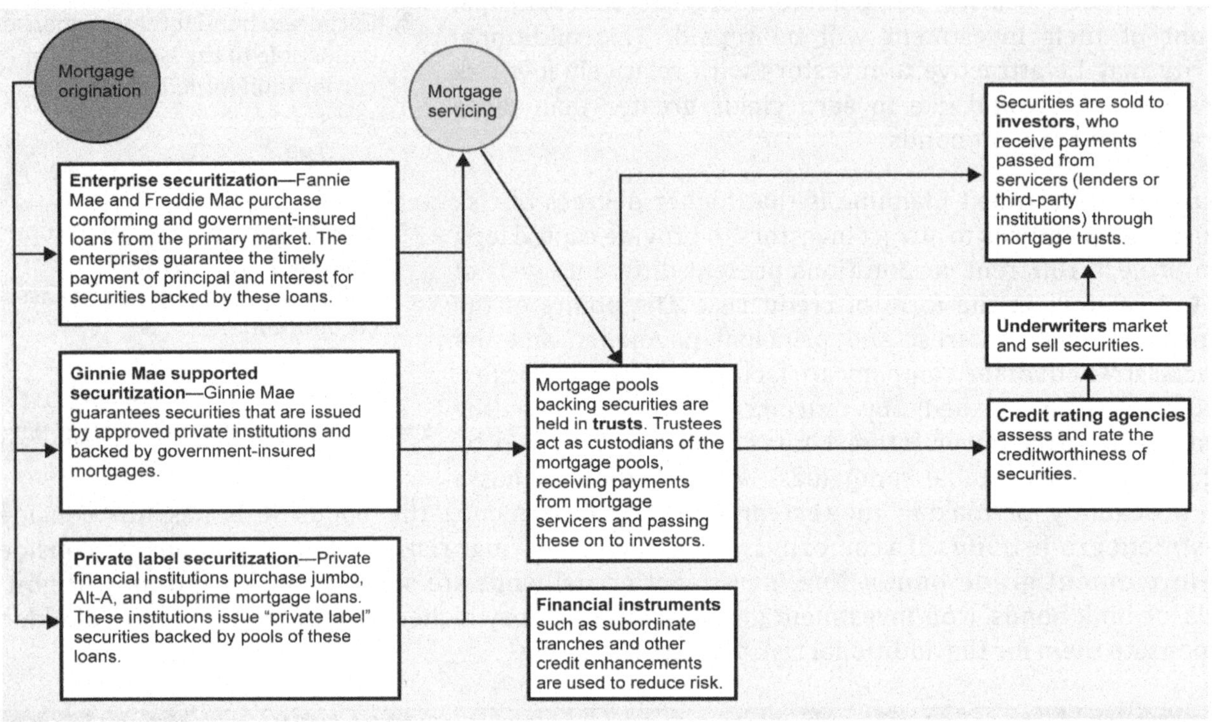

Source: GAO. | GAO-15-185

Unlike government issued or government sponsored mortgage-backed securities, which pool mortgages together and pass through all payments (interest, principal, and prepayments) to investors, CMOs typically split the anticipated payments on the underlying pool of mortgages into various **tranches** that have different repayment periods. The most basic type of CMO structure is referred to as a sequential pay offering. In this type of CMO, each tranche receives regular interest payments, but the principal payments are only made to the first tranche until that tranche is completely paid off (i.e., the debt is retired). After the debt for the first tranche is retired, then the principal payments will be paid to the second tranche until it is fully retired. This process continues until the final tranche is completely paid. In some respects, a CMO is similar to the Treasury STRIPS discussed earlier in this chapter. The CMO's ability to create different tranches from one underlying pool of mortgages provides flexibility for investors that is not available with traditional mortgage-backed securities.

Example 7.13

Marcy has a five-year investment horizon and decides to purchase a collateralized mortgage obligation issued by a national financial institution. The CMO has multiple tranches with maturities of five, ten, and twenty-five years. Marcy selects the five-year tranche and expects to receive interest payments for five years and then the return of her principal at maturity. Marcy should be aware that she is exposed to prepayment risk, which means she might receive her principal payments before her five-year time horizon is completed.

Another benefit of the split of the investment pool into various tranches is that investors with different risk propensities can choose the tranche that best meets their risk-return needs while still benefiting from investing in a pool of mortgage-backed securities. The tranches with shorter maturities expose the investor to less interest rate risk and reinvestment rate risk than the tranches with longer maturities. However, the tranches with longer maturities likely have higher interest rates. The exhibit below illustrates the structure of a CMO.

Exhibit 7.10 | CMO Tranche

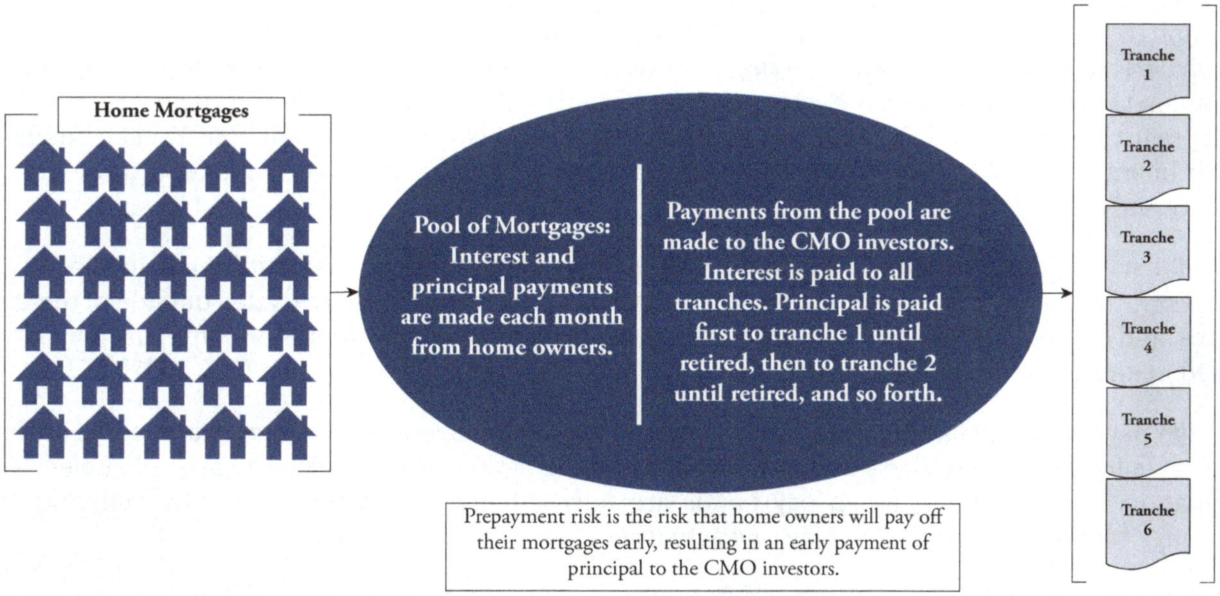

SOVEREIGN BONDS

Bonds issued by foreign governments and corporations can be used by U.S. investors to further diversify risk exposure in an investment portfolio and receive potentially higher returns. In addition to the traditional risks that are associated with bond investments, foreign bonds add another layer of risk - the risk of currency fluctuations, sometimes referred to as **exchange-rate risk**. As currencies strengthen and weaken with respect to each other, the actual return a bond investor receives in their own local currency can vary greatly.

Quick Quiz 7.7

1. CMOs are collateralized by a pool of mortgages.
   a. True
   b. False
2. CMOs eliminate risk for investors.
   a. True
   b. False
3. CMOs typically split payments into various tranches with different repayment periods.
   a. True
   b. False

True, False, True.

Foreign bonds come in three primary forms: U.S. dollar denominated bonds (Yankee bonds); Eurodollar bonds; and foreign pay, or non-dollar-denominated bonds.

U.S. dollar denominated bonds (Yankee Bonds) are bonds issued by foreign governments and companies that state the principal amount, interest rate, coupon, purchase price, and maturity amount in U.S. dollars. These bonds permit U.S. investors to purchase foreign bonds without incurring currency fluctuation, or exchange rate risk. Yankee bonds are traded in the United States on organized exchanges and over-the-counter markets, which requires them to be registered with the U.S. Securities and Exchange Commission (SEC). Issuers of Yankee bonds tend to be financially secure, established companies, and as a consequence the bonds tend to be of a high quality and are highly rated.

Eurodollar bonds are issued by foreign governments and corporations that state the principal amount, interest rate, coupon, purchase price, and maturity amount. These bonds are traded outside of the United States, and consequently are not subject to SEC registration. Eurodollar bonds are often used by foreign-based institutional investors.

Foreign pay, or non-dollar denominated bonds, are issued by foreign governments and corporations in their own local currency. These bonds are traded outside of the United States, and are not subject to SEC regulation. Purchasers of foreign pay bonds are fully subject to exchange rate risk, and changes in exchange rates can substantially affect the actual return earned on the bond.

The interest earned on foreign bonds is subject to tax in the jurisdiction where the bond was issued. U.S. investors who purchase foreign bonds also have to pay tax to the United States (and, possibly, to state and local governments) on income earned on foreign bonds but can claim the foreign tax paid as a credit or as a deduction when completing their own federal income tax return.

PROMISSORY NOTES

Promissory notes are private transactions, usually between individuals or between individuals and institutions, that create a fixed-income security for the holder. When a promissory note is created, the maker (the person borrowing the money) promises to pay the holder of the note the principal amount at maturity, as well as interest on the principal amount in periodic payments, or upon maturity of the note (referred to as a balloon note). While not formally traded on securities exchanges, it is possible to sell an interest in a promissory note if the holder of the note needs liquidity. Promissory notes are commonly used by individuals and businesses who need access to financing but do not have the ability to access that financing from the financial markets.

When an individual purchases a home subject to a mortgage (a mortgage is a security interest in the real property underlying the loan that is used to protect the interest of the lender), a promissory note is also created. The promissory note specifies the repayment terms, and, upon repayment, the lender releases the mortgage, or security interest, in the underlying property since the note has been satisfied in full. As discussed earlier in this chapter, these types of promissory notes, along with the mortgages, are packaged into pools and then sold to investors in the form of mortgage-backed securities. These are issued by or guaranteed by the government or as collateralized mortgage obligations (CMOs).

While promissory notes are not bonds in the classic sense, the risks and rewards associated with promissory notes are similar to those associated with bonds. Promissory notes are frequently used in personal wealth and financial planning to achieve various wealth transfer and tax objectives.

GUARANTEED INCOME CONTRACTS (GICS)

A **guaranteed income contract (GIC)** is a fixed-income security similar to a certificate of deposit that is sold primarily to large, institutional investors such as pension plan providers. Like certificates of deposits (CDs), GICs pay a specified rate of return for a fixed period of time. While the dollar amount invested tends to be large (most GICs are issued for $1 million or more), GICs present very low credit risk for the purchaser because the contract is issued by a large financial institution (typically an insurance company), which invests that money (typically in very low risk fixed-income securities, such as government bonds, government sponsored or backed bonds, and high quality corporate bonds) at a spread above the guaranteed rate of return paid on the contract. Furthermore, every state has a guarantee fund that compensates investors in GIC contracts for their losses in the event that the issuing financial institution does not meet its obligations under the contract. Purchasers of GIC contracts are typically able to receive higher rates of return than are available in money-market type instruments with little more than a nominal increase in risk.

CONVERTIBLE BONDS

A **convertible security** is a hybrid security that allows the holder to acquire shares of common stock from the issuing company by exchanging the currently held security under a specific formula. Similar to an option contract, the holder's ability to convert the current security into common stock is a right that the holder has, not an obligation. Effectively, a convertible bond is a corporate bond with a call option to purchase the issuing company's stock at a specific price. Whether the investor takes advantage of the conversion feature hinges on the value of the stock.

Convertible bonds provide the investor with a steady stream of cash flows and the ability to participate in the potential growth of the underlying company, without the downside risk of a company's common stock. Because the conversion feature is attractive to investors, it allows the issuing company to offer bonds to the market with a lower coupon rate and yield. The investor purchasing the bond receives the lower stream of coupon payments as well as a call option to convert the bond to common stock. In some cases, a company may be able to issue common stock at a higher price through convertible bonds than it might by issuing the common stock to the market.

A convertible bond specifies the number of shares the bondholder will receive if the bond is converted or exchanged for stock. The **conversion ratio** is the number of shares of common stock of the issuing company that can be acquired by exchanging the convertible security. The **conversion price** is the price that is paid for each share of common stock acquired through the conversion of the convertible security. The conversion price equals the par value of the bond divided by the conversion ratio.

$$\text{Conversion Price} = \frac{\text{Par value of the convertible bond}}{\text{Conversion ratio}}$$

Bondholders have to decide whether or not they want to convert the bond to common stock. The conversion value is helpful in making this decision. The **conversion value** equals the conversion ratio multiplied by the market price for the stock.

$$\text{Conversion Value} = \text{Conversion ratio} \times \text{market price of stock}$$

Chapter 8 discusses valuation of bonds in great detail. The value of a convertible bond is influenced by the stream of cash flows from the bond, as well as the conversion value. Therefore, the minimum value of a convertible bond is the greater of the conversion value or the value of the bond without the conversion feature. The value of the bond without the conversion feature is referred to as an option-free bond.

Market conversion price represents the cost of each share of stock obtained through the conversion. This market conversion price equals the market value of the convertible security divided by the conversion ratio.

$$\text{Market Conversion Price} = \frac{\text{Market value of convertible security}}{\text{Conversion ratio}}$$

The market conversion price is a useful threshold for the stock price. Whenever the stock rises above this price, the convertible bond should also increase in price.

Generally, convertible bonds are issued such that the bondholder will pay a premium over market value for the underlying stock. In other words, the market conversion price is higher than the market price of the underlying stock. The **market conversion premium** equals the difference between the market conversion price and the current market price.

$$\text{Market Conversion Premium} = \text{Market Conversion Price} - \text{Current Stock Price}$$

The market conversion premium is effectively the per share cost of the option to buy the underlying stock above the current market price for the stock.

Example 7.14

Rouge Industries (RI) issues a ten-year convertible bond with a coupon rate of 5% and a par value of $1,000. The yield to maturity is 6.38% and the current bond price is $900. The bond's conversion ratio is 40 and the current market price of RI's stock is $20. RI pays no dividends.

- The conversion price = $1,000/40 = $25.

  Each bondholder has the right but not the obligation to convert one bond into 40 shares of stock at $25 per share.

- The conversion value = 40 * $20 = $800.

  The conversion value is less than the price of the bond, so the bondholder would not exercise the option to convert. If the stock price increased to $23, the conversion value would increase to $920 and the bondholder might consider exercising the option to convert. As the stock price continues to increase, the value of the option also increases.

- The market conversion price = $900/40 = $22.50.

  The market conversion price is a type of break-even price for the bondholder. The conversion option becomes valuable when the stock price exceeds the market conversion price.

- The market conversion premium is $22.50 - $20.00 = $2.50.

The following exhibit illustrates the price of a convertible bond for a range of stock prices.

Exhibit 7.11 | Convertible Bond Price

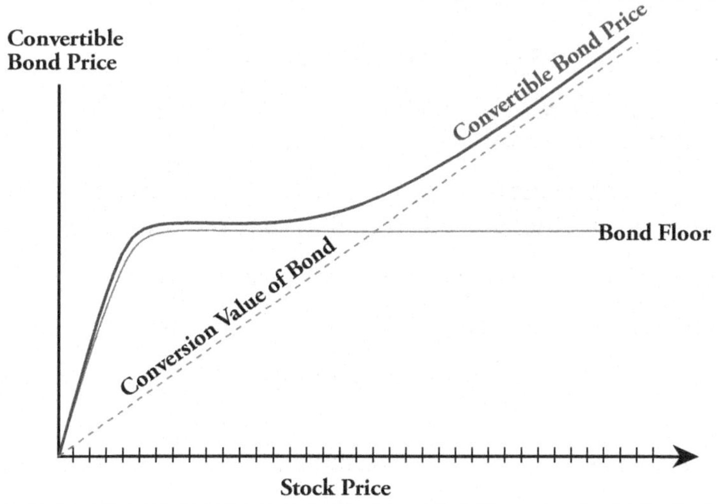

As the stock price increases, so does the value of the convertible security. As the stock price increases higher and higher, the value of the convertible bond converges to the price of the underlying stock. If the stock price is relatively low, then the bond should trade based on the bond's straight value. However, if the stock of the company decreases too much, then it indicates the business is in serious trouble. As such, the company may not be able to service the debt and the value of the bond may decrease to almost zero.

Many convertible bonds are issued with call features. The call feature is a benefit to the issuer, who can call the bond issue if interest rates decrease. Call features decrease the value of the convertible security. If the bond is called when the conversion value is less than the call value, then the bondholder accepts the call value. If the bond is called when the conversion value is greater than the call value, then the bondholder converts the bond into common stock.

SUMMARY

Summary of key points:

- Bonds are debt instruments that typically make semi-annual coupon payments and repay the final par value of the bond at maturity.
- The U.S. bond market is made up of Treasuries, corporate, and municipal bonds, as well as mortgage-backed securities and savings bonds.
- Fixed-income securities are often used in conjunction with equities in portfolios.
- Bonds may be issued with a variety of features, including call options, convertible features, zero coupons, and may be secured or unsecured.
- Municipal bonds have favorable tax treatment. Investors must calculate the tax equivalent yield to compare municipal yields to corporate yields.
- Treasury notes and bonds can be combined and stripped so that the periodic cash flows create zero-coupon bonds.
- Mortgage-backed securities are backed by mortgages on real property. These securities have added risks, including prepayment risk.
- Moody's and S&P rate bonds based on their default risk.
- Convertible bonds can provide upside potential for bondholders if the underlying stock increases above the market conversion value.
- Collateralized mortgage obligations are bonds issued by financial institutions that pool mortgage together and divide the pool into specific tranches to make them more attractive to investors.
- Bonds are issued by corporations to finance wealth increasing projects.
- Bonds are issued by federal and local governments to finance budget deficits.
- Bonds are issued by federal agencies to support a specific class of borrower, such as a homeowner.
- Bondholders are generally exposed to both credit risk and interest rate risk.

DISCUSSION QUESTIONS

SOLUTIONS to the discussion questions can be found exclusively within the chapter. Once you have completed an initial reading of the chapter, go back and highlight the answers to these questions.

1. Describe the difference between short and long-term debt securities.

2. Explain the main reason that Treasury bills will almost always sell for a discount.

3. Identify the common features of a long-term bond and discus how each impacts the price of the bond.

4. Distinguish between secured and unsecured bonds and identify which will most likely have a higher yield to maturity.

5. Describe the embedded option in a callable bond and discuss one critical reason any bondholder would want to own such a bond.

6. Describe the various types of Treasury securities.

7. Distinguish between general obligation bonds and revenue bonds.

8. Compare investment grade with non-investment grade bonds.

9. Discuss the significance of tranches in collateralized mortgage obligations.

10. Describe convertible bonds and discuss one critical reason any bondholder would want to own such a bond.

MULTIPLE CHOICE PROBLEMS

A sample of multiple choice problems is provided below. Additional multiple choice problems are available at money-education.com by accessing the Student Practice Portal.

1. Money market securities are:
   a. Readily marketable.
   b. Not very volatile.
   c. Highly liquid.
   d. All of the above.

2. Commercial paper is most likely issued by:
   a. The Federal Reserve bank.
   b. Commercial banks.
   c. Large, well-known companies.
   d. A securities exchange.

3. A Treasury bond has an ask price of 107.04 and a bid price of 107.00. What is the dollar price a buyer expects to pay?
   a. $1,070.00.
   b. $1,070.40.
   c. $1,071.13.
   d. $1,071.25.

4. The primary difference between Treasury notes and bonds is:
   a. Maturity.
   b. Default risk.
   c. Coupon rate.
   d. Taxability.

5. The price of a bond that a buyer would pay is equal to:
   a. The asked price plus accrued interest.
   b. The asked price less accrued interest.
   c. The bid price plus accrued interest.
   d. The bid price less accrued interest.

QUICK QUIZ EXPLANATIONS

Quick Quiz 7.1

1. False. By June 2021, there was more than $50 trillion of fixed-income securities in issue.
2. False. Treasury bills do not make interest payments.
3. True.
4. False. MMDAs and CDs have identical tax treatments, but commercial paper tax treatment depends on whether it is sold before the maturity date.

Quick Quiz 7.2

1. True.
2. True.
3. True.
4. False. Debentures are unsecured bonds.
5. True.

Quick Quiz 7.3

1. False. Treasury notes are issued up to 10 years.
2. True.
3. True.

Quick Quiz 7.4

1. True.
2. False. CMOs are created by private investment firms.
3. True.
4. True.

Quick Quiz 7.5

1. False. The reverse is true. Revenue bonds expose investors to more risk than general obligation bonds.
2. False. Even though there is no federal income tax on interest from a muni bond, there may be capital gains tax on the sale of a municipal bond.
3. True.

Quick Quiz 7.6

1. True.
2. True.
3. True.

Quick Quiz 7.7

1. True.
2. False. Investors in CMOs are still subject to risk in the form of interest-rate risk, reinvestment rate risk, and prepayment risk.
3. True.

8

FIXED-INCOME SECURITIES - ANALYSIS

LEARNING OBJECTIVES

1. Calculate the value of a bond based on coupon rate, yield to maturity, and maturity.*
2. Calculate the current yield, yield to maturity, and yield to call for a bond.*
3. Evaluate whether a taxable bond or a municipal bond is more appropriate based on determining the tax equivalent yield.*
4. Explain the most significant risks that impact fixed-income securities.
5. Understand the most common yield curve theories.*
6. Explain how changes in interest rates affect fixed-income securities.*
7. Use duration to determine the price sensitivity of a bond or bond portfolio.*
8. Explain the concepts of immunizing bond portfolios.*
9. Describe the limitations of duration and how convexity is a benefit to investors.*
10. Compare passive and active bond portfolio management strategies.

**Ties to CFP Certification Learning Objectives*

INTRODUCTION

Fixed-income securities are those in which the issuer makes an explicit promise to pay the lender interest and principal. The interest payments are almost always referred to as **coupon payments** and these are made at regular intervals over the life of the bond. Essentially, the issuer promises to make interest-only payments over a long term and then return the par value of the bond to the bondholders on the maturity date.

Bonds provide investors with an excellent alternative to other types of investment securities and can be used to diversify equity portfolios or provide income to individuals who are in need of a stream of cash flows. Although bonds generally have lower expected returns than equity investments, they are generally less risky than equities and provide higher returns than bank certificates of deposit, savings accounts, and other lending alternatives.

Key Concepts

1. The value of a bond is the present value of all future cash flows.
2. The discount rate used to value bonds is the yield to maturity.
3. Asset-backed securities contain more uncertainty regarding cash flows than regular bonds.
4. Zero-coupon bonds do not pay interest during the term of the bond.

This chapter discusses the valuation of, as well as the risks associated with, fixed-income securities. Also discussed are return calculations and the concepts surrounding the volatility of bonds when interest rates change. Finally, a brief discussion of passive and active fixed-income management is discussed.

VALUATION OF FIXED-INCOME SECURITIES

A bond is a fixed income security in which the issuer promises to make regular interest payments coupled with a final principal payment. The value of any bond is the present value of these cash flows. Consider a firm that promises to make annual interest payments of $100 over a five-year period coupled with a principal payment of $1,000 at the end of year five. The cash flows received by the investor will be as follows:

Year 1	Year 2	Year 3	Year 4	Year 5
$100	$100	$100	$100	$1,100

To calculate their present value, these cash flows must be discounted at the bond's required return. If the required return for this bond was 10%, the present value of each cash flow would be as follows:

$$\frac{\$100}{1.10}+\frac{\$100}{1.10^2}+\frac{\$100}{1.10^3}+\frac{\$100}{1.10^4}+\frac{\$1{,}100}{1.10^5}$$

$$= \$90.91 + \$82.65 + \$75.13 + \$68.30 + \$683.01$$

$$= \$1{,}000$$

An investor who purchases the bond at $1,000 and holds it until maturity will therefore earn a 10% return. This return is known as the yield to maturity and will be covered in detail in a later section. A bond with a yield to maturity equal to its coupon rate, as is the case here, will always trade at its par value. Note that almost all bonds are issued in increments of $1,000 principal amount.

Rather than calculating the present value of each individual cash flow as above, it is much quicker to price a bond using a financial calculator. In this case the inputs would be:

PMT	=	$100
FV	=	$1,000
N	=	5
i	=	10%
PV	=	$1,000

Example 8.1

Mardale Farms (MF) issues a 20-year, annual pay bond that offers an 8% coupon rate. MF needs $10 million to purchase new tractors and build a new barn and stables for its horses. The yield to maturity on these bonds is 8.5%. Calculate how many bonds MF needs to issue to cover the expenditure required.

The initial step is to calculate the price at which MF can issue a $1,000 par value bond given a required return of 8.5%. The cash flows on the bond are as follows:

Years 1 - 19	Year 20
$80	$1,080

Each of these cash flows needs to be discounted to their present value at 8.5%. Using a financial calculator, the inputs required are:

PMT	=	$80
FV	=	$1,000
N	=	20
i	=	8.5%
PV	=	$952.68

Note the price of this bond is less than the par value of the bond, which means the bonds sell for a discount. MF is offering its bondholders an 8% annual coupon rate, but the bondholders, based on current risk conditions, are requiring a return of 8.5%. The bondholders are not satisfied with the 8% coupon rate, so they agree to buy the bonds but at a price less than par value. When the coupon on a bond is lower than the required return, that bond will always be issued at a discount.

Now the number of bonds that must be issued can be calculated. Given required proceeds of $10 million and a price of $952.68 per $1,000 par value bond, MF must issue 10,497 bonds ($10m/$952.68). Had the coupon rate matched the market rate, the bond price would have been $1,000 and MF would only have had to issue 10,000 bonds.

The yield to maturity on bonds is a function of their risk and market conditions, and is constantly changing, meaning bond prices are also constantly changing. The changes can be so dramatic that bond prices can move far away from their par values. Bonds can either sell at a discount, such as shown in **Example 8.1** or at a premium. The determination of premiums and discounts is shown in **Exhibit 8.1**.

Exhibit 8.1 | Relationship Between Coupon Rate and YTM

Bond Selling At:	Relationship:		
Par	Coupon Rate	=	Yield to Maturity
Discount	Coupon Rate	<	Yield to Maturity
Premium	Coupon Rate	>	Yield to Maturity

ADDITIONAL BOND PRICING ISSUES

Yield to Maturity (YTM)

Yield to Maturity is defined as the required return on the bond and is determined by both macro-economic factors and those factors that are unique to the issuer. Macro factors include the general level of interest rates, inflation, and economic growth. Unique factors include default risk, time to maturity on the bonds, and event risk.

The YTM is calculated as the internal rate of return of the bond's cash flows. It therefore equates the present value of the bond's promised cash flows to its current price.

By convention, it is stated as an annual, simple rate, but most corporate bonds pay interest semi-annually. When using the YTM to price these bonds, the semi-annual rate must be used.

Example 8.2

Harris Farms issues a 40-year bond with an annual coupon rate of 8.2% but pays interest every six months. The yield to maturity on the bonds is 7.6%.

Compute the price of the bond:

The semiannual payment is $41 over 80 semi-annual periods. The stated YTM of 7.6% is an annual rate, and must be divided by two (as there are two semi-annual periods in a year) before it can be used to price the semi-annual pay bond. The correct rate to use is therefore 3.8% (7.6%÷ 2). The bond price inputs are shown below:

PMT	=	$41
FV	=	$1,000
N	=	80
i	=	3.8%
PV	=	$1,074.95

Using the YTM to Price Zero-Coupon Bonds

Zero-coupon bonds are issued with a coupon rate of zero percent, which means bondholders receive only the principal payment at maturity.

Example 8.3

Organic Farms issued a 30-year zero-coupon bond with a yield to maturity of 6.4%.

Compute the price of the bond:

Since there are no annual or semi-annual coupon payments, the price can be computed as follows:

PMT	=	$0
FV	=	$1,000
N	=	60
i	=	3.2%
PV	=	$151.08

Note the semi-annual convention is used for zero-coupon bond pricing even though it might not be initially obvious. To compare zero-coupon bonds with coupon paying bonds, the semi-annual compounding assumption must be applied. Also, note the zero-coupon bond sells at a deep discount.

Using the YTM to Price Step-Up Bonds

Step-Up Bonds are issued with increasing coupon rates, which means bondholders can expect to receive interest payments that rise over time. Many step up bonds have one step up during their lives, but some bonds have multiple steps.

Example 8.4

Rooster Egg Farm issues a 10-year bond that offers a 6.2% coupon rate for years 1 through 4, followed by a 6.4% coupon rate for the reminder of the bond's life. The yield to maturity on this bond is 7%.

Compute the price of this bond:

Since the coupon payments are not represented as an ordinary annuity, the expected cash flows are a series of consecutive but unequal payments. To compute price, the cash flow function on the calculator is appropriate. Inputs are shown below.

CF_0	=	\$0
CF_1	=	\$31
N	=	8
CF_2	=	\$32
N	=	11
CF_3	=	1,032
i	=	3.5%
NPV	=	\$950.49

Note the interest payment is \$31 for 8 total semi-annual payments, followed by eleven \$32 payments. The final payment of \$1,032 includes both the final coupon payment and the \$1,000 principal payment. Since the yield to maturity exceeds both step up coupons, this bond sells for a discount.

Callable Bonds

Callable bonds are those with an embedded call option that gives the issuer the right but not the obligation to repurchase the bonds before they mature under certain circumstances. Callable bonds behave exactly like bonds without embedded options in that they pay regular coupons and a final principal payment. The option becomes valuable only during times of falling interest rates. Most callable bonds have a deferred call feature in that the bonds are not callable until a specified date in the future. For example, a firm issuing a thirty-year callable bond may not be able to call the bonds for the first twelve years. Consider the following example.

Example 8.5

Sanford Farms issues a callable bond with a coupon rate of 8% over 25 years. The yield to maturity of the bonds when issued was 8% but falls over the next several quarters. Today, the yield to maturity is 5%. Sanford is paying 8% to its bondholders but could issue new bonds at the much lower rate of 5%. The call feature allows Sanford to repurchase its bonds at par value, plus perhaps the next semi-annual coupon payment. Sanford will very likely fund the bond repurchase with a new bond issue that will carry the lower 5% coupon rate, thus providing substantial savings on its interest payments.

The pricing of callable bonds is typically done in one of two ways. The first of which is to divide the callable bond into its two components:

1. the plain option-free component, and
2. the call option itself using the following equation:

Price of Callable Bond = Price of the Option Free Bond - Call Option

The second more complex way is to use an interest rate tree to model possible paths that interest rates could take in the future and then use time value of money principles to value the bond.

Regardless of which method is used, the price of a callable bond will be less than the price of an option free bond because the issuer compensates bondholders for assuming interest rate risk and that compensation takes the form of a lower price. The risk of course to bondholders is that rates will fall and they will receive only the par value of the bond instead of the premium price on the option free bond.

Quick Quiz 8.1

1. YTM in the basic bond valuation model is equivalent to IRR.
   a. True
   b. False
2. A 10-year zero-coupon bond yielding 4.5%, compounded semi-annually should be priced at $640.82.
   a. True
   b. False
3. There is more certainty of cash flows from a mortgage-backed security than from a corporate bond.
   a. True
   b. False

True, True, False.

Asset-Backed Securities

Asset-backed securities, such as **mortgage-backed securities** and collateralized mortgage obligations, contain more uncertainty than option-free bonds with regard to their cash flows. First, coupon payments and repayment of principal are based on payments made by the mortgagers who often have the right to prepay principal. Prepayments cause the schedule of expected cash flows to change, which changes the value of the security. The second issue related to asset-backed securities concerns the potential for defaults. While default risk also exists with corporate bonds, it is based on the risk associated with the issuing corporation. In a mortgage-backed security with a large pool of mortgages, it is likely that some of the mortgages will result in default. In such a case, the cash flows are impacted, causing the value of the security to change. Each of these issues must be incorporated into the projection of expected cash flows and, therefore, incorporated into the valuation of the asset-backed securities. Mortgage-backed securities and collateralized mortgage obligations were discussed in the previous chapter.

MEASURING BOND RETURNS

Bondholders expect to be compensated in the form of interest payments, capital gains, and the reinvestment of interest payments. Each of the following return measures considers one or more of these income components.

Current Yield (CY)

The current yield of a bond is a measure of the bondholder's return if the bond is purchased and held for one year. It is simply the ratio of annual income over the current market price of the bond. Bonds that sell for discounts tend to have higher current yields than those that sell at premiums.

Example 8.6

Wisconsin Farms issues a ten-year bond with a 10% coupon rate and a current price of $850. The current yield can be computed as follows:

$$\text{Current yield} = \frac{\text{Annual coupon payment in dollars}}{\text{Current market price}}$$

$$\text{Current yield} = \frac{\$100}{\$850} = 0.1176 = 11.76\%$$

The current yield is useful for determining the income that can be earned on the purchase of a bond over the short term. It is a good first way to evaluate bond returns, but it does not measure the return if the bond is held until it matures or if the bond is called. It also ignores the value of reinvested coupon payments. Therefore, other return measures are much more useful.

Yield to Maturity

The **yield to maturity** explicitly measures the return to bondholders if the bond is held until its maturity date. It assumes the coupon payments are reinvested, that the bond does not default or is called by the issuer, and that premiums or discounts are properly reflected in the return measurement. The relationship between the YTM, coupon rate and current yield which depends on the price of the bond as illustrated in **Example 8.7**.

Example 8.7

Bonds A and D are selling at a discount, Bonds B and E are selling at par, and Bonds C and F are selling at a premium. The actual coupon rate, YTM and current yield are provided to help illustrate the relationship between the three measures. The first chart fixes maturity and the coupon rate. The second chart fixes maturity and YTM.

Type of Bond	Bond	Maturity	Coupon	PV	YTM	Current Yield	Order
Discount	A	5	6%	$881.31	9%	6.8%	YTM > CY > CR
Par	B	5	6%	$1,000.00	6%	6.0%	CR = CY = YTM
Premium	C	5	6%	$1,138.33	3%	5.3%	CR > CY > YTM

Key Concepts

1. Current yield measures the cash flows received in a year as a percentage of the current value of the fixed-income security.
2. YTM equates the cash inflows to the cash outflows. YTM is the discount rate that equates the PV of the future cash inflows and the price paid.
3. There is a relationship between the current yield, the coupon rate and the YTM depending on whether a bond is selling at a premium, discount or par.
4. The yield to call calculation typically incorporates a shorter maturity and a higher FV in the calculation.
5. Almost all bonds pay interest semi-annually, although a few make annual or even monthly payments.

Type of Bond	Bond	Maturity	Coupon	PV	YTM	Current Yield	Order
Discount	D	5	6%	$918.89	8%	6.5%	YTM > CY > CR
Par	E	5	8%	$1,000.00	8%	8.0%	CR = CY = YTM
Premium	F	5	10%	$1,081.11	8%	9.2%	CR > CY > YTM

Example 8.8

Huntfield Farms has a bond outstanding that matures in 20 years. The bond pays an annual coupon of 6.7% and its current market price is $952. The yield to maturity can be computed using a financial calculator as follows:

PMT	=	$67
FV	=	$1,000
N	=	20
PV	=	-$952
i	=	7.159%

Make certain the PV is entered as a negative value. Since the bond sells at a discount, the yield to maturity must exceed the coupon rate. A bondholder purchasing this bond today for $952 expects to earn 7.159% over the next 20 years by receiving the coupon payments, reinvesting them at 7.159%, and then receiving the final $1,000 principal payment.

Most bonds pay interest semi-annually, which makes the yield to maturity calculation slightly more complex.

Example 8.9

McAdoo Farms issues a bond that pays interest on June 30 and December 31 every year for the next 25 years. The coupon rate is 5.7% and the current price of the bond is $1,069.51. The yield to maturity can be computed using a financial calculator as follows:

PMT	=	$28.50
FV	=	$1,000
N	=	50
PV	=	-$1,069.51
i	=	2.6%

Note the semi-annual coupon payment is one-half of $57 while N is twice the time to maturity, as there are 50 semi-annual payment periods during the bond's 25-year life. The interest rate calculated per semi-annual payment period is 2.6%, but by convention the YTM will be stated annually as 5.2% (2 x 2.6%). Students can also change the P/YR button on the financial calculator from 1 to 2 when pricing semi-annual bonds, but that method is not recommended because students might forget to change that setting back to 1 to solve other bond pricing and time value of money problems.

Example 8.10

Trevor Farms issued a forty-year bond exactly ten years ago, which means there are 30 years until the bond matures. The coupon rate on the issue date was 8.4%, Trevor Farms pays interest every six months, and the yield to maturity was 8.4% making the issue price exactly $1,000. In the past decade, general interest rates have been falling, and the current market price of this Trevor Farms bond is $1,107. The yield to maturity can be computed as follows:

PMT	=	$42
FV	=	$1,000
N	=	60
PV	=	-$1,107
i	=	3.75%

Again, the calculator output is the semi-annual yield to maturity, which means it should be multiplied by 2 to obtain the annual yield to maturity on this bond of 7.5%. Also, note the bond sells for a premium so they yield to maturity must be less than the coupon rate.

Yield to Call

The **yield to call** is the return a bondholder would earn if the bond is held until its first deferred call date. Recall that the call option will typically only be exercised during periods of declining interest rates. Also, recall that as rates fall, bond prices will rise. The bad news for bondholders of callable bonds is that they are only promised a maturity payment of $1,000. Issuers realize this and generally offer a premium to bondholders when called. The premium is usually equal to the next semi-annual coupon payment.

Most municipal bonds are callable as are many corporate bonds. Treasury bonds, however, typically do not have the call feature.

Example 8.11

Johnson Farms issues a fifty-year callable bond that cannot be called for the next twenty years. The current market price is $925, the coupon rate is 4.6%, and interest is paid semi-annually. The bonds can be called for par value plus $23, or 102.3% of par. Calculate the yield to maturity and the yield to call.

Yield to Maturity (YTM)

PMT	=	$23
FV	=	$1,000
N	=	100
PV	=	-$925
i	=	2.51%

Double that semi-annual yield to maturity to obtain 5.02%

Yield to Call

PMT	=	$23
FV	=	$1,023
N	=	40
PV	=	-$925
i	=	2.64%

Double that semi-annual yield to call to obtain 5.28%. Note that N is much less than the maturity date on the bond and that future value includes one semi-annual coupon payment.

Note that the yield to call exceeds the yield to maturity. This will be the case when the bond sells at a discount. If the bond sells for a premium, the yield to call will be less than the yield to maturity.

Comparing Corporate Returns and Municipal Bond Returns (Tax Free)

The taxable bond market and the tax-exempt bond market make up the United States bond market. The **taxable bond market** consists of U.S. Treasury bonds, U.S. government agency bonds, and corporate bonds. The **tax-exempt bond market** consists of bonds issued by municipalities, including states, counties, cities, and parishes. The exemption from federal income tax is why municipal bonds are referred to as tax exempt. Interest from bonds issued by these municipalities is exempt from federal income tax, and in some cases, also exempt from state income tax. Interest from U.S. Treasury securities is subject to federal income tax, but is not subject to state income tax. Corporate bond interest and interest derived from U.S. agency bonds are subject to both federal and state income tax. Since the various types of bonds have different income tax treatments, it is necessary to compare yields for different bonds on a consistent basis. This comparison can be performed on either an after-tax basis or a pretax basis.

An investor can convert a municipal bond yield to an equivalent taxable yield using the following formula:

$$\textbf{Tax Equivalent Yield (TEY)} = \frac{\textbf{Tax-exempt yield}}{\textbf{1 – marginal income tax rate}}$$

Example 8.12

Tonya, who is in the 40% combined federal and state income tax bracket, is considering the purchase of a Big State municipal bond that is offering a 5% yield, while comparable credit-worthy taxable corporate bonds are offering a yield of 7.5%. To determine which bond is preferred, based on yield, Tonya could determine the pretax yield for the municipal bond, as illustrated:

$$\text{TEY} = \frac{0.05}{1 - 0.40} = 0.0833 = 8.33\%$$

Since the pretax equivalent yield equals 8.33%, the municipal bond yield of 5% is preferable to the taxable corporate bond yield of 7.5%. The comparison can also be made on an after-tax basis by multiplying the taxable yield of the corporate bond by the difference between 1 and the marginal tax rate, as follows:

$$\text{After-tax yield} = 0.075 \times (1 - 0.40) = 0.045 = 4.5\%$$

Since the 5% tax-free municipal yield is greater than the 4.5% after-tax corporate bond yield, the municipal bond appears to be the better choice, based on yield. A third method of comparison is to determine the equilibrium income tax rate (the indifference point) of the investor. This rate is the marginal tax rate at which the yield of the taxable bond is equal to the yield of the municipal bond. Using the example above, the equilibrium income tax rate equals 33%:

$$\textbf{Pretax yield} = \frac{\textbf{Tax-exempt yield}}{\textbf{1 - marginal tax rate}}$$

$$(1 - \text{marginal tax rate}) = \frac{\text{Tax-exempt yield}}{\text{Pretax yield}}$$

$$(1 - \text{marginal tax rate}) = \frac{0.050}{0.075}$$

$$(1 - \text{marginal tax rate}) = 0.6667$$

$$\text{marginal tax rate} = 0.3333 (33\%)$$

Since the equilibrium income tax rate is 33%, investors in a marginal income tax bracket that exceeds 33%, such as Tonya, will want to invest in municipal bonds, while those investors in a tax bracket below 33% will be better off with taxable corporate bonds.

Tax-exempt entities will rarely have a sensible reason to purchase municipal bonds instead of taxable bonds because pre-tax yields on taxable securities almost always exceed the yields on tax-exempt securities of similar risk levels. Similarly, municipal bonds should not be used in tax-deferred accounts, such as IRAs and 401(k) plans because when earnings are distributed, the earnings are subject to ordinary income tax rates. The yields on municipals will generally be lower than yields on taxable bonds.

Example 8.13

Corinthia is in the 32% federal and 8% state tax brackets, and is not subject to the 3.8% federal Net Investment Income Tax (discussed in Chapters 7 and 17). She has the option to buy a muni bond issued by a municipality outside of her state of residence yielding 3% or a Treasury bond yielding 4.5%. Which one is better from an after-tax yield perspective?

The after-tax yield is equal to the taxable yield x (1 - the tax bracket), using the taxes that are paid for each bond. The municipal bond is taxed at the state level since she is not a resident of the state. The Treasury bond is taxed only at the federal level.

After-tax yield of the municipal bond = 3% x (1 - 0.08) = 2.76%

After-tax yield on Treasury bond = 4.5% x (1 - 0.32) = 3.06%

The Treasury bond will provide a higher after-tax yield.

Tax exempt bonds can also be compared to taxable bonds by calculating a tax equivalent yield, which is calculated by dividing the tax exempt yield by (1 - marginal tax rate).

For example, if Corinthia lived in the state issuing the municipal bond yielding 3%, its tax equivalent yield would be 5% (3/0.6).

A taxable bond would therefore need to generate a yield of 5% to match the municipal bond's tax exempt yield of 3%.

Exhibit 8.2 depicts tax equivalent yields for various municipal yields at the seven different federal tax rates. For example, if a municipal bond has a five percent yield and the investor's marginal tax rate is 37 percent, then the tax equivalent yield equals 8.446 percent.

Exhibit 8.2 | Tax Equivalent Yield Chart[1]

	Municipal Yield				
	1%	2%	3%	5%	10%
Federal Tax Rate	Tax Equivalent Yield				
10.0%	1.111%	2.222%	3.333%	5.556%	11.111%
12.0%	1.136%	2.273%	3.409%	5.682%	11.364%
22.0%	1.282%	2.564%	3.846%	6.410%	12.821%
24.0%	1.316%	2.632%	3.947%	6.579%	13.158%
32.0%	1.471%	2.941%	4.412%	7.353%	14.706%
35.0%*	1.634%	3.268%	4.902%	8.170%	16.340%
37.0%*	1.689%	3.378%	5.068%	8.446%	16.892%

**Note: investors in the 35% and 37% tax bracket are subject to the 3.8% Net investment Income Tax (discussed in Chapters 7 & 17), so the tax brackets used in the TEY calculations are 38.8% and 40.8% respectively.*

Example 8.14

Consider how Elwyn, who is in the 32% marginal federal income tax bracket, would fare investing in the following alternatives. Assume that capital gains and dividends are taxed at 15%, that there is no state or local tax, and that he plans to hold all investments for two years:

	Municipal Bond	Corporate Bond	Corporate Stock
Percent return from interest or dividends	5%	6%	1%
Percent return from capital appreciation	10%	10%	15%
Pre-Tax Total Return	15%	16%	16%
After-Tax Return Calculations:			
• Municipal Bonds: [5% + (10% x (1 - 0.15))]	13.5%		
• Corporate Bonds: [6% x (1 - 0.32) + 10% x (1 - 0.15)]		12.58%	
• Stock: [16% x (1 - 0.15)]			13.6%
Rank in order of after-tax return for Elwyn	**2**	**3**	**1**

The calculations in the example above assume that the income from the municipal bonds is non-taxable, and that the taxpayer is not subject to the 3.8 percent Net Investment Income Tax on interest income or any portion of the capital gains. Under current federal tax law, long-term capital gains and qualifying dividends are taxed at a potentially highest rate of 20 percent, but short-term capital gains are taxed at

1. Federal tax rates are updated for TCJA 2017.

ordinary income rates. The holding period for long term is at least one year and a day. The 32 percent income tax bracket equates to a 15 percent capital gains rate for long-term capital gains.

The **marginal income tax rate** represents the percent of income earned that would be paid as income tax, whether at the federal or state level. The calculation of the marginal income tax is not always straight forward. Consider the tax treatment of income from the following types of bonds:

Type of Bond - Subject to Income Tax	Federal	State
Corporate Bonds	Yes	Yes
Treasury Bonds	Yes	No
Municipal bonds issued by a state other than the investor's state of residence	No	Yes
Municipal bonds issued by the investor's state of residence	No	No

As discussed in Chapter 17, taxpayers may use the standard deduction or itemize deductions when calculating their federal taxable income. Because state income tax is deductible as an itemized deduction, taxpayers need to determine the marginal tax rate after considering the tax benefit of paying state income tax. In other words, to the extent that a taxpayer pays a higher state income tax attributable to investment income, it would create a higher income tax deduction on the federal return. TCJA 2017 placed a cap on the deductibility of state and local taxes (SALT) of $10,000. Investors in general and particularly those who live in high income tax states might look to the municipal bond market for allowable tax breaks. Therefore, to accurately calculate the marginal tax rate, consideration must be given to the type of bond as well as the taxpayer's income tax situation. Taxpayers in states such as Texas and Florida do not have state income tax, while other states have very high state income tax rates.

Quick Quiz 8.2

1. Jack paid $971.27 for a 5% semiannual coupon bond that is callable in 6 years at 103. The YTC for this bond equals 3%.
   a. True
   b. False
2. The tax equivalent yield for a municipal bond yielding 3% at a tax rate of 25% is 4%.
   a. True
   b. False

False, True.

Mutual fund families offer various types of municipal bond funds (muni funds) that appeal to different investors. Single-state muni funds attempt to diversify by investing in bonds exclusively from a specific state, such as Louisiana. These state specific mutual funds generate taxable income that is not subject to federal or state income tax for investors who are residents of the state. Multi-state muni funds will often have an objective of delivering the highest muni returns while diversifying across many states. Because these funds have bonds from various states, the mutual fund must report muni income (on a percentage basis) to investors on a state by state basis so that they can determine the amount of income that is subject to state income tax.

Example 8.15

Freida, who lives in Louisiana, invests $100,000 in the Wonderland Muni Fund (WMF). The fund invests in bonds from most states in the U.S. attempting to generate high yields. Freida has muni income of $3,000 from her investment this year. The $3,000 is not subject to federal income tax, however the income will be taxable at the state level except to the extent it is derived from bonds from Louisiana. Assuming 10% of the income is from Louisiana bonds, then $300 will not be subject to Louisiana state income tax.

RISKS OF FIXED-INCOME SECURITIES

Even though bonds are thought of as being less risky than equity securities, they do carry risks, some of which can be substantial. The risks can be divided into two general components: market risks and issuer risks. **Market risks** are exposures to general economic conditions, such as inflation and changes in interest rates. **Issuer risks** are exposures that are unique to each firm or government entity issuing the bonds, such as default risk. These risks are discussed below.

Market Risks	Issuer Risks
Interest Rate Risk	Default Risk
Reinvestment Rate Risk	Call Risk
Purchasing Power Risk	Liquidity Risk
Exchange Rate Risk	Spread Risk

Market Risks

Interest Rate Risk

Interest rate risk is the variability in bond prices due to changes in yields. This risk can be substantial, especially for longer term bonds and during periods when rates are volatile. Recall the inverse relationship between bond prices and their yields; when rates rise, the price of all bonds will fall. Consider the following example.

Example 8.16

Reggie buys a Littlefoot Farms twelve-year bond with a 10% coupon rate at par value (assume annual coupon payments). Reggie is concerned about yield volatility and wonders how the value of his bond will change if yields increase or decrease by 2%.

The table below illustrates Reggie's interest rate risk.

Price at Purchase Date		Price if Yields Rise to 12%		Price if Yields Fall to 8%	
PMT	= $100	PMT	= $100	PMT	= $100
FV	= $1,000	FV	= $1,000	FV	= $1,000
N	= 12	N	= 12	N	= 12
i	= 10%	i	= 12%	i	= 8%
PV	= $1,000	PV	= $876.11	PV	= $1,150.72

Falling bond yields are beneficial to Reggie as the value of his bond increases by approximately $150 but decreases by approximately $125 when the yield rises. The uncertainty surrounding future yield paths is interest rate risk.

Exhibit 8.3 is an illustration of the inverse relationship between yields and prices.

Exhibit 8.3 | Relationship Between Bond Price and Yield

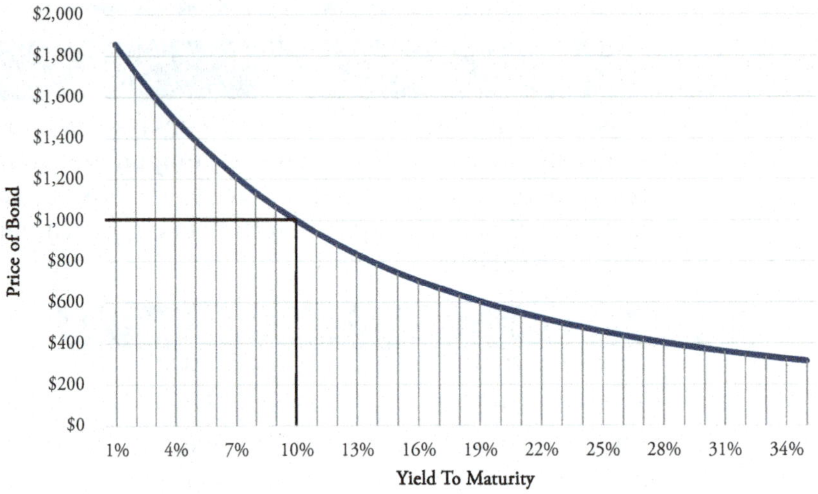

Example 8.17

Arlene buys two annual-pay bonds issued by Capital Farms: They both have 10% coupon rates and have identical yields of 10%, which means both have market prices of $1,000. Bond 1 matures in 5 years, while Bond 2 matures in 30 years. Arlene is worried about a spike in rates and how that change will impact the price of each bond. The new bond price after a change in yields of both bonds to 12% is shown below:

Bond 1		Bond 2%	
PMT	= $100	PMT	= $100
FV	= $1,000	FV	= $1,000
i	= 12%	i	= 12%
N	= 5	N	= 30
PV	= $927.90	PV	= $838.90

Note that a spike in yields of 2% is bad news for Arlene in that both of her bonds lose value. Bond 1 loses approximately $72 while Bond 2 loses over $160 in value. Longer term bonds have greater interest rate risk.

Reinvestment Rate Risk

Reinvestment rate risk is the uncertainty surrounding the rate at which investors are able to reinvest their coupon payments. An investor will only achieve the YTM if all coupons can be reinvested at that YTM for the life of the bond.

Example 8.18

Wilson buys ten six-year bond issued by Green Farms. The bond has a coupon rate of 8% that is paid annually, and a yield to maturity of 9%, which prices the bond at $955.14. Wilson hopes to use the future value of the bond when it matures to use as a down payment on a lake cottage. Wilson reinvests every annual coupon payment at 9% and then receives the final principal payment at the end of six years. The future value of that reinvestment, also known as the terminal value of the bond is computed as follows:

PMT	=	$80
i	=	9%
N	=	6
PV	=	$0
FV	=	$601.87

Sum the future value of the coupon payments and the $1,000 principal payment to obtain a terminal value of $1,601.87. Since Wilson purchased ten bonds, he will have $16,018.70 for the down payment on his cottage.

Note that the initial cost of the ten bonds was $9,551. Over six years, growing this to a terminal value of $16,018 results in a holding period return of 67.7 percent over six years. [(16,018/9551) -1]. This equates to an annual return of nine percent. This was achieved because the calculation assumed a reinvestment rate of nine percent (i = 9%). If the reinvestment rate increases or decreases, the terminal value will change in the same direction as the rate change. Higher reinvestment rates imply greater terminal values. Since those future reinvestment rates are unknown, the terminal value of the bond is subject to changing interest rates. This is reinvestment rate risk. In **Example 8.18**, Wilson might have much less or much more than $16,018 at the end of six years, depending on the path that interest rates take over the time period.

Key Concepts

1. Interest rate risk is the risk that changes in market yields will negatively impact the value of a bond.
2. Default risk is the risk that a bond issuer will not make scheduled coupon or principal payments.
3. Reinvestment rate risk is the risk that coupon payments cannot be reinvested at the YTM over the life of the bond.
4. Call features allow the bond issuer to call back a bond if interest rates drop, enabling the issuer to lower their cost of debt.
5. Investors who own international bonds are exposed to risks from politicians and foreign exchange markets.

Purchasing Power Risk

Purchasing power risk is the possibility that inflation will erode the real value of an investment. All investors are exposed to this type of risk, especially bondholders, and is particularly harmful when changes in the consumer price index are higher than anticipated. For example, a bondholder who purchases a bond with specific terminal value expectations will suffer when the rate of inflation exceeds the coupon rate. Consequently, investors search for financial securities that offer some type of inflation protection, such as Treasury Inflation Protected Securities, or commodities such as gold or physical investments such as real estate.

Purchasing power risk is a market risk that can be managed through security selection but not through diversification. Inflation tends to reduce both corporate bond and stock prices because it will reduce a firm's profit margins unless it can pass along those higher input costs to customers and clients.

Foreign Exchange Risk

Foreign exchange risk is the variability in cash flows when foreign investments are repatriated back to the domestic currency. Currency values change constantly and can substantially impact the total return on a fixed income investment in a foreign country.

Example 8.19

Carla purchases a zero-coupon bond issued by Montreal Farms for CAD 440. The current rate of exchange is USD 0.85/CAD, which means Carla pays USD 374 for the bond. After two years, Carla decides to sell her bond at its current price of CAD 455, but the exchange rate has changed to USD 0.80/CAD. Carla only receives USD 364, giving her a total loss of USD 10 and a return of -2.7%, even though there was a 3.4% appreciation in the value of her bond.

Political Risk

Related to foreign exchange risk is political risk, in which foreign governments can seize a firm's assets, can place restrictions on repatriation, and impose laws and regulations that reduce the value of a foreign investment.

Issuer Risks

Credit Risk

Credit risk is the chance bondholders will not receive the promised cash flows in full or in a timely manner. Credit risk generally takes three forms: default risk, downgrade risk, and spread risk.

Default Risk

Default risk is the specific risk that the issuer defaults on the coupon payments or the principal payment. Recall that firms issue bonds to finance positive net present projects and expect to repay the bonds using operating cash flows. If those cash flows are insufficient to make the debt service payments, bondholders suffer. When a bond goes into default, the firm is forced in bankruptcy court and a judge will require the executives of the firm to sell long term assets to pay off the bondholders. Consequently, the likelihood that all payments will be made depends on the financial health of the firm plus the overall general health of the economy. A host of ratings agencies, such as Moody's, provide valuable information to bondholders regarding the prospects each issuer has of making all its promised payments.

Default risk can be managed with the help of the ratings agencies and some common investing sense. For example, investors who are highly risk-averse will most likely choose bonds that Moody's identifies as 'investment grade' or choose default risk-free Treasuries. On the other hand, there is a large market for 'speculative grade' bonds and highly distressed securities, which are attractive to bondholders seeking higher yields. Fixed income investors, of course, take advantage of diversification to reduce the total risk of investing in bonds.

Downgrade Risk

Downgrade risk is the chance that a bond will be downgraded by one of the ratings agencies causing bond prices to fall.

Example 8.20

A bond issued by Forrest Farms enjoys a double A rating by a ratings agency, placing the bond in the upper level of the investment grade category. The bond has a market price of $991. Over the next six months, the profitability of Forrest drops because of intense competition, a spike in wages, and a drop in commodity prices. The financial health of Forrest is a concern to the ratings agency who, after a thorough re-evaluation of the current financial statements, estimates of future interest rate paths, and predictions of profitability decide that the default risk of Forrest has increased. The ratings agency announces a drop to a single A rating, which causes the price of the bond to fall to $965.

Downgrades are usually caused by substantial changes in firm specific information but are also related to general economic and industry conditions.

Spread Risk

Spreads are important measuring tools for bondholders. Typically, a basic spread is the simple difference between the yield on a risk-free security and the yield on the bond in question. For example, when U.S. five-year treasuries yield four percent and a five-year corporate bond yields six percent, the spread is two percent or 200 basis points. **Spread risk** is the possibility that spreads unexpectedly widen causing bond prices to fall.

Example 8.21

A financial analyst collects fixed income market data on the following two bonds:

	Wilshire Farms Bond	Treasury Bond
Maturity Date	10 Years	10 Years
Yield to Maturity	8.6%	4.4%
Price	$895	$1,206
Spread	4.2%	N/A

A few months later, the analyst observes changes in the U.S. economy, as well as firm-specific information regarding Wilshire, that causes the Treasury yield to increase to 4.6% and the yield on the Wilshire bond to decrease to 8.2%. The credit spread narrows to 3.6%, the Treasury bond price falls to $1,189, and the Wilshire bond rises to $920. Bondholders are willing to pay a higher price for the Wilshire bond because its credit risk, relative to the risk-free Treasury security, has fallen.

Call Risk

Call risk is related to interest rate risk in that the call feature on a bond will only be used when interest rates fall as issuers want to reduce their total interest payments by refinancing at lower rates. Falling rates have two consequences for callable bondholders. Initially, they reduce terminal values because the coupon payments are reinvested at lower rates and second, the price of callable bonds has an upper limit equal to the call price. Consequently, callable bonds have higher yields to maturity and sell for lower prices than similar option-free bonds. Callable bonds also inject additional uncertainty into the expected timing of the bond's cash flows because bondholders are unable to predict when the call will be used with any degree of accuracy.

Liquidity Risk

Liquidity risk is the risk associated with the breadth and depth of the fixed income market. For issues with a substantial number of buyers and sellers, such as the secondary market for treasuries and well-known established brand name companies, liquidity risk is quite low. For issues with a limited number of buyers, such as low credit rated bonds, liquidity risk can be substantial. For these low liquidity markets, sellers are may be forced to sell bonds at a discount to their intrinsic value.

TERM STRUCTURE OF INTEREST RATES

Yield Curves

A yield curve shows the relationship between yields and time to maturity. The most popular of these yield curves is the Treasury yield curve, which depicts current yields for Treasury securities. The yield curve is generally upward sloping indicating that yields on longer-term bonds are higher than yields on shorter-term bonds. However, there have been times when the structure of interest rates has caused the yield curve to be shaped differently. The three yield most common curves include the upward sloping (normal), flat, and downward (inverted), shaped yield curves as shown in **Exhibit 8.4**.

Key Concepts

1. Yield curves graphically depict market yields or interest rates for a range of bond maturities.
2. The most common yield curves are upward sloping, downward sloping, and flat.
3. Yield curve theories attempt to explain the shape of yield curves.

Exhibit 8.4 | Traditional Yield Curve Shapes

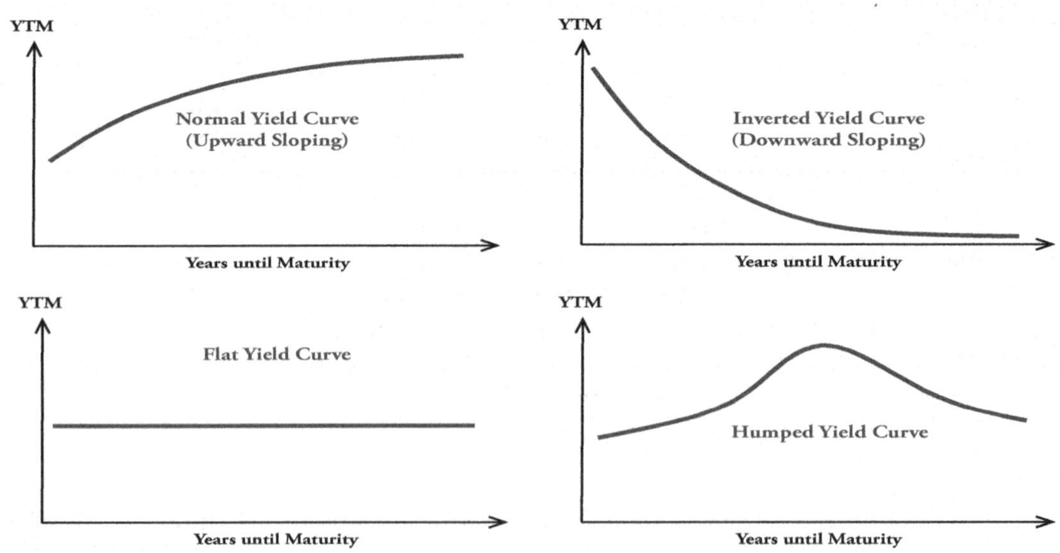

The Treasury yield curve is often used as a benchmark for other fixed-income securities. The Treasury yield curve is an effective benchmark for pricing bonds and determining yields of bonds in other sectors since it is not impacted by credit risk or liquidity risk. The backing and full faith of the U.S. government eliminates credit risk, and the size of the Treasury market, which the largest and most actively traded bond market, eliminates liquidity risk.

The traditional method for valuing or pricing non-Treasury bonds has been to use the yield on the Treasury yield curve for the appropriate maturity, plus a premium for the additional risks. There are arguments, however, that this method has certain inherent weaknesses.

For example, when constructing a yield curve, it is important to ensure that the bonds used all have identical characteristics except for their maturity. Bonds with different coupon rates, for example, would likely have different yields even if they had the same maturity.

An alternative way to consider the valuation of bonds is to consider them as a series of individual cash flows with each cash flow being viewed as an independent zero-coupon bond. For example, Bond A (from the previous paragraph) could be viewed as 20 separate and distinct zero-coupon bonds and Bond B could be viewed as a single zero-coupon bond. These individual cash flows should then be valued based on market yields for zero-coupon Treasuries with similar maturities.

Quick Quiz 8.3

1. A yield curve that has higher long-term rates than short-term rates is called an inverted yield curve.
   a. True
   b. False
2. The pure expectations theory states that long-term rates are comprised of current and expected short-term rates.
   a. True
   b. False
3. Supply and demand play a key role in the market segmentations theory.
   a. True
   b. False

False, True, True.

Yield Curve Theories

There are several theories that attempt to explain the shape of the yield curve. These include the pure expectations theory, the liquidity theory, the preferred habitat theory, and the market segmentation theory.

The Pure Expectations Theory

The pure expectations theory is based on the concept that longer-term rates, are based on expected future short-term rates. In other words, longer term rates should indicate the market's perception of which direction interest rates will be moving. For example, an upward sloping yield curve would indicate that future short-term rates would be increasing; a flat yield curve indicates that future short-term rates will remain constant; and a downward, or inverted, yield curve represents the expectation that short-term rates will be declining. This concept can be illustrated with the following example.

Example 8.22

Assume that the 1-year rate equals 6% and the 2-year rate equals 8%. Under this assumption, an investor willing to invest for a period of two years could receive a return of 8% for each of the two years, whereas the investor who was only willing to invest one year would receive 6%. There is a 2-percentage-point difference in the returns that the 2-year investor will receive in the first year as compared to the return for the 1-year investor. Under the expectations theory, the reason that an investor would receive 8%

over two years and only 6% for one year is that the market expects short-term interest rates to increase in one year. In other words, the 8% rate for two years actually consists of the 1-year rate of 6% and the 1-year rate one year from today. This future 1-year rate turns out to be 10.04 percent, as follows:

Future Value of 2-Year Bond = 1.08 x 1.08 = $1.1664 (PV=$1, N=2, i=8, PMT=0, FV=$1.1664)	The investor should have 16.64% more than the initial investment at the end of 2 years.
Future 1-Year Rate = 1.1664 ÷ 1.06 = 1.1004 – 1.00 = 10.04%	Since the 1-year rate equals 6%, the future 1-year rate must equal 10.04%.
Proof = 1.06 x 1.1004 = 1.1664	A rate of 6% for the first year plus a rate of 10.04% for the second year is equal to a 2-year rate of 8%.

One weakness of this theory is that it does not reflect the inherent increased risk or uncertainty in longer-term bonds. There is clearly more uncertainty with a 2-year bond than with a 1-year bond. In the above example, the theory explains that the 2-year return of eight percent results from a six percent return the first year and a 10.04 percent return the second year. Based on this theory, it seems reasonable that an investor with a 1-year time horizon would purchase the 2-year bond to earn eight percent for the first year and then sell it at the end of one year. However, there is no guarantee that the bond could be sold at a specific price at the end of one year, which introduces the element of risk into the decision. As a result, an investor with a 1-year time horizon might choose the 1-year bond instead of the 2-year bond, even though the return for the 1-year bond is lower. Therefore, it seems as though the forward rate, in our example 10.04 percent, may consist of a risk premium for the increased term as well as expectations of higher future interest rates.

The Liquidity Preference Theory

According to the liquidity preference theory, investors prefer certainty and expect to be compensated for uncertainty. This theory is based on the expectations theory, but goes on to incorporate a liquidity premium into the model. Under this theory, investors require premiums for the increased exposure to interest rate risk inherent in long-term bonds. Based on this theory, yield curves are generally upward sloping, reflecting higher premiums for longer-term bonds.

Key Concepts

1. Bond prices are inversely related to bond yields.
2. Prices for longer-term bonds are more volatile than for shorter-term bonds when interest rates change.
3. Higher coupon bonds are less sensitive to interest rate changes than lower coupon bonds.
4. The percent decrease in the price of a bond for a given increase in market yields will be less than the percent increase in the price of the same bond for an equal decrease in market yields.

The Market Segmentation Theory

According to the market segmentation theory, interest rates for varying maturities are determined by supply and demand. Institutions may have liabilities that are short term, intermediate term, or long term and want to match the maturity of their assets with the maturity of their liabilities. As a result, certain types of institutions lend and borrow in different segments of the yield curve. This results in a separate market for short-term borrowings, intermediate-term borrowings, and long-term borrowings. Each market has its own balance between supply and demand. Therefore, based on the supply and demand in each maturity market, the yield curve can be any shape. For example, a number of pension plans could have a need for five-year bonds, thus the demand at five years is greater than the supply, causing a decrease in the yield at five years, which may create a kink in an otherwise smooth yield curve.

The Preferred Habitat Theory

The preferred habitat theory, similar to the market segmentation theory, states that financial institutions have certain maturity preferences for their investments as they seek to match the term of their liabilities. However, this theory states that these institutions sometimes shift their maturities or duration if the premiums for the switch are significant enough. Therefore, it is possible to have any shape yield curve under this theory.

BOND PRICE VOLATILITY

Bond prices fluctuate with changes in interest rates. However, bond prices vary by different amounts depending on the coupon rate and maturity of the bond, as well as the direction of interest rate changes.

In 1962, Burton G. Malkiel wrote his seminal paper, *Expectations, Bond Prices, and the Term Structure of Interest Rates*, in which he discusses the relationship between YTM and bond prices.[2] In this paper, he identifies and discusses five theorems regarding the relationship between YTM and bond prices. These five theorems document how bonds are impacted by changes in market interest rates as well as coupon rate and maturity. **Exhibit 8.5** outlines these five theorems.

Exhibit 8.5 | Malkiel's Theorems

Theorem 1	Bond prices move inversely to bond yields.
Theorem 2	For a given change in yield, longer-term bond price changes are greater than changes for shorter-term bond prices.
Theorem 3	The percent change in price described in Theorem 2 increases at a diminishing rate as bond maturity increases.
Theorem 4	Price movements resulting from equal absolute (or, what is the same, from equal proportionate) increases and decreases in yield are asymmetric; i.e., a decrease in yields raises bond prices more than the same increase in yields lowers prices.
Theorem 5	The higher the coupon carried by the bond, the smaller the percentage price fluctuation for a given change in yield except for one-year securities and consols.[1]

1. Consols are a form of a perpetual bond issued in England. Perpetual bonds do not have a fixed maturity and would be comparable to a preferred stock in terms of cash flows.

Bond Prices Move Inversely to Changes in Yields

There is an inverse relationship between movements in prevailing market interest rates and bond prices. As market rates or yields increase, bond prices will decrease. This relationship is essentially interest rate risk and was discussed earlier in the chapter.

2. Burton G. Malkiel is a professor of economics from Princeton, who is famous for his book entitled, *A Random Walk Down Wall Street.*

Longer-Term Bonds Are More Volatile Than Shorter-Term Bonds

Longer-term bonds are subject to more price change when interest rates change as compared to shorter-term bonds. A 30-year bond is more volatile than a 10-year bond.

Example 8.23

Bond A is a 5-year bond with a 10 percent coupon rate. Bond B is a 30-year bond also with a 10 percent coupon rate. Since Bond B has a longer maturity, it should be more volatile when interest rates change.

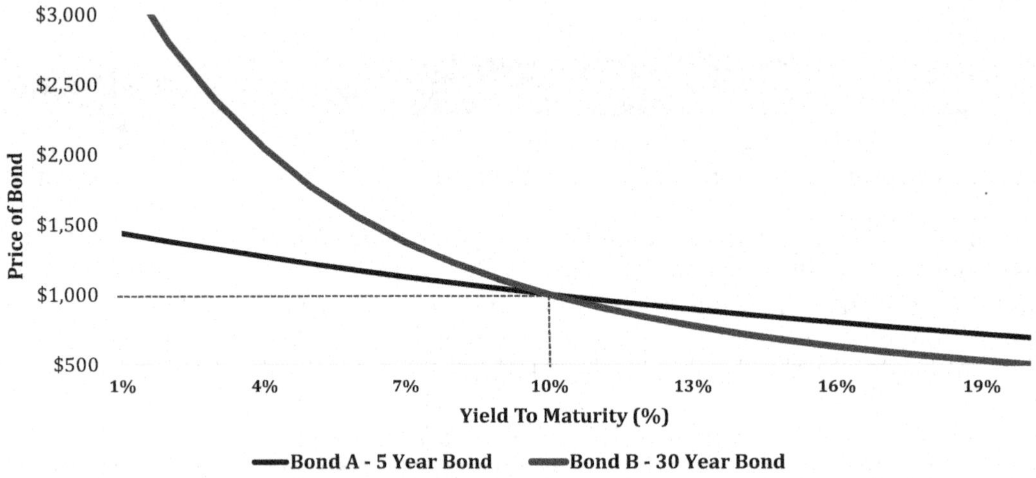

Notice that Bond B does in fact change more than Bond A when interest rates change. At a YTM of 10 percent, the price of both bonds is equal to $1,000. When interest rates decrease, the price of Bond B increases more than the price of Bond A. When interest rates increase, the price of Bond B decreases more than the price of Bond A. However, the increases and decreases are not symmetrical.

Example 8.24

The chart below illustrates changes in the value of 5% coupon bonds initially priced at par.

A	B	C	D	E	F	G	H
Term of the bond	Price of 5% coupon bond yielding 5%*	$ gain if market yield decreases to 4%	% Δ in gain from prior period (1 yr to 2 yrs, 25 yrs to 30 yrs, etc.)	The % Δ in bond price from drop in market yield to 4%	Price of 5% coupon bond yielding 6%*	$ loss if market yield increases to 6%	The % Δ in bond price from increase in market yield of 1%
1	$1,000.00	$9.71		1.0%	$990.43	($9.57)	-1.0%
2	$1,000.00	$19.04	96%	1.9%	$981.41	($18.59)	-1.9%
3	$1,000.00	$28.01	47%	2.8%	$972.91	($27.09)	-2.7%
5	$1,000.00	$44.91	60%	4.5%	$957.35	($42.65)	-4.3%
10	$1,000.00	$81.76	82%	8.2%	$925.61	($74.39)	-7.4%
15	$1,000.00	$111.98	37%	11.2%	$902.00	($98.00)	-9.8%
20	$1,000.00	$136.78	22%	13.7%	$884.43	($115.57)	-11.6%
25	$1,000.00	$157.12	15%	15.7%	$871.35	($128.65)	-12.9%
30	$1,000.00	$173.80	11%	17.4%	$861.62	($138.38)	-13.8%

** Semi-annual coupon payments.*
Note: The Greek letter Delta (Δ) means change

Each of the columns in the chart above is explained below:

- Column A: Term of the bond being compared.
- Column B: The price of each bond – all are at par because the YTM equals the coupon rate.
- Column C: The increase in the bond price (gain), in dollars, assuming interest rates decrease from 5% to 4%.
- Column D: The percent increase in the gain from Column C by comparing a longer-term bond to the next shorter-term bond in the exhibit. The percent increase in the gain for the 2-year bond compared to the 1-year bond is 96%. The increase from the 5-year bond to the 10-year bond is 82%, whereas the increase from the 25-year bond to the 30-year bond is only 11%. This decreasing change is the essence of Malkiel's Theorem 3, which states that the percent change in price described in Theorem 2 increases at a diminishing rate as bond maturity increases.
- Column E: The percent increase in the bond due to a decline in interest rates of 1%. Notice that the percent change in the value of the bond is much greater for the longer-term bonds than for the shorter-term bonds. This column illustrates Malkiel's second theorem.
- Column F: The price of each bond assuming interest rates move from 5% to 6%. This change in the value of the bond illustrates Malkiel's Theorem 1.
- Column G: The change in the price of each bond assuming interest rates move from 5% to 6%.

- Column H: The percent change in the price of each bond assuming interest rates move from 5% to 6%. Comparing Column H to Column E illustrates Malkiel's Theorem 4, which states that the percent change is asymmetric for an equal increase or decrease in interest rates. For the 30-year bond, a 1% decrease in yield increases the value of the bond by 17.4%, whereas a 1% increase in yield decreases the value of the bond by 13.8%.

Lower Coupon Bonds Are More Volatile

Bonds with higher coupon rates have smaller percentage price fluctuations for a given change in yield compared to bonds with lower coupon rates. Given this fact, zero-coupon bonds should be the most volatile.

Example 8.25

Consider the following:

A	B	C	D	E	F
Coupon Rate*	**Price of a 20-year bond yielding 8%**	**Price of bond if market yield increases to 9%**	**% Δ in price from the market yield increase to 9%**	**Price of bond if market yield decreases to 7%**	**% Δ in price from the market yield increase to 9%**
10%	$1,197.93	$1,092.01	-8.8%	$1,320.33	10.2%
8%	$1,000.00	$907.99	-9.2%	$1,106.78	10.7%
6%	$802.07	$723.98	-9.7%	$893.22	11.4%
4%	$604.14	$539.96	-10.6%	$679.67	12.5%
2%	$406.22	$355.94	-12.4%	$466.12	14.7%
0%	$208.29	$171.93	-17.5%	$252.57	21.3%

** Semi-annual coupon payments.*
Note: The Greek letter Delta (Δ) means change

Each of the columns in the chart above is explained below:

- Column A: The coupon rate for each bond being compared.
- Column B: The price of each bond priced to yield 8%.
- Column C: The price of each bond if the YTM increases to 9%.
- Column D: The percent change in the price of the bond from an increase in interest rates from 8% to 9%. Notice that the percent change for the zero-coupon bond is greater than the change for the coupon-paying bonds. As the coupon rate (Column A) decreases, the volatility of the bond price increases for an equal change (from 8% to 9%) in interest rates.
- Column E: The price of each bond if the YTM decreases to 7%.
- Column F: The percent change in the price of the bond from a decrease in interest rates from 8% to 7%. Notice that the change for the zero-coupon bond is greater than the coupon-paying bonds. As the coupon rate decreases, the volatility of the bond price increases for an equal change in interest rates. Also, the rate of change is asymmetric for gains compared to losses for an equal change in interest rates. The gain will always be greater than the loss.

Malkiel's theorems are very helpful in understanding how bond prices will move based on changes in prevailing interest rates and the underlying characteristics of the bond. Ultimately, the price of a bond is attributable to three factors – YTM, coupon rate, and the term of the bond.

It can be somewhat challenging to keep all five of Malkiel's theorems in mind when considering the volatility of a bond. Fortunately, these three factors can be used to determine **duration**, which provides an indication of the volatility or sensitivity to interest rate changes for bonds and bond portfolios. Duration is discussed in the following section.

Bond Price Convergence

A bond's price is subject to the relationship between the coupon rate, YTM, and term for that particular bond. Bonds with a coupon rate in excess of the YTM sell at a premium, while bonds with a coupon rate below the YTM sell at a discount. Bonds in which the YTM and coupon rate are equal sell at par value. However, all bonds, whether sold at a premium or a discount, converge to par value as they approach maturity.

Exhibit 8.6 depicts prices over a ten-year period for three seven percent coupon bonds. The premium bond is priced to yield six percent, the discount bond is priced to yield eight percent, and the par bond is priced to yield seven percent.

Quick Quiz 8.4

1. A 30-year, zero-coupon bond is more volatile than a 10-year, 4% coupon bond.
   a. True
   b. False
2. A 10-year, 3% coupon bond is more volatile than a 10-year, 5% coupon bond.
   a. True
   b. False
3. As the time remaining to maturity decreases, so does the difference in the price between premium bonds and discount bonds that have the same coupon rate.
   a. True
   b. False
4. When interest rates change, bond prices change inversely. The percent change in price is the same, whether the interest rates increase or decrease.
   a. True
   b. False

True, True, True, False.

Exhibit 8.6 | Bond Price Convergence

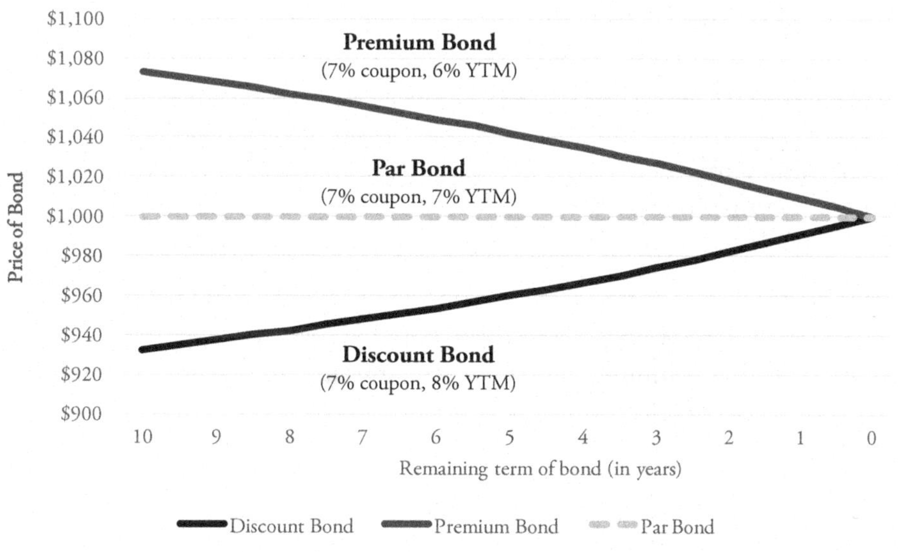

When the bonds have ten years until maturity, there is a $140 difference between the value of the premium bond and the value of the discount bond. This difference in price decreases over the ten years until finally the prices of the bonds converge to par at maturity. Investors are only willing to pay $1,000 for a bond on the day it matures, as that is the cash flow expected from the issuer of the bond.

DURATION, IMMUNIZATION, AND CONVEXITY

The concept of **duration**, developed by Frederick Macaulay in 1938, provides a time-weighted measure of a fixed-income security's cash flows in terms of payback.[3] There are three important uses for duration, which include:

1. Providing a measure of a bond's volatility;
2. Estimating the change in the price of a bond based on changes in interest rates; and
3. Immunizing a bond or bond portfolio against interest rate risk.

Most savvy bond investors acknowledge that it is insufficient to evaluate a bond based on its yield alone. The bond should also be evaluated based on the timing of its cash flows. The calculation of duration allows investors to evaluate both factors in a single metric.

Key Concepts

1. Duration is a weighted measure of payback.
2. Modified duration is used to determine the percent change in the price of a bond or bond portfolio for a specific change in prevailing interest rates.
3. Duration is a linear measure of the curvilinear bond price-yield relationship.
4. Duration assumes parallel shifts in the yield curve.
5. A bond or bond portfolio can be initially immunized if the Macaulay duration of the bond or bond portfolio matches the investor's time horizon.
6. Convexity is the degree to which the bond price-yield relationship is curvilinear.

Calculating Duration (Macaulay)

There are several methods for calculating duration including Macaulay duration, modified duration, and effective duration. The following formula is one method for calculating Macaulay duration:

$$D = \frac{\sum_{t=1}^{n} \frac{CF_t(t)}{(1+k)^t}}{\sum_{t=1}^{n} \frac{CF_t}{(1+k)^t}}$$

n = Number of periods until maturity
CF_t = Cash flow that occurs in period t
k = Yield to maturity
t = Time period

The denominator is the market price of the bond, defined as the present value of future cash flows. The numerator is the sum of each discounted cash flow adjusted for the period in which it occurs.

3. Frederick Macaulay was a Canadian economist who introduced the concept of duration. He received his undergraduate and masters degrees from the University of Colorado and his Ph.D. from Columbia University.

Example 8.26

The duration for a 10-year bond that pays a 10 percent coupon annually and is yielding 10 percent can be calculated as follows:

(A) Period	(B) Cash Flow	(C) PV Factor*	(D) PV @ 10%	(E) PV x Period
1	$100.00	0.9091	$90.91	$90.91
2	$100.00	0.8264	$82.64	$165.29
3	$100.00	0.7513	$75.13	$225.39
4	$100.00	0.6830	$68.30	$273.21
5	$100.00	0.6209	$62.09	$310.46
6	$100.00	0.5645	$56.45	$338.68
7	$100.00	0.5132	$51.32	$359.21
8	$100.00	0.4665	$46.65	$373.21
9	$100.00	0.4241	$42.41	$381.69
10	$1,100.00	0.3855	$424.10	$4,240.98
			$1,000.00	$6,759.02

$$\textbf{(F)}\quad \textbf{Duration} = \frac{\$6{,}759.02}{\$1{,}000.00} = \textbf{6.76 years}$$

** The PV Factors are at 10%.*

The calculation of duration requires five broad steps.

Step 1: List the periods relevant to the bond (A). In the above example, there are ten periods associated with the bond.

Step 2: List the cash flow for each period (B). The cash flows will consist of coupon payments and/or principal payments.

Step 3: Calculate the present value of each of the cash flows. This can be done by multiplying column B by column C. Column C lists the present value factors used to discount a future cash flow back n periods.

Step 4: Multiply column A by column D. For example, in the third period, 3 is multiplied by $75.13, which equals $225.39.

Step 5: Divide the sum of column E by the sum of column D. The result of this fifth step is the duration in years (F).

Duration can be calculated on a periodic basis to accurately account for semi-annual coupon payments by listing each semi-annual period and cash flow. This adjustment will result in an answer in terms of periods, which can be converted into years simply by dividing by two (for semi-annual payments).

It is important to realize that duration for a bond or bond portfolio will change over time. This change results from changes in market yields and remaining time until maturity.

Another method of estimating Macaulay duration is to use the following closed-end formula:

$$\text{Dur} = \frac{1+k}{k} - \frac{(1+k)+T(C-k)}{C[(1+k)^T - 1]+k}$$

C = Coupon rate (as a decimal)
k = Yield to maturity (as a decimal)
T = Time until maturity (in periods)

Example 8.27

The calculation of this formula can be illustrated using the information in **Example 8.26**:

$$\text{Dur} = \frac{1+0.10}{0.10} - \frac{(1+0.10)+10(0.10-0.10)}{0.10[(1+0.10)^{10} - 1]+0.10}$$

$$\text{Dur} = 11 - \frac{1.10}{0.25937}$$

$$\text{Dur} = 11 - 4.24$$

$$\text{Dur} = 6.76 \text{ years}$$

Remember the closed end formula is just an estimate, but is attractive to many students who like shortcuts. Many professionals, however, use the efficient spreadsheet shown in **Example 8.27** which makes the shortcut less attractive. It should be noted that duration for a bond will change as interest rates and time change. Therefore, it is not a static number.

Duration as a Measure of a Bond's Volatility

Duration provides investors with a method of easily comparing the volatility of one bond with that of another bond, or bond portfolio. Very simply, bonds with higher durations are more volatile when interest rates change than bonds with lower durations. Therefore, the volatility of bonds increases as duration increases. The three main factors that impact a bond's duration are coupon rate, maturity, and yield to maturity.

Coupon Rate

There is an inverse relationship between a bond's coupon rate and its duration, which is consistent with Malkiel's Theorem 5. The duration of a bond cannot exceed the maturity of a bond. Generally, the duration of a bond is less than its term to maturity unless it is a zero coupon bond. Macaulay duration for a zero coupon bond is equal to its maturity.

Duration decreases when the coupon rate increases because the investor is receiving cash flows faster, decreasing the time the investor must wait to be paid back the initial investment. A quicker payback means a shorter duration and thus, less volatility. Note that a bond that pays back principal before the bond's maturity will have a lower duration than one that pays off principal at maturity. Two examples are bonds with sinking funds and callable bonds.

Maturity

There is a direct relationship between a bond's maturity and its duration. Bonds with greater maturities have longer durations. The increase in duration, however, occurs at a decreasing rate.The following example illustrates this point.

Example 8.28

Durations for a bond with a 3% coupon and an 8% YTM, calculated for maturities ranging between one year and 30 years.

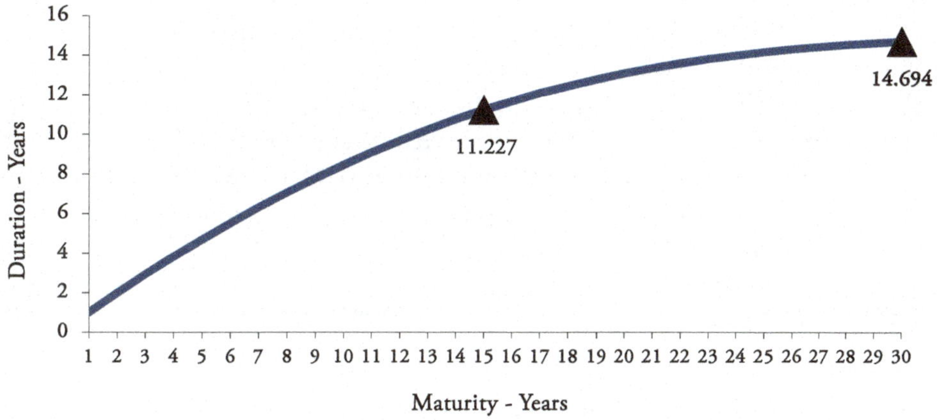

As illustrated, duration is directly impacted by maturity at a decreasing rate. In this example, the duration for a maturity of 15 years is approximately 11.2 years, while the duration for a maturity of 30 years is only 14.7 years.[4] Although the actual maturity doubled (15 years to 30 years), the duration of the bond increased by only 3.5 years. It should also be noted that the coupon rate impacts the degree to which the duration changes, as will the YTM.

Yield to Maturity

Generally, yield to maturity (YTM) is inversely related to duration. When the YTM is increased for a coupon bond, the duration will decline. As stated above, the duration of a zero-coupon bond is its term to maturity, therefore, its duration is unaffected by changes in the YTM.

4. Duration was calculated assuming annual coupon payments.

Exhibit 8.7 | Macaulay Duration Summary

> Macaulay duration can be thought of as a time-weighted payback period. Bonds with greater durations are more sensitive to interest rate changes. Characteristics of Macaulay duration:
>
> 1. The duration of a coupon bond will always be less than its maturity because of the weights given to the intermediate cash flows.
> 2. There is an inverse relationship between coupon and duration. Bonds with higher coupons have lower durations. For example, the duration of an 8% bond with twenty years to maturity is less than the duration of a 5% coupon bond with twenty years to maturity. Note: the duration of a zero-coupon bond always equals its maturity.
> 3. There is a positive relationship between duration and time to maturity. The duration of an 8% coupon bond with twenty years to maturity is greater than the duration of an 8% coupon bond with 15 years to maturity.
> 4. There is an inverse relationship between duration and yield to maturity. As YTM increases, duration decreases.
> 5. Sinking funds and call provisions can change the duration of a bond.

Modified Duration

Another important application of duration is its use in determining the expected price change in a bond or bond portfolio based on changes in interest rates. It should be clear that as interest rates change, bond prices change in the opposite direction. Fixed-income investors are concerned with the exposure to interest rate risk. Modified duration is used as an estimate of the percentage change in the price of a bond based on its duration and the change in market interest rates.

Modified duration is a "modified" version of Macaulay duration. Modified duration is a linear approximation of the price-yield relationship. It is a useful tool to approximate the impact that a small change in interest rates has on the value of a non-callable bond. It is equal to Macaulay duration divided by 1 plus the current yield to maturity divided by the number of payments in a year.

$$\textbf{Modified Duration} = \frac{\textbf{Macaulay Duration}}{1 + \dfrac{\textbf{Current YTM}}{\textbf{\# pmts in a year}}}$$

As the formula below describes, the estimated change in the price of a bond equals the duration of a bond divided by one plus the YTM and multiplied by the change in interest rates. The negative sign reflects the inverse relationship between bond prices and changes in interest rates.

$$\frac{\Delta P}{P} = \frac{-D}{1 + YTM} \times \Delta YTM$$

$\Delta P/P$ = Percentage change in the price of a bond

D = Macaulay Duration of the bond

YTM = Yield to maturity for the bond

ΔYTM = Change in YTM as a decimal

Example 8.29

A ten-year bond with a 10% coupon rate that sells for par value has a duration of 6.76 years. Investors in the bond market are expecting yields to fall over the next few days. The price change in the bond if yields decrease by 1% (100 basis points) is closest to:

$$\frac{\Delta P}{P} = \frac{-D}{1 + YTM} \times \Delta YTM$$

$$\frac{\Delta P}{P} = \frac{-6.76}{1 + 0.10} \times (0.09 - 0.10)$$

$$\frac{\Delta P}{P} = -6.1455 \times -0.01$$

$$\frac{\Delta P}{P} = 0.06145 = 6.145\%$$

Based on the above formula, the price of the bond should increase by approximately 6.15 percent. This estimation of the price change of a bond is very useful in analyzing the exposure that a bond portfolio has to interest rate risk. Based on this estimate, we would expect the new price of the bond to be \$1,061.45 (\$1,000 x 1.06145).

Effective Duration

Effective duration is a direct measure of the sensitivity of a bond to changes in interest rates. It represents the approximate percentage change in the value of a bond for a given change in yields. A simple way to calculate effective duration is as follows:

$$\textbf{Effective Duration} = \frac{\textbf{(Price if yield declines)} - \textbf{(Price if yield increases)}}{\textbf{(2)(Initial price)(Decimal change in yield)}}$$

Example 8.30

Consider an 8-year, 6% coupon, semi-annual bond currently priced to yield the prevailing market interest rate of 6 percent (\$1,000). If market rates were to increase by 50 basis points (0.5%) to 6.5%, the new price would be \$969.19. If market rates were to decline by 50 basis points to 5.5%, the new price would be \$1,032.01. Note that the decimal yield change in this example is 0.0050.

$$\text{Effective Duration} = \frac{(\$1{,}032.01) - (\$969.19)}{(2)(\$1{,}000.00)(0.0050)} = 6.282 \text{ years}$$

Effective duration accommodates changing cash flows that result from embedded options (for example, callable bonds and putable bonds) whereas modified duration assumes that cash flows remain constant.

Example 8.31

An 8-year, 6 percent coupon, semi-annual bond is currently priced to yield the prevailing market rate of 6 percent ($1,000.00). The bond is callable at 105. If market rates were to increase by 100 basis points to 7 percent, the new price of the bond would be $939.53. If market rates were to decline by 100 basis points to 5 percent, the new price would be equal to $1,065.28. However, because the bond is callable, the call price of 105 acts as a ceiling. Investors are unlikely to pay more than 105 if the bond could be called at any point in time at 105. Therefore, the highest price for the calculation is $1,050.00. Note that the decimal yield change in this example is 0.010.

$$\text{Effective Duration} = \frac{(\$1{,}050.00) - (\$939.53)}{(2)(\$1{,}000.00)(0.010)} = 5.5235 \text{ years}$$

The call option has caused the effective duration to drop to 5.5235.[5]

Modified duration and effective duration can both be used to estimate changes in the price of a bond or bond portfolio. However, effective duration can accommodate bonds with embedded options.

Portfolio Duration

Bond investors rarely own only one bond. Bondholders generally own diversified fixed income portfolios, which helps mitigate any unsystematic risks. The duration of a portfolio of bonds is equal to the weighted average of the durations of bonds included in the portfolio.

$$\textbf{Portfolio duration} = w_1D_1 + w_2D_2 + \ldots + w_nD_n$$

w_n = the percentage of the bond portfolio that the market value for bond n represents
D_n = the duration for bond n
n = number of bonds in the portfolio

Example 8.32

Max owns three bonds in his $6,000 bond portfolio, as follows:

Bond	FMV	Duration
A	$1,000.00	3.0
B	$2,000.00	4.5
C	$3,000.00	5.0

The duration of his portfolio is 4.5 years, calculated as follows:

$$\frac{1}{6}(3.0) + \frac{2}{6}(4.5) + \frac{3}{6}(5.0) = 4.5$$

The weighted duration of the portfolio equals 4.5 years.

5. The effective duration using a 100 basis point change and no call option is 6.2875. This number is not much different than the effective duration calculated using the 50 basis point change in the prior example.

Example 8.33

Lucas owns Bonds A, B, C, and D in his portfolio. After calculating the duration of each bond, he is able to determine that the overall duration of the portfolio equals 10 years, as follows:

Bond	Quantity	Price	YTM	Coupon*	Maturity	Duration	Portfolio Value	Portfolio %	Weighted Duration**
A	400	$308.32	4%	0%	30	30.000	$123,328	17.55%	5.26
B	300	$1,000.00	5%	5%	8	6.786	$300,000	42.68%	2.90
C	200	$949.24	5%	4%	6	5.435	$189,848	27.01%	1.47
D	100	$896.92	8%	4%	3	2.879	$89,692	12.76%	0.37
							$702,868	**100.00%**	**10.00**

**Assumes annual payments*
*** Equals duration times portfolio %*

Effective duration can be used in lieu of Macaulay duration. The weighted portfolio effective duration indicates the volatility of the bond portfolio based on a specific change in interest rates. The weighted duration for the bonds Lucas owns equals 10 years, which means that the value of the bond portfolio should change by approximately 10% for every 100 basis point change in prevailing interest rates.

Limitations of Duration

Bond duration is a useful tool for investors evaluating the interest rate sensitivity of a bond or bond portfolio. However, it also has several limitations. It is important to understand the limitations as well as the benefits of duration.

Duration Pricing Error

Duration is the first derivative of the bond price equation. It is a line that is tangent to the bond price graph. However, because it is a straight line, it is not a perfect estimation of the true price change a bond will incur assuming rates change. This difference is because duration assumes the relationship between price and yield is linear when in fact the bond price-yield line is curvilinear. Consider the exhibit below.

Quick Quiz 8.5

1. A 30-year, zero-coupon bond yielding 4.375% has a duration of 27.5 years.
   a. True
   b. False
2. A 10-year, 3% coupon bond has a duration that is less than 10 years.
   a. True
   b. False
3. A 10-year, 3% coupon bond has a longer duration than a 10-year, 5% coupon bond.
   a. True
   b. False

False, True, True.

Exhibit 8.8 | Duration Pricing Error

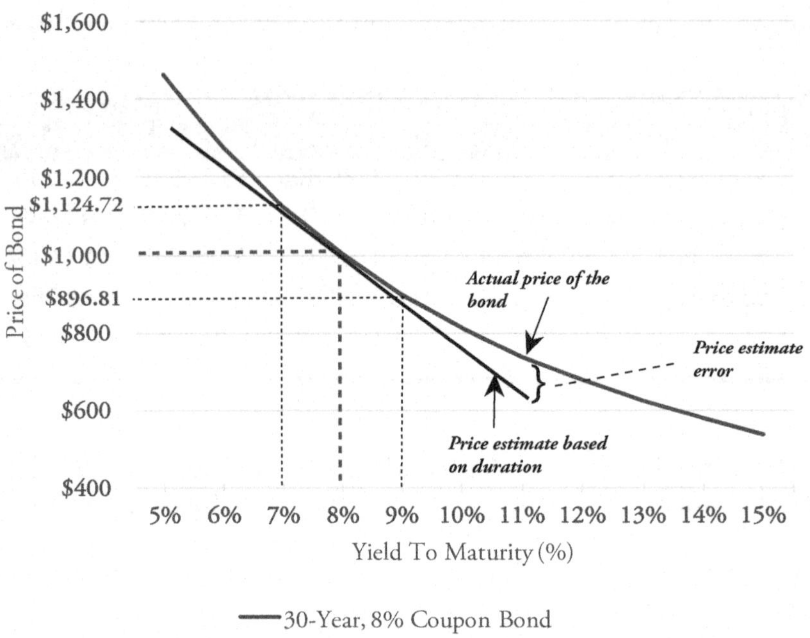

The curved line in the exhibit above represents a 30-year, eight percent coupon bond priced at various YTMs. The straight line represents the price estimated using duration. As depicted, duration is effective for relatively small changes in interest rates, but is less effective for larger changes. The difference between the lines is the pricing error and is attributable to the curvature of the bond's price-yield line. The curvature of this line is due to the bond's convexity, which is discussed later in this chapter.

Yield Curve Risk

As discussed earlier, the effective duration of a bond portfolio can be calculated as the weighted average duration of the bonds that make up the portfolio. This portfolio duration can then be used to estimate the price change for the portfolio in response to a change in yields. However, in the (likely) case where the portfolio contains bonds with different maturities, the estimate will only be accurate if the yield changes by the same amount for every maturity. This is known as a parallel shift, as the **yield curve** shift upwards or downwards for an increase or decrease is identical at every maturity.

Yield curve risk is the risk of a non-parallel shift in the yield curve. In this case, yields for different maturities change by different amounts, the yield curve will change shape, and as a result the weighted average duration for a portfolio may provide an inaccurate estimate of the resulting change in the portfolio's price.

Example 8.34

Byron owns the following bonds that make coupon payments annually, currently worth $4,000.

Bond	Coupon (%)	Maturity (Years)	Yield (%)	Par Value ($)	Duration	Modified Duration
1	6.00	3	6.00	$1,000	2.833	2.673
2	6.25	6	6.25	$1,000	5.184	4.879
3	6.50	21	6.50	$1,000	12.019	11.285
4	6.75	29	6.75	$1,000	13.436	12.586
			Total	$4,000		

Assume there is a parallel shift in the yield curve of +50 basis points. A parallel shift in the yield curve results in an equal change in the yield for all maturities. In this case, yields for all maturities increase by 50 basis points. How sensitive is the value of Byron's portfolio to an increase of 50 basis points? As can be seen below, the value of Byron's portfolio drops by $151.36 ($4,000.00 - $3,848.64).

Bond	Coupon (%)	(Years)	Maturity Yield (%)	Original Par Value ($)	New Yield (%)	New Bond Price
1	6.00	3	6.00	$1,000	6.50	$986.75
2	6.25	6	6.25	$1,000	6.75	$975.98
3	6.50	21	6.50	$1,000	7.00	$945.82
4	6.75	29	6.75	$1,000	7.25	$940.09
					Total	$3,848.64

The change in bond price estimated by duration is based on the assumption of parallel shifts in the yield curve. However, not all shifts are perfectly parallel, which can impact the precision with which duration accurately measures change in bond price as interest rates change.

To estimate the change in the price of the portfolio using the modified duration formula, the portfolio duration can be determined by calculating the weighted average modified duration for the four bonds. However, since the bonds are each selling at par, the portfolio modified duration equals the simple average of the modified duration for the four bonds. In this case, the portfolio modified duration equals 7.856 years.

The estimated percentage change in the value of the portfolio = -7.856 x 0.005 = -3.928%.
The estimated dollar change in the value of the portfolio = -3.928% x $4,000 = -$157.12

The actual change equals $151.36, while the estimated change using duration equals $157.12. The error is only about 0.16%. In other words, duration adequately estimated the change in the portfolio value based on a 50 basis point change in prevailing interest rates.

Example 8.35

Consider a **nonparallel shift** in the yield curve, in which the market interest rate change varies across maturities. As previously mentioned, when market interest rates change, the shift in the yield curve is typically nonparallel. In this case, the 3-year yield increases by 10 basis points, the 6-year yield increases by 20 basis points, the 21-year yield increases by 25 basis points and the 29-year yield increases by 45 basis points. The portfolio value in this case declines by $94.19 ($4,000 - $3,905.81).

Bond	Coupon (%)	(Years)	Maturity Yield (%)	Original Par Value ($)	New Yield (%)	New Bond Price
1	6.00	3	6.00	$1,000	6.10	$997.33
2	6.25	6	6.25	$1,000	6.45	$990.30
3	6.50	21	6.50	$1,000	6.75	$972.36
4	6.75	29	6.75	$1,000	7.20	$945.82
					Total	**$3,905.81**

The key point to remember is that portfolios have different exposures depending on how the yield curve shifts. Since duration is calculated assuming parallel shifts in yields, it will not accurately predict the change in the value of a portfolio of bonds with multiple maturities when interest rates change.

Example 8.36

Consider the following two portfolios, each with $100.00 of assets.

Asset	Portfolio A	Portfolio B
4-year zero-coupon bond	$50	$0
17-year zero-coupon bond	$0	$100
30-year zero-coupon bond	$50	$0

Recall that the duration of a zero-coupon bond is equal to its maturity. Also recall that the duration of a portfolio of bonds is equal to the weighted-average of the durations of the bonds that makeup the portfolio.

The duration of Portfolio A is calculated as follows:
(0.50)(4 years) + (0.00)(17 years) + (0.50)(30 years) = 17 years

The duration of Portfolio B is calculated as follows:
(0.00)(4 years) + (1.00)(17 years) + (0.00)(30 years) = 17 years

Note that the duration of Portfolios A and B are equal. As such, the price change that results from a parallel shift in the yield curve (that is, the 4-year, 17-year, and 30-year rates all change by the same percent) will be the same for Portfolio A and Portfolio B. However, if the change in yields is not parallel (i.e., a non-parallel shift in the yield curve) then the change in the value for Portfolio A will not be equal to the change in the value for Portfolio B.

While duration is very useful, it has its limitations. It is important for investors to understand how duration is calculated and what it represents so they understand its potential risks and limitations.

Using Duration to Immunize Bond Portfolios

Interest rate risk is one of the primary concerns of fixed-income investors, as well as for managers of fixed-income portfolios. The concern is that an increase in interest rates will result in a decrease in the value of bonds and bond portfolios. However, there is another aspect to the relationship between bond prices and interest rates that must be considered. When interest rates increase, the coupon payments received can be reinvested at higher interest rates, thus offsetting the decline in the value of the bond. The effect of interest rates on bond prices and reinvested coupon payments is illustrated in the following exhibit.

Exhibit 8.9 | The Effect of Interest Rates

Interest Rates Move	Value of Bond (Inverse to interest rates)	Value of Reinvested Coupon Payments (Move is direct to interest rates)
↑	↓	↑
↓	↑	↓

As illustrated above, when interest rates increase, the value of bonds decline, but the value of reinvested coupon payments increase. Similarly, as interest rates decline, bond prices increase and the value of reinvested coupon payments decreases. This offsetting relationship is the basis for immunizing a bond or bond portfolio against interest rate risk.

Immunization is the concept of minimizing the impact of changes in interest rates on the value of the investment. The goal of immunization is to protect the bond portfolio from interest rate fluctuations and reinvestment rate risk. Immunization should provide a stable compound rate of return that equals the calculated YTM at the purchase of the bond, despite interest rate fluctuations. The portfolio is considered immunized if the realized rate of return is at least as great as the computed YTM calculated at inception. Another way to think of immunization is that a bond portfolio is immunized when the actual future value is at least as great as was expected at inception.

A bond portfolio is defined as being initially immunized at the point of duration. Therefore, if an investor matches the duration of a bond portfolio to the time horizon of their goal, then the portfolio is initially immunized. This matching of duration to the time horizon of the goal can be easily accomplished with a zero-coupon bond. An investor who needs cash in ten years can simply purchase a ten-year, zero-coupon bond and hold it to maturity. The zero-coupon bond will eliminate all reinvestment

Quick Quiz 8.6

1. The price of a bond with a modified duration of 4.5 years should increase by approximately 2.25% if the prevailing yields decrease by 50 basis points.
   a. True
   b. False
2. Modified duration is a perfect measure of changes in the price of a bond based on changes in interest rates.
   a. True
   b. False
3. Bonds can be initially immunized at the point of duration.
   a. True
   b. False
4. Convexity measures the error between the actual change in the price of a bond when interest rates change and the estimate based on duration.
   a. True
   b. False

True, False, True, True.

rate and interest rate risk at the point of duration. Regardless of what happens to interest rates, the investor will have $1,000 in ten years when the bond matures. However, an appropriate zero-coupon bond may not always be available. Fortunately, ordinary coupon bonds can also be effectively immunized (albeit not as easily as zeros). Consider the following example.

Example 8.37

Kylie purchases a 10-year bond with a coupon rate of 8 percent, paid annually. The yield on the bond equals 10% and the duration of the bond matches Kylie's time horizon of approximately seven years. Kylie is concerned that fluctuations in interest rates may adversely affect the amount of cash that she expects to receive in seven years.

At the end of seven years, Kylie should have a total value of $1,709.23, assuming interest rates remain steady at 10 percent. The $1,709.23 consists of the reinvested coupon payments ($758.97) plus the sales proceeds of the bond ($950.26) at year seven.

Assuming Interest Rates Remain at:		Interest Rates Change to the Following:			
	10%	8%	9%	11%	12%
Coupon Payment Reinvested					
PMT	$80.00	$80.00	$80.00	$80.00	$80.00
i	10.00%	8.00%	9.00%	11.00%	12.00%
n	7.000	7.000	7.000	7.000	7.000
FV@7years	**$758.97**	**$713.82**	**$736.03**	**$782.66**	**$807.12**
Proceeds of Bond Sales @ Year 7					
FV	$1,000.00	$1,000.00	$1,000.00	$1,000.00	$1,000.00
PMT	$80.00	$80.00	$80.00	$80.00	$80.00
i	10.00%	8.00%	9.00%	11.00%	12.00%
n	3.000	3.000	3.000	3.000	3.000
PV@7years	**$950.26**	**$1,000.00**	**$974.69**	**$926.69**	**$903.93**
Reinvested Coupon Payments	$758.97	$713.82	$736.03	$782.66	$807.12
Bond Sale Proceeds	$950.26	$1,000.00	$974.69	$926.69	$903.93
Total@7years	**$1,709.23**	**$1,713.82**	**$1,710.72**	**$1,709.35**	**$1,711.05**

The example illustrates the concept of immunization. Because the future value at the point of duration (seven years) for interest rates of 8%, 9%, 11%, and 12% is at least as great as the future value if the interest rates had remained at 10 percent, this bond is considered immunized for this range of interest rates. Therefore, an investor who needs cash in seven years could use this bond as a method of minimizing his exposure to interest rate risk.

It should be noted that matching the duration to the investor's cash need only immunizes the portfolio against initial changes in interest rates and is only effective for a parallel shift in interest rates. It therefore follows that immunization is not effective for non-parallel shifts in interest rates. As time passes the "immunized" bond portfolio will need to be rebalanced so that the duration and remaining time continue to match. Rebalancing should be done once or twice per year. If rebalancing is performed more frequently than twice per year, the transactions costs may minimize any benefit derived through rebalancing.

Convexity

Convexity is a measure of the curvature of the price of a bond along a spectrum of yields. It can be used to provide a more precise measure of expected changes in the price of a bond than duration alone. Convexity is the second derivative of the equation for the price of the bond. While calculus is beyond this text, the formula below is an approximation for convexity.[6]

$$\text{Convexity} = \frac{P_+ + P_- - 2P_0}{P_0(\Delta Y)^2}$$

P_0 = Price of the bond as of today, before any change in Y
P_+ = Price of the bond based on an increase in interest rates equal to Y
P_- = Price of the bond based on an decrease in interest rates equal to Y
Y = Yield to maturity

The impact of convexity on the price of the bond can be estimated with the following formula.

$$\text{Convexity \% } \Delta \text{ in price} = \frac{1}{2}(\text{Convexity})(\Delta Y)^2$$

Example 8.38

Consider the 30-year, 8% coupon bond discussed earlier in the chapter. Assume it is priced to yield 8%. At that yield, the duration for the bond equals 12.158 years. The modified duration equals 11.257, which is found by dividing duration by one plus the YTM.

Assume interest rates increase by 1% (100 basis points). Modified duration can be used to estimate the change in the price of the bond:

$$\text{Percent } \Delta \text{ in price} = \frac{-D}{(1+Y)}(\Delta Y) = \frac{-12.158}{(1+0.08)}(0.01) = -11.257\%$$

The estimated price of the bond based on modified duration has an error of approximately $9.38 as follows:

- Current price = $1,000
- Estimated price = $1,000 x (1 - 0.11257) = $887.43
- Actual price of bond at 9% YTM = $896.81
- Actual change in the price of the bond = 10.32%
- Difference between estimate and actual = $9.384

6. Formula for approximate convexity is from Bond Markets, Analysis and Strategies, by Frank J. Fabozzi.

The adjustment for convexity can be calculated as follows:

$$\text{Convexity} = \frac{P_+ + P_- - 2P_0}{P_0(\Delta Y)^2} = \frac{\$896.81 + \$1{,}124.72 - 2(\$1{,}000)}{(\$1{,}000)(0.01)^2} = 215.336$$

$$\text{Convexity \% } \Delta \text{ in price} = \frac{1}{2}(\text{Convexity})(\Delta Y)^2 = \frac{1}{2}(215.336)(0.01)^2 = 0.01077$$

Modified duration + convexity adjustment = -11.257% + 1.077% = -10.18%

The predicted price with convexity adjustment = $1,000 x (1 – 10.18%) = $898.20, which is very close to the actual price change for the bond.

While duration is effective as a measure of interest rate sensitivity for bonds, it works best with small changes in interest rates and with parallel shifts in the yield curve. Convexity is the curvature of the bond price-yield relationship and can be used to provide more precision to the price sensitivity of a bond to changes in market interest rates.

Different bonds have varying levels of convexity. Investors prefer bonds with more convexity over those with less convexity. When interest rates decrease, bonds with more convexity increase in price more than bonds with less convexity. When interest rates increase, bonds with more convexity decrease in price less than bonds with less convexity. The chart below depicts the relationship between coupon rate, YTM and maturity on duration and convexity.

Exhibit 8.10 | Relationship between Coupon Rate, YTM, and Maturity

Bond Feature	Duration	Convexity
Coupon rate	Inverse ↑↓	Inverse ↑↓
Yield to maturity	Inverse ↓↑	Inverse ↓↑
Maturity	Direct ↑↑	Direct ↑↑

BOND PORTFOLIO MANAGEMENT STRATEGIES

There are two broad categories of bond portfolio management strategies, active and passive. Fixed-income investors must decide whether to employ the use of one, the other or both. Passive bond management generally involves indexing, while there are many active strategies. Some investors choose to index a core element of their bond portfolio, and use active management to attempt to enhance the performance of the portfolio returns.

Passive Strategies

Generally, passive investment strategies involve indexing. Indexing involves replicating an index by purchasing all of the bonds that make up the index. Naturally, the bonds need to be in the same proportion as reflected in the index. While indexing is not conceptually difficult to understand, it provides several important advantages over active strategies. Most of these advantages apply to both fixed-income investments as well as equities. These advantages include diversification, lower management cost, reduced transaction costs, and better performance.

Indexing provides instant diversification through the process of buying the bonds to replicate the index. As with equities, diversification is important in the management of fixed-income portfolios so that unsystematic risks are eliminated or at least minimized. An indexed mutual fund provides access to various issuers, market segments, and durations.

Replicating an index requires a different skill set than does active management. Passive indexing requires knowledge of index construction, weighting schemes, and various replication methods. One glaring characteristic of all passive funds is that they have lower asset management fees and trading costs, which lessens the drag on performance.

Key Concepts

1. The two categories of bond portfolio management strategies are passive and active.
2. Passive strategies generally involve indexing.
3. Active strategies often take advantage of expectations about changes in interest rates.

In terms of performance, index mutual funds perform better than many if not most actively managed funds, especially after considering management fees and 12b-1 fees.[7] Active funds may beat an index periodically but will also have periods of under-performance versus the index. Index funds provide consistent returns relative to an index because index funds replicate the holdings of the index.

While index strategies have advantages, fully replicating the index is not required to effectively replicate the characteristics of the bond index. In addition, index strategies can also be enhanced by modifying characteristics of an index to try and increase returns or reduce risk. For example, a portfolio might be established to take advantage of higher yields from certain credit sectors or from longer or shorter term bonds. The important point to keep in mind is that an enhanced index can create more attractive features or characteristics than the original index itself.

Active Strategies

Fixed-income portfolio managers can create value in many ways. Many active strategies are based on the portfolio manager's expectations about the future. For example, when managers expect interest rates to decline, they increase the duration of a portfolio. If interest rates actually decrease, the portfolio will increase more than if the duration was shorter. Similarly, if portfolio managers expect interest rates to increase, they typically reduce the duration of the portfolio to protect from losses to the portfolio. While an entire text could be devoted to the discussion of active fixed-income management, we have included only a few techniques to help illustrate some of the value additive strategies.

Consider the exhibit below, which shows the yield on 10-year Treasury securities from 1962 through 2019. Since the 1980s, rates have been steadily declining, reaching historic lows in the last decade. Fixed-income portfolio managers have an opinion on whether these rates, as well as the other rates on the Treasury yield curve will continue to decline or whether they will likely increase. As we have discussed, these future changes in rates will impact the value of fixed-income securities.

7. 12b-1 fees are service and distribution fees charged by mutual funds and are discussed in Chapter 12.

Exhibit 8.11 | 10-Year Treasury Constant Maturity Rate

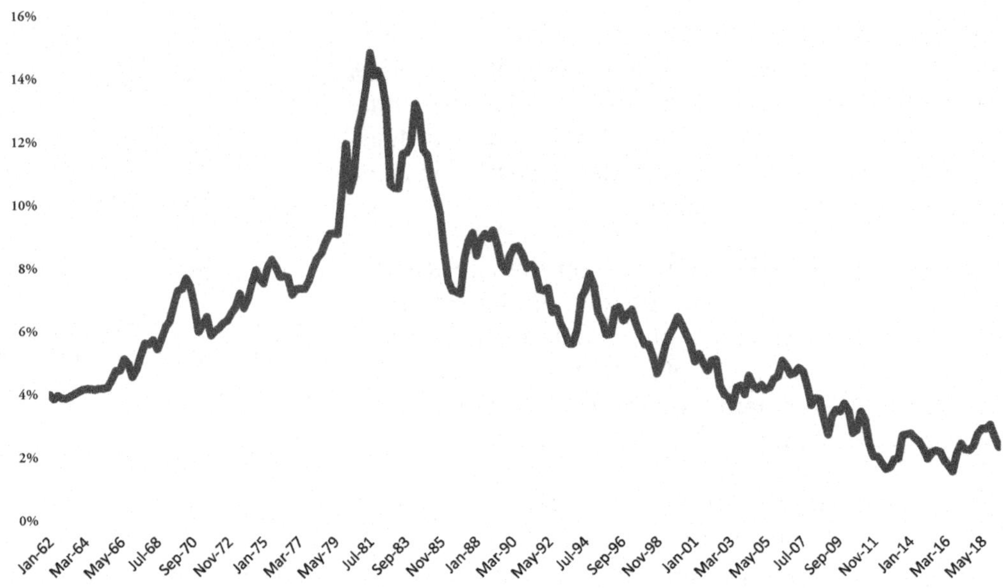

Yield Curve Strategies

As discussed earlier in the chapter, a yield curve is a graphical reflection of the prevailing market interest rates for bonds at various maturities. A normal yield curve is upward sloping such that longer term bonds have higher yields than shorter term bonds. Other yield curves include flat, inverted and even humped. Humped yield curves depict higher intermediate yields compared to short and long-term yields.

Bond managers often anticipate a shift in the yield curve. The shift might be a parallel shift in which all yields are expected to increase the same number of basis points. Alternatively, the yield curve might twist such that the curve becomes steeper or flatter. A steeper yield curve has higher long-term rates than short-term rates. A flatter curve reflects minimal yield differences between long and short-term bonds.

Depending on what a bond manager expects in terms of shifts in the yield curve, they may engage in one of three yield curve strategies. These strategies are referred to as the ladder strategy, the barbell strategy, and the bullet strategy. These names are in reference to how the strategy appears, as illustrated in **Exhibit 8.12**.

Exhibit 8.12 | Yield Curve Strategies

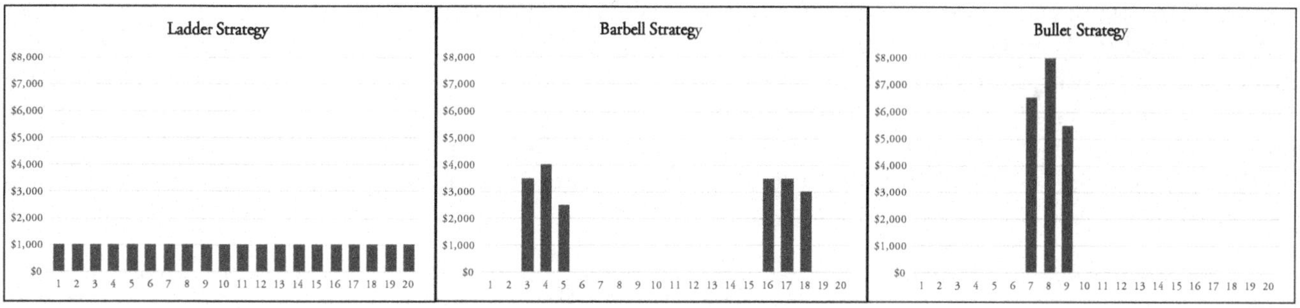

The Ladder Strategy

The ladder strategy is accomplished by establishing a portfolio of bonds with staggered maturities. For example, $20,000 of bonds could be purchased with maturities ranging from one to ten years for a total portfolio of $200,000. The shorter maturity bonds would be less subject to price fluctuation and, therefore, would reduce the overall portfolio interest rate risk. This approach provides two advantages. First, since there is a combination of long-term and short-term bonds in the portfolio, the laddered portfolio will provide higher yields during normal upward sloping yield curve environments than a portfolio consisting entirely of short-term bonds. Second, because one bond matures each year, cash is available to the investor. Furthermore, the funds from the maturing bond may be used to purchase another bond with a 10-year maturity that will maintain the original structure of the bond portfolio and minimize the risk of increasing interest rates. One important disadvantage of the laddered approach is that it reduces flexibility of the portfolio because all bonds may need to be liquidated in the event that the manager wishes to restructure the portfolio.

The Barbell Strategy

Under the barbell strategy, one-half of the portfolio is invested in shorter-term bonds, while the other half of the portfolio is invested in longer-term bonds. This approach creates a structure that has the appearance of a barbell. For example, a $200,000 fixed-income portfolio might be invested with $100,000 in 5-year bonds and $100,000 in 15-year bonds. The barbell strategy provides the advantage of only selling one group of bonds in the event that the structure of the portfolio needs to be changed due to changing interest rates. This strategy will not maintain its original structure because each year the maturity of the two groups of bonds will decline by one. Under this strategy, it is costly to maintain the original structure of the bond portfolio since the entire portfolio must be liquidated.

The Bullet Strategy

When investors purchase a series of bonds with similar maturities that are focused around one point in time, it is considered a bullet strategy. The bullet strategy is one in which the average maturity declines by one each year and may be effective in matching duration to the cash needs of an investor. Like the barbell strategy, to maintain the original structure, the entire portfolio must be liquidated, possibly resulting in significant transaction costs.

Riding the Yield Curve

Riding the yield curve is a strategy that is designed to take advantage of the normal yield curve structure in which long-term yields are higher than shorter-term yields. This technique is a "buy and hold" strategy that works when long-term rates are higher than short-term rates. The investor or money manager purchases long-term bonds and holds them for a period of time, but less than maturity. As the bond "travels down the yield curve," it will increase in value compared with newly issued bonds with the same maturity because the long-term bond was yielding a higher rate of return when it was originally purchased. The risk associated with this strategy is that interest rates will increase, instead of decrease, thus causing the value of the bond to decline.

Example 8.39

Assume that the market yields for a 5-year, 10-year, and 15-year bond are 1%, 1.5% and 2%, respectively. Seth buys a 15-year bond at par yielding 2%. If he holds the bond for ten years and yields remain the same, then he could sell the bond at a premium. He would have paid $1,000 for the bond when it was issued since it was at par. At 5 years, the bond will be worth $1,048.53 (n = 5, i = 1%, pmt = $20, fv = $1,000). Therefore, he gains $48.53, which equates to a YTM of 2.435%. That YTM is higher than if he were to hold the bond until maturity.

Bond Swapping

Fixed-income portfolio managers have opportunities to exchange one bond for another bond to benefit the portfolio. Bond swapping is the process of selling one debt instrument and replacing it with another. There are a variety of types of bond swaps with varying objectives. Often, the goal of a bond swap is to increase the overall rate of return.

Substitution Swap

Substitution swaps involve exchanging bonds with identical characteristics (including credit rating, maturity, coupon interest payment, call feature, etc.) selling for different prices. This price difference is an arbitrage opportunity and will only last until the lower priced bond is bid upward. These opportunities arise when there are temporary market imperfections.

Several risks associated with substitution swaps should be considered:

- The bonds may not be perfect substitutes for each other.
- The gain may not be sufficient to cover any required transaction costs.
- The workout time, which is the time it takes for the bonds prices to equal each other, may be longer than originally expected. This will reduce the realized yield for the swap.

Intermarket Spread Swap

Intermarket spread swaps involve the exchange of similar bonds from two different market sectors. These sectors might be the Treasury market and the corporate market, or the Treasury market and the agency bond market. The goal of this type of swap is to capitalize on the spread between two similar bonds.

An example of an intermarket spread swap is when investors swap Treasury securities for corporate bonds. Historically, the spread between Treasuries and corporate bonds fluctuates with the business cycle. Treasuries are largely considered default risk free. Corporate bonds have default risk, which increases when the economy is struggling and decreases when the economy is booming. Historically, the spread between Treasuries and corporates decreases when the economy is strong and increases when the economy is weak. When the economy is weak, investors require more return for accepting the higher potential default risk.

Example 8.40

Consider the following two bonds:

- Bond A: Ten-year corporate bond yielding 5.0% (coupon 5%) selling at par.
- Bond B: Ten-year Treasury note yielding 4.5% (coupon 2%) selling at a discount.

There is currently a 50-basis point spread between the yield for Bond A and Bond B. Assume that the historical spread for these bonds is 70 basis points. Because the 50-basis point spread (0.05 - 0.045) between A and B is historically small, then there is an opportunity to benefit from a spread swap. There are several ways in which the spread could return to its historical level of 70 basis points:

- Bond A's yield could increase (i.e., from 5% to 5.2%).
- Bond B's yield could decrease (i.e., 4.5% to 4.3%).
- Bond A's yield could increase while Bond B's yield decreases.

If any of the three possibilities occur, the swap benefits the investor. However, there is always the possibility that the yield on the bonds moves in the opposite direction than anticipated, causing the portfolio to incur losses.

Rate Anticipation Swap

Rate anticipation swaps are designed to take advantage of expected changes in market interest rates. As discussed, bond prices move inversely with interest rates. If rates are expected to increase, long-term bonds should be swapped for short-term bonds. Rising interest rates cause the value of long-term bonds to decrease more than the value for short-term bonds because long-term bonds are more sensitive to changes in interest rates. If rates are expected to decline, long-term bonds should be purchased to capitalize on the price increases for these bonds.

Pure Yield Pickup Swap

A pure yield pickup swap is designed to increase the yield through a swap. This swap involves exchanging a lower YTM bond with a higher YTM bond. Typically, these bonds have very similar characteristics except for the coupon rate.

Tax Swap

There is a saying that investors should not "let the tax tail wag the dog." In other words, investors should not be focused on tax issues at the expense of making sound financial decisions. However, managing taxable income and gains is a prudent element of asset management. Tax swaps are motivated by making use of unrecognized capital losses. An investor might sell a bond with a built-in capital loss for the purpose of recognizing the loss for tax purposes. That investor might then use the proceeds to repurchase a similar bond for a similar price. The result of this type of swap is to accelerate a tax loss or recognize a tax loss, which can be used to offset other capital gains.

Example 8.41

Pedro owns a bond that is priced at $800. He originally purchased the bond for $1,000. If he sells the bond for $800, it generates proceeds of $800 (assuming no transaction costs) plus a capital loss of $200. The capital loss might be worth $30 to $60, depending on the rate for the capital gains. Pedro could then use the proceeds to repurchase a similar bond for $800 and make use of the tax savings until maturity. It is likely that there will be a capital gain upon maturity.

Careful consideration should be given to current tax laws. For example, the wash sale rule will disallow the capital loss that the tax swap generated if the identical security is purchased within thirty days before or after the sale. This rule is designed to prevent taxpayers from maintaining their current positions and simultaneously recognizing a capital loss. Wash sale rules are easily avoided in the case of fixed-income securities by substituting a bond with similar or the same characteristics (i.e., coupon, term, quality, etc.) as long as it is from a different issuer.

There are certainly other strategies that fixed-income portfolio managers may employ to increase the yield or YTM for their portfolios. The techniques above are a sample of some of the more common ones.

SUMMARY

Summary of key points:

- The price of a bond equals the present value of the bond's cash flows, discounted at the prevailing market yield.
- Current yield, yield to maturity, and yield to call are important measures of a bond's return.
- Tax equivalent yields help investors compare yields for taxable bonds and municipal bonds.
- Interest rate risk, default risk, reinvestment rate risk, and call risk are important risks that impact bond investors.
- Yield curves are graphical representations of prevailing market interest rates.
- Bond prices are inversely related to bond yields.
- Long-term bonds are more volatile than short-term bonds.
- Duration is a weighted measure of payback that is used to estimate the volatility of a bond or bond portfolio.
- Immunization occurs when changes in the price of a bond are offset by reinvested coupon payments when interest rate fluctuations occur.
- Passive and active strategies are two categories of bond portfolio management strategies.

Quick Quiz 8.7

1. Indexing bond portfolios provides immediate diversification and lower management fees compared to actively managed bond portfolios.
   a. True
   b. False
2. Three yield curve strategies are the ladder strategy, the barbell strategy, and the bullet strategy.
   a. True
   b. False
3. A rate anticipation swap is used to take advantage of recent changes in interest rates.
   a. True
   b. False
4. Tax swaps are no longer permitted.
   a. True
   b. False

True, True, False, False.

DISCUSSION QUESTIONS

SOLUTIONS to the discussion questions can be found exclusively within the chapter. Once you have completed an initial reading of the chapter, go back and highlight the answers to these questions.

1. Explain how the value of a bond is calculated based on expected cash flows.
2. Describe the relationship between coupon rate, current yield, and yield to maturity as it relates to bonds selling at, below, or above par value.
3. Explain the differences in calculating YTM and YTC.
4. How should returns for Treasury, corporate, and municipal bonds be compared?
5. Describe default risk and interest rate risk.
6. Describe the impact of a bond's maturity and coupon rate on its interest rate risk.
7. What is duration and how is it used?
8. If Parker has a $4 million bond portfolio with a duration of 4 and an average YTM of 5%, how will it be impacted by a 100 basis point increase in interest rates?
9. Discuss the limitations of duration.
10. What are the keys to using duration to immunize a bond portfolio?
11. Differentiate passive and active bond portfolio strategies.

MULTIPLE CHOICE

A sample of multiple choice problems is provided below. Additional multiple choice problems are available at money-education.com by accessing the Student Practice Portal.

1. The Anderson bond is a 5% coupon bond with semi-annual coupon payments that matures in 10 years. If the YTM for this bond is 4%, what is the value of the bond?
    a. $1,081.11.
    b. $1,081.76.
    c. $1,124.35.
    d. $1,125.03.

2. Zola is considering purchasing a 35-year bond that is selling for $500. What is the YTM for this bond if it has a 2% coupon, paid semi-annually?
    a. 5.00%.
    b. 5.03%.
    c. 5.06%.
    d. 5.09%.

3. Winston is considering purchasing an 8-year bond that is selling for $700. What is the current yield for this bond if it has a 6% coupon, paid semi-annually?
    a. 8.57%.
    b. 9.32%.
    c. 10.17%.
    d. 11.92%.

4. Addison bought a bond with a modified duration of 11.20. By approximately what percentage will the bond price change assuming interest rates increase by 90 basis points?
    a. -11.20%.
    b. -10.08%.
    c. +10.08%.
    d. +11.20%.

5. Elton decides to invest $3 million in short-term fixed-income securities with an average duration of 3 years and $3 million in longer-term fixed-income securities with an average duration of 7 years. What type of strategy is Elton using?
    a. Intermarket spread strategy.
    b. Bullet strategy.
    c. Barbell strategy.
    d. Long-short strategy.

QUICK QUIZ EXPLANATIONS

Quick Quiz 8.1

1. True.
2. True.
3. False. Mortgage-backed securities have prepayment risk, whereas corporate bonds do not.

Quick Quiz 8.2

1. False. The YTM is 3%. The current yield equals $40 divided by the current price ($1,070.66), which equals 3.7%.
2. True.
3. True.
4. True.

Quick Quiz 8.3

1. False. It is a normal or upward sloping yield curve.
2. True.
3. True.

Quick Quiz 8.4

1. True.
2. True.
3. True.
4. False. The increase in price will be greater than the decrease in price.

Quick Quiz 8.5

1. False. It has a duration of 30 years.
2. True.
3. True.

Quick Quiz 8.6

1. True.
2. False. Modified duration is an approximation of the change in the price of a bond for a given change in interest rates. It is not a perfect measure.
3. True.
4. True.

Quick Quiz 8.7

1. True.
2. True.
3. False. A rate anticipation swap is used to take advantage of expected changes in interest rates.
4. False. Investors must avoid the wash sale rules when using a tax swap.

9

EQUITY SECURITIES - INTRODUCTION

LEARNING OBJECTIVES

1. Understand how dividends, capital appreciation, voting rights, maintaining ownership percentage, and liability contribute to the meaning of "ownership" investments.
2. Describe the types of equity securities.*
3. Define common stock and preferred stock and explain how they are alike and how they differ.*
4. List the types of foreign securities available to investors and the characteristics of each type.*
5. Discuss systematic and unsystematic risks that are inherent to equity securities.*
6. Identify and compare the markets in which equity securities are traded.
7. List the market indexes and averages that provide information to investors on the overall movement and performance of the securities markets.
8. Explain the primary characteristics of a good benchmark as a measure of a security's performance.*
9. Describe the ways in which an investor can measure the return of a security.*
10. Differentiate between taking a long position and a short position when purchasing equity securities.
11. List and differentiate the types of orders used to purchase shares of common stock.

**Ties to CFP Certification Learning Objectives*

INTRODUCTION

Equity securities play a significant role in investment strategy, largely due to their historically high level of returns. Equity returns have been higher than most other asset classes over a long period of time. The S&P 500 index, for example, has returned an average annual compound rate of return in excess of 10 percent over the last 30 years (Dec 1990 - Dec 2020), assuming dividends are reinvested.

A $1,000 investment at the beginning of this period would be worth approximately $17,600 at the end of 2020. An investment of $10 per month over that period would be worth approximately $17,700.

However, equity securities and the companies they represent have significant risks, including large swings in valuation and the potential for bankruptcy and liquidation.

Key Concepts

1. Equity investing has produced higher returns than most other asset classes over long periods of time.
2. Corporations obtain their legal authority from individual states.
3. Shareholders of common stock have the right to receive dividends, the right to vote, the right to limited liability and the right to assets in liquidation.

This chapter will explain the basic concepts of equity-type investments, their risks, and how equity securities are traded. The following chapter will discuss the analysis of equity investments, covering both fundamental and technical analysis. Valuation of equity securities is covered in Chapter 11: Equities Securities - Valuation.

CASE STUDY 9.1

ENRON

Enron was the "darling" of Wall Street in the 1990s. Enron was an American energy company based in Houston, Texas that had revenues in excess of $100 billion, a market cap in excess of $60 billion and was trading at an extremely high price to earnings ratio (PE) of 70. Shortly after these performance highs, the company filed for bankruptcy protection after being investigated for fraud by the Securities and Exchange Commission (SEC). Investors may have had huge returns or may have had massive losses, depending on when they purchased and when they sold Enron stock. Today, the company is out of business, which is the ultimate risk of owning equity securities.

BASIC CONCEPTS OF OWNERSHIP-TYPE INVESTMENTS

What Ownership Means

As discussed in Chapter 2, the two general types of investment securities are lending securities and ownership securities. Lending securities, which are investments with interest payments made to the investor (lender) for the use of the loaned funds, were discussed in Chapters 7 and 8. Ownership securities are securities that represent some form of ownership interest in a company or corporation.[1] Corporations are artificial, legal entities whose creation and operation are controlled by individual state statutes. To become a corporation, a business must incorporate within a state. As part of the incorporation process and as one method of raising capital, a corporation issues shares of common stock. Holders of these shares have certain rights and benefits, including the right to receive dividends, the right to vote on corporate issues, the right to limited liability, and finally, the right to ultimate distribution of assets in the event of liquidation. Shareholders also have a claim on the income generated by the assets of the company.

Key Concepts

1. Dividends are an important source of cash flow for investors.
2. The payout ratio is the percent of earnings paid out in the form of dividends.
3. A holder of stock receives a declared dividend if the holder is the owner on the date of record.
4. Dividend yield is the annual dividend divided by the current share price.
5. Stock splits are simply large stock dividends.

Numerous risks are inherent in owning common stock, including bankruptcy. These risks were discussed in Chapter 3. The primary reason investors are willing to accept these risks is that equities have earned significantly higher total returns than other types of investments over long periods of time. These total returns consist of two primary sources - dividends and capital appreciation. Dividend yield is the return attributable to dividend payments. Total return includes both dividend yield and capital appreciation.

1. The word "company" is used in consideration of other entity forms – partnerships, LLCs, etc., that are not "corporations."

There are three methods of holding equity securities. Equity investors can have a **physical certificate**, which represents ownership of equity shares. The second method is what is referred to as **street name** registration. Street name registration is when the security is registered in the name of the investor's brokerage firm on the issuer's books, and the brokerage firm holds the security for the investor in "book-entry" form. "Book-entry" simply means that the investor does not receive a certificate. Instead, the broker keeps a record in its books that the investor owns that particular security. With **Direct registration**, the security is registered in the investor's name on the issuer's books, and either the company or its transfer agent holds the security in book-entry form.

Exhibit 9.1 | Three Methods of Owning Equity Securities

	Advantages	Disadvantages
Physical Certificate	• The company knows how to reach the investor. • Pledging of securities as collateral may be easier with actual certificates.	• Significantly more time consuming to sell securities. • Lost certificates are replaced at a fee.
Street Name Registration	• Easy to buy and sell and make use of limit orders. • Brokers provide safe keeping of certificates. • Investors can borrow from the broker in the form of a margin account.	• Investors generally do not receive annual reports directly from the company.
Direct Registration	• Annual reports and other information are provided directly by the company to the investor. • Companies often provide dividend-reinvestment plans (DRIPs) that benefit shareholders.	• Less flexibility when buying and selling. No limit orders.

Exhibit 9.2 is a copy of an actual stock certificate. There are several important details on stock certificates.

1. Stock certificate number – each stock certificate will have a unique number.
2. Number of shares – the certificate will indicate the number of shares that are represented by the certificate.
3. CUSIP – CUSIP stands for Committee on Uniform Securities Identification Procedures. A CUSIP number identifies most financial instruments, including stocks of all registered U.S. and Canadian companies, commercial paper, and U.S. government and municipal bonds. The CUSIP system facilitates the clearance and settlement process of securities. CUSIP numbers consist of nine characters (including letters and numbers) that uniquely identify a company or issuer and the type of financial instrument. A similar system is used to identify foreign securities (CUSIP International Numbering System or CINS).[2]

2. When an estate tax return (Form 706) is filed, it must contain a list of securities owned by the decedent with their corresponding CUSIP numbers.

Exhibit 9.2 | Stock Certificate

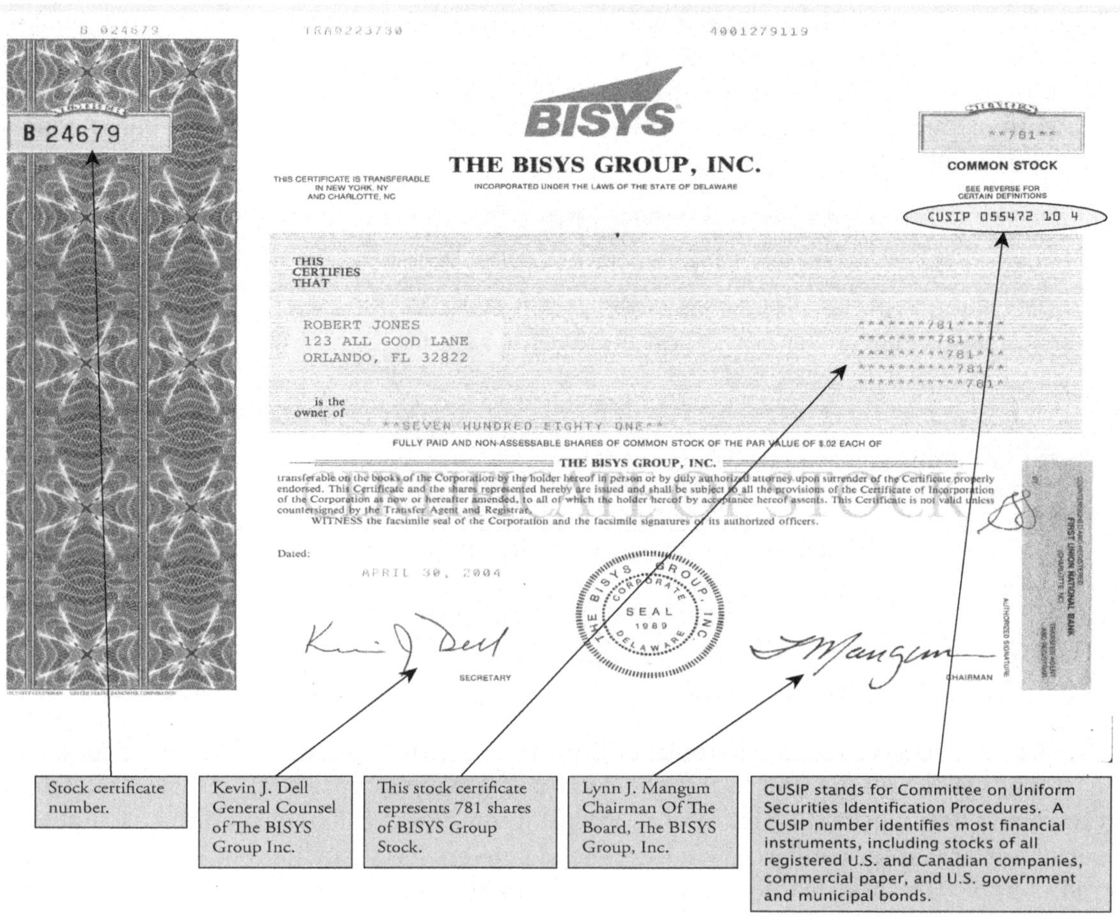

Dividends

Companies develop and offer products and services to fill the needs of customers and are in the business of offering these products and services in such a way as to generate a financial profit. Annual profits or earnings for common stocks are reported in total, but are also reported in terms of earnings per share of common stock. **Earnings per share (EPS)** represents the accounting profit of the company on a per share basis.

Public companies with a simple capital structure are only required to report basic EPS. A simple capital structure is one that does not contain any potentially dilutive securities. These are securities that may result in the issue of additional common shares, which in turn could potentially reduce (dilute) basic EPS.

Basic EPS is calculated as net income after preferred dividends divided by the weighted average number of common shares that have been outstanding for the year.

$$\textbf{EPS} = \frac{\textbf{Net Income - Preferred Stock Dividends}}{\textbf{Weighted Average Number of Common Shares Outstanding}}$$ [3]

3. Net Income - Preferred Stock Dividends = Earnings Available to Common Shareholders.

Example 9.1

Colin Corporation (Colin) had net income this year of $3,141,375 and will pay $160,000 in preferred dividends to preferred shareholders. At the beginning of the year, Colin had 200,000 common shares outstanding. On October 1st, Colin issued another 50,000 shares of common stock. The weighted average number of outstanding common shares equals 212,500 as follows.

Portion of The Year	Shares Outstanding (A)	Portion of the Year (B)	Weighted Shares (A) x (B)
Jan - Sept.	200,000	¾	150,000
Oct. - Dec.	250,000	¼	62,500
			212,500

EPS for Colin this year equals $14.03 as follows:

$$\text{EPS} = \frac{\text{Net income - preferred stock dividends}}{\text{Weighted average number of common shares outstanding}}$$

$$\text{EPS} = \frac{\$3{,}141{,}375 - \$160{,}000}{212{,}500} = \$14.03$$

Complex capital structures include potentially dilutive securities such as convertible bonds, convertible preferred stock, stock options and warrants. Public companies with complex capital structures are required to report both basic EPS and diluted EPS. Diluted EPS is calculated on the assumption that all dilutive securities are either converted (in the case of convertible securities) or exercised (in the case of share options and warrants) leading to an increase in the number of common shares in issue, and potentially an increase in net income. Any potentially dilutive securities that would increase EPS are anti-dilutive, and their conversion or exercise is not taken into account in the calculation.

To check whether a convertible security is anti-dilutive, compare the increase in net income as a result of the conversion to the number of common shares issued. If the increase in net income per share issued is greater than basic EPS, then the security is anti-dilutive.

To check whether a share option or warrant is anti-dilutive, compare its exercise price to the average share price for the year. Financial reporting standards require diluted EPS to be calculated using the 'Treasury Stock Method" which makes the assumption that all proceeds from the exercise of the option or warrant are used to repurchase shares in the open market at the average price for the year. Hence if the exercise price is higher than the average share price for the year, more shares could be repurchased than would be issued, and the share option or warrant is anti-dilutive.

Example 9.2

Sam's Stoked Snowboards, Inc. (SSS), a publicly traded company, has the following characteristics for the current year:

- Market value: $250 million
- Average market price: $50 per share
- Shares outstanding: 5 million
- Outstanding options: 200,000
- Average exercise price for options: $10
- Average tax rate: 25%[4]
- Net income: $25 million
- Debt of $10 million with an average cost of 5%, which is convertible into 200,000 shares

$$\text{Basic EPS} = \frac{\$25 \text{ million}}{5 \text{ million}} = \$5.00$$

Diluted EPS requires consideration of whether the share options and convertible bonds are dilutive. The 200,000 options have an exercise price of $10 per share which is lower than the average market price of $50, and hence they are dilutive. The total proceeds from issuing 200,0000 shares at an exercise price of $10 would be $2 million. To correctly calculate diluted EPS using the treasury stock method, it is assumed the $2 million proceeds are used to repurchase shares at the average price of $50, meaning the company could repurchase 40,000 shares, leaving a net increase of 160,000 shares from the exercise of the options. These 160,000 shares are added to the shares in issue in the denominator.

The bonds are convertible into 200,000 shares. If the bonds were converted, the company would no longer have to pay interest on them. Currently the interest on the debt equals $500,000. However, because interest is deductible, the net benefit to SSS equals $375,000 ($500,000 x (1 – 25% tax rate)).

Saving this interest represents an increase in net income of $1.875 per share issued ($375,000 for 200,000 shares issued). As this is less than the $5.00 basic EPS, the convertible bonds are dilutive. As a result, $375,000 is added to net income in the numerator of the diluted EPS calculation, and 200,000 shares are added to the denominator.

$$\text{Diluted EPS} = \frac{\$25 \text{ million} + \$375{,}000}{5 \text{ million} + 160{,}000 + 200{,}000} = \$4.73$$

The diluted EPS figure of $4.73 is lower than the basic EPS figure of $5.00 due to the impact of converting and exercising all of SSS's dilutive securities.

4. Federal rate of 21% plus state income tax rate.

When company revenues exceed expenses, companies have positive earnings or net income. A company has two choices with regard to any positive earnings. These earnings can be reinvested into the business in the form of new or existing projects, or paid out to the owners or shareholders of the corporation.[5] These payments to shareholders are referred to as cash dividends and typically signal that the company is financially healthy. Cash dividends also reduce the uncertainty of cash flows from an investment from an investor's point of view. Larger cash dividends, however, could also signal to the market that the company is struggling to find projects that generate a high enough return to justify investment.

From a theoretical standpoint, the company should reinvest additional earnings in new or existing projects if it is able to earn returns that are higher than shareholders could earn on their own. If there are no projects that meet the return requirement, then companies should pay the additional cash to shareholders in the form of dividends. The **payout ratio** equals a company's dividend payments divided by its earnings and provides information about the long-term sustainability of a company's dividend payments and policy.

$$\text{Payout Ratio} = \frac{\text{Dividends per Share}}{\text{Earnings per Share}}$$

Example 9.3

Colin Corporation (Colin) declares and pays a $1 common dividend (per share) each quarter of the year. Total annual dividends are $4 per share. Assume its EPS is $12. Colin's payout ratio equals 33.33%.

$$\text{Payout Ratio} = \frac{\$4}{\$12} = 33.33\%$$

Colin's payout ratio means that it retains 66.7% of its earnings and pays out 33.3% to shareholders as a dividend. Even if earnings decline, Colin should be able to maintain the $4 annual dividend payment per share of common stock because it only represents one-third of its current earnings.

CASE STUDY 9.2

MICROSOFT AND APPLE

In June 2021 Microsoft (MSFT) had a market capitalization in excess of $1.8 trillion but was eclipsed by Apple (AAPL) which became the first $2.0 trillion company in August 2020. Both companies had tremendous growth rates over a long period and historically did not pay dividends. Instead, earnings were reinvested to fuel growth or held as cash to deal with unexpected costs. However, Microsoft began paying dividends in 2003 and in 2012 Apple recommenced dividend payments for the first time since 1995. For the period 2016 to 2020 Microsoft's payout ratio averaged over 40%, while Apple's was slightly lower, averaging approximately 25%.

5. This excludes the idea that management may decide to pay it to themselves. It assumes management is fully and adequately compensated.

A lower payout ratio suggests that the dividend payments are more sustainable as they represent a small percentage of a company's EPS. Higher payout ratios suggest that a company does not have suitable alternative projects in which to invest. Payout ratios in excess of 100 percent occur when a company pays out more in cash dividends than it earns.

Companies may pay out more than 100 percent of earnings for a few reasons. In some cases, a company may have a substantial amount of cash, and thus may make dividend payments in excess of earnings. More often, however, a company may pay out more than 100 percent of its earnings to protect its dividend payments and dividend policy to shareholders. These situations are typically "red flags" to investors and may indicate serious issues with the operating performance of the company. In an attempt to protect its dividend payments, a company may even borrow funds or use available cash on the balance sheet.

The percent of income retained by a company is called its **retention ratio**. The retention ratio equals 1 minus the payout ratio or the difference between net income and dividend payments divided by net income.

$$\text{Retention Ratio} = \frac{\text{Net Income - Dividends}}{\text{Net Income}}$$

$$\text{Retention Ratio} = 1 - \text{Payout Ratio}$$

Dividend Payment Dates

Four dates are important when discussing the payment of a dividend. These dates are:

1. **The dividend declaration date** - The date when the board of directors declares a dividend payment. This action creates an obligation for the company to make a dividend payment.
2. **The ex-dividend date** - The ex-dividend date is generally set one business day before the date of record. Ex-dividend means that the stock trades "ex" or without the dividend distribution. If a stock is currently valued at $100 and the company declares a $5 dividend, then the stock should theoretically decline in value by $5 to a price of $95 on the ex-dividend date. From an economic standpoint, the shareholder is in the same position after the ex-dividend date as before. Prior to the dividend, the shareholders owned stock worth $100. After the dividend payment, the shareholders own shares of stock worth $95 and have a right to $5 in cash per share of stock owned. The day before the ex-dividend date is the last day the stock can be purchased in order to receive the dividend payment. Investors who purchase stock on the ex-dividend date or after will not receive the dividend payment. Instead, the seller of those shares will receive the dividend.

Quick Quiz 9.1

1. It is impossible to have a dividend payout ratio exceeding 100%.
   a. True
   b. False
2. A stock paying a quarterly dividend of 28 cents and trading for $56 has a dividend yield of 2%.
   a. True
   b. False
3. Mr. James sells his XYZ stock on July 15, three days before the date of record but after the date of declaration. Mr. James will receive the dividend.
   a. True
   b. False
4. A 25% stock dividend is expected to lower the price of a stock to 80% of its original price.
   a. True
   b. False

False, True, False, True.

3. **The record date** - When a company declares a dividend, it sets a date of record. The date of record is the date the company determines who owns the company stock for the purpose of receiving the dividend. If an investor bought the stock prior to the ex-dividend date, then he or she will be reflected as a common stock holder. The difference in time is due to the time it takes to settle stock trades. Generally, it takes two days after the execution of the purchase of a share of stock for the trade to settle.

4. **The payment date** - The **date of payment** is the date on which the dividend will actually be paid. Remember that the dividend will be paid to those who owned the shares as of the date of record. Anyone who sells his or her shares on or after the ex-dividend date will receive the dividend payment.

Example 9.4

Delle, Inc. declares a dividend on October 25th and sets the date of record as November 5th. The ex-dividend date is one business day before the date of record, which is November 4th. The date of payment is set as November 11th.

Date of Declaration October 25th	Day Before Ex-Date November 3rd	Ex-Dividend Date November 4th	Date of Record November 5th	Date of Payment November 11th

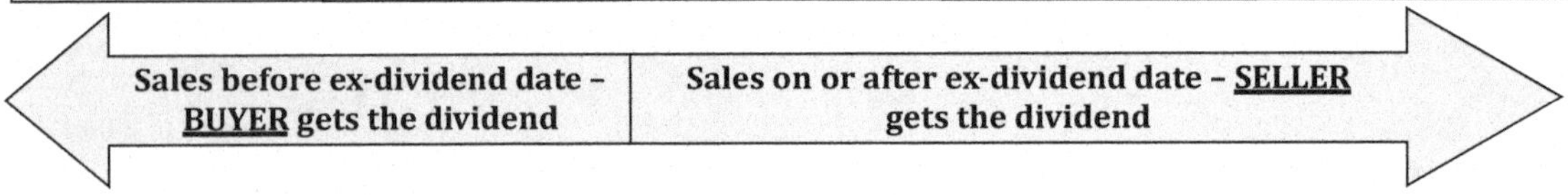

An investor who purchases the stock by November 3rd will be entitled to receive the dividend scheduled for payment on November 11th. An investor of Delle, Inc. stock who sells the stock on the ex-dividend date or after will also receive the dividend.

Dividend Yield

A company's dividend yield shows the annual divided payment as a percentage of the current share price. It shows investors how much income they are likely to receive as a percentage of the price they would have to pay to buy the stock. The formula for dividend yield is:

$$\text{Dividend Yield Percentage} = \frac{\text{Total Annual Dividends per Share}}{\text{Stock Price per Share}}$$

Example 9.5

Rome Company stock pays a $2 dividend each quarter. The stock is currently trading at $80 per share. Therefore, the dividend yield equals 10% ($8 ÷ $80). Naturally, the dividend yield will fluctuate as the price of the stock increases or decreases. If Rome Company increases to $100 per share, then the yield will decline to 8% presuming the dividend remains $2 per quarter.

Extraordinary Dividends

Extraordinary dividends, sometimes referred to as special dividends, are those dividend payments issued by a company that are outside of it's normal dividend policy. This type of dividend is paid out of cash that has been accumulated on the company's balance sheet. Many companies issued extraordinary dividends at the end of 2012, ahead of an expected increases in the federal income tax rates for dividends and capital gains, so that their shareholders could benefit from current lower tax rates.

DRIPs (Dividend Reinvestment Plans)

Dividend reinvestment plans, commonly referred to as DRIPs, are plans offered by companies that allow investors to purchase shares directly from the company, as opposed to through a broker. These plans allow investors to receive dividends in cash or to automatically reinvest the cash dividends in the company's stock. This automatic reinvestment allows DRIP participants to accumulate more shares over time. Each of these new shares will receive dividends and subsequent appreciation, which allows for significant compounding over time. From an income tax perspective, the dividends that are declared and reinvested are taxable in the year in which they are distributed (or reinvested).

Example 9.6

Marcie invests $9,000 in ABC's DRIP for her son, Linus. Marcie originally purchased 100 shares at $90 per share. Assuming ABC stock increases at an annual rate of 6% and pays a $2.00 dividend that increases at 2% per year, Linus will have over $50,000 in 25 years. The value of this investment will be approximately 16% higher than if the dividends were not reinvested.

Stock Dividends & Stock Splits

Instead of paying cash dividends, a company may instead declare a stock dividend. **Stock dividends** are shares or partial shares granted to shareholders based on ownership. For example, a company might declare a stock dividend of 0.1 shares (1 tenth of a share) for each share owned (10% stock dividend). A shareholder who owned 100 shares before the stock dividend would have 110 shares after the stock dividend. Theoretically, a stock dividend should not have any impact on the market value of the company in total, or the value of each individual shareholder's holding. There has been no change in the fundamental value of the company so the increase in the number of shares in issue should result in a proportional decrease in the value per share. In practice, however, the market price does not always respond in exactly this way.

A small stock dividend is generally less than 20 percent to 25 percent of the outstanding shares prior to the issuance of the dividend. A large stock dividend is a distribution of more than 20 percent to 25 percent of the outstanding shares prior to the issuance of the divided. There are differences between the financial accounting treatment of small stock dividends, large dividends, and stock splits, which are larger and are discussed below.

Example 9.7

Assume Frame Industries, which is trading at a market value of $100 per share, declares a 10% stock dividend. Also assume that Frame has one million shares of common stock outstanding. The market value of the company equals $100 million. After the 10% stock dividend, there will be 1.1 million shares outstanding and Frame's market value should remain the same. Therefore, the stock price for Frame should decrease from $100 per share to $90.91 per share. Shareholders are not enriched by the declaration of a stock dividend or stock split. They should simply have more shares trading at a lower price.

Stock splits are similar in concept to stock dividends, except they involve a larger number of new shares. A stock split increases the number of issued and outstanding shares of stock and also decreases the par value of the stock, whereas stock dividends do not impact par value per share.[6] A 2-for-1 stock split doubles the number of shares and reduces the par value per share in half. A 3-for-1 stock split triples the number of shares and reduces the par value per share to one-third.

Often, a company will declare a stock split when it perceives that its stock price (per round lot of 100 shares) is too high for the types of investors it seeks to attract. For example, a company might issue a two-for-one stock split, which means that each shareholder will receive two shares for each share owned. The stock split doubles the outstanding shares and should result in the market price per share decreasing by half. Theoretically, the market capitalization should remain the same.

Key Concepts

1. Generally a company's dividend policy remains constant over time.
2. Price appreciation of a stock is less reliable and predictable than dividend income.
3. Common shareholders have many rights, often including voting, limited liability, and maintaining ownership percentages.

Most shares of stock are bought and sold in lots of 100 shares. These lots of 100 shares are called **round lots**. By lowering the price of each share of stock, a stock split may increase the number of potential investors willing to purchase round lots of a company's stock. Of course, in the current trading environment, investors can purchase almost any number of shares using their on-line accounts. This makes a round-lot motivation for executing a stock split less likely.

Investors should be aware that the tax basis in each share of stock will change proportionally after a stock dividend or a stock split. The total basis, which is the amount of money that has been invested in the stock, does not change. However, the total tax basis must be spread over a larger number of shares.

Example 9.8

Apple split one more time after 2014, in 2020 with a 4 to 1 split.

Apple Inc stock has split five times since its initial public offering on December 12, 1980 at a price of $22 per share. The following table illustrates the historical split dates, the total shares as of 2022 and the basis per share.

Year	Description	Shares	Basis/Share
1980	Purchase IPO shares	1,000	$22.00
1987	2-for-1 split	2,000	$11.00
2000	2-for-1 split	4,000	$5.50
2005	2-for-1 split	8,000	$2.75
2014	7-for-1 split	56,000	$0.393
2020	4-for-1 split	224,000	$0.098

Note, the basis for an investor who purchased 1,000 shares in 1980 would still have the same $22,000 basis today.

6. The par value of common stock is the value assigned to the stock on the issuing corporation's balance sheet. It is typically a small value, such as $0.10 per share, and is not related to market value.

A **reverse stock split** occurs when a company wants to reduce the number of outstanding shares of corporate stock. A reverse stock split reduces the number of shares and increases the share price proportionately. Companies may use a reverse stock split so that the price of the stock increases in an attempt to avoid delisting on stock exchanges. Stocks that trade with a stock price below $1 are subject to delisting, which can result in the stock price dropping significantly as it is no longer visible to investors.

Example 9.9

Citigroup announced a 1:10 reverse stock split effective after the close of trading on May 6, 2011. If Laura owned 10,000 shares before the split, she would own 1,000 shares after the reverse stock split. If Laura had bought her shares at $40 per share, then she would have paid $400,000 plus a transaction fee. Assuming her transaction fee was $100, her tax basis equals $400,100, which does not change after the stock split. However, her tax basis will change from $40.01 to $400.10 per share of Citigroup.

Capital Appreciation

A company must choose how to use the earnings it generates. Even if a company is highly profitable, it may choose to retain its earnings and invest in additional projects. Assuming the capital projects are successful and the company generates additional net income, the company's stock price should increase. Investors in this type of company receive their return in the form of appreciation of the stock, which is referred to as capital appreciation. Apple is a good example of a company that historically did not pay dividends, but generated significant stock appreciation. **Exhibit 9.3** shows the price appreciation in Apple's share price (which is adjusted for stock splits) over a seventeen year period when it did not pay dividends.[7]

Exhibit 9.3 | Apple Stock Price

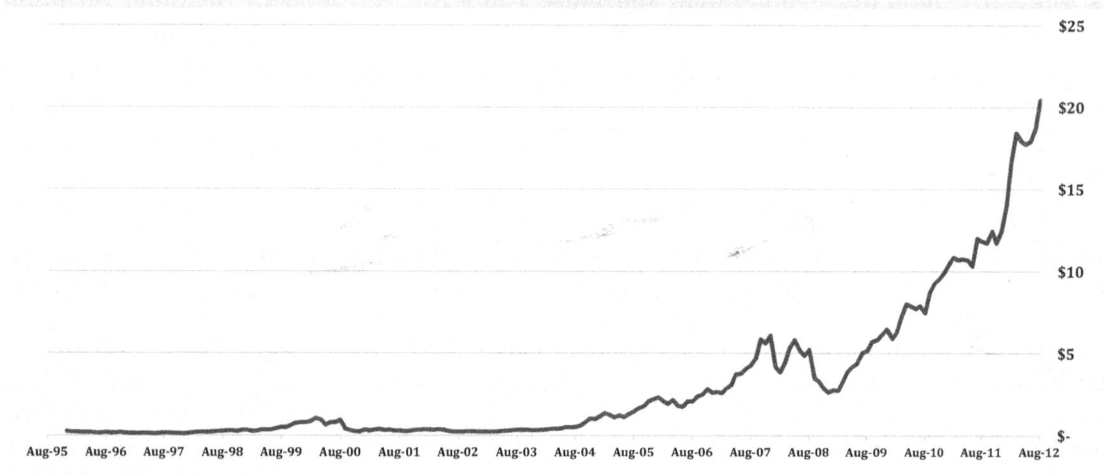

Shareholder View of Dividends vs. Capital Appreciation

There are two primary differences between dividend income and capital appreciation that need to be considered before answering the question, "Which is better?" The two primary differences between

7. Apple paid dividends in the late 1980s and early 1990s, but did not pay dividends again until 2012.

dividend income and capital appreciation are the differential income tax treatment and the differences in risk between the two income types.

Since 2003, most dividends are taxed at the same rate as long-term capital gains in the year in which the dividend payment is received.[8] Most companies that pay dividends do so on a quarterly basis, which results in taxable dividend income for shareholders each year.

The income tax rates for long-term capital gains range from zero percent to 20 percent.[9] Appreciation in the price of a stock is taxed as a capital gain, but is taxed only when the stock has been sold. If a stock is held for 20 years, then the capital gain income will be taxable only when the stock is ultimately sold. Therefore, from a tax standpoint, capital gains may be preferred over dividend income due to the deferral of taxation.

Although income from capital appreciation is preferable from a tax standpoint, for some investors dividend income may be preferable from a risk standpoint.

Once the dividend is paid, there is no further uncertainty attached to it and the investor is free to spend or invest it. Capital gains, however, are not realized until the stock is sold. A stock can lose several years' worth of capital appreciation in just a few days of volatile trading. In addition, dividend policies for the majority of companies tend to be stable, making the stream of dividend income more predictable than potential capital gains.

> **Quick Quiz 9.2**
>
> 1. Some investors prefer capital appreciation rather than dividends.
>   a. True
>   b. False
> 2. The choice of appreciation versus dividend income is often influenced by income tax policy.
>   a. True
>   b. False
> 3. The rights of shareholders include the right to receive a dividend, the right to vote for board seats, and the obligation to vote in person at annual meetings.
>   a. True
>   b. False
>
> True, True, False.

Investors with high liquidity needs might therefore value the certainty of dividend income over the prospect of riskier capital gains. Those with long-term investment horizons and lower immediate liquidity requirements have a higher risk tolerance and may be willing to take on the higher risk of waiting on capital appreciation in the hope of seeing a larger return.

Voting

In addition to the right to returns from dividend income and capital appreciation, owners of common stock have the right to vote on corporate matters. These voting rights include the right to vote for the board of directors and the right to vote on corporate issues, such as certain mergers and acquisitions.

Voting can take the form of straight voting or cumulative voting. **Straight voting (statutory voting)** authorizes one vote per share of common stock and is the most common form of voting. **Cumulative voting** allows one vote per share times the number of seats on the board of directors. Cumulative voting is used to protect minority shareholder interests. In addition, voting can be done in person or by proxy. **Proxy voting** involves sending a written authorization to an agent to cast the vote for the shareholder.

8. For dividends to be taxed at the long-term capital gain rates, they must be qualified dividends.
9. Note that these rates do not take into consideration the 3.8% net investment income tax for years after 2013. Tax rates for capital gains were not changed in the TCJA 2017.

Maintaining Ownership Percentage

Some companies permit owners to maintain their ownership percentage in the event of any new offering of their stock. For example, an investor who owned 10 percent of a company might be given the right to purchase 10 percent of any new stock offering. This right allows the owner to maintain his or her ownership percentage and is known as a **preemptive right**.

Liability

Because corporations are separate legal entities, they are responsible for all of their debts and claims arising from all sources. As a result, shareholders are protected from personal liability for corporate obligations. The corporation legally shields the personal assets of the shareholders from personal liability for the liabilities or actions of the corporation.

CASE STUDY 9.3

DEEPWATER HORIZON

In 2010, an explosion occurred on the Deepwater Horizon drilling rig in the Gulf of Mexico. This explosion resulted in an under water oil leak that became the largest oil spill in the history of the petroleum industry. BP Inc., which is one of the world's leading integrated oil and gas companies, was the primary operator of the Deepwater Horizon rig and was responsible for paying billions of dollars to those who were impacted by the massive oil spill and billions in fines to the U.S. Government. At no point were the shareholders of BP exposed to the liabilities as a result of the actions of the corporation.

In some cases, however, courts may hold shareholders liable for the debts or actions of their corporation. This shifting of responsibility is called **piercing the corporate veil**. It occurs infrequently and generally with small closely held corporations. Typically, piercing the corporate veil occurs in the context of a lawsuit in which the corporation does not act as a separate entity and acts more as an extension of the individual shareholders. It may also occur if the entity is undercapitalized or if fraud or injustice are involved.

CASE STUDY 9.4

DEWITT TRUCK BROKERS V. W. RAY FLEMMING FRUIT CO.

In Dewitt Truck Brokers v. W. Ray Flemming Fruit Co., 540 F.2d 681 (4th Cir. 1976), the court agreed that the district court's decision to pierce the corporate veil should be upheld and that Flemming should be held personally liable. W. Ray Flemming Fruit Co. was an agent for growers to sell produce. Flemming Company owed Dewitt money for transportation of goods, which it did not pay. Flemming had personally told Dewitt that he would pay them if his company failed to pay. Dewitt sued Flemming personally. The district court agreed to pierce the corporate veil. The reason for the decision was that the company, which was substantially undercapitalized, never held shareholder meetings and Flemming was the only one that was paid from the company. Additionally, Flemming simply took money from the company for his personal use. In short, he did not operate the entity as a separate entity from himself.

Liquidation

When a corporation terminates and liquidates, for any reason, the common shareholders have a right to the remaining assets (net of liabilities) in the corporation. If assets are distributed to common shareholders, the shareholders will receive those assets on a prorated basis based on their ownership interest.

Corporations can be voluntarily or involuntarily dissolved. Voluntary dissolutions occur based on the vote of shareholders. Involuntary dissolutions typically occur through a court proceeding, such as bankruptcy.

A corporation that is going to be dissolved must comply with state dissolution laws and distribute assets in an orderly manner based on various preferences. Secured creditors are the first to be paid from the assets of a company. Secured creditors are owed a debt from the company and have a claim on specific assets of the company, such as equipment or machinery. To the extent that there are sufficient assets in the company, secured creditors will be fully satisfied before unsecured creditors are paid for the debts they are owed. Unsecured creditors may include banks, taxing authorities, employees, partners, or suppliers. Once creditors are satisfied, preferred stock holders will next receive funds. Finally, if there are any assets left, common stockholders will receive their proportion of the assets remaining based on their ownership interest.

Quick Quiz 9.3

1. Straight voting protects minority shareholders.
   a. True
   b. False
2. The right to maintain your proportional interest is called the preemptive right.
   a. True
   b. False
3. The shareholders in a corporation have limited liability.
   a. True
   b. False

False, True, True.

Example 9.10

James and Robin want to go into business together and run a taco truck. They establish a corporation in the state of Louisiana named JRRJ, Inc. James contributes $15,000 in cash and $5,000 of equipment to JRRJ. Robin contributes $30,000. They both plan on working in the business and agree that James will own 40% of the business and Robin will own 60% of the business. They agree that they need additional capital and borrow $60,000 from their Grandpa Mike.

With the help of their parents and grandpa, James and Robin successfully operate the taco truck for three years. At that point, they decide they want to do something different. Over the last three years, they have repaid Grandpa Mike $10,000 of principal. They sell the taco truck for $95,000, because it is in great shape and is outfitted with high quality kitchen equipment. Assume that after the sale of the taco truck they have cash of $250,000 in the bank. As part of dissolving the corporation, they must pay back their creditors. In this case it is Grandpa Mike, to whom they owe $50,000. Paying him leaves them $200,000 to distribute to themselves (shareholders). Robin and James will receive $120,000 and $80,000, respectively, along with having received a lifetime of business experience and other important lessons.

TYPES OF EQUITY SECURITIES

Equity securities are typically thought of as common stock. However, there are other types of equity securities that are discussed within this section, including preferred stock, treasury stock and classified common stock.

> **Key Concepts**
>
> 1. There are a wide variety of ways to classify common stock.
> 2. Other than common stock, equity types include preferred, treasury, and classified stock.

Common Stock

Common stock represents an ownership interest in a company. If the company is financially successful, the investor will receive positive returns from the investment. However, if the company does not perform well, the value of the common stock will most likely decline. Since there are thousands of companies, classification systems have been developed to categorize equity securities. One such classification system is based on the type of the stock. This classification system includes defensive stocks, cyclical stocks, blue-chip stocks, growth stocks, income stocks, interest-sensitive stocks, value stocks, new economy stocks, and tech stocks.

Defensive Stocks

As discussed in Chapter 3, stocks are subject to systematic risk. Macroeconomic factors cause markets to rise and fall over time, but not all stocks are affected to the same extent. Defensive stocks are less volatile than the market, their low beta means they post only moderate gains during economic booms but hold up well during recessions. Many of these companies provide products and services that are necessary for everyday life, such as food, health care and household products. Thus, the demand for these products is not adversely affected by changing economic cycles. Since the relative demand for these products does not change, the demand for these products is considered inelastic. A good example of a product that is classified as a necessity is toothpaste. In times of economic boom, consumers are unlikely to significantly increase their consumption of toothpaste. Similarly, demand should remain stable in a recession.

Defensive stocks are usually found in the following industries: utilities, beverages, retail food, confectionery, pharmaceutical, healthcare, and consumer staples.

Cyclical Stocks

Cyclical stocks tend to prosper during expanding economic times and tend to do poorly during contracting business cycles. When the economy is growing, demand strengthens, and these companies are able to make large profits. When the economy is in a downturn, these companies are hurt by declines in demand and are less profitable. In recessions, cyclical companies begin cost cutting measures to improve the operating efficiency and earnings and, as a result, these companies end up in a healthy financial position for the next economic upturn. Companies regarded as cyclicals usually have large investments in plant and equipment and, therefore, have high fixed costs. Cyclical stocks are commonly found in sectors providing goods and services that are tied to the performance of the economy such as: automobiles, cement, paper, airlines, railroads, machinery, steel.

Because these stocks typically perform well when the economy is expanding and perform poorly when the economy is contracting, cyclical stocks are highly correlated with the overall stock market. In addition, these stocks typically have higher betas than the overall market.

Blue-Chip Stocks

Stocks issued by highly regarded investment-quality companies are called blue-chip stocks. These companies tend to be older, well-established companies that maintain their ability to pay dividends both in years the company has earnings and in years the company has losses. These companies are generally leaders in their respective industries. They tend to offer investors quality investments with both steady dividend streams and relatively consistent growth and capital appreciation. Examples of blue-chip stocks include Proctor & Gamble, Home Depot, ExxonMobil, Wal-Mart, IBM, Apple, Amazon, Coca-Cola, and Johnson and Johnson.

Although blue-chip companies are by definition high-quality, sound financial companies, are they good investments? The answer to this question depends on a variety of issues related to the particular company. However, some good companies may be poor investments. This distinction occurs because the price for quality companies may be so high that it makes the investment a poor decision.

Growth Stocks

Growth stocks represent ownership in companies who have demonstrated above average growth when compared to their peers or the industry as a whole. High revenue or earnings growth and the potential for sizeable capital gains mean that these stocks are often characterized by high Price to Earnings (P/E) ratios.

Those strong earnings and the potential for further growth make growth stocks an attractive investment opportunity, but there also downsides to owning a growth stock. In order fuel the high growth, earnings must be reinvested and hence many growth companies do not pay out dividends. Apple, for example, grew significantly between 1995 and 2012 but did not pay out any dividends in that entire seventeen-year stretch.

A lack of dividends leaves investors relying on uncertain future capital appreciation for gains, rather than a steady income stream. This may not be suitable for those with short-term liquidity needs.

Emerging growth stocks differ from growth stocks in that they are smaller and younger companies who have survived their start-up period and are on the cusp of expansion and growth. Whilst the potential for capital appreciation from emerging growth stocks is large, the associated risk is similarly high, large market swings can put extreme pressure on a young companies' ability to survive.

Income Stocks

Some stocks are attractive because they make large divided payments relative to other companies in the economy. Often these companies are in the mature phase of their industry life cycle and pay out a significant percentage of their earnings in the form of dividends (high payout ratio). These stocks generally appreciate moderately, but the companies continue to be profitable and grow over time (usually at the GDP growth rate). Johnson & Johnson (JNJ) has been a favorite stock for investors seeking a steady income stream for many years. In 2021 the company had a dividend yield over two percent and a payout ratio of over 70 percent.

Interest Sensitive Stocks

The performance of some companies is significantly affected by changes in interest rates. Their stocks are considered interest sensitive stocks. For example, the housing industry is more productive and has more demand when interest rates are low, in part, because it is less expensive for consumers to purchase homes. When interest rates increase, the cost of purchasing homes goes up, causing the demand for new homes to decline. These trends also affect lumber, plumbing, furnishing, and household equipment companies. Rising interest rates cause the cost of debt to increase; therefore, companies that have large amounts of debt have increasing interest expense. These companies, like consumers, have the opportunity to refinance their debt during low interest rate periods.

Companies that are significantly affected by interest rates include: insurance companies, savings and loans, commercial banks, telephone companies, utility companies, and home construction companies.

Value Stocks

Stocks trading at prices that are low based on their historical earnings and current asset value are referred to as value stocks. These securities tend to have low price-to-earnings ratios and tend to be currently out of favor in the market. Value investors attempt to find these high quality companies temporarily undervalued by the market in hopes that the market will ultimately recognize their true value, and the stock's price will increase. A value stock may also have a very strong balance sheet in which a large percentage of the market capitalization is supported by cash and other liquid and non-liquid assets the company owns.

Warren Buffett, who is one of the most famous investors, is classically a value investor. He looks for securities with prices that are artificially low based on his perception of the company's intrinsic value. In his 2008 Chairman's letter to Berkshire Hathaway Inc. shareholders, Buffet wrote:

> "Long ago, Ben Graham taught me that 'Price is what you pay; value is what you get.' Whether we're talking about socks or stocks, I like buying quality merchandise when it is marked down."

Buffet's quote epitomizes the value approach to investing.

New Economy Stocks

During the early part of the year 2000, the term "new economy stocks" became popular. This new term was used to describe the stocks within the technology industry that were expected to benefit greatly from the popularity and mainstreaming of the Internet. These companies included companies selling products to consumers directly over the Internet, such as Amazon, eBay, Yahoo!, and numerous others, some of which are now out of business. In addition, companies providing access to the Internet, such as cable companies and telephone companies, were benefiting from the new economy. Providers of computer hardware, such as Cisco Systems, were seeing tremendous growth and prosperity due to the demand for Internet systems.

Within a short time period, these companies and many more have benefited from the Internet. The media hype on Internet and technology stocks led many to believe that we had entered a new era and that traditional methods of valuation were somehow outdated and out of touch with the new economy. During the latter part of 2000 and in 2001, the euphoria of the Internet and technology stocks dissipated and the markets took a nosedive, losing more than 60 percent of their market capitalization. Investors found that despite the hype, traditional valuation models do work. Those valuation models are primarily driven by cash flows available to shareholders.

Tech Stocks

Tech stocks include stocks in the technology sector that are involved in the research, development, and distribution of goods and services. Industries within the technology sector include: computer hardware and storage, IT services and consulting, software, communications equipment, and semiconductors.

From May 2006 to May 2016, the S&P 500 index increased in value over 60 percent. During this same time, the technology sector increased by more than 120 percent. While the technology sector was not the very best performing sector, it was one of the better ones.

Socially Responsible and Impact Stocks

Some investors choose to include in their portfolio only stocks of companies that support the investor's moral and ethical beliefs, or choose to avoid owning the stocks of companies that do not support their moral or ethical beliefs. For example, an investor may choose to avoid companies that produce or sell addictive substances such as tobacco, alcohol, gambling, or marijuana companies. As an alternative to filtering out certain types of companies, a socially responsible investor may actively seek companies that support the investor's social, moral, or religious beliefs, or companies that invest substantially in their communities. In recent years there has been an increased interest in "impact investing." Impact investing focuses on the stocks of companies that have a positive measurable social or environmental impact, such as companies that produce sustainable agriculture, renewable energy, and affordable housing. Well known companies included in the S&P Global 1200 ESG (Environmental, Social, and Governance) Index include Microsoft, Apple, Amazon, Johnson & Johnson, Exxon Mobile Corp, and Nestle.

Market Cap Classification

In addition to the classifications discussed above, there are other ways to classify equity securities. Equities can be segregated by:

1. Sectors of the economy (healthcare, energy, technology)
2. Size or market capitalization (large-cap, mid-cap, small-cap)
3. Domestic versus foreign

While the amounts have changed over the years, the structure remains the same when classifying equities based on market capitalization. **Market capitalization** is defined as the outstanding shares for a company times the current share price. If a company has 50 million shares that are trading at a price of $25 per share, then the market capitalization equals $1.25 billion. The market capitalization of a company determines whether it is classified as a large-cap, mid-cap, or small-cap stock.

Large-cap stocks are generally defined as companies with a market capitalization of at least $10 billion. Within this category are companies that have market capitalizations in excess of $200 billion. These companies are often referred to as **mega caps**. As of mid-2021, Apple's (AAPL) market cap exceeded $2 trillion while Google's parent company Alphabet's (GOOG) total market cap was over $1.6 trillion, putting them both firmly in the mega-cap category. In the retail sector, Home Depot (HD) had a market cap of over $300 billion, again qualifying as a mega-cap stock, whereas its competitor in the home improvement space, Lowes (LOW),

> ### Quick Quiz 9.4
>
> 1. Defensive stocks are generally less affected by changes in the economy than other stocks.
>   a. True
>   b. False
> 2. Cyclical stocks tend to lead or follow the economy.
>   a. True
>   b. False
> 3. Value stocks are usually out of favor stocks with low PE ratios.
>   a. True
>   b. False
>
> True, True, True.

sat at $130 billion, towards the top of the large-cap classification. At the same date retail giant WalMart (WMT) had a market capitalization of nearly $300 billion, classifying it as a mega-cap, while its large-cap competitor Target (TGT) had a market cap nearer $115 billion. All of these mega- and large-cap companies are dominant in their industries.

CASE STUDY 9.5

APPLE

Beginning in 2013, Apple began repurchasing its stock from shareholders. From 2013 through 2016, it used more than $100 billion in cash to repurchase stock. In isolation, this should have increased the price per share. However, the markets do not function in isolation and over this time the stock has both increased and decreased significantly. In May 2018, Apple announced that it would increase its share repurchase program to $310 billion.[1]

1. Source: Apple Press Releases

Mid-cap stocks are generally defined as companies with market capitalizations in excess of $2 billion, but less than $10 billion. These companies are generally fairly well established, but do not have the size or market share of large-cap stocks. Investors expect the returns for mid-cap stocks to exceed the returns for large-cap stocks and to be less volatile than returns for small-cap stocks. Bed, Bath & Beyond with a market cap in mid-2021 of $3.5 billion is an example of a mid-cap stock in the retail sector.

Exhibit 9.4 | Market Capitalization

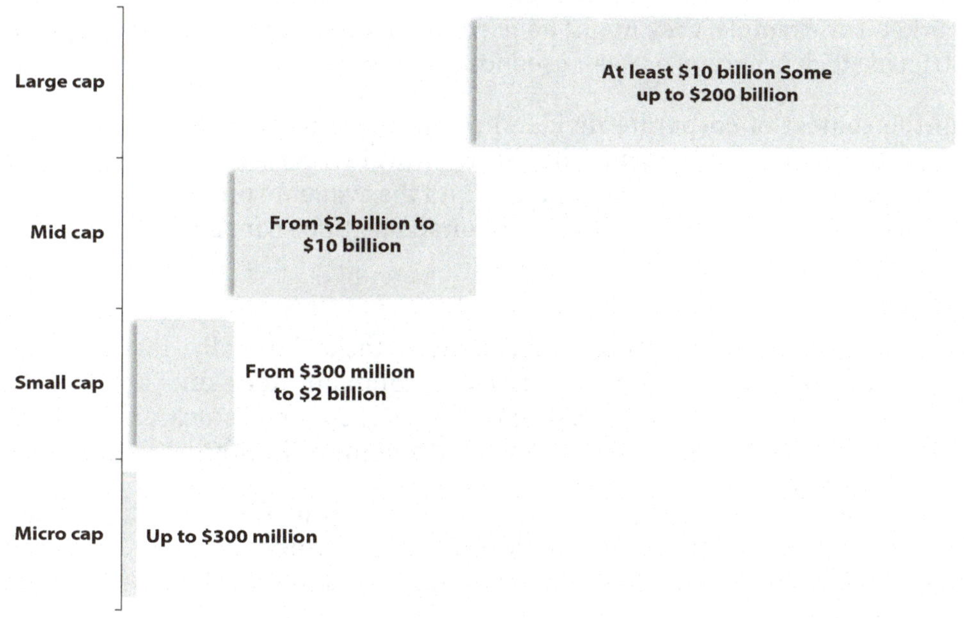

Small-cap stocks are generally defined as companies with market capitalizations less than $2 billion. Within this category are stocks with a market capitalization of less than $300 million. These are often referred to as **micro-cap stocks**. In some cases, companies with a market capitalization of less than $50 million are referred to as nano cap stocks. Small cap stocks are often younger companies that are positioned earlier in the industry life cycle and have great growth potential. However, these stocks tend to be riskier than those with higher capitalization, with many going out of business in the short to intermediate term. Rite Aid, the U.S. based retail drug store chain is a well known small-cap company with market cap in mid-2021 of just over $1 billion.

Treasury Stock

Treasury stock is stock repurchased by a corporation from its shareholders and held in its treasury. A company will typically repurchase its own stock when it believes that the stock is undervalued by the market. The result of a repurchase initiative is to reduce the number of outstanding shares in the market. Companies that engage in this type of buyback program often have excess cash on their balance sheets. Buybacks act as selective dividends as those investors wishing to leave the company sell stock and those believing in the long run prospects retain the stock.

The effect of this type of buyback program on the balance sheet of a company is a reduction in cash, no change in liabilities and a reduction in owner's equity. Assuming earnings remain constant, EPS should increase since the same amount of net income is being spread over a smaller number of outstanding shares. The overall impact on the total value of the firm should be minimal, but the share price should increase since the cash flow per share is increasing.

Once purchased, treasury shares are kept by the corporation and may be used for purposes other than resale in the market. For example, they might be used as part of a compensatory employee stock option program, a restricted stock program, or even used for mergers and acquisitions.

As discussed in the context of corporate dividend programs, if a company has projects that have the potential for high returns, then the company should generally invest excess cash in those projects. When a company has more cash than required to adequately fund the available projects, a company may decide to engage in dividend programs, repurchase programs, or acquisitions (or some of each).

Classified Stock

Companies may have more than one class of common stock. Generally, the benefits and rights of shareholders are the same for the various classes of common stock and are based on ownership percentage. However, companies can create multiple classes of common stock, each with a different set of rights. These differences might include varying dividend amounts or different voting rights.

While some large publicly traded companies, such as Ford Motor Company, have multiple classes of shares, it is not exclusive to large companies. Small privately held companies may also issue class A shares and class B shares. Often this is done to preserve voting rights and control for the family owning the business.

Exhibit 9.5 | Excerpt From Facebook's IPO Prospectus

"We have two classes of common stock, Class A common stock and Class B common stock. The rights of the holders of Class A common stock and Class B common stock are identical, except voting and conversion rights. Each share of Class A common stock is entitled to one vote. Each share of Class B common stock is entitled to ten votes and is convertible at any time into one share of Class A common stock. The holders of our outstanding shares of Class B common stock will hold approximately 96.0% of the voting power of our outstanding capital stock following this offering, and our founder, Chairman, and CEO, Mark Zuckerberg, will hold or have the ability to control approximately 55.9% of the voting power of our outstanding capital stock following this offering."

Stock Spin-Offs

Companies may use free cash flow to engage in mergers and acquisitions. Often, these acquisitions are undertaken for the purpose of controlling another aspect of a company's supply chain, to roll up a competitor, or to control distribution of its product offering. Over time, however, companies can become too big to react to changes in the markets in which they operate. In addition, these large companies often become significantly more bureaucratic and less entrepreneurial. They can become "too diversified" and are no longer able to create innovative products. In these cases, management may make the decision to spin-off a successful division or subsidiary of the company.

The purpose of this type of strategy is to create value for shareholders and involves distributing the shares of the subsidiary to the existing shareholders of the company. In some cases, the company that is spun off may increase in value relative to the parent company. Often, the smaller spin-off has more freedom and autonomy to pursue growth strategies. There will be more visability of financial information for the spin-off because, as a separate entity, it must provide financial statements to shareholders. In addition, there may be more transparency for the new firm in terms of value and opportunity.

From a tax perspective, shareholders must prorate their tax basis between the two companies. As part of a spin-off, the company will provide basis information to the shareholders so that they can keep track of their tax basis information.

CASE STUDY 9.6

HEWLETT-PACKARD (HP)

1934: After graduating as electrical engineers from Stanford University, Bill Hewlett and Dave Packard become close friends.

1938: HP creates its first product for Walt Disney.

1957: HP goes public.

1961: HP is listed on NYSE.

1980: HP introduces its first personal computer, the HP-85.

1981: The initial introduction of the HP12C calculator. This is HP's longest and best selling calculator.

2002: HP and Compaq merge.

2014: HP is 75 years old.

2014: HP announces it will split into two publicly traded companies: Hewlett Packard Enterprise and HP Inc.

The purpose of the HP split in 2014 was to create better operating environments for both entities and ultimately increase shareholder value. Time will tell as to whether or not this strategy is successful.

Shareholders in the HP split received shares of both companies. The separation occurred by means of a pro rata distribution to HP Co. shareholders of 100% of the outstanding shares of Hewlett Packard Enterprise. Each HP Co. stockholder received one share of Hewlett Packard Enterprise common stock for every one share of HP Co. common stock held on October 21, 2015, the record date for the distribution. Consequently, the separation provided HP Co. stockholders with ownership interest in both HP Inc. (stock ticker HPQ) and Hewlett Packard Enterprise (HPE). These shares can now be traded independently. For example, if a shareholder held 100 shares of HPQ (HP Co.) before the separation, he or she would now hold 100 shares of HPQ and 100 shares of HPE.

On November 2, 2015, the day of the HP split, the average opening/closing trading prices were $13.15 for HP Co. and $14.74 for Hewlett Packard Enterprise. Based on these share prices, HP shareholders would split their tax basis between the two new companies with 47.15% to HP Co. and 52.85% to Hewlett Packard Enterprise.

At various points in time, mergers and acquisitions become in vogue. At other times, spin-offs become popular among large firms. Ultimately, both strategies are intended to create shareholder value. In some cases, that goal is achieved. However, in many other cases, it turns out to be a waste of time and resources.

Preferred Stock

Preferred stock has characteristics of both fixed-income and equity securities. Shareholders of preferred stock generally receive preferential dividends each year equal to a stated percentage of the par value of the stock if the corporation declares them. For instance, a $100 par, 5.5 percent issue of preferred stock pays a dividend of $5.50 each year for each preferred share owned. The corporation must generally satisfy these preferred dividend payments each year before paying any dividend to the common shareholders. If the corporation is required to pay any unpaid preferred dividends from prior years before paying a dividend to common stockholders, the preferred stock is referred to as **cumulative**.

Example 9.11

Denton Company has decided to distribute $100,000 as cash dividends. It has 20,000 shares of common stock outstanding and 2,000 shares of preferred stock. The preferred stock has a par value of $100 and receives an 8% dividend that is noncumulative. Assume that preferred dividends have not been paid for two years. The chart below illustrates the distribution of cash between common and preferred shareholders.

	Shares	Dividend
Preferred stock, $100 par value, 8% dividend	2,000	$16,000
Common stock ($15 par value)	20,000	$84,000
Total		**$100,000**

The dividend to the common stock shareholders equates to a dividend of $4.20 per share. Assuming that the preferred stock is cumulative, then the distribution of the dividend payments would be as follows:

	Shares	Dividend
Preferred stock dividends in arrears	2,000	$32,000
Preferred stock, $100 par value, 8% dividend	2,000	$16,000
Common stock	20,000	$52,000
Total		**$100,000**

With cumulative preferred, the company must make up any unpaid dividends before paying any dividends to the common shareholders. As a result, the common dividend equals $2.60 per share instead of $4.20 per share.

Preferred stock may also be **participating**, meaning that preferred shareholders share in the profits of the corporation. With participating preferred, the preferred shareholders receive dividend payments first. Then, holders of common stock receive dividends equal (in percent terms) to the amount paid to the preferred shareholders. Additional funds for dividends are then allocated between the participating preferred and common shareholders according to stock agreements.

Example 9.12

Assume the same facts as in **Example 9.11**. Assume that Denton is distributing $100,000 as a cash dividend. However, assume that the preferred stock is fully participating and cumulative and there have been no dividends to preferred shareholders in two years. The following chart illustrates the allocation of the dividend payments:

	Total Par Value	Dividend
Preferred stock dividends in arrears	$200,000	$32,000
Preferred stock dividend @ 8%	$200,000	$16,000
Common stock dividend @ 8%	$300,000	$24,000
Preferred stock participating dividend @ 5.6%	$200,000	$11,200
Common stock participating dividend @ 5.6%	$300,000	$16,800
		$100,000

In this example, the preferred dividends are made up prior to any dividends being paid for the current year because the preferred stock is cumulative. Next, the preferred dividend is paid based on its 8% dividend. Then a common stock dividend is paid that is proportional based on par value. The preferred stock has a par value of $200,000. The common stock has a par value of $300,000. Therefore, the preferred stock makes up 40% of the par value and thus, shares in 40% of the participating profits. The common stock makes up 60% of the par value and thus, shares in 60% of the participating profits. The first three payments above total $72,000, which leaves $28,000 of participating profits. These are divided 40% to preferred and 60% to common.

Preferred stock has a preferential right in liquidation over common shareholders to the assets of the corporation equal to the par value of the stock. This right must be satisfied before the common shareholders receive any assets upon liquidation or acquisition. However, secured and unsecured creditors must be paid before preferred shareholders receive any assets of the corporation.

Convertible preferred stock has a conversion right that allows holders to redeem or trade in their preferred stock for a specified number of common shares. Convertible preferred stock provides the safety of a fixed-income security with the growth potential of a common stock.

Exhibit 9.6 | Examples of Preferred Stock

Company	Ticker Symbol	Market Price	Annual Dividend	Dividend Yield
The Goldman Sachs Group, Inc.	GS-PK	$29.34	$1.59	5.43%
JP Morgan Chase & Co.	JPM-PC	$28.33	$1.50	5.29%
Allstate Corp	ALL-PB	$26.98	$1.28	4.74%
MetLife, Inc.	MET-PA	$25.99	$1.01	3.90%

Source: preferred-stock.com June 7, 2021.

Preferred stock may also be issued with an embedded call feature. Callable preferred stock allows the issuing company to call the stock from the shareholder at a premium above par value. This type of feature is a benefit to the issuing company. Just as with callable bonds, the company can lower the cost of capital by exercising the call in the event that interest rates have dropped below the rates on the outstanding preferred stock. Since this call feature does not benefit investors, callable preferred stock generally has higher yields than non-callable preferred stock to attract investors who wish to take this risk.

Recall that preferred stocks are similar to bonds. They are sometimes thought of as a hybrid investment security. The value of preferred stock is primarily based on the cash flows or dividend payments and the prevailing interest rates. When evaluating preferred stock, it is important to understand whether the company has the ability to pay the preferred dividends. Rating agencies, such as Moody's, evaluate preferred stock in addition to bonds. These ratings can help determine the level of risk inherent in a preferred stock issue. Calculations of value for preferred stock are discussed in Chapter 11.

There are several types of preferred stock, which may or may not receive favorable tax treatment on dividend payments. Many preferred stock dividends are qualified and therefore receive favorable tax treatment and are taxed at the same rates as long-term capital gains. Other preferred stock dividends are not qualified and do not receive this favorable tax treatment.

Foreign Securities

Although the financial markets in the United States are the largest in the world, as measured by market capitalization, they only represent approximately half of the world financial market capitalization.[10] The other half of all publicly traded companies are outside of the United States. As a result, **foreign securities** may provide significant opportunities to United States investors for several reasons.

First, securities outside the U.S. have substantial return potential. Many of the countries outside the U.S. are less developed and, therefore, provide opportunities for significant growth. Second, the degree of efficiency found in foreign markets is likely less than that of the US markets, with the exception of the established exchanges in locations such as London, Tokyo, and Shanghai. Emerging markets, however, might provide substantial opportunities to trade mis-priced securities. Third, foreign securities provide benefits of diversification. The returns and movements in the equity markets of most foreign countries are not highly correlated with those of the U.S. market. Therefore, adding foreign asset classes to a portfolio may increase the efficiency of the portfolio.

Foreign securities are generally classified as being from developed countries or emerging markets. Foreign developed countries include countries such as Canada, Japan, England, and France. Emerging markets include those countries with significant growth potential, but that are currently underdeveloped. Examples of emerging markets include Argentina, Brazil, Chile, Taiwan, and Venezuela. The returns from emerging market countries are generally less correlated to the returns of the U.S. market than that of developed countries. However, the returns of emerging markets can be extremely volatile.

There are currently several methods for U.S. investors to invest in foreign securities. These include purchasing American Depositary Receipts, foreign shares on foreign stock exchanges, international iShares and investing in international mutual funds, international ETFs, and international closed-end funds. **American Depositary Receipts (ADRs)** are one of the easiest methods of acquiring individual foreign securities. They are certificates issued by U.S. banks representing ownership in shares of stock of

10. See Credit Suisse Global Investment Returns Yearbook 2019.

a foreign company that are held on deposit in a bank in the firm's home country. ADRs are denominated in U.S. dollars and pay dividends in U.S. dollars. Although they are denominated in U.S. currency, they do not protect holders from exchange rate risk. Changes in currency rates between the firm's currency and the U.S. dollar will be reflected by a change in the value of the ADR.

ADRs are considered "cross listed" since the foreign shares are listed on the U.S. stock exchange as well as the foreign exchange. One of the benefits of ADRs is that the foreign company must satisfy the requirements of U.S. exchanges including compliance with U.S. GAAP (Generally Accepted Accounting Principles) and certain disclosure and reporting requirements.[11]

Foreign Mutual Funds and ETFs

Today, numerous mutual funds and ETFs have the objective of investing internationally. These foreign funds provide investors with one of the easiest methods of investing in foreign markets in the context of a diversified portfolio. These foreign funds have a variety of objectives, including investing in companies from specific regions of the world to investing in foreign securities with varying market capitalization. Global funds invest in securities throughout the world, while foreign and international funds strictly invest outside the United States. Mutual funds are discussed in detail in Chapter 12.

Foreign Closed-End Funds

Foreign closed-end funds provide the same basic benefits as foreign mutual funds. However, because closed-end funds trade on exchanges, they do not have the cash inflow and outflow that mutual funds frequently experience. This fixed capitalization allows managers of closed-end funds to invest in less liquid securities without fear that investors will wish to liquidate their positions, forcing the manager to liquidate the illiquid securities in the portfolio.

Purchasing Foreign Shares on Foreign Stock Exchanges

Direct purchasing of foreign securities on foreign exchanges is more difficult than indirect purchasing. However, with the advance of technology, the process has become simpler. Establishing a brokerage account in a foreign country or using a foreign branch of a U.S. broker are both methods that can be used to purchase foreign shares on foreign exchanges. These foreign transactions require completion in the local currency. In addition, monitoring direct foreign investments is more difficult than monitoring a mutual fund.

Today, many companies have products that are sold throughout the world. These international companies have great opportunities in new international markets, but are also subject to the economic ups and downs throughout the world. Apple, for example, sells its iPhone in many countries outside of the United States. If sales for a new product in one part of the world are lower than expected, it can put negative pressure on the value of the company. Thus, today, investors have the ability to invest in domestic securities, foreign securities, or international securities, either directly or indirectly via mutual funds or ETFs.

11.Companies can also use IFRS (International Financial Reporting Standards).

EQUITY MARKETS AND BENCHMARKS

Typically, the discussion of investing in equity securities means investing in publicly-traded equity securities. However, there are investors who specialize in investing in equity securities that are private, rather than publicly traded. This section addresses publicly-traded equity securities, which provide many advantages over other types of securities. These securities are available to purchase and are marketable, meaning that they can be sold rapidly at the available market price. In contrast to fixed-income securities, publicly-traded equity securities have historically earned far greater returns. In fact, stocks have had a better long-term investment return than any other asset class. However, it is interesting to note that less than one percent of all companies are publicly traded. In fact, according to the U.S. Census, there are approximately 5.7 million firms in the United States with employees.[12]

Key Concepts

1. There are advantages to going public.
2. Most companies are not publicly traded.
3. Markets include the primary, secondary, third and fourth markets.

Of these, less than 5,000 firms are publicly traded. In addition, the number of publicly-traded firms has decreased significantly over the last twenty years.

The Wilshire 5000 Total Market Index (Wilshire 5000) attempts to measure the performance of all publicly traded firms in the United States. In 1998, the Wilshire 5000 included 7,562 companies, while only 3,500 on March 31, 2021.[13]

The decrease in the number of publicly-traded firms is due, at least in part, to governmental compliance requirements, including those that are part of Sarbanes-Oxley.[14] Sarbanes-Oxley (often referred to as SOX), was intended to provide protection for investors after several high profile bankruptcies resulting from fraud and accounting. One of these, Enron, was highlighted earlier in the chapter.

Initial Public Offering

In an **initial public offering (IPO)**, a corporate entity offers its shares for sale to the general investing public for the first time. Commonly referred to as "going public" or "floating", an IPO is a method of raising equity in the primary markets by reaching a wide range of potential investors. Once the shares have been issued, they will be available for trading between investors in the secondary market. Although public companies are subject to additional auditing and reporting requirements, the liquidity provided by the secondary markets is just one of several advantages of raising capital via an IPO.

12. 2012 County Business Patterns and 2012 Economic Census & http://www.census.gov/econ/susb/data/susb2012.html
13. https://wilshire.com/Portals/0/analytics/indexes/fact-sheets/wilshire-5000-fact-sheet.pdf
14. On July 30, 2002, President Bush signed into law the Sarbanes-Oxley Act of 2002, which he characterized as "the most far reaching reforms of American business practices since the time of Franklin Delano Roosevelt." The Act mandated a number of reforms to enhance corporate responsibility, enhance financial disclosures and combat corporate and accounting fraud, and created the "Public Company Accounting Oversight Board," also known as the PCAOB, to oversee the activities of the auditing profession.

Advantages of Going Public

Raising Capital (Cash)

Cash raised from an IPO may be used to fund projects, acquisitions, or buyouts of original shareholders as a liquidity event. In many cases, owners of companies that go public will cash out part of their ownership as part of the IPO process. However, many companies use the infusion of cash from a public stock offering to execute a growth strategy, which might include a series of acquisitions, or increased focus on new product development.

Example 9.13

Facebook, which has more than 1 billion daily active users, held its initial public offering (IPO) on Friday, May 18, 2012. It was one of the biggest technology company IPOs of all time, raising $16 billion for the company and valuing it at over $100 billion. As part of its equity structure, Facebook has a duel class structure, with Class A shares and Class B shares. Class A shares receive one vote per share, while Class B shares, held only by Facebook insiders, receive 10 votes per share. This duel class structure allows the operators of the business to have more control. Ford Motor Company and Google are two other companies with similar duel class structures. As of the beginning of June 2021, Facebook's market capitalization was in excess of $950 billion.

Creating Currency and Liquidity

One of the advantages of a public company is that the market value of the company, as well as each share of stock, is known to everyone. Going public creates a stock that is liquid and that can be used as "currency" with acquisitions. Owners of companies that may be acquired are more interested in a public security, as opposed to shares of a privately held firm. Of course, owners are also interested in the security that has the ultimate amount of liquidity, cash.

In Mark Zuckerberg's letter in Facebook's IPO filing, he wrote the following: "We're going public for our employees and our investors. We made a commitment to them when we gave them equity that we'd work hard to make it worth a lot and make it liquid, and this IPO is fulfilling our commitment. As we become a public company, we're making a similar commitment to our new investors and we will work just as hard to fulfill it."

Creating Awareness and Credibility

Public companies receive more attention than private companies. As part of the IPO process, a company receives a significant amount of press. This increased awareness can have positive effects on the sales for a company. Public companies also have the perception of being more credible than private companies. In part, this perception is due to the increased reporting and transparency required of public companies.

Disadvantages of Going Public

While these benefits are compelling, there are disadvantages to going public. Below is a list of some of the disadvantages or challenges to being a public company.

Exposure

Public companies are just that, public. While this can be beneficial in terms of marketing, it has its downside in terms of required disclosures. All public companies must file annual and quarterly reports with the SEC. Officer compensation and stock ownership changes must be reported as well. In addition, any scandals, whether they relate to product issues or personnel issues, are likely to be covered by the media.

Stock Prices and Shareholder Value

Public companies face far more pressure from external stakeholders than private companies. Shareholders who invested either in the primary or secondary market demand returns, and equity analysts scrutinize every available piece of information about the company to try and quantify what those returns may be. This scrutiny often leads to a short-term focus as management tries to deliver the results shareholders' demand. In cases like Enron, this can lead to illegal reporting practices and artificially inflated share prices.

A lack of external shareholders, and a much lower external reporting burden means private companies are often able to spend more time focusing on their long-term goals.

Loss of Control

Issuing shares, whether to the public or other entities, will result in a reduction in the level of control for existing shareholders due to the dilution of their shareholding. In some cases, such as Ford, UPS, and Facebook, the original shareholders created multiple classes of stock to help maintain voting control over the businesses. The share class that the owners retained has more voting rights than the shares issued to the public.

Compliance and Reporting Costs

Public companies are required to file quarterly and annual reports with the SEC, as well as file other reports. Financial statements must be closed quickly after the end of each month, quarter, and year. In addition, financial statements must be audited by a public accounting firm. The costs for these audits and the teams of finance and accounting personnel required for all the reporting generally total in the millions of dollars.

Exhibit 9.7 | Advantages & Disadvantages of Going Public

Reasons to go Public	Consequences of Going Public
• Raise capital • Create currency and liquidity • Create awareness and credibility	• Exposure • Pressure to increase stock price • Loss of control • Compliance and reporting costs, including disclosures

While there are advantages and disadvantages, often the most compelling reason to take a company public is the additional capital that can be raised from the issuance of stock. Given that less than one percent of companies are public, it stands to reason that there must be funding from other sources for the other 99 percent of companies. These other funding sources include bank lending, venture capital, private equity, and crowdfunding, a method of raising small amounts from a large number of investors that has grown in popularity over the last decade.

CASE STUDY 9.7

UNITED PARCEL SERVICE (UPS)

With more than 400,000 employees and revenue that exceeds $50 billion per year, UPS is the largest shipping company in the world. UPS is incorporated in Delaware and has been in business since 1907. Despite being in business for more than 100 years, UPS did not become a publicly-traded company until 1999. On November 10, 1999, in what was, at the time, the largest Initial Public Offering (IPO), UPS offered 109.4 million shares on the NYSE, with an IPO stock price of $50. Based on this price, UPS had a market capitalization in excess of $80 billion on its first day as a publicly traded company.

UPS has two classes of stock. UPS Class B common stock is traded on the New York Stock Exchange under the symbol "UPS." UPS Class A shares are not publicly traded. The difference between A shares and B shares is the voting rights. Class A shares have 10 votes per share, and Class B shares have one vote per share. Class A shares are held by UPS employees and retirees; they are not publicly traded.

Employees had been able to buy Class A shares in years prior to the IPO. Going public greatly benefited the employees, such as managers, who had been with the company for many years. The proceeds from the IPO were to be used to buy back Class A shares from the employees, managers, retirees, foundations and families who are heirs of the late James Casey, who founded the company in 1907. In addition, the intent of going public was to create a liquid security, UPS stock, that would be able to be used in acquisitions.

UPS offers a DRIP (Dividend Reinvestment Plan) for both Class A and B shares. These plans allow investors to purchase UPS shares directly from UPS without the aid of an investment broker. In addition, the program allows for automatic reinvestment of dividends.

Primary Market

The primary market is the place where securities are initially offered to the public. These security offerings are in the form of initial public offerings, commonly referred to as IPOs. IPOs allow businesses and entrepreneurs access to capital markets. Business owners may issue additional shares to the public to raise capital for the expansion and growth of their businesses. While an IPO dilutes the ownership of existing shareholders, it can provide the capital and resources to dramatically expand the business.

Underwriting

To issue shares to the public, companies enlist the assistance of investment bankers to underwrite the stock issue. In the process of underwriting an IPO, the investment banker may assume some of the risk associated with selling the securities to the public. For example, an investment banker might agree to purchase an issue for $12 per share and then attempt to resell the issue to the public for $13 per share. This $1 profit is referred to as an underwriter's spread. In addition, underwriters often help the issuing firm determine its financial needs and the best investment vehicle to achieve the needed funds. Underwriting can take one of several forms. These forms of underwriting include firm commitment, stand-by underwriting, best efforts, and private placement.

Exhibit 9.8 | Facebook IPO Prospectus (Page 1)

Filed Pursuant to Rule 424(b)(4)
Registration No. 333-179287

PROSPECTUS

421,233,615 Shares

facebook

CLASS A COMMON STOCK

Facebook, Inc. is offering 180,000,000 shares of its Class A common stock and the selling stockholders are offering 241,233,615 shares of Class A common stock. We will not receive any proceeds from the sale of shares by the selling stockholders. This is our initial public offering and no public market currently exists for our shares of Class A common stock.

We have two classes of common stock, Class A common stock and Class B common stock. The rights of the holders of Class A common stock and Class B common stock are identical, except voting and conversion rights. Each share of Class A common stock is entitled to one vote. Each share of Class B common stock is entitled to ten votes and is convertible at any time into one share of Class A common stock. The holders of our outstanding shares of Class B common stock will hold approximately 96.0% of the voting power of our outstanding capital stock following this offering, and our founder, Chairman, and CEO, Mark Zuckerberg, will hold or have the ability to control approximately 55.9% of the voting power of our outstanding capital stock following this offering.

Our Class A common stock has been approved for listing on the NASDAQ Global Select Market under the symbol "FB."

We are a "controlled company" under the corporate governance rules for NASDAQ-listed companies, and our board of directors has determined not to have an independent nominating function and instead to have the full board of directors be directly responsible for nominating members of our board.

Investing in our Class A common stock involves risks. See "Risk Factors" beginning on page 12.

PRICE $38.00 A SHARE

	Price to Public	Underwriting Discounts and Commissions	Proceeds to Facebook	Proceeds to Selling Stockholders
Per share	$38.00	$0.418	$37.582	$37.582
Total	$16,006,877,370	$176,075,651	$6,764,760,000	$9,066,041,719

We and the selling stockholders have granted the underwriters the right to purchase up to an additional 63,185,042 shares of Class A common stock to cover over-allotments.

The Securities and Exchange Commission and state regulators have not approved or disapproved of these securities, or determined if this prospectus is truthful or complete. Any representation to the contrary is a criminal offense.

The underwriters expect to deliver the shares of Class A common stock to purchasers on May 22, 2012.

MORGAN STANLEY *J.P. MORGAN* *GOLDMAN, SACHS & CO.*

BofA MERRILL LYNCH *BARCLAYS* *ALLEN & COMPANY LLC*

CITIGROUP *CREDIT SUISSE* *DEUTSCHE BANK SECURITIES*

RBC CAPITAL MARKETS *WELLS FARGO SECURITIES*

May 17, 2012

Exhibit 9.9 | Twitter IPO Prospectus (Page 1)

Filed Pursuant to Rule 424(b)(4)
Registration No. 333-191552

70,000,000 Shares

Twitter, Inc.

Common Stock

This is an initial public offering of shares of common stock of Twitter, Inc.

Prior to this offering, there has been no public market for the common stock. The initial public offering price per share is $26.00. Our common stock has been approved for listing on the New York Stock Exchange under the symbol "TWTR".

We are an "emerging growth company" as defined under the federal securities laws and, as such, may elect to comply with certain reduced public company reporting requirements for future filings.

See "Risk Factors" beginning on page 16 to read about factors you should consider before buying shares of the common stock.

Neither the Securities and Exchange Commission nor any other regulatory body has approved or disapproved of these securities or passed upon the accuracy or adequacy of this prospectus. Any representation to the contrary is a criminal offense.

	Per Share	Total
Initial public offering price	$ 26.000	$1,820,000,000
Underwriting discount(1)	$ 0.845	$ 59,150,000
Proceeds, before expenses, to Twitter	$ 25.155	$1,760,850,000

(1) See the section titled "Underwriting" for a description of the compensation payable to the underwriters.

To the extent that the underwriters sell more than 70,000,000 shares of common stock, the underwriters have the option to purchase up to an additional 10,500,000 shares from Twitter at the initial public offering price less the underwriting discount.

The underwriters expect to deliver the shares against payment in New York, New York on November 13, 2013.

Firm Commitment

With a firm commitment, the underwriter purchases the entire issue of securities at a specific price then attempts to resell it at a higher price. This arrangement shifts all of the risk to the underwriter. If the issue cannot be resold at a price above the purchase price, the underwriter will lose money on the transaction. Often, a syndicate of underwriters is established to spread the potential risk. With this type of arrangement, the issuing company knows ahead of time how much money the offering will raise. This type of underwriting is classically done with very high quality companies.

Stand-By Underwriting

Stand-by underwriting is when an underwriter purchases the remaining securities at a predetermined price after an initial offering (usually to existing shareholders/owners). The predetermined price is referred to as a subscription price and is lower than the stock's market price.

Best-Efforts

Under a best-efforts agreement, the underwriter sells as much of the issue as possible, and the remainder is returned to the issuing company. No risk is shifted to the underwriter. This arrangement occurs when the issuing company is confident that the issue will be sold or the underwriter is concerned about the financial stability of the company.

Investment banks will also form a syndicate of underwriters to mitigate the risk of the IPO. Each of the firms in the syndicate will sell part of the stock offering.

Exhibit 9.10 | Types of Underwriting

Type of Underwriting	Risk to Issuing Company	Risk to Underwriter
Firm commitment	Minimal risk as underwriter is responsible for placement of the shares.	Underwriter takes on the full risk of selling the securities.
Stand-by underwriting	Minimal risk as underwriter agrees to sell securities after initial offering (generally to existing shareholders).	Underwriter takes on risk of selling remaining securities after initial offering.
Best efforts underwriting	The risk to the issuing company is that some of the shares are not able to be sold or placed.	The underwriter takes on minimal risk with best efforts underwriting.

Exhibit 9.11 | IPO Historical Statistics

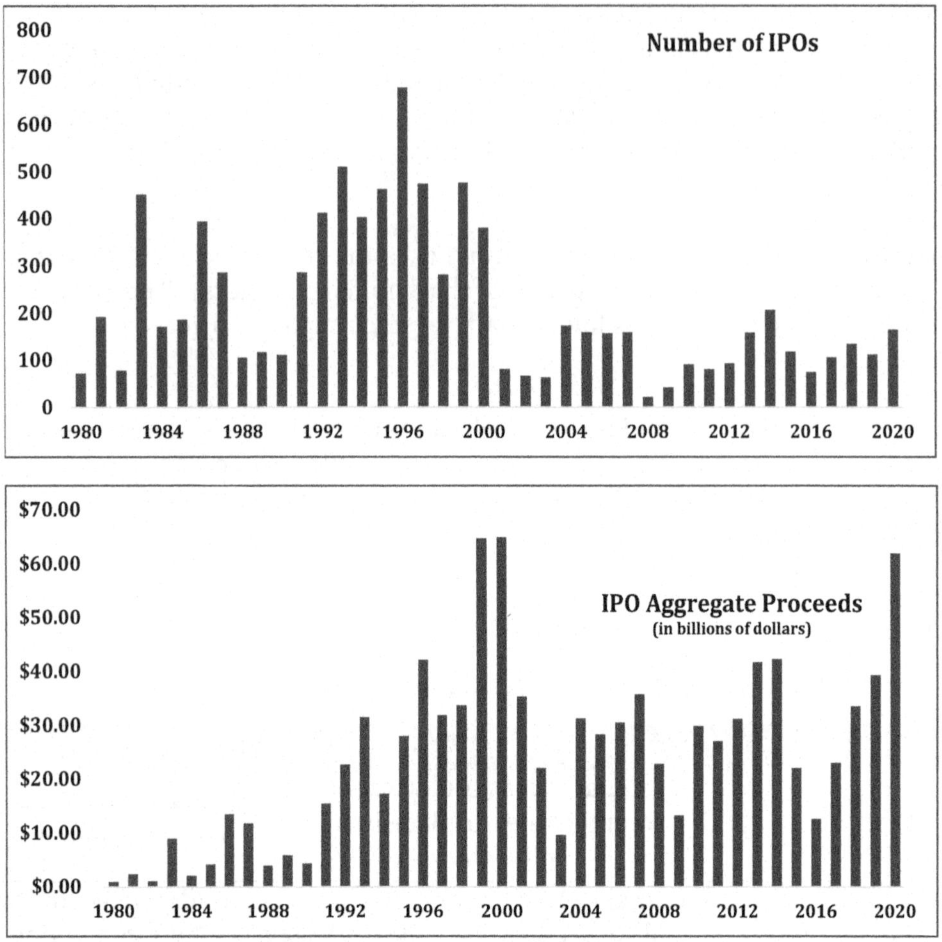

Source: https://site.warrington.ufl.edu/ritter/ipo-data/

Private Placement[15]

A securities offering exempt from registration with the Securities Exchange Commission (SEC) is sometimes referred to as a **private placement** or an unregistered offering. Under the federal securities laws, a company may not offer or sell securities unless the offering has been registered with the SEC or an exemption from registration is available. The main attraction of a private placement is the lack of registration requirements associated with an IPO. It is, therefore, less expensive and less time consuming. Generally, the issue can be placed quickly and at a low cost. Underwriters help find investors and receive a finder's fee or commission ranging from 0.25 percent to 1.5 percent. Bonds have been the most common privately placed issues.

Under Regulation D, the SEC has two rules that issuers often rely on to sell securities in unregistered offerings. These rules are 504 and 506.

15. https://www.investor.gov/additional-resources/general-resources/glossary/regulation-d-offerings

Rules 504 and 506[16]

Rule 504 permits certain issuers to offer and sell up to $10 million of securities in any 12-month period. These securities may be sold to any number and type of investor, and the issuer is not subject to specific disclosure requirements. Generally, securities issued under Rule 504 will be restricted securities, unless the offering meets certain additional requirements. Restricted securities may not be able to be sold for a period of time (at least 6 months or a year) and they may be more difficult to sell if the company is private. Information about a private company is not typically available to the public, and a private company may not provide adequate information for the owner of restricted shares to be able to sell the shares to a potential buyer. The restricted status of the securities may also transfer to a subsequent buyer. For these reasons, it may be difficult to attract buyers.

Under Rule 504, companies may sell non-restricted securities if the company sells exclusively according to state law exemptions that permit general solicitation and advertising, so long as the company sells only to **accredited investors**.

An individual will be considered an accredited investor if he or she:

- has an individual net worth, or joint net worth with the person's spouse (or spousal equivalent), that exceeds $1million (excluding the value of the primary residence) at the time of the purchase.
- has income exceeding $200,000 in each of the two most recent years or joint income with a spouse (or spousal equivalent) exceeding $300,000 for those years and a reasonable expectation of the same income level in the current year.
- is a director, executive officer, or general partner of the company selling the securities.
- is an individual who holds a FINRA Series 7 (General Securities Representative) license, Series 65 (Investment Advisor Representative) license, or Series 82 (Private Securities Offering Representative) license and is in good standing.
- is a natural person who is a "knowledgeable employee" of the private fund issuer of the securities being offered or sold.
- With respect to investment in a private fund, a natural person who is a "knowledgeable employee" of the fund.
- SEC- and state- registered investment advisors.
- is a family client of a family office with at least $5 million in assets under management.

An unaccredited individual investor is one who does not fit into one of the above categories. There are also a range of entities that qualify as accredited investors including Indian tribes, government bodies, and entities organized under the laws of foreign countries, owning investments in excess of $5 million, that were not formed for the specific purpose of acquiring the securities being offered.

An unlimited amount of money may be raised in offerings relying on one of two possible Rule 506 exemptions. An issuer relying on Rule 506(b) may sell to an unlimited number of accredited investors, but to no more than 35 non-accredited investors. However, the non-accredited investors in the offering must be financially sophisticated or, in other words, have sufficient knowledge and experience in financial and business matters to evaluate the investment. This sophistication requirement may be satisfied by having a purchaser representative for the investor who satisfies the criteria. Purchasers of securities offered under Rule 506(b) receive restricted securities which cannot be resold for six months or a year.

16.Rule 505 was repealed.

In addition to reduced cost, private placements avoid the registration requirements of the SEC and the public access to information that occurs when conforming to SEC requirements. Although private placements are limited to 35 non-accredited investors, there is no limit to the number of accredited investors. Investors need to be careful before investing in securities and should conduct their own due diligence. Consider the enforcement action by the SEC in Case Study 9.8.

CASE STUDY 9.8

SEC ENFORCEMENT

Between 2014 and 2016 the Securities and Exchange Commission filed a total of 143 actions against 144 respondents as part of the Municipalities Continuing Disclosure Cooperation (MCDC) Initiative. All actions involved municipal issuers who had used offering documents that contained 'materially false statements or omissions about their compliance with continuing disclosure obligations'.

The SEC found that between 2010 and 2014, the 22 underwriting firms violated federal securities laws by selling municipal bonds using offering documents that contained materially false statements or omissions about the bond issuers' compliance with continuing disclosure obligations. The SEC also found that the underwriting firms failed to conduct adequate due diligence to identify the misstatements and omissions before offering and selling the bonds to their customers.

Crowdfunding

Over the last several decades there has been a massive amount of disintermediation in many industries. Today, consumers are able to buy direct from manufacturers and have access to enormously greater amounts of information to make smarter decisions; and through these changes, transaction costs have been reduced. Consider an example of buying a car today with the information available to consumers.

Example 9.14

Bart decides he wants to purchase a two-year old Porsche 911. He looks at the inventory at his local Porsche dealership, but there are none that match his criteria. In years past, Bart might have been out of luck. However, today, he can search the entire country for the car he wants. He finds one in Ohio and is able to haggle with the dealership based on all of the cars for sale on the market, which is easy to find on the internet. Once he and the dealership agree on a price, he has funds wired from his bank to the dealership and has the car shipped to his residence in Florida for a few hundred dollars.

Crowdfunding generally refers to a financing method in which money is raised through soliciting relatively small individual investments or contributions from a large number of people. Over the last few years, crowdfunding websites in the United States have proven a popular way by which to solicit charitable donations and to raise funds for artistic endeavors like films and music recordings.[17]

17. These include entities such as Kickstarter and GoFundMe.

Exhibit 9.12 | Kickstarter

Kickstarter is one of the more popular crowdfunding platforms. As of June 2021, Kickstarter:

- had raised more than $5.8 billion,
- funded over 200,000 projects, and
- had more than 19 million backers.

Projects funded through Kickstarter include games, design, technology, film, music, publishing and more.

On November 16, 2015, the Securities and Exchange Commission (SEC) adopted new rules and forms to permit companies to offer and sell securities through crowdfunding. Based on these rules, the general public now has the opportunity to participate in the early capital raising activities of start-up and early-stage companies and businesses.

The SEC crowdfunding rules created a framework for facilitating crowdfunding transactions. This framework includes a type of intermediary called a **funding portal,** which allows the general public to participate in crowdfunding transactions. Both funding portals and broker-dealers can act as intermediaries in crowdfunding transactions. However, a funding portal is prohibited from:

- Offering investment advice or recommendations;
- Soliciting purchases, sales or offers to buy the securities displayed on its platform;
- Compensating employees, agents, or other persons for such solicitation or based on the sale of securities displayed or referenced on its platform; or
- Holding, managing, possessing, or handling investor funds or securities.[18]

Anyone can invest in a crowdfunding securities offering. Because of the risks involved with this type of investing, however, individuals who do not qualify as accredited investors are limited in terms of how much they can invest during any 12-month period. The limitation on how much can be invested by non-accredited investors depends on two factors: the individual's net worth and annual income. The amount that can be invested, along with the net worth and annual income limits, are now indexed every five years by the SEC to reflect inflation.

If either the annual income or the net worth for an investor is less than $107,000, then during any 12-month period the investor can invest up to the greater of either $2,200 or 5% of the greater of the annual income or net worth.

If both the individual's annual income and net worth are equal to or more than $107,000, then during any 12-month period the individual can invest up to 10 percent of annual income or net worth, whichever is greater, but not to exceed $107,000.

Example 9.15

Arturo, an accredited investor, has an annual income of $30,000 and a net worth of $400,000. Since he is an accredited investor, he is not subject to limits on his investment.

18.FINRA maintains a list of all FINRA funding portal members on its website at http://www.finra.org/about/funding-portals-we-regulate.

Example 9.16

Katarina, a non-accredited investor, has an annual income of $300,000 and a net worth of $80,000. Since her net worth is less than $107,000, she can invest the greater of $2,200 or 5% of the greater of the annual income or net worth, which equals $15,000 (5% of $300,000).

Example 9.17

Dean, a non-accredited investor, has an annual income of $400,000 and a net worth of $600,000. Since his annual income and net worth are greater than $107,000, he can invest up to 10% of annual income or net worth, whichever is greater, but not to exceed $107,000. In this case, this amounts to $60,000 (10% of $600,000).

As discussed above, individuals can only invest in a crowdfunding offering through an online platform, such as a website or a mobile app, of a broker-dealer or a funding portal. Companies may not offer crowdfunding investments to individuals directly—they must use a broker-dealer or funding portal.

The chart below reflects the original crowdfunding limits and the current limits that have been increased due to the inflation adjustments for investor limits, and an update to the maximum aggregate amount an issuer can sell:

Regulation Crowdfunding Rule	Original Amount	Rounded Inflation Adjusted Amount
Maximum aggregate amount an issuer can sell under Regulation Crowdfunding in a 12-month period (Rule 100(a)(1))	$1,000,000	$5,000,000
Threshold for assessing investor's annual income or net worth to determine investment limits (Rule 100(a)(2)(i) and (ii))	$100,000	$107,000
Lower threshold of Regulation Crowdfunding securities permitted to be sold to an investor if annual income or net worth is less than $107,000 (Rule 100(a)(2)(i))	$2,000	$2,200
Maximum amount that can be sold to an investor under Regulation Crowdfunding in a 12-month period (Rule 100(a)(2)(ii))	$100,000	$107,000

The SEC's crowdfunding rules apply to "emerging growth companies," which are defined in the JOBS Act as an issuer with total annual gross revenues of less than $1 billion. This limit is also subject to indexing and is currently $1.07 billion.

The primary market is critical for companies to be able to raise needed capital. However, the secondary market provides vital benefits to investors that enhance their willingness to participate in the primary market.

Special Purpose Acquisition Companies (SPACs)

One disadvantage of an IPO is the time it takes a private company to get to market, which can often be more than six months. In addition, regulatory requirements prohibit the company from marketing itself to the public during the later stages of the process.

Both issues are addressed to a certain extent through the use of **Special Purpose Acquisition Companies (SPACs)**. A SPAC is initially formed as a shell company with no underlying business or operations. Its only significant asset is the cash it raises from investors. As a result, the SPAC will usually obtain a public listing relatively quickly. Once listed, the SPAC uses its cash to acquire a private company.

Once acquired, the SPAC merges with that company, effectively fast tracking it through the normal IPO process. As the target company itself was not seeking an IPO, it is not subject to rules restricting it from advertising to potential investors. This allows the target to continue to court investors even after it has been identified as the target of a SPAC acquisition.

The advantage for the sponsor of the SPAC usually comes in the form of the right to buy a stake in the target company at a deeply discounted price. For investors, this can result in a dilution of their holding and reduce returns. It is therefore key for investors to review the prospectus of the SPAC to identify any such provisions.

The other more obvious risk for investors is that when investing in a SPAC they are putting their faith in its management. There is no valuation exercise that can be performed to forecast potential returns, as the SPAC has no revenue or cash flow generating activities. Typically a SPAC will sell units at a fixed price of $10, and once listed trade at or very near that price until the target company is acquired.

An investor's due diligence should therefore be focused on the track record and skill of the SPAC management team to assess whether they believe a successful acquisition is likely to be made. The SPAC prospectus may outline a sector that it is aiming for, but investors will still need to fund the SPAC before a target is named.

To offset this risk, SPACs typically contain provisions that allow investors to withdraw their initial investment if no target, or in the investor's view an unsuitable target, is found. Investors may also have warrants giving them the right to buy more shares in the target company once the acquisition is made.

Exhibit 9.13 shows the growth in SPAC issues between 2012 and 2020. Issues in the first half of 2021 alone topped $106 billion, easily eclipsing the amount raised in all of 2020.

Exhibit 9.13| SPAC issuance 2012 – 2020

Year	SPAC IPOs	SPAC Proceeds ($M)
2021	341	106,448
2020	248	83,361
2019	59	13,600
2018	46	10,750
2017	34	10,048
2016	13	3,499
2015	20	3,902
2014	12	1,750
2013	10	1,447
2012	9	490

The most popular sectors were those focused on new technology and new or emerging industries. In May 2019 for example Social Capital Hedosophia, a SPAC that had previously raised $600 million through the issue of 60 million $10 units, merged with Virgin Galactic, taking Richard Branson's private space tourism venture public and raising around $800 billion for the company.

Secondary Market

The secondary market is where investors buy and sell securities that have been previously issued in the primary market. The secondary market provides liquidity to the capital markets and allows for the free trade of public securities. The secondary market's role is critical as it provides liquidity for investors as well as real time information about equity values.

The secondary markets consist of securities exchanges, such as the New York Stock Exchange (known as the Big Board), the London Stock Exchange, and NASDAQ. These exchanges house the buying and selling of securities that are listed on the particular exchange. This buying and selling represents the primary function of the secondary market.

Quick Quiz 9.5

1. One of the advantages of going public is liquidity.
   a. True
   b. False
2. The primary market is where securities are initially offered to the public.
   a. True
   b. False
3. The secondary market consists of exchanges.
   a. True
   b. False
4. Individuals are limited in the amount they can invest through crowdfunding.
   a. True
   b. False

True, True, True, True.

Third and Fourth Markets

The third market consists of over-the-counter trading of equity shares that are listed on an exchange. This market is especially important when the exchange is not trading a security and for trading outside the normal operating hours of the exchange.

This trading is conducted by large institutional investors, such as pension funds and mutual funds, without the use of brokers. Instead, these transactions are handled by dealers who are not part of the organized exchanges and are usually conducted at lower fees compared to those of the general public.

The fourth market is comprised of traders who trade without the help of brokers or dealers. They trade directly with other interested parties. These traders make use of electronic communication networks (ECNs) such as Instinet, which began in 1969, to find other interested parties with whom to trade.[19] Most of these traders are institutional type investors who are interested in trading large volumes of securities.

MARKET INDEXES AND AVERAGES

Key Concepts

1. Indexes provide a benchmark for asset manager performance.

2. There are price-weighted, market-weighted, and equal weighted indexes.

A stock market index is a composite value of a certain group of stocks and is used as a measure of the performance of the overall market or of stocks trading on a particular exchange. The purpose of a market index or average is to provide information to investors and investment advisers concerning the overall movement and performance of the securities markets, as well as the overall economy. Since most securities are positively correlated with their respective indexes, most securities tend to increase when their index is increasing and decrease when their index is decreasing. When the index is increasing, it can be presumed that there are positive economic results from companies that make up the index. Ultimately, the value of a company is driven predominately by earnings and cash flows generated by the business coupled with changes in economic conditions.

Indexes are used to provide a benchmark for asset manager performance. Investors understand whether their portfolios increased or decreased in terms of dollars, but need a benchmark to help to evaluate the performance of a portfolio manager. Assume an investor's portfolio decreases in value. That fact does not in and of itself provide any information about how well the asset manager performed. It could be that the loss the investor experienced is not as severe as the performance would have been without the asset manager. Indexes provide comparative information upon which managers can be graded.

Indexes that are used as benchmarks must be suitable for comparison with the investment manager's investment style. If a small-cap manager is compared to the S&P 500 index, which encompasses U.S. large-cap equities, the comparison is flawed.

There are various ways to create an index. Indexes may differ in terms of how the components are weighted and whether or not dividends impact the index value. Below is a discussion of price-weighted, market capitalization-weighted, and equal-weighted indexes.

Price-Weighted Index

The constituents of a price-weighted index are weighted based solely on their price; hence the resulting weightings do not take into account their total market capitalization. The index is initially constructed by adding together the price of each individual constituent in the numerator and dividing by the number of constituents in the index as the denominator. The Dow Jones industrial average is a popular price-weighted stock market index.

19. Instinet is now part of the Nomura Group.

There are several issues that impact a price-weighted index that must be accommodated by modifying the denominator. If a company has a stock split, the price of the stock will decrease and the number of shares will increase. With a 2-for-1 split, the price theoretically will decrease by 50 percent and the number of shares will double. A stock split will not change the market capitalization for the company or the value of the company. However, the drop in price of the shares will impact a price-weighted index unless the denominator is adjusted. The denominator must also be adjusted in the event that one of the component stocks is replaced in the index. Consider the following example.

Example 9.18

Assume Companies A, B, and C represent a price-weighted index (average) and have current market prices of $25, $80, and $100, respectively. The following illustration demonstrates the adjustment required to the denominator when Company A's stock splits (2-to-1) and when Company B is replaced with Company D (market price of $50).

Company	Original	Co. A's Stock Splits	Co. B is Replaced with Co. D
A	25.00	12.50	12.50
B	80.00	80.00	-
C	100.00	100.00	100.00
D	-	-	50.00
Numerator	**205.00**	**192.50**	**162.50**
Denominator	**3.00**	**2.82**	**2.38**
Average	**68.33**	**68.33**	**68.33**

As illustrated, when Company A's stock splits, the denominator must be reduced from 3 to 2.82 so as to not impact the average. Similarly, when Company D replaces Company B, the denominator must be adjusted to 2.38. This process must continue as these types of changes occur.

Market Capitalization-Weighted (or Cap-Weighted) Index

A cap-weighted index is impacted by changes in the market value or market capitalization of the component securities. The index value is determined by dividing the total current market value of the component stocks by market value of the component stocks from the base year, the year in which the index began. Similar to price-weighted indexes, cap-weighted indexes must be modified over time as companies are added to or deleted from the index. It should be noted that larger companies, in terms of market capitalization, have a bigger impact on the index than smaller companies. This gives the index a 'momentum' tilt. Most of the cap-weighted indexes are float-adjusted, meaning the market capitalization is adjusted to reflect only the shares that are available to purchase on open markets. Those that are unavailable for purchase, for example those owned by the company founders, are excluded. Market cap-weighted indexes are the most widely used indexes. Two of the more popular cap-weighted indexes are the S&P 500 and the Wilshire 5000 indexes.

Equal-Weighted Index

Equal-weighted indexes are equally weighted regardless of the size of the component companies. Each of the companies represents the same percent of the total as all other companies on the index. An example of an equal-weighted index is the Rydex S&P 500 Equal Weight exchange traded fund and the NASDAQ 100 Equal Weighted Index.

There are numerous indexes that cover various segments of American equities, as well as indexes that cover equities around the world. In addition, there are multiple ways to create an index or average. Below are some of the more common ones.

Fundamental Weighted Index

Fundamental weighted indexes use a fundamental metric such as book value, earnings or dividends to weight constituents. Unlike a market-cap weighted index, a fundamental weight gives the index a 'value' tilt. For example, in a fundamental index based on earnings, stocks with high earnings to price ratios would be weighted more heavily than they would be in a cap-weighted index. A high earnings to price ratio means a low PE ratio, hence the term 'value' tilt.

An example of a set of fundamental weighted indexes is the Russell RAFI™ Index Series.

Dow Jones Industrial Average

The Dow Jones Industrial Average (DJIA) is probably the best-known financial index in the United States. It is a price-weighted average of thirty leading industrial stocks used to measure the status of the equity market. The thirty stocks included in the DJIA as of June 2021 are identified in **Exhibit 9.14**. As a comparison, the DJIA components from 2019 are also included. The ones highlighted are no longer included in the DJIA.

Exhibit 9.14 | DJIA Stocks

#	As of June 2021	Ticker	As of April 2019
1	3M Co.	MMM	3M Co.
2	American Express Co.	AXP	American Express Co.
3	Amgen Inc.	AMGN	Apple Inc.
4	Apple Inc.	AAPL	Boeing Co.
5	Boeing Co.	BA	Caterpillar Inc.
6	Caterpillar Inc.	CAT	Chevron Corp.
7	Chevron Corp.	CVX	Cisco Systems Inc.
8	Cisco Systems Inc.	CSCO	Coca Cola Co.
9	Coca Cola Company	KO	Dow Inc.
10	Dow Inc.	DOW	Exxon Mobil
11	Goldman Sachs Group Inc.	GS	Goldman Sachs Group Inc.
12	Home Depot Inc.	HD	Home Depot Inc.
13	Honeywell International Inc.	HON	Intel Corp.
14	International Business Machines Corp.	INTC	International Business Machines Corp.
15	Intel Corp.	IBM	Johnson & Johnson
16	Johnson & Johnson	JNJ	JPMorgan Chase & Co.
17	JPMorgan Chase & Co.	JPM	McDonald's Corp.
18	McDonald's Corp.	MCD	Merck & Co. Inc.
19	Merck & Co. Inc.	MRK	Microsoft Corporation
20	Microsoft Corporation	MSFT	Nike Inc.
21	Nike Inc.	NKE	Pfizer Inc.
22	Procter & Gamble Company	PG	Procter & Gamble Company
23	Salesforce.com Inc.	CRM	Travelers Companies Inc.
24	Travelers Companies Inc.	TRV	United Technologies Corp.
25	UnitedHealth Group Inc.	UNH	UnitedHealth Group Inc.
26	Verizon Communications Inc.	VZ	Verizon Communications Inc.
27	Visa Inc.	V	Visa Inc.
28	Walgreens Boots Alliance Inc.	WBA	Walgreens Boots Alliance Inc.
29	Walmart Inc.	WMT	Walmart Inc.
30	Walt Disney Co.	DIS	Walt Disney Co.

The DJIA, which began in 1896, consists of widely held and traded blue-chip companies. Although these companies are often leaders in their industries, the composition of the average does change over time, as reflected in the exhibit above. These changes have resulted in a divisor that is not only less than 30, it is significantly lower than 1.0. In fact, as of June 2019, the divisor equaled 0.15188516925198.

As with all equity indexes, the DJIA historical returns vary tremendously from year to year. Below are the ten best and worst annual returns.[20]

20.www.tradingninvestment.com

Exhibit 9.15 | DJIA Ten Best & Worst Annual Returns

Year	Close	Percentage Change	Year	Close	Percentage Change
1933	99.90	66.69%	1931	77.90	-52.67%
1928	300.00	48.22%	1907	58.75	-37.73%
1908	86.15	46.64%	2008	8,776.39	-33.84%
1954	404.39	43.96%	1930	164.58	-33.76%
1904	69.61	41.74%	1920	71.95	-32.90%
1935	144.13	38.53%	1937	120.85	-32.82%
1975	852.41	38.32%	1974	616.24	-27.57%
1905	96.20	38.20%	1903	49.11	-23.61%
1958	583.65	33.96%	1932	59.93	-23.07%
1995	5,117.12	33.45%	1917	74.38	-21.70%
Average of 10 Best Years		+ 42.97%	Average of 10 Worst Years		-31.97%

Standard & Poor's 500 Index

The Standard & Poor's Index (S&P 500) has traditionally been the most widely used measure of the U.S. large capitalization market by academics and financial professionals. It consists of 500 U.S. equities chosen for market size, liquidity, and industry group representation. These 500 stocks are represented by the sectors described in **Exhibit 9.16.** [21]

Exhibit 9.16 | S&P 500 Index Sectors

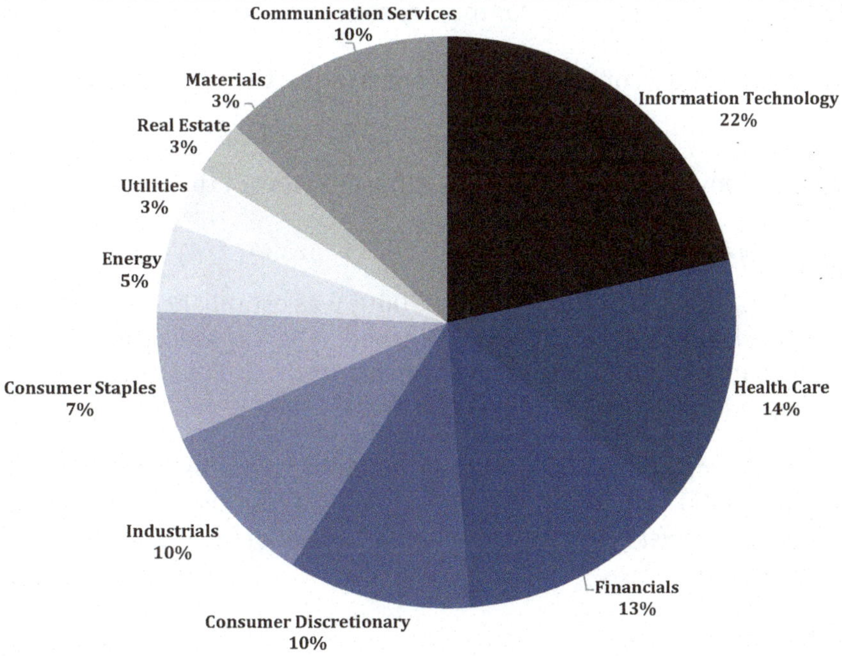

Based on GICS sectors:
The weightings for each sector of the index are rounded to the nearest tenth of a percent, therefore, the aggregate weights for the index may not equal 100% (as of October, 31, 2018).

21.us.spindices.com/indices/equity/sp-500

The S&P 500 index was created in 1957 and was the first U.S. market cap-weighted stock index. To be included in the index, companies must be based in the United States and have a market capitalization of at least $8.2 billion. **Exhibit 9.17** includes the top ten companies in the S&P 500 based on index weight.

Exhibit 9.17 | S&P 500 Top Ten Companies[22]

Apple Inc.	AAPL	Information Technology
Microsoft Corp	MSFT	Information Technology
Amazon.com Inc	AMZN	Consumer Discretionary
Facebook Inc A	FB	Information Technology
Alphabet Inc A	GOOGL	Information Technology
Alphabet Inc C	GOOG	Information Technology
Berkshire Hathaway B	BRK.B	Financials
JP Morgan Chase & Co	JPM	Financials
Tesla, Inc.	TSLA	Auto & Truck Manufacturers
Johnson & Johnson	JNJ	Health Care

In addition to the S&P 500 index, Standard & Poor's maintains numerous other U.S. indexes, some of which are below:

- S&P MidCap 400 Index – benchmark for mid-sized companies.
- S&P SmallCap 600 Index – benchmark for U.S. small-cap companies.
- S&P 500 Top 50 – consists of the largest 50 companies from the S&P 500 index.
- S&P 900 Index – consists of the companies that make up the S&P 500 index and the S&P MidCap 400 index.
- S&P Composite 1500 – combines the S&P 500 index, the S&P MidCap 500 index, and the S&P 600 index.

Each of these indexes provides investors with a different view of the U.S. equities market.

Wilshire 5000 Index

The Wilshire 5000 Total Market Index (Wilshire 5000) was established in 1974 and named for the nearly 5,000 equities it consisted of when it was launched. The capitalization-weighted index attempts to measure the performance of all publicly-traded firms in the United States. In 1998, the Wilshire 5000 included 7,562 companies, while only 3,500 on March 31, 2021.[23]

Wilshire Associates also maintains other indexes, including the Wilshire 4500 and numerous style-based indexes. The Wilshire 4500 consists of the Wilshire 5000 less the companies included in the S&P 500 index. The various style indexes consist of a particular subset of the Wilshire 5000, such as large-cap value stocks or small-cap growths.

22. As of June 14, 2021.
23. https://wilshire.com/Portals/0/analytics/indexes/fact-sheets/wilshire-5000-fact-sheet.pdf

Russell U.S. Indexes

FTSE Russell offers a broad range of U.S. indexes used by investors to gauge investment performance. Three of the more common Russell indexes are:

- Russell 1000
- Russell 2000
- Russell 3000

The Russell 3000 represents the complete U.S. market. The Russell 1000 and 2000 indexes are components of the Russell 3000. The Russell 1000 represents the large-cap market and the Russell 2000 represents the small-cap market. These indexes are market cap-weighted indexes and often used by institutional investors as a benchmark for investment performance.

The Russell 3000E index includes the 4,000 largest U.S. companies. The Russell indexes include the following companies ranked based on market capitalization, with the #1 company having the largest market capitalization:

- Russell 3000E – Companies #1 – 4,000
- Russell 3000 – Companies #1 – 3,000
- Russell 1000 – Companies #1 – 1,000
- Russell 2000 – Companies #1,001 – 3,000
- Russell 2500 – Companies #500 – 3,000
- Russell Microcap Index – Companies #2,001 – 4,000

Exhibit 9.18 | FTSE Russell Indexes

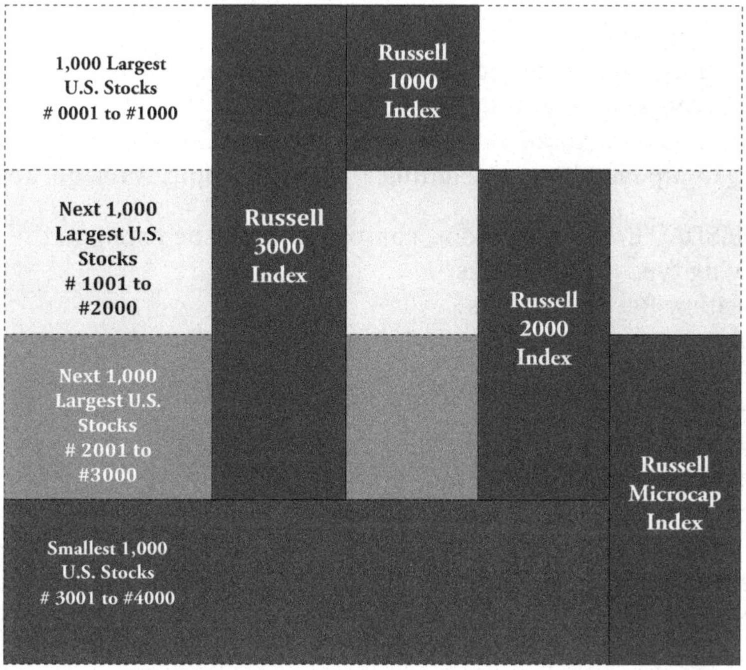

Barron's 400 Index

The Barron's 400 index was first launched in September 2007 and was jointly created by Barron's and MarketGrader. The concept of the index is that it "collects the most fundamentally sound and attractively priced stocks from all corners of the market, using a proven and disciplined stock-selection process." The purpose of the Barron's 400 is not to provide a representation of the market as a whole. Instead, it is intended to provide a list of 400 of the most fundamentally sound companies for investors.

MSCI EAFE Index

The MSCI EAFE Index is designed to track the performance of large and mid-cap securities from Europe, Australasia and the Far East, which is the basis for the index name. Stocks included in the index are from the following 21 developed markets:

1. Australia	8. Hong Kong	15. Norway
2. Austria	9. Ireland	16. Portugal
3. Belgium	10. Israel	17. Singapore
4. Denmark	11. Italy	18. Spain
5. Finland	12. Japan	19. Sweden
6. France	13. Netherlands	20. Switzerland
7. Germany	14. New Zealand	21. United Kingdom

The index is often used as a benchmark for foreign asset managers and is also used as the basis for ETFs and other financial products. As of May 31, 2021, the index had more than 840 constituents (stocks). Some of the largest are Nestle, Toyota, Unilever and Astrazeneca.

NASDAQ Composite Index

The NASDAQ Composite Index is a market capitalization-weighted index that includes more than 3,000 equities listed on the NASDAQ stock market. Unlike many indexes, the NASDAQ Composite Index includes companies that may be headquartered outside the United States. Very well known companies are included in the NASDAQ Composite Index, including Microsoft, Apple, Amazon, and Google.

To be included in the NASDAQ Composite Index, companies must be listed on the NASDAQ stock market and be one of the following types of securities:

- American Depositary Receipts (ADRs)
- Common Stock
- Limited Partnership Interests
- Ordinary Shares
- Real Estate Investment Trusts (REITs)
- Shares of Beneficial Interest (SBIs)
- Tracking Stocks

Closed-end funds, convertible debentures, exchange traded funds, preferred stocks, rights, warrants, units and other derivative securities are not included in the index.

Benchmarks

The indexes discussed above can be used for comparison with a portfolio's results to evaluate the manager's performance. Although many investors use comparisons with other managers as a measure of performance, benchmarks should have certain characteristics. The characteristics of a good benchmark include the following:

- **Unambiguous.** The composition and weighting of the components of the benchmark must be clearly delineated.
- **Investable.** The option to invest in the benchmark is available.
- **Measurable.** It should be possible to calculate the benchmark's return on a relatively frequent basis.
- **Appropriate.** The benchmark must be consistent with the manager's investment philosophy and style.
- **Reflective of current investment opinions.** The manager has current investment knowledge of the securities that make up the benchmark.
- **Specified in advance.** The benchmark should be constructed before the beginning of the evaluation period.

Quick Quiz 9.6

1. The S&P 500 Index is a price-weighted index.
   a. True
   b. False
2. The Dow Jones Industrial Average (DJIA) is a market cap index.
   a. True
   b. False
3. The Wilshire 5000 is a price-weighted index.
   a. True
   b. False

False, False, False.

These six properties improve the usefulness of a benchmark as an investment management tool and allow for a better measure of a portfolio manager's performance.

INVESTING IN EQUITY SECURITIES

Investors can profit from trading equity securities by either buying stock or selling stock. In addition, investors may use margin accounts to increase the leverage associated with the investment. These topics are discussed in this section, along with the types of orders that can be placed when investing in equity securities.

Key Concepts

1. A long position is a purchase of stock.
2. A short position is a sale of stock.
3. Dividends, if declared, must be paid to the owner of the stock by the short seller.
4. Investors can pay 100% cash or borrow on margin to buy securities.

Long Positions

The most prevalent type of position investors take is referred to as a long position. A **long position** is the purchase of a stock in hopes that it will appreciate over time. If a stock is purchased for $45 and is later sold for $100, then the stock has increased, resulting in a monetary gain of $55.

Mutual funds and other asset managers generally buy securities based on the belief that the securities will increase in value over the expected holding period. Some investors and asset managers may attempt to profit by taking a short position.

Short Positions

Investors can benefit in the market when they find securities that they believe are overvalued. A **short sale** allows the investor to benefit from the decline in the value of a security. A short sale is accomplished by selling shares that are not owned by the investor. This transaction is accomplished by borrowing shares of stock from a broker. Once the shares are sold in the market, the investor is credited with the proceeds from the sale. However, the investor must, at some point, replace the borrowed shares. This replacing of shares is known as covering the short position and is accomplished by purchasing the shares in the market and replacing the shares that were borrowed.

The short sale will be profitable if the shares can be purchased at a price less than the price at which the shares were sold. If the stock appreciates after the shares are sold short, then the investor will lose money. Short sales have unlimited risk as there is no limit on how high the price of a stock could go.

Example 9.19

Serena has evaluated Ace stock over the last 18 months and believes that it is significantly overvalued. Serena sells 100 shares of Ace short at a price of $150 per share. This trade generates proceeds of $15,000. When the stock gets to $100 per share, Serena buys back the 100 shares and covers the short position. This short sale generates a gain for Serena of $5,000, not including any borrowing costs or brokerage commissions.

Brokerage firms typically lend stock to customers who engage in short sales using the firm's own inventory, the margin account of another of the firm's customers, or another lender. Regardless of the source, the shares must be returned at some point in the future. To cover the short position, the shares are purchased in the open market and returned to the lender. The price of a volatile stock may be pushed upward when short positions are covered. Short selling is considered a more advanced trading approach and is only available to investors with margin accounts, which is discussed in the next section.

Uptick Rule

The Securities and Exchange Commission (Commission) adopted Rule 10a-1 (short sale rule) under the Securities Exchange Act of 1934 at a time when the securities markets had less trading volume and simpler trading strategies than current markets. This rule became known as the **uptick rule** as it required that a short sale must occur on an uptick or zero plus tick. An uptick occurs when the price of a security increases. A zero plus tick is a zero tick which has been proceeded by a plus tick or uptick. The purpose of these rules was to curb short selling that could manipulate or depress the market for a security.[24]

These rules regarding short selling remained largely unchanged for 60 years. However, today, short selling is instrumental to a growing number of sophisticated investment models and instruments. For example, short sales are used to hedge option positions and to engage in a variety of arbitrage strategies. Short selling is also integral to other trading and investment strategies that are not tied to individual securities, but involve baskets of securities. The restrictions in the uptick rule may inject unnecessary inefficiencies into such trading strategies. Based on these and other issues, the SEC eliminated the uptick rule in 2007.

24.www.sec.gov/rules/concept/34-42037.htm

After the financial crisis in 2008, the SEC began to seek input on reinstating a form of the uptick rule. In 2010, the SEC adopted an alternative uptick rule, which is designed to restrict short selling from further driving down the price of a stock that has dropped more than 10 percent in one day.[25]

Example 9.20

If ABC stock trades at the following prices in one day: $45.00, $44.50, $44.50, $41.00, $41.50, $41.50, $42.00, then a short sale could not occur under the old uptick rules until the stock price moved from $41.00 to $41.50.

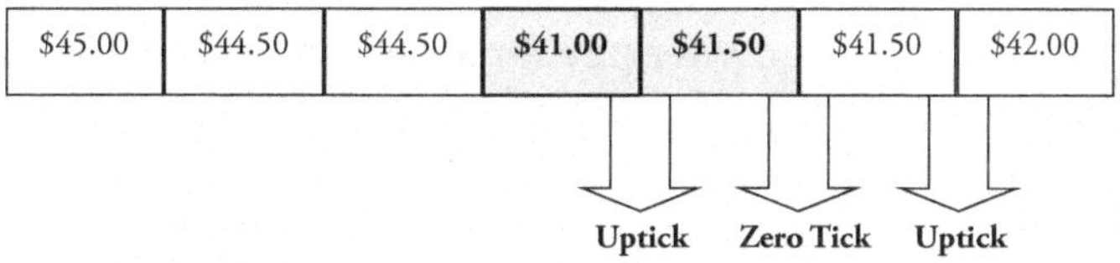

The price of $41.50 represents the first uptick in the series. The second trade at $41.50 represents a zero tick or zero plus tick.

Dividends on Stocks Sold Short

Another issue concerning short sales is that of dividend payments that occur before closing the short position. A short sale involves borrowing stock and selling it in the market. At the time of a short sale, two investors believe that they own the same shares of stock. The person who bought the shares as well as the person from whom the shares were borrowed. Both believe they are entitled to receive any dividend payments for the stock. However, the company declaring the dividend will only recognize one owner (the third party who purchased the shares in the market) and will only make one dividend payment. Therefore, it is the responsibility of the short seller to make up the other dividend payment to the party from whom the stock was originally borrowed.

Example 9.21

Danny has evaluated Tanner stock over the last 18 months and believes that it is significantly overvalued. Danny sells 100 shares of Tanner short at a price of $150 per share. This trade generates proceeds of $15,000. Before he covers the short position, Tanner declares and pays a $2.00 dividend per share. Danny must pay the dividend to the owner from whom the shares were borrowed. When the stock gets to $100 per share, Danny buys back the 100 shares and covers the short position. This short sale generates a gain for Danny of $5,000, not including any borrowing costs, brokerage commissions, or the dividend payment. After considering the dividend payment, Danny's gain equals $4,800 ($5,000 less $200).

25.In 2010, the Commission adopted Rule 201 of Regulation SHO. Rule 201 restricts the price at which short sales may be affected when a stock has experienced significant downward price pressure.

MARGIN ACCOUNTS

When an investor opens a brokerage account, it is either a cash account or a **margin account**. Cash accounts require that all securities purchased by the investor be paid for in full without any indebtedness. If a cash account is fully invested in securities, then the only way to purchase additional securities is to add cash to the account or sell some of the current securities to generate cash. In contrast, margin accounts allow the investor to borrow funds from the broker to purchase additional securities without adding cash to the account. Margin accounts provide investors with flexibility and the ability to leverage the account.

Margin accounts require that the account owner pay for a certain percentage of the cost of an investment. The margin percentage that is established for the purchase of a security is referred to as the **initial margin**.

The Federal Reserve Board determines the margin requirements, which is 50 percent in 2022. Investors must put up 50 percent of their investment in cash, although some brokerages will lend up to 70 percent for special clients.

Example 9.22

Sharna buys a stock for $50 and the price of the stock rises to $75. If she purchased the stock in a cash account, she would have a 50% return – $25 return on a $50 investment. However, if she used a margin account, then her return would equal 100% because she only put up 50% of the initial purchase price. The remainder of the purchase price would have been borrowed from the broker. This example provides an illustration of the leverage available in a margin account. In reality, Sharna would have interest on the loan from the broker which would reduce her dollar return and her rate of return.

In addition to the amount that must be initially put up by the investor, the investor must maintain an equity position in the account that equals or exceeds the **maintenance margin**. The maintenance margin is typically 35 percent, which means that the equity in the account must equal or exceed 35 percent. If the equity in the account drops below the maintenance margin, then the account holder receives a margin call from the broker. A margin call is a request for funds to restore the account equity to the maintenance margin.

Quick Quiz 9.7

1. Jayne bought 100 shares of ING for $10 each. She has a long position.
   a. True
   b. False
2. Maya was a short seller of ABC stock. Before she closed her position ABC declared and paid a dividend of $1 per share. Maya will have to pay $1 per share to the lender of the stock.
   a. True
   b. False
3. Javier buys XYZ on margin where the price is $150. Javier puts up $75. Assume the maintenance margin is 40%. If the price of XYZ falls to $120, Javier will get a margin call.
   a. True
   b. False

True, True, True.

Determining the Price for a Margin Call

An investor's equity is defined as the market value of the securities in the account less the outstanding debt. The equity percentage equals the account equity divided by the market value of the securities. The price at which a margin call is received occurs when the equity percentage drops below the maintenance margin.

The price (or account value) when a margin call will be received can be determined by setting the equity percentage equal to the maintenance margin, as follows:

$$\frac{\text{Account Value} - \text{Debt}}{\text{Account Value}} = \text{Maintenance Margin}$$

The account value at which the investor would receive a margin call can be found by rearranging this equation.

$$\text{Account Value} = \frac{\text{Debt}}{1 - \text{Maintenance Margin}}$$

Example 9.23

Dwayne purchases one share of Healthy Eats Company for $104. He uses a margin account with a 50 percent initial margin for the purchase and is concerned about receiving a margin call. If the maintenance margin equals 35 percent, then Dwayne will receive a margin call if the stock falls below $80, as illustrated below:

$$\text{Account Value} = \frac{\$104 - \$52}{1 - 0.35} = \$80$$

If the stock price falls by more than 23.08% [(104 - 80)÷104], a margin call will occur.

[1-(debt percentage ÷ (1-MMR))]

[1-(0.5 ÷ (1-0.35))] = 23.08%

Determining How Much to Put Up to Restore the Account Equity

If the stock or account drops below the price at which there is a margin call, the account owner must deposit sufficient funds to restore the account equity to the maintenance margin. This amount can be determined by asking two questions.

1. How much equity does the broker require?
2. How much equity does the investor currently have?

Example 9.24

Using **Example 9.23**, assume that Healthy Eats Company drops in value from $104 to $70 due to a contamination issue (e.g., Salmonella). In this case, Dwayne would be required to put up $6.50 per share ($24.50 - $18.00).

Required Equity		Current Equity	
Current Value of Stock	$70.00	Current Value of Stock	$70.00
Equity %	x 35%	Loan Amount	- 52.00
Required Equity	**$24.50**	**Equity**	**$18.00**

The investor must maintain an equity position of 35 percent, which is the given maintenance margin. Because the price of the stock is currently $70, Dwayne must have $24.50 ($70 x 35%) of equity in his account. To determine Dwayne's current equity position, subtract the outstanding debt from the value of the stock. Since his current equity position equals $18, and he must have $24.50 of equity, Dwayne must fund the account with the difference of $6.50 per share.

In this example, Dwayne has lost approximately 65% of his investment. He began with $52 in equity at the initial purchase of the stock. When the stock drops to $70, he has lost $34, which equates to a loss of 65.39%.

Investors should be aware of the risks inherent in margin accounts. During significant drops in the market, investors have lost enormous amounts of wealth and been unable to meet margin calls. This occurred during the early 2000s "dot com" bubble and during the 2008 financial crisis. Brokerage firms set the initial and maintenance margins, which they can change at any time.[26] In addition, brokerage firms can sell securities to meet margin requirements without contacting the investor. Investors are not required to be given an extension of time to meet a margin call.

Margin accounts are very common and provide investors with flexibility in terms of being able to execute trades and make investments without having to wait on depositing cash into the account. However, buying securities on margin has more risk than most investors are really aware of.

The following example illustrates the impact of a margin account on the calculation of holding period return.

Example 9.25

Colie bought 1,000 shares of Nike at $20 per share using her margin account, which allows her to borrow funds from her broker. The initial margin equals 60%, which means that Colie has to put up 60% of the purchase price while 40% of the purchase price can be purchased using borrowed funds. She was charged 10% margin interest annually from her broker. One year later she sold the 1,000 shares of Nike for $55 per share. During the year, Nike declared and paid a dividend of $1 per share. Colie's holding period return equals 293.33%, as follows:

$$\text{HPR} = \frac{\text{Sales Price + Dividend} - \text{Purchase Price} - \text{Interest}}{\text{Equity}}$$

$$\text{HPR} = \frac{\$55 + \$1 - \$20 - (10\% \text{ interest} \times \$20 \text{ initial price} \times 40\% \text{ borrowed})}{\$20 \times 60\%} = 293.33\%$$

Colie's return is magnified because she borrowed money from the broker to purchase the stock. Therefore, her investment was only $12 per share, while her return was $36 per share, less the interest of $0.80 per share (10% x $20 x 40%). Notice that the calculation is done on a per share basis. While the calculation can be performed based on the total cash invested, it is often easier to calculate it on a per share basis.

26. The Federal Reserve Board, FINRA, and securities exchanges, including the New York Stock Exchange (NYSE), regulate margin trading. Most brokerage firms also establish their own more stringent margin requirements. Under Federal Reserve Board Regulation T, investors can borrow up to 50 percent of the total purchase price of a stock for new, or initial, purchases. Under FINRA Rule 4210, investor's equity must not fall below 25% of the current market value of securities in the brokerage account.

TYPES OF ORDERS

When purchasing equity investments, it is important to understand the different types of orders that can be used to acquire and sell shares of common stock. The three standard types of orders are:

- Market orders
- Limit orders
- Stop orders

Orders typically expire daily, unless otherwise specified. Options for extending the time an order is open are also discussed below.

Key Concepts

1. There are market, limit, and stop orders.
2. Orders expire each day unless otherwise specified.
3. Round lots are 100 shares or increments of 100 shares.
4. Odd lots are less than 100 shares.

Market Order

The majority of orders are market orders. In fact, 75 to 80 percent of all orders have traditionally been market orders, and these orders have the highest priority. A **market order** is an order to buy or sell a security at the best current market price. These orders must be filled prior to other types of orders being considered. While these are the fastest orders, they do not have limits or a specific price and, therefore, are subject to the fluctuations and time lines of the market.

It is possible that an investor places a market order to buy when the stock is trading at $22.00 per share, and the order is filled at a price higher than when the order was placed – such as $22.10 or $22.20. This might occur because there are more buy orders than sell orders, which causes the market price to increase.

Limit Order

The objective of a limit order is to acquire or sell a security at a specific price; typically, one that is better than the market price at the time the order is placed. The **limit order** price acts as a ceiling for purchases and as a floor for sales, and the order will be held until filled or canceled. Limit orders are maintained in chronological order. Higher priced purchase limit orders take priority over lower priced purchase limit orders. Even if the price for the stock is below (or above) the limit order, there is no guarantee that it will be filled.

Example 9.26

Ethan, a shrewd investor, has analyzed all the relevant financial information and has determined that the intrinsic value of Ashby Corporation stock is $45 per share. While the stock is trading between $48 and $50, he places a limit order at $45. This type of order will assure that if the order is filled to purchase shares of Ashby Corporation, Ethan's price will be no higher than $45. If Ashby continues to trade above $45, Ethan's order will not be filled.

Stop Orders

Investors typically use stop orders to limit losses or protect gains. There are several types of stop orders. These include:

- Stop-loss orders
- Stop-limit orders
- Trailing-stop orders

Stop-Loss Orders

Stop-loss orders are used to protect investors from large losses. If the market price reaches a certain point, the stop order will turn into a market order. For instance, an investor who is long in a security might place a stop order at 10 points below the current market price to protect the appreciation of the stock against serious declines in market price. Likewise, these orders can be used to limit losses in connection with short sales.

Example 9.27

Conrad purchased Roland, Inc. for $29 per share. It is now trading at $73 per share. He has an unrealized gain of $44 per share. If Conrad is concerned about the price of the stock declining, he can place a stop order at $70. If the stock price drops to $70, a market order is placed immediately. However, because it is a market order, it may be filled at a price slightly below $70 per share. The stop loss order protects his profit position from a serious decline in value.

Stop-Limit Orders

A **stop-limit order** is an order to buy or sell a stock that combines the features of a stop order and a limit order. Once the stop price is reached, a stop-limit order becomes a limit order that will be executed at a specified price (or better). The benefit of a stop-limit order is that the investor can control the price at which the order can be executed.

The stop price and the limit price for a stop-limit order do not have to be the same price. For example, a sell stop-limit order with a stop price of $3.00 may have a limit price of $2.50. Such an order would become an active limit order if market prices reach $3.00, although the order could only be executed at a price of $2.50 or better.

Example 9.28

If Rose owns 5,000 shares of Pete's Pretzels, which is selling for $35 per share, and she is concerned about the price dropping, she may want to place a stop-limit order. If she places the order "sell 5,000 shares at $32 stop, $30 limit," and the price drops to $32, the broker will attempt to sell the stock for $32 but will not sell below the $30 limit order.

Trailing-Stop Orders

Trailing-stop orders allow an investor to place a stop order that trails the current stock price a specific dollar amount or a specific percentage of the market price. This order is held by the broker until the trigger is reached and then sent to the marketplace to be filled. The primary benefit of a trailing stop order is that it maintains proximity to the current market price and does not have to be canceled and re-entered as the price of the stock varies. Trailing-stop orders can be entered as stop-loss orders or stop-limit orders.

Example 9.29

Drago owns 1,000 shares of Apollo Stock, which he purchased several years ago at $22.00 per share. Apollo is currently trading at $100 per share. Drago would like to protect his gain and decides to place a trailing-stop loss order at 5% below the bid price. A couple weeks later, the stock increases in price and is trading at $120 per share. At this price, his stop-loss order would be triggered if the stock dropped to $114 per share. If Apollo stock moved from $120 per share to $150 per share, then the stop-loss order would be triggered if the stock pulled back to $142.50. Thus, the trailing stop-loss order is activated at 95% of the high share price.

Time Limitations and Special Orders

Investors have many options when it comes to choosing when or over what time an order will be placed. These options allow investors to pick when they will buy or sell securities giving them a significant amount of control over their trades.

- **Day orders** are good until the end of the current day's market close. Orders placed after the market has closed remain in effect until the end of the following day.
- **Good till canceled (GTC) orders** remain in effect until they are filled or until the investor cancels the order. Brokerage firms may establish limits on how long GTC orders can remain in place. Many cancel them automatically after 30, 90, or 120 days.
- **Fill-or-kill (FOK) orders** are either executed immediately in their entirety or canceled. This order does not allow for partial completion of the order.
- **All-or-none (AON) orders** are similar to FOK orders in that they are orders to buy or sell a stock that must be executed in its entirety, or not executed at all. However, unlike the FOK orders, AON orders that cannot be executed immediately remain active until they are executed or canceled.
- **Immediate or cancel (IOC) orders** are similar to FOK orders except they can be partially filled. IOC orders require all or part of the order to be filled immediately. Otherwise, the order, in full or in part, will be canceled.

Quick Quiz 9.8

1. Limit orders account for 50% of all order.s
   a. True
   b. False
2. A limit order may or may not be filled.
   a. True
   b. False
3. A stop order is really a stop-loss order for downside protection.
   a. True
   b. False

False, True, True.

Order Size and Pricing

Secondary stock markets depend on efficient execution of trades. Managing millions of trades on a daily basis is far easier and quicker if trades are in standard sizes. Every exchange will designate a standard number of shares as a round lot. Typically, a **round lot** equates to 100 shares of a security. Any trade with fewer than 100 shares is deemed an odd lot. Commissions for round lots have traditionally been less expensive than commissions for odd lots. Institutional investors almost always purchase shares in round lots. However, non-institutional investors often prefer to buy odd lots so that they can allocate a limited amount of investment dollars. Assume an investor wanted to invest $5,000 in Google, which is trading close to $800 per share and $5,000 in Southern Company, which is trading close to $50 per share. In this case, she would have about six shares of Google and 100 shares of Southern Company. The Southern Company trade is a round lot, while the Google trade is an odd lot.

Investors need to be aware that there are two market prices listed for stocks. These prices are the bid price and the ask price. The **bid price** is the price a security dealer is willing to pay for a security - the price an investor gets if she sells. The **ask price** is the price someone is willing to sell a security - the price an investor pays if she buys a security. The bid-ask spread is the difference between the two prices. This spread will generally be less for liquid securities that are traded frequently, whereas the spread will be larger for illiquid securities that are thinly traded.

This type of difference in pricing is not uncommon. For example, automobiles have various prices depending on if the car is being sold to a private party, traded-in, or purchased from a dealer.

Brokerage Industry

Thirty or forty years ago, stock transactions had to be executed with the assistance of stock brokers. Prior to 1975, commissions were fixed and brokers differentiated themselves based on services. Today, those same transactions can be executed in seconds using a computer, or for that matter, a smart phone, at a fraction of the cost they were in the past.

The brokerage industry has gone through a process of disintermediation and transformation. The services of executing trades have been commoditized such that brokers have been forced to change their business model from that of a transaction based business to more of an advice based business. Today, brokers are now typically referred to as financial advisers, wealth managers, or something similar. In offering more holistic solutions, they help clients accumulate and manage wealth, as well as plan for life events such as weddings, college education, and retirement.

SUMMARY

Summary of key points:

- Despite being subject to large fluctuations in value, equity securities are an important asset class due to their high returns over time.
- Ownership of common stock entitles shareholders to certain rights, including the right to receive dividends, the right to vote on corporate issues, the right to limited liability, and finally, the right to ultimate distribution of assets in the event of liquidation. Shareholders also have a claim on the income generated by the assets of the company.
- Shareholders can hold their ownership in physical certificates issued by the company, in street name with their broker, or directly with the issuing company.
- Earnings per share (EPS) represents the accounting profit of the company on a per share basis. EPS equals the difference of net income and preferred dividends divided by the weighted average number of common shares outstanding.
- Companies with complex capital structures must report both EPS and diluted EPS, which accounts for potential new common shares.
- The payout ratio equals the percentage of earnings that are paid out as dividends to shareholders. Large payout ratios are often unsustainable and suggest potential problems.
- The percent of earnings that are not paid out as dividends is referred to as the retention ratio.
- The key dates for dividends are the dividend declaration date, the ex-dividend date, the record date, and the payment date.
- Dividend yield equals annual dividends per share divided by stock price per share.
- Stock dividends and stock splits result in an increase in total common shares, but no fundamental change in the enterprise value of the firm.
- A reverse stock split reduces the total number of outstanding common shares.
- Round lots consist of 100 shares of stock.
- A DRIP is a dividend reinvestment plan. These company plans permit shareholders to automatically reinvest dividends back into company stock as soon as the dividends are paid.
- Capital appreciation is an increase in the value of an equity security in terms of market price.
- Common stock shareholders have the right to vote. Voting may be straight or cumulative.
- The preemptive right permits shareholders to maintain their ownership percentage with any new offerings of stock.
- Shareholders are generally protected from personal liability for any lawsuits against their corporation. Exceptions to this general rule are called piercing the corporate veil.
- There are various types of common stock, including defensive stocks, cyclical stocks, blue-chip stocks, growth stocks, income stocks, interest sensitive stocks, value stocks, and tech stocks.
- Stocks are categorized in terms of their size: mega-cap stocks, large-cap stocks, mid-cap stocks, small-cap stocks, and micro-cap stocks.

- Treasury stock is stock that is repurchased by the corporation from the shareholder.
- Corporations may have more than one class of stock. The different classes will generally have different rights, such as voting.
- Preferred stock has characteristics of both fixed-income securities and equity securities and receives preferential dividends each year equal to a stated percent of par value. Cumulative preferred stock requires that all previous unpaid preferred dividends be paid prior to paying any dividends to common shareholders. Participating preferred stock participates in profits of the company once the preferred dividends have been paid along with an equal common dividend.
- American Depositary Receipts (ADRs) are one of the easiest methods of acquiring individual foreign securities. They are certificates issued by U.S. banks representing ownership in shares of stock of a foreign company that are held on deposit in a bank in the firm's home country. ADRs are denominated in U.S. dollars and pay dividends in U.S. dollars.
- Only a small percentage of U.S. firms are publicly traded. The total number has been decreasing over the last 20 years.
- An IPO is the first offering of stock to the public. Going public has many advantages as well as disadvantages.
- The primary market is where securities are initially offered to the public. The secondary market is where investors buy and sell securities from other investors.
- Indexes are used to gauge the performance of securities markets. There are price-weighted, market capitalization, and equal-weighted indexes. Well known indexes include the Dow Jones Industrial Average, the S&P 500, the Wilshire 5000, the Russell 2000, and the EAFE index.
- Equity investors can take long or short positions in stocks. A long position is one that benefits when the price of the stock increases. A short position is one that benefits when the price of the stock decreases. Shorting entails selling borrowed stock and replacing it with stock purchased in the market at some future date.
- Margin accounts allow investors to borrow money from a broker to leverage their investments. Leverage will magnify gains and losses. Margin calls result from too little equity in a security and require the investor to put up additional funds to restore their equity position.
- Market orders, which are the most common type of order, are orders to buy or sell a security at the best current market price. These orders have priority over other types of orders (e.g., limit or stop orders).
- Limit orders are intended to limit the price at which a security is bought or sold.
- There are several types of stop orders, which are used to limit loses or protect gains.
- There are always two prices for securities: the bid price and the ask price. The bid price is the price a security dealer is willing to pay for a security. The ask price is the price at which someone is willing to sell a security.

DISCUSSION QUESTIONS

SOLUTIONS to the discussion questions can be found exclusively within the chapter. Once you have completed an initial reading of the chapter, go back and highlight the answers to these questions.

1. Discuss why investors choose equities.
2. Explain why cash dividends are important.
3. Identify similarities and differences in stock dividends, stock splits, and reverse stock splits.
4. Is a cash dividend or capital appreciation more valued by shareholders?
5. Identify common stock shareholders rights.
6. What is the difference between a cyclical and a defensive stock?
7. What is the primary reason for a company to go public?
8. What is the difference between a price-weighted index and a cap-weighted index?

MULTIPLE-CHOICE PROBLEMS

A sample of multiple choice problems is provided below. Additional multiple choice problems are available at money-education.com by accessing the Student Practice Portal.

1. Which of the following is not correct regarding cash dividends?
    a. They typically signal that the company is financially healthy.
    b. They reduce uncertainty.
    c. They are beneficial for investors who have a preference for current income.
    d. They impose no tax liability on the shareholders who receive them.

2. All of the following are correct regarding stock splits except:
    a. The market price per share of stock is reduced after the split, generally proportional to the split.
    b. The number of outstanding shares is increased to reflect the stock split.
    c. The tax basis in each share of stock remains the same after a stock split.
    d. Ownership remains proportionally unchanged.

3. An individual stockholder reinvests dividends under a company's dividend reinvestment plan (DRIP). The reinvestment dividends are:
    a. Not ever taxable to the shareholder but do change the taxable basis of shares.
    b. Taxable to the shareholder in the year of the reinvestment as capital gains.
    c. Taxable to the shareholder in the year declared and reinvested.
    d. Taxable income that is deferred until the sale of the stock.

4. Acme, Inc. has net earnings of $2.1 billion this year. It has 700 million shares of common stock outstanding, and it paid 25 cents per share per quarter this year as a dividend. Which of the following is correct?
    a. The retention ratio cannot be determined based on this information.
    b. The payout ratio equals 12.5%.
    c. The payout ratio equals 33.33%.
    d. The payout ratio equals 66.67%.

5. A dividend reinvestment plan (DRIP) is a(n):
    a. Optional investment plan, provided by brokerage firms, allowing shareholders to automatically reinvest dividend payments in additional shares of the firm's stock.
    b. Optional investment plan, provided by large corporate firms, allowing shareholders to automatically reinvest dividend payments in additional shares of the firm's stock.
    c. Mandatory investment plan, provided by brokerage firms, in which shareholders are automatically reinvesting dividend payments in additional shares of the firm's stock at a reduced price.
    d. Mandatory investment plan, provided by large corporate firms, in which shareholders automatically reinvest dividends into additional shares of the firm's stock at a reduced price.

QUICK QUIZ EXPLANATIONS

Quick Quiz 9.1

1. False. The payout ratio could be the result of previous earnings or a form of liquidation.
2. True.
3. False. He needed to hold the stock until the ex-dividend date or after.
4. True.

Quick Quiz 9.2

1. True.
2. True.
3. False. Shareholders can vote by proxy.

Quick Quiz 9.3

1. False. Cumulative voting protects minority shareholders.
2. True.
3. True.

Quick Quiz 9.4

1. True.
2. True.
3. True.

Quick Quiz 9.5

1. True.
2. True.
3. True.
4. True.

Quick Quiz 9.6

1. False. It is a market-cap weighted index.
2. False. The Dow Jones Industrial Average (DJIA) is a price-weighted index.
3. False. The Wilshire 5000 is a cap-weighted index.

Quick Quiz 9.7

1. True.
2. True.
3. True. $75/0.60 = $125 point of margin call.

Quick Quiz 9.8

1. False. Market orders make up 75-80% of all orders.
2. True.
3. True.

10
EQUITY SECURITIES - ANALYSIS

LEARNING OBJECTIVES

1. Differentiate between technical analysis and fundamental analysis and understand the framework used in doing fundamental analysis.*
2. Analyze companies using the techniques for fundamental analysis.*
3. Understand the importance of ROE and ROA in security analysis.*
4. Critically evaluate most of the techniques used in technical analysis as well as the claims made for these techniques.*
5. Decide what role, if any, technical analysis might play when investing.*
6. Appreciate the purpose and contributions of economic analysis.*
7. Describe industry analysis and how it is used.*
8. Demonstrate a basic understanding of fundamental analysis and why it is used.*
9. Calculate financial ratios and describe how financial statement analysis is used to gauge the financial well being of a company.*
10. Use various financial measures to assess a company's performance, and explain how the insights derived from the basic input for the valuation process.*
11. Describe the key attributes of technical analysis, including some popular measures and procedures used to assess the market.*
12. Differentiate cyclical and stable industries.*
13. Identify factors that may affect the performance of an industry.*
14. Differentiate between (1) a current ratio and the quick ratio, (2) accounts receivable turnover and the average collection period, and (3) gross profit margin, operating profit margin, and net profit margin.*
15. Identify which ratios are a primary interest to short-term creditors, long-term creditors, and stockholders.*
16. Apply ratios to analyze the financial statements of a firm.*
17. Compare a firm's ratio with other firms in its industry.*
18. Be able to trace the effects of a change in a firm' s financial statements on the analysis of the statements.*

**Ties to CFP Certification Learning Objectives*

INTRODUCTION

What is the value of an equity security? How does one identify a security that has great return potential? How much should an investor be willing to pay for expected future cash flows? What market and economic variables impact the expected future returns of an investment? Financial analysts, portfolio managers, institutional investors, and individual investors face these questions each day.

Investors face the daunting task of estimating an asset's value based upon an analysis of variables believed to be related to future cash flows, through comparisons with similar assets, or through fundamental analysis. The purpose of equity analysis is to collect and process enough relevant information so that an investor can make a decision as whether to buy, hold, or sell common or preferred stock.

There are two general approaches to asset selection: fundamental analysis and technical analysis. Fundamental analysis attempts to determine the value of a security based on expected future cash flows.

Future cash flows are projected by analyzing a firm's financial statements. Analysts conduct a thorough industry analysis to gain an understanding of the industry's characteristics and conditions. Fundamental analysts also appraise overall market and economic conditions. The fundamental research analyst searches for undervalued good companies, characterized by superior management, brand name product lines, effective governance structures, and the ability to generate sustainable cash flows. The irony of fundamental analysis is that good companies cannot be undervalued all the time. Consequently, good companies will not always warrant buy recommendations by research analysts.

Those who believe in technical analysis believe that supply and demand for stocks determine stock prices, and that fundamental tools (financial statements, industry, and economic analyses) are of secondary importance. They believe that changes in the supply and demand for stocks lead to trends that influence asset prices. Further, they believe that trend analysis is useful in predicting future asset prices.

It is common for investment firms to employ both fundamental and technical analysts. This chapter focuses on the elements of both fundamental and technical analysis and their possible influences on stock price behavior. The following chapter discusses equity valuation models.

FUNDAMENTAL ANALYSIS

Fundamental analysis is the process of determining the intrinsic value of a firm or security and then comparing it to the market price. Determining this intrinsic value requires an understanding of the fundamental characteristics of the company as well as the economic environment and industry in which it operates

Bottom-Up versus Top-Down Approaches

There are two approaches used in fundamental analysis when evaluating securities in relation to their industries and the overall economy. The bottom-up approach begins with the company, later fitting it into an industry and from there into the overall economy. The top-down approach, which is favored by many financial analysts and portfolio managers, takes the opposite approach by beginning with an analysis of the global economy. The objective of both approaches is to use fundamental analysis to identify firms in which to invest or divest.

Key Concepts

1. There are two approaches to asset selection: fundamental and technical analysis.
2. Two approaches used in fundamental analysis are top down and bottom up.
3. Economic analysis includes an analysis of GDP, inflation, interest rates and unemployment.
4. Federal policy includes fiscal and monetary policy.

Bottom Up Approach

Analysts who prefer to begin their asset selection process by evaluating individual companies use the bottom up approach. Analysts typically utilize fundamental analysis to identify firms which are more likely to produce higher-than-expected cash flows. The bottom up approach is a strategy to analyze individual firms based on their intrinsic values or on the basis of their relative values. By comparing these fundamental metrics to market values or peer groups, analysts can often times locate mis-priced securities. Elements of the bottom up approach include a focus on the financial health of the company and an evaluation of the firm's product line offerings. General economic and industry conditions, while important as part of the portfolio decision process, are of secondary consequence to the analyst using the bottom up approach. This approach supports the idea that an undervalued company can be expected to outperform both the market and the peer group even if it operates in an industry that is expected to underperform. The bottom up analyst must pay close attention to the tendency of this approach to generate less than ideal portfolio diversification. The sample of undervalued securities might include firms that are concentrated in certain industries or geographic regions. The portfolio might contain securities that have similar economic or risk characteristics. Overall, however, the bottom up approach can be used to great effectiveness in asset selection.

Top Down Approach

Analysts who prefer to begin their asset selection process by evaluating the macro economy use the top down approach. Fundamental analysis is applied to the entire economy to determine its current state as well as an economic forecast of key variables that will have an impact across a wide range of companies. Included in this analysis is a measure of government influence and political risks. By identifying economic strengths and weaknesses, top down analysts hope to identify firms that will most likely benefit from those conditions. For example, if the United States Department of Labor reports a substantial increase in wages for construction workers, those firms operating in that industry will likely experience a drop in margins unless it can pass along those input price increases to the consumer. On the other hand, if the United States government is planning on improving its military by upgrading aircraft and battleships, then companies in the defense industry will very likely experience increases in cash flows over the long term.

Quick Quiz 10.1

1. Fundamental analysis makes a buy or sell decision on securities based on historical prices.
   a. True
   b. False
2. The two approaches to fundamental analysis are the top-down and bottom-up approaches.
   a. True
   b. False

False, True.

The second step of the top-down approach is to identify those industries that will likely benefit from the current and forecasted conditions. Industries differ in their reaction to economic cycles and changes in behavior of market participants such a labor, suppliers, and customers. For example, if an analyst believes that the economy is contracting and headed towards a recession, then it may be appropriate to identify industries that are characteristically defensive in nature (i.e., industries that tend to do well during a recession). Or, if it is believed that interest rates are likely to rise, then using the top-down approach, the analyst may avoid certain industries that have historically struggled in high interest rate environments (such as home builders).

After the analyst has identified the most attractive industries, attention is then focused on specific companies within the industry. The goal is to identify the best companies in the most attractive industries or sectors of the economy.

Fundamental analysis is the core of both the bottom-up and the top-down approach to equity evaluation. Although the bottom-up approach can also lead to considerable returns, a thorough analysis from the top is more likely to result in a well-performing portfolio and to prevent the analyst from overlooking major factors that pose a risk to the invested capital (such as a lack of diversification across the portfolio).

Economic Analysis

To conduct a thorough equity analysis, one must understand the macroeconomic environment in which all companies operate. General economic developments have significant influences on the returns of many individual assets. As an investor or investment adviser, it is critical to have a grasp of historical and current economic variables in order to gain insight into how these forces impact various segments of the economy.

To a large extent, economic activity greatly impacts the opportunities and threats to a firm. Each industry is affected differently based on a given set of economic data. Some of the most important economic variables to consider include gross domestic product (GDP), inflation, employment statistics, interest rates, consumer spending, industrial production, and government debt to GDP ratio. Other important considerations in today's economy include commodity prices and geopolitical events.

Gross Domestic Product

Gross Domestic Product (GDP) is a measure of the total output of an economy. It is the total value of goods and services that are produced within a country in a certain period. U.S. GDP was over $20 trillion in 2020. Real U.S. GDP has increased at an average of nearly 3.5 percent per year since 1930. U.S. GDP is calculated in both current (nominal) dollars and real dollars. Real GDP measures the value of all the goods and services produced expressed in the prices of a base year. The exhibit below illustrates the growth in U.S. GDP in terms of real dollars during the first two decades of the 21st century.

Calculating GDP

One method of calculating GDP is via the expenditure approach. In this method, the sum of final goods and services produced in the economy is measured as the sum of four components, C, I, G, and Xn. C is consumer spending for new, final goods and services. I is gross private domestic investment. G is government spending, and X_n is total exports minus total imports.

$$GDP = C + I + G + X_n$$

Where:
C = Expenditures on personal consumption
I = Gross domestic investment from private sources
G = Expenditures by government
X_n = Net exports which is exports less imports

Note that only the final value of goods and services should be included in output. Hence, if a lumber yard sells raw materials to a furniture store for $800,000, and the furniture store turns the lumber into furniture and sells it for $1.2 million, only the $1.2 million is included in GDP. Including the lumber sale would double count some of the revenue.

Exhibit 10.1 | Growth in U.S. GDP in Both Current and Real Dollars

Year	% Change Real $	Year	% Change Real $
2001	1.0	2011	1.5
2002	1.7	2012	2.3
2003	2.8	2013	1.8
2004	3.9	2014	2.3
2005	3.5	2015	2.7
2006	2.8	2016	1.7
2007	2.0	2017	2.3
2008	0.1	2018	2.9
2009	-2.6	2019	2.3
2010	2.7	2020	-3.4

Source: http://www.bea.gov/National/Index.htm

Also relevant to economic analysis is the rate of change in GDP. Many analysts believe the optimal GDP growth rate is between 2.5 percent and 3 percent. When observed GDP growth rates fall within that range, the economy is expanding in a sustainable manner and generally providing businesses the opportunity to increase their sales, profitability and cash flows. If the growth rate is below than that range, the economy is not healthy and not providing its workers and consumers with the strength required for labor productivity and stable prices. Of course, negative GDP growth rates mean the economy is at risk of a recession. On the other hand, GDP growth rates that are too high are typically not sustainable and increase the threat of asset bubbles. When GDP falls outside the range, there are additional interest rate implications. When GDP is too high or at least perceived to be too high, it may signal a surging economic growth rate that needs to be tamed by the Federal Reserve raising short term interest rates. When the GDP growth rate is too low, it may signal the Federal Reserve might lower short term interest rates and lower the cost of borrowing for businesses.

Quick Quiz 10.2

1. A top-down approach is more likely to produce a well diversified investment portfolio.
   a. True
   b. False
2. High GDP growth is often followed by higher interest rates.
   a. True
   b. False

True, True.

Exhibit 10.2 | Real GDP Implications

Real GDP	Suggests in the Future:
Higher than long run average	Higher interest rates: Negative for consumer durables, housing and auto industry.
Lower than long run average	Low interest rates: Positive for consumer durables, housing and auto industry.
Recession	Defensive industries such as food, alcohol and tobacco may be appropriate.

Inflation

The **inflation** rate expresses the general level of price changes in the economy. One tool used to measure inflation is the **consumer price index (CPI)**. The Federal Reserve Board attempts to keep inflation at a "healthy" low level. High inflation rates are associated with overheated economies where the demand for goods and services is higher than the production capacities, which puts upward pressure on prices.

Inflation, as measured by the consumer price index, has historically averaged two to three percent per year. The change in the consumer price index is nothing more than the change in the cost of a basket of goods and services from one year to the next.

Both top down and bottom up analysts are highly sensitive to changes in inflation, but in slightly different ways. Top down analysts evaluate the effect of inflation on general economic performance and use it to find companies that can adapt to changing price levels. For example, companies with brand name product lines are more able to pass along increases in input prices to their customers than other firms. Bottom up analysts, however, typically use inflation as one of the inputs to determine the company's weighted average cost of capital.

Exhibit 10.3 | Historic Inflation Rates

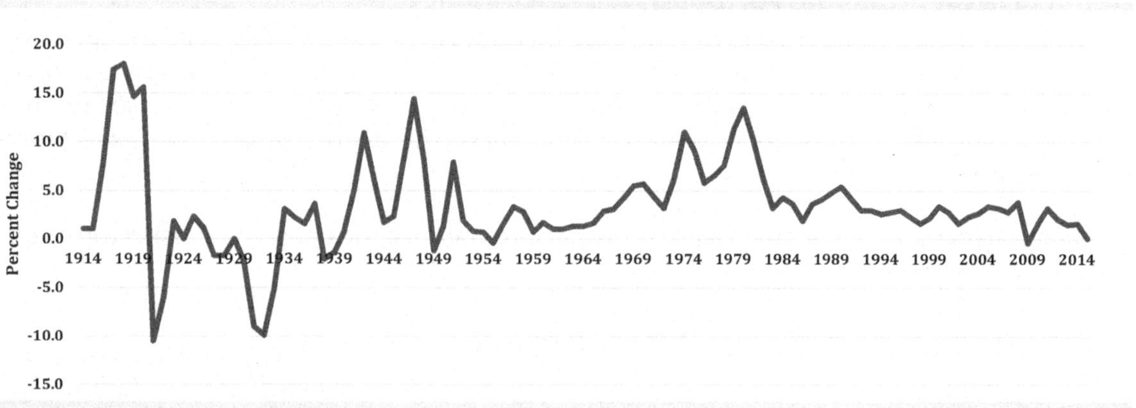

http://data.bls.gov/pdq/SurveyOutputServlet

Employment Statistics

The **unemployment rate** expresses the percentage of people in the workforce who are seeking but do not have a job. The lower the unemployment rate, the closer the economy is to operating at full capacity. The rate of unemployment is a key figure for assessing economic conditions.

The rate is calculated by dividing the number of persons unemployed by the number of persons in the labor force.

Some unemployment is both expected and necessary in an efficient labor market. In the United States, full employment is usually considered to be approximately 95 percent of the labor force. High rates of unemployment, however, usually indicate a problem with growth in the economy.

Full employment levels signal to both top down and bottom up analysts that firms are finding wealth-increasing projects and need more workers to capture higher levels of a growing market. Top down analysts will use labor statistics to determine which sectors of the economy will benefit most from higher employment levels. Bottom up analysts will evaluate the productivity of each firm to determine which is best suited to capture productivity gains.

Interest Rates

Interest rates are key economic variables as they directly affect the value of assets, investments, and the willingness of consumers to both borrow and spend. Most assets and investments are valued at the present value of their future cash flows. Higher interest rates mean cash flows are discounted at higher rates, resulting in lower present values, and fewer attractive investment opportunities.

Higher rates also increase the opportunity cost of consumption, as the interest consumers miss out on by spending rather than holding on to cash increases. As a result, some consumers will choose to save rather than spend. Additionally, as rates rise financing purchases becomes more expensive and demand for housing and high-priced consumer durables (e.g., cars) falls.

Many firms rely on borrowing to finance both operations and growth opportunities. Consequently, as interest rates increase, so does the firm's cost of financing. Additionally, higher interest expenses may result in lower profitability, which in turn may also drag down stock prices.

Additional Critical Economic Variables

The federal government collects and releases data on almost any conceivable economic, but some of the more important ones include consumer spending which provides a sense of the propensity of individuals to spend their income. Industrial production data reveals the willingness of businesses to invest for the future. Government debt ratios provide information about the degree of leverage used by the federal government to finance budget deficits.

Highly skilled financial analysts can discern which economic variables play the most critical roles in their current fundamental analysis.

Federal Government Policy and Its Influences

The federal government can influence the economy through fiscal and monetary policy. Fiscal policy is the spending, taxation and debt management policies of the government, while monetary policy deals with the government's ability to control the money supply and interest rates.

Key Concepts

1. What is monetary policy?
2. Identify and define the four tools that are used to implement monetary policy.
3. Distinguish between fiscal policy and monetary policy.
4. Identify the two tools that government can use to implement fiscal policy.

Monetary Policy

Monetary policy represents the intended influence on the money supply and interest rates by the central bank of a country. In the United States, the central bank is the Federal Reserve. The Federal Reserve system is composed of the Board of Governors and twelve regional Federal Reserve Banks.

The Federal Reserve has three primary goals:

1. Maintain price levels
2. Maintain long-term economic growth
3. Maintain full employment

The Federal Reserve accomplishes its goals by influencing money supply and interest rates. If GDP is slowing and unemployment is increasing, the Federal Reserve may want to stimulate or expand the economy. In an effort to expand the economy, it may ease monetary policy by increasing the money supply. This increased supply should put downward pressure on interest rates. Interest rates represent the cost of borrowing money, so when the money supply is abundant, the cost to borrow is low and encourages consumers to borrow money to buy houses and cars. Alternatively, if the Federal Reserve believes the economy is growing too quickly and inflation is showing signs of increasing or is actually increasing, the Federal Reserve may **tighten** monetary policy by decreasing the supply of money, which should increase short-term interest rates and slow consumer spending.

There are four primary tools that can be used to implement monetary policy. The four tools are:

1. Reserve Requirement
2. Discount Rate / Federal Funds Rate
3. Open Market Operations
4. Excess Reserve Deposits

Reserve Requirement

The Federal Reserve has historically required that banks maintain a certain percentage of their deposits on hand, in the form of cash known as their **reserve requirement**. A simplified bank's balance sheet might appear as follows:

Exhibit 10.4 | Bank Balance Sheet

Assets	Liabilities
Loans	Deposits
Cash	

Banks receive deposits that are applied to checking accounts, savings accounts, money market accounts, and Certificates of Deposit. Those deposits actually represent liabilities since the bank owes those funds to its depositors. A bank creates an asset when it uses deposits to lend funds to businesses and consumers for commercial or personal purposes. A bank also maintains a percentage of deposits as available cash for future loans or to meet the reserve requirement. Historically, the reserve requirement for banks (as set by the Federal Reserve), was effectively 10 percent.[1] For every $10 in deposits, a bank could lend $9 and keep $1 in cash to meet the reserve requirement. However, in response to the COVID-19 pandemic, the Federal Reserve Board reduced reserve requirements to zero percent, eliminating the reserve requirement for all depository institutions, as of March 26, 2020. The board announced that it has no plans to re-impose reserve requirements, but retains the right to do so in the future if warranted by a change in economic conditions.

Historically, the Federal Reserve would increase or decrease the reserve requirement, which would have a direct impact on the money supply and ultimately influence interest rates. If the Federal Reserve's monetary policy was to tighten the money supply, it would increase the reserve requirement, causing banks to maintain more deposits in the form of cash and have less funds available for loans. Since there were fewer funds available for loans, the money supply would decrease and interest rates increase.

1. In the past, reserve requirements for banks were tiered, based on net transaction accounts. As of January 16, 2020, banks with less than $16.9 million in accounts were not required to maintain a minimum reserve level. The reserve requirement for banks over $16.9 million up to $127.5 million was 3 percent. Banks with over $127.5 million were required to maintain a 10 percent reserve. (https://www.frbservices.org/resources/central-bank/faq/reserve-account-admin-app.html)

Alternatively, if the Federal Reserve's monetary policy was to ease the money supply, it would decrease the reserve requirement. Banks would maintain fewer deposits in the form of cash and increase the funds available for loans. Since there were more funds available for loans, the money supply would increase and interest rates decrease.

Exhibit 10.5 | Monetary Policy

Monetary Policy	Reserve Requirement	Money Supply	Interest Rates
Tighten	Increase	Decrease	Increase
Ease	Decrease	Increase	Decrease

Discount Rate

The **discount rate** is the interest rate that the Federal Reserve charges financial institutions for short-term loans. When borrowing from the Federal Reserve institutions go to the discount window, a term which dates back to the days when borrowers would send a representative to the Federal Reserve's bank window to borrow funds. Borrowing is now accomplished electronically, but the term discount window is still used.

The Federal Reserve sets the discount rate and the rate is increased or decreased based on the Federal Reserve's monetary policy. The discount rate represents the overnight borrowing rate that banks are charged for funds used to meet their reserve requirement or other liquidity issues. The discount rate is typically 100 basis points (or 1%) higher than the rate banks charge each other to borrow.

When the Federal Reserve tightens monetary policy, the discount rate increases. If the Fed eases monetary policy, they are going to decrease the discount rate.

The bank-to-bank lending rate is the **federal funds rate** (also known as the overnight rate). It is important to be able to differentiate between the discount rate and federal funds rate. The supply and demand of funds is an important consideration when federal funds rates are negotiated between banks. If a number of banks have reserve deficiencies and a few banks have excess reserves, the federal funds rate is likely to increase, since the demand for funds is higher than the supply. If a number of banks have excess reserves and a few banks have reserve deficiencies, the federal funds rate is likely to decrease. Since the discount rate is usually higher than the federal funds rate, the Federal Reserve is known as the bank of last resort. However, as a result of the COVID-19 pandemic, on March 16, 2020 the Federal Reserve implemented a strategy to improve liquidity and stability in the banking system by reducing the targeted spread between the discount rate and the federal funds rate to zero - 0.25 percent, thereby encouraging active use of the discount window.

Quick Quiz 10.3

1. Monetary policy represents the government's position on whether to expand or contract the economy by using taxation and government spending.
   a. True
   b. False
2. The discount rate is the interest rate that the Federal Reserve charges financial institutions for short-term loans.
   a. True
   b. False

False, True.

Open Market Operations

Through open market operations, the Federal Reserve can directly influence the money supply and interest rates. **Open market operations** is the process by which the Federal Reserve buys or sells U.S. Treasury securities such as T-bills, notes, and bonds. This process is done electronically with the Federal Reserve crediting or debiting financial institution's transactions. Only about 10 percent of the country's money supply is in the form of bank notes or cash; the rest is maintained electronically.

If the Federal Reserve's monetary policy is to tighten, then it will sell U.S. Treasury securities and reduce the deposits held by banks at the Federal Reserve. When deposits are decreased, the money supply decreases and interest rates are likely to increase.

Exhibit 10.6 | Open Market Operations

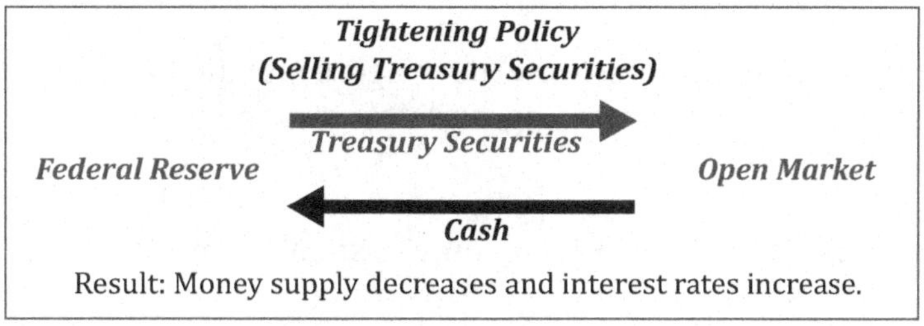

Excess Reserves

Banks must maintain a minimum level of cash reserves (based on the amount of their deposits), which is determined by the reserve requirement. The cash reserves are on deposit with the Federal Reserve. **Excess reserves** represent the amount of cash or deposits with the Federal Reserve in excess of the minimum amount required. Prior to 2008, it was disadvantageous for financial institutions to keep cash in excess of their reserve requirement on deposit with the Federal Reserve because there was no return on that capital. Institutions were more inclined to keep reserve deposits at minimum levels and instead took risks by lending the excess reserves to generate higher returns.

The Financial Services Regulatory Relief Act of 2006 established that on October 1, 2011, the Federal Reserve could begin paying interest on cash balances financial institutions have on deposit at the Federal Reserve. The Economic Stabilization Act of 2008 changed the effective date from October 1, 2011 to October 1, 2008. The impact of the Federal Reserve paying interest on deposits is that financial institutions have an incentive to keep excess reserves on deposit with the Federal Reserve. The Federal Reserve now has the ability to increase or decrease the interest rate paid on excess reserves to help control the money supply.

If the Federal Reserve's policy is to slow down or contract the economy, it increases the interest rate paid on excess reserves. This creates an incentive for institutions to keep cash on deposit with the Federal Reserve, as opposed to making risky loans.

Quick Quiz 10.4

1. If the Federal Reserve's monetary policy is to tighten the money supply, then it sells U.S. Treasury securities (open market operations) to reduce the deposits held by banks at the Federal Reserve.
   a. True
   b. False
2. A change in tax laws is a change in fiscal policy.
   a. True
   b. False

True, True.

If the Federal Reserve's policy is to stimulate or expand the economy, it decreases the interest rate paid on excess reserves. This creates an incentive for financial institutions to lend money and grow the money supply. As a result of the Federal Reserve's move to zero percent required reserves in March 2020, all bank reserves are currently excess reserves.

Fiscal Policy

Fiscal policy is exerted by Congress as a means of expanding or contracting the economy. Congress uses taxes and government spending to implement fiscal policy. Congress has the same three goals the Federal Reserve has, which are to:

- Maintain price levels
- Maintain long-term economic growth
- Maintain full employment

Fiscal policy is an attempt to either stimulate or reduce aggregate demand within a country. Fiscal policy is implemented using three tools: taxes, spending, and deficit management.

Tax Policy

When tax rates decrease, consumers have more income to spend on products and services. As consumers demand more products and services, consumer spending increases causing aggregate demand to increase. Congress controls taxes through income tax rates, deductions, and credits. Congress is likely to decrease tax rates when fiscal policy is to expand the economy. Alternatively, when taxes increase, consumers have less income to spend on products and services. As consumers demand fewer products and services, consumer spending decreases, causing aggregate demand to decrease or slow down. Congress is likely to increase taxes when fiscal policy is to contract the economy.

Exhibit 10.7 | Fiscal Policy Tax Impact

Tax	Fiscal Policy
Decrease	Expand
Increase	Contract

Spending

Government spending has a direct impact on aggregate demand (AD), as seen in the Keynesian definition of aggregate demand:

$$AD = C + I + G + (X-M)$$

However, as well as the direct impact of government spending (G), there is also an indirect impact. Some of the dollars invested will be used by households for consumption (C), which further increases AD. Spending on infrastructure may also reduce unemployment.

A disadvantage of using government spending to boost aggregate demand is that it may lead to, or increase, a government's budget deficit. This can happen when government spending is greater than the tax revenues it earns. For example, in a recession tax revenues tend to be lower due to falling corporate profits. If the government tries to combat the recession by boosting AD through spending, the amount spent is likely to exceed those revenues, which may result in, or increase, the budget deficit.

The only way to finance a deficit is to print more money, which has serious inflation implications, or borrow. Increasing levels of government borrowing can have negative consequences for the rest of the economy. Given a finite level of loanable funds, interest rates are likely to rise, and businesses and consumers may be 'crowded out', i.e., unable to borrow due to a lack of available funds, or forced to borrow at higher interest rates. Reduced private sector borrowing can lead to slower economic growth, reducing the effectiveness of the government's attempt to combat the recession.

An expanding economy is characterized by an increase in demand for goods and services, which most likely results from increases in disposable income. When consumers are willing to spend more, producers are willing to produce more of those goods and services. As output increases, GDP increases and the unemployment rate decreases, as firms are hiring more employees to meet the demand for the firm's products. If GDP continues to increase, inflation in the form of higher prices for goods and services begins to increase. Higher prices are the result of consumer spending and high demand for a limited supply of products and services. In response, the Federal Reserve may tighten monetary policy by reducing the money supply and increasing interest rates, in an effort to slow consumer spending and GDP growth. A financial planner that is knowledgeable regarding the business life cycle can anticipate the direction of the economy and assist the client with informed decisions accordingly.

Deficit Management

Deficit spending is a concept that is most often applied to local or federal government budgets. Consumers and businesses can engage in deficit spending but only for short periods of time. When cash outflows exceed cash inflows, the possibility of insolvency and bankruptcy arises for individuals and companies. For governments, however, deficit management is critical in honoring the explicit interest and principal promises made to the bondholders. Deficits for federal governments can be beneficial. For example, if a fiscal policy of deficit spending is chosen in an unstable economy, such as a deep recession or depression, the deficit increase can be worth the risk. However, if deficit spending is related to overspending or failure to follow a budget, then the risks associated with deficit spending are not reasonable. In the latter case, fiscal policy should include a cut in spending (including a reduction in expenses, if necessary) to meet budget constraints.

Business Cycles

Every market economy is subject to changes in the rate of economic growth. In times of expansion, the economy tends to grow across all sectors when the growth rate in GDP exceeds the optimal range by a substantial amount. It has the added effect of lowering unemployment rates. Unfortunately, these positive developments tend to slow down over time and finally, after having reached a peak, lead to a contraction, or recession, where GDP growth is close to zero or even negative, which means the economy is shrinking.

The National Bureau's Business Cycle Dating Committee maintains a chronology of the U.S. business cycle. The chronology identifies the dates of peaks and troughs that frame economic recession or expansion.

Key Concepts

1. There are cyclical (leaders, coincident, and laggers) and defensive industries.
2. Industries go through a life cycle from development to decline.
3. Porter uses five forces to describe the competitive structure of an industry and a firm's position.

A **recession** is a significant decline in economic activity spread across the economy, lasting more than a few months, normally visible in real GDP, real income, employment, industrial production, and wholesale-retail sales. A recession begins just after the economy reaches a peak of activity and ends as the economy reaches its trough. Between trough and peak, the economy is in an expansion. Expansion is the normal state of the economy; most recessions are brief and they have been rare in recent decades.[2]

Exhibit 10.8 | Business Cycles

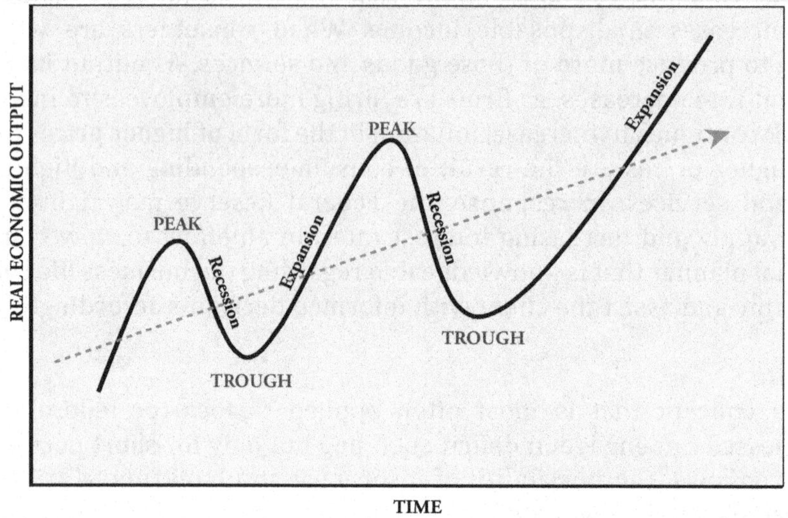

Business cycles are very difficult to predict because they do not follow a regular pattern and vary in length. According to the National Bureau of Economic Research there were thirty-four documented business cycles (measured from peak to peak) that occurred from 1854 through 2020. The shortest business cycle length was 17 months, the longest was 146 months. The average business cycle was fifty-nine months long.

Economists can use a range of leading, coincident, and lagging indicators to help forecast the growth or contraction of an economy. These indicators, however, cannot predict external shocks such as the COVID-19 pandemic in 2020 that drastically impacted global economic activity. Such shocks occur randomly and cannot be predicted or controlled.

Quick Quiz 10.5

1. An expansion phase in the business cycle is characterized by an increase in consumer spending resulting in higher output by firms.
   a. True
   b. False
2. The business cycle goes from trough through recession.
   a. True
   b. False

True, True.

Although expansion and contraction cycles represent the general health of the economy, there are pronounced differences in how various industries are affected. Cyclical industries rely heavily on a positive economic framework to generate profits. Examples of cyclical industries are producers of durable consumer goods such as cars or appliances. Purchases of these goods can be deferred during a recession, which makes sales particularly sensitive to macroeconomic conditions. Defensive industries, in contrast, do not rely on a positive economic stage. Sales in these industries are relatively stable even in times of recession because their products satisfy essential consumer needs. Examples of defensive industries include food, food processing, tobacco, pharmaceuticals, and public utilities.

2. Source: http://www.nber.org/cycles/jan08bcdc_memo.html

INDUSTRY ANALYSIS

For any given time period, the rates of return from various industry groups are likely to be significantly different. Industry analysis can be an effective tool to identify the best-performing industries. Since rates of return vary widely over time, simple extrapolation of historical results is unlikely to be effective. Thus, a more thorough analysis of industry conditions is necessary to identify the most promising industries.

Industry analysis is commonly performed with the help of two widely used models. The **industry life cycle** helps us to identify the development stages of industry groups, while **Porter's model of the five competitive forces** helps determine an industry's long-term attractiveness.

Industry Life Cycle

Industries go through five characteristic stages throughout their lives. The stages differ primarily by the patterns of growth and the measures of profitability that are exhibited. The analyst needs to be able to determine the correct stage of development of an industry in order to make sound predictions about the future financial performance of companies within the industry.

Exhibit 10.9 | Life Cycles

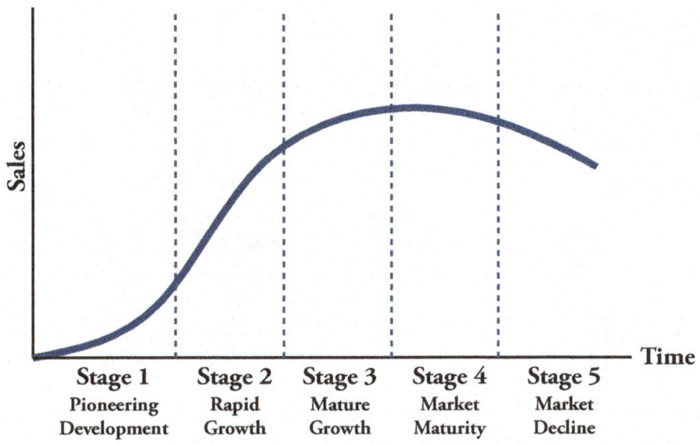

Pioneering Development

During this stage sales growth is modest, and profit margins are small or negative. The market is small and underdeveloped, and development costs may be large. It is not yet obvious how the market will develop, which in connection with high development costs constitutes considerable risk for companies within the industry.

Rapid, Accelerated Growth

A market has developed and demand is becoming substantial. There is limited competition, so profit margins are high. The industry is working to rapidly build its productive capacity. The combination of accelerated sales growth and higher profit margins can cause earnings to explode.

Mature Growth

In this phase, output capacity is catching up with demand. Although growth may exceed that of the overall economy, industry growth is no longer accelerating. Recent high growth and profitability have attracted competitors, causing margins to stabilize and profitability to decelerate.

Stabilization and Market Maturity

This is probably the longest stage in the industry life cycle. Industry growth matches overall economic growth. Good management becomes more important in this state to achieve greater profitability. Returns on investment trend toward the cost of capital.

Deceleration of Growth and Decline

Sales growth declines due to shifts in demand or substitute products. Profit margins continue to decline, and returns on capital are low. Investors starve the industry of capital in search of more attractive investments.

Porter's Five Competitive Forces

According to Michael Porter, a professor at Harvard Business School and the founder of the modern strategy field, there are five forces that describe the state of competition in an industry, and the resulting potential for profit in that industry. The five forces identified by Porter are:

1. Rivalry Among Present Competitors
2. Threat of New Entrants
3. Threat of Substitute Products
4. Bargaining Power of Buyers
5. Bargaining Power of Suppliers

Exhibit 10.10 | Porter's Five Competitive Forces

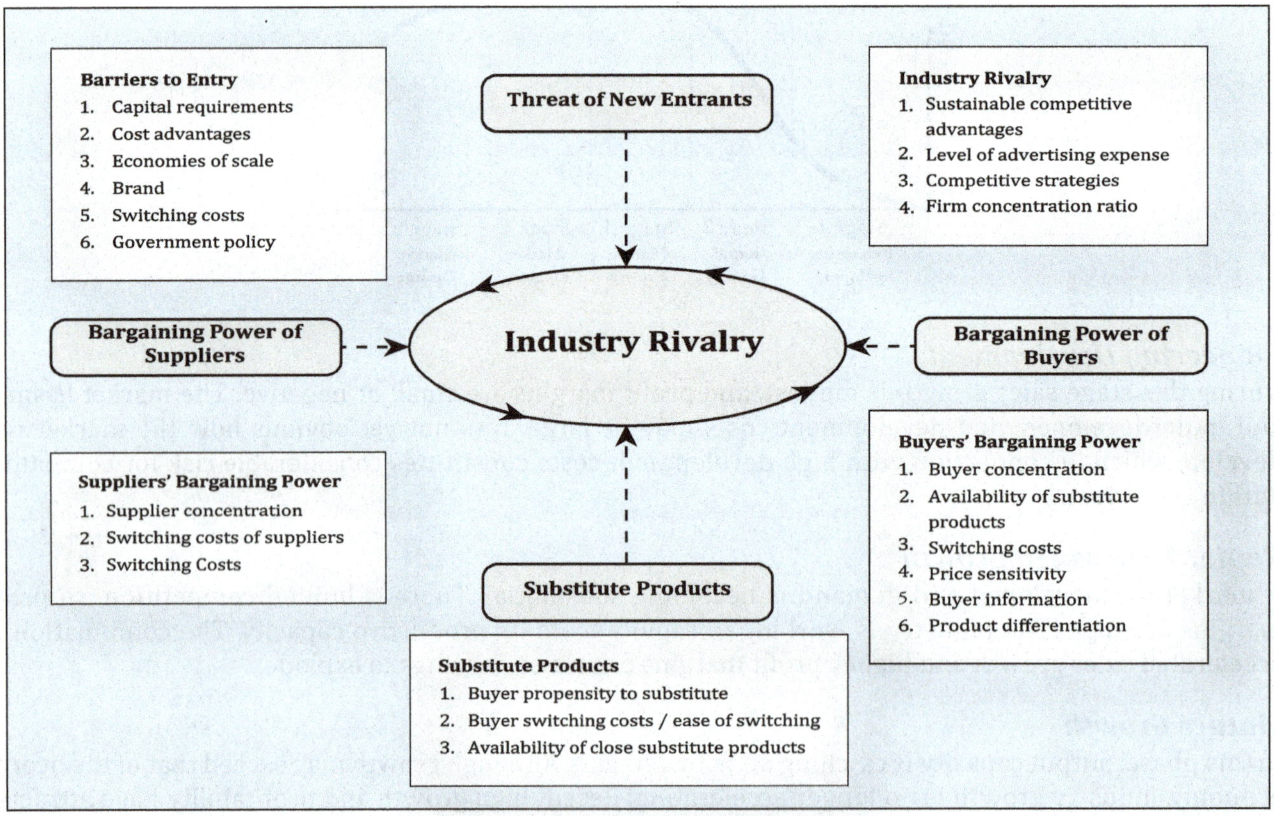

Rivalry Among Present Competitors

Rivalry occurs among companies in the same industry that produce products that are close substitutes for each other. Rivalry tends to increase under the following conditions:

- There are several players of equal size participating in the industry and there is no dominant firm in the industry.
- Market share battles occur due to slow growth.
- Firms in capital intensive industries that are characterized by high fixed costs tend to produce high outputs even when demand is low. This creates downward pressure on prices, which leads to increased competition. These industries are generally less profitable than low-investment industries.
- Exit barriers such as labor agreements may cause an uncompetitive company to remain in the industry.

Threat of New Entrants

The second force to consider when assessing an industry is the threat of new entrants to the market. New competitors trying to gain market share will increase rivalry within the industry. These barriers make entry more difficult:

- Low prices relative to costs make economies of scale and learning effects very important and give existing players an advantage.
- High investments required in capital intensive sectors.
- Government regulation.

Threat of Substitute Products

Almost all products and services have some kind of substitute. The key is to determine how well each product provides for its demand. For example, cars and trains are alternate forms of transportation, but cars offer greater flexibility in terms of destinations and travel times. However, trains offer passengers the benefit of being able to relax and enjoy the ride. As another example, glass, plastic, and aluminum are all effective methods of holding liquids.

Quick Quiz 10.6

1. Rapid growth follows mature growth.
   a. True
   b. False
2. Substitute products is one threat in Porter's five forces.
   a. True
   b. False

False, True.

Bargaining Power of Buyers

Any industry's buyers are always looking for lower prices, better quality, and added services. The buyer's bargaining power to achieve these goals depends mainly on the quantities demanded and the resulting percentage of sales the buyer represents.

Bargaining Power of Suppliers

Suppliers exercise their bargaining power mostly through increased prices. This force is especially strong when there are only a few suppliers to several different industries and the costs of changing the supplier are high. In recent years many companies have established partnerships with their suppliers that have often resulted in reduced costs, higher quality of products and distribution, and reduced risk of supply.

Example 10.1

An equity research analyst is investigating the Bath Towel industry and writes a report to be distributed to financial advisers throughout her firm. The report most likely will contain the following components:

A. The analyst's first step will be to gather knowledge of the current state of the industry from a wide range of sources including reports distributed by the industry-leading firms, federal and state government statistics, and information distributed by reputable financial news outlets. For example, the analyst will certainly be interested in identifying industry trends in product development, the financial ratios and overall economic position of the key firms in the industry, and expected growth rates for the Bath Towel market. From this research, the analyst will obtain a first indication of the relative value of the industry compared to other industries.

B. The second step is to construct a microeconomic analysis of the product lines offered by the industry. This includes an estimate of supply and demand conditions, an analysis of the industry supply chain, and predictions of total industry revenues and expenses. For example, innovations in allergy-free and anti-bacterial towels could lead to substantial increases in demand for towels. In addition, the prices of inputs in the towel production process should be monitored. From this research, the analyst will continue to uncover information that will add to her assessment of relative value.

C. The next step is to apply Porter's Five Forces model, which is arguably the most critical part of an industry analysis. The initial evaluation of the supply chain in the second step provides the basis for evaluating the bargaining power of buyers and suppliers. For example, the analyst must become knowledgeable in the farming, energy, and water industries because bath towels are generally made from cotton or polyester, which is produced from petroleum, water, and coal. The analyst also must be knowledgeable in the travel industry as hotels are one of the largest consumers of bath towels. The analysis continues with an evaluation of the threat of new firms entering into the industry as well as a prediction on whether substitute products can capture any significant market share. Finally, the relationship between and among the firms in the industry must be evaluated, including a measure of their degree of rivalry.

D. The final step is to dissect recent trends in the industry, including political, entertainment, and sports influences on the product lines. For example, hand towels used by basketball coaches during televised games has increased the demand for these items. One coach would chomp on the towel during tense moments, one coach had the towel draped over their shoulder, and another coach used their towel to cover a rip in their pants during a game. These moments are sometimes critical in determining the future success of a product.

Company Analysis

Having assessed the overall economic situation and having determined attractive industries to invest in, the next step in fundamental analysis is to determine which companies provide the best investment opportunities by analyzing data of particularly promising firms.

Fundamental or quantitative analysis at the company level is the process by which investors analyze corporate financial statements and try to determine the value of a particular stock. Financial statements include an income statement, balance sheet, statement of retained earnings, and statement of cash flows. All information contained within financial statements provides insight into the operations and profitability of a firm. A limitation of financial statement analysis is that the analysis is conducted using historical financial information. That is, historical financial information is used to gain insight as to future events. However, past performance is no guarantee of future performance.

To gain insight into certain patterns in the financial history of a company, financial statements from a period of several quarters or years are needed rather than just the latest reports. The objective is to estimate the volatility and the growth of both revenues and profits. The volatility helps determine the level of risk associated with a company while growth rates give hints about the future performance of the company and investment.

Using absolute values to compare financial data across time periods can be difficult and inconclusive. Comparing financial statement values of different firms can also be even more challenging. For example, one company might have debt of $52.7 million and interest charges of $4.3 million. Another firm may have debt of $4 million and interest charges of $380,000. The figures alone do not indicate which company is in a better position to service its debt. One reasonable solution to this problem is to compare one firm's ratios against the ratios of its competition. Coupled with a trend analysis, the comparison should provide sufficient information to determine if the firm's ratios are acceptable.

Key Concepts

1. Company analysis includes ratio analysis.
2. Liquidity ratios measure coverage of short-term liabilities.
3. Asset management ratios measure efficiency.
4. Leverage ratios measure long-term solvency.
5. Profitability ratios measures the ability of a firm to generate earnings.
6. The DuPont formula disaggregates return on equity.
7. SWOT analysis is a strategic planning tool.

However, the burden of debt, and the company's ability to service its debt, can be evaluated by comparing total debt to the firm's assets and its interest payments to its operating income. This is the essence of ratio analysis. Ratio analysis is an important tool that can be used for comparative analysis. It enables the analyst to compare key financial values across industries and companies and to predict future performance through trend analysis.

Financial Analysts

Many firms in the investment business such as brokerage firms, investment banks, or mutual funds employ vast numbers of financial analysts who observe and analyze events relevant to the financial markets on a day-to-day basis. The reports they write cover everything from general economic data to detailed information on single companies. For most publicly traded firms they also sum up their findings in a rating that expresses how good an investment a certain stock is. These ratings generally range from "strong buy" over "buy," "hold," "sell" to "strong sell." Summaries of these reports or at least the stock ratings can be found on the internet. Refer to the next section for web addresses and other sources.

Sources of Information

The vast majority of information used in a thorough industry analysis is publicly available and relatively easy to access.

Annual Reports

Every publicly traded company has to file an annual report, known as a 10-K, with the Securities and Exchange Commission (SEC). The 10-K contains audited financial statements as well as management's outlook regarding the company's operations and information about products, lawsuits, competition, executive compensation, and risks to the company. In addition to the 10-K, every company also has to prepare quarterly reports, called 10-Q's. These reports, current and historical, can be found in the EDGAR database on the SEC website (www.sec.gov). Most companies also produce a more "glossy" version of their annual report that they send out to their stockholders. These reports can generally be found under the investor relations section on the company website.

Finance Websites

Websites like Yahoo! Finance (finance.yahoo.com) or MSN Money (moneycentral.msn.com) have become very useful sources of financial information over the last few years. They offer a wide range of data on every publicly-traded company, such as historical and current prices, charts, key financial data, ratios, company news, and even analyst reports. Furthermore, these websites present information on different industries and sectors of the economy.

S&P Stock Report and S&P Industry Analysis

Standard & Poor's is one of the leading financial market analysis firms. One of their core products is the S&P Stock Report, which covers several thousand U.S. and international stocks. The analyses also include ratings from other analysts. The industry analysis, which is issued quarterly, contains in-depth coverage of all relevant industries.

Value Line Investment Survey

Covering thousands of stocks, the Value Line Investment Survey offers financial data, ratios, forecasts, and ratings along with a narrative describing each company's current situation and outlook. It also includes analyses of several different industries and offers listings of the best and worst performing stocks in several categories.

Quick Quiz 10.7

1. Threats are external in a SWOT analysis.
   a. True
   b. False
2. If a firm increases its debt, as part of its capital structure, it will increase its operating leverage.
   a. True
   b. False

True, False.

SWOT Analysis

SWOT (Strengths and Weaknesses, Opportunities and Threats) analysis is a strategic planning tool to help assess the operating strength and quality of companies. Strengths and weaknesses are internal to a firm, such as earnings growth, new product lines, management, and cost structure. Opportunities and threats are external forces that impact the firm, including the current state of the economy and the industry environment. These forces have generally been taken into account in the economic and industry analysis. However, the SWOT analysis is not only a structured summary of previous results; it also takes into account internal company facts that determine the position of a firm in its industry. **Example 10.2** is for ValueTech, Inc., a fictitious company that will be used as an example in the ratio analysis discussion.

Example 10.2

Value Tech is a medium sized firm that was started 25 years ago after its founders developed a code that helped financial institutions more closely monitor the credit risk of their mortgage customers. Over time, Value Tech expanded its technology services to include a variety of adaptations that were highly useful and valuable to all types of financial institutions. Five years ago, it developed a unique distributed ledger technology, but has been unable to advance it beyond the original offering because of intense competition, increasing input prices, and a non-competitive cost structure. Value Tech has been able to consistently generate revenues and cash flows above its competitors.

Value Tech is recognized as a reliable and a highly qualified tech consultant. The company's founders have recently decided to retire and pass the leadership positions to their children and other relatives. The interest rate on its long-term debt is higher than its competitors.

The current state of the economy includes a substantial drop in inflation, an uptick in consumer confidence, and an expected increase in the supply of tech-related college graduates. The financial services industry is currently characterized by an increase in demand for block chain technology and mobile-related apps for their customers.

2018 SWOT Analysis For ValueTech, Inc.	
Strengths: • Revenue and cash flow growth higher than the industry average • Management with track record of being successful • Brand name recognition • Reputation for quality services and products • Pioneer in distributed ledger technology	**Opportunities:** • Falling interest rate environment • Increase in consumer confidence • Expected reduction in inflation • Hire new college graduates
Weaknesses: • Cost structure higher than competitors • Outdated technologies • Retirement of founders • High interest rate on debt	**Threats:** • New competition to the marketplace • Rapidly changing technologies • Increasing input prices • Shifts in preferences by financial institutions

RATIO ANALYSIS

There are several key things to consider when conducting ratio analysis:

1. A benchmark or reference point is needed. A single value of a ratio for one single period does not give insight into the financial or operating situation of a company. For a ratio to be meaningful, it must be compared to historical values and/or forecasts. Moreover, financial ratios vary significantly between different industries, thus they can only be interpreted meaningfully in a comparison with an industry average and variance.
2. Individual ratios are much more meaningful when they are used in combination with other ratios to fully understand the financial performance of a company. In addition, ratios should be computed over several time periods to determine strengths and weaknesses.
3. Year-end values may not be representative. Certain account balances that are used to calculate ratios may increase or decrease at the end of the accounting period because of seasonal factors. Such changes may distort the value of the ratio. One way to solve this problem is to use average values, which can be calculated using quarterly data.
4. Ratios depend on the accounting methods chosen. Ratio analysis uses numbers from financial statements that were built using certain accounting methods. Not all companies obtain their numbers in the same way, and different accounting choices may result in significantly different ratio values.

Exhibit 10.11 and **Exhibit 10.12** contain financial information for ValueTech Inc., which will be used throughout this section to illustrate the various ratios.

Exhibit 10.11 | ValueTech Inc.'s Statement of Income and Expenses

Consolidated Income Statement for ValueTech Inc. For the Period Ended December 31, 2018	
Operating Revenues	**$ Million**
Net Sales	$97,640
Cost of Goods Sold	$70,360
Operating Expenses	
General and Administrative Expenses	$12,120
Research and Development Expenses	$5,500
Depreciation	$2,360
Other Expenses	$2,900
Operating Income	$4,400
Other Income	$90
Earnings Before Interest and Taxes (EBIT)	$4,490
Interest Expense	$360
Taxable Income	$4,130
Taxes	$1,440
Net Income	$2,690
Allocation of Net Income	
Dividends	$1,020
Addition to Retained Earnings	$1,670

Exhibit 10.12 | ValueTech Inc.'s Balance Sheet

Statement of Financial Position ValueTech, Inc. Balance Sheet as of 12/31/18					
ASSETS[1] ($ MILLION)			**LIABILITIES AND NET WORTH**		
Current Assets			**Current Liabilities[2]**		
Cash and Marketable Securities	$16,220		Debt Due for Repayment	$4,340	
Receivables	$19,500		Accounts Payable	$17,330	
Inventories	$7,750		Other Current Liabilities	$3,210	
Other Current Assets	$980		**Total Current Liabilities**		**$24,880**
Total Current Assets		**$44,450**			
			Long-Term Liabilities		
Fixed Assets			Long-Term Debt	$2,840	
Tangible Fixed Assets			Other Long-Term Liabilities	$4,550	
Property, Plant, & Equipment	$9,640		**Total Long-Term Liabilities**		**$7,390**
Intangible Fixed Assets			**Total Liabilities**		**$32,270**
Goodwill	$8,750				
Other Intangible Assets	$4,240		**Shareholder's Equity**		
Total Fixed Assets		**$22,630**	Common stock & other paid-in capital	$19,750	
			Retained Earnings	$15,060	
			Total Shareholder's Equity		**$34,810**
Total Assets		**$67,080**	**Total Liability and Shareholder's Equity**		**$67,080**

1. Assets are stated at fair market value.
2. Liabilities are stated at principal only as of January 1, 2019 (prior to January payments).

Liquidity Ratios

Liquidity is defined as a company's ability to meet current obligations as they fall due. Poor current asset management can lead to liquidity issues and the inability to meet the current portion of long-term debt obligations can even lead to bankruptcy. A liquid asset is one that can easily be traded in a market and thus be converted to cash. To determine whether or not a company has sufficient liquidity, the analyst commonly calculates two different liquidity ratios.

Current Ratio

The most important liquidity ratio is the current ratio, which is calculated by dividing current assets by current liabilities. The current ratio indicates how well ValueTech's current liabilities (obligations) are covered by its current assets.

$$\text{Current Ratio} = \frac{\text{Current Assets}}{\text{Current Liabilities}} = \frac{\$44{,}450}{\$24{,}880} = 1.79$$

Current assets include cash, marketable securities, accounts receivable, inventories, and other current assets. ValueTech's current liabilities consist of long-term debt due for repayment, accounts payable, and other current liabilities. There can be further balance sheet positions that are considered current liabilities, such as short-term notes payable, accrued wages, and accrued taxes.

ValueTech's current ratio of 1.79 indicates that current liabilities are covered by current assets (the current ratio is greater than 1). The company could liquidate all current assets at 56 percent (1/1.79 = 0.558) of its book value and still pay off all its current liabilities.

Quick Ratio

The quick ratio, sometimes also called the acid test ratio, is similar to the current ratio except that only the most highly liquid current assets are considered. Inventories are unfinished or unsold products that cannot normally be converted to cash as easily and fast as other current assets and perhaps only at a price well below their book value. Removing inventories and other less liquid assets leads to a more conservative insight into a company's liquidity position because it only takes current assets into consideration that can easily be converted to cash.

$$\text{Quick Ratio} = \frac{\text{Cash + Short Term Marketable Securities + Accounts Receivable}}{\text{Current Liabilities}}$$

$$\text{Quick Ratio} = \frac{\$16{,}220 + \$19{,}500}{\$24{,}880} = 1.44$$

With a quick ratio of 1.44, ValueTech can pay off all its current liabilities without having to liquidate its inventories or the assets in the "other current assets" category.

Asset Management Ratios

Asset management ratios measure how effectively a company is using its assets to generate sales. These ratios are sometimes referred to as efficiency ratios, asset utilization ratios, or activity ratios.

Total Assets Turnover Ratio

The total assets turnover ratio measures how effectively a company uses all of its assets to generate sales. It is the ratio of sales to total assets.

$$\text{Total Asset Turnover Ratio} = \frac{\text{Sales}}{\text{Total Assets}} = \frac{\$97{,}640}{\$67{,}080} = 1.456$$

This ratio indicates that ValueTech is generating $1.456 in sales for every dollar that they have invested in total assets.

Inventory Turnover Ratio

Another frequently used asset management ratio is the inventory turnover ratio. The inventory turnover ratio is calculated by dividing the cost of goods sold by the average inventory, where average inventory is equal to (beginning inventory + ending inventory) divided by two.

$$\text{Inventory Turnover Ratio} = \frac{\text{Cost of Goods Sold}}{\text{Average Inventory}}$$

Assuming that ValueTech's beginning inventory was equal to the ending inventory of $7,750:

$$\textbf{Inventory Turnover Ratio} = \frac{\$70{,}360}{\$7{,}750} = 9.08$$

Roughly speaking, each item in ValueTech's inventory is sold and restocked 9.08 times per year. A low value of this ratio can indicate that the company is holding too much inventory. However, a large inventory might be needed in industries with high fluctuations of demand to be able to satisfy all potential customers willing to buy the company's products. Unnecessarily large inventories can be a problem because they are a form of invested capital that could be used in a more productive way.

Days Sales Outstanding

This ratio, also referred to as Average Collection Period, tells the analyst how long it takes a company on average to collect cash from sales on credit. It is calculated by dividing average receivables by average sales per day. Assuming that ValueTech's beginning receivables were equal to ending receivables of $19,500:

$$\textbf{Days Sales Outstanding} = \frac{\text{Average Receivables}}{\text{Average Sales per Day}} = \frac{\text{Average Receivables}}{\text{Annual Sales/365}}$$

$$\frac{\$19{,}500}{(\$97{,}640/365)} = 72.90 \text{ days}$$

ValueTech's average collection period is 72.90 days. This means that it takes the company more than two months to collects cash from sales on credit. This could be a sign that some of the customers are either not very creditworthy, or that the firm's credit policy is too liberal. It is also possible that this is both the company and the industry average.

Financial Leverage Ratios

Financial leverage ratios, or debt ratios, provide an indication of the long-term solvency of the firm. Unlike liquidity ratios, which are concerned with short-term assets and liabilities, financial leverage ratios measure the extent to which the firm is using long-term debt. When comparing these ratios across multiple companies or to industry averages, it is important to be consistent with the classification of certain balance sheet positions as debt or equity. For example, some analysts may treat items such as long-term leases and deferred tax liabilities as debt, where others may not.

Debt Ratio

The ratio of total debt to total assets is called the debt ratio. It expresses the percentage of all funds that have been provided by creditors. Total debt can be calculated by including all current liabilities as well as long-term debt. As an alternative, the debt ratio can be calculated using only long-term debt. The key when using ratios to compare companies is to ensure they have been calculated in the same way.

$$\textbf{Debt Ratio} = \frac{\text{Total Debt}}{\text{Total Assets}} = \frac{\$32{,}270}{\$67{,}080} = 48.11\%$$

With a debt ratio of 48.11 percent, about one-half of ValueTech's total assets have been financed by creditors. Creditors prefer low debt ratios because a lower debt ratio means a lower risk of losses for creditors in the event of a liquidation. On the other hand, equity holders might prefer higher debt ratios because positive financial leverage can boost the performance of the company and enable it to generate higher earnings. One reason is that the interest portion of debt service payments is deductible for federal income tax purposes.

Quick Quiz 10.8

1. Ratio analysis is generally useful when compared over time and with industry averages.
   a. True
   b. False
2. The quick ratio does not include inventory in current assets.
   a. True
   b. False
3. Inventory turnover is an efficiency ratio.
   a. True
   b. False

True, True, True.

Profitability Ratios

Profitability ratios measure the success of the firm at generating profits. In a way these ratios reflect the results of all financing and operating activities of the firm, which were analyzed separately by all the ratios introduced earlier.

Gross Profit Margin

The gross profit margin is a measure of the gross profit earned on sales. The gross profit margin considers the firm's cost of goods sold, but does not include other costs.

$$\text{Gross Profit Margin} = \frac{\text{Sales - Cost of Goods Sold}}{\text{Sales}}$$

$$\frac{(\$97{,}640 - \$70{,}360)}{\$97{,}640} = 27.94\%$$

ValueTech's gross profit margin is 27.94 percent.

Profit Margin

The profit margin measures the percentage of each sale that results in net income. As with other profitability measures, higher profit margins are preferred.

$$\text{Profit Margin} = \frac{\text{Net Income}}{\text{Sales}} = \frac{\$2{,}690}{\$97{,}640} = 2.76\%$$

ValueTech's profit margin is 2.76 percent. As with all other ratios, the profit margin should be compared historically to similar companies in the same industry.

Return on Assets (ROA)

Return on assets is a measure of how effectively the firm's assets are being used to generate profits.

$$\text{ROA} = \frac{\text{Net Income}}{\text{Total Assets}} = \frac{\$2{,}690}{\$67{,}080} = 4.01\%$$

ValueTech has an ROA of 4.01 percent. It is not uncommon for analysts to use operating income (Earning Before Interest and Taxes or EBIT) in place of net income in computing this ratio. This approach enables the analyst to better compare ROA figures for companies with different levels of financial leverage and tax situations.

Return on Common Equity (ROE)

Return on equity (ROE) is a useful ratio for shareholders as it measures not only the amount of income generated by the company, but also the resources that were used to generate it. Whereas net income simply states the return as an absolute figure, ROE shows the return generated relative to the amount of equity that was used to generate it. Net income is the appropriate measure of return to use in ROE as it represents the amount of profit generated each year that can be distributed to equity holders, or added to retained earnings in equity (which will help fuel growth).

$$ROE = \frac{\text{Net Income}}{\text{Shareholders Equity}} = \frac{\$2{,}690}{\$34{,}810} = 7.7\%$$

ValueTech has an ROE of 7.7 percent. ROE is the best single measure of performance because it reflects all the effects of the other ratios. Although investors generally like higher ROEs, it is important to determine which factors influenced the value. Higher leverage, for example, increases ROE but also increases risk at the same time. A company's management could also sacrifice future growth in favor of a higher current ROE by cutting research and development expenses. It can be misleading to judge an investment solely on its ROE without looking at the overall general financial situation of a company.

ROE can be used to determine a company's sustainable growth rate (g). A company's **sustainable growth rate** is the maximum growth rate for a company, while maintaining its capital structure. The sustainable growth rate is impacted by ROE and the company's payout ratio.

> ***Quick Quiz 10.9***
>
> 1. The debt ratio is debt divided by equity.
>   a. True
>   b. False
> 2. Gross profit margin is gross profit divided by net income.
>   a. True
>   b. False
> 3. Profit margin, asset turnover and financial leverage are DuPont components.
>   a. True
>   b. False
>
> False, False, True.

$$g = ROE \times (1 - \text{Payout Ratio})$$

Essentially, the more earnings a company retains and reinvests back into the company, the higher the potential growth rate.

DuPont Formula

The DuPont formula is a method of disaggregating ROE into three basic components. This process can be insightful as to the components that are either contributing to ROE or hindering ROE. ROE is broken into these three components: profit margin, asset turnover, and financial leverage.

$$ROE = \frac{\text{Net Income}}{\text{Sales}} \times \frac{\text{Sales}}{\text{Total Assets}} \times \frac{\text{Assets}}{\text{Equity}}$$

When broken down into its components, analysts can gain better insight into the impact of each factor on ROE. This analysis is especially enlightening when viewed over time.

$$ROE = \frac{\$2{,}690}{\$97{,}640} \times \frac{\$97{,}640}{\$67{,}080} \times \frac{\$67{,}080}{\$34{,}810}$$

$$ROE = 2.76 \times 1.456 \times 1.927 = 7.7\%$$

Degree of Leverage (Operating, Financial, and Total Leverage)
A company's net income is exposed to two major types of risk, business risk and financial risk. Financial risk results from taking on debt and can be analyzed by calculating a company's degree of financial leverage. Business risk can be broken down into sales risk – which is the risk that sales of a product may fall, and operating risk which is measured by the degree of operating leverage.

The degree of operating leverage (DOL) is dependent on what percentage of a company's operating costs are fixed as opposed to variable. The higher the percentage of fixed costs, the higher the degree of operating leverage. It is defined as:

$$\text{DOL} = \frac{\text{\% Change in EBIT}}{\text{\% Change in Sales}} = \frac{\text{Sales - Variable Costs}}{\text{EBIT}} = \frac{Q(P-V)}{Q(P-V)-F}\text{, where}$$

V = variable costs per unit sold
F = total fixed operating costs
P = average sales price per unit sold
Q = quantity of units sold
EBIT = earnings before interest and taxes

This is because an increase in sales increases variable operating costs but not fixed costs. So, for a company facing mostly fixed costs, increasing sales leads to only a small increase in costs, and the resulting percentage increase in EBIT is much larger than that in sales.

Assuming COGS is the only variable cost for ValueTech, the DOL is over 6 times.

$$\text{DOL} = \frac{\text{Sales - V}}{\text{EBIT}} = \frac{\$97{,}640 - \$70{,}360}{\$4{,}490} = 6.08$$

Thus, a 10 percent increase in sales would result in a 60 percent increase in EBIT. For example, if ValueTech's sales increase by $9,764 and variable costs (COGS) are 72 percent, then EBIT should increase by $2,734 (28% x $9,764). The impact on EBIT is a 60 percent increase from a 10 percent increase in sales.

While operating leverage impacts earnings before interest and taxes, financial leverage impacts earnings after interest and taxes, which represents earnings available to shareholders. Financial leverage is accomplished through borrowing and is a result of a firm's capital structure. The degree of financial leverage (DFL) is defined as the percent change in earnings per share (EPS) resulting from a given percent change in EBIT.[3] ValueTech's DFL equals 1.087.

$$\text{DFL} = \frac{\text{\% Change in EPS}}{\text{\% Change in EBIT}} = \frac{\text{EBIT}}{\text{EBIT} - \text{Interest Expense}} = \frac{\$4{,}490}{\$4{,}490 - \$360} = 1.087$$

The leverage a firm obtains via its operating cost structure (operating leverage) and through its capital structure (financial leverage) can be combined into degree of total leverage (DTL).

$$\text{DTL} = \text{DOL} \times \text{DFL} = 6.08 \times 1.087 = 6.61$$

ValueTech's degree of total leverage equals 6.61, based on its operating leverage and its financial leverage.

3. If a firm pays a preferred dividend, then the formula has to be modified. In such a case, the denominator equals EBIT – Interest Expense – (Preferred Dividend / (1-Tax Rate)).

Market Value Ratios

Market value ratios give insight into how the market and other investors perceive a company's risk and future prospects. In order to calculate the different market value ratios, it is necessary to collect data about the stock of the company. **Exhibit 10.13** contains information about ValueTech Inc.'s stock at some point in the future.

Exhibit 10.13 | ValueTech Inc.'s Stock

Share price	$22
Earnings per share (EPS)	$1.67
Expected EPS growth	5%
Dividend per share	$0.42
Number of shares issued and outstanding	1,500,000,000

Price/Earnings Ratio (PE Ratio)

The PE ratio expresses how much investors in the market are willing to pay for a dollar of reported profits. The PE ratio is calculated by dividing the stock's price per share by its earnings per share. Some analysts believe that a low PE ratio is an indication that a stock is undervalued. The PE can be compared historically and to other firms in the same industry.

$$\text{PE Ratio} = \frac{\text{Price per Share}}{\text{Earnings per Share}} = \frac{\$22.00}{\$1.67} = 13.2$$

Price/Earnings to Growth Ratio (PEG Ratio)

The PEG ratio compares a stock's PE ratio to the expected growth of that stock's earnings per share. The PEG ratio is calculated by dividing the stock's PE ratio by the expected annual growth rate of its earnings per share. Some analysts believe that a low PEG ratio, like a low PE ratio, is an indication that a stock is undervalued.

$$\text{PEG Ratio} = \frac{\text{PE Ratio}}{\text{Expected EPS Growth}} = \frac{13.2}{5} = 2.64$$

Book Value per Share

Book value per share (BVPS) is the theoretical value of the amount shareholders would receive if the firm decided to fully liquidate. In reality, book value per share is a measure of the value of the ownership portion of the balance sheet. It is commonly used to determine whether a firm's stock price is under or overvalued. If the book value exceeds the current market value, then the firm is undervalued.

$$\text{Book Value} = \frac{\text{Shareholders Equity}}{\text{Shares Outstanding}} = \frac{\$34{,}810{,}000{,}000}{1{,}500{,}000{,}000} = \$23.21$$

Price-to-Book Ratio

The price-to-book ratio expresses how much investors in the market are willing to pay for a dollar of book value. In other words, this ratio expresses the value that the market places on the book value of this company.

$$\text{Price to Book Ratio} = \frac{\text{Share Price}}{\text{Book Value per Share}} = \frac{\$22.00}{\$23.21} = 0.95$$

Dividend Policy Ratios

Dividend Yield

The dividend yield is how much a company pays out in dividends relative to the company's stock price. The dividend yield is calculated by dividing dividends per share by the price per share.

$$\text{Dividend Yield} = \frac{\text{Dividend per Share}}{\text{Share Price}} = \frac{\$0.42}{\$22.00} = 1.91\%$$

The dividend yield only measures one source of return for the shareholder. To determine the total return of an investment, changes in the share price have to also be considered.

Payout Ratio

The payout ratio expresses the percentage of earnings paid out to the shareholders in the form of dividends. A company can either pay out its profits as dividends or retain profits in order to internally finance new projects for future growth.

$$\text{Payout Ratio} = \frac{\text{Dividend per Share}}{\text{Earnings per Share}} = \frac{\$0.42}{\$1.67} = 25.1\%$$

TECHNICAL ANALYSIS

Technical analysis is another method that may help determine the price at which an investor should buy, sell, or hold an individual equity security. This method is guided by the principles of supply and demand. Technical analysts attempt to determine the demand for an asset (stock) by observing the movements in past prices and volume. Technical analysis is based on the belief that past movements in the asset will help to predict future patterns and prices.

> ***Key Concepts***
>
> 1. Technical analysis is driven by supply and demand.
> 2. Technical analysis uses tools like volume, breadth, advance decline line, short interest, odd lot trading and charting.

Technical analysts believe that both rational and irrational investor decisions influence the demand for assets, and that the interaction of demand and supply determines asset prices. Technical analysts believe that patterns in investor behavior persist and are predictable. Once a pattern is established, prices tend to follow that pattern. If technical analysts can identify the trend, then they can execute trades and exploit the trend for economic gain.

Comparison with Fundamental Analysis

Fundamental analysts focus on economy, industry, and company specific variables that impact asset value. Much of the primary fundamental data comes from a firm's financial statements. The premise of fundamental analysis is that through analysis of these variables, one may uncover assets that are undervalued. This makes them attractive assets to purchase. Specifically, the fundamental analyst uses the data to estimate future cash flows, develop an appropriate discount rate to reflect market conditions and risk, and then discounts the cash flows to determine the asset's intrinsic value. The intrinsic value is compared to the market price of the asset to determine whether or not the asset is a good investment. The time frame used to evaluate the market using fundamental analysis is generally longer than the time frame used by technical analysts. Technical analysts often make trades based on short-term (days, hours, and minutes) price and volume data.

Technical analysis largely ignores the fundamentals. One premise of technical analysis is that asset prices reflect everything that is known about the market, including market "psychology," and company, industry, and economic factors. Because information related to all of the factors has already been priced into the assets, technical analysts do not study each factor. Instead, they study the trends that are generated by the interaction of the factors. Technical analysis focuses primarily on the supply and demand of securities in the market to determine the direction the market is likely to take. Technical analysts do not care why assets increase or decrease in value; they simply try to profit from the trends.

Technicians use several tools to identify and predict patterns in the market. Technical analysts look at broad economic variables, stock trading history, trading volume, short interest, odd lot trading and patterns formed by historical stock prices. Technical indicators include market volume, breadth, short interest and odd lot trading. In addition, charting is used to predict buy and sell price points.

Tools of Technical Analysis

Market Volume

Market volume is simply the total number of shares traded during the course of a day. Market volume is based upon supply and demand of securities, and it provides technical analysts with insight as to the market's strength or weakness. The total market volume on an up or down day indicates the strength of the market. The market is considered strong (and positive) when volume increases in a rising market. The market is also considered strong (and negative) when volume decreases in a falling market. A weak market is one in which market volume increases in a falling market, or rises in a market decline. Market volume is an indicator of investor sentiment.

Breadth of the Market

The breadth of the market (or market breadth) measures the number of advancing stocks versus declining stocks. An advancing stock is one that closes at a price higher than the previous day's close. A declining stock is one that closes at a price below its closing price from the previous day. Market breadth measures the difference between the number of advancing and declining issues. Technical analysts use this measure to assess the direction of the market. The greater the spread between the number of advancing and declining issues, the stronger the market and more positive the outlook. Conversely, a narrowing spread (an increasing number of declining issues) might indicate bearish sentiment in the market, and an impending negative outlook.

Advance-Decline Line

The advance-decline line (A/D line) is a graphical depiction of periodic change in advancing and declining issues on an exchange. Each point on the chart is determined by taking the difference between the number of advancing and declining stocks, most often for the previous trading day, although intraday analyses are common. The formula used to determine the advance-decline line is as follows:

A/D Line = (# of Advancing Issues - # of Declining Issues) + Previous A/D Line Value

For example, if the number of S&P 500 stocks that have increased in price is 400, and the number that decreased in value is 100, then the value reported for that day is 300. That value (300) is then added to previous A/D line value and plotted on the chart.

This technical indicator may be used to assess the strength of a current trend. For example, an upward sloping A/D line suggests a positive outlook as the number of advancing issues is greater than the number of declining issues. However, as the slope of the line flattens, fewer firms are posting price increases, relative to firms that have price declines. This may be a sign that markets are slowing and a trend reversal may occur.

Exhibit 10.14 | Advance - Decline Line

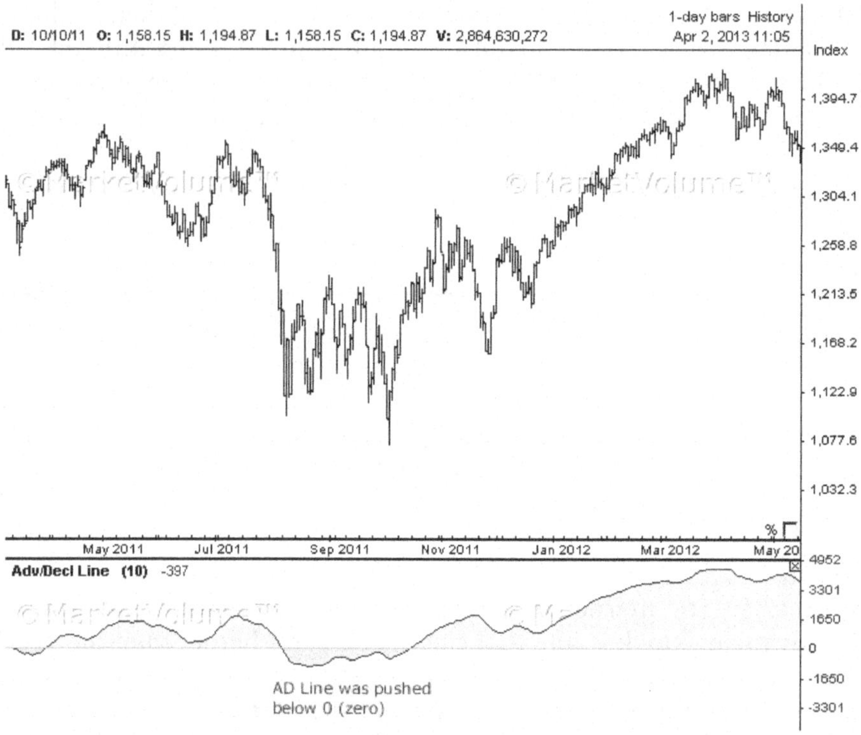

Used with Permission from marketvolume.com

Short Interest

Recall that in the traditional short sell strategy, an investor does not own the assets that he wants to sell. He borrows the assets from a broker, sells them, and hopes that the price of the underlying asset decreases. The investor closes the short position by repurchasing the borrowed shares. The short seller profits if the share prices decline. Short interest simply measures the total number of shares currently sold short on a particular market, such as the NYSE or NASDAQ.

Short sales are most often executed by sophisticated investors, so the level of short interest is thought to reveal the sentiment of those investors. Short sellers profit with market declines, so an increase in short selling activity may indicate negative sentiment regarding present market conditions. However, because every short position must eventually be closed (shares must be re-purchased), a short sale also represents latent future demand for stock. When short interest becomes increasingly large by normal standards, the market may view this as a bullish signal. The demand for shares, driven by the buying activity to close the short positions, may have a positive effect on stock prices.

Alternatively, when the level of short interest is low, this could be an indicator that the market is over-bought and primed for a correction. The total amount of short interest can be found in publications such as Barron's or the Wall Street Journal.

Odd Lot Trading

A round lot is a trade, either buy or sell, that is equal to 100 shares. Institutional investors often trade shares in 100 block increments. An odd lot is a trade in any amount less than 100 shares. Most odd lot trades are made by individual investors. Individual investors trade in odd lots primarily because of capital constraints (limited financial resources) associated with purchasing in large 100-share blocks.

Sophisticated investors view the average individual investor as being unsophisticated and unable to accurately time the beginning or end of market trends. So, the odd-lot indicator suggests that when the number of odd lot purchases begins to far exceed the number of odd lot sales, it may be time to sell. The "odd 0" missed the signal to buy and have entered the market late. The market may be over-bought. Alternatively, when the number of odd lot sales far exceed the number of odd lot purchases, it may indicate an over-sold market, which is a buy signal. Odd lot trading is a contrarian indicator for technical analysts. In other words, those employing this concept tend to do the opposite of what unsophisticated investors are doing.

According to Nasdaq's chief economist, Phil Mackintosh, higher priced stocks have substantially more add lot trades than lower priced stocks. Mackintosh even suggests that odd lot quotes might even be more efficient in determining the best price in the market at any given time during the trading day.[4]

Charting

The Dow Theory, which was initially developed by Charles Dow, is the foundation for several of the tools and methods used by technical analysts today. Charles Dow was the first editor of the Wall Street Journal and co-founder of Dow Jones and Company.

According to the theory, there are three types of price movements, or trends, observed in the market. The premise of the Dow Theory is that trend behavior signals the end of both bear and bull markets. The first type of price movement is a primary trend. Primary trends are long-term trends observed in the markets. These trends can signify a bull market (long-term trend is increasing) or a bear market (market is decreasing). Primary trends last anywhere from one to four years.

The second type of price movement is a secondary movement. Intermediate movements of this type represent a temporary change, or technical correction. The time frame for secondary movements is generally less than two months. The third type of movement is called a ripple. A ripple is a very small change and may occur simultaneously with both primary and secondary movements.

Once a primary trend is established, asset prices tend to move in that direction. The primary trend will be supported by the same directional movement in both the Dow Jones Industrial Average (DJIA) and the Dow Jones Transportation Average (DJTA). The primary trend will continue until the trend is reversed, as evidenced by both the DJIA and the DJTA. Specifically, the primary trend terminates when the secondary movements in the DJIA are confirmed by secondary movements in the DJTA.

4. https://www.nasdaq.com/articles/two-charts-show-how-smart-traders-use-odd-lots-compress-spreads-high-priced-stocks-2019-06.

Exhibit 10.15 | Dow Jones Industrial Average and Dow Jones Transportation Average

Bar Charts

One of the more popular charts used by technical analysts is the bar chart. The charts are easy to develop and interpret. A bar chart plots the high, low, and closing price of a stock for a particular unit of time (day, week, month, etc.). Incremental prices are represented on the vertical axis. Units of time make up the horizontal axis. The bar chart provides a visual tool to identify trends as well as price volatility.

Exhibit 10.16 displays a bar chart for Apple. The chart covers the period from October 17, 2016 through December 16, 2016. For each trading day, the vertical bar represents the trading range for Apple stock on that day. The perpendicular mark on each bar represents the closing price.

Exhibit 10.16 | Apple Bar Chart and 50-Day Moving Average

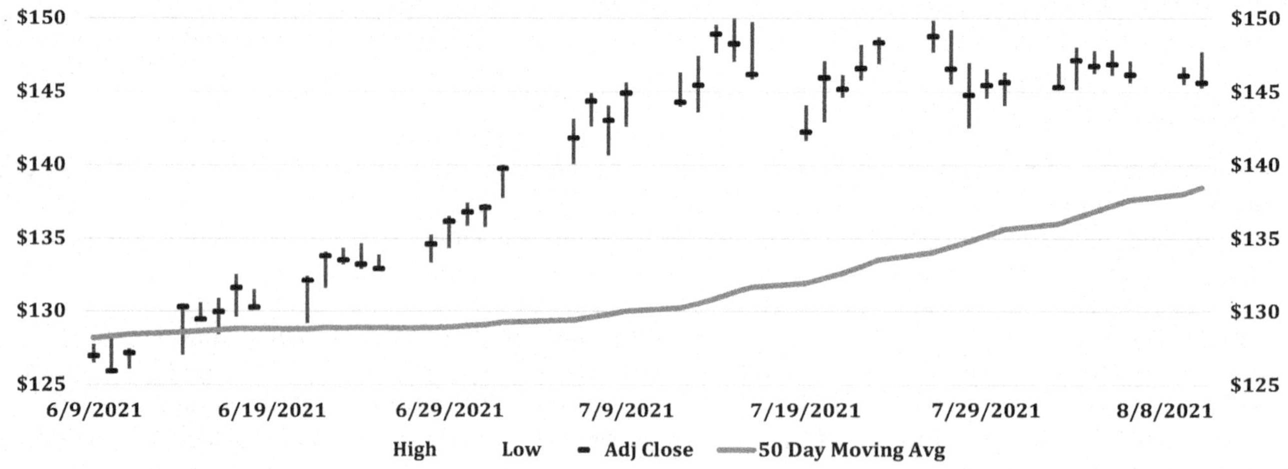

Moving Average

Daily price charts often show considerable short-term volatility. The volatility may be important for short-term investing, but in the long run this volatility is often inconsequential. It is thought to be nothing more than a "ripple." For long-term forecasts and trend identification, it is best to ignore short-term volatility.

A tool that smooths out minor, short-term variation in price changes is the moving average. The moving average is a useful indicator of long-term trends. A moving average is an arithmetic mean of stock prices. For example, a 10-day moving average calculates the average price over the previous ten trading days. As each day passes, the price from the most distant trading day (in the range) is dropped, and the price from the recent trading day is added. There are always ten prices used to determine the average. The prices used in the calculation "move" or shift forward by one day each trading day.

Moving averages are often calculated over periods from 10 to 200 days. Moving averages calculated using longer periods are better for identifying trends and reversals.

Refer again to **Exhibit 10.16**. Also plotted on that chart is the 50-day moving average. Note the smoothness of the 50-day moving average line, relative to the sporadic daily price activity of the stock.

The following exhibit illustrates how to calculate a moving average. Seven days of data are provided in the table. The prices for the first five days are added and divided by five. This calculation equals the moving average for Day 5.

Exhibit 10.17 | 5-Day Moving Average

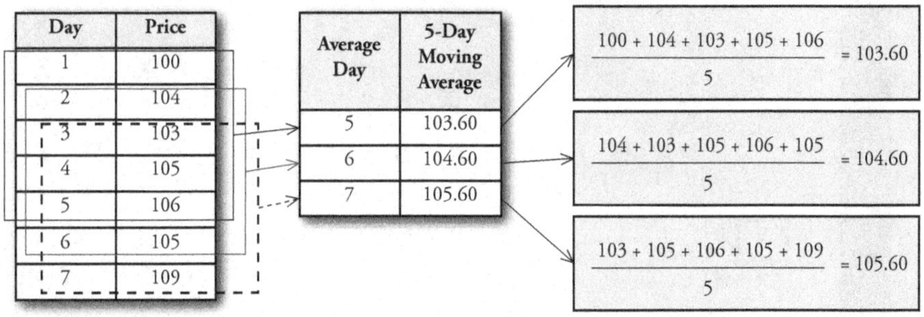

The calculation of the moving average for Day 6 drops the price for Day 1 and adds the price for Day 6. Notice that the average increases by 1.00. The difference between the price for Day 1 of 100 and the price for Day 6 of 105 is five. Dividing this difference by five results in an average increase of 1.00.

The calculation of the moving average for Day 7 drops the price for Day 2 and adds the price for Day 7. Notice that the average increases by 1.00. The difference between the price for Day 2 of 104 and the price for Day 7 of 109 is five. Dividing this difference by five results in an average increase of 1.00.

Note that the moving average shows less volatility than the actual series of daily prices.

Point and Figure Charts

Point and figure charts are popular technical analysis tools that help to identify price trends. These visual tools have been used for many years. There is no time dimension on a point and figure graph. The chart follows a column format with price represented on the vertical axis. Price reversals are represented on the horizontal axis. Minor price changes are not recorded; rather, only significant price changes are plotted on the chart.

On the charts, price movements are denoted by Xs and Os. A price increase is recorded by placing an X in the box on the chart. Each box has a box size. This is a setting that determines the amount a stock that must change in price before the price change is recorded. For example, if the box size is two, then only price changes greater than or equal to $2 are recorded. Another important setting is the reversal amount. This setting determines the opposite price change that is necessary before a reversing trend is documented on the chart.

Example 10.3

The point and figure chart below uses a 2-point box size and reversal amount also equal to $2. Assume that the stock has been actively trading, increasing from $36 to $48 (see second column). The last positive trade occurred at a price of $48 (note the X in the box). Following that trade, the price fell from $48 to $46. The drop by $2 reflects the start of a reversing trend. Since the asset changed in value by the required reversal amount, a "O" is placed the next column (column 3) to represent $46. Assume that over the course of the next several weeks, the stock gradually fell from $46 to $38. Only trades that changed in price by at least $2 were recorded on the chart. The trend reversed again when the stock price rose again to $40 per share.

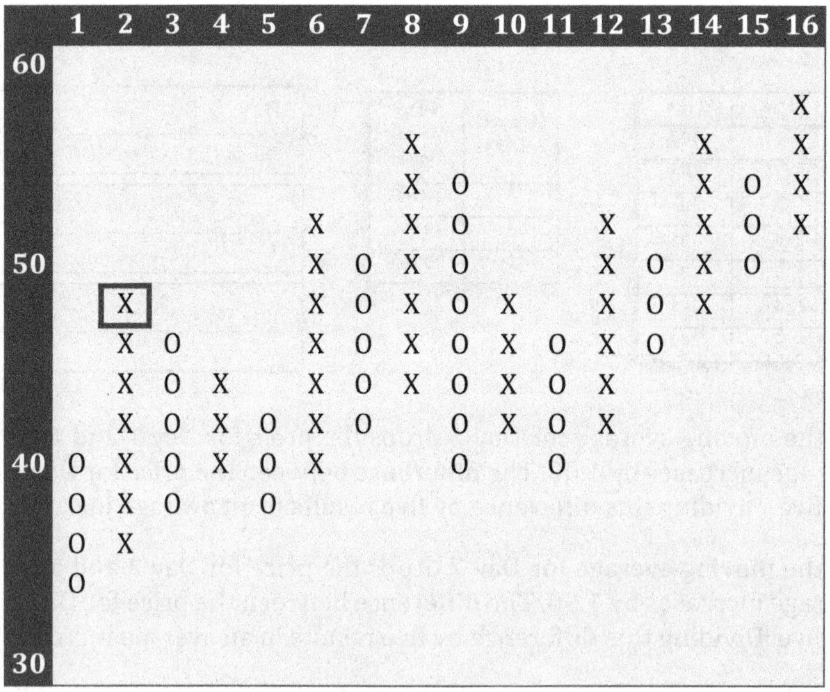

Remember that there is no standard time element represented on point and figure charts. Each column represents a trend, and the length of the trend can vary from intraday to days, weeks, or months. In addition to identifying price trends, point and figure charts also help to identify support and resistance levels.

Support and Resistance Levels

Charts can be useful tools to help investors make important trading decisions. Not only does a chart visually show stock movements over time, they also help identify support and resistance levels.

Support levels indicate the floor price below which an asset is not expected to trade. When a stock is trading near its support level, most investors expect the stock price to increase. At the support level, demand for the stock drives the price higher. Similarly, resistance levels represent a "ceiling" for the stock price trading range. When an asset sells near the ceiling, investors may believe that asset value has peaked and will likely fall.

Assume that a chartist has plotted stock price movement over time. The stock has fluctuated significantly over the last twelve months. In spite of the volatility, the investor observes that the stock never falls below $62 and never rises above $78. As the price nears $62 in the future, the investor may decide to buy the asset as it is unlikely that the price will fall below this support level. Similarly, if the price of the asset increases to the $78 range, the investor may decide to sell the asset. It is unlikely that the resistance level will be crossed.

Quick Quiz 10.10

1. Technical analysis incorporates fundamental analysis.
   a. True
   b. False
2. The advance-decline is positive if upward sloping.
   a. True
   b. False
3. If short sales are up it is initially a negative sign.
   a. True
   b. False
4. If odd lot purchase to sales decline, that is a positive.
   a. True
   b. False

False, True, True, True.

Refer to the bar chart for Eli Lilly & Company. During the period of observation, there is a noticeable resistance level at approximately $78 per share. A support level can be seen at approximately $62 per share.

Exhibit 10.18 | Eli Lilly Support

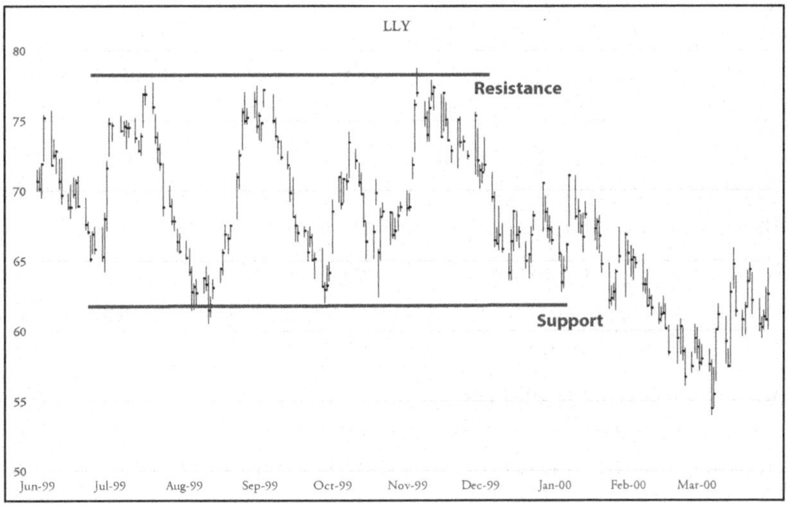

SUMMARY

Summary of key points:

- Fundamental analysis is the process of using publicly available information regarding a financial security's cash flows to estimate the intrinsic value of the security.
- There are two approaches to performing a solid fundamental analysis: bottom-up and top-down approaches.
- The bottom-up approach is an analysis of individual firms that issue financial securities. The goal of the bottom-up approach is to find undervalued securities based on intrinsic values or relative valuation measures.
- The top-down approach is a sequential analysis of the macro economy, of specific industries, and then finally of the individual securities that are a part of the highest growing industries. The goal of the top-down approach is to find undervalued securities based on industry and general economic conditions.
- Economic analysis is a thorough investigation of the relevant economic factors that tend to impact the value of specific securities. Factors include GDP, inflation, interest rates and unemployment rates.
- Monetary policy is one of two ways that federal governments exercise control or influence over the inflation, supply, economic growth, and employments levels. The Federal Reserve in the U.S. has four primary tools for monetary policy: reserve requirements, discount rate, open market operations, and excess reserve deposits.
- Fiscal policy is one of two ways that federal governments exercise control or influence over inflation, supply, economic growth, and employments levels. The U.S. Congress has the ability to spend and tax, and these are the two tools for fiscal policy.
- Business cycles are defined by periods of economic growth in which companies are expanding revenues, cash flows and asset size. This period is followed by a leveling off of growth rates and then a subsequent decline in economic activity. The economy eventually recovers and begins growing again. The four stages are expansion, peak, recession, and trough.
- Industry analysis is an investigation of an entire industry to determine industry trends, patterns and the industry life cycle. The stages of the life cycle are pioneering development, rapid growth, mature growth, market maturity, and market decline.
- Porter's competitive forces defines the competitive structure of an industry and includes rivalry among present competitors, threat of new entrants, threat of substitute products, bargaining power of buyers, and bargaining power of suppliers.
- Company analysis, sometimes referred to as security analysis, is a fundamental or quantitative analysis of a specific company in which financial statements are evaluated, corporate leadership skills are observed, and a prediction of future profitability and cash flows are made.
- Financial analysts use information to make the various types of analyses from annual reports, finance websites, reports made by financial organizations, and perform a SWOT analysis assessing the strategy of individual companies.

- SWOT analysis is a strategic planning tool that assesses the operating strengths, weaknesses, opportunities and threats to a business.
- Ratio analysis is a tool to evaluate the financial performance of a business by examining its reported financial statements. A complete ratio analysis includes to calculation of the specific ratio as well as an observation of trends and a comparison against industry competitors.
- Liquidity ratios measure a firm's ability to convert its short-term assets into cash to meet short-term obligations. Important ratios include the current ratio and the quick ratio.
- Asset management ratios measure a firm's ability to generate revenues from the purchase of its assets. Important ratios include the total asset turnover and inventory turnover.
- Financial leverage ratios measure a firm's ability to manage its capital structure. A debt ratio will magnify returns and losses.
- Profitability ratios measure a firm's ability to generate a profit. Important ratios include the return on assets and the return on equity.
- The DuPont formula is a compartmentalization tool to show the important components of the return on equity. The three parts are profit margin, asset turnover, and leverage.
- The degree of operating leverage measures the sensitivity of a firm to changes in sales and operating income.
- The degree of financial leverage measures the sensitivity of a firm to change in operating income on earnings per share.
- The degree of total leverage is a combination of the degrees of operating and financial leverage.
- Market value ratios measure the relationship between a company's stock price and important financial data. Important market value ratios include the price-to-earnings ratio, the price-to-book-value ratio, and the dividend yield.
- Technical analysis is a tool that uses historical stock price or volume data to estimate future stock pricing patterns. Important tools of technical analysts include market volume, the advance-decline line, and short interest.
- Support and resistance levels are important components of technical analysis and are used to define reasonable ranges for future stock prices.

DISCUSSION QUESTIONS

SOLUTIONS to the discussion questions can be found exclusively within the chapter. Once you have completed an initial reading of the chapter, go back and highlight the answers to these questions.

1. Explain the difference between fundamental and technical analysis.
2. What are the most important economic variables to consider when conducting an economic analysis as part of fundamental analysis.
3. Explain fiscal and monetary policy and why they are important in an economic analysis.
4. Describe the business cycle.
5. Compare and contrast cyclical industries with defensive industries.
6. Describe the life cycle for the normal industry identifying each important stage.
7. What are Porter's five forces and what do they reveal to us?
8. Explain the DuPont formula.
9. Identify the tools of technical analysis.
10. Explain the importance of profitability ratios.

MULTIPLE-CHOICE PROBLEMS

A sample of multiple choice problems is provided below. Additional multiple choice problems are available at money-education.com by accessing the Student Practice Portal.

1. During a period of recession/contraction, which of the following would be true?
   a. The supply of goods and services would increase.
   b. Interest rates would increase.
   c. Unemployment rates would decrease.
   d. Inflation would decrease.

2. Which of the following is a fiscal policy tool used by Congress that influences the money supply and interest rates?
   a. Prime Lending Rate.
   b. Open Market Operations.
   c. Discount Rate.
   d. Debt Management.

3. Which firm has high operating leverage? One with:
   a. High fixed costs and low variable cost.
   b. High fixed cost and high variable cost.
   c. Low fixed cost and low variable cost.
   d. Low fixed cost and high variable cost.

4. A firm has operating leverage if it uses which of the following?
   a. Long-term debt.
   b. An equal amount of debt and equity.
   c. Fixed costs.
   d. High variable costs.

5. Which of the following amplifies EPS?
   a. Degree of operational leverage.
   b. Degree of financial leverage.
   c. Both of the above.
   d. Neither of the above.

QUICK QUIZ EXPLANATIONS

Quick Quiz 10.1

1. False. This is the definition of technical analysis. Fundamental analysis is the process of determining the intrinsic value of a security.
2. True.

Quick Quiz 10.2

1. True.
2. True.

Quick Quiz 10.3

1. False. This is the definition of fiscal policy. Monetary policy is the intended influence on the money supply and interest rates by the central bank of a country.
2. True.

Quick Quiz 10.4

1. True.
2. True.

Quick Quiz 10.5

1. True.
2. True.

Quick Quiz 10.6

1. False. Market maturity follows mature growth. Rapid growth is right before mature growth.
2. True.

Quick Quiz 10.7

1. True.
2. False. If a firm increases its debt as part of its capital structure, it will increase financial leverage but not its operating leverage.

Quick Quiz 10.8

1. True.
2. True.
3. True.

Quick Quiz 10.9

1. False. The debt ratio equals total debt divided by total assets.
2. False. Gross profit margin equals gross profit divided by sales, not net income.
3. True.

Quick Quiz 10.10

1. False. Technical analysis largely ignores fundamental analysis.
2. True.
3. True.
4. True.

11

EQUITY SECURITIES - VALUATION

LEARNING OBJECTIVES

1. Understand the basics of equity analysis and valuation.*
2. Distinguish between a good company and a good investment.
3. Apply time value of money concepts to the valuation of equity securities.*
4. Identify the relevant cash flows in equity valuation models, including dividends and cash flows.*
5. Understand and apply the dividend discount model.*
6. Learn the circumstances under which the fair market value model is appropriate.*
7. Calculate a firm's sustainable growth rate.*
8. Compute a firm's required rate of return using the dividend discount model.*
9. Compute the value of equity using the two-stage dividend discount model.*
10. Compute the value of equity using the H Model.*
11. Identify the relevant variables used to determine free cash flow to equity.*
12. Use free cash flows in the dividend discount model to estimate the value of an equity security.*
13. Understand and apply relative valuation models.*
14. Distinguish among price-to-earnings, price-to-cash flow, price-to-book, and price-to-sales ratios.*
15. Understand the relationship among payout ratios, retention ratios, and growth rates.*

**Ties to CFP Certification Learning Objectives*

INTRODUCTION

The purpose of equity analysis and valuation is to evaluate investment alternatives and produce a recommendation to buy or sell a security. An individual security (or market sector) is analyzed in terms of its intrinsic value, which is its theoretical value based on **fundamental analysis**. If the intrinsic value of a security is determined to be greater than its current price, then the investor might consider buying it because it is undervalued. Alternatively, if the investment's intrinsic value is less than the current price, the investor should consider selling the security if it is owned. If the security is significantly overvalued by the market, then the investor might consider selling the security short or removing it from the portfolio.[1]

It is important to understand the difference between a great company and a great investment. A great company will generally deliver high quality competitive products or services, have a highly skilled management team, be well positioned in the market place, and generate free cash flow to shareholders, as well as various other characteristics. Just because a company is a great company does not mean that it is a great investment. It could simply be overvalued for a variety of reasons, including short-term fluctuations occurring entirely because of changing market conditions. A great investment is a great company that can be purchased at or below its **fair market value**.

Valuation of a firm utilizing fundamental analysis relies on long-run forecasts of the economy, the industry, and the company's financial statements. These inputs in the analysis are used in determining the company's prospects for the future. A company's future prospects are critical to investors in determining the intrinsic value of a security. These future prospects are important as they influence expectations of earnings and dividends.

1. Remember that "shorting" a security is the process of selling borrowed shares and then buying the shares in the market sometime in the future to replace the borrowed shares. If the security goes down in value, then the short seller will have a profit.

Example 11.1

In May 2015, Apple was trading above $130 per share. In May 2016, the stock was trading close to $90 per share. That decline represented a drop of more than 30% of the value of Apple stock in a twelve-month period. Why did this occur? The simple answer is that investors changed their expectations about future Apple product sales and earnings. Investors believed that the stock was overvalued. In August of 2017, Apple was trading around $160 per share and had increased to over $225 per share in August of 2018. By fall 2018, Apple's total market value exceeded $1 trillion because of its long-term success and the investor expectations that it will continue to provide excellent products.

Example 11.2

In July 2016, Nintendo launched the Pokemon Go app and the U.S. listed shares increased almost 100% to approximately $33 per share. This increase was in anticipation of higher revenue, earnings, and cash flow in the future. By March 2018, the stock was nearly $60 per share. However, the share price fell sharply when Nintendo released a statement clarifying that it only owned 32% of the Pokemon company and had already factored projected revenues into its forecasts. This shows the importance of a thorough analysis when determining the intrinsic value of stock.

The **top-down** process of fundamental analysis begins with a macro analysis of the economy before moving to industry analysis, and finally company analysis.

Equity can be valued using several different approaches. However, most valuation models are based on the concept of discounted cash flows. In some cases, valuation is based on dividends paid out by the stock, whereas other methods attempt to determine a value based on free cash flows to the shareholders.

As discussed, shareholders of a company have a right to profits or earnings after expenses are paid. Free cash flow is defined as the cash available to be potentially paid out to shareholders after expenses are paid and other investments in the operation of the company are made.

Dividend valuation models rely solely on dividend streams, or dividends expected to be received in the future. These dividend valuation models are based on modifications to the standard discounted cash flow model. As such, the model is only as accurate as estimates of expected future dividends and the other variables in the model.

Earnings valuation models are a variation of the dividend discount model, in which earnings are substituted as the main "cash flow" stream for valuation. Earnings valuation models may also call for a determination of a price-earnings ratio or some multiplier of earnings to determine value. Other models may reduce earnings to actual cash flows as opposed to accounting earnings. Some models rely on long-run historical relationships between market price and sales per share or market price and book value per share. This chapter discusses several valuation models and methods.

Key Concepts

1. Describe a firm that operates as a going concern.
2. Discuss the difference between absolute and relative valuation measures.
3. Explain how to estimate fair market value for a firm that is in bankruptcy proceedings.
4. Discuss why it is difficult to estimate fair market value of assets and liabilities.

VALUATION OF EQUITY SECURITIES

The method used to value a company is dependent on whether or not it is considered a going concern. Going concern is the term used to describe a business that is operating and expected to continue operations indefinitely. Companies that are not going concerns cannot be valued based on discounted cash flows as they are not expected to occur far into the future. These firms must be valuated based on liquidation value or some other method.

Valuation of Common Stock for Going Concerns

There are two broad types of valuation models for common stocks considered to be **going concerns**:

1. Absolute valuation models
2. Relative valuation models

An absolute valuation model is used to identify a common stock's intrinsic value, which is the stock's value assuming a complete understanding of the financial characteristics of that company and its future returns. Present value models are the most widely used type of absolute approach to common stock valuation. **Present value models** (sometimes referred to as discounted cash flow models) provide a point estimate of future cash flows to the investor discounted at an appropriate discount rate to today. This estimate can then be compared to the current stock price for the determination of buy, sell, or hold decisions.

Quick Quiz 11.1

1. Stock values and bond values can be estimated using the present value approach even though they have different types of cash flows.
   a. True
   b. False
2. If the market price of a firm's stock is less than its intrinsic value, the stock is most likely to be overvalued.
   a. True
   b. False

True, False.

Example 11.3

J.J. estimates the value of Jackson Brothers Inc. (JBI) to be $100. The market price for JBI is currently $87. Based on the valuation, it appears that the market is undervaluing JBI and it appears to be a potential buying opportunity for J.J. This estimate of a higher intrinsic value may indicate that the stock is undervalued or that the estimate does not take into consideration a factor or factors that the market is considering.

Present value models use future cash flows as the basis for the valuation. These projected cash flows may be dividends or free cash flows to the shareholders. Common shareholders have an equity ownership claim on the balance of the cash flows generated by the company after payments have been made to senior claimants such as bondholders and preferred stockholders. Cash flows at the company level are called free cash flows or residual income. Free cash flows are those cash flows that result from operations but take into consideration necessary reinvestments into capital assets and other working capital necessary to continue as a going concern.

The present value approach to valuing common stock is similar to that used to value bonds. However, the approach is simpler for bonds because barring default and the presence of embedded options, the future cash flows the bond will pay out are known with certainty. For a typical fixed coupon bond, the prospectus will outline the coupon payments that will be made over its life, and the principal that will be paid back at maturity. Risk-free interest rates, plus an appropriate spread, can also be used to discount those cash flows back to present value.

Common stock, however, has no maturity date and no obligation to pay out cash flows. Even dividends that may be paid to shareholders are discretionary. As a result, present value models used for equity typically have to make assumptions about future cash flows. In the simplest dividend discount model, a dividend stream which grows at a constant rate indefinitely is used as the cash flow, and the appropriate discount rate is estimated using the capital asset pricing model.

Relative valuation methods estimate or determine a common stock's value by comparing it to values of other similar companies. These comparable companies are generally in the same or similar industries and are often competitors. This method is based on the law of one price, which states that two assets that have identical characteristics and cash flows should also have the same value. Relative valuation methods typically use price multiples. The most common price multiple is the price earnings multiple or PE ratio. The PE ratio is simply the ratio of a company's stock price divided by the company's earnings per share. It provides an indication of the price investors are willing to pay for a dollar's worth of earnings from that company. Other relative valuation methods include the price-to-book ratio (PB), the price-to-sales ratio (PS) and the PE to growth ratio (PEG). These will be discussed later in this chapter.

Quick Quiz 11.2

1. The fair market value approach is appropriate for natural resource firms.
   a. True
   b. False
2. The calculation of fair market value ignores the effects of any preferred stock outstanding.
   a. True
   b. False

True, False.

Valuing Companies without Using the Going Concern Assumption or for Natural Resource Companies

When a company is not a going concern, it cannot be valued based on discounting a continuing stream of cash flows. If the value of the company is not based on the cash flow to shareholders, then the value is generally based on the net assets owned by the company. This valuation approach is accomplished by determining the fair market value (FMV) of the company's assets and then the FMV of the company's liabilities. This difference equals the FMV of the company. The FMV of the company must be reduced by any preferred stock rights to determine the value to common shareholders, which can then be divided by the outstanding shares of common stock to determine the per-share value.

Example 11.4

Premier Typewriters, Inc. (PTI) is shutting down operations due to a dramatic decline in the demand for typewriters. PTI is not insolvent and has the following assets and liabilities, stated at FMV:

Assets	FMV	Liabilities	FMV
Land	$4.5 million	Accounts payable	$0.5 million
Inventory	$0.0 million	Long-term debt	$2.5 million
Equipment	$2.3 million		
Cash	$1.0 million		
Accounts receivable	$1.2 million		
Total	**$9.0 million**	**Total**	**$3.0 million**

PTI cannot be valued based on future operations as it is shutting down and will no longer have future sales or earnings. However, the company can be valued based on its current assets and liabilities. Its assets are worth a total of $9 million and it has debt of $3 million. Based on these values, it is worth a net of $6 million. The balance sheet reflects a value of zero for inventory, because the inventory is obsolete and worthless.

A similar approach can be used for valuing natural resource companies such as those with oil reserves, mineral reserves or timber reserves. The valuation equals the current market price for the proven reserves less the cost to extract and sell those reserves. One interesting component of using fair market value for natural resource companies is that their cash flows are highly dependent on commodity prices. For example, shares in a gold mining company will fall if the price of gold drops substantially. Once again, liabilities and any preferred rights must be subtracted to arrive at the value for common shareholders. Finally, this value is divided by the outstanding common shares to determine the per common share value.

PRESENT VALUE MODELS

The value of most assets is based upon the cash for which the asset can be sold or the cash that the asset can generate in the future.[2] Present value models are important models for determining the value of assets that generate future cash flows, such as bonds, common stocks, and preferred stocks. These models discount the future cash flows at appropriate discount rates to determine the current or present value of the future cash flows.

The present value concept is based on the premise that the value of any asset is equal to the benefits or returns expected to be received from that asset over the holding period. In the case of common stock, these returns are cash flows in the form of dividends or the proceeds from a sale of the common stock. In considering cash flows as they occur over time, it is important to keep in mind that a dollar received in the future is less valuable than a dollar received today. Therefore, when evaluating a stream of expected future cash flows, an appropriate discount rate, which will reduce the future value to a present value, must be applied to each flow. The sum of the present values of each future cash flow is the estimated value of the common stock. The discount rate applied to the cash flows may be the same discount rate for all cash flows. Alternatively, different discount rates can be applied to different cash flows (such as those that are far in the future).

Keep in mind that accurately projecting cash flows available to common stock ownership is both difficult and uncertain. Cash flows to common stock are far more uncertain than bond cash flows. The first step is to identify the relevant cash flows to be used in equity valuation. The three most common inputs are dividends, free cash flows, and residual income.

Basic Present Value Model

The basic **present value model** has been discussed previously in the text. However, it is worth revisiting as it is the basis for most valuation models.

$$p_0 = \frac{CF_1}{(1+k)^1} + \frac{CF_2}{(1+k)^2} + \ldots + \frac{CF_t}{(1+k)^t}$$

2. Other factors that may impact the value of an asset include transaction costs, storage costs, etc.

P_0 = The value of the security today.
CF_t = The cash flow for period t.
k = The discount rate based on the type of security and the risk level of the investment.
t = The number of cash flows to be evaluated.

The model states that the value of a security today is equal to its future cash flows (CF_t), discounted at an appropriate discount rate (k) based on the security's level of risk.

Example 11.5

Neo is attempting to determine the value of Arc stock. Arc pays an annual dividend of $4 and Neo believes that he can sell the stock at the end of three years for $90. He also believes that a discount rate of 14% is appropriate. Based on these factors, the value of the stock is $70.03.

$$PV = \frac{\$4}{(1+0.14)^1} + \frac{\$4}{(1+0.14)^2} + \frac{\$94}{(1+0.14)^3} = \$70.03$$

If Arc were currently trading in the secondary market for $52 per share, then Neo should consider buying it as its intrinsic value of $70.03 is greater than its current market value. However, if Arc were trading at $80 per share, then Neo should avoid adding Arc to his portfolio, should consider selling the stock if he owned it, and might even consider shorting it.

Dividend Discount Model (DDM)

The **dividend discount model** calculates the present value of a company's estimated future dividend payments. While not all stocks pay dividends, most of the companies that are part of the S&P 500 do. For companies that retain 100 percent of earnings, dividend discount models are not appropriate.

Dividend discount models are most suitable when a company is a dividend paying company and there is an established dividend policy that bears an understandable and consistent relationship to the company's profitability.

There are a handful of S&P 500 companies (approximately 50) that have consistently increased their dividends over the last 25 years. Clorox, Coca Cola, and Johnson and Johnson are just a few that have historically rewarded shareholders by increasing their dividends regularly. These companies are called **dividend aristocrats**. Consistency of earnings or dividend payments provides a sense of certainty and hence lower risk.

Key Concepts

1. Describe the sustainable growth rate for a firm.
2. Discuss the similarities and differences between pricing common and preferred shares.
3. Discuss the advantages the two-stage dividend discount model has over the one developed by Myron Gordon in the 1950s.
4. Compare and contrast the two-stage model with the H Model.

Constant Growth Dividend Model

The most common dividend discount model is the **constant growth dividend model**, also known as the Gordon Growth Model, as it was published by Myron J. Gordon in 1956. The constant growth model assumes dividends grow at a constant growth rate (g) for the foreseeable future. To value this perpetuity with growth, the next dividend payment (D1) is simply divided by the required return (k) less the constant growth rate (g).

$$V_0 = \frac{D_1}{(k - g)}$$

V = value or price per share
D_1 = the dividend per share one period from today
k = investor's required return
g = the dividend growth rate

Example 11.6

Lissette is considering whether to buy Parker stock, which is currently trading at $72 per share. Parker Inc. is currently paying a three dollar per share dividend. Assume that the growth rate of the dividend is 4% and the Lissette's required return is 8%. The value of the stock equals $78.00 per share as follows:

$$V = \frac{\$3(1 + 0.04)}{(0.08 - 0.04)} = \$78.00$$

Notice that D_1 was not provided in the problem. The current dividend equals $3 per share. The current dividend is D_0. The dividend one period from today equals the dividend today multiplied by one plus the growth rate (g) of the dividend.

Should Lissette buy the stock? The stock is selling in the market for $72 per share and Lissette believes it is worth $78 per share. Therefore, this stock is undervalued and should be considered for purchase.[3]

The constant growth dividend model has several assumptions that limit the application and accuracy of this valuation model. These limitations include:

- The required return must be greater than growth rate of the dividend.
- The dividend stream is growing and expected to grow at a constant rate.

The model is highly sensitive to small differences in the required rate of return or the dividend growth rate. For example, changing the growth rate of the dividend in the above example from 4% to 5% will increase the value of the stock by more than 34%, from $78 per share to $105 per share. The calculation for the new value is as follows:

$$V = \frac{\$3(1 + 0.05)}{(0.08 - 0.05)} = \$105.00$$

3. Why should the stock only be considered for purchase? Even when the stock is undervalued, it may not be the best stock or the best investment at the time.

As the investor's required return approaches the growth rate of the dividend, the value of the stock will increase exponentially. The exhibit below illustrates the increase in the value as the required return in the example above approaches 5%.

Required rate of Return	8.0%	7.5%	7.0%	6.5%	6.0%	5.5%	5.4%	5.3%	5.2%	5.1%
Equity Value	$105	$126	$158	$210	$315	$630	$788	$1,050	$1,575	$3,150

As indicated above, the model does not work if the required return is less than or equal to the growth rate of the dividend payment.

Example 11.7

The required rate of return for XYZ stock is 9%. The dividend for XYZ stock is currently $6.50 per share with a growth rate of 5%. The value of XYZ equals $170.63 as follows:

$$V = \frac{\$6.50(1 + 0.05)}{(0.09 - 0.05)} = \$170.63$$

Compare this to the value of XYZ assuming the dividend has zero growth, i.e., XYZ simply pays out the current dividend of $6.50 for the foreseeable future:

$$V = \frac{\$6.50(1 + 0.00)}{(0.09 - 0.00)} = \$72.22$$

By subtracting the value of the current dividend stream without growth from the value for the stock assuming a 5% growth rate for the dividend stream, the resulting value of the growth of the dividend stream equals $98.41 ($170.63 - $72.22). This demonstrates that, the value of the stock is significantly impacted by the growth of the future dividend payments.

The next step is to develop a model to estimate the firm's growth rate in dividends. In theory, dividends can only grow if the firm's operating cash flows increase, unless the firm funds the growth via external financing. In the absence of a bond or equity issue, the sustainable growth rate in dividends is a function of the percentage of earnings reinvested back into the firm and the firm's return on equity. It is the maximum rate of growth a firm can achieve using internally generated funds. Hence the sustainable growth rate (g) can be calculated as:

$$\mathbf{g = ROE \times Retention\ Ratio}$$

Example 11.8

Parrish Breads Inc (PBI) recently paid a dividend of $3.81 and reported earnings per share of $10.32. PBI also reported an ROE of 11.2% and its shareholders require a rate of return of 9.6%. Determine the sustainable growth rate and then use it to estimate the price of the shares.

$$g = 0.112 \times \frac{10.32 - 3.81}{10.32} = 0.0707$$

$$V = \frac{\$3.81(1.0707)}{(0.096 - 0.0707)} = \$161.24$$

PBI can grow by approximately 7% without having to issue any new securities. As such, the value of the shares depends on the firm's ability to generate an accounting profit (ROE) and the percentage it reinvests back into its existing product lines (63%). Note the two extreme cases: When a firm pays out all of its earnings in dividends, the growth rate is zero. When it pays no dividends, the growth rate is the return on equity.

The constant growth dividend model can also be used to derive the assumed required rate of return for the dividend stream when the investor has the current dividend and the market value of the stock along with the dividend growth rate. The formula is simply rearranged algebraically. Consider the following example.

Example 11.9

Anna is trying to determine the implicit required rate of return for Beat stock. The current dividend of Beat stock is $2 and the dividend growth rate is 5%. The current price of the stock is $42. The constant growth dividend model can be rewritten as follows to be solved for required return.

$$r = \frac{D_1}{P} + g, \text{ where P is the current price of the stock}$$

$$r = \frac{\$2(1.05)}{\$42} + 0.05 = 10\%$$

In this case, the implicit required rate of return built into the stock price is 10%. If Anna has a required rate of return less than 10%, then this stock will look attractive to buy.

The constant growth dividend model is appropriate for valuing stocks that pay a dividend with a stable growth rate. The model is simple and clear and is useful for understanding the relationship between price, growth, required rate of return, and payout ratio. However, it is highly sensitive to the assumed dividend growth rate and the required rate of return. It is also not applicable for stocks that pay no dividend, or those that have an unstable growth rate in dividends.

Preferred Stock & Perpetuities – Zero Growth

The constant growth dividend model discussed above can be modified to value preferred stock. Preferred stock generally pays a fixed dividend that remains constant into the future. Because these cash flows continue indefinitely at the same amount, preferred stock is referred to as a perpetuity. The constant growth model is modified for a zero-growth dividend stream, as follows.

Begin with the constant growth model:

$$V = \frac{D_0(1+g)}{(k-g)}$$

Substitute 0 in for g:

$$V = \frac{D_0}{k}$$

By substituting zero for g, the formula for valuing a perpetuity simplifies to the dividend divided by the discount rate.

Quick Quiz 11.3

1. The price for a firm that pays a constantly growing dividend will increase when the shareholder's required return increases.
   a. True
   b. False
2. The required return on equity must exceed the dividend growth rate in the constant growth dividend models.
   a. True
   b. False

False, True.

Example 11.10

ABC preferred stock is paying an annual dividend of \$4.00 per share. If the required rate of return equals 10%, the value of ABC preferred is \$40.00. This value is calculated by dividing \$4.00 by 0.10.

Two-Stage Dividend Discount Model

One criticism of the constant growth dividend model is that it assumes constant growth rates over indefinite time periods. For most firms, this assumption is not too realistic, as many firms change their dividend growth rates over time. The **two-stage dividend growth model** allows for growth rates to change. This is especially relevant for a firm that uncovers a high growth opportunity that will last for only a few years, after which the firm will return to its more normal growth rate. The constant growth dividend model can be modified to allow for two stages of growth. The first stage is an initial period of growth, which is typically not stable and often higher than the growth rate for the second phase. The initial phase is often easier to predict as it is not as far into the future. It should be noted that the initial phase of growth does not have to be positive. This period of growth could be low, or even negative, which might indicate a period of building or investment in the company. The second phase will be a period of steady growth. The value of the stock is based on the formula below.

$$V_0 = \sum_{i=1}^{n} \frac{D_t}{(1+k)^t} + \frac{P_n}{(1+k)^n}$$

V = value or price of the stock

D_t = the dividend per share for period t

k = required return of the investor

P_n = price of the stock at time-period n based on the constant growth dividend model (terminal value)

n = the time period for the initial phase

The cash flows during the initial growth period are discounted individually. The cash flows during the constant growth period can be valued using the constant growth model discussed above. The value of these constant growth cash flows is often referred to as the **terminal value**. Consider the example below:

Example 11.11

Stark, Inc. creates a new revolutionary reactor and expects that its dividend will increase significantly over the next few years. Beyond the initial growth period, Stark expects that its dividend will increase at 5% per year indefinitely. Assuming the required return equals 14%, what is the value of a single share of Stark stock? The exhibit below depicts the expected increase in growth of Stark's dividends over the next six years.

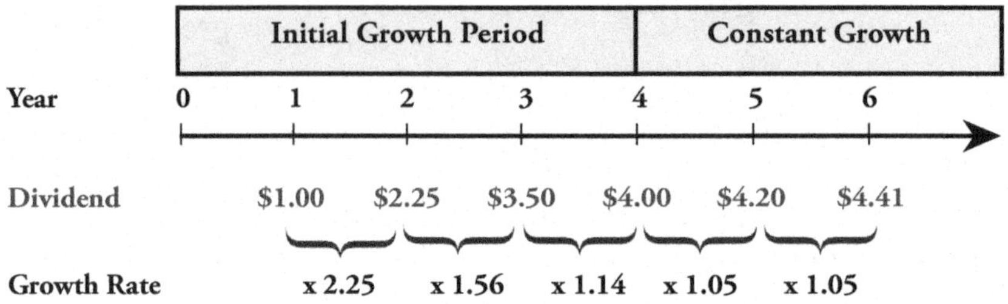

The terminal value is determined at year 4, from which there is constant growth of 5%. The value of the stock at year 4 equals $46.67, as follows:

$$V = \frac{D_1}{(k - g)}$$

$$V = \frac{\$4.20}{(0.14 - 0.05)} = \$46.67$$

The model calls for D_1. If the value of the stock is being valued at year 4, then D_1 is the dividend in year 5, which is $4.20. Based on the above terminal value of $46.67, the cash flows that must be discounted to determine the intrinsic value of the stock are as follows:

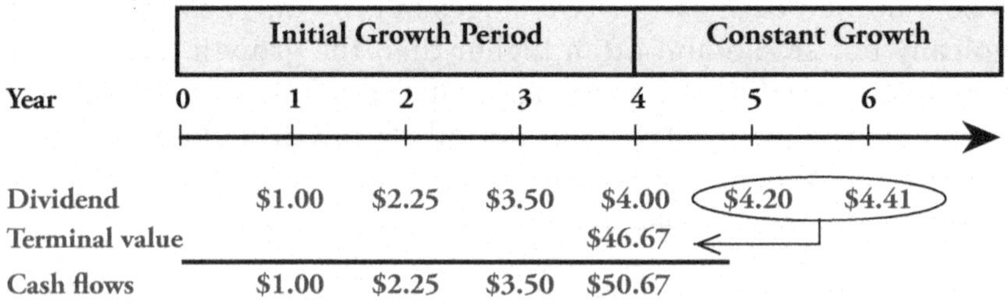

$$PV = \frac{\$1.00}{(1 + 0.14)^1} + \frac{\$2.25}{(1 + 0.14)^2} + \frac{\$3.50}{(1 + 0.14)^3} + \frac{(\$4.00 + \$46.67)}{(1 + 0.14)^4} = \$34.97$$

The discounted future cash flows equal $34.97. This value consists of the forecasted dividends in years 1 through 4 plus the terminal value. The terminal value at period 4 equals $46.67. Discounted to period 0, the terminal value equals $27.63. Therefore, approximately 79% of this value is attributable to the discounted terminal value.

The terminal value represents the future dividend stream beyond year 4. Changes in the underlying assumptions may have small or large impacts depending on the variable that changes.

Consider the following:

- Assuming the expected growth rate of the dividend stream was only 4% instead of 5%, the value of Stark would drop $3.00 to $31.97.
- Assuming the expected growth rate of the dividend stream was 6% instead of 5%, the value of Stark would increase by $3.75 to $38.72.
- Assuming the required return is 12% and the dividend growth rate remains at 5%, the value of Stark would increase by $10.88 to $45.85.

This two-stage methodology can be applied to cash flows that consist of dividends or free cash flows to shareholders. As near-term cash flows are more reliably forecasted than those far out into the future, the two-stage model is flexible enough to accommodate multiple growth factors. The two-stage model can also be adapted to a multi-stage model to accommodate more than two growth phases.

H-Model

One of the main weaknesses in the two-stage growth model is the reliance on an abrupt and dramatic change in dividends. In reality, firms do not change their dividend payments substantially unless a major event dictates a large increase or reduction in dividend payments. Rather, firms like to offer shareholders a smooth dividend policy with changes occurring gradually over time to reflect changes in profitability.

Quick Quiz 11.4

1. The H Model and the two-stage model make identical assumptions regarding dividend growth rates.
   a. True
   b. False
2. The two-stage dividend discount model relies on the stock's terminal value estimation.
   a. True
   b. False

False, True.

To account for gradual dividend changes, financial analysts use the **H Model**, which takes the form:

$$V = \frac{Div_0 \times (1 + ag)}{k - ag} + \frac{Div_0 \times H \times (hg - ag)}{k - ag}$$

Div_0 = The firm's current dividend
ag = The firm's long-term average growth rate
k = The required return on equity
H = The half-life of the transition time from high growth to low growth
hg = The firm's short-term high growth rate

Example 11.12

Matthews Tire Company (MTC) is expecting its current dividend of $1.16 to grow considerably over the next eight years after it acquires a major competitor. The high growth rate is expected to be 18% but will gradually decline to its normal average rate of 4%. MTC's shareholders require a 9.2% return.

Use the H Model to value MTC's shares.

$$V = \frac{1.16 \times (1.04)}{0.092 - 0.04} + \frac{1.16 \times 4 \times (0.18 - 0.04)}{0.092 - 0.04} = 35.69$$

MTC will experience a gradual decline in its growth rate in dividends from 18% down to 4% over an eight-year period (half life of four years). The H Model values MTC at $35.69. The H Model works fairly well when the time period is relatively short and the difference between the two growth rates is relatively low.

Valuation Using Free Cash Flows

A dividend discount model is not always the best choice for valuing a stock. Common situations where other approaches may be more suited include:

1. the company is not paying dividends
2. the company pays a dividend, but it is significantly different (generally lower, but not always) from the firm's ability to pay dividends
3. the investor is valuing the company from a control point of view[4]

In these situations, an analyst may instead choose to calculate the present value of future free cash flow to equity instead of dividends. If dividends are zero, or not reflective of the company's ability to distribute cash flows, free cash flow to equity may provide a more accurate valuation. In addition, a free cash flow to equity model has the advantage of reflecting a control perspective.

Dividend discount models assume the future cash flows received by an investor are simply the dividends the firm pays. This is true for minority investors who have no say in the firm's dividend policy. However, if the valuation is being carried out from a control perspective, free cash flows are a more relevant metric than dividends. A investor who controls a firm also controls all the free cash flows that it generates. In this case, a free cash flow model is more appropriate.

Free cash flow to equity (FCFE) is the cash flow available to the company's common shareholders after the firm has met all of its capital spending requirements and paid off debt and preferred stockholders.

Key Concepts

1. Describe the importance of non-cash expenses in the free cash flow to equity calculation.
2. Discuss how free cash flow to equity can help value a firm in a control situation.
3. Compare and contrast each price multiple.
4. Explain why price-to-earnings and price-to-sales are different relative measures.

4. Publicly-traded stock is valued as a minority interest because no single investor typically has more than 50% of the stock, which is a controlling interest. When a public company's stock is purchased in an acquisition, the acquiring company will generally pay a control premium, which is a premium above the market price that reflects the value of controlling the company.

Although different analysts may calculate slightly different versions of FCFE, the formula below shows the typical steps required to calculate FCFE from Net Income.

Free Cash Flow to Equity

+	Net Income
+	Depreciation and Amortization (Add back non-cash expenses)
-	Capital Expenditures (Cash that is reinvested back into the company)
-	Changes in Net Working Capital (Working Capital = Current Assets – Current Liabilities)
+	New Bond Issues or Bank Loans
-	Debt Repayments
=	Free Cash Flow to Equity

The formula starts with net income which includes some non-cash expenses such as accounting depreciation and amortization. These non-cash expenses are added back (non-cash income would be removed) to turn the net income figure into a cash flow.

Next, the cash a company must reinvest in its fixed assets and working capital must be deducted, as this is not 'free' to be distributed to equity holders. Finally, interactions with providers of debt are taken into account. Any cash raised via debt issues during the year is added (debt repayments would be deducted) and interest paid on outstanding debt is deducted.

Once FCFE has been calculated, it can be used in a discounted cash flow model to value a firm. In addition to FCFE, this will require a growth rate for FCFE (or more than one growth rate if a two-stage model is to be used) and the firm's cost of equity to use as the discount rate.

Quick Quiz 11.5

1. Free cash flow to equity will increase when a firm issues new bonds.
   a. True
   b. False
2. A free cash flow to equity model is not appropriate for firms that do not pay dividends.
   a. True
   b. False

True, False.

Example 11.13

DC Car Wash is a successful family-owned business. The matriarch of the family has decided to sell the business to a national company that operates multiple automobile services. To determine if the bid DC has received is fair, the family has asked Preston, their financial manager, to determine a value based on its cash flows. Preston collects the following information from DC's financial statements for the current year:

Profit Before Tax	$400,000
Changes in Working Capital	$25,000
Loan from Gibraltar Bank	$75,000
Payment of Principal on Real Estate Loans	$12,000
Purchase of Long-Term Assets	$15,000
Depreciation Expense	$33,000
Taxes Paid	$54,000

DC has experienced a constant growth rate in its cash flows of 4.2% annually, and there is no reason to believe the acquiring firm can exceed that rate after the takeover. The cost of equity for similar businesses is 11.9%.

To determine a market value for DC based on cash flows, the first step is to compute free cash flow to equity.

Profit Before Tax	$400,000
Taxes Paid	$54,000
Net Income	$346,000
Depreciation Expense	$33,000
Capital Expenditures	$15,000
Change in WC	$25,000
New Bank Loan	$75,000
Debt Repayments	$12,000
FCFE	$402,000

The current FCFE is $402,000. To determine market value, use the discounted cash flow model:

$$\text{Value} = \frac{\$402{,}000 \times 1.042}{0.119 - 0.042} = \$5{,}440{,}051$$

The total market value of the car wash in $5,440,051. To obtain the firm's stock price, simply divide by the number of outstanding shares.

Example 11.14

Assume Spectra Inc. has FCF per share of $9.00 this year and that FCF is expected to increase at 3.5% for the foreseeable future. If the cost of equity is 12%, then the value of Spectra equals $109.59 as follows.

$$V = \frac{\$9.00(1 + 0.035)}{0.12 - 0.035} = \$109.59$$

If the stock is currently trading in the market for $92 per share, then the stock is currently undervalued and may be considered a buy. If the stock were trading at $135 per share, then the stock is overvalued.

RELATIVE VALUATION METHODS (PRICE MULTIPLES)

Relative valuation models are not a new or unusual concept. They are based on the law of one price, which is an economic theory that states that identical assets should sell for identical prices. The FMV of a home is generally based on "comps," which are the sales prices of comparable properties. If a home owner is selling her house (House A) and a similar house (House B) just sold for $200,000, then her house is likely to sell at or around $200,000. There are naturally exceptions. If House A has better perceived features and amenities, then it is likely to sell for a premium over House B. However, those amenities are not likely to double the price of the house. Rather, they are likely to cause the house to sell at a premium. The types of amenities that might increase the value of a house include a pool, an updated kitchen and bathroom, and smart home technology.

Similarly, some investors estimate the value of a common stock based on comparison to other companies. They may use these relative valuation methods instead of, or in addition to, focusing on dividends or free cash flows. These relative valuation methods are generally referred to as multiples. The most common of these multiples is the **price-to-earnings** multiple or PE Ratio. Other multiples used include price-to-book, price-to-sales, and the PEG ratio.

When using relative measures, investors should compare a company's ratio or ratios to similar companies or an average of peer group companies. Generally, these comparisons will be made within an industry. Making relative valuation even more challenging is the possibility that perceived similar firms are actually quite different. For example, according to Hoover's, Johnson and Johnson operates three business segments: medical devices, pharmaceuticals, and consumer goods. Hoover's lists Colgate Palmolive and Pfizer as its top competition, but CP does not sell medical devices and Pfizer does not compete in the same consumer market as Johnson and Johnson.

PE Ratio

The price-to-earnings ratio is likely the most widely used relative measure of value. It relies on the concept that earnings are the key measure of value for any financial security. As discussed, shareholders are entitled to the earnings of a company. It follows that the higher the earnings for a company, the more valuable the company. The PE ratio is essentially the amount of money that investors are willing to pay for a single dollar of earnings. If the PE ratio for a company is 10, then investors are willing to pay $10 for every dollar of earnings. If the company is expected to earn $3.50 per share, then the company should be selling for $35 per share. Below is a chart that illustrates historical PE ratios.[5]

Exhibit 11.1 | S&P Equity Index Historical PE Ratios

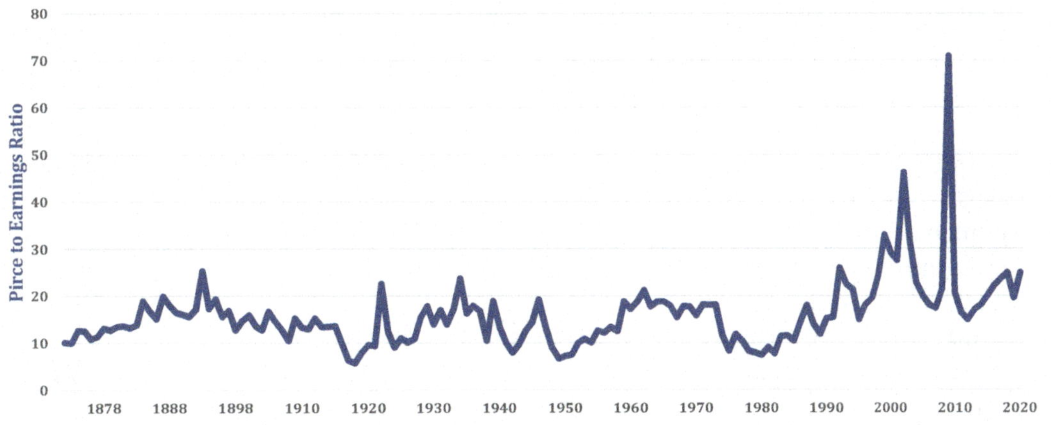

The exhibit above illustrates at least two important points. First, investors go through periods of irrational exuberance. Yes. That term is the name of Robert Shiller's book. However, it seems quite appropriate. It means that investors periodically get caught up in the momentum of the stock market and basically pay far too much for stocks. The values of stocks during these periods are not rational. The second point that

5. Source: Robert Shiller – online stock market data used in his book, *Irrational Exuberance*, 2000.

is illustrated is that historic PE ratios typically fall within a range with a floor of approximately five and a ceiling of approximately 25. There can be substantial variations, however, and the average appears to trend upwards. This range is nothing more than an average. A single security may reasonably trade above or below this range. A diversified portfolio, however, should generally not have an average PE ratio that is far outside these ranges.

$$\text{PE Ratio} = \frac{\text{Current Market Price per Share}}{\text{Earnings per Share}}$$

Current market price per share is simply the current price of the stock trading in the market.

Often, earnings per share (EPS) is a trailing 12 months of earnings or the most recent four quarters of earnings. This PE ratio is referred to as the **trailing PE ratio**. PE ratios, however, can also be based on expected 12 months of earnings. This PE ratio is referred to as the forward PE ratio or **leading PE ratio**. The trailing PE ratio is based on historical data, while the leading PE ratio is based on expectations.

When investors use the PE ratio, they typically evaluate the PE ratio in comparison to the market, as well as other possible investments. In some cases, a firm with tremendous growth prospects may justifiably have a relatively high PE ratio.

Fundamental PE Ratio

A firm's PE ratio can also be compared to its fundamental PE ratio to judge whether it appears to be correctly priced. The fundamental PE ratio can be derived from the constant growth dividend model:

$$P_0 = \frac{D_1}{(k - g)}$$

Divide both sides by earnings:

$$\text{PE Ratio} = \frac{(D_1 \div E)}{k - g} = \frac{\text{Payout Ratio}}{k - g}$$

If this fundamental PE ratio is higher than the actual PE ratio, it could be an indication that the stock is undervalued. The fundamental PE ratio calculation also highlights the three key inputs that impact its value:

1. The payout ratio of the firm – remember that sustainable growth decreases as the payout ratio increases.
2. The required return:
   - The required return is a measure of the return investors demand for the level of risk inherent within the security.
   - As the required return goes up, the PE ratio goes down.
   - The required return is influenced by the risk-free rate of return, inflation and a risk premium that accounts for the specific risk of the specific security.
   - The required return can be estimated by using the capital asset pricing model.[6]
3. The expected growth rate of dividends:
   - As the growth rate of dividends increases, so does the PE ratio.
   - Recall that sustainable growth equals the retention rate times ROE. Dividend growth potential is driven largely by earnings growth.

6. The formula for the capital asset pricing model is: $E(R) = R_f + ß(R_m - R_f)$.

Example 11.15

Topo, Inc. is a stock that has a dividend payout of 75%, a required return of 12%, and a dividend growth rate of 8%. Based on this information, the fundamental PE ratio for Topo is 18.75, as follows:

$$\text{PE Ratio} = \frac{75\%}{12\% - 8\%} = 18.75$$

It is expected that Topo will earn $4.00 per share next year. Based on the PE ratio, Topo should be valued at $75.00 per share.

Example 11.16

Karli is attempting to value Powell Enterprises based on an average PE ratio for its industry. Karli has found three similar companies with PE ratios of 14, 23, and 20. The average PE ratio for these comparable companies is 19. Powell has EPS of $4.00 this year and expects EPS to be $4.50 next year. The expected value of Powell next year equals $85.50 per share, which is determined by multiplying the average PE ratio of 19 by the expected EPS of $4.50.

A low PE ratio may be interpreted as an indication of an undervalued company. However, it may also indicate earnings growth is expected to be lower in the future.

Another potential problem with the PE ratio is that it is based on accounting earnings and not cash flow. While earnings for a company appears to be relatively straight forward, that simply is not the case. Companies have accounting policies (governed by GAAP - generally accepted accounting principles) that may cause earnings to be artificially high or relatively conservative.

Additionally, the PE ratio does not make any sense when earnings are negative. Therefore, it can only be used with companies that have positive earnings.

The PEG Ratio

The **PEG ratio** is calculated as a company's PE ratio divided by the growth rate of its expected earnings.

$$\textbf{PEG Ratio} = \frac{\textbf{PE Ratio}}{\textbf{EPS Growth}}$$

The PEG ratio is a relative measure of a stock's PE ratio per unit of EPS growth and a measure of the company's relative valuation. A lower PEG ratio, all else equal, implies a better value or more of an undervalued stock given its earnings expectations. Consider the following example.

Example 11.17

Leaf Company has a PE ratio of 15 and earnings growth of 20 percent per year. Branch Company has a PE ratio of 36 and earnings growth of 30%. The PEG ratio for Leaf and Branch are 0.75 and 1.2, respectively. The conclusion that can be drawn from the PEG ratio is that Branch is overvalued on a relative basis compared to Leaf. It is obvious that Branch is expected to grow at a higher rate than Leaf. However, the PE multiple is even higher on a relative basis, which is why Branch's PEG ratio is higher than Leaf's PEG ratio.

A low PE ratio may make a stock appear to be a good buy. By incorporating the company's EPS growth rate, however, calculating the PEG ratio may provide a much different conclusion. A high PEG ratio may reveal that while a company appears to be undervalued based on a low PE ratio, it is actually overvalued based on the PEG ratio.

Example 11.18

Assume the same facts in the above example. The market prices for Leaf and Branch are currently $45 and $72 respectively, with an EPS of $3.00 and $2.00 respectively. Based on the expected 20% growth rate for Leaf, its stock price should be $111.97 in five years, assuming the PE ratio remains the same. Based on the growth rate for Branch, its stock price should be $267.33 in five years. Thus, the total return is significantly higher for Branch than for Leaf.

Time Period	Firm	Price	EPS	PE Ratio	EPS Growth	PEG Ratio
0 (Today)	Leaf	$45.00	$3.00	15	20	0.75
5 Years	Leaf	$111.97	$7.46	15	20	0.75
	Total Return	**149%**				
0 (Today)	Branch	$72.00	$2.00	36	30	1.2
5 Years	Branch	$267.33	$7.43	36	30	1.2
	Total Return	**271%**				

This example illustrates that even though Leaf has a lower PEG ratio, Branch turns out to be the better investment.

Like all multiples, the PEG ratio has its limitations. Fore example, it does not take into consideration the underlying risk of the individual company. The PEG ratio also assumes a linear relationship between PE ratio and growth rates. However, growth in earnings compounds over time.

Price-to-Sales Ratio

The **price-to-sales ratio** is calculated as the company's total market price divided by its total sales. This ratio indicates the amount of money that the market is willing to pay for each dollar of revenue. One of the obvious problems with this ratio is that it does not address earnings, which is a fundamental driver of value. Assuming companies have similar profit margins, however, the ratio can be an effective tool for comparing industry rivals.In terms of accounting manipulation, sales or revenue is more difficult to manipulate than earnings, especially over long periods. GAAP requires specific procedures be followed for public companies to recognize revenue – effectively, the revenue must be earned by the company to be able to be reported. While the timing of revenue recognition can be manipulated, any advantage is generally only experienced in a single accounting period.

The price-to-sales ratio can also be used when earnings are negative. The biggest drawback, however, is that it fails to address operational efficiency, earnings, or cash flow. The PS ratio became popular during the 1990s when many technology and Internet firms had negative earnings. Analysts began using this metric to evaluate firms that had little or no history of generating positive net income. The idea was that these firms would eventually become profitable, but in the meantime, the PS ratio was used as a substitute for the more traditional PE ratio. This decision contributed to the asset bubble that burst at the end of the decade. The financial markets learned a valuable lesson that the ability to generate revenues was not was not necessarily related to the ability to generate positive earnings.

Price-to-Cash-Flow Ratio

Financial analysts are wary of the price-to-earnings ratio because it may not completely reveal the firm's ability to generate cash flow. After all, the goal of any business is to invest in wealth maximizing projects. One way to accomplish this goal is to find projects that generate sustainable cash flows over extended periods of time. The price-to-cash-flow ratio has many advantages over other relative valuation measures. Cash flow is less apt to be manipulated than earnings. It is also better than sales as it addresses the real value from a firm, which is cash flow. Despite some of the positive differences, it is used less frequently by investors compared to the PE ratio. This maybe because information on the cash flow generated by a firm during the year is not as readily available as the earnings or sales figures.

Quick Quiz 11.6

1. A high price-to-earnings ratio indicates the firm is likely undervalued.
   a. True
   b. False
2. Low price-to-book ratios are typical for undervalued firms.
   a. True
   b. False

False, True.

Price-to-Book Ratio

The **price-to-book ratio** is calculated as the ratio of the current market price to the book value of stockholders' equity, as measured on the balance sheet. For companies where book values and market values are similar, such as banks, this ratio has at least historical significance. If the value of the ratio is 1.0, then the book value is equal to the market value and vice versa. If this valuation measure is used it should be compared both to the company's price-to-book ratio over a long period of time and to industry competitors over that same period.

Stockholder's equity is the difference between assets and liabilities on a balance sheet. Book value for assets represents the historical value when those assets were acquired or placed into service. It is important to remember that the book value is not fair market value. The book value of liabilities represents the outstanding balance.

Firms with low price-to-book ratios are often thought of by analysts to be undervalued. This is mostly because it provides an indication that the firm's stock is offering a rate of growth that is not expensive. On the other hand, a low PB ratio could simply mean the company is financially unsound.

Example 11.19

Moyer Energy Company seeks to expand its operations by acquiring a natural gas firm located in the southeast portion of the United States. There are three firms that meet the initial criteria for a takeover and have similar price-to-earnings ratios. To further evaluate them, Moyer collects relative value data that is summarized in the table below:

Firm	PCF	PS	PB
Apple Energy Company	2.6	4.2	5.6
Peach Natural Gas Inc	1.2	1.1	3.2
Blueberry Industries	3.4	5.9	7.9

Moyer is most likely to select Peach as the best choice for acquisition based on the relative measures. Blueberry is probably eliminated first because it has the highest price-to-cash-flow ratio and the highest price-to-book ratio, indicating that it is not a value stock. The next step is to eliminate Apple because it has a much higher price-to-book ratio than Peach, which has the best ratios among the three firms. Peach looks more like it is undervalued than the other two energy firms.

CJD Enterprises

CJD is a successful growth company. Below is the income statement for the years 20X1 through 20X5. A new management team was put in place in 20X0 and has helped drive the growth over the last five years. This management team expects continued growth over the next four years.

CJD is an example that will help illustrate how an investor might forecast the next four years to determine an expected stock price in 20X9.

Exhibit 11.2 | CJD Enterprises Income Statement

(in millions)	20X1	20X2	20X3	20X4	20X5
Revenue	$475	$618	$772	$926	$1,121
COGS	$57	$73	$89	$104	$123
Profit Margin	$418	$545	$683	$822	$997
SGA Expenses	$372	$405	$441	$480	$523
Pre-Tax Income	$46	$140	$242	$342	$474
Net Income (after tax)	**$32**	**$98**	**$169**	**$240**	**$332**
Shares of common stock	50	60	75	80	80
EPS	$0.64	$1.63	$2.26	$2.99	$4.15
Stock Price	$20.38	$32.25	$49.90	$69.17	$90.63
PE Ratio	31.65	19.78	22.11	23.10	21.84
Market Cap	1.02B	1.93B	3.74B	5.53B	7.25B

This example is not complete as there is no balance sheet or cash flow statement. However, the income statement can be used to help forecast the next four years.

Vertical and horizontal analysis are the two types of analysis that were previously introduced. Each method provides insight into trends for the business. Consider the following exhibits.

Exhibit 11.3 | CJD Enterprises Vertical Analysis

Vertical Analysis	20X1	20X2	20X3	20X4	20X5
Revenue	100.00%	100.00%	100.00%	100.00%	100.00%
COGS	12.00%	11.75%	11.50%	11.25%	11.00%
Profit Margin	88.00%	88.25%	88.50%	88.75%	89.00%
SGA Expenses	78.32%	65.61%	57.17%	51.81%	46.68%
Pre-Tax Income	9.68%	22.64%	31.33%	36.94%	42.32%
Net Income (after tax)	**6.78%**	**15.85%**	**21.93%**	**25.86%**	**29.62%**

Vertical analysis converts all items on the income statement to a percentage of revenue. There are a few trends that are revealed. COGS, which is short for cost of goods sold, holds fairly constant at 11 percent to 12 percent of sales. The trend for COGS is favorable. Based on this trend, we might forecast a constant COGS of 11 percent.

SGA expenses, which includes selling, general and administrative expenses, are declining as a percentage of revenue. As revenue is increasing, SGA is a smaller percentage of revenue.

Exhibit 11.4 | CJD Enterprises Horizontal Analysis

Horizontal Analysis	20X2	20X3	20X4	20X5
Revenue	30.00%	25.00%	20.00%	21.00%
COGS	27.29%	22.34%	17.39%	18.31%
Profit Margin	30.37%	25.35%	20.34%	21.34%
SGA Expenses	8.92%	8.91%	8.75%	9.03%
Pre-Tax Income	203.87%	73.03%	41.48%	38.61%
Net Income (after tax)	**203.87%**	**73.03%**	**41.48%**	**38.61%**

Horizontal analysis, which may also be called year-over-year analysis, reveals the growth in each line item on the income statement from the prior year. In this case, 20X1 is the base year, which means that it does not reflect a growth rate.

Revenue grew 30 percent from 20X1 to 20X2 and appears to be continuing to grow at or around 20 percent per year. Based on this trend, we can forecast the growth continuing. However, an analysis of the overall economy as well as CJD's market share and market size would have to be considered to make this forecast reasonable. If CJD had a 90 percent market share, it is unlikely that growth would continue at 20 percent per year, unless the overall market was also growing at 20 percent per year.

From the horizontal analysis, it appears that SGA expenses are growing at a fairly steady rate from one year to the next. While it appears that nine percent is a reasonable estimate for SGA expenses, a more conservative adjustment is to increase the year-over-year SGA growth rate to 10 percent.

While it is important to understand the basis for expected growth, this forecast will rely on the short analysis above. Based on this short analysis, a forecast can be created for the next few years. The assumptions for the forecast include:

1. The forecast period will consist of four years: 20X6 to 20X9.
2. Revenue will continue to grow at 20% per year.
3. COGS will remain steady at 11% of revenue.
4. SGA expenses will grow each year at 10%.
5. Income tax will remain at 30%.
6. The PE ratio will remain steady at 22.
7. Shares of common stock remains at 80 million shares.

Following is the forecast for the next four years. Numbers in blue are forecasts.

Exhibit 11.5 | CJD Enterprises Projected Income Statement

	20X1	20X2	20X3	20X4	20X5	20X6	20X7	20X8	20X9
Revenue	$475	$618	$772	$926	$1,121	$1,345	$1,614	$1,937	$2,324
COGS	$57	$73	$89	$104	$123	$148	$178	$213	$256
Profit Margin	$418	$545	$683	$822	$997	$1,197	$1,436	$1,724	$2,068
SGA Expenses	$372	$405	$441	$480	$523	$575	$633	$696	$766
Pre-Tax Income	$46	$140	$242	$342	$474	$621	$803	$1,027	$1,302
Net Income (after tax)	**$32**	**$98**	**$169**	**$240**	**$332**	**$435**	**$562**	**$719**	**$912**
Shares of common stock	50	60	75	80	80	80	80	80	80
EPS	$0.64	$1.63	$2.26	$2.99	$4.15	$5.44	$7.03	$8.99	$11.40
Stock Price	$20.38	$32.25	$49.90	$69.17	$90.63	$119.64	$154.64	$197.76	$250.71
PE Ratio	31.65	19.78	22.11	23.10	21.84	22.00	22.00	22.00	22.00
Market Cap	1.02B	1.93B	3.74B	5.53B	7.25B	9.57B	12.37B	15.82B	20.06B

Based on the above assumptions, NI increases from $332 million in 20X5 to $912 million in 20X9, which represents an increase in EPS from $4.15 to $11.40 over the same period. Based on this higher EPS and a PE ratio of 22, the expected stock price in 20X9 is approximately $250. This increase in stock price represents a compound annual growth rate (CAGR) of 28.96 percent.

SUMMARY

Summary of key points:

- Two broad types of common stock valuation models for going concerns are absolute and relative valuation models.
- Absolute common stock valuation models compute the firm's intrinsic value based on the present value future cash flows. Important absolute valuation models include the dividend discount model.
- Relative common stock valuation models compare a firm's stock price to other similar companies. Important relative valuation models include the price-to-earnings ratio.
- To value a company that is not operating as a going concern, the difference between the fair market value of the assets and the fair market value of the liabilities is estimated.
- The basic present value model estimates cash flows the security is likely to pay and then discounts them at an appropriate interest rate to find value.
- The dividend discount model computes value as the present value of an infinite growing dividend stream.
- The constant growth dividend model was developed by Myron Gordon in the mid 1950s.
- A firm's dividend growth rate can be estimated using the retention ratio and the firm's return on equity.
- Preferred stock can be valued using a zero-growth rate assumption in the dividend discount model.
- A two-stage dividend discount model assumes that a firm's dividends grow at different rates during a high growth period that is followed by an infinite normal growth period.
- The terminal value of a stock is the expected future selling price in the two-stage dividend discount model.
- The H Model is a dividend discount model in which dividends change gradually from a high growth rate to a low normal growth over a period of years.
- For firms that do not pay dividends or for firms that pay dividends that are substantially different from its earnings, free cash flow can be used as an input variable in a present value model to estimate intrinsic value.
- Free cash flow to equity is the amount of cash available to the common shareholders after the free cash flow to the firm has been determined and the firm's bondholders and preferred shareholders have been paid.
- The price-to-earnings ratio is the most commonly used relative valuation measure. Price divided by earnings for one firm is compared to PE ratios of other firms to judge relative value.
- The PEG ratio is a firm's PE ratio divided by its EPS growth rate. Lower PEG ratios imply undervaluation.
- The price-to-sales ratio is the ratio of a firm's stock price to its revenues per share.
- The price-to-cash-flow ratio is the ratio of a firm's stock price to its cash flow per share.
- The price-to-book ratio is the ratio of the firm's stock price to its book value of equity per share.

DISCUSSION QUESTIONS

***SOLUTIONS** to the discussion questions can be found exclusively within the chapter. Once you have completed an initial reading of the chapter, go back and highlight the answers to these questions.*

1. Explain how companies can be valued using the dividend discount model.

2. Discuss when it is appropriate to value a company using a fair market value model.

3. Explain the relationship between the required return and expected growth rates in the dividend discount model.

4. Define an undervalued firm in the context of its intrinsic value.

5. Discuss the critical input variables a financial analyst must use in order to estimate a company's sustainable growth rate.

6. Describe the difference between using dividends and free cash flows in discount valuation models.

7. Identify the main reason that the H Model is used to value a firm.

8. Describe how an investor can value a firm with substantial growth for a few years followed by more normal growth afterwards.

9. Explain the concept of free cash flow to equity.

10. Compare and contrast PE, PS, PCF, and PB ratios.

MULTIPLE CHOICE QUESTIONS

A sample of multiple choice problems is provided below. Additional multiple choice problems are available at money-education.com by accessing the Student Practice Portal.

1. After examining a tech firm's cash flows, its executive leadership, and its likelihood of becoming a takeover target, a research analyst estimates the intrinsic value for this firm to be $64.50. The current market price on the NASDAQ exchange is $61.10. The analyst is most likely to recommend:
    a. Shorting the shares.
    b. Selling the shares that are already owned.
    c. Buying the shares.
    d. Increasing allocation in the tech sector.

2. Which is most accurate regarding a firm's common stock dividend policy?
    a. Dividend payments are discretionary and can fluctuate over time.
    b. Dividend payments represent a legal obligation to the shareholders.
    c. Dividends are paid until the maturity date of the outstanding equity.
    d. Dividends are an expense appearing on the firm's income statement.

3. Relative valuation models least likely include:
    a. Price-to-equity multiple.
    b. Price-to-book multiple.
    c. Dividend discount model.
    d. Price-to-sales multiple.

4. Patch Software is expected to pay its first dividend in exactly one year of $0.25 per share. The growth rate in dividends is expected to be 4.5% and Patch's shareholders require 13.8%. The stock value is closest to:
    a. $2.42.
    b. $2.69.
    c. $2.84.
    d. $3.11.

5. Free cash flow to equity in the current year will most likely increase when a firm:
    a. Has substantial capital expenditures.
    b. Issues bonds.
    c. Increases its investment in net working capital.
    d. Experiences a decline in net income.

QUICK QUIZ EXPLANATIONS

Quick Quiz 11.1

1. True.
2. False. When the price is less than intrinsic value, the stock price will likely rise as investors become aware that it is undervalued.

Quick Quiz 11.2

1. True
2. False. The FMV of the company must be reduced by any preferred stock rights to determine the value to common shareholders.

Quick Quiz 11.3

1. False. There is an inverse relationship between prices and interest rates, and this holds true in the dividend discount models.
2. True.

Quick Quiz 11.4

1. False. The two-stage model assumes growth rates change dramatically from one period to the next, while the H Model allows for a gradual decline in dividend growth rates.
2. True.

Quick Quiz 11.5

1. True.
2. False. One of the great advantages in using the FCFE model is that it can be applied to almost any firms, especially those that do not pay dividends.

Quick Quiz 11.6

1. False. Higher PE ratios mean the market assigns a high value to the earnings of the firm. This is more likely an indication of overvaluation.
2. True.

12
INVESTMENT COMPANIES

LEARNING OBJECTIVES

1. List the four types of investment companies and describe how each functions.*
2. Identify who regulates investment companies.*
3. Describe the income tax treatment of earnings from investment companies.*
4. Discuss the various fees charged by mutual fund companies.*
5. Describe the three classes of load fund shares.*
6. Explain how fund expenses impact fund performance.*
7. Discuss the advantages and disadvantages of mutual funds.*
8. List and discuss the types of mutual funds.*

**Ties to CFP Certification Learning Objectives*

INTRODUCTION

Investment companies provide investors with easy access to capital markets, whether they are investing thousands or millions of dollars. These investors include individuals and institutional investors, such as retirement plans. In 2020, more than 58 million households (representing 46% of households) owned mutual funds.[1]

Exhibit 12.1 | Investment Company Net Assets by Type

U.S. Investment Company Type	Total Net Assets 12/31/2020
Mutual Funds	$23.9 Trillion
Exchange-Traded Funds	$5.4 Trillion
Closed-End Funds	$279 Billion
Unit Investment Trusts	$78 Billion

Source: 2021 Investment Company Fact Book

An **investment company** issues and invests in financial securities. It invests the money it receives from investors on a collective basis, and each investor shares in the profits and losses of the company in proportion to their interest in the investment company. The performance of the investment company is based on the performance of the underlying securities and other assets that the investment company owns.[2]

There are four basic types of investment companies discussed in this chapter:

1. Unit investment trusts (UITs)
2. Closed-end funds (known as closed-end companies)
3. Exchange-traded funds (ETFs)
4. Mutual funds (known as open-end companies)

Assets in investment companies have increased tremendously since the mid 1990s, as reflected in the following chart.

1. ICI.org: 2021 ICI Factbook.
2. SEC - http://www.sec.gov/answers/mfinvco.htm

Exhibit 12.2 | Investment Company Assets by Type 1999 - 2020

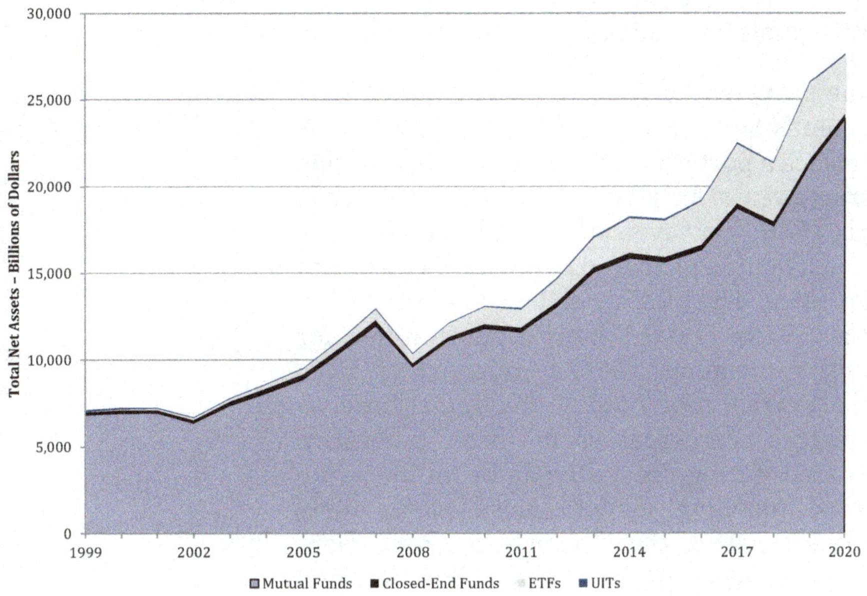

Source: ICI.org 2021 Fact Book

Investment company assets have grown from under $8 trillion in 2000 to over $27 trillion at the end of 2020. Most of the growth and most of the assets in investment companies have come from mutual funds, as opposed to UITs, closed-end funds, and ETFs. However, the number of ETFs has grown a lot in the last few years as well as the ETF assets.

Most individuals are initially exposed to investing in financial markets through their employers and the retirement benefits offered to them. Employees typically have little knowledge of retirement and investment planning when they begin employment, but learn of the importance and relevance of mutual funds as they age. Over time, some employees become experts in understanding capital markets and financial planning, but some remain less informed.

Key Concepts

1. Understand the characteristics of investment companies.
2. Differentiate between UITs, ETFs, closed-end and open-end mutual funds.
3. Know the size of investment company assets.
4. Summarize the tax treatment of investment companies.

The lack of understanding is mostly a result of the previous predominance of employer-funded retirement plans, such as defined benefit plans. These plans became very popular after World War II, when employers offered pension plans that would guarantee a benefit to employees upon retirement and throughout the remainder of their lives. Under these conditions, employees could ignore risk, asset allocation, and security selection. Employers were exposed to the risk of promising to fulfill future obligations and were, therefore, exposed to the risks and uncertainties inherent in retirement planning and asset management. In addition, employers were responsible for determining investment strategies for all their employees as a group. This arrangement worked well as long as the fund performed to match the return objectives of the pool and employees remained with the company until they retired.

The significant disadvantage, of course, is the plans are typically not portable when the employee accepts a position with a different employer. In recent years, consequently, employers have begun offering different types of retirement plans in which the employee has complete control and ownership of the plan. As a result, individuals have gained a greater understanding of the mutual fund industry.

The relevant income provided by pension plans coupled with the federal government's Social Security program have always been intended to replace a portion of the income earned during the employee's working years. As inflation became a problem in the 1970s and early 1980s, however, employers reduced their commitment to defined benefit plans and began a slow switch to defined contribution plans. The ERISA and Revenue Acts passed by Congress in the 1970s created more opportunities for appropriate retirement planning. The Revenue Act of 1978 created the 401(k) plans that have become so popular because of their tax advantages. Participation in these innovative retirement plans soared during the 1990s and continues into the current financial planning model. These plans allow employees to contribute part of their income to a retirement fund and have direct influence on both asset allocation and security selection. Defined contribution plans offer the additional advantage of encouraging employees to take ownership of their expected retirement lifestyle. Of course, the ownership includes the risk-taking function as well. In effect, there has been an amazing shift in funding risk as well as the risk of outliving one's assets (called **superannuation**) from employers and plan sponsors to individuals who are generally not well equipped to understand or manage these risks.

Quick Quiz 12.1

1. As of the end of 2017, there was more than $18 trillion invested in investment companies.
   a. True
   b. False
2. The largest percentage of investment company assets are invested in ETFs.
   a. True
   b. False
3. Most investment companies are structured in such a way as to be nontaxable entities.
   a. True
   b. False

True, False, True.

The link between retirement planning and employment has also led more individuals to become more aware of financial planning and the consequences of being financially unprepared for retirement. Originally, President Roosevelt signed the Social Security Act of 1935 to create government retirement planning, but the average life expectancy for individuals retiring back then was less than a decade. Today, those retiring even at age 67 can often be expected to live for twenty or even thirty years. In fact, one in ten individuals retiring today will live beyond the age of 95. Extended life expectancies place significant pressure on retirement portfolios to perform well beyond their original intentions.

For many reasons, including retirement planning, individual investors have increased their appetites for equity securities and generally purchase these through investment companies, most of which are mutual funds. The institutions that provide investing services offer a variety of advantages for the average individual investor. Investment companies offer an inexpensive and indirect way to gain exposure to a host of financial securities, including equity and fixed-income securities. The funds tend to be highly diversified and are characterized by ease of entry and exit. Investors must educate themselves about the traits of investment companies because they are not perfect investment vehicles, and they do have some disadvantages.

The four types of investment companies are discussed in the next section.

INVESTMENT COMPANY CHARACTERISTICS

An investment company (IC) operates as a business that purchases, holds, and manages financial investments for its clients. Essentially, an IC invests capital on behalf of its customer base, who then share in the profits and losses of the underlying financial assets. ICs raise capital by disclosing the fund's purpose and issuing shares to the investing public. ICs then use the proceeds of the issue to purchase securities in the various markets throughout the world. For example, an IC fund manager might craft a prospectus that informs investors that she will purchase equity shares in large cap firms that operate globally and trade on multiple exchanges. Only institutional and individual investors who are interested in those types of investments will provide capital to the fund manager. As such, the IC fund manager is able to raise huge amounts of capital and offer its shareholders the benefits of diversification and economies of scale. Of course, the IC will generate a positive return to its owners if the underlying assets appreciate in value.

Investment companies avoid taxation issues by becoming registered investment companies (RIC) through Internal Revenue Code Section 851. The basic idea is that if the IC receives interest payments, dividend payments, or capital gains, it is tax exempt at both federal and local levels by simply distributing the payments to its shareholders. RICs act merely as channels (or flow-through entities), thus creating a tax liability for its shareholders, who must report capital gains and cash payments to the IRS and local tax agencies. Each shareholder's tax liability is a function of the proportion of ownership it has in the fund.

ICs are regulated by the Securities and Exchange Commission and the Investment Company Act of 1940, as well as other legislation passed in the 1930s and 1940s.

IRS Code 851 requires the following for ICs to be considered tax exempt:

1. The RIC must generate at least 90% of its income from dividends, coupon or interest payments, and capital gains.
2. The RIC must distribute at least 90% of its taxable income to its shareholders.
3. The RIC must invest at least 50% of its total assets in cash, cash equivalents, or securities.
4. The RIC must not exceed a maximum of 25% of its total assets invested in the securities of any one issuer, unless the securities are issued by specified government entities.

In general, there are four types of investment companies covered in this chapter:

1. Unit investment trusts
2. Exchange-traded funds
3. Closed-end funds
4. Open-end investment companies (mutual funds)

Exhibit 12.3 | Fund Type Comparison

	Unit Investment Trust	Open-End Investment Company	Closed-End Investment Company	Exchange-Traded Fund
Common name	Unit trust	Mutual fund	Closed-end fund	ETF
Capitalization	Fixed	Constantly changing	Fixed	Changes over time
Management of investments	Passive; portfolio is fixed	Active; portfolio changes	Active; portfolio changes	Generally passive; some active ETFs
Purchases	Units offered by trust require a prospectus	Prospectus required; each sale is an offering by the fund	After initial offering, buying on exchanges through a broker does not require a prospectus	Bought on exchanges through a broker at or near NAV
Sales	Units are redeemable with a trust at NAV	Shares are redeemed by a fund at NAV, no trading on exchanges	Shares trade on exchanges above or below NAV; shares are not redeemable	Sold on exchanges through a broker at or near NAV
Transaction costs	Sales charges by fund	Sales charges by fund	Commission to broker	Commission to broker

UNIT INVESTMENT TRUSTS

Key Concepts

1. Discuss how funds are invested passively in a UIT.
2. Compare the maturity and distributions for stock UITs and bond UITs.

Unit investment trusts (UIT) are baskets of securities formed much like the traditional mutual fund. UITs can invest in equity securities, fixed-income securities, derivative securities, and almost any financial security that has a liquid secondary market. The traditional UIT, however, invests solely in bonds. These are still by far the most common of all unit investment trusts. When compared to other funds offered by investment companies, UITs have characteristics that make them unique. Recent innovations include UITs that invest in many different types of bonds, including mortgage backed securities, global fixed-income securities, and corporate bonds, in addition to the traditional UIT investment in government securities.

When UITs are formed, the securities are purchased according to the stated objectives described in the prospectus and held until maturity. For UITs that contain only fixed-income securities, the maturity date is usually determined using the longest-term bond. For UITs that contain equity securities, however, the maturity date is determined at the fund's inception. Some UITs have maturities as short as five years, but many have twenty-five-year maturity dates. Most UITs are passively managed and any cash payments made by the securities in the trust are immediately passed through to the investors. The cash payments include coupon payments made by fixed-income securities, dividends paid by equity securities, and any principal payments. In some cases, the dividend payments in an equity UIT can be reinvested in additional shares.

UITs make a one-time public offering via the following steps:

1. A financial institution or broker/dealer (known as a sponsor) decides to create a unit investment trust.
2. The sponsor either purchases or contracts to purchase a portfolio of securities.
3. The sponsor deposits the securities or the contract with a trustee.
4. The trustee creates unit certificates for the sponsor that reflect ownership.
5. A financial expert assigns a value of the portfolio on a specific date.
6. Shares are sold to the investing public.

Many UIT sponsors maintain a secondary market, which allows investors in the UIT to sell part or all of the shares to the sponsor and for new owners to participate in the portfolio. The secondary market improves the attractiveness of the UIT by making it more liquid with trading occurring at the fund's net asset value.

Quick Quiz 12.2

1. UITs often make a public offering twice per year for each fund.
   a. True
   b. False
2. UITs are generally passively managed.
   a. True
   b. False
3. Municipal bond UITs pay out interest and principal as it is received.
   a. True
   b. False

False, True, True.

Advantages of investing in UITs include diversification, exposure to many asset classes, income, and liquidity. Some view the passive nature of UITs to be a major disadvantage, but others see it as a way to track specific benchmarks. The large drawback to UITs, however, is that owners pay a sales charge, a lump sum organizational cost, and annual expenses that include trustee fees.

EXCHANGE-TRADED FUNDS (ETFs)

Exchange-traded funds (ETFs) are portfolios of securities that are created through the use of unit investments trusts or through a general fund. ETFs are historically passively managed with the sponsor selecting the securities to be included in the portfolio. The securities are identified to mimic the performance of a commonly used benchmark, such as the Standard and Poor's 500 Index or a specific sector, such as the Vanguard Healthcare ETF. ETFs have expanded to include emerging markets, high yield municipal securities, and REITs. The initial ETFs were named according to their benchmark reference index, such as SPDRs (S&P Depositary Receipts) and QQQ (NASDAQ 100 Index).

Key Concepts

1. Explain how ETF shares are sold to the public.
2. Differentiate the timing of a sale of ETF shares with the timing of a sale of mutual fund shares.
3. Assess the typical expense ratio for ETFs.

Exhibit 12.4 | ETFs as Defined by the SEC

Exchange-traded funds, or ETFs, are investment companies that are legally classified as open-end companies or UITs, but they differ from traditional open-end companies and UITs in the following respects:

1. ETFs do not sell individual shares directly to investors and only issue their shares in large blocks (blocks of 50,000 shares, for example) that are known as "Creation Units."
2. Investors do not purchase Creation Units with cash. Instead, they buy Creation Units with a basket of securities that mirrors the ETF's portfolio. Those who purchase Creation Units are frequently institutions.
3. After purchasing a Creation Unit, an investor often splits it up and sells the individual shares on a secondary market. This process permits other investors to purchase individual shares (instead of Creation Units).
4. Investors who want to sell their ETF shares have two options: (1) they can sell individual shares to other investors on the secondary market, or (2) they can sell the Creation Units back to the ETF. In addition, ETFs redeem Creation Units by giving investors the securities that comprise the portfolio instead of cash. So, for example, an ETF invested in the stocks contained in the Dow Jones Industrial Average (DJIA) would give a redeeming shareholder the actual securities that constitute the DJIA instead of cash. Because of the limited redeemability of ETF shares, ETFs are not considered to be-and may not call themselves-mutual funds.

ETFs are created in the following manner:

1. A financial institution (known as the sponsor) creates the ETF, identifies its investment objectives and decides on security selection and organizational fees.
2. An authorized participant purchases the shares described in the ETF or borrows them from an institutional investor such as a pension fund.
3. The authorized participant transfers the shares into the ETF and receives **creation units**, which are typically 50,000 share blocks. The exchange is known as an in-kind transfer.
4. The authorized participant sells shares to investors or makes a market for them so they can be traded on a stock market.

Authorized participants are large enough to offer shares of ETFs on stock exchanges, acting as market makers or specialists on the exchange. The attractiveness for investors is that ETFs can be traded throughout the day. There are typically no trading restrictions on ETFs, which means they can be purchased on margin and be a part of short selling strategies.

Quick Quiz 12.3

1. ETF shares can only be sold at the end of the trading day.
   a. True
   b. False
2. ETFs are generally actively managed.
   a. True
   b. False
3. One of the advantages of ETFs is the low expense ratios for these funds.
   a. True
   b. False
4. ETFs could be used to build a diversified portfolio.
   a. True
   b. False

False, False, True, True.

ETF market prices should theoretically be equal to its net asset value, but short-term fluctuations in supply and demand conditions will cause slight differences between the two values. When the minor disequilibrium exists, ETFs will trade at premiums or discounts. Arbitrage by authorized participants (AP) will keep the price differential quite small. For example, if the NAV of an ETF were $100 and its market price were $98, the authorized participant would buy the ETF shares in the open market and exchange them for the underlying securities in the ETF. The AP could then sell the securities for a $2 gain, less any transaction costs. On the other hand, if the NAV of an ETF is EUR 200 and its market price were EUR 203, the authorized participant would purchase the securities in the ETF in the open market and exchange them for additional creation shares in the ETF. It could then sell the shares for a EUR 3 gain, less any transaction costs. The reliance on and the legalities of the arbitrage opportunities are the conditions that distinguish ETFs from other investment companies.

ETFs are relatively new innovations with the first one having been introduced on the American Stock Exchange in 1993. The first ETF was the SPDR and became very popular as an appropriate alternative to index mutual funds. Most ETFs are passively managed, tracking an index or an industry, but some are actively managed. In the 1990s, investors appreciated the low expense characteristics of ETFs compared to mutual funds, but demand for active management led to the introduction of actively managed ETFs in the 2010s. Investors can now use ETFs as a platform to either mimic an index or attempt to beat one.

ETFs typically have low expense ratios, as low as 11 basis points for passively managed funds, but increase to 200 or even 300 basis points for actively managed ETFs. Some investors purchase ETFs through a broker, which may add commissions and maybe even other transactions fees to the total cost. Passive ETFs by definition have low turnover and are not subject to any cash on hand limitations. In addition, the existence of a liquid secondary market for ETFs means no requirement for redemptions by the shareholders. Finally, taxable distributions from ETFs are relatively low. Many investors use ETFs to build their entire portfolios, some use them to construct only their portfolio cores, while others use them to add value to their existing portfolios.

The global ETF market has grown from around $2 billion in total assets in the mid-1990s to over $3.4 trillion by the end of 2020.[3] In addition, Statista reports the existence of almost 7,500 ETFs globally in 2020. Both of these data points suggest ETFs have grown at a substantial rate as compared to other investment companies, both in awareness and in investable assets. **Exhibit 12.5** depicts the growth of ETFs compared to mutual funds in the U.S.

Exhibit 12.5 | U.S. ETF and Mutual Fund Assets

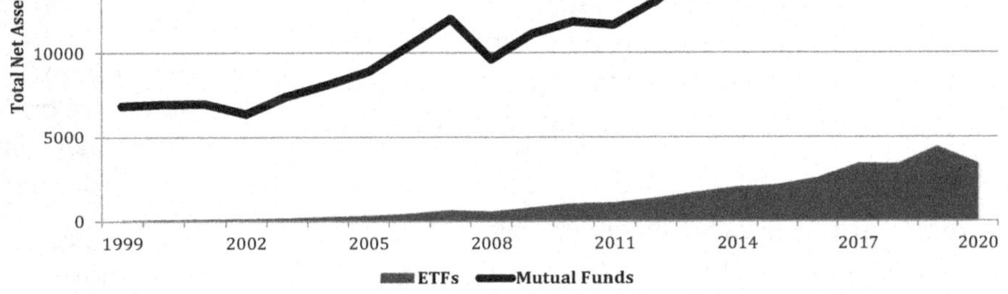

Source: ICI.org 2021 Fact Book

3. Investment Company Institute (ici.org).

CLOSED-END INVESTMENT COMPANIES

Closed-end funds (CEFs) are investment companies that combine the advantages of ETFs and regular open-end mutual funds. CEFs invest in a basket of securities but typically raise capital through an initial public offering. They have a fixed number of shares, which means the market price will depend on short-term economic conditions for those shares. Like ETFs, CEFs can trade at premiums or discounts, compared to NAV. Unlike ETFs, the variance between the market price and the CEF's net asset value can be substantial. CEFs lack the involvement of authorized participants, who play such a significant role in supply and demand conditions in the ETF world.

Key Concepts

1. Describe how a closed-end fund is created.
2. Explain why the shares of closed-end funds generally do not trade at their NAV.
3. Identify the factors that affect the price at which the shares of closed-end funds trade.

CEFs trade in the secondary market on stock exchanges, and their prices change throughout the trading day. The transparency of exchange trading makes it simple to compute the market value of the securities in the fund. Sometimes, a CEF becomes popular, and its market price rises well above its net asset value. Other times, a CEF is out of favor with the marketplace, and its price falls well below the net asset value. Many financial researchers view the size of CEF premiums or discounts as a measure of market sentiment.

Once CEFs raise their initial capital, additional shares are not issued to the public. This makes CEF capitalization fixed as compared to open-end mutual funds, which continuously raise capital and redeem shares simultaneously. Consequently, CEF managers have significant flexibility in asset selection and allocation decisions. Because capital is fixed, CEF managers are able to invest in securities that may have different risk or liquidity characteristics than the securities selected by other investment companies.

The first CEF in the United States was created by the Boston Personal Property Trust in 1893 and there were various forms of CEFs until the legislation during the great depression, including the Investment Company Act of 1940. The growth of investment companies began around the turn of the century, but they became very popular during the 1980s. CEFs, however, have not enjoyed the great surge in use as compared to other investment companies. This lack of dramatic growth is probably due to the fact that CEF managers are not able to raise their fees as easily as other investment company managers. With fixed capitalization, superior performance cannot be rewarded with increased fees charged to shareholders. This explains at least partially why there are so many closed-end funds with wide ranges of expense ratios.

Quick Quiz 12.4

1. A closed-end mutual fund rarely trades at NAV.
   a. True
   b. False
2. There are far more open-end than closed-end mutual funds.
   a. True
   b. False
3. Shares for both ETFs and closed-end funds are traded on the secondary exchange.
   a. True
   b. False

True, True, True.

CEFs invest in almost any financial security available in secondary markets. Fixed-income CEFs invest in bonds issued by governments, municipalities, agencies, quasi-government entities, and corporations. The bonds can have embedded options such as puts, calls, and conversion features. Equity CEFs invest in domestic, international, and emerging market equity securities. Of course, the CEF manager can invest in any combination of these securities, as long as the objective is stated clearly in the prospectus.

An equity dual purpose CEF is a fund that divides its shareholders into two classes, one that is scheduled to receive dividend payments and one that is scheduled to receive capital gains. Slicing the fund into two components allows investors to select whether they want to receive income or price appreciation, but not both.

CEFs offer some interesting advantages, mainly an efficient investing opportunity in which the manager can remain fully invested in diversified portfolios. There are no cash requirements for the manager. CEFs trade on exchanges, which means they can be bought or sold throughout the trading day, plus they can be bought at a discount and sold at a premium. Finally, CEF managers use leverage to magnify returns. Of course, leverage also magnifies losses, so investors must be careful to identify the borrowing tendencies of the CEF fund manager.

OPEN-END INVESTMENT COMPANIES (MUTUAL FUNDS)

Open-end investment companies are the most common type of investment company used by investors to gain equity exposure. They are open-ended because the fund manager continually accepts new capital and continually redeems shares to the investing public, which means that total capitalization changes constantly. This investment company type is most frequently referred to as a mutual fund. In general, mutual funds are created by financial institutions or mutual fund families, although almost anyone can start one. A mutual fund family is a set of funds run by a single institution. The funds within the family typically will have a range of different objectives and hence suit different investor needs. Investing in a fund that is part of a family benefits an investor, as transferring assets between funds should involve minimal or no fees. It should be noted, however, that any taxable gains will still be assessed on assets sold as part of the transfer. Investors generally purchase shares in mutual funds directly from the investment company, although shares can also be purchased through a broker.

One key feature of mutual funds is that they are valued daily according to the fund's **net asset value**, which is computed as follows:

$$\text{Net Asset Value} = \frac{\text{Market Value of Assets} - \text{Market Value of Liabilities}}{\text{Total Outstanding Shares}}$$

NAV is calculated at the end of every trading day and is the value of the shares that investors buy or sell. There is no separate 'price' for mutual funds.

A mutual fund's net asset value depends on the prices of the individual securities contained in the fund, its liabilities, and the number of shares distributed to the fund's owners. As such, NAVs increase when the performance of the fund's assets rise and when its liabilities decrease. However, the open-ended nature of mutual funds means that the number of shares outstanding tends to increase daily, putting pressure on the rising NAV. Investors may also face an initial sales charge and perhaps other commissions when buying mutual funds from a broker.

Exhibit 12.6 | Mutual Fund Structure

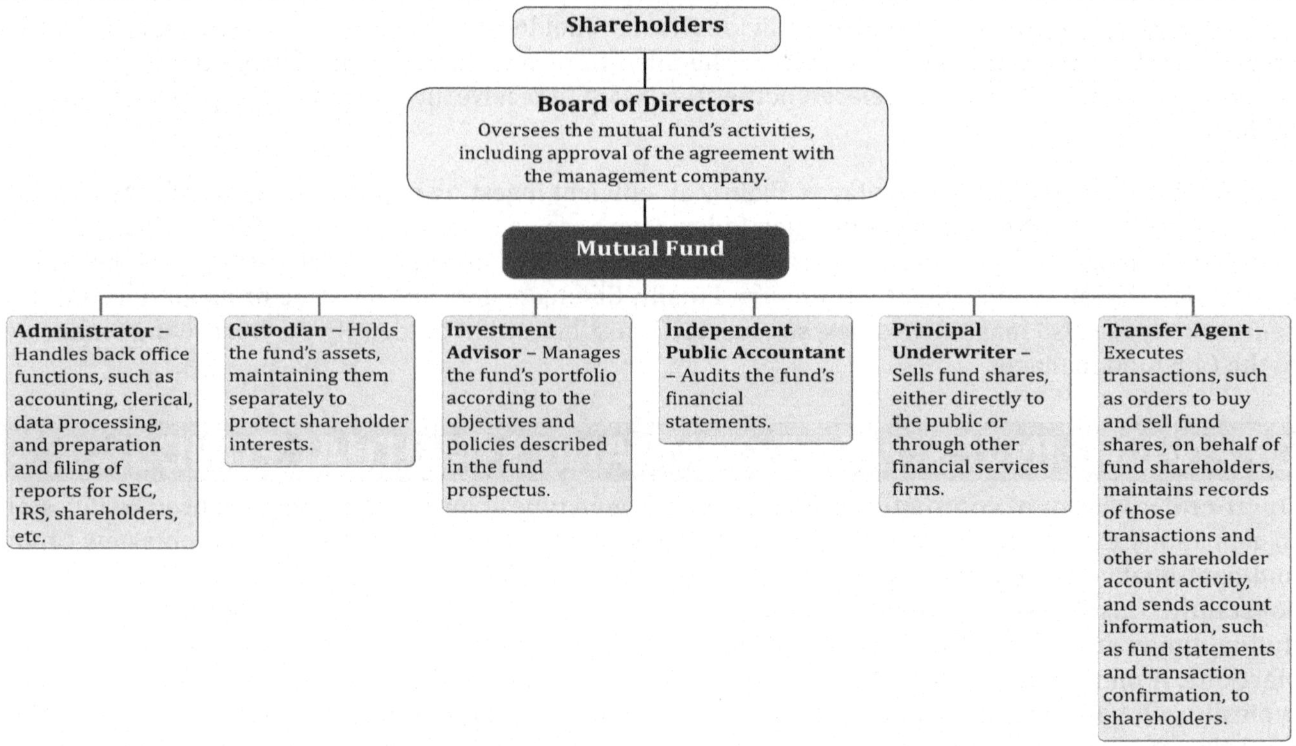

Exhibit 12.6 shows a typical organizational structure for mutual funds. Each function of the mutual fund is important, but shareholders are most interested in the investment adviser. The adviser is often just one individual but can be a team of advisers. Frequently referred to as mutual fund managers, they are responsible for the performance of the fund as they make asset selection, asset allocation, and timing decisions.

Key Concepts

1. Describe why open-end funds are called open-end.
2. State the methods of purchasing shares of an open-end fund.

Each mutual fund has its own board of directors who oversee the entire family of funds' managers and performance. Independent directors of registered investment companies play a critical role in overseeing funds' operations and protecting the interests of their shareholders. In an effort to control conflicts of interest between funds and their investment advisers, Congress required that at least 40 percent of a fund's board be composed of independent directors. Congress intended to place independent directors in the role of "independent watchdogs," to furnish an independent check upon the management of funds and provide a means for the representation of shareholder interests in fund affairs.

MUTUAL FUND FEES AND COSTS

Investment advisers and money managers charge fees for their professional services. Investment companies incur expenses that they tend to pass on to customers in addition to trading fees, regulatory fees, and sales commissions. The two broad categories of fees are sales charges (known as loads) and operating expenses. Each mutual fund has expenses associated with its daily operations, such as rent, electronic access to markets, and employee wages. Some mutual funds additionally charge a sales commission to shareholders when they purchase shares in the fund. The sales charges can be paid at the original purchase and can include charges during sales of shares. Many mutual funds, however, do not charge any sales fees and are known as **no-load funds**. The investment professionals who operate no-load funds usually include asset-based fees as part of their operating expenses.

Key Concepts

1. Mutual funds may have loads, sales charges, 12b-1 fees, management fees, expense ratios, and transaction costs.
2. Fees and expenses have a significant impact on long-term mutual fund performance.
3. Sales charges may be reduced or eliminated depending on the amount of the investment into a fund.

Loads or Sales Charges

Front-End Load

Sales commissions that are charged at the time investors purchase shares of the fund are **front-end load** charges. They are usually paid as a percentage of the original investment. These commissions are typically advertised as the cost paid to a commission-based broker in exchange for their expertise in locating the appropriate funds for the client. Many funds have relatively low front-end load charges, but some loaded mutual funds have sales commissions that can exceed eight percent (FINRA limits sales loads to a maximum of 8.5%). Investors must use traditional marginal cost and marginal benefit analysis to make the decision to purchase mutual funds that charge commissions.

Example 12.1

Greta makes an initial investment into the Mountain Mutual Fund (MMF) in the amount of $10,000. MMF has a front-end load of 5%. Greta will essentially pay her broker $500 for finding MMF for her as the most appropriate fund available to meet her risk and return objectives. Her net investment in MMF will then be $9,500. One important investment issue for Greta is that MMF will have to earn 5.26% to return her $9,500 net investment into the $10,000 total investment.[4]

Another issue for Greta is that when she makes additional investments in MMF, she will most likely be subject to sales commissions again on the new investment amounts. These sales charges place considerable drag on her total portfolio performance.

4. 500/9500 = 0.0526 or {10,000/9,500} - 1 = 0.0526.

Back-End Load and Redemption Fees

Some mutual funds charge sales commissions when investors redeem their shares. Known as **back-end loads** this fee structure is designed to encourage shareholders to remain in the fund over the long term. Back-end loads can be a flat fee, but the majority of them charge a decreasing rate over time. For example, many funds charge a five percent fee if the fund is sold during the first year and four percent if sold during the second year. The rate often declines to zero percent if the fund is held for five years or longer.

Back-end loads are sometimes referred to as contingent deferred sales charges and usually appear in mutual funds that offer at least two classes of shares. For example, Class A shares may have a front-end load while Class B shares may have a back-end load.

Redemption fees are slightly different than back-end commissions. Some funds charge redemption fees whenever shareholders sell all or part of their ownership in the fund. The objective of charging redemption fees is to discourage frequent trading by shareholders that might be disruptive to the financial goals of the fund. The SEC limits redemption fees to two percent in most situations.

Typically, a fund calculates the amount of a back-end sales load based on the lesser of the value of the shareholder's initial investment or the value of the shareholder's investment at redemption. For example, if the shareholder initially invests $10,000, and at redemption the investment has appreciated to $12,000, a back-end sales load calculated in this manner would be based on the value of the initial investment ($10,000) not on the value of the investment at redemption. Investors should carefully read a fund's prospectus to determine whether the fund calculates its back-end sales load in this manner.

Example 12.2

Cisco invests $20,000 in the Driskill Fund (DF) and $10,000 in the Gentry Fund (GF). Both funds charge a 4% back-end load. Cisco decides to sell both funds after six months to help finance the purchase of a fishing vessel. DF has risen in value to $21,700 while GF has fallen in value to $9,600.

Cisco will pay $800 on the DF sale and $384 on the GF sale.[5]

Public Offering Price

The price an investor must pay for a share in a mutual fund that has a sales charge is known as the public offering price (POP). It will be higher than the net asset value of the fund due to the sales charge.

Example 12.3

Valentina is looking to purchase shares in a mutual fund that currently has a net asset value per share of $12.50. However, the public offering price she sees is $13.09.

The difference between the NAV and POP is caused by the sales charge. It is calculated as:

$$\% = \frac{\text{POP - NAV}}{\text{POP}} = \frac{13.09 - 12.50}{13.09} = 0.045$$

The sales charge is 4.5%. The NAV of $12.50 is net of that 4.5% charge, hence it is only 95.5% of the POP. To calculate the POP from the NAV of $12.50, divide it by 0.955.

5. 0.04 × 20,000 = 800; 0.04 × 9,600 = 384. Note the sales fee is based on the lower of the original investment or the current value of the investment.

Other Mutual Fund Fees and Costs

12b-1 Fees

Mutual funds rely on attracting new investors to increase their asset bases. Mutual fund managers consequently market their investment expertise by advertising to the broad investing public. They also incur distribution costs, printing expenses, and compensation fees paid to brokers who sell their funds. These and other shareholder services costs are covered by **12b-1 fees**, which are outlined in the Investment Company Act of 1940.

> **Quick Quiz 12.5**
>
> 1. Front-loads reduce the amount invested.
>   a. True
>   b. False
> 2. 12b-1 fees are applied annually, if at all.
>   a. True
>   b. False
>
> True, True.

There are essentially two parts to the 12b-1 Rule. The first is the 12b-1 distribution fee, which cannot exceed 0.75 percent of the net asset value of the shares. The second is the 12b-1 service fee, which cannot exceed 0.25 percent. The distribution fee pays the brokers who maintain the relationship with shareholders in the fund and are paid as either up front commissions or trailing commissions over several years. Typical commission percentages are between 25 percent to 45 percent of the fees generated and are paid by the mutual fund to the adviser.

Potential 12b-1 fees are one percent (100 basis points) for each fund. Many investors believe the 12b-1 fee arrangement is good for shareholders as it reduces the need for front-end loads. Others claim it reduces the potential return for shareholders as 12b-1 fees reduce performance.

Example 12.4

Seth's investment adviser recommends the Getty Fund (GF) as part of the construction of his overall portfolio. GF is a no-load mutual fund with a 50 basis point 12b-1 fee structure. The adviser charges 35% for the recommendation. Seth invests $1,000,000, which means $5,000 will be the 12b-1 fee. Of that amount, $1,750 will be paid to the adviser.

Management Fees

Management fees are all direct expenses incurred in the management of the fund, including compensating the portfolio fund manager. A large portion of the management fee tends to be the cost of hiring the investment team and providing them with appropriate incentives to encourage retention. Management fees are typically around 0.25 percent to 0.50 percent (25 to 50 basis points) and are included in the mutual fund's expense ratio.

Expense Ratio

Expense ratios include management fees, 12b-1 fees, operating expenses, administrative fees, and other expenses based on asset size necessary to run the fund, such as rent, computer costs, and cash flows paid on borrowed securities. Expense ratios exclude commissions, brokerage costs, and portfolio transaction costs. Expense ratios are deducted from the market value of the assets on a daily basis.

There is generally a one-to-one tradeoff of expense ratios and mutual fund performance. In other words, every one percent increase in expense ratios reduces portfolio performance by that same one percent. All investors should be aware of their fund's expense ratio and be willing to make allocation decisions based on changing expense ratios.

Example 12.5

Daisy invests $10,000 in the Plant Fund (PF), which earns 11% during the subsequent year. PF has a 1% expense ratio with no 12b-1 fees. At year's end, Daisy's investment is worth $11,000.

Daisy's sister, Iris, invests $10,000 in the Botany Fund (BF), which also earns 11% during the subsequent year. BF has a 2% expense ratio, which includes 1% in 12b-1 fees. At year's end, Iris's investment is worth $10,900.

The difference in performance is due solely to the extra 1% Iris is paying in expense ratio. A $100 difference on a $10,000 investment over one year translates into a $11,230 difference (20%) in 20 years, as calculated below.

	Daisy	Iris
PV	$10,000	$10,000
N	20	20
i	10%	9%
PMT	$0	$0
FV	$67,275	$56,044

Transaction Costs

There are several types of transaction costs that can reduce realized returns for mutual funds. Included in this category are brokerage costs, spread costs, and market-impact costs, which can range from one percent to two percent per year and are excluded from the expense ratio computation.

Brokerage costs result from the purchase and sale of securities within the mutual fund. Investors have a difficult time in precisely calculating this cost, but note that higher portfolio turnover rates indicate higher brokerage costs. Some funds have very high turnover rates, sometimes in excess of 100 percent. Recall that a 100 percent turnover rate implies the fund has completely different securities at the end of a period than it did at the beginning. Other funds, however, have lower turnover rates, which implies the manager pursues a buy and hold strategy rather than a strategy of significant asset allocation changes.

Bid-ask spreads are differences between prices at which market makers are willing to purchase shares and prices for which they are willing to sell. For example, consider a share of stock with a bid price of $100 and an ask price of $101. The bid-ask spread is $1 and represents the total revenue generated by the market maker. Bid-ask spreads pose natural obstacles to performance for all investors as markets could not exist without them. Suppose prices rise over time and the bid is $119 and the ask is $120. Portfolio managers who buy shares at the $101 ask price will face the prospect of selling them in the future at the $119 bid price. The trade generates a 17.8 percent return on what could appear to be a 20 percent investment return if spreads are ignored.

Market-impact costs are substantial price changes in a specific security that result mostly from large trades, but also occur during initial public offerings. This cost is more of an issue for thinly traded stocks and perhaps large positions in specific securities due to the size of the fund.

Commissions and Soft Dollar Arrangements

Portfolio managers can buy and sell securities through a broker using an 'execution only' style order. This trading agreement tends to have a lower commission cost because the broker is only executing the trade and not providing any other services. Portfolio managers can also pay for extra services from the broker, such as market research on specific securities, industries, or economies. If those services are included the extra commission fees paid are known as **soft dollars**. Some mutual fund shareholders are willing to agree to pay the higher commission so their portfolio manager has more access to financial information and therefore can make better security selections. Soft dollars have been under intense scrutiny during the 2010s but many funds still use them. These types of fee arrangements must be disclosed to all shareholders.

Discounts on Loads and Commissions

Mutual funds and brokerage firms offer discounts on services under certain circumstances. Mutual funds often offer discounts on front-end sales charges for larger investments. Each investment level is a '**breakpoint**'. For example, a mutual fund might charge a front-end load of six percent on all purchases up to $50,000, but reduce the load when an investor makes larger purchases. Mutual funds can even eliminate the load altogether if the purchase amount is large enough.

Exhibit 12.7 | Breakpoint Schedule

Investment Amount	Front-End Sales Load
Less than $25,000	5.00%
$25,000 but less than $50,000	4.25%
$50,000 but less than $100,000	3.75%
$100,000 but less than $250,000	3.25%
$250,000 but less than $500,000	2.75%
$500,000 but less than $1 million	2.00%
$1 million or more	0.00%

As depicted in the **Exhibit 12.7**, an investment of $50,000 would require a load of 3.75 percent, while a substantially larger investment of $1,000,000 is not subject to a load at all. This declining load schedule encourages investors to provide more capital to the fund manager. Some mutual funds will allow an investor to qualify for the minimum load with only a commitment to invest the minimum amount required. For example, if an investor were willing to commit $1,000,000 within one year's time, most funds that offer discounts would be willing to waive the load. The fund, however, is very likely to require a **letter of intent (LOI)**. Even though the LOI is not a legal and binding contract, funds are typically willing to honor them in good faith. In addition, some funds allow family members to pool capital so they can take advantage of the discount. All investors should inquire about breakpoints before paying sales charges.

Quick Quiz 12.6

1. An international equity fund will likely have a higher expense ratio than a domestic money market fund.
   a. True
   b. False
2. A 1% difference in expense ratio can produce substantial difference in overall performance over a long period.
   a. True
   b. False.

True, True.

Purchasing mutual funds within a brokerage account, rather than directly from the fund family, provides a level of convenience and ease of access. It allows investors to construct portfolios and evaluate their performance within one account. Brokerage firms have arrangements with many mutual fund families that permit the purchase of funds without a transaction fee (commission). Not all brokerage firms, however, have these arrangements with all funds, which means there might be transaction fees associated with the purchase of a particular mutual fund.

Example 12.6

Beibei wants to invest in PIMIX, a multi-sector bond fund from the PIMCO fund family with a focus on maximizing current income. Beibei can invest directly with PIMCO, which has a minimum investment of $1 million. Alternatively, he can purchase it in a brokerage account, such as Fidelity, E*TRADE, or Schwab. However, even if PIMIX is offered by all of the brokerage firms, it may not be offered in the same way. For example, three brokerage firms A,B, and C may offer different minimum investment levels and different transaction fees.

	Firm A	Firm B	Firm C
Minimum Investment	$100,000	$1 million	$100,000
Transaction Fee	$49	$19	$76

It is important to understand that the underlying investment is the same whether it is purchased directly from the mutual fund family or whether it is purchased through a brokerage firm. For investors who have sizable balances in a brokerage firm, they can often have their broker purchase the mutual fund shares and waive the transaction fee. This is because brokers prefer the investor keep their money at the brokerage firm, as opposed to removing it from the account.

Investors can also avoid or minimize loads or transaction costs by using a financial adviser who has a relationship with a brokerage firm or firms. Using an adviser might benefit the shareholder in the long run, especially if the arrangement between the adviser and the brokerage firm results in out-performance.

MUTUAL FUND CLASSIFICATION

Open-end mutual funds are typically classified as being either with or without a sales commission or a load. Funds with loads may charge a front-end or back-end load, but no-load funds charge neither. The main difference between the two is the amount of the original investment that flows into the securities held by the fund. For a no-load fund, a $100 investment goes directly to the portfolio manager and is invested in the fund's securities. A loaded fund with a five percent front-end load takes $5 to pay the broker and the remaining $95 is invested in the fund's securities.

Load versus No-Load Funds

The Securities and Exchange Commission requires that any fund charging either a front-end or back-end sales charge must be classified as a loaded fund. In addition, any fund that has a 12b-1 fee that exceeds 0.25 percent must be advertised by the fund manager as a loaded fund.

No-load funds are usually purchased by investors without the need for a broker. The fund family directly sells shares in the no-load fund to the investing public. No-load funds have no sales commissions and can have relatively low 12b-1 fees (less than 0.25%), but have expense ratios sufficient to recapture the fund's operating expenses.

Classes of Load Fund Shares

Funds with loads offer their shareholders different classes of shares that reflect different fee structures. There are significant differences among the various classes, so shareholders should make certain they invest in the most appropriate class for them. There is no specific standard for determining class types and the number of classes, but most create three separate classes.

Key Concepts

1. There are load and no-load mutual funds.
2. Load funds may be further classified to class A, B, or C.
3. Expenses impact performances.
4. Expense ratios vary with the type of mutual fund.

Class A Shares

Purchasing Class A shares typically means investors pay a sales commission up front. Class A shares operate as a front-end loaded mutual fund, with discounts available for breakpoints and letters of intent for committed purchases. Class A shares might have lower 12b-1 fees and a lower expense ratio.

Class B Shares

Purchasing Class B shares typically does not include paying a front-end load, but there will be a back end commission or a deferred redemption fee. In addition, they very likely charge a higher expense ratio than Class A shares. Most Class B shares have a conversion feature in which the shares convert to Class A after a specified time period. There are no breakpoints for Class B shares.

Class C Shares

Purchasing Class C shares will not involve paying a front-end load, but will have a relatively lower back-end load. Many Class C shares will waive the back-end load if the fund is held for longer than one year. Class C ownership does not offer discounts, breakpoints, or conversions, and they tend to have higher expense ratios.

Class I Shares

Purchasing Class I shares requires a substantial initial investment that can typically be made only by institutional investors. Class I shares have much lower expense ratios, often less than one-half the ratio of the Class A shares. Fund managers make these shares available to large institutional investors such as pension funds, insurance companies, and endowments. The low expense ratio is very attractive to institutions that have strict fiduciary responsibilities to their clients.

Which Share Class is Best?

The best class of shares for an investor depends on the circumstances, including the type of fund, the exact fees, and the expected holding period for the investment. Class A shares are generally best for a long-term holding period. Even though the front-end load is high, the lower 12b-1 fee will make up for it over a longer time period. Class C shares are generally best if the investment time horizon is short (1 to 2 years). Class B shares tend to be better for time horizons in the middle, such as five to seven years. However, the actual impact of fees is relative to the returns from the fund.

Exhibit 12.8 | Mutual Fund Share Classes

	Class A	Class B	Class C	Class I
Access Restricted	No	No	No	Yes. Requires large investment or relationship with adviser.
Front-End Load	Yes. Can be reduced from breakpoint discounts.	N/A	N/A	N/A
Back-End Load	N/A	Yes. Declining.	Yes. Usually 1% within the first year.	N/A
12b-1 Fee	Yes. Lower than Class B & C shares.	Generally higher than Class A shares.	Generally higher than Class A shares.	N/A
Converts to Class A Shares	N/A	Yes. This occurs after a specified number of years.	No	N/A

Many fund families have additional classes of shares that have a variety of meanings. As a result, investors should carefully review the prospectus of each fund to determine the actual fees that are being charged to shareholders for each class of shares for a particular fund. FINRA has a 'Fund Analyzer' tool on its website that investors can use to compare performance of various classes of specific mutual funds over time.[6]

It is important to consider that mutual fund families with loads and 12b-1 fees use these fees to pay advisers to promote their funds. Investors have several choices in terms of how they pick mutual funds:

1. They can use advisers who help the investor pick mutual funds and are compensated through loads and 12b-1 fees.
2. They can use advisers who help the investor pick no-load mutual funds and are compensated based on an hourly fee, fixed fee, or based on the assets under management.
3. They can do the research themselves and pick the funds they feel are appropriate.

Quick Quiz 12.7

1. A shares are the cheapest in the long run for loaded shares.
   a. True
   b. False
2. B shares revert to A shares after a number of years.
   a. True
   b. False

True, True.

In each of the three cases, the investor is paying for the advice, either directly or indirectly, through research and time. It is also important to realize the impact of fees on the long-term performance of the investor's assets.

Expense Ratios for Different Types of Funds

Expense ratios for mutual funds range from just a few basis points (0.20%) to several hundred basis points (over 2%). Investors must be aware of the expense ratio for funds they are considering, but they must also be aware that there is much more to fund investing than comparing expense ratios. Investors

6. FINRA states that it is an independent, not-for-profit organization authorized by Congress to protect America's investors by making sure the securities industry operates fairly and honestly.

should find funds that have the same objectives as they do, then choose the funds with the lowest expense ratios. Those investors who just want to match market returns will find index funds with very low expense ratios. On the other hand, investors who prefer active management will find funds that have much higher expense ratios. Actively managed funds incur significant research costs, tend to have higher portfolio turnover, and follow sophisticated asset allocation and selection strategies that are much more costly than passively managed funds. For this reason, funds that include international equities tend to have higher expense ratios because of the extra research needed to locate potential securities, the lack of accurate financial data, and incomplete markets.

ADVANTAGES OF MUTUAL FUNDS

Mutual funds are attractive to a wide variety of investors because they offer benefits that trading fixed income and equity securities does not. The primary reasons investors use mutual funds are to realize the benefits of diversification and to have professionals manage their capital. Other advantages are mostly related to efficiencies that fund managers have access to that escape individual investors.

Key Concepts

1. The advantages of mutual funds include diversification and professional management.
2. Low initial investment is an advantage of mutual funds.

Low Initial Investment

To attract investors that do not have a large amount of capital available, most mutual funds have low initial investment requirements. Over one-half of all funds permit initial investments as low as $1,000.[7] Investors gain exposure to hundreds of equity and fixed-income securities for one low price. In fact, some funds allow investors to purchase shares with an initial investment as low as $250 if they commit to regular deposits from a bank account through wire transfers. Fidelity came out with several zero minimum mutual funds in 2018. Most funds also have provisions for retirement accounts that lower the initial deposit even further.

Exhibit 12.9 | Mutual Fund Minimum Investment Requirements

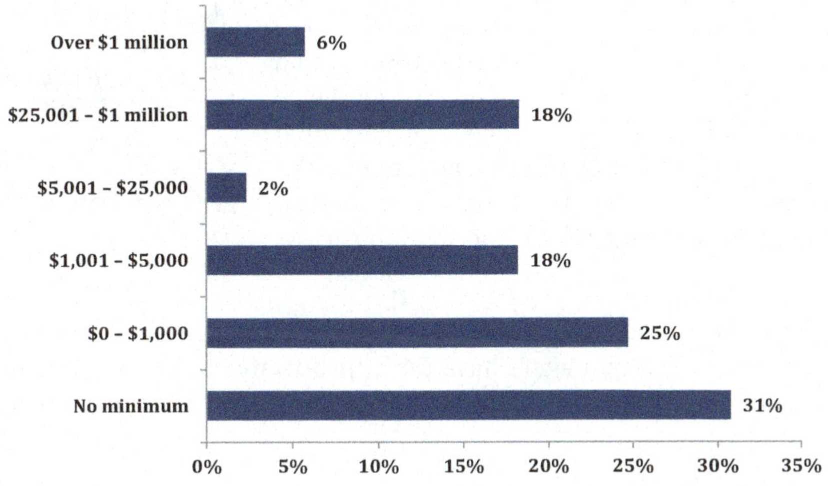

Source: Morningstar as of 8/21/21

7. Morningstar research as of August 18, 2021.

Diversification

Most investors know the benefits of diversification include a significant reduction in risk. Only an irrational investor would hold a portfolio that is not well-diversified. Mutual funds, therefore, are popular with investors because they offer a quick and efficient way to achieve diversification benefits. With low initial investments, investors have access to ownership in mutual funds that consist of hundreds or even thousands of securities. For example, the Vanguard Total Stock Market Index Fund owns over 3,900 securities as of 2021. Its minimum investment is only $3,000 while offering broad global diversification. Fidelity's Total Market Index Fund has a minimum investment of zero dollars, an expense ratio of 15 basis points (0.15% or 0.0015), and had over 3,700 holdings as of June 2021.

Ease of Access

Mutual funds can be purchased through hundreds of outlets, which include indirect purchases through financial institutions and brokers and direct purchases from the mutual fund family. Financial institutions typically have relationships with a single or sometimes multiple mutual fund families, which means it is almost as easy to purchase funds through a bank as it is to open a checking account. It is just as simple and easy to purchase funds directly from the fund family itself. Investors have access to online applications, which can be sent to the family along with a check or wire transfer. Modern technology allows investments in mutual funds to be as quick and painless as purchasing many consumer goods and services.

Professional Management

Mutual fund managers have extensive investment backgrounds, knowledge, and experience. They tend to have a variety of undergraduate degrees, from finance and general business to psychology and mathematics. Many of them have graduate degrees with the most common being the master of business administration. In addition, many have earned professional recognition, such as the Chartered Financial Analyst® designation. Mutual fund managers have professional experience that has trained them to continuously evaluate the performance of the securities in the fund, to use statistical software for efficient portfolio construction, and to monitor the fund's outcomes.

Quick Quiz 12.8

1. Most mutual funds require a minimum investment of at least $10,000.
   a. True
   b. False
2. Mutual funds are one of the most efficient ways to achieve diversification with a relatively small investment.
   a. True
   b. False
3. Professional management is one of the benefits of mutual funds.
   a. True
   b. False
4. The management fee charged by mutual funds can be deducted as an itemized deduction subject to the 2% AGI limit.
   a. True
   b. False

False, True, True, False.

Some funds are managed by individuals, others by a team of managers, but in either case, mutual fund investors can have confidence that managers have the appropriate backgrounds to manage their money. Of course, one important decision for mutual fund investors is to choose between having one fund manager or a team.

Mutual fund managers typically have research departments at their disposal to help provide institutional support for all the decisions that must be made. Some fund managers do not have this elaborate type of support, but they make arrangements with financial institutions to gain access to all the market reports and data they need.

Tax Efficiency of Management Fees

The management fees of a mutual fund are part of its expense ratio. Mutual funds offer a tax benefit that separately-managed accounts (SMAs) do not.[8] Prior to the Tax Cuts and Jobs Act of 2017 (TCJA 2017), investment advisory fees and other advisory fees were deductible as an itemized deduction subject to the two percent of AGI limit. However, TCJA 2017 suspended this deduction for years after 2018.

The entire management fee for a mutual fund is removed before there are any distributions made to the fund shareholders. Consequently, investors receive the full tax benefit of paying management fees, while they no longer receive the full benefit from SMAs or other actively managed portfolios.

Liquidity

Mutual fund managers have a constant flow of capital into and out of the fund. The nature of an open-end fund means that investors can purchase shares daily. Out of fairness and some SEC regulations, mutual funds must also provide opportunities for shareholders to redeem shares. This process also occurs daily, which means mutual funds maintain significant levels of liquidity. Mutual fund investors simply inform the manager how many shares they want redeemed and the fund manager sells those shares. The price of the sale is the net asset value at the end of the day in which the sell order was placed. There is significant liquidity in the mutual fund market.

Transaction Cost Efficiency

Mutual funds enjoy the benefits of economies of scale because of their size. The economies occur at the trade level because hundreds if not thousands of shares are bought and sold at a time. This makes transaction costs significantly lower than shareholders could possibly hope for if they traded with a traditional broker. Technology advances with online trading, however, have significantly reduced the cost of trading for all investors. Nevertheless, mutual funds offer both explicit and implicit transaction cost efficiency for their shareholders.

Range of Mutual Fund Products

Investors generally have goals that include growth, income, capital preservation, and tax efficiency. The mutual fund industry is well-equipped to handle those and many other additional investor objectives. Even the most selective investor should be able to find a fund or set of funds that meet their risk and return objectives.

Services

Mutual fund investors receive a list of services and benefits that help them manage their accounts and reach their investment objectives. The first and most fundamental service provided by the fund is the report on the performance of the fund coupled with the unique aspects of the shareholder's position in the fund. Years ago, fund managers would send quarterly and annual reports to investors in the mail regarding net asset values, performance, shares owned, and distributions. They still do this, but most investors have easy access to the fund's online services, which includes all of these items plus many others.

8. SMAs or separately managed accounts are portfolios that are managed by professional money managers, taking into consideration the needs of an individual investor. The assets within the SMA are owned directly by the investor, as opposed to indirectly in a mutual fund. SMAs have several advantages over mutual funds: control of security sales, such as tax harvesting, as well as clear transparency – knowing what securities are in the portfolio.

Mutual funds also offer regularly scheduled purchases and withdrawals. It is very easy to link the bank account of the investor to the fund, making one-time trades and periodic purchases or withdrawals seamless. This service provides fund shareholders the opportunity to increase or decrease their investment in the fund whenever they choose and to take advantage of dollar cost averaging by making periodic investments. Many investors prefer to have a portion of their monthly income invested in funds, while others prefer to make periodic withdrawals to meet periodic obligations. Mutual fund investors can arrange this schedule with ease.

Mutual funds also offer additional services that make investing convenient for their shareholders. These handy services include the opportunity to reinvest coupon income, dividend income, and even capital gains. Many funds attach the ability to write checks or access a debit card through one of their funds. Since most funds offer these services, investors now expect them and expect their convenience levels to improve over time.

DISADVANTAGES OF MUTUAL FUNDS

While mutual funds possess a wide range of benefits, they are not always the perfect investing vehicle. Investors should be aware of the pitfalls and obstacles that mutual funds present. The most glaring is relative poor performance and the incurrence of fund expenses.

Key Concepts

1. There are disadvantages to mutual funds including fees, loads and expenses.
2. There are more mutual funds than individual stocks.

Poor Relative Performance

Many mutual funds are actively managed, meaning the fund management team believes it can outperform the market. Active management is the process of performing market research, identifying under or overvalued securities, taking positions in those securities, and rotating asset allocation to take advantage of market mispricing. Each active fund manager will have a specific objective and will attempt to beat a relevant benchmark. The problem with active management is that the empirical evidence indicates most funds underperform their benchmarks. This poor relative performance is most observed during bull markets. In addition, large cap funds tend to perform the worst because of the high amount of trading and information available on large cap companies. Fund expenses reduce performance and it seems the majority of active managers cannot overcome this natural deficit. Finally, there is some evidence that small cap funds and international funds are best at beating the market, but this is likely only true because those markets are not as efficient.

Investors should always measure performance on a risk-adjusted basis. Metrics such as a fund's standard deviation, R-squared, and beta are readily available. These are good measures of risk to which mutual fund investors are exposed and should be used to measure risk-adjusted performance. Investors should also be cognizant of a fund's Sharpe ratio.

Passive mutual funds, however, should replicate their benchmark performance. The most common passively managed funds are those that track a broad stock market index, such as the Standard and Poor's 500 Index. The problem with passive funds is that the expense ratio will by definition reduce performance below that of the benchmark. However, as implied above, passive or index funds outperform most actively managed funds, after taking expenses into consideration.

Control Issues

While mutual funds provide professional investment management, it is the fund manager that chooses the securities in the portfolio and decides on how to allocate them. Each mutual fund has stated objectives outlined in the prospectus, but the objectives allow the manager a good degree of flexibility to make decisions. This means that the investor's risk and return objectives might not be exactly consistent with those of the overall fund. In addition, buy and sell decisions have tax implications and the tax liabilities that arise from the decisions made by managers tend not to be optimal for every shareholder.

Fees, Loads, and Expenses

Mutual fund managers and the supporting mutual fund industry do not perform their services for free. Investors pay a variety of management fees, commissions, and other operating expenses, and these necessarily reduce investment performance. Many funds charge a sales load that may be five percent or higher, and many funds have expense ratios in excess of two percent. As these costs accelerate, more pressure is placed on fund managers to perform and most of them are not up to the challenge, at least in terms of beating their benchmark index.

Quick Quiz 12.9

1. Mutual funds can be sold throughout the trading day.
   a. True
   b. False
2. Mutual funds with high turnover are more likely to have more built-in gains than mutual funds with lower turnover.
   a. True
   b. False

False, False.

Cash Reserves

Since mutual fund managers accept new purchases and redeem shares daily, they need to retain a significant amount of cash on hand. This puts a drag on the portfolio as the capital available to the fund is never fully invested, and the cash held earns a minimal or even zero return. Some fund managers use futures contracts to reduce the need for having available cash and to reduce the cash drag, but positions in futures contracts have their own set of risks shareholders might not be willing to bear.

No Insurance

There is no federal government guarantee of mutual fund investments, as there is for deposits made at financial institutions with FDIC insurance.

Market Impact

Since mutual funds trade large blocks of shares, they need to take into account their market impact. Large volume trades can impact bid and ask prices, resulting in higher asks and hence increased purchase prices, and lower bids which decrease sales proceeds.

Choice of Many Funds

The 2021 Investment Company Fact Book states that at the end of 2020 there were over 7,500 mutual funds available to investors. For some, there are simply too many choices, and it can be quite confusing to decide which ones best serve their investment objectives.

Classification System

Because there are so many mutual funds, the industry has begun to classify funds according to their investment objectives. Equity funds tend to be classified into one of three fundamental categories:

Income, capital gains, and aggressive growth. Within these classes, sub categories include large cap, mid cap, small cap, high and low dividend yields, value, and then an extension into global and emerging market securities. All these classifications can be quite confusing for investors, especially since some mutual funds fall into multiple categories. It can be difficult for investors to find the right fit for their objectives.

Tax Inefficiencies

Mutual funds that hold securities for long periods of time during bull markets have built-in gains in the portfolio. For new shareholders, these gains pose a potential tax liability when the securities are sold, even though the new shareholders have not benefited from the price appreciation. The timing and amount of the tax is a burden for shareholders, who should make themselves aware of any unrealized gains in the fund before they buy.

TYPES AND OBJECTIVES OF MUTUAL FUNDS

There are four main types of mutual fund categories:

1. Money market funds
2. Fixed-income funds
3. Equity funds
4. Hybrid funds

Equity funds dominate the market with over one-half of all funds.

Key Concepts

1. Explain the basic differences between the various categories of mutual funds.
2. Identify the major risks of fixed-income mutual funds and equity funds.

Exhibit 12.10 | Allocation of Types of Mutual Funds[9]

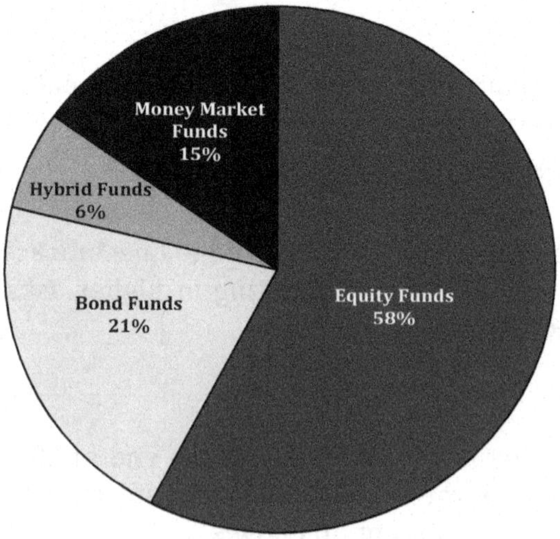

9. ICI.org: 2021 Investment Company Fact Book.

Money Market Mutual Funds

Money market securities are those that mature in one year or less and typically do not pay any intermediate cash flows. As such, they almost always trade at a discount from their maturity values.

Some of the more popular money market instruments include:

- Treasury Bills
- Commercial Paper
- Bankers' Acceptances
- Negotiable Certificates of Deposit
- Repurchase Agreements
- Short-Term Municipal Debt

Each of these can be purchased by investors, either through brokers or through the issuing entity. For example, Treasury bills can be purchased directly from the U.S. Treasury Department with only a minimum investment of $100. On the other hand, commercial paper and negotiable certificates of deposits can only be purchased with minimum investments of $100,000. Bankers' acceptances have additional trading limitations and repurchase agreements are almost exclusively traded among large institutions. With the exception of treasuries, buying money market securities is very difficult for individual investors to do.

Money market securities offer many advantages for individual investors, and the financial services met the demand by introducing money market mutual funds (MMMF) in the early 1970s. From their inception, fund managers have preferred investing in securities with two to three months maturity to ensure liquidity but also to adhere to the Securities and Exchange Commission's rule that the average maturity of the securities in the fund must be 90 days or less.

Most fund shareholders view their MMMF holding as storage for cash with better expected returns than offered by other financial institutions. These funds do not have loads at either front or back ends and do not charge redemption fees. They do, however, include management fees. Because these funds offer check writing and wire transfer services, investors can transfer funds into and out of their MMMFs with ease. Many investors, especially high net worth investors, use MMMFs for tax purposes. Tax-exempt MMMFs typically invest in municipal securities. Investors should remember to use taxable funds for their retirement accounts, such as 401(k) plans or their individual retirement accounts (IRAs), as these accounts are tax exempt and taxable MMMFs will have higher yields than tax-exempt MMMFs. Taxable funds invest in almost any other short-term security, but some invest solely in Treasuries.

There was substantial growth in the industry in the late 1970s and early 1980s because interest rates were relatively high and investors could earn significant returns without taking much risk. In fact, MMMF returns during that time period were far greater than yields offered by commercial banks. This interest rate advantage has generally occurred over their history. Over time, interest rates gradually declined, but MMMFs have maintained their popularity, even in the face of a near zero interest rate environment during the 2010s.

MMMFs offer very low risk for investors coupled with high liquidity. Net asset values for every fund are set to $1.00 at the end of every trading day. To accomplish this, fund managers use unique valuation methods, but this changed in 2016 when the Securities and Exchange Commission adopted rules that force institutional funds to allow the NAV to fluctuate around that magic $1.00 amount. Funds with retail individual shareholders can still use the old $1.00 rule. The new rule seeks to maintain more transparency in the mutual fund market. Even though MMMF investors are exposed to little default risk and little interest rate risk, they still must concern themselves with reinvestment risk and loss of purchasing power.

Fixed-Income Mutual Funds

Fixed-income securities are issued by governments, agencies, or corporations and have maturity dates from five to thirty (or more) years. Fixed-income securities make regular coupon payments and then return the par value at maturity. Fixed-income investors, consequently, purchase bonds for their income and their capital gains. Bondholders are exposed to default risk, interest rate risk, inflation risk, reinvestment risk, and sometimes option risk.

Fixed-income mutual funds were created to help investors manage each of these risks. Fund managers typically purchase the following types of bonds:

- Treasury Notes and Bonds
- Investment Grade Corporate Bonds
- High Yielding Corporate Bonds
- Mortgage Backed Securities
- Inflation Protected Bonds
- Long-Term Municipal Debt

Because bond mutual funds are well-diversified, investing in them typically exposes investors to very little default risk, especially if the fund invests in high quality fixed-income securities. Investors are only exposed to option risk if the fund purchases bonds with embedded options.

The primary source of risk from, investing in fixed-income mutual funds is interest rate risk. When yields rise, the prices of the underlying bonds fall. During a rising interest rate environment, most bonds that have traditional convex price-yield relationships experience price drops. The implication is that the majority of the bonds will lose value when interest rates rise.

During the decade of the 1980s, and 1990s, the Federal Reserve Bank utilized an anti-inflation policy, which resulted in falling interest rates for much of those twenty years. Bond funds, as one might guess, experienced relatively high total returns. During the 2010s, however, interest rates were so low, there was no room for falling rates and performance has been average.

Exhibit 12.11 | Rates of 1-Year U.S. Treasury Securities

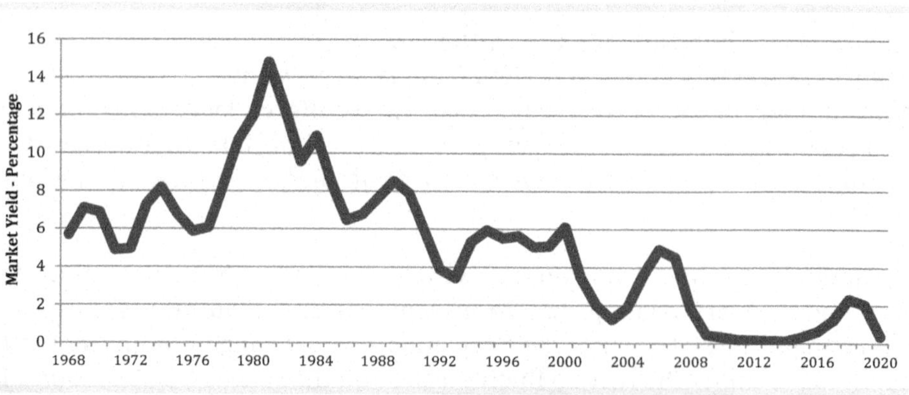

Source: Federal Reserve Board

Example 12.7

The Walnut Foundation (WF) invests solely in fixed-income mutual funds to meet its future obligations. WF grants college scholarships to talented students who declare Conservation and Wildlife Management as their major. WF has a committed semi-annual cash outflow to pay tuition expenses, and it prefers investing in bonds with higher coupon payments.

Martin is WF's financial adviser, and his research suggests the economy is moving from a low interest rate environment to a much higher one. Martin has identified five fixed-income mutual funds for WF, and the monthly distributions have been sufficient to cover all WF's cash outflow needs. WF has been approached by the local university to donate a substantial amount of capital to help construct a new building for the university's newly created College of Environmental Science. WF considers this opportunity but would have to sell a portion of its investment in bond funds for the donation.

WF is exposed to the common risks facing all bondholders. First, an increasing interest rate environment will reduce the value of each one of WF's fixed-income funds. When yields rise, bond prices fall, and the degree of price drop depends on the level of interest rate risk to which each fund is exposed. Interest rate risk for bonds and bond funds is typically measured by its duration. There is no doubt that the longer it waits to sell one of its funds, the more likely the net asset value of the fund is to fall, if Martin is correct in his prediction. This is a delicate decision, one that is similar to a stock market investor trying to time the market.

There is some good news, however, in a rising rate market. The monthly distributions WF receives can now be reinvested at higher yields. This is also true for any bonds maturing in the fund or called during a time period. The fund manager will be able to purchase new bonds at relatively lower prices, thus generating higher expected returns.

Fixed-income mutual funds are exactly like other mutual funds in that they charge for providing professional investment services. For example, Vanguard Total Bond Market Index Fund (Admiral Shares) has no loads, no 12b-1 fees, no distribution fees, and an expense ratio of 0.05 percent (5 basis points), of which 0.04 percent is the management fee. As of 2021, this fund had a minimum investment requirement of $3,000. The stated objective of the fund is to provide a broad exposure to US investment grade bonds.

Funds that are designed to mimic the performance of an index should have lower expense ratios than actively managed funds. The passive approach does not require the time and research requirements to search for undervalued securities or expensive asset models to achieve efficient diversification. The majority of fixed-income funds have expense ratios of less than one percent, with actively managed and international funds having expense ratios at the higher end.

Exhibit 12.12 | Types of Mutual Funds

Types of Mutual Funds

- **Domestic Equity**
  - Capital appreciation funds seek growth of capital; dividends are not a primary consideration.
    - **Growth** funds invest primarily in common stock of growth companies, which are those that exhibit signs of above-average growth, even if the share price is high relative to earnings/intrinsic value.
    - **Sector funds** seek capital appreciation by investing in companies in related fields or specific industries.
    - **Alternative strategy** funds seek to provide capital appreciation while minimizing risk by employing long/short, market neutral, leveraged, or inverse strategies.
  - Total return funds seek a combination of current income and capital appreciation by investing in equity securities.
    - **Value funds** invest primarily in common stock of value companies, which are those that are out of favor with investors, appear underpriced by the market relative to their earnings/intrinsic value, or have high dividend yields.
    - **Blend funds** invest primarily in common stock of both growth and value companies or are not limited to the types of companies in which they can invest.
- **World Equity**
  - **Emerging markets** funds invest primarily in companies based in less-developed countries.
  - **Global equity** funds invest primarily in equity securities traded worldwide, including equity securities of U.S. companies.
  - **International equity** funds must invest in equity securities of companies located outside the United States, and cannot invest in U.S. companies' stocks.
  - **Regional equity** funds invest in companies that are based in a specific part of the world.
- **Hybrid Funds**
  - **Asset Allocation funds** seek high total return by investing in a mix of equities, fixed-income securities, and money market instruments.
  - **Balanced** funds invest in a specific mix of equity securities and bonds with the the objective of conserving principal, providing income, and achieving long-term growth of both principal and income.
  - **Flexible portfolio** funds are designed to provide high total return by investing in common stock, bonds and other debt securities, and money market securities. The portfolio may hold up to 100 percent of any one of these types of securities and may easily change, depending on market conditions.
  - **Income-Mixed** funds invest in a variety of income producing securities, including equities and fixed-income securities. They seek a high level of current income for shareholders. Capital appreciation is not a primary objective.
  - **Alternative strategies** funds seek to provide capital appreciation while minimizing risk by investing in a mix of equity and fixed-income securities while employing long/short, market neutral, leverage, inverse, or commodity strategies.
- **Bonds**
  - **Investment grade** funds seek current income by investing primarily in investment grade debt securities. These funds may be short-term, intermediate-term, or long-term focused.
  - **High yield** funds seek current income by investing two-thirds or more of their portfolios in lower-rated corporate bonds (Baa or lower by Moody's and BBB or lower by Standard and Poor's rating services).
  - **Government bond** funds pursue an objective of high current income by investing in taxable bonds issued, or backed, by the U.S. government. These funds may be short-term, intermediate-term, or long-term focused.
  - **Multisector bond** funds seek to provide high current income for their shareholders by investing predominantly in a combination of domestic fixed-income securities, including mortgage-backed securities and high yield bonds, and may invest up to 25 percent in bonds issued by foreign companies and governments.
  - **Municipal bond** funds invest primarily in municipal bonds of a single state or across various states. The bonds are exempt from federal income tax as well as state taxes for residents of that state.

Equity Mutual Funds

According to the Investment Company Institute, there was over $24 trillion invested in U.S. open-end mutual funds by investment companies at the end of 2020. Over 50 percent of this amount was invested in equity mutual funds. The total amount is approximately equal to the size of the U.S. economy as measured by gross domestic product. The vast amount of funds flowing into mutual funds reflects the tremendous demand for long-term investing in the equity ownership of publicly held corporations.

Exhibit 12.12 shows the wide range of investment objectives in the equity fund market. For investors with long or short-term horizons, there are so many funds from which to choose. Notice from the exhibit that investors generally search for income or capital gains or a combination of the two. The various slices of those general objectives are available for investors with more sophisticated goals. **Exhibit 12.13** shows the breakdown in total fund assets under management as of the end of 2020 and 2019.

Exhibit 12.13 | How Mutual Funds are Invested

Total Net Assets of Mutual Funds (in billions)	December 2020		December 2019	
Long-Term				
Equity				
• Domestic Equity	9,524		8,439	
• World Equity	3,205		2,937	
		12,729		11,376
Hybrid		1,620		1,579
Bond				
• Taxable Bond	4,337		3,890	
• Municipal Bond	877		814	
		5,214		4,704
Total Long-Term		**19,563**		**17,659**
Money Market				
• Taxable Money Market	4,228		3,494	
• Tax-Exempt Money Market	105		138	
Total Money Market		4,333		3,632
Total		**23,896**		**21,291**

Source: Investment Company Factbook 2021

Equity mutual fund managers obviously invest capital in equity securities. The equity asset class has historically enjoyed higher long-term returns than either the fixed-income class or the money market class. Equity funds are a natural fit for investors seeking long-term growth plus income. Equity funds have gained prominence in the era of retirement-focused investors, especially since the mid 1970s with the creation of the individual retirement account (IRA) and the early 1980s with the creation of 401(k) plans. Since that time period, investors have had easy access to equity exposure through these funds and with low minimum investment requirements, there popularity is unlikely to decline.

The higher returns are only achieved because equity securities tend to have more risk than other financial securities. The most commonly cited risk in the stock market is known as market risk or systematic risk, defined as the variability in returns due to changes in economic factors. Examples of economic factors include changes in the size of the economy, interest rates, energy prices, unemployment rates, and global conflicts. When any of these and other systematic risk factors change, the prices of financial securities and therefore net asset values of mutual funds also change. Extreme U.S. stock market examples include financial market crises in 2008, 1987,1929, and the volatility experienced during the pandemic of 2020. Systematic risk is measured by beta. The other component of risk is known as unsystematic risk, which can be virtually eliminated through diversification. Consequently, index funds have no unsystematic risk. Sector or focused funds and almost any fund that is actively managed, however, may have more than just a small amount of unsystematic risk.

Quick Quiz 12.10

1. There is more money invested in bond funds than equity funds.
   a. True
   b. False
2. Actively managed funds should have higher expense ratios than passively managed funds.
   a. True
   b. False.
3. Market risk is the primary risk for equity mutual funds.
   a. True
   b. False

False, True, True.

The unsystematic component can be divided into three parts:

- Company risk results from the uncertainties surrounding the management of each firm in the fund. These include poor decision making or unethical behavior by executives, loss of competitive advantages, unexpected changes in operating cash flows, and increases in the firm's weighted average cost of capital.
- Concentration risk is the uncertainty surrounding the mutual fund holdings. Active fund managers frequently make asset selection and allocation bets in which large concentrations are held in just a few stocks, making the fund poorly diversified. When those stocks underperform, it significantly affects the performance of the fund.
- Liquidity risk is the uncertainty over the redemption of shares, especially during times of severe market stress.

Equity mutual fund investors should be aware of both systematic and unsystematic risks. All fund investors should demand diversification from their managers, at least to the degree that it's consistent with the objectives stated in the fund's prospectus. This is a non-issue for index fund investors. For investors in actively managed funds or funds that target a specific industry, they should identify which unsystematic risk factors are likely to be present in the fund and decide if they are comfortable taking those risks.

Hybrid or Balanced Funds

Hybrid funds invest in a combination of money market, fixed-income, and equity securities. The idea is to provide investors with a balanced exposure to all types of mutual funds. Of course, investors could always buy equity funds, fixed-income funds, and money market funds individually and as part of a fund portfolio, but may investors like the convenience of owning just one balanced fund.

Hybrid funds are generally categorized in the following manner:

- Low risk, with a majority invested in high-grade bonds, low-risk money market securities, and a few equity securities in well-established companies.
- Moderate risk, with an equal balance of fixed-income and equity securities.
- High risk, with a majority invested in equity securities.

Hybrid funds became more popular when fund families began offering target retirement date funds. Specific allocations are recommended for a worker who has 40 years until retirement, and these would be quite different for one who will retire in ten years. As a result, hybrids became a popular part of individual's retirement plans.

SUMMARY

Summary of key points:

- Investment companies, which include mutual funds, closed-end funds, exchange-traded funds (ETFs), and unit investment trusts (UITs), provide investors easy access to capital markets, professional management, and instant diversification. Forty-six percent of households have investments in one or more types of investment company.
- The transition from defined benefit plans to defined contribution plans has fueled the exposure to investment companies.
- Investment companies invest capital in various types of securities on behalf of shareholders and are flow-through entities that pass income along to shareholders. Investment companies offer many objectives, such as growth or income.
- Unit investment trusts typically have a fixed capitalization, passive management, and a fixed termination date.
- Exchange-traded funds are relatively inexpensive, passively managed portfolios that trade on the secondary exchanges like equity securities and offer index or sector exposure to investors.
- Closed-end funds are generally funded through an initial offering, have a fixed number of shares, and typically trade at a discount or premium to NAV.
- Mutual funds are the most popular type of investment company in terms of assets under management and always trade at NAV.
- There are various fees and expenses for mutual funds, including sales charges, operating expenses, 12b-1 fees, and management fees. These fees have to be carefully considered prior to investing in a fund, along with whether it is a load or no-load fund.

DISCUSSION QUESTIONS

SOLUTIONS to the discussion questions can be found exclusively within the chapter. Once you have completed an initial reading of the chapter, go back and highlight the answers to these questions.

1. What are investment companies?
2. What are the four types of investment companies?
3. What is net asset value (NAV)?
4. What type of investment company has the largest invested assets?
5. Why is it important for individuals to invest on their own behalf?
6. Discuss the tax treatment of investment companies (IC).
7. Describe a unit investment trust (UIT).
8. Describe ETFs.
9. Describe closed-end funds (CEF).
10. Describe open-end investment companies (mutual funds).
11. Explain the difference between front-end loads and back-end loads.
12. What are 12b-1 fees used for?
13. What does a mutual fund's expense ratio include?
14. Explain how discounts on front-end sales charges work.
15. List several advantages of mutual funds.
16. List several disadvantages of mutual funds.
17. Determine which class of shares is the best for an investor based on their holding period.
18. Mariah is considering adding the Alpha Equity Fund (AFE) to her portfolio, but has to choose between A shares, B shares, or C shares. She expects the fund will generate a return of 10 percent annually. Below are the details of the three share classes. Determine which class of shares is the best for Mariah based on her holding period of 2 years and a $500,000 investment.

Class	Load (Redemption Fee)	12b-1 Fee	Conversion
A Shares	5% front load	25 basis points	N/A
B Shares	5% declining redemption fee*	100 basis points	Converts to A Shares after 5 years
C Shares	1% redemption fee	100 basis points	No Conversion
* 5% fee for redemption within the first year, 4% fee within the second year, 3% fee within the third year, 2% fee within the fourth year, and 1% fee within the fifth year.			

MULTIPLE-CHOICE PROBLEMS

A sample of multiple choice problems is provided below. Additional multiple choice problems are available at money-education.com by accessing the Student Practice Portal.

1. Mutual fund expense ratios include all of the following except?
   a. Management fees.
   b. 12b-1 fees.
   c. Operating expenses.
   d. Investment losses.

2. Which of the following investment companies is most likely characterized by continual ability to redeem shares?
   a. Closed-end fund.
   b. Open-end fund.
   c. Unit investment trust.
   d. Exchange traded fund.

3. Which of the following statements concerning a unit investment trust is correct?
   a. It has an unmanaged portfolio.
   b. It usually consists of common stocks.
   c. It is most appropriate for young people.
   d. It requires constant management attention.

4. Open-end funds and closed-end funds are similar except for:
   a. Capitalization.
   b. Objectives.
   c. Regulation.
   d. Investment management.

5. Leon is considering a mutual fund that invests only in technology companies. What is the best term for this type of fund?
   a. Equity Fund.
   b. Growth Fund.
   c. Momentum Fund.
   d. Sector Fund.

QUICK QUIZ EXPLANATIONS

Quick Quiz 12.1

1. True.
2. False. The largest percentage of investment company assets are invested in mutual funds.
3. True.

Quick Quiz 12.2

1. False. A UIT usually has only one initial public offering.
2. True.
3. True.

Quick Quiz 12.3

1. False. ETF shares can be sold anytime during the trading day.
2. False. ETFs are generally passively managed but some are actively managed.
3. True.
4. True.

Quick Quiz 12.4

1. True.
2. True.
3. True.

Quick Quiz 12.5

1. True.
2. True.

Quick Quiz 12.6

1. True.
2. True.

Quick Quiz 12.7

1. True.
2. True.

Quick Quiz 12.8

1. False. Most have a minimum of $1,000 or less. Some even have zero minimums.
2. True.
3. True.
4. False. The fee reduces taxable income, so it is effectively an adjustment for AGI (above-the-line deduction).

QUICK QUIZ EXPLANATIONS

Quick Quiz 12.9

1. False. Mutual funds can only be sold at the end of the day after the close of the market.
2. False. The statement is just the opposite of what is correct.

Quick Quiz 12.10

1. False. More money is invested in equity funds.
2. True.
3. True.

13

INVESTMENT COMPANY - ANALYSIS

LEARNING OBJECTIVES

1. Understand that asset allocation is the most important factor in determining long-term variation in portfolio returns.
2. Understand that asset allocation is selected based on the goals, objectives, and risk tolerance of the investor.*
3. Realize that a mean variance optimization model is used to identify efficient portfolios.*
4. Understand that portfolios once chosen must be monitored and rebalanced when necessary.*
5. Understand that a mutual fund prospectus identifies the fund objective, the investment policy and strategy, management and tenure, historical performance, portfolio turnover, fees and expenses, and risk of investing.
6. Be aware that there are no-load and load funds. For load funds, there are various share classes, such as A, B, C, and I shares, each with distinct fees and expenses.
7. Understand that no-load simply means no sales charges up front or deferred. However, there are management fees and other fees that make up total annual operating expenses.
8. Understand that two measures of risk used in measures of performance are beta and standard deviation.*
9. Understand that there are three common measures of performance: Jensen's Alpha (an absolute measure) and Sharpe and Treynor (both relative measures).*
10. Be able to distinguish between Sharpe (standard deviation is the risk measure) and Treynor (beta is the risk measure).*
11. Understand that R^2 (the coefficient of determination) provides insight into the type of risk inherent in a mutual fund and may impact the use of certain performance measures for a mutual fund.*
12. Understand how mutual funds can be used to implement an investment plan once an asset allocation is complete.*
13. Explain how professional investment advisers select mutual funds for inclusion in a portfolio.*
14. Discuss how the information in a mutual fund's prospectus can assist an analyst in evaluating that fund.
15. Describe the way modern portfolio theory statistics provide insight into a mutual fund's risk-return characteristics.
16. Describe the issues to consider when managing portfolios of mutual funds.

**Ties to CFP Certification Learning Objectives*

INTRODUCTION

Investment companies provide many services that investors use to achieve their financial goals. Mutual funds, exchange-traded funds, and even unit investment trusts (UITs) are easy to purchase, easy to sell, and relatively easy to manage. The challenge for investors is to sift through the myriad of possible investment opportunities, especially since there are so many differences in objectives, expense ratios, and management styles. Most individuals own mutual funds rather than equity shares directly, and a great majority of workers have mutual funds as part of their retirement portfolios. These financial assets are extremely important to all investors.

The investment process is discussed in this chapter, helping investors decide which funds are optimal for them. The process begins with fund selection, moves to fund allocation, and ends with implementation. The role of professional investment advisers as part of the process is addressed.

ASSET ALLOCATION USING MUTUAL FUNDS

In a landmark study published in the Financial Analysts Journal in 1986, investment advisers Gary Brinson, Randolph Hood, and Gilbert Beebower (BHB) show that asset allocation is the most important factor that determines the long run variation in pension plan returns. BHB show that investment advisers should focus most of their research on the allocation decision and less research on market timing or security selection. In fact, BHB show that over 90 percent of the variability in pension plan returns is explained by the asset allocation decision.

Key Concepts

1. Describe the process of choosing mutual funds for an investor portfolio.
2. Explain the importance of asset allocation in the determination of portfolio returns.
3. Define mean-variance analysis models and explain how they are used to find efficient portfolios.

Mutual funds can and should be part of an investment strategy that enables investors to achieve their financial goals. The allocation decision identifies the proportional investments of each fund. For example, simple strategies include a 40 percent fixed-income and 60 percent equity security allocation for an investor with moderate risk tolerance. More complex examples include a division of the fixed-income component into investment grade corporate debt, agency debt, and federal government debt, with an equity division into small cap, large cap, and emerging markets. The process can get even more complex when investors consider bond duration, sector shifting, and the impact of global diversification. The allocation decision is even more critical when investors own several funds.

Steps in the Investment Process

The steps in the investment process are outlined below. These should occur with or without a financial adviser.

1. Collect relevant information, including specific cash outflow obligations, the number of dependents, income needs, size of investable assets, and any aspirations each investor might have.
2. Identify the investor constraints, including any liquidity needs, time horizon issues, tax liabilities, and anything unique to each investor. This step should include any behavioral biases the investor might have.
3. Compute both the return and risk objectives. This should include a measure of expected inflation and perhaps an estimate of the investor's acceptable standard deviation or beta.
4. Identify the appropriate funds to be included in the portfolio. Each should be consistent with the risk and return objectives.
5. Identify the appropriate allocation for each fund.
6. Monitor the portfolio for performance, compare against the objectives and relevant benchmarks, evaluate portfolio and fund reports, and collect feedback for future benefit.

Example 13.1

Rory and Paulina Gill have been married for ten years and are in their early 40s. The Gills have no children and a combined income of $90,000. They inherited some money and have $45,000 of investable assets. Brianna is their financial adviser who guides the couple through their risk and return objectives. Brianna determines they have average risk tolerance and average return objectives. Brianna suggests a 30% allocation to fixed-income securities with the remainder allocated to equity. Brianna recommends the following allocation:

Equities	70%	Fixed Income	30%
Large-Cap Value	10%	Taxable Corporate Bonds	20%
Large-Cap Growth	20%	International Bonds	10%
Mid-Cap Growth	20%		
International Large Cap	20%		

This allocation is weighted toward equity large-cap funds, which is consistent with the Gill's average risk and return objectives. At this point, specific funds within the allocation recommended by Brianna will have to be identified. There are so many funds from which to choose, Brianna and the Gills should not have much difficulty finding funds that fit their objectives and also provide the services they need. This is probably a reasonable allocation, but notice that the allocation in each fund is either 20% or 10%. It is easy for a financial adviser or an investor to simply round to the nearest 10th percentile, but this approach may not be optimal.

Mean Variance Optimization

In 1952, Harry Markowitz developed a model that is used even today as the basis for finding optimal allocations for portfolio management. The model assumes that investors consider only two factors when making investments, namely the investment's expected return, measured by its mean, and its risk, measured by its variance.

In addition, all investors are assumed to be risk averse. Meaning that investors need the promise of higher expected returns to take on extra risk. As a result, investors choose portfolios that have the highest return for a given level of risk, or the lowest risk for a given level of return.

A portfolio that has the highest possible return for a given level of risk is known as an efficient portfolio. With knowledge of every asset's expected return, risk and correlation with other assets, a financial adviser can calculate asset allocations that result in efficient portfolios.

With knowledge of the individual's risk and return objectives, the adviser can then recommend a specific efficient portfolio for that investor.

Example 13.2

Rory and Paulina Gill have a return objective of 8.8% and a maximum variability allowed in the portfolio of 15%. Their financial adviser, Brianna, has identified a family of funds that fits the needs of the Gill couple. Using the Markowitz optimization model, Brianna derives the following allocation to achieve those goals.

The Big Valley (BV) Family of Mutual Funds

	Allocation	Expected Return	Variability
BV Diversified Large-Cap Growth and Value Fund	34%	8.1%	14.9%
BV Mid-Cap Dividend Fund	17%	9.3%	16.3%
BV Global Equity Fund	19%	11.8%	17.4%
BV High Quality Bond Fund	22%	6.8%	7.5%
BV Global Bond Fund	8%	9.5%	12.9%

The weighted average return on this portfolio is 8.83%, which meets the return objective for the Gill couple. Their maximum variability is exceeded by only two funds and they have less than 20% allocation each. The variability calculation of the portfolio would include the correlations between and among each fund, so the portfolio risk would be less than the maximum. This illustrates the benefits of diversification.

To compute mean-variance optimal allocations, it is necessary to collect data for each fund, including historical returns, historical volatility as measured by standard deviation, and the correlations between and among all funds. It is the correlation coefficients that will determine how diversified the portfolio is.

The relevant data is easy to find, as many financial websites provide asset prices for various financial securities, and net asset values for mutual funds. The investor or adviser, however, must decide on the frequency of data to use. Many academic researchers use daily prices but many practitioners use monthly prices. Once the data has been gathered, practitioners will typically use proprietary software to calculate the means, standard deviations and correlations required for the optimization process.

Some advisers use data taken from the funds directly and some use data from index proxies. For example, price and return data from the S&P 500 may be used as a proxy for the performance of large-cap equities. Once this data has been used to derive the optimal large-cap equity allocation, the adviser finds a mutual fund that replicates the performance of the index. The challenge with this method is to make certain the fund actually performs like the index. Advisers can do this by careful observation of the correlation between the fund and the index. If the correlation coefficient between the fund and the index remains high over time, the adviser can be confident the two are moving in tandem. If there is a divergence, then the adviser will have to decide whether to find another fund as a substitute.

If the funds chosen closely represent the relevant indexes upon which the **mean-variance optimization model** was based, then the actual portfolio should perform as expected. However, a fund's risk and return profile may change over time, so it is crucial to monitor its performance and make adjustments as necessary.

Portfolio Performance Report

The final step in the investment process is critical for the successful implementation of an investment policy. Each portfolio decision regarding selection and allocation should be monitored on an almost continual basis because financial security prices rise and fall over time. These market changes should be monitored to make certain the securities remain appropriate for the client and that their risk characteristics do not place them outside the range of acceptable variability. Effective monitoring includes reading and scrutinizing fund reports each time they are published, whether it is annually or more regularly. Among the more important characteristics shown in the reports are the fund's standard deviation, beta, and geometric returns over one, three, and five-year horizons. These statistics should be compared against the benchmarks that were chosen at the beginning of the time period and assessments made about the fund performance in both absolute and relative terms.

The adviser should complete the process by crafting a report on the client's portfolio performance, which would include many references to the fund reports. The adviser would compare the return objective to the realized portfolio return as well as important measures of risk. Goals for the upcoming year would be finalized.

Mutual Fund Selection by Professional Investment Advisers

The selection of appropriate mutual funds begins with the investor's risk and return objectives. The investment adviser is responsible for matching these objectives with funds that have similar goals. For example, an investor who desires regular income and who has low risk tolerance and a low return objective would most likely choose an investment grade fixed-income fund. From that starting point, the adviser can find additional funds that satisfy other investor objectives. The ideal fund would be one that has a low expense ratio, relatively low turnover, high quality historical performance, and risk characteristics that are consistent with the investor's objectives.

Example 13.3

Freddie has a return objective of 8% with average risk tolerance. His financial adviser has identified the following possible mutual funds to satisfy Freddie's goals.

Fund	Expected Return	Risk Level
A	5.6%	Moderate
B	6.8%	Low
C	8.3%	Moderate
D	9.1%	Moderate to High
E	12.6%	High

Fund C is the most appropriate one for Freddie because it is the only one that meets both the return objective of 8% and the average risk tolerance objective. Freddie's financial adviser should then examine other aspects of Fund C to make sure it is efficiently run. If not, then the adviser should search for other funds that would meet Freddie's objectives.

Professional money managers use well-known mutual fund data bases to search for appropriate funds. Morningstar® is a popular independent source of mutual fund information, but many fund families, such as Fidelity, offer similar data services. There is a wealth of information contained in these data bases that advisers can use to narrow their search.

For example, on the Fidelity web page, a search for equity natural resources sector funds that have a 4-star rating from Morningstar with average returns and average expense ratios produces two possible funds that meet both requirements.[1]

There are even more screening possibilities, such as Sharpe Ratios, minimum investment requirements, and size. The benefit of using these services is that they are likely to be accurate and they are easy to use while producing quick results.

Quick Quiz 13.1

1. Asset allocation may account for 90% or more of the long-term variation in portfolio returns.
   a. True
   b. False
2. A mean-variance optimization model is used to identify efficient portfolios.
   a. True
   b. False

True, True.

THE FUND PROSPECTUS

Mutual funds use a document called a **prospectus** to disclose information about the fund to investors. The SEC requires mutual funds to include important information in the prospectus, including the fund's:

- investment objectives,
- strategies for obtaining those objectives,
- primary risks,
- fees and expenses, and
- historical performance.

Key Concepts

1. Explain how professional portfolio managers use databases of fund information to narrow the selection of funds.
2. Understand what is in a mutual fund prospectus.

Mutual funds are required to provide a copy of the fund's prospectus to investors before or with the delivery of fund shares. However, investors should read the prospectus prior to making an investment decision.

Mutual Fund Objective

A mutual fund's objective will be stated in its prospectus. Funds generate returns for investors via capital appreciation and income generation, and the majority of mutual funds state one of these two sources of return as their objective. More specific objectives include stable income, high total return and aggressive growth. Some funds even combine those goals. As well as being stated in its prospectus, a fund's objectives can also be found in summaries provided by Morningstar® and other financial services companies.

Equity funds are typically split into large cap, mid cap, and small cap and then further divided by growth, value, or income.

1. The Morningstar ratings rank funds based on their risk adjusted returns. On its ranking system, five stars is best (highest return for the level of risk undertaken) and one is the worst. Search was as of August 19, 2021.

Exhibit 13.1 | Morning Star Style Box™

The Morningstar Style Box™

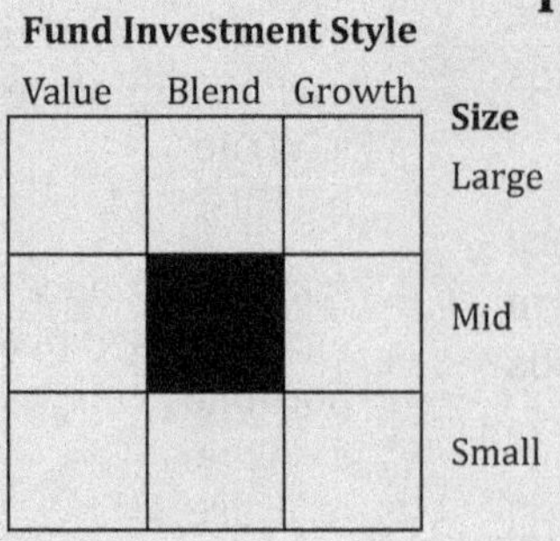

The Morningstar Style Box is a nine-square grid that depicts the investment style for a mutual fund. The investment styles are based on approach and size. The approach, which is represented by the columns, is either value, blend, or growth. The size of the companies in which the mutual fund invests in is represented by the rows. The size labels are large, mid, and small. These represent large-cap, mid-cap, and small-cap companies.

The Morningstar® Style Box is a well-known description of the combination of size and style. Investors can quickly look at the style box for a specific fund to determine if it fits their general objectives. For example, investors who desire a blend of growth and value for medium sized firms will select funds that Morningstar® places in the center box of the grid.

For fixed-income mutual funds, the prospectus includes the type of bonds likely to be included in the fund, the credit risk expectations, and perhaps even mention of the desired maturities or duration of the portfolio. Many fixed-income funds simply state the manager will invest in bonds of any maturity but will manage interest rate risk. The duration and maturity information is important for investors so they can assess how much the fund value will vary in response to changing interest rates.

Investors will attempt to identify funds in which the stated objective matches their investment goals. For example, retired investors are much more likely to seek income than their youthful counterparts. Both sets of investors, however, seek to avoid significant tax liabilities. Retired investors generating income to cover their living expenses pay a higher tax rate than growth investors who pay the lower capital gains rate. In both cases, the prospectus should be clear regarding the implementation of the investment strategy so investors can prepare a tax plan.

Quick Quiz 13.2

1. A mutual fund prospectus includes a fund's goals, strategies, risks, fees, expenses, as well as past performance.
   a. True
   b. False
2. An equity income fund seeks long-term growth through stocks that pay dividends.
   a. True
   b. False

True, True.

Investment Policy and Strategy

Once a fund has established its primary objectives, it outlines the principal strategies that are intended to achieve those objectives. The design includes the manner in which securities will be categorized as appropriate for the fund and whether the selection is quantitative or qualitative based. The prospectus might provide ranges on allocations and whether the securities of foreign based firms are allowed. For example, a fund might indicate it will purchase equity shares in firms that represent a broad diversification with a focus on risks that are similar to a particular index, but whose companies have potential for higher than average growth rates. The prospectus is also likely to identify maximum or minimum allocations. For example, the fund might suggest that U.S. large-cap equities will comprise at least 85 percent of the portfolio at all times. There will most likely be a section outlining the restrictions of the fund, such as no derivative securities will be used.

Exhibit 13.2 | Sample Prospectus Objectives

T. Rowe Price Equity Income Fund's Objective

"The fund seeks a high level of dividend income and long-term capital growth primarily through investments in stocks." This objective provides some insight. However, more information can be found under principal investment strategies. Below is an excerpt from this section of the prospectus:

The fund will normally invest at least 80% of its net assets (including any borrowings for investment purposes) in common stocks, with an emphasis on large-capitalization stocks that have a strong track record of paying dividends or that are believed to be undervalued. The fund typically employs a "value" approach in selecting investments. Our inhouse research team seeks companies that appear to be undervalued by various measures and may be temporarily out of favor but have good prospects for capital appreciation and dividend growth.

Wasatch Small Cap Growth Fund's Objective:

"The Fund's primary investment objective is long-term growth of capital. Income is a secondary objective, but only when consistent with long-term growth of capital. Currently, we do not expect the Fund's investments to generate substantial income." Under Principal Strategies, the prospectus discusses the focus of the fund's investment strategy, including the size of the companies that the fund invests in, as well as the bottom-up fundamental analysis approach.

Harbor Commodity Real Return Strategy Fund's Objective

"The Fund seeks maximum real return, consistent with prudent investment management." This objective provides very little information. However, investors can find additional information under the Principal Investment Strategy section, in which it states:

"The Fund seeks to achieve its investment objective by investing under normal market conditions in commodity-linked derivative instruments backed by a portfolio of inflation-indexed securities and other fixed-income instruments. Rather than invest directly in physical commodities, the Fund employs an enhanced index strategy. The commodity-linked derivative instruments in which the Fund primarily invests are linked to the Bloomberg Commodity Index Total ReturnSM (the "Commodity Index"), which is intended to provide the Fund with exposure to the investment returns of the commodities markets as represented by the Commodity Index without the Fund investing directly in physical commodities. Commodities are assets that have tangible properties, such as oil, metals and agricultural products. Commodity-linked derivative instruments in which the Fund may invest include commodity index-linked notes, swap agreements (including currency swaps, interest rate swaps, total return swaps, credit default swaps and others, in which the Fund may be either the buyer or the seller), commodity options, futures and options on futures."

It goes on in this section to let investors know that it may engage in short selling and may invest in common and preferred stocks, as well as convertible securities.

Exhibit 13.2 illustrates the variety of investments objectives for three different funds. Notice that dividends, capital growth, and real returns are mentioned as three goals. Short discussions on principal strategies, minimum allocations, and benchmarks are also included.

Manager Tenure

Fund managers typically have undergraduate or graduate business degrees, and many hold professional designations, such as the Chartered Financial Analyst® designation. The educational history of fund managers is important in evaluating their background and likelihood of good performance. These details can be found in the prospectus, along with the length of time the manager has been in charge of the fund. It is important to recognize how long the current fund manager has been operating the fund in addition to recognizing that some funds are managed by a team of individuals. Knowledge of these facts will allow an investor to evaluate whether a fund's superior performance is due to the manager, the analysts, the research, or the approach of the fund.

Key Concepts

1. Understand the importance of manager tenure, historical performance and portfolio turnover.
2. Be able to explain fees and expenses of mutual funds.
3. Be able to distinguish the various classes of load funds.

Total Annual Returns

Each year, the fund updates its historical performance and provides the details in the prospectus. Historical returns over one-year, five-year, and ten-year periods are normally shown, although funds can also report performance over almost any period they wish. Total returns include dividends, interest, and capital gains and are computed as geometric returns.[2] The return on the benchmark or relevant index is also provided to allow investors to make direct comparisons. Risk-adjusted measures of performance are typically not included, which forces investors to find this information on their own or to rely on an investor services firm. For example, a fund might outperform its index by 25 basis points, but display three times as much volatility as the index. In this case the extra return is likely a result of taking on more risk, rather than manager skill. It is for this reason that well informed investors will seek out data on risk-adjusted, as well as absolute, returns.

Example 13.4

The Turbocharge Fund (Turbo) is managed by Ricky "Risk-taker" Robinson. During the last three years, the S&P 500 had annualized returns of 10%, while Turbo had returns of 13%. It looks like Ricky did a great job. However, it turns out that he simply invested in the S&P 500 index using borrowed funds (leverage). This strategy "turbocharged" the returns. However, there was no great skill for Ricky. Instead, he had higher returns for higher risk. If the market had decreased in value, then the Risk-taker's losses would have been greater than the market losses on a percentage basis.

2. Recall that the geometric return is equivalent to the IRR.

Portfolio Turnover

The process of buying and selling securities inside a mutual fund has implications for both expenses and taxes. A fund with a pure buy and hold strategy will have few sell transactions. A fund with a short-term time horizon will have many sell transactions which can result in significant capital gains and will result in significant trading costs. Strategies that involves higher portfolio turnover may impose higher tax liabilities on investors who have no control over the timing of the trades. Short-term capital gains may have a different tax treatment than long-term capital gains and remove ordinary income depending on which country they are generated in. Consequently, managers with higher turnover ratios tend to cause investors to pay taxes sooner than they might prefer.

Remember that investors face both federal and local income taxes. Some states have relatively high state income tax rates, which makes turnover even more important to shareholders living in those states. High portfolio turnover is only good for investors if the securities purchased outperform the ones that were sold and if the realized gain surpasses the marginal tax rate of the investor. Investors should be aware of the turnover in each taxable fund, but can be less concerned using tax-deferred accounts. Pension plans and individual retirement accounts are not subject to any taxation until the investor begins receiving income after retirement. For these types of accounts, turnover is less important from a tax perspective but equally important from an expense perspective. **Turnover** is typically defined as the ratio of the lesser of purchases or sales to average daily assets.

$$\text{Turnover} = \frac{\text{Lesser of Asset Purchases or Sales}}{\text{Average Daily Assets}}$$

Example 13.5

Hightower Endowment Fund (HE) considers two equity mutual funds to add to its portfolio of funds. HE collects data summarized in the following table.

	Average Daily Assets	Purchases	Sales
GY Growth Fund	$300	$360	$275
FT Growth and Income Fund	$450	$120	$110

$$\text{Turnover}_{GY} = \frac{275}{300} = 0.917$$

$$\text{Turnover}_{FT} = \frac{110}{450} = 0.244$$

The FT Fund has significantly less turnover than GY, and if this is important to Hightower Endowment Fund, then it will likely select FT if the other critical variables are consistent with its policy statement.

It should be noted that high turnover can result in larger distributions of short-term capital gains. Unlike long-term capital gains that receive preferential tax treatment, short-term capital gains are taxed as ordinary income.

Fees and Expenses

The fee and expense section of the prospectus usually follows the objectives and provides a table as an outline. There are two parts to the table, the first being a list of shareholder fees, including sales fees, purchase fees, account fees, and redemption fees. The second part shows the annual operating expenses, including the management fee, any 12 b-1 fees, and other relevant expenses. An example showing how the fees reduce total return typically follows the table.

Exhibit 13.3 illustrates the fees and expenses charged by the Dodge and Cox Income Fund and the Income Fund of America.

Exhibit 13.3 | Fee and Expense Comparison[3]

	Dodge & Cox Income Fund (as of 5/1/21)	American Funds The Income Fund of America (as of October 1, 2020)				
Fees and Expenses		A Shares	F-1 Shares	F-2 Shares	F-3 Shares	C Shares
Maximum sales charge (load) imposed on purchases (as a % of offering price)	None	5.75%	None	None	None	None
Maximum deferred sales charge (load) (as a % of the amount redeemed)	None	1.00%	None	None	None	1.00%
Maximum sales charge (load) imposed on reinvested dividends	None	None	None	None	None	None
Redemption or exchange fees	None	None	None	None	None	None
Annual Fund Operating Expenses						
Management Fees	0.40%	0.22%	0.22%	0.22%	0.22%	0.22%
Distribution and/or service (12b-1) fees	None	0.25%	0.25%	None	None	1.00%
Other expenses (transfer agent, custody, accounting, legal, etc.)	0.02%	0.10%	0.16%	0.15	0.04%	0.10%
Total Annual Fund Operating Expenses	0.42%	0.57%	0.63%	0.37%	0.26%	1.32%

3. Source: American Funds. Class F-1, F-2, F-3 and 529-F-1 shares are designed for investors who choose to compensate their financial professional based on the total assets in their portfolios, rather than commissions or sales charges. This arrangement is often called an "asset-based" or a "fee-based" program. Class F-1, F-2, F-3 and 529-F-1 shares do not have an up-front or a contingent deferred sales charge (CDSC). Class F-2 shares also do not carry a 12b-1 fee but may have slightly higher administrative expenses than Class F-1 shares. These expenses will vary among the funds. Class F-3 shares do not carry 12b-1 or sub-transfer agency fees.

Dodge and Cox is a no-load fund, while the Income Fund of America charges sales fees on some share classes. Investors comparing these two funds should note the following differences:

- Dodge and Cox does not have a 12 b-1 fee.
- The 12 b-1 fee for the Class A shares is 25 basis points, which is far lower than the 100 basis point fee for C shares. American Funds eliminated Class B shares.
- The 12 b-1 fee is part of the operating expenses.
- Investors will find in another part of the prospectus that the Class C shares are not convertible to Class A shares.
- Class F shares are designed for investors who choose to compensate their financial professional based on the total assets in their portfolios, rather than commissions or sales charges.

Risks of Investing

Each mutual fund identifies the types of risks to which the fund is subject based on the fund's stated strategy and types of investment purchased by the manager. The exhibit below is a summary of risks identified in several different prospectuses.

Exhibit 13.4 | Summary of Investment Risks

• General market risk	• Credit risk
• Inflation risk	• Call risk
• Stock market risk	• Derivative risk
• Security selection risk	• Liquidity risk
• Small-cap risk	• Mortgage backed security risk
• Management risk	• Emerging market risk
• Interest rate risk	• Leverage risk

It is important for investors to understand the implications of being exposed to each type of risk as well as how each risk will influence performance. For example, general market risk results from the underlying economy, which makes changes in macro economic variables critical in determining fund returns. Stock market risk is a subset of market risk but includes operational risks such as the possibility of circuit breakers being triggered during periods of market stress. Call risk is specific to instruments that contain a call provision. Derivatives risk results from the exposure to any derivative instrument. Leverage risk includes the consequences of financial distress. Ultimately, the fund is exposed to the same risks as the underlying investments.

Buying and Selling Shares

Mutual funds permit investors to purchase shares through almost any means available to them. The old fashioned check by regular mail is still accepted, but most investors use wire transfers and links to their bank accounts to buy shares. When investors decide to redeem their shares, they can always choose to receive a check in the mail, but most will simply have the funds deposited into a bank account. Similar options are available for retirement accounts. Most funds provide investors with the choice of transacting over the phone or through their websites.

Minimum Initial Investment

Most mutual funds have minimum investment requirements and most are relatively low. For example, the Vanguard family typically requires only an initial deposit of $3,000 while the Janus family has one of only

$2,500. Of course, many funds will waive that minimum investment requirement if the investor agrees to make regularly scheduled purchases. Alternatively, there are funds intended to attract higher wealth individuals by making their minimum investment requirement much higher, some in the hundreds of thousands of dollars and some much higher still.

Example 13.6

PIMCO's Income Fund Institutional Class shares (PIMIX) require a minimum initial investment of $1,000,000. This fund is available in other share classes and with other minimums through various brokers. However, the institutional class has the lowest fees and the highest minimum.

Investor Services

Mutual funds offer a range of services to assist investors, such as the ability to schedule automatic purchases or redemptions, phone and internet support through chat functions, and online reports. While the information contained in the prospectus is seemingly exhaustive, it is not a complete information set. Investors should rely on professional research firms such as Morningstar®. These firms provide summaries of the statistics used in modern portfolio theory to assess a firm's relative value and performance. Of course, investors can always perform fundamental analysis on the fund to uncover information themselves.

Quick Quiz 13.3

1. Portfolio turnover (PT) is calculated by dividing total purchases during the year by average daily assets.
   a. True
   b. False
2. Investors should automatically sell a mutual fund when the fund manager leaves.
   a. True
   b. False

False, False.

Although the prospectus provides much information needed to make an informed investment decision, the **Statement of Additional Information (SAI)** provides more detailed disclosures and generally includes information about:

1. the history and description of the fund;
2. fund officers and directors; and
3. other topics.

Mutual funds must provide this document to investors upon request. The SAI can also be found by searching the SEC's Electronic Data Gathering, Analysis, and Retrieval ("EDGAR") database.

MODERN PORTFOLIO THEORY STATISTICS

Modern portfolio theory (MPT) is a set of principles, ideas, and theoretical models developed to help investors make efficient and informed portfolio decisions. MPT statistics are highly relevant for mutual fund investors and are used by financial advisers to provide valuable insights into specific funds. Some of the more important MPT stats are discussed below.

Correlation Coefficient (R)

The correlation coefficient (frequently noted as "R") between two variables indicates the strength and direction of their relationship. When two mutual fund returns have a high positive correlation, it means that their returns tend to move together in response to changing economic information. On the other hand, when two mutual funds have a correlation close to zero, their returns are close to being independent. The returns on assets with a negative correlation tend to move in opposite directions in response to changing economic conditions. The strength and direction of correlation provides a great deal of information about the movement of the returns on two funds, but it provides no information about the cause of those movements.

Key Concepts

1. Understand that modern portfolio theory (MPT) and statistics provide insight into a fund's risk-return characteristics.
2. Explain MPT statistics including R^2 and beta.

Correlation coefficients range from negative 1.0 to positive 1.0. When a fund and an index have perfectly positive correlation, the returns vary together and move in the same direction. For example, the Vanguard 500 Index fund should have a correlation coefficient of 1.0 when compared against the S&P 500 Index. In reality, the correlations between index funds and the index itself are slightly less than 1.0 due to the expenses of the fund and any cash drag. Investors use correlations as one way to determine if the fund being examined closely resembles an index. Alternatively, when a fund and an index have perfectly negative correlation, the returns vary together but in opposite directions. For example, the Rydex Inverse S&P 500 Shares should have a correlation coefficient of -1.0 when compared to the S&P 500 index because Rydex shorts every stock in the index. Again, factors such as fund expenses mean the correlation is unlikely to be exactly -1.0.

COEFFICIENT OF DETERMINATION (R^2)

The coefficient of determination (**R-squared** or R^2) is calculated by squaring the correlation coefficient. R-squared is useful to financial analysts as it measures how well the variation in one variable (the dependent variable) explains the variation in another (the independent variable). As with the correlation coefficient, R-squared is not useful as a measure of performance. Funds with a high R-squared may still perform badly. Instead, it is used to assess how much of the price movement in one asset can be explained by the movements in another.

In the mutual fund world, the independent variable is usually the return on an index or a benchmark, and the dependent variable is the return on the mutual fund. If the R-squared is zero, then changes in the index have no power in explaining the changes in the mutual fund. A zero R-squared might occur if the index is the NASDAQ Composite Index and the fund is one that invests solely in short-term commercial paper. On the other hand, an R-squared of 100 percent means the changes in the index perfectly explain the changes in the mutual fund. An R-squared of 100 percent might occur if the index is the S&P 500 Index and the fund is the Vanguard 500 Index Mutual Fund.

Most funds do not have an R-squared at the extreme ends like the two examples discussed briefly above. Suppose the LG Growth Fund has an R-squared of 90 percent against the S&P 500 Index. The implication is that 90 percent of the variability in the LG Growth Fund can be explained by the variability in the S&P 500 Index, which makes 10 percent of the variability unexplained.

The difference must be attributed to other factors, such as security selection or asset allocation.

An additional interpretation is that the fund has 90 percent systematic risk and 10 percent unsystematic risk, which would include business risks, operating risks, and leverage.

When selecting funds, investors should avoid adding those that have similar R-squared to existing funds as they tend to add little value. Finding funds with a lower R-squared tends to increase diversification. Of course, R-squared should be used with other MPT statistics to locate the most appropriate funds for each investor.

Example 13.7

Nedra is a high net worth investor who owns the Gray Broad Equity Fund which has a correlation coefficient of 0.98 with the S&P 500 Index. Nedra is considering adding another fund to her portfolio to increase its diversification and is deciding between the Orange Growth Fund and the Purple Equity Fund. Nedra believes both funds will satisfy her risk and return objectives and is confident their low expense ratios will continue into the future. Both fund managers have excellent backgrounds and track records, so Nedra will add the fund that will provide more diversification to her Gray Broad Equity Fund.

Fund	Correlation to the S&P 500 Index
Orange Growth	0.83
Purple Equity	0.51

The Purple Equity Fund is likely to be more appropriate for Nedra because it has a low R-squared (0.51 × 0.51 = 0.26), much lower than Orange Growth's R-squared of 0.689. The Purple Equity Fund will add significantly more diversification than the Orange Growth Fund and is therefore, more appropriate for Nedra.

A fund's R-squared is also useful if a proxy was used to represent an asset class in a mean-variance optimization model. For example, if the S&P 500 index was used as a proxy for large-cap equity, the funds used to fill the allocation must have a high R-squared with that index. Both an S&P 500 index fund and an actively managed fund with a high R-squared compared to the S&P 500 would be good choices to fill the large-cap allocation.

Beta

The systematic risk of a portfolio is measured by its beta, which has its roots in statistical analysis. Any beta in regression analysis is simply the slope of the line, but in financial research, its meaning is much more specific. Formally, **beta** is defined as the ratio of the covariance between a fund and an index divided by the variance of the index.

For example, the level of systematic risk between the Purple Equity Fund and the S&P 500 Index might be:

$$\text{Beta} = \frac{\text{Covariance}_{\text{Purple, S\&P 500 Index}}}{\text{Variance}_{\text{S\&P 500 Index}}} = \frac{0.0304}{0.0225} = 1.351$$

The numerator represents the co-movement between the fund and the index while the denominator represents the total volatility of the index. By definition, the beta of the benchmark index is 1.0 (as the covariance of the index with itself is equal to its variance). Funds with a beta greater than 1.0 have more systematic risk than the index, and those with a beta of less than 1.0 have less systematic risk than the index.

Recall that systematic risk can be defined as the variability in mutual fund returns due to changes in economic factors. This means that a fund with a beta of 1.2 will be more sensitive to changes in economic variables than a fund with a beta of 0.8. For example, if there is an unexpected increase in interest rates, equity prices are likely to fall, and the fund with a beta of 1.2 will experience a much greater decline in net asset value than the fund with a beta of 0.8.

Diversified mutual funds tend to have betas that are close to 1.0 indicating they have an average amount of systematic risk. The beta analysis, however, should be coupled with the R-squared of the fund. If the beta is close to 1.0 and the R-squared is close to 100 percent, then the fund is highly diversified and beta captures almost all of the risk to which the fund is exposed. If, however, the fund has a beta close to 1.0 and the R-squared is 50 percent, then there is risk to which the fund is exposed that is not captured by beta. Consequently, beta should only be used as an investment tool for mutual funds if the fund's returns are correlated with the market index.

PERFORMANCE MEASURES

It should be clear that risk-adjusted returns are much more helpful than simple realized returns, especially for mutual fund shareholders trying to find the right investment among the thousands of funds available to them. There are three excellent measures of risk-adjusted returns, including Jensen's alpha, the Sharpe Ratio, and the Treynor Ratio.

Key Concepts

1. Note the difference in absolute versus relative measures of performance.
2. Differentiate the three measures of performance Jensen, Sharpe and Treynor.

Jensen's Alpha

The Capital Asset Pricing Model (CAPM) was developed in the mid 1960s independently by Jack Treynor, William Sharpe, John Lintner, and Jan Mossin. Only Sharpe was awarded the Nobel Prize in Economic Science for this research, however, in 1990. Lintner and Mossin were both deceased by 1990, and Treynor did not publish his research until well after 1990.

Investors can use CAPM to calculate an expected return for either an individual stock or a portfolio. CAPM is a simple model that uses only the risk-free rate, the market return and the stock or fund's level of systematic risk to calculate the expected return. The formula is as follows:

$$R_p = R_f + \beta(R_m - R_f)$$

R_p = Expected return on the portfolio (fund)

R_f = Risk-free rate of return

β = Beta of the portfolio

R_m = Expected return on the market portfolio

Michael Jensen developed an absolute measure of fund manager performance in 1968, known as Jensen's alpha, which is simply the difference between the CAPM-generated expected return and the actual return on the fund.

The formula for Jensen's alpha is often written as follows:

$$\alpha = R_p - [R_f + \beta(R_m - R_f)]$$

Example 13.8

The Arctic Fund has a beta of 1.14 and its manager, Willis, has a long tenure of good performance. During this past year, Arctic Fund has generated a return of 10.2%, while the benchmark S&P 500 Index was expected to return 9.8%. At first glance, it might seem that Arctic has outperformed its benchmark. To complete the analysis, however, Jensen's alpha should be computed. Using a risk-free rate of 2.8%, alpha is:

$$\alpha = 0.102 - [0.028 + 1.14(0.098 - 0.028)] = -0.0058$$

Since the alpha is less than zero, it appears as though Willis did not in fact outperform the benchmark on a risk-adjusted basis. Willis exposed the fund to higher risk than that of the index and earned a higher return than the index, but his performance on a risk-adjusted basis was not superior.

Jensen's alpha is used to evaluate the performance of fund managers and was actually Michael Jensen's original purpose in 1968.

Positive alphas indicate better than expected performance, negative alphas indicate worse than expected performance, and zero alphas indicate the fund performed as expected.

Obviously, investors should seek fund managers that have positive alphas. They must be careful, however, as historical positive alphas do not guarantee future positive alphas.

Investors should also be careful since the alpha performance measure relies on beta as the appropriate measure of systematic risk. Recall that the beta for a fund with a low R-squared might not be a reliable measure of systematic risk. Investors should combine their understanding of beta and R-squared when making decisions using Jensen alpha.

Another important input is the market return. This is calculated using a benchmark index, and it is crucial that an appropriate benchmark is chosen. For example, if an energy fund has an alpha of 1.1 percent, but its beta against the S&P 500 Index is only 0.40, then alpha is not a complete description of that performance. The alpha for the energy fund should be computed against a broad energy index. In this case, the R-squared is likely to be high and a performance evaluation is more reliable. Unfortunately, many alphas are computed using the S&P 500 Index, even when it is not a good match. **Exhibit 13.5** illustrates this issue.

Exhibit 13.5 | Reliability of Alpha

Fund A		Fund B	
Alpha	0.7	Alpha	1.2
Beta	1.3	Beta	2.0
R-Squared	95	R-Squared	32

Since Fund A has a high R-squared, its alpha is quite reliable. Fund B, on the other hand, has a low R-squared, so its alpha can be ignored or highly discounted when making comparisons.

It should be clear that Fund A's alpha is positive and the alpha for Fund B, while also positive, is unreliable because its R-squared is only 32 percent. This suggests that 68 percent of the variability in returns is not explained leading to significant amounts of unsystematic risk.

Example 13.9

Lars Ranta is a financial analyst trying to find the most appropriate index to use as an input variable in his modern portfolio toolbox. Ranta identifies two funds shown in the following tables:

Sky Fund	S&P 500 Index	Russell 3000 Index
α	75 basis points	160 basis points
β	1.16	1.09
R^2	95	96

Star Fund	S&P 500 Index	Russell 2000 Index
α	-380 basis points	90 basis points
β	1.27	1.01
R^2	81	95

Sky Fund is a large-cap value fund, which means the S&P 500 Index is the more likely benchmark. Sky's R-squared is not notably different using either index as the market return. The R-squared of 95 against the S&P 500 index indicates a high correlation with the index and that the overwhelming majority of the risk in the fund is systematic. With a beta of 1.16, Ranta can conclude the Sky Fund has about 16% more relative volatility than the index and can be confident the fund manager has outperformed the index on a risk-adjusted basis as evidenced by the positive 0.75% alpha.

Star Fund is a small-cap blend fund, which normally is compared against the Russell 2000 index. The first thing Ranta should note is the difference between R-squareds. Against the Russell 2000, the R-squared is 95 while only 81 against the S&P 500 Index. This is the first indication that the appropriate benchmark is the Russell 2000. In addition, a beta of 1.01 against the Russell 2000 is the second data point indicating that the Star Fund behaves almost exactly like the Russell 2000. Ranta can reasonably conclude the Star fund manager has outperformed the Russell 2000, instead of lagging behind the S&P 500 Index.

Sharpe Ratio

In 1966, William Sharpe developed what he called the 'reward to variability' ratio as a relative measure of performance. It became known as the **Sharpe ratio** over time, especially after Sharpe was awarded the Nobel Prize. The formula compares the portfolio's excess return, that is the return in excess of the risk-free rate, and its total risk. The resulting ratio shows the units of excess return per unit of risk. The higher the ratio, the better the relative performance. The ratio uses the excess return because an investor should be able to generate the risk-free return without taking on any risk.

$$\textbf{Sharpe Ratio } (S_p) = \frac{R_p - R_f}{\sigma_p}$$

S_p = Actual return of the portfolio

R_p = Actual return of the portfolio

R_f = Risk-free rate of return

σ_p = Standard deviation of the portfolio

Example 13.10

Mary Jo Thomas manages the Thomas Endowment Fund and has generated a total return over the past year of 15.4%. The standard deviation of the Thomas Fund is 22.4% while the risk-free rate is 4.3%. Using the Sharpe ratio formula:

$$S_{\text{Thomas Fund}} = \frac{0.154 - 0.043}{0.224} = 0.4955$$

A Sharpe ratio of 0.4955 is a measure of reward to variability, which means that Thomas has produced 0.4955 units of excess return for every unit of total risk taken. As with many ratios, the Sharpe ratio is difficult to interpret in isolation, so it is standard practice to compare ratios of different funds to determine which one is superior on a risk-adjusted basis.

Example 13.11

Consider the following four funds with their respective Sharpe ratios:

Fund	Sharpe Ratio
Super Growth Fund	1.31
High Growth and Income Fund	1.18
Light Speed Growth Fund	0.63
Moon 500 Index Fund	0.91

Based solely on Sharpe ratios, the Super High Growth Fund outperforms each of the other three funds and the Light Speed Growth Fund clearly is the worst performer. An investor comparing the three growth funds might select both Super Growth and High Growth and Income if the other modern finance tools indicate such an investment is warranted.

The general benefit of using Sharpe is that the input of total risk in the denominator means there are no limitations on the level of systematic risk as can be found in Jensen's alpha and beta. This means that any fund can be compared to any other fund using Sharpe.

Quick Quiz 13.4

1. Jensen, Sharpe and Treynor use beta as their risk measure.
   a. True
   b. False
2. Jensen's alpha is an absolute measure of performance.
   a. True
   b. False
3. The Sharpe ratio and the Treynor ratio are both relative measures of performance.
   a. True
   b. False

False, True, True.

Treynor Ratio

Jack Treynor developed a 'risk to volatility' ratio that measures the relative performance of a portfolio. Treynor developed this model in the mid 1960s after reading some of the research by Sharpe. The only difference between the Sharpe and **Treynor ratios** is the denominator, as Treynor uses beta instead of standard deviation.

$$\textbf{Treynor Ratio } (T_p) = \frac{R_p - R_f}{\beta_p}$$

T_p = Treynor ratio

R_p = Actual return of the portfolio

R_f = Risk-free rate of return

β_p = Beta of the portfolio

Example 13.12

Carl Lock manages a portfolio for a non-profit organization. Lock typically invests in value stocks but has some exposure to growth stocks. Lock has generated a total return over the past year of 11.2%. The beta of the portfolio is 1.07 while the risk-free rate is 2.3%. Using the Treynor ratio formula:

$$T_{Lock} = \frac{0.112 - 0.023}{1.07} = 0.0832$$

A Treynor ratio of 0.0832 is a measure of reward to volatility, which means that Lock has produced 0.0832 units of return for every unit of systematic risk taken. This is another tough one to interpret, so it is standard practice to compare ratios of different funds to determine which one is superior on a risk-adjusted basis.

Example 13.13

Consider the following four funds with their respective Treynor ratios:

Fund	Treynor Ratio
Super Growth Fund	0.031
High Growth and Income Fund	0.043
Light Speed Growth Fund	0.012
Moon 500 Index Fund	0.055

Based solely on Treynor ratios, the Moon 500 index fund is clearly the best performer and Light Speed is the worst performer. Coupling Sharpe with Treynor would most likely rule out investing in the Light Speed Growth Fund as both ratios are inferior to the other three.

One caveat with Treynor is that investors should be aware of the limitations of using beta as a measure of risk. Therefore, investors should use Treynor in conjunction after consideration of beta and R-squared.

Example 13.14

Assume that Monica wants to select a large cap mutual fund to add to her investment portfolio. Also assume that she will choose from the following seven funds. Which one(s) would you recommend for her? Why?

R squared of 100 indicates it is an index fund.

Beta of 1.08 suggests a fund that is 8% more volatile. However, the standard deviation is 36% higher than the market (15.3/11.25).

An Alpha of -4 means that the actual return was 4% lower than its expected return.

R squared of 37 indicates a low correlation to the index and 63% unsystematic risk.

	500 Index	PGI	MSIG	FOTC	DCS	COP	MIIGF
Alpha	-0.20	4.20	2.40	1.20	-4.00	5.62	1.88
Beta	1.00	0.92	1.08	1.21	1.09	0.49	0.77
R-Squared	100	79	63	66	92	37	47
Standard Deviation	11.25	11.56	15.30	16.69	12.82	9.02	12.61
Mean 3 Yr Return	11.49	15.26	14.78	14.93	8.28	11.57	10.63
Sharpe Ratio	1.02	1.28	0.98	0.92	0.68	1.25	0.86
Stock %	100%	96%	94%	99%	99%	133%	75%
Net Assets	26B	1B	794m	9B	55B	83m	11m

The net assets of this fund are extremely low at $11 million.

Fund	Sharpe Ratio	Fund	Alpha
PGI	1.28	COP	5.62
COP	1.25	PGI	4.20
500 Index	1.02	MSIG	2.40
MSIG	0.98	MIIGF	1.88
FOTC	0.92	FOTC	1.20
MIIGF	0.86	500 Index	-0.20
DCS	0.68	DCS	-4.00

A stock percentage that exceeds 100% implies the fund is leveraged and thus, subject to greater risk.

Monica is looking for a fund for the large-cap allocation of her portfolio, which is likely based on her risk tolerance and a mean variance optimization model. The large-cap fund should be consistent with the benchmark used in the optimization, which we will assume is the S&P 500. The MPT statistics for the funds in the chart above are based on the S&P 500 index.

Based on the discussion above, the S&P 500 index fund is a reasonable selection. However, it is worth considering the other fund choices.

PGI - This fund ranks high with the Sharpe ratio and Alpha. It is almost fully invested in equities and has a reasonably high R-squared. The fund's R-squared of 79 means that 79% of the change in the value of the fund is attributable to changes in the market (as measured by the S&P 500).

MSIG - This fund does not have as high a Sharpe ratio or alpha. Based on its R-squared value, it has a lower correlation with the S&P 500. The statistics for this fund illustrate a potential issue with the use of beta. The fund's beta of 1.08 indicates that the fund is 8% more volatile than the market. However, the standard deviation is 36% higher than the standard deviation of the market, as measured by the 500 Index fund.

As a result, the fund ranking based on Alpha is higher than the ranking based on Sharpe. The reason for this outcome is that the R-squared is 63, meaning that only 63% of the change in the fund is attributable to changes in the market.

FOTC - This fund has a similar ranking based on both performance measures. However, it does not have one of the higher risk adjusted returns, as measured by either Alpha or Sharpe. In addition, its R-squared is lower than that of PGI.

Key Concepts

1. A mutual fund that has a dramatic change in its asset base may perform differently than it has in the past.
2. Performance for mutual funds and other portfolios is driven by investment managers. When the manager of a fund changes, investors should consider the implications.
3. Funds that shift from one investment style to another may not be a good choice for implementing a strategic asset allocation.

DCS - This fund has the lowest risk-adjusted returns based on both performance measures. An alpha of -4 means that the actual return was 4% less than the expected return based on its risk, as measured by beta. The fund is also quite large at $55 billion.

COP - This fund's alpha stands out as the highest, along with a very high Sharpe ratio. However, the other factor that should stand out is the percent of stock, which exceeds 100%. This implies that the fund is leveraged and therefore, subject to greater risk. The R-squared of 37 should also gain attention. This fund is interesting, but is not likely a good choice for a large-cap fund that is being used as part of an asset allocation strategy. It turns out that this fund is allocating 57% of the portfolio to utility stocks.

MIIGF - One of the factors that should stand out is that the net assets of the fund are only $11 million. That amount is extremely low for a mutual fund. In addition, the R-squared is extremely low given the objective for the fund.

Given the full discussion of the funds, the two funds that Monica should consider are the PGI fund and the 500 Index fund.

It should be noted that other factors should be considered when selecting mutual funds. These factors might include the mutual fund's approach to building the portfolio, the organization of fund or fund family, as well as the consistency of the approach over time.

ISSUES FOR THE MANAGEMENT OF MUTUAL FUNDS

The final step in the investment process is the monitoring of the portfolio. The funds in the portfolio were chosen because they met the risk and return objectives of the investor. After implementing the allocation strategy, it is critical to monitor the progress of each fund in the portfolio to make certain the fund is continuing to meet the objectives of the investor.

Changing Asset Size

Because of the nature of price variability together with the daily cash inflows and outflows of mutual funds, the total size of the assets is very likely to change dramatically over time. Mutual funds that perform well generally receive an influx of capital while funds that perform poorly generally lose capital. The size of the fund should be monitored for basic changes in the dynamics of the fund. For example, a small-cap fund is in danger of becoming a mid-cap fund if it is very successful and inflows are high. In addition, most funds place limits on the amounts or percentages that can be invested in any one stock or group of stocks within an industry. A small-cap fund manager might really like a specific company but could be prevented from investing the inflows in that stock because of prospectus restrictions. Similar problems exist for mid-cap and large-cap funds, so the size issue is universal and might prevent the fund manager from investing efficiently.

Style Drift

Problems can arise over time if there is a shift by the fund manager from one style to another. For example, a value manager might be permitted by the policy statement to have between 10 percent and 30 percent allocation to growth securities. If the allocation at the beginning of the year is 10 percent, but increases to 20 percent or 30 percent, even for a short period of time, then the style has changed and along with it, the risk structure of the fund.

Funds must be monitored for their level of diversification over time as a result of style changes. A blended fund that looks like the S&P 500 Index at the beginning of the year could become a growth or value fund by the end of the year.

Example 13.15

Whitney is a sophisticated financial adviser. She is helping Lindsay, her client, with the implementation of an asset allocation strategy in which Lindsay will invest 10 percent of her funds in a small-cap fund. Whitney is considering either Fund A or Fund B for the small-cap allocation. The historical information about the size of the companies each fund has been investing in over the last six years is included in the following table:

Fund	Year 1	Year 2	Year 3	Year 4	Year 5	Year 6
A	SCG	SCV	MCB	MCV	SCV	MCG
B	SCB	SCB	SCB	SCV	SCB	SCB

SCG - Small-cap growth	MCG - Mid-cap growth
SCV - Small-cap value	MCV - Mid-cap value
SCB - Small-cap blend	MCB - Mid-cap blend

As is obvious from the table above, Fund A's manager is not as disciplined as Fund B's manager in terms of investing fund assets in small-cap companies. Fund A's manager invests in small-cap funds in some years, but invests in mid-cap companies in other years. This "style drift" may be due to the size of the asset base for Fund A or it may be that Fund A's manager is pursuing what he believes are the best investment alternatives. However, if Lindsay wants 10 percent of her portfolio invested in small-cap funds, then Fund B may be a better choice.

Below is visual representation of the same information using Morningstar's style box.

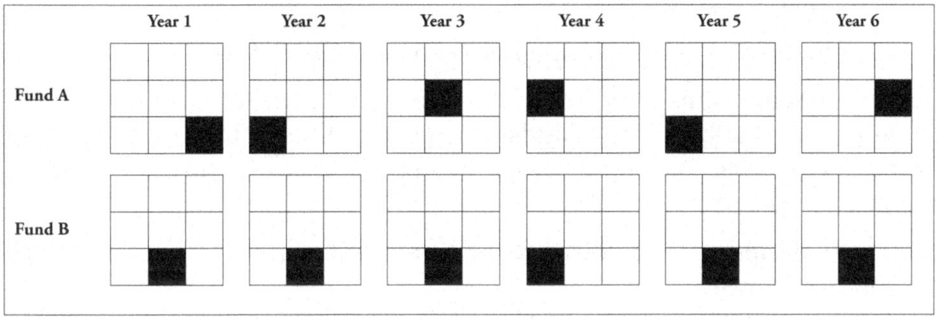

It is important to keep in mind that Fund A may actually be a better performing fund or a better choice. It is also important to realize that style drift is only one factor in making a decision about a fund.

Manager Changes

Successful managers often switch mutual funds over time and poor managers are sometimes relieved of their duties. It is important as part of the monitoring process that investors are aware of any managerial changes.

Remember that many funds are managed by teams and the team composition can change. In addition, fund managers can take on new responsibilities with existing funds or new funds. Any of these changes can affect the performance and risk structure of the fund.

Built-In Capital Gains

All investors should be aware of the capital gains that are built into a fund. When these gains are realized, they trigger a tax liability that must be paid by fund shareholders at the end of the year. It is especially important for a new shareholder to be aware they can be responsible for a tax liability even if the net assets of the fund falls. This often happens when an investor purchases mutual fund shares in the fourth quarter of the year and the fund distributes income and gains toward the end of the year. Effectively, the investor has taxable income with no economic gain.

Quick Quiz 13.5

1. Style drift is the term to describe an asset manager who changes from small-cap value to small-cap growth and then back again depending on economic conditions.
   a. True
   b. False
2. A large-cap mutual fund with a Sharpe ratio equal to the market Sharpe ratio and a low R-squared is a good choice for a strategic asset allocation based on a mean-variance optimization model.
   a. True
   b. False

True, False.

SUMMARY

Summary of key points:

- Investment companies offer shareholders many services and are easy to buy and sell. However, there are so many of them that it can be challenging to find ones that meet the objectives of an investor.
- Asset allocation accounts for the majority of variability in a portfolio.
- Mean variance optimization is often the basis for finding an optimal asset allocation. Inputs for this model include historical returns (or expected returns), historical volatility (as measured by standard deviation), and the correlation between and among the assets or asset classes.
- Mutual fund selection begins with an investor's risk and return objectives. A professional money manager then searches for mutual funds that fit with these objectives. There are many search criteria that can be used, including return objectives, risk measures, as well as MPT statistics (Sharpe, alpha, etc.).
- The mutual fund prospectus provides information about a fund's objectives, strategies, risks, fees, expenses, and past performance.
- The types of risk that might be included in a prospectus include market risk, inflation risk, security selection risk, small-cap risk, management risk, interest rate risk, credit risk, call risk, derivative risk, liquidity risk, prepayment risk, and leverage risk.
- Correlation ranges from -1 to +1. R^2 ranges from 0 to 100% and provides insight into the percent of change for a mutual fund that can be explained by changes in the market. This statistical measure also provides insight into whether beta is reliable or not.
- Beta is a measure of a mutual fund's systematic risk, relative to the market.
- Alpha is an absolute measure of performance that equals the difference between the actual return for a mutual fund and the expected return based on the CAPM.
- Sharpe and Treynor, as discussed in Chapter 5, are relative measures of performance. The primary difference is the measure of risk that is used in each of the measures.
- When managing mutual funds for an investor, it is important to monitor changing asset size for the fund, style drift, manager changes, as well as turnover.

DISCUSSION QUESTIONS

SOLUTIONS to the discussion questions can be found exclusively within the chapter. Once you have completed an initial reading of the chapter, go back and highlight the answers to these questions.

1. Explain the process of using mutual funds to implement an investment plan once an asset allocation has been completed using a mean variance optimization model and a risk tolerance tool for the investor.

2. What are the types of inputs that go into a mean variance optimization model?

3. What is the purpose of a mutual fund prospectus?

4. Describe how portfolio turnover is calculated and impacts performance and taxation.

5. Does manager tenure matter in terms of evaluating fund performance?

6. Describe the usefulness of alpha as a performance measure for mutual funds.

7. Sharpe and Treynor are both relative measures of performance that are used to evaluate the risk-adjusted performance of comparable funds. Should the two measures result in the same rankings?

8. How might the changing of a mutual fund's asset base impact performance?

MULTIPLE-CHOICE PROBLEMS

A sample of multiple choice problems is provided below. Additional multiple choice problems are available at money-education.com by accessing the Student Practice Portal.

1. Which of the following is an advantage of an index equity mutual fund as compared to a managed equity fund?
   a. Index funds have lower operating costs because of less stock trading.
   b. Index funds generally have better portfolio managers.
   c. Index funds engage in more research than managed funds.
   d. Index funds generally have less systematic risk compared to actively managed equity funds.

2. Monica purchased 100 shares of NOLA mutual fund at a price of $25 per share at the beginning of the year and paid a front-end load of 4.5%. The securities in the fund increased in value by 11% during the year and the fund's expense ratio was 1.2%. What was Monica's annual return for this year assuming she were to sell at year end?
   a. 4.50%.
   b. 4.85%.
   c. 5.30%.
   d. 9.80%.

3. An analyst collects the following data for two mutual funds, given a risk-free rate of 5%:

Fund	Return	Standard Deviation	Beta
1	12%	16%	1.160
2	13%	18%	1.326

   Which of the following is most accurate?
   a. Fund 1 has the higher Sharpe ratio.
   b. Fund 2 has the higher Treynor ratio.
   c. Fund 1 has the lower Sharpe ratio.
   d. Fund 2 has the lower Treynor ratio.

4. Jeremiah is a portfolio manager who consistently obtains a high Sharpe ratio. His forecasting ability is which of the following?
   a. Above average.
   b. Average.
   c. Below average.
   d. Irrelevant to his Sharpe ratio.

5. Active managers in contrast with passive portfolios attempt to construct risky portfolios with securities that have:
   a. A higher Sharpe ratio than an index fund.
   b. A lower Sharpe ratio than an index fund.
   c. The same Sharpe ratio as an index fund.
   d. A Sharpe ratio greater than 1.0.

QUICK QUIZ EXPLANATIONS

Quick Quiz 13.1

1. True.
2. True.

Quick Quiz 13.2

1. True.
2. True.

Quick Quiz 13.3

1. False. PT is calculated by dividing the lesser of total purchases or sales during the year by average daily assets.
2. False. The investors should understand how the fund makes investment decisions. Often, there may be co-managers and research analysts who help make investment decisions. However, the departure of a prominent manager should be evaluated.

Quick Quiz 13.4

1. False. Sharpe uses standard deviation.
2. True.
3. True.

Quick Quiz 13.5

1. True.
2. False. The fund should have a relatively high R-squared so that it performs like the index that was used to develop the asset allocation.

14
DERIVATIVE SECURITIES: FUTURES & SWAP CONTRACTS

LEARNING OBJECTIVES

1. Understand the value of a derivative security and that they can be used for speculation or hedging.*
2. Understand that derivatives tend to be risky and highly leveraged.*
3. Differentiate between forward contracts and futures contracts.*
4. Discuss the importance of organized exchanges for buying and selling futures contracts.*
5. Compare market orders and limit orders.*
6. List the specific terms of a standardized futures contract.*
7. Justify the process of marking to market.
8. Describe initial margin and maintenance margin.
9. Determine whether a short hedge or a long hedge is appropriate for a given situation.*
10. Describe a perfect hedge and discuss why perfect hedges are extremely rare.
11. Explain the relationship between the spot price and the futures price.
12. Describe how to close a futures contract.
13. Illustrate a plain vanilla swap.
14. Summarize currency swaps.

**Ties to CFP Certification Learning Objectives*

DERIVATIVES

Financial securities are valued based on the promised cash flows made by the issuer. Derivative securities are no different, with the exception that they are created mostly by secondary market participants. Whereas stocks and bonds are issued by corporations and governments in the primary market, derivatives are written by investors. Consequently, derivative securities are valued based on the terms of the derivative contract. Derivatives include forward and futures contracts, option contracts, and swap contracts. Derivatives can be traded on organized exchanges or in over-the-counter markets and the terms are set by the participants. For example, a swap contract is an exchange of cash flows generated by two underlying financial assets, such as the yield on a fixed rate bond and the yield on a floating rate bond. A futures contract obligates the buyer to purchase an underlying asset sometime in the future while it obligates the seller to deliver that same underlying asset.

A **derivative** is a financial security or asset whose value is derived from the value of an underlying security or asset (e.g., coffee, oil). For example, the price of coffee futures contracts varies based on changes to the current price of coffee. While derivatives have the potential for large gains or losses, they also provide benefits to investors, such as hedging and increased leveraging. Derivatives are limited only by the imagination of financial product designers. Included in this chapter are forward, futures, and swap contracts.

Key Concepts

1. A derivative is a financial security whose value is derived from the value of an underlying security or asset (e.g., coffee).
2. Derivatives can be used for speculation or hedging.
3. Common derivatives include futures, forwards, options, and swaps.
4. Leverage is a key feature of derivatives.
5. Futures contracts can be used to mitigate risk.
6. Derivatives provide a certain level of trading efficiency.

CASE STUDY 14.1

AMERICAN INTERNATIONAL GROUP (AIG)

AIG was founded after WWI and operated for many years as a general insurance company. AIG expanded its services to include life, health, fire, and other types of insurance and by the 1980s was even offering pollution and political insurance contracts. AIG also expanded globally.

In the early 2000s, AIG began selling credit default swaps (CDS). These derivative securities are essentially insurance contacts in which a bondholder makes regular payments to AIG in return for a promise to pay the bondholder the principal amount on the bonds in the event the issuer defaults. AIG only wrote CDS's on investment grade bonds which of course were perceived to have very little risk of default. The CDS market became so popular that many institutional investors bought and sold the CDS's rather than the bonds themselves, such was the extent of the liquidity in the CDS market. In fact, AIG's revenues and profitability soared during the early 2000s because virtually none of the bonds defaulted and AIG was able to 'keep' all the premiums without having to make any payments. Over time, AIG became less and less careful about the credit risk of the underlying assets on which the credit default swaps were written. It wrote tens of billions of dollars of CDS's on mortgage related securities. Of course, many financial professionals believe the crisis of 2008 began in the mortgage market, and when these bonds began to default, AIG was forced to pay out. It learned quickly that it did not have the funds to meet all of its obligations.

The larger problem was that many money market funds and equity mutual funds held AIG's short-term debt and equity, in addition to the billions of dollars in credit default swaps. If AIG were to go bankrupt, its financial distress would spill over to financial markets in general and potentially cause a significant recession or even depression. Consequently, the U.S. federal government stepped in and bailed out AIG with a loan of almost $200 billion. In March of 2009, AIG reported a net loss of approximately $60 billion causing the DJIA to fall to just one-half its value from two years earlier.

The fascinating end of the storyline is that AIG recovered fairly quickly and was able to repay the federal government the entire amount of the loan plus an extra $23 billion. The government was able to avoid a major recession by executing this bailout.

Derivative securities are legal and bonding financial contracts between two or more parties. They take many forms from the simple example of a forward contact to the highly complex agreements in the exotic derivatives market. A **forward contract** is a financial agreement between two parties to trade an underlying asset in the future at an agreed upon rate. Forward contacts are typically designed to meet the specific needs of both parties. **Futures contracts**, on the other hand, are standardized forward contacts that trade in a highly liquid secondary market and require daily settlement. Examples of futures contracts include commodity futures such as lumber and coffee and financial futures contracts such as the S&P 500 Index. **Swap contracts** are agreements between two parties to exchange cash flows at regular intervals in the future. Popular swaps include plain vanilla interest rate swaps and equity swaps. **Option contracts** give the buyer the right but not the obligation to buy or sell an underlying asset at a date, or possibly several dates, in the future. One attractive feature of an option contract is that it gives the owner the right to do nothing and allow the option to lapse. This right is valuable to the owner, as they can walk away if exercising the option would result in a negative payoff. Common option contracts include stock options, currency options, and index options.

Derivatives have received a significant amount of bad press in light of the subprime mortgage "meltdown" during 2008, due to the huge losses systematically important institutions experienced in derivatives trading. However, derivatives have several advantages compared to other securities in addition to having their own set of risks. Derivatives must be utilized only after a complete due diligence is performed. Many of the losses incurred during the 2008 crisis were due to the failure to understand and manage the inherent risks of derivatives. Derivatives help provide for a complete market, allow for speculation, leveraging, hedging or reducing risk.

> **Quick Quiz 14.1**
>
> 1. The value of a derivative is not related to the value of the underlying security.
>   a. True
>   b. False
> 2. Derivatives can be used to decrease risk as well as increase risk.
>   a. True
>   b. False
> 3. Derivatives help to create a market with more choices for investors.
>   a. True
>   b. False
>
> False, True, True.

In economics, a complete market is one in which a complete set of outcomes is attainable through the construction of a portfolio of existing assets, real or financial. The Federal Reserve defines a complete market as, "a system of markets in which every agent is able to exchange every good, either directly or indirectly with every other agent." While the financial markets are not perfectly complete, derivatives significantly help to make the markets more complete. This market completeness provides asset managers with more control in designing the risk and return characteristics of their portfolios.

Investors can (and often do) lose a significant amount of money trading futures as derivatives are risky assets. Given an investor with the appropriate amount of knowledge, skill, and training, however, derivative securities offer an efficient way of either speculating on, or hedging the risk of, price movements in a range of financial and non-financial assets from commodities to currencies and even the weather.

Leverage is a key feature of derivatives. With a relatively small amount of capital, a larger asset can be controlled through the purchase (or sale) of the derivative. The amount of capital required to take a position with a derivative is much less than is necessary to purchase the underlying securities. This built-in leverage of derivative contracts is what causes many to lose a significant amount of money while trading, but it also allows investors to have exposure to certain assets with a small amount of funds. This leverage magnifies both gains and losses.

FUTURES CONTRACTS

According to the U.S. Commodity Futures Trading Commission (CFTC), trading commodity futures and options is a volatile, complex and risky venture that is rarely suitable for individual investors or "retail customers." Many individuals lose all of their money and can be required to pay more than they initially invested. These are the opening comments on the CFTC website under consumer protection. However, despite the potential for financial disaster, futures contracts provide an important role for speculators and investors. This section discusses the basics of futures contracts, including the components of a futures contract agreement, futures exchanges and trading contracts, hedging using futures contracts, futures prices, closing futures contracts, and the tax treatment of futures contract gains and losses.

Key Concepts

1. Futures contracts are standardized except for the market price.
2. Forward contracts are private agreements and are not standardized nor traded on exchanges.
3. Futures contracts are bought and sold on exchanges and provide more liquidity than forward contracts.

Introduction to Futures Contracts

Throughout history, humans have always been exposed to price risk, especially in the food market. In the period after the Revolutionary War, farmers would harvest their crops, sell as much as they could, and use the remaining harvest for their own personal consumption. This period was characterized by substantial amounts of waste and significant amounts of uncertainty regarding prices. To combat the issue, The Chicago Board of Trade was formed and offered the first formal forward commodity contact. These contracts allowed farmers and grain processing companies to agree on a price to trade in the future. Standardization of the contracts soon followed and along with it, a surge in trading activity.

Today, a **forward contract** is a legal agreement between two parties to buy or sell a specific asset at a specified future time, which is agreed to today. Forward contracts are not standardized or traded on exchanges. Rather, they are private agreements between two parties that are negotiated between the buyer and the seller. At the origination of the forward contract, the value is zero. However, as the value of the underlying commodity changes, the value of the contract increases for one party and decreases for the other party. The sum of the changes is zero. This type of situation is referred to as a zero-sum game, whereby one party's gains are offset by the other party's losses.

A **futures contract** is similar to a forward contract, but it has several important differences. A futures contract is a standardized agreement between two parties to make (sell) or take delivery (buy) of a contract of a specific commodity of a specified quality at a future time, place, and unit price. One contract specifies all the details agreed to by the buyer and the seller.

The buyer of a futures contract is taking on the obligation to buy the underlying asset at the expiration of the futures contract at the specified price in the contract.

The seller of a futures contract is taking on the obligation to sell the underlying asset at the expiration of the futures contract at the specified price in the contract.[1]

1. It should be noted that most futures contracts do not result in delivery of the underlying asset. Generally, gains and losses are settled daily, and contracts are closed out prior to expiration.

Whereas forward contract terms vary due to negotiation between the parties to the contract, futures contracts are facilitated through exchanges and are standardized. For example, coffee futures contracts are standardized in the following manner.

Exhibit 14.1 | Characteristics of a Coffee Futures Contract

Contract Unit	37,500 pounds of coffee
Price Quotation	U.S. Dollars per pound
Minimum Price Fluctuation	$0.0005 per pound
Listed Contracts	Trading is conducted in the March, May, July, September, and December cycle for the next 23 months.
Settlement Method	Financially Settled

The ability to negotiate the specific details of a forward contract so that they fit the exact needs of the two parties involved is extremely valuable to those parties. However, the terms of the forward contract may or may not appeal to third parties. Consequently, there is little secondary market trading for forward contracts, which lessens their liquidity levels and makes them less attractive to some investors. The standardization of futures contracts stimulates trading and allows for increased liquidity compared to forward contracts, as those standardized features are likely to appeal to a much wider range of investors.

Exhibit 14.2 | Futures Contracts vs. Forward Contracts

Futures Contract	Forward Contract
Standardized contract	Customized contract
Exchange-traded	Over-the-counter trading
Daily settlement (marked to market)	Settled at expiration
Delivery of underlying asset rarely occurs	Delivery of underlying asset generally occurs
Highly liquid contract	Illiquid contract

One additional attractive feature regarding the use of futures contracts is the ability to take advantage of leverage opportunities. This feature is particularly true for financial futures contracts, such as the S&P 500 Index futures contract. **Exhibit 14.3** contrasts the purchase of an exchange traded fund designed to mimic the S&P 500 Index with a long position on an S&P 500 Index futures contract.

Exhibit 14.3 | Leverage Comparison

Buy an ETF	Buy an ETF on 50% Margin	Buy S&P 500 Futures on Margin
Buy $500,000 of SPY (S&P 500 ETF). This investment has zero leverage and requires $500,000 of capital.	Buy $500,000 of SPY (S&P 500 ETF) on margin. This investment provides a 2-to-1 leverage. It controls the same asset as the first choice but with only $250,000 of capital.	Buy S&P 500 Futures on Margin. This investment provides more than 20 times leverage with only $55,000 of capital. It has approximately the same exposure to the S&P 500 index as the SPY ETF.*

* The initial margin at the time of writing was $55,000. However, this margin will change over time.

Exhibit 14.3 illustrates the amount of leverage available through the futures market. Futures exchanges use the term 'performance bond', which are identical to margin requirements. Performance bonds are often between three and 12 percent of the futures contract value. Futures contracts allow for investors to control a relatively large asset value with a relatively small amount of capital. Performance bonds are required by both buyers and sellers and represent good-faith money to ensure the ability of the parties to meet day-to-day obligations of holding the futures position. Positions are marked to market on a daily basis, such that profits and losses are reflected in buyers' and sellers' accounts daily. In many cases, positions are marked to market on a twice-daily basis - in the morning and in the afternoon.

Example 14.1

Marcus is a coffee trader who lives in Costa Rica and Brazil at various times during the year. He believes that the price of coffee is on the rise due to the recent drought and other harsh weather conditions. If coffee production is in fact lower, then the price will increase based on the relationship between supply and demand. Marcus is a speculator. Marcus takes the long position in one coffee futures contract, which will benefit him if prices rise. Coffee futures contracts have the following characteristics:

- Contract Size: 37,500 pounds
- Deliverable Grades: Arabica Coffee
- Current (spot) Price: 120.00 (this equates to $1.2000 per pound)
- Futures Price: 122.15 (this equates to $1.2215 per pound)
- Initial Margin: $4,500
- Maintenance Margin: $3,000

Assuming he wants to go long in one coffee futures contract, he must put up the initial margin of $4,500. The contract value equals $45,806.25 ($1.2215 per pound x 37,500 pounds). He is able to control an asset worth $45,806.25 with an investment of only $4,500. This ability to control such a large asset with such a small initial margin is why futures contracts have so much leverage.

Assuming the price of the coffee contract increases to 136.00, the contract value will equal $51,000, which is a gain of $5,193.75. This gain represents more than a 100 percent return on his investment.

If, on the other hand, the future price dropped to 105.00, he will have lost more than 100 percent of his investment. The maintenance margin is the minimum equity that must be maintained for the futures contract to avoid having to put up additional funds. As a result of the price decrease, his equity (initial margin plus gains and losses) is completely wiped out and he must put up additional capital to cover his losses and to restore his equity.

As **Example 14.1** illustrates, futures contracts, and derivatives in general, provide great opportunities to speculate on future prices. In addition, the futures market provides insight into the expected prices of commodities in the future, a concept known as price discovery. If futures prices six months or twelve months out are significantly higher, there must be an underlying reason, such as an expected change in supply or demand.

The leverage built into derivatives contracts exposes market participants to extra risk, but these markets can also be used to mitigate a variety of risks. Futures contracts are frequently used by both suppliers and consumers of commodities and financial securities to lock in future prices. This removes price risk, i.e. the uncertainty as to the price that will be paid and received in the future. For example, farmers are exposed to substantial price fluctuations when selling their harvest. If a farmer grows a crop and the price drops by 10 percent, it can be financially devastating, mostly because farmers rely on commodity prices to repay loans used to finance the purchase of farming equipment. Futures contracts provide an opportunity for farmers, and others, to hedge against fluctuations in the price of commodities. Consider the following example.

Example 14.2

Rennie is a coffee farmer who lives in Costa Rica and sells her coffee to support her family. She is concerned that the price of coffee may drop due to an increase in coffee production. If coffee production increases, then the price of coffee will decrease based on the relationship between supply and demand. Rennie is a hedger. She decides to go short (sells a futures contract) in a coffee futures contract, which has the following assumed characteristics:

- Contract Size: 37,500 pounds
- Deliverable Grades: Arabica Coffee
- Current (spot) Price: 122.15 (this equates to $1.2215 per pound)
- Futures Price - 6 months: 125.15
- Initial Margin: $4,500
- Maintenance Margin: $3,000

Rennie's crop, which is expected to yield 75,000 pounds of coffee, will be harvested in six months. She wants to assure herself that she can sell it for approximately the current market price of $1.2215 per pound. The futures price is currently $1.2515 per pound. Therefore, she sells two six-month contracts at 125.15. These futures contracts assure Rennie that she can 'lock-in' a specific price in six months, which is $1.2515 per pound. The value of Rennie's futures position is:

Value = 2 × 37,500 pounds × $1.2515 = $93,862.50

This is the total 'lock-in' amount that Rennie will receive in six months, whether spot coffee prices rise or fall. Suppose changes in the coffee market cause spot prices to either rise to $1.75 per pound or fall to $1.11 per pound. The calculations below show the results of the hedge under both conditions. Note the price of coffee in the spot market will converge to the futures price of coffee on the maturity date of the contract because the two markets converge. That is, the spot market results in immediate delivery as does the futures market when the contract is maturing.

If the spot rate is $1.75 on maturity date of the contract:

- Rennie sells her coffee in the spot market and receives: $1.75 × 75,000
  = $131,250.00
- Rennie loses on her short futures position: ($1.2515 – $1.75) × 2 × 37,500
  = -$37,387.50

Rennie's net position: $93,862.50

If the spot rate is $1.11 on maturity date of the contract:

- Rennie sells her coffee in the spot market and receives: ($1.11 × 75,000) = $83,250.00
- Rennie wins on her short futures position: ($1.2515 – $1.11) × 2 × 37,500 = +$10,612.50

Rennie's net position: $93,862.50

The hedge works perfectly for Rennie, as she will receive a total of $93,862.50 regardless of the path that coffee prices take, not just the two possible prices shown in the table above. The reason for the perfect hedge is two-fold: The contract matures on the exact same date Rennie wants to sell her coffee and the assets are identical in both markets.

As the two previous examples illustrate, derivatives provide opportunities for both speculators and hedgers. In addition, they help to provide a more complete financial market.

A final advantage of derivatives is that they provide a certain level of trading efficiency. Derivatives can often be purchased with less capital and at lower transactions costs than attempting to purchase (or sell) the underlying securities or assets.

Futures Exchanges

Futures contracts are traded on organized exchanges. These exchanges have many advantages, including liquidity, transparency, access to account information, and financial safeguards. With the breadth of futures offerings, exchanges attract millions of participants, speculators, hedgers, and asset managers. Millions of contracts are traded on a daily basis, providing a sizable amount of liquidity to the futures markets.[2] **Exhibit 14.4** depicts some of the futures contracts that are available. This list is far from complete as there are often multiple variations in types of products, such as wheat or oil.

Exhibit 14.4 | Example of Selected Futures Contracts Across Selected Sectors

Agriculture	Energy	Equities	FX	Interest Rates	Metals
Dairy	Crude oil	S&P 500	Euro FX	Eurodollar	Gold
Corn	Natural gas	NASDAQ 100	Japanese Yen	10-Year T-Note	Silver
Soybeans	Electricity	Nikkei/Yen	Mexican Peso	5-Year T-Note	Copper
Wheat	Ethanol	Dow	British Pound	2-Year T-Note	Platinum
Milk		S&P –Midcap 400	Australian Dollar	U.S. Treasury Bond	Palladium
Oats		S&P 500 – Energy Sector Index	Russian Ruble		Steel
Rice		S&P 500 – Health Care Sector Index	Swiss Franc		Uranium
Cocoa			South African Rand		Aluminum
Coffee					Zinc
Cotton					Iron ore
Cheese					
Sugar					
Live cattle					
Hogs					

2. CMEGroup.com

Transparency is an important part of any system of exchange. Trading futures contracts is highly transparent in terms of pricing and volume. Comprehensive trade information is available and distributed from the exchanges in real-time and available to futures traders.

Asset managers, hedgers, and speculators make decisions quickly, and futures exchanges allow instantaneous access around the world. Trades are executed almost immediately, which allows for quick reactions to changes in economic situations and opportunities.

Futures contracts have an inherently high degree of leverage, which enhances gains and magnifies losses. Although this presents a high degree of financial risk, some traders embrace it and use derivative instruments to deliberately leverage their portfolios.

Key Concepts

1. Futures exchanges have many advantages for investors.
2. There are market orders and limit orders.
3. The clearing house provides for an efficient and effective market.

However, all traders want to minimize counter-party risk, i.e. the risk that the counter-party is unable to fulfill the obligations of the contract. To achieve this, exchanges provide a clearing service, which acts as the middleman for all trades. As a clearing house, it becomes the buyer for every seller and the seller for every buyer. The clearing house provides financial safeguards for the market and manages and maintains performance bonds. The clearing house ensures trades meet certain requirements and that investors can satisfy their financial obligations in the event their investments lose money. While there is transparency in terms of volume and price, trades are anonymous such that buyers of a contract will not know the seller and sellers will not know the buyer.

Exhibit 14.5 | Clearing House Functions

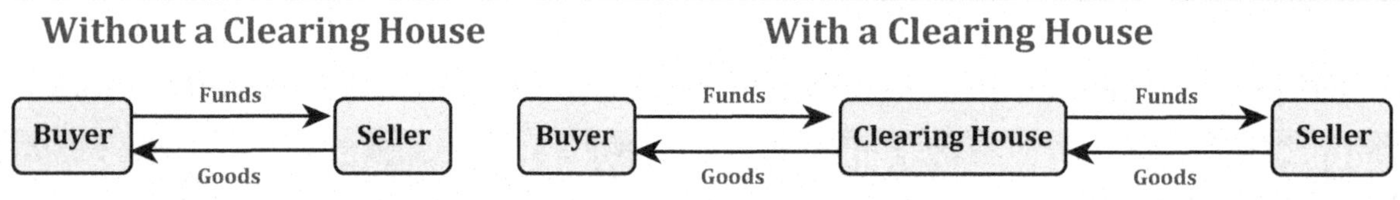

Price Limits

Leverage is a key attribute of futures contracts. As a result, even small amounts of price volatility for an underlying commodity can result in enormously large gains and losses for futures traders. As a result of this potential volatility and the potential for price manipulation, futures exchanges impose daily price limits for futures contracts. Trading during a single day cannot result in the price of the commodity increasing beyond the up limit or decreasing below the down limit. These limits provide the market with time to settle down. Exchanges have used these limits since 1988.

The securities and futures exchanges have procedures for coordinated cross-market trading halts if a severe market price decline reaches levels that may exhaust market liquidity. These procedures, known as market-wide circuit breakers, may halt trading temporarily or, under extreme circumstances, close the markets before the normal close of the trading session. The purpose of these circuit breakers is to stop volatility attributable to panic in the market and allow time for traders to "settle down."

Types of Orders

Buying or selling a futures contract requires the investor to place an order to buy or sell the contract. The investor executes the order as a market order or a limit order. The type of order determines whether the trade (the order to buy or sell) is executed and at what price.

Market orders are filled by the broker at the next available price in the market. Market orders are almost always filled, but there is no control over the price at which the order is filled.

Limit orders indicate to the broker that the buy or sell order must be filled only if the futures contract reaches a specific price. For example, a limit sell order for a coffee futures contract at a price of $120 instructs a broker to sell at a price of $120 or better. Limit orders may or may not be filled, depending on the limit order price relative to the market price. In addition, the limit order must specify the time period over which the broker is instructed to fill the order. This time period might be a day, a week, a month, or might be placed as "good 'til cancel." A good 'til canceled order remains open until it is filled or until the trader cancels the order.

Futures Contract Agreements

Futures contracts, by definition, are standardized. These agreements have specific terms, which include:

- Contract size
- Contract value
- Tick size
- Price limits
- Margin requirements
- Mark-to-market

Contract Size

Each futures contract represents a specific standardized size that does not change, known as the **contract size**. For example, a coffee contract represents 37,500 pounds of coffee. A corn contract represents 5,000 bushels of a specific type of corn. The E-mini S&P 500 futures contract size is always $50 times the price of S&P 500 index.

These contract sizes allow traders to easily determine how many contracts they may need for their trading objectives. For example, if a corn farmer wants to hedge 100,000 bushels of corn, he will need to sell 20 contracts (100,000 bushels divided by the contract size of 5,000 bushels).

> ***Key Concepts***
>
> 1. Specific terms of a futures contract are standardized.
> 2. Futures contracts are marked to market on a daily basis.
> 3. There are two margins for futures contracts: initial and maintenance margin.

Contract Value

The value of a futures contract is called the **contract value** or **notional value**, and is determined by multiplying the size of the contract by the current price. For example, if coffee is currently priced at $1.20 per pound, the value of one contract equals $45,000 ($1.20 x 37,500). The value of the E-mini S&P 500 futures contract equals $50 times the price of the S&P 500 index. If the index is currently 4,500, then the contract value equals $225,000 ($50 x 4,500).

Tick Size

The price of futures contracts change in specific increments. The smallest price change for a futures contract is called the **tick size**. The smallest amount that the price of a particular contract can fluctuate is called a tick, which is different for each type of futures contract. For a coffee contract, the tick size is $0.0005 per pound, which translates into a contract price change of $18.75 (37,500 x $0.0005 per pound).

Price Limit

Some futures markets impose **price limits**, which are limits in daily price fluctuations. These price limits help to manage volatile price fluctuations. The purpose of imposing a daily price limit is to prevent prices moving so much that a trader's performance bond or margin no longer covers their losses.

Margin Requirements

Both buyers and sellers must deposit funds with a broker when buying or selling futures contracts, known as **margin requirements**. The **initial margin** (also known as a **performance bond**) is the amount of money that must be put up by the buyer and seller of a contract to initiate the trade. The funds are held by the broker but earn interest while they are held. The purpose of the funds is to ensure that traders can meet their financial obligations for the contracts they have bought or sold. As the value of the underlying commodity or security changes, it increases or decreases the trader's equity, either above or below the initial performance bond that was deposited. Brokers often permit futures traders to meet their margin requirements with securities rather than cash. For example, brokers may permit investors to have Treasury securities or equity securities on hand to meet the performance bond requirements. However, the value of the assets will not be dollar-for-dollar for purposes of margin requirements. A broker might give an investor credit for 90 percent of the value of Treasury securities.

Maintenance Margin

The **maintenance margin** is the minimum amount of equity that must be maintained by the investor (futures trader) in their account. If the equity in the account drops below this level, the investor will generally receive a margin call and be required to add additional funds to the account to increase equity back up to the initial margin level.

Mark-to-Market

Mark-to-market is a practice that all futures contracts follow on a daily basis. It is designed to allocate gains and losses occurring during the day to the accounts of buyers and sellers to ensure that all traders can meet their financial obligations for the contracts they have bought or sold. At the end of each day, a settlement price for each contract results in gains for one party to a contract and losses to the other. Gains are added to a trader's account and increase the equity in the account. Losses are subtracted from a trader's account and decrease equity in an account. The initial equity in a trader's account originates from the performance bond deposited to enter into the initial futures contract position. In the event that losses reduce the performance bond below the maintenance margin, the trader may receive a margin call, which is a call for additional funds to restore equity in the trader's account.

Settlement Price

The **settlement price** is the average of the prices that a futures contract trades for immediately before the close of trading for a specific day. It is the price that is used to calculate gains and losses for the mark-to-market practice.

Margin Call

A **margin call** requires a futures trader to increase the equity in their trading account due to the recognition of losses. This requirement generally occurs as part of the mark-to-market practice and helps to ensure that traders can meet their financial obligations for the contracts they have bought or sold.

Example 14.3

Assume the following:

Contract Specifications for a British Pound Currency Futures Contract	
Initial Margin Requirement (assumed)	$1,500
Maintenance Margin (assumed)	$1,100

On Monday morning, an investor takes a long position in a British Pound futures contract that matures in three weeks. At the close of trading on Monday, the account gains $200. At Tuesday close, the account has further gains of $100. At Wednesday close, the account loses $250. At Thursday close the account again falls, this time $900. At Friday close, the account loses $200. The chart below details the daily settlement process for the week.

Time	Cash Flow
Monday Morning	Investor deposits $1,500 as the initial margin.
Monday Close	Balance in account is $1,500 + $200 = $1,700.
Tuesday Close	Balance in account is $1,700 + $100 = $1,800.
Wednesday Close	Balance in account is $1,800 - $250 = $1,550.
Thursday Close	Balance in account is $1,550 - $900 = $650. This is below the maintenance margin, therefore the investor receives a margin call and must deposit $850: $1,500 - $650 = $850. The account balance is $1,500.
Friday Close	Balance in account is $1,500 - $200 = $1,300.

Example 14.4

Jack and Zach are 28-year-old twins who both trade futures contracts. While they have a close brotherly relationship, they have always held opposite opinions on many subjects. They agree that the price of coffee is likely to change over the next several months. Jack believes the price will increase due to demand, influenced by medical research, which he says is conclusive. Zach believes the price will decrease because the weather and climate will produce larger crops of coffee. Based on their respective beliefs, Jack purchases (takes a long position) ten coffee contracts and Zach sells (takes a short position) ten coffee contracts. Below are the details for one contract:

- Contract Size: 37,500 pounds
- Deliverable Grades: Arabica Coffee
- Current (spot) Price: 120.00 (this equates to $1.2000 per pound)
- Futures Price - 6 months: 123.50
- Initial Margin: $4,500
- Maintenance Margin: $3,000

Before entering into their respective positions, Jack and Zach must each put up $4,500 per contract as a performance bond (initial margin).

Below is a chart of possible daily price changes over a four-day period per contract.

Day	Futures Price	Δ in Futures Contract Price	Jack's Daily Gain (Loss)	Jack's Cumulative Gain (Loss)	Jack's Equity Position	Zach's Equity Position	Sum for Jack & Zach
Day 1	123.5000				$ 4,500.00	$ 4,500.00	$ 9,000.00
Day 2	121.4000	-2.1000	$ (787.50)	$ (787.50)	$ 3,712.50	$ 5,287.50	$ 9,000.00
Day 3	119.6000	-1.8000	$ (675.00)	$ (1,462.50)	$ 3,037.50	$ 5,962.50	$ 9,000.00
Day 4	127.7500	8.1500	$ 3,056.25	$ 1,593.75	$ 6,093.75	$ 2,906.25	$ 9,000.00

Change from Day 1 to Day 2: 121.40 - 123.50 = -2.10

37,500 pounds x -$0.021 = -787.50

The change from Day 2 to 3 represents a price drop of 1.4%, but Jack's equity drops by 18%.

Zach will receive a margin call because his equity falls below the maintenance margin of $3,000.

This chart illustrates the futures price of coffee over four days. The change in the futures price impacts the value of the ten contracts as well as Jack and Zach's positions. The change in the futures price during the first two days does not result in a margin call. However, on Day 4, the price increases and results in Zach having to increase his performance bond. Notice that the value of Jack and Zach's positions always equals $9,000. This relationship is why futures contracts are referred to as a zero-sum game. As one party gains, the other will lose the same amount.

It should also be noted that a rather small change in the value of the commodity results in a significant change in the value of the funds invested. The futures price for coffee increased on Day 4 from $119.60 to $127.75, which is a 6.8% increase. The value of Jack's investment increased by 100%, from $3,038 to $6,094. The leverage built into each contract means that small changes in commodity prices result in large changes in the value of a futures contract.

Futures Contract Positions

Speculators and hedgers can take long or short positions in futures contracts. Purchasing a contract for future delivery is termed a long position (take delivery). Selling a contract for future delivery is called a short position (make delivery). Like stocks, a long position increases in value if the underlying security or commodity increases in value; whereas, a short position increases in value if the underlying security or commodity decreases in value.

Hedging is one of the primary uses of derivatives and involves entering into a futures contract position that is the opposite to the position held in the underlying asset. The purpose of hedging is to reduce risk from fluctuating commodity prices. The short hedge and the long hedge are discussed below.

The Short Hedge

If a farmer grows and sells wheat, he or she has a long position in wheat since the farmer benefits when the price increases. If the price of the wheat declines, the farmer loses money. Therefore, the farmer is subject to the price changes in the commodity wheat. To eliminate their risk exposure to price fluctuations, the farmer can use a short hedge.

To use a short hedge, the farmer must take a short position in wheat by selling a wheat contract. Once the farmer has both a long position (their wheat crop) and a short position (the futures contract), the farmer has eliminated the risk of price fluctuations. If the price of wheat increases, the value of their crop increases. If the price of wheat declines, the value of the futures contract increases.

Key Concepts

1. A short hedge is frequently used by a commodity producer. A long hedge is frequently used to guard against commodity price increases.
2. Perfect hedges are difficult to achieve.

Example 14.5

Assume the following facts:

- The cash or spot price for a bushel of wheat is $3.00.
- The September futures price for wheat is $3.10.

A producer who expects to harvest and sell wheat at the end of September can either wait and see what the spot price is at that date, or hedge the position by selling (shorting) a September futures contract at a price of $3.10. If the spot price falls to $2.80 at end of September, a producer who hedged the position would be $0.30 per bushel better off than one who remained unhedged. The hedged producer can deliver the wheat to settle the futures contract and receive $3.10, or sell in the spot market for $2.80 and collect $0.30 from the long side of the futures contract. Either way the hedged producer collects $3.10.

If the spot price is $4.00 at the expiry of the futures contract, the hedged producer is $0.90 worse off than one who remained unhedged. The hedged producer is obligated to sell her wheat for $3.10 to the long side of the futures contract, or alternatively sell the wheat for $4.00 in the spot market and pay the long $0.90. Either way, once again, by hedging the producer had locked in proceeds of $3.10.

The Long Hedge

The long hedge works similarly to the short hedge with the exception that the long hedge involves a user or consumer of a commodity who is concerned that the price may increase. Paper manufacturers and furniture makers both purchase and use wood as a raw material. If the price of wood or lumber increases, their cost of goods sold increases and their net income decreases. If the price of lumber declines, they benefit. Thus, they have a short position in lumber since they profit from its decline. To limit the risk of price fluctuations, these paper manufacturers and furniture makers need to take a long position, which can be accomplished with a futures contract.

Example 14.6

Jayden's Lumber Company (JLC) expects to harvest 330,000 board feet of lumber in exactly three months. Universal Construction Company (UCC) expects to need 330,000 board feet of lumber in three months for a specific project.

The spot price of lumber is $370 per 1,000 feet while the three-month futures contract price is $380 per 1,000 feet. The standard amount of the contract is 110,000 board feet.

JLC and UCC can both use the futures contract to hedge their positions. JLC takes the short position, agreeing to deliver the lumber in three months, while UCC takes the long position, agreeing to purchase the lumber in three months. They each lock in the future price of the commodity and agree to exchange 330,000 board feet of lumber at $380 per feet. The total amount of the contract is $125,400. Regardless of the spot price in three months, the two parties have agreed to trade at $380, thus substantially reducing if not eliminating price risk.

One alternative to hedging using futures contract would be to purchase the lumber today at $370. However, there are carrying costs, such as interest and storage, which must be considered. The buyer would have to pay for the materials today instead of in the future. This outflow of cash results in interest that would be paid on borrowed funds or interest forgone on invested funds. In addition, the buyer would have to pay for the storage of the lumber until it is needed for production.

Other Hedging Concerns

A **perfect hedge** occurs when all of the risk of buying or selling a commodity is fully offset by a futures contract. Because contracts have predetermined quantities, it may be impossible to create a perfect hedge using a standardized futures contract. For example, if a farmer produces 275,000 bushels of cotton and cotton futures specify 50,000 bushels of cotton per contract, then it is impossible to perfectly hedge against price fluctuations. This farmer will have to either over hedge or under hedge. The farmer could sell five futures contracts to hedge 250,000 bushels of cotton or could sell six futures contracts to hedge against 300,000 bushels of cotton. Usually, the farmer hedges in the direction that he or she feels price will most likely move (an imperfect hedge).

Additional concerns for a perfect hedge include the underlying asset and the maturity of the contract. If the underlying asset of the futures contract does not identically match the commodity that is being hedged, price fluctuations between the assets may vary. However, it is likely that they will be similar and highly correlated.

If the expiration date of the futures contract does not correspond with the date that the commodity is to be purchased or sold, a perfect hedge does not exist. The inability to match time horizons also subjects the hedger to the risks of price fluctuations.

Futures Contract Prices

Commodity and other futures contract prices constantly change. The **spot price** is the price of a commodity or asset to be delivered today. The spot price is also called the cash price or the current price.

The **futures price** is the price at which two parties agree to exchange a commodity or a financial asset at some point in the future. The difference between the spot and futures price is known as the **basis**. The basis for a far term contract is typically much higher than for a near term contact. In fact, as the maturity date of the futures contract approaches, and hence the contract term decreases, the spot and futures prices will converge. This occurs essentially because the spot market and the futures market become the same market. For example, a one-month futures contract on corn might have a futures price of $3.15 and a spot price of $3.00. Over time, both the spot and futures prices will change but will converge on the final day of the contract. A trader could buy corn in the spot market for immediate delivery or take the long position, which would also result in immediate delivery because the contract matures at the end of that day. If a trader could buy corn in the spot market on the final day of the contract at $3.25 and short the futures contract at $3.30, the trader would earn an arbitrage profit. This is not very likely to occur in an efficient market.

Key Concepts

1. Spot price is the cash price or current price.
2. Carry costs of a futures contract may include storage, insurance, transportation, and financing costs.
3. Basis is the spot price minus the futures price.
4. Spread describes the relationship between two futures prices.

There are several theories regarding the relationship between spot prices and futures prices. One of the more common ones deals with commodity prices and carrying costs. The theory is that futures prices for a commodity are equal to the spot price plus the cost to carry. There are four basic types of carrying costs: storage, insurance, transportation and financing. Some or all of the carrying costs may apply in a particular scenario.

Example 14.7

Assume the spot price of apples is $10 per bushel and the one-month futures price of apples is $12 per bushel. The cost of carry which includes financing and storage is $2 per bushel. The two markets are in equilibrium. If the futures price were $15 per bushel, however, an arbitrage opportunity would exist. An investor could purchase apples in the spot market for $10 per bushel, enter a futures contract to sell the apples for $15, while storing them for one month at a cost of $2 per bushel. The arbitrage profit is $3 per bushel.

Like spot prices and futures prices, a similar relationship exists between two futures prices. Assume the one-month futures price for apples is $12 per bushel and assume the two-month futures price for apples is $16 per bushel. In this case, an investor could buy a one-month contract and sell a two-month contract, netting a profit of $2 ($4 less carry cost of $2) without risk and after paying $2 of carry cost for one month.

Example 14.8

Assume the spot price of crickets is $100 for 2,000 crickets and the one-year futures price is $103. Money market returns are 3% annually. The two markets are in equilibrium. If the money market return were 5%, however, an arbitrage opportunity would exist. An investor could short crickets in the spot market and invest the proceeds at 5% while simultaneously taking the long position in the futures contract for $103. In one year, the money market account has a value of $105, the investor takes delivery of the crickets and uses the proceeds to cover the short position in the spot market. The arbitrage profit is $2.

Of course, there are no futures markets for apples or crickets, but the examples illustrate the importance of the relationship between the money market, the spot market, and the futures markets. They must be in equilibrium or arbitrageurs will take advantage of those pricing failures.

The above examples illustrate how investors can take advantage of an imbalance in the relationship between the spot price and the futures price for a given commodity.

Another theory of futures prices is that they are impacted by expected future spot prices. This theory allows for futures prices that are lower than the current spot price.

The term **spread** is used to describe the relationship between two futures prices. A spread equals the difference between the two futures prices. The two futures prices may be for the same commodity, such as December Wheat and February Wheat, or it may be for different commodities, such as corn and wheat.

Quick Quiz 14.2

1. Futures contracts and forward contracts are similar, but differ in terms of standardization and liquidity.
   a. True
   b. False
2. Futures exchanges have margin requirements and a system of marking-to-market for the purpose of ensuring traders can meet their financial obligations.
   a. True
   b. False
3. Contract value, which is also know as the notional value, is determined by multiplying the size of the contract by the current price.
   a. True
   b. False

True, True, True.

Closing a Futures Contract

A futures contract is a standardized agreement between two parties to make or take delivery of a contract of a specific commodity of a specified quality at a future time, place, and unit price. As such, many futures contracts call for the delivery of the actual commodity identified in the contract. The delivery should meet the quality and other specifications that are required for the commodity in the contract. It should be noted that deliveries are rare and only represent a small percentage of all contracts. In most cases, deliveries are not made. Instead, some contracts are settled in cash and most contracts are closed with offsetting contracts.

When a contract is cash settled, the party who has suffered a loss pays the party who has made a gain. For example, if a trader was long on an oil futures contract at a price of $85 and at expiry the price was $80, she has lost $5 per barrel. Rather than purchasing the oil for the contracted price of $85, she can simply pay the short $5 per barrel and buy oil in the spot market (if indeed she has a need for the underlying oil) for $80. The short side of the contract receives the $5 and can sell their oil for $80 a barrel in the spot market.

Cash settlement allows traders to take positions in commodity futures without owning or delivering the underlying asset. Additionally, some futures contracts call for cash settlement. For example, S&P 500 futures contracts call for cash settlement as it is not practical to 'deliver' the index.

To close a position using offsetting contracts, a trader takes the opposite position in the contract that they already hold. For example, a trader who is long a September oil futures contract at $85 can close the position by taking a short September oil futures contract. The gain or loss is calculated using the difference between the original price and the price of the offsetting contract. If the trader closed out by taking a short position at $80, she has lost $5 per barrel.

Another way to close a futures contract is to follow a procedure that is known as exchange for physicals. Exchange for physicals is a process by which two traders, one with a short position and one with a long position, agree to complete the transaction off the exchange floor. To complete this transaction, the seller makes delivery and the buyer takes delivery. They privately negotiate the price and terms and must notify the exchange so that both traders are shown to be out of the market.

Tax Implications of Futures Contracts (1256 Contracts)

1256 contracts include any regulated futures contract, any foreign currency contract, any non-equity option, any dealer equity option, and any dealer securities futures contract. Any gain or loss with respect to a section 1256 contract shall be treated as:

- short-term capital gain or loss, to the extent of 40 percent of such gain or loss, and
- long-term capital gain or loss, to the extent of 60 percent of such gain or loss.

Quick Quiz 14.3

1. A corn farmer is concerned about corn prices dropping. Therefore, he should enter into a long hedge.
   a. True
   b. False
2. The spot price less the futures price equals the basis.
   a. True
   b. False
3. Most futures contracts are settled by delivering the underlying commodity.
   a. True
   b. False

False, True, False.

Because most 1256 type contracts are traded in relatively short time frames, this treatment is favorable to taxpayers as the holding period for long-term capital gain treatment is one year.

SWAPS

This section provides a basic introduction to swaps, including the types of swaps, mechanics and applications for swaps.

A **swap** is an over-the-counter agreement between two or more parties to exchange future sets of cash flows. Swap agreements define the terms of the agreements, including the dates of payments and the methodology that is to be used to determine the payments. The future payments may be fixed or may change (float or fluctuate) based on changes in interest rates, exchange rates, or other variables.

As with futures and forward contracts, both parties are obligated to perform in the future in accordance with the requirements set out in the swap agreement. The two primary types of swaps are interest rate swaps and currency swaps. Interest rate swaps are agreements whereby the counterparties agree to exchange future cash flows. For one of the parties, the cash flows are fixed amounts. For the other party, the cash flows float based on market interest rates. The term floating simply means that the interest payments change from one period to another based on changes in an underlying interest rate or some other variable. Currency swaps are agreements to exchange cash flows in different currencies.

One of the reasons that a company would engage in an interest rate swap is to better manage interest rate risk. Interest rate risk is the risk that changes in interest rates (up or down) will have an adverse effect on the value of assets. Consider the following examples.

Example 14.9

Duncan Bank (DB) is primarily a mortgage lender and is concerned about its interest rate risk. Its balance sheet has the following attributes:

	Assets	- Liabilities	= Equity
Composition	Consist of mortgage loans with an average term of 26 years and an average interest rate of 6%. Very few ARMs.*	Consist of short-term deposits that earn an average rate of 2%.	Equals the difference between assets and liabilities.
Duration	Longer term	Shorter term	
Interest	Primarily fixed	Primarily floating	

** ARM = adjustable rate mortgage. The interest rate for an ARM fluctuates based on changes in interest rates.*

The duration of Duncan Bank's assets and liabilities is mismatched. As discussed in Chapter 8, duration is a measure of interest rate sensitivity. DB's fixed income assets have a longer duration than the floating rate liabilities. Therefore, the asset side of DB's balance sheet is more sensitive to interest rate changes than the liability side. In addition, DB has a different type of interest rate for its assets than for its liabilities. Its assets have a fixed rate of interest, while its liabilities are subject to a floating rate.

Assume that interest rates increase. The value of the asset side of the balance sheet decreases because the interest rates are fixed and the value is inversely related to changes in interest rates. The impact of rising rates on liabilities is to increase the liabilities side of the balance sheet because the rates are floating. Duncan Bank will have to increase the rate at which it pays deposits. Thus, an increase in interest rates will have a negative impact on the equity of the bank, as assets go down and liabilities go up. As a simple example, if average rates rise by 1% DB still receives the fixed 6% on its assets, but now pays an average of 3% on deposits. The spread between assets and liabilities decreases from 4% to 3%, and DB's equity will decrease.

Key Concepts

1. A swap is an agreement to exchange future sets of cash flows or currencies.
2. Swap parties are called counter parties.
3. A plain vanilla swap is a swap of a fixed interest payment for a floating rate payment.
4. Currency swaps involve the exchange of cash flows in different currencies.

DB could manage this exposure to interest rate risk by entering into a swap, for example by paying a fixed rate and receiving floating to better match their cash inflows to the floating rate outflows.

It is important to realize that over time, as mortgages are paid off and replaced with higher interest rate mortgages, equity should increase. However, there is a negative impact to increases in interest rates that should be actively managed.

If interest rates go down, liabilities go down resulting in an increase in equity. However, too much of a drop in interest rates causes people to consider refinancing their loans at a lower rate of interest.

Example 14.10

Jacob Life Insurance (JLI) is a life insurer that is concerned about its interest rate risk. JLI's balance sheet has the following attributes:

	Assets	-	Liabilities	=	Equity
Composition	Consist primarily of a fixed-income portfolio from life insurance premiums.		Consist of life insurance policy death benefit obligations and annuity payments from death benefits.		Equals the difference between assets and liabilities.
Duration	Term varies		Longer term		
Interest	Primarily floating		Primarily fixed		

The duration of JLI's assets and liabilities is somewhat mismatched. However, JLI has more control over the duration of the asset side of its balance sheet. JLI also has a different type of interest rate for its assets than for its liabilities. Its assets have a floating rate of interest, while its liabilities are subject to a fixed rate.

Assume interest rates increase. The value of the asset side of the balance sheet decreases because the value is inversely related to changes in interest rates. However, the impact of the change will be dependent upon the duration of the fixed-income assets in its portfolio. Any cash flows from interest or principle from the bond portfolio will be reinvested at higher rates. The impact of rising rates on liabilities is to decrease the liabilities side of the balance sheet because the rates are fixed. JLI will not have to increase the rate at which it pays annuities.

If interest rates were to go down, it would cause the liabilities to go up resulting in a decrease in equity. Assets would go up in value offsetting the decrease. However, depending on the duration of the assets and liabilities, it might cause a positive or negative impact to equity. JLI could manage this exposure to interest rate risk by entering into a swap, for example by paying a fixed rate and receiving floating to better match their cash outflows to the floating rate inflows.

As the two examples above illustrate, different companies have different types of interest rate assets and liabilities, and these differences can impact the firm's equity. Firms attempt to manage these interest rate differences (fixed versus floating) by using interest rate swaps.

Plain Vanilla Swap

The most basic and common type of swap is a plain vanilla interest rate swap. In this type of swap, two parties agree to swap or exchange interest rate payments, one of which is fixed and one of which is floating. One counterparty agrees to make interest payments at a predetermined fixed rate of interest on a set amount of principal, referred to as notional principal. The other counterparty agrees to make interest payments based on a floating rate of interest calculated on the same notional principal amount. By using this plain-vanilla swap, a firm can transform a liability or an asset from a fixed interest rate instrument to a floating interest rate instrument.

In a plain vanilla swap, notional principal is not exchanged, nor are the interest payments. Rather, only the differences in the interest payments are exchanged. If ABC owes $10 million and XYZ owes $11 million, then XYZ would simply pay ABC the net of $1 million.

Floating rates were historically referenced to one of the LIBOR rates. LIBOR stands for London Interbank Offered Rate and was calculated as an average rate at which banks would offer to lend money to other banks. However, due to a change in bank behavior and the ease with which LIBOR can be manipulated, in 2018 the UK Financial Conduct authority decided to end the requirement that its panel banks participate in the interest rate submission process that forms LIBOR.

As a result, it is gradually being replaced as a reference rate. In July 2021 for example, U.S. inter-dealer brokers began using the secured overnight financing rate (SOFR) as a reference rate in swaps instead of LIBOR. In addition, the Federal Reserve Board has instructed banks to cease using LIBOR as a reference rate in new contracts by the end of 2021. For the moment, swaps may use LIBOR or SOFR as a reference rate for the floating leg. The floating rate leg of a swap might be equal to the reference rate chosen, or it might equal the reference rate plus or minus a spread to reflect counterparty risk.

Example 14.11

Assumptions:

- Fixed rate payer: Delta
- Fixed rate: 5%, annually
- Floating rate payer: Gamma
- Floating rate: 6-month LIBOR, paid annually
- Notional amount: $100 million
- Maturity: 3 years
- LIBOR rates at the start of years 1, 2, and 3: 5%, 5.5% and 4%

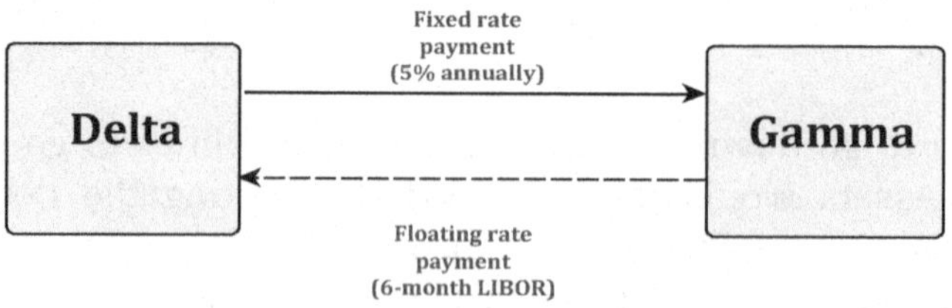

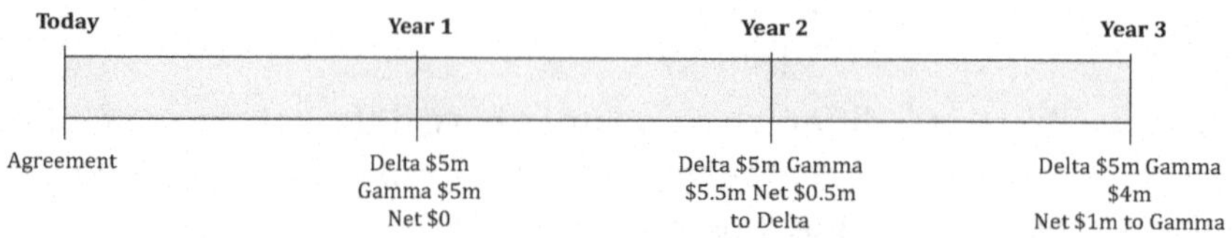

In this agreement, Delta will pay Gamma 5% of the notional amount each year. This amount equates to $5 million, or 5% of $100 million. Gamma will pay Delta the 6-month LIBOR rate times the notional amount. In a typical plain vanilla swap, payments at each settlement date are based on the reference rate at the start of the period. In this case the swap is using LIBOR, so the payment at the end of year 1 will be based on LIBOR at the start of year 1, which is 5%. Note that as a result the payment due at the first settlement date will be known at the inception of the swap. The schedule of payments over the life of the swap will be as below:

- Year 1 - The LIBOR rate is the same as the fixed rate. Therefore, there is no payment from either party.
- Year 2 - The LIBOR rate is 5.5%, which equates to a $5.5 million payment to Delta. However, the payments will net out and Gamma will simply pay the difference of $0.5 million.
- Year 3 - The LIBOR rate is 4%, which equates to a $4 million payment to Delta, which is less than the $5 million from Delta. Therefore Delta will pay the difference of $1 million.

Currency Swaps

Unlike interest rate swaps where the notional principal is never actually exchanged, currency swaps involve the exchange of principal and interest payments in one currency for principal and interest payments in another currency. At the inception of the swap the exchange rate between the two currencies will be identified and used to calculate the equivalent amount of principal in each currency that will be exchanged. At the expiry of the swap, those principal amounts will be swapped back. At each settlement date both parties will pay interest on the currency they received at the start of the swap, and receive interest on the currency they loaned out. These payments cannot be netted as they would be in an interest rate swap as they are made in different currencies. The interest rates in a currency swap may be fixed or floating. For example, both parties may pay a fixed rate, both may pay a floating rate or, as with an interest rate swap, one rate may be fixed and one floating.

Example 14.12

Michigan Ice Company (MIC) intends to expand its operations to Nuuk Greenland. MIC hopes to couple Greenland's clean water supply with its unique ice making machines to better compete with the U.S. domestic ice companies. MIC is aware that Greenland remains an autonomous country of the Kingdom of Denmark even though it has its own form of government.

Arctic Packaging Company (APC) is a Danish firm that intends to expand its operations to South Carolina. APC believes it can compete with U.S. packing companies because of a newly developed way to make shoe boxes.

Both firms need to borrow to finance their expansions and maintain a comparative advantage in their domestic credit markets. Both firms will use a currency swap to help in this process.

MIC can borrow in the U.S. at 6% while APV can borrow in Denmark at 8%. The current spot rate between the USD and the DKK is USD 0.1613/DKK. The notional principal of the swap is USD 10 million.

The currency swap is one of the only swap types in which the principal amounts are exchanged at the swap initiation and at its maturity date.

Before the swap is initiated:

- Michigan Ice obtains a credit line of USD 10 million at 6%.
- Arctic Packaging obtains a credit line of DKK 61,996,280 at 8%.

After the credit lines have been established, the two firms essentially agree to make each other's interest rate payments.

Michigan Ice will use the DKK 61,996,280 to expand into Greenland and then pay DKK 4,959,702 in annual interest payments.

Quick Quiz 14.4

1. In a fixed/floating interest rate swap, each party will make an interest payment to the other at every settlement date.
   a. True
   b. False
2. Interest rate swaps are often used to convert a fixed set of cash flows to a floating set of cash flows.
   a. True
   b. False
3. Currency swaps involve the counterparties exchanging principal amounts in each currency at the beginning and the end of the contract.
   a. True
   b. False

False, True, True.

Arctic Packaging will use the USD 10,000,000 to expand its operations into the U.S. and then pay USD 600,000 in annual interest payments.

At the end of the swap, the two firms will again swap principal amounts. Michigan Ice will repay the DKK 61,996,280, and Arctic Packaging will repay USD 10,000,000.

This Michigan Ice example is a simple fixed for fixed swap, but currency swaps can be much more complex. For example, the annual or semi-annual swap payments could be tied to the relative value of the currencies.

Other types of swaps include equity swaps, which can be fixed for floating or even floating for floating. In an equity swap, investors agree to exchange returns on equity securities or indexes for a fixed or floating interest rate payment based on a reference rate.

Example 14.13

Grace is a wealthy small business owner who inherits $20 million of equity in the Ranger Company (RC) from her grandmother who was an executive at RC for many years. The grandmother kindly asked Grace to hold on to the shares for at least five years. Grace is worried that her inheritance is not diversified and learns about equity swaps from her financial adviser. Grace becomes aware that she can keep ownership of her shares to honor her grandmother's wishes while simultaneously using an equity swap to diversify.

Grace decides to swap the fixed dividend payment she receives from her RC position for the returns on a broad equity index. The swap will be settled quarterly. Details of both positions are outlined below.

Grace currently owns 300,000 shares of RC which pays a fixed dividend of $2.50 per share. Her total quarterly dividend is $187,500.

Grace selects a notional amount on the swap of $5,000,000. Grace agrees to pay a fixed rate of 3.75% and receive the actual return on the index from one quarter to the next.

The net payments between Grace and the financial institution offering her the swap depends on the relative performance of the broad index. Net payments are shown in the table below with different possible returns to the index over the next four quarters:

	Quarter 1	Quarter 2	Quarter 3	Quarter 4
Possible Equity Index Return	6%	2%	12%	-4%
Fixed Payment	-$187,500	-$187,500	-$187,500	-$187,500
Floating Payment	+$300,000	+$100,000	+$600,000	-$200,000
Net Payment	+$112,500	-87,500	+$412,500	-$387,500

It should be obvious equity swaps are not appropriate for every investor. The net payments have high volatility, but they do serve to convert a fixed payment into a floating payment. There is no doubt the swap contract has exposed Grace to the equity market risks and that she has diversified her investment in RC. The extra variability in her returns plus the simple fact that if the index drops in value, she loses on both ends of the swap (last quarter) makes equity swaps only appropriate for those that completely understand the risks and are capable of bearing them.

SUMMARY

Summary of key points:

- A derivative is a financial security or asset whose value is derived from the value of an underlying security or asset (e.g., coffee, oil). While derivatives have the potential for large gains or losses, derivatives help provide for a complete market, allow for speculation, leveraging, hedging or reducing risk.
- A futures contract is a standardized agreement between two parties to buy or sell a specific commodity (e.g., coffee or lumber) or other asset in a specified quality at a future time, place, and unit price. Options contracts give the buyer the right (but not the obligation) to buy (call option) or sell (put option) the underlying security (e.g., Apple stock) for a specified price within a specified period of time. A forward contract is a legal agreement between two parties to buy or sell a specific asset at a specified future time, which is agreed to today. Forward contracts are not standardized or traded on exchanges. Rather, they are private agreements between two parties that are negotiated between the buyer and the seller.
- Futures exchanges have many advantages, including liquidity, transparency, access to account information, and financial safeguards. With the breadth of futures offerings, exchanges attract millions of participants, speculators, hedgers, and asset managers, as well as offering clearing house functions to ensure contract fulfillment.
- Futures contracts have specific terms, including contract size, value, tick size, price limits, and margin requirements.
- Both buyers and sellers must deposit funds with a broker when buying or selling futures contracts, known as margin requirements. The initial margin (also known as a performance bond) is the amount of money that must be put up by the buyer and seller of a contract to initiate the trade. The funds are held by the broker but earn interest while they are held. The purpose of the funds is to ensure that traders can meet their financial obligations for the contracts they have bought or sold.
- Hedging is one of the primary uses of derivatives and involves entering into a futures contract position that is the opposite position than is currently held. The purpose of hedging is to reduce risk from fluctuating commodity prices.
- 1256 type contracts are marked to market at the end of each year with defined gain and loss percentages.
- A swap is an over-the-counter agreement between two or more parties to exchange future sets of cash flows. There are interest rate swaps, currency swaps and equity swaps.

DISCUSSION QUESTIONS

SOLUTIONS to the discussion questions can be found exclusively within the chapter. Once you have completed an initial reading of the chapter, go back and highlight the answers to these questions.

1. What is a derivative?
2. Define a futures contract.
3. Define an option agreement.
4. Describe the impact of leverage on derivatives.
5. Describe a forward contract.
6. What are the benefits of futures exchanges?
7. Explain how price limits for futures contracts work.
8. Describe market orders and limit orders.
9. How is a futures contract value determined?
10. Explain a performance bond.
11. What is the process of mark-to-market?
12. Differentiate between long and short positions with a futures contract.
13. Describe a short hedge and a long hedge.
14. Describe 1256 contracts and their tax treatment.
15. What is a swap agreement?
16. Describe a plain vanilla swap.
17. Describe a currency swap.
18. Describe equity swaps.

MULTIPLE CHOICE

A sample of multiple choice problems is provided below. Additional multiple choice problems are available at money-education.com by accessing the Student Practice Portal.

1. Which of the following types of contracts are traded on exchanges in the United States?
    a. Executive contracts.
    b. Forward contracts.
    c. Spot contracts.
    d. Futures contracts.

2. An individual buyer and seller of lumber may enter into a customizable sales transaction that will occur nine months from today. This type of contract is typically called a:
    a. Buy/Sell agreement.
    b. Forward contract.
    c. Lumber contract.
    d. Sales contract.

3. Liquidity can be defined as the ability to transact quickly and efficiently without a substantial impact to the price of the underlying asset. Which of the following transactions is the LEAST liquid?
    a. Buying or selling an exchange-traded fund (ETF).
    b. Buying or selling an E-mini S&P 500 futures contract.
    c. Buying or selling a car.
    d. Buying or selling a house.

4. Futures trading in the U.S. is regulated by:
    a. The Securities and Exchange Commission (SEC).
    b. The Federal Reserve (FED).
    c. The Commodity Futures Trading Commission (CFTC).
    d. The U.S. Trade and Tariff Board (UTTB).

5. Which of the following factors are important when selecting a futures contract to trade?
    a. Volatility.
    b. Contract size (dollar value of the contract).
    c. Liquidity.
    d. All of the above.

QUICK QUIZ EXPLANATIONS

Quick Quiz 14.1

1. False. The value of a derivative is directly related to the value of the underlying security.
2. True.
3. True.

Quick Quiz 14.2

1. True.
2. True.
3. True.

Quick Quiz 14.3

1. False. He should enter into a short hedge, which involves selling a futures contract. Selling a futures contract is equivalent to an agreement to sell the corn in the future.
2. True.
3. False. In reality, very few futures contracts are settled through delivery.

Quick Quiz 14.4

1. False. Only the difference in the interest payments is paid by one party to the other party of the agreement.
2. True.
3. True.

15

DERIVATIVES SECURITIES: OPTION CONTRACTS

LEARNING OBJECTIVES

1. Know that options are derivative instruments.*
2. Discuss the difference between a buyer (holder) of an option and a seller (writer) of an option.*
3. Identify the four basic option positions.*
4. Describe how options can be used for speculating or hedging.*
5. Identify how to determine option profitability, protective calls, and collars.*
6. Differentiate among stock options, stock index options, interest rate options, and currency options.*
7. Describe an option premium. *
8. Describe a strike price.*
9. Describe the phrase "in the money."*
10. Explain intrinsic value.*
11. Describe time value as it relates to options.*
12. Explain covered and naked options.*
13. Discuss the difference between American and European options.*
14. Identify the difference between a market order and a limit order.*
15. Know that most options are short (9 months) but LEAPs may be up to three years.*
16. Describe the different option strategies such as straddles, strangles, strips and straps.*
17. Discuss the characteristics of a warrant.*
18. Discuss how to value options, the binomial option pricing model, and the Black-Scholes model.*
19. Describe the nature of the put-call parity model.*

**Ties to CFP Certification Learning Objectives*

INTRODUCTION

"Keep your options open" is an expression that implies there is value in having choices. Financial options are derivative securities that derive their value from an underlying security. Options, like other derivatives, are bought and sold by investors. The buyer of the option has the right to do something. The seller of the option is obligated to do something. There are two types of options: calls and puts.

1. **Call options** - Gives the owner the right, but not the obligation to purchase the underlying security at a predetermined price over a specified period of time.
2. **Put options** - Gives the owner the right, but not the obligation to sell the underlying security at a predetermined price over a specified period of time.

Key Concepts

1. Describe the rights and obligations for buyers and sellers of option contracts.
2. Differentiate between a call option and a put option.
3. Explain the reasons that an investor or speculator might enter into an option contract.

Example 15.1

Jordan is interested in owning Peach Hardware (PH) common stock because she expects a substantial price increase over the next few months. Jordan has two choices to gain ownership of the shares: She can buy the shares, or she can buy a call option on the shares.

The shares are priced at $100 per share and a call option that gives her the right but not the obligation to buy the shares at $100 sells for $2. To buy the shares, Jordan needs to invest $100, but to buy the option, all she needs is $2.

To illustrate the difference between the two choices, suppose that after a few months when the option expires, PH trades at $145. If Jordan bought the shares at $100 and then sold them at $145, she would have made $45 as a capital gain. If Jordan had instead bought the call option, she would be able to exercise her right to buy at $100. Jordan could buy PH for $100 and then immediately sell the shares for $145. Her profit would be $45 minus the $2 she spent on the option or $43. The stock purchase required an initial investment of $100 to generate a profit of $45, while the call purchase required an initial investment of only $2 to generate a profit of $43. The return on Jordan's stock investment is 45% while her return on the option investment is an astonishing 21,500%. This outcome demonstrates the benefit of leverage.

Suppose, on the other hand, that PH trades at $72 when the option expires. If Jordan bought the shares at $100 and then sold them for $72, she would have lost $28. If Jordan had bought the call option instead, she would allow the option to expire and the loss in the options market would be her total initial investment of $2. The return on Jordan's stock investment is -28% while her return on the option investment is a -100%. This outcome demonstrates the downside of leverage.

In both cases, whether Jordan owned the shares or the option, she benefited when the price of PH rose and suffered when the price of PH fell. Note that if she purchased the option, the share price has to rise by $2 to cover the purchase price before she starts to make gains.

There are many reasons to purchase or sell options. All derivatives help to create a more complete financial market. Option contracts frequently offer a way to obtain exposure or limit exposure to an underlying asset that either cannot be constructed with long or short positions in the asset or cannot be economically implemented. There are many strategies that can be used with options alone or in conjunction with other positions. However, the primary motivations for using options are as follows:

- Options offer a cost-efficient way to speculate on price movements of underlying assets.
- Options help to hedge or reduce risk exposure of other investments or portfolios.
- Options can be used to reduce transaction costs.
- Options can be used to reduce or delay the tax exposure of an underlying asset.

Quick Quiz 15.1

1. If Morgan purchased a put option on XYZ stock with an exercise price of $100, she might exercise that option if the stock price exceeds $100.
   a. True
   b. False
2. Options can be used to reduce risk.
   a. True
   b. False

False, True.

OPTION TERMINOLOGY

There are a significant number of terms that are important to understand when studying option contracts. Many of these terms are defined within this section and should help in understanding option positions, strategies, and valuation.

Key Concepts

1. Compare American and European options.
2. Categorize options as in-the-money, at-the-money, or out-of-the-money.
3. Separate the value of an option into its intrinsic value and its time value.

American vs European Options - The terms American option and European option refer to when the option can be exercised. American options can be exercised anytime up until the point of expiration. European options can only be exercised at expiration. The added flexibility of the American option means that it will be priced equal to, or possibly higher than, an otherwise identical European option. Most options traded in the markets are American options. However, European options are somewhat easier to analyze and are available from financial services firms.

At-the-money - An option is at-the-money when its exercise price equals the market price for the underlying security for both calls and puts. Note that this term is not referring to the buyer or seller, but rather to the option contract.

Buyer - The buyer, or holder, of an option contract purchases the right to buy (call option) or sell (put option) the underlying security from or to the writer of the contract. The buyer pays the premium to the writer (seller). The buyer takes a long position in the option contract while the seller (writer) takes a short position.

Exercise - Options provide the holder or buyer with the right to buy or sell the underlying security at the strike price (exercise price). Exercising the option means compelling the seller of the contract to sell the underlying security for a call option or to buy the underlying security for a put option.

Expiration - The point in time at which the buyer's rights under the call or put contract terminate.

In-the-money - A call option is in-the-money when its exercise price is below the market price for the underlying security. A put option that is in-the-money has an exercise price that is above the market price for the underlying security. Note that this term is not referring to the buyer or seller, but rather to the option contract.

Intrinsic value - The intrinsic value of an option is the minimum price at which an option will trade. It equals the difference between the current underlying asset price and the exercise price. The total value of the option consists of two parts: the intrinsic value plus the time value of the option. The intrinsic value can never be less than zero. The intrinsic value of a call option equals the stock price minus the strike price, but no less than zero. The intrinsic value of a put option equals the exercise price minus the stock price, but no less than zero.

Moneyness - A term that is used to describe the relationship between the strike price of an option and the current trading price for the underlying security. The three terms that are part of moneyness are in-the-money, at-the-money, and out-of-the-money.

Offsetting order - An offsetting order is one that an investor uses to effectively close out an option position. For the holder (buyer) of an option, an offsetting order will write (sell) the same call or put option. For the writer (seller) of an option, an offsetting order must buy the same call or put option.

Option contract - A standard option contract represents 100 shares but is quoted on a per share basis.

Out-of-the-money - A call option that is out-of-the-money has an exercise price that is above the market price for the underlying security. A put option that is out-of-the-money has an exercise price that is below the market price for the underlying security. Note that this term is not referring to the buyer or seller, but rather to the option contract.

Payoff - The positive difference between the strike price and the underlying security price upon exercise of the option. Calculated as (S - X) for a call option and (X - S) for a put option. Zero if the option is not exercised. Note that the calculation of the payoff excludes the premium paid or received.

Premium - The cost of the option. The premium is the amount of money that must be paid by the buyer to the seller of the option contract for the right to buy or sell the underlying security. The premium consists of the intrinsic value plus the time value of the option.

Quick Quiz 15.2

1. European options can only be exercised at expiration.
   a. True
   b. False
2. A put option is in-the-money if the stock price is below the strike (exercise) price.
   a. True
   b. False
3. Assume a call option has a strike price of $100 and the underlying stock price is $108. If the time value of the option is $4, then the option should be priced at $10.
   a. True
   b. False

True, True, False.

Profit (or loss) - An investor's total gain or loss on their option position including the payoff and premium paid or received.

Strike price - Also known as the exercise price. The strike price is the price at which the option holder (buyer) can exercise the option. For a call option, the strike price represents the price at which the buyer can purchase the underlying security. For a put option, it represents the price at which the buyer can sell the underlying security.

Time value - The time value equals the difference between the market value of the option contract and its intrinsic value.

Writer - The writer, also known as the seller, of an option contract is obligated to either sell (call option) the underlying security at the specified price in the contract or buy (put option) the underlying security at the specified price in the contract. The writer receives the premium for this obligation and has a short position in the contract.

OPTION POSITIONS

There are two sides to each call and put option contract, the buyer or owner of the contract and the seller or writer of the contract. The buyer of the option has a long position in the option, and the seller has a short position. Therefore there are four basic option positions:

1. Long call
2. Long put
3. Short call
4. Short put

Key Concepts

1. Summarize the motivation for buying or selling a call option or a put option.
2. Explain the profit and loss potential for each of the four option contract positions.
3. Identify the option position(s) with unlimited loss potential.

It is important to realize that gains from one position are losses to the other side of an option contract. Because of this relationship, options are considered a zero-sum game. A **zero-sum game** is an economic situation in which the sum of the gains and losses from all contracts total zero. The exhibit below summarizes the primary motivations an investor might have for entering into each of the four option positions.

Exhibit 15.1 | Motivations for the Four Option Positions

	Call	Put
Long (Buy)	An investor purchases a call option in hopes that the stock will increase in value. Generally done to participate in the upward move of a security.	A put is generally purchased in expectation of a downward move in the underlying price of the security. In addition, puts are often purchased to provide downside protection for currently held long positions in the underlying security.
Short (Sell)	Sellers of options are motivated by the income that is generated from the premium and will often reinvest that income as a hedge against unfavorable price movements of the underlying asset. A call option is often written on a stock that has recently hit a new high and is not expected to continue to rise in price. The investor hopes that the stock price will remain steady or decline. If the stock rises, then the seller may be required to deliver the stock to the option buyer. The seller would receive the exercise price as the sales price in addition to the premium for writing the option.	Sellers of options are motivated by the income that is generated from the premium and will often reinvest that income as a hedge against unfavorable price movements of the underlying asset. Puts are often written on stocks that have recently made new lows in price. The investor hopes that the stock price will rise. However, if the stock declines, the stock may be "put" to the seller of the option. The seller will have to buy the stock at the exercise price but will also receive the premium for writing the option.

Exhibit 15.2 illustrates the profit or loss for the four option positions, including when the options are in-the-money, at-the-money, and out-of-the-money.

Exhibit 15.2 | Profit & Loss Diagrams

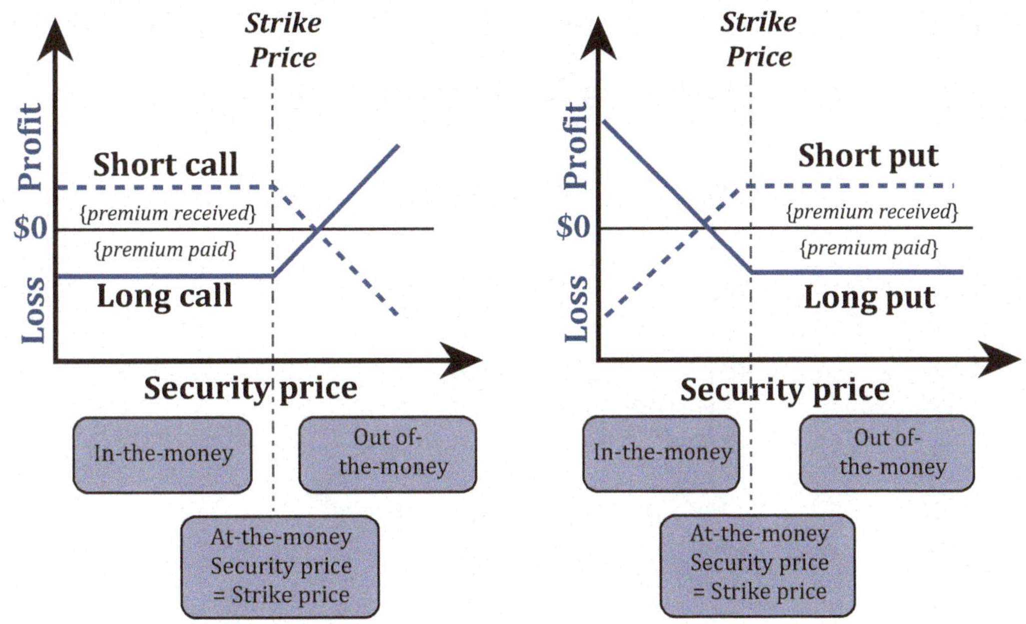

Exhibit 15.3 summarizes the profit and loss for each of the four option positions. Notice that the profit or loss for opposite positions are equal. This outcome should be the case since options are a zero-sum game.

Exhibit 15.3 | Option Contract Profit and Loss Summary Chart

Contract Position	Maximum Gain	Maximum Loss
Buy a call option (long call)	Unlimited (**S** minus **X** minus **P**)	Premium
Sell a call option (short call)	Premium	Unlimited (**S** minus **X** minus **P**)
Buy a put option (long put)	Limited (**X** minus **P**)	Premium
Sell a put option (short put)	Premium	Limited (**X** minus **P**)

Where:

- S - price of underlying security
- X - exercise or strike price of the option
- P - premium

Long Call

Investors purchase call options to participate in the upward movement of an underlying security. Call options give the holder (buyer) the right (but not the obligation) to purchase the underlying security for a specified price within a specified period of time. For that right, the buyer must pay a premium.

Consider the following graph of the profit and loss for a long call option (the purchase of a call option).

Exhibit 15.4 | Long Call Option Profit and Loss

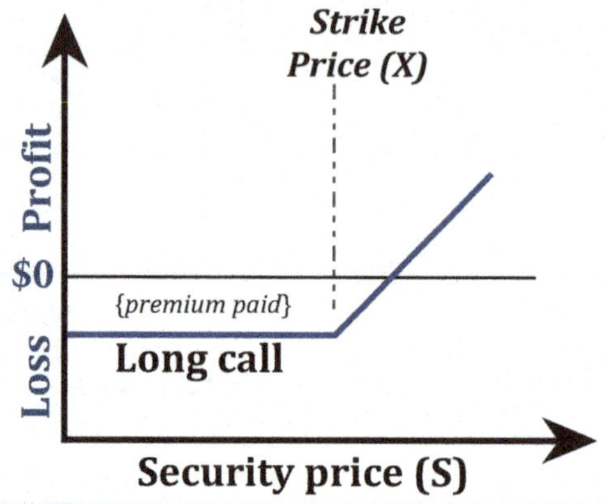

The profit or loss on a long call position is calculated using the payoff and the premium paid.

The payoff will be positive for the option holder if the option is exercised. This will occur for a call option when the price of the underlying security is higher than the strike price. In this case the holder has the right to buy the security at the lower strike price and could sell it immediately at the higher market price. The payoff is therefore equal to the underlying price (S) less the strike price (X).

If the underlying security price is lower than the strike price, exercising a call option would result in a negative payoff. The holder will avoid this by simply allowing the option to lapse. In this case the payoff is zero.

The payoff on a call option is therefore the greater of zero or (S -X).

The profit or loss on a long call position is calculated by deducting the premium the long had to pay to purchase the option from the positive payoff.

Profit or loss = Payoff – Premium

Exhibit 15.4 illustrates the profit or loss at various prices for the underlying security.

When the underlying security is priced below the strike price (X), the option is allowed to lapse. The payoff is zero, and the loss to the long is the premium paid.

When the underlying security is priced above the strike price (X), the option is exercised. The payoff to the long is (S – X) and the profit or loss is the payoff less the premium paid. Note that until the payoff is large enough to cover the premium paid, the long will still take an overall loss. This is reflected in the diagram where the profit line is upward sloping, but still below the horizontal $0 profit axis.

The line crosses the axis at the **breakeven price**. This is the price at which the long makes zero profit, i.e., breaks even. For the long call, this is the strike price (X) plus the premium. At this point the positive payoff is just enough to offset the premium paid.

Maximum Gain

Once the underlying security price moves above the strike price, the long call makes a profit or loss of (S – X – P). As the underlying security price (S) can keep increasing without any upper limit, the maximum gain for the long call position is unlimited.

Maximum Loss

The maximum loss to a long option position is always equal to the premium. This is because the long will never exercise an option that would lead to a negative payoff. When the option is out-of-the-money, the long simply allows the option to lapse and loses the premium.

Example 15.2

Donald buys a call option with a strike price of $50 and a premium of $10. The chart below illustrates graphically and numerically the gain or loss based on purchasing the call option depending on the stock price at or before expiration.

Call Options

Call options - Give the holder (buyer) the right (but not the obligation) to purchase the underlying security for a specified price within a specified period of time.

Option cost per share	$10
Strike price	$50
Break even stock price	$60

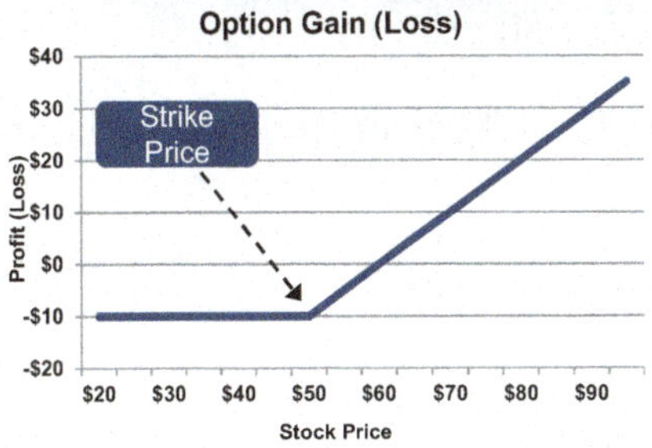

Stock Price	Intrinsic Value	Option Gain (Loss)
$20	$0	-$10
$25	$0	-$10
$30	$0	-$10
$35	$0	-$10
$40	$0	-$10
$45	$0	-$10
$50	$0	-$10
$55	$5	-$5
$60	$10	$0
$65	$15	$5
$70	$20	$10
$75	$25	$15
$80	$30	$20
$85	$35	$25
$90	$40	$30
$95	$45	$35

If the stock remains below $50, the strike price, then Donald will not exercise the option and he will lose $10, the premium he paid. However, if the stock increases above $50, then he breaks even at $60 (the gain of S-X-P = 60 - 50 - 10 = 0) and has a gain above $60. The breakeven price of $60 equals the exercise price plus the premium (X+P). At a stock price of $90, he will have a gain of $30. This is calculated as S-X-P, which equals $90-$50-$10=$30.

It is worth noting how the long call compares with the purchase of the underlying security as they have similar gain potential but different loss potential.

Example 15.3

Consider the facts in the prior example as illustrated below.

Long Call vs. Long Stock

The long call and the long stock have similar profit profiles, but different loss profiles. The gap between the gain lines equals the premium for the option.

Price at which stock is purchased	$50
Option cost per share	$10
Strike price	$50
Break even stock price	$60

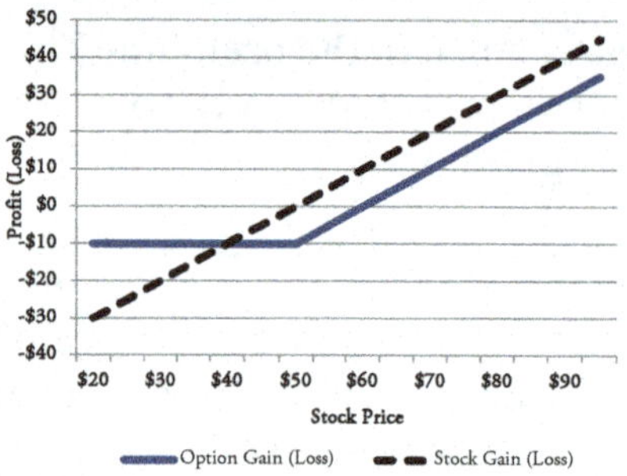

Stock Price	Stock Gain (Loss)	Intrinsic Value	Option Gain (Loss)
$20	-$30	$0	-$10
$25	-$25	$0	-$10
$30	-$20	$0	-$10
$35	-$15	$0	-$10
$40	-$10	$0	-$10
$45	-$5	$0	-$10
$50	$0	$0	-$10
$55	$5	$5	-$5
$60	$10	$10	$0
$65	$15	$15	$5
$70	$20	$20	$10
$75	$25	$25	$15
$80	$30	$30	$20
$85	$35	$35	$25
$90	$40	$40	$30
$95	$45	$45	$35

Notice that the gain from the long stock and the long call are similar. The difference is due to the premium paid for the call option. The loss for the option is limited to the premium paid, while the loss on the long stock could be as much as the price at which the stock was purchased in the event that the stock price were to fall to zero.

Short Call

Investors often write or sell call options to generate premium income on securities that they believe are fully valued or overvalued and are not expected to increase in price. Consider the following graph of the profit and loss for a short call option (the sale of a call option).

Exhibit 15.5 | Short Call Option Profit and Loss

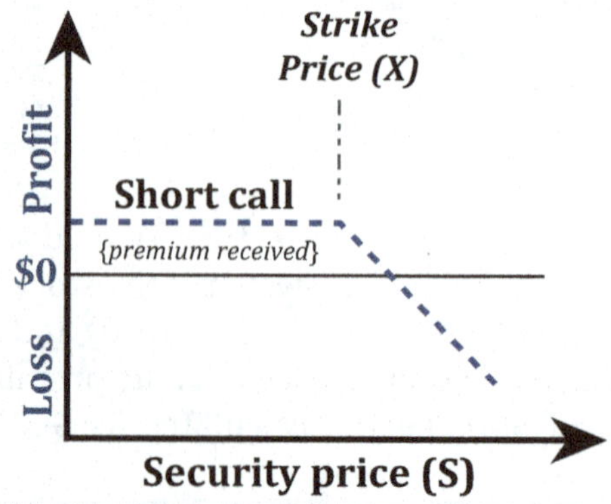

The profit or loss on a short call position is calculated by using the premium received and the payoff.

The payoff will be positive for the option holder if the option is exercised. This will occur for a call option when the price of the underlying security is higher than the strike price. In this case the holder has the right to buy the security at the lower strike price and could sell it immediately at the higher market price. The payoff is therefore equal to the underlying price (S) less the strike price (X).

If the underlying security price is lower than the strike price, exercising a call option would result in a negative payoff. The holder will avoid this by simply allowing the option to lapse. In this case the payoff is zero.

The payoff on a call option is therefore the greater of zero or (S -X).

The profit or loss on a short call position is calculated by deducting the payoff from the premium the short received for writing the option.

Profit or Loss = Premium - Payoff

Exhibit 15.5 illustrates the profit or loss at various prices for the underlying security.

When the underlying security is priced below the strike price (X), the option is allowed to lapse. The payoff is zero, and the profit to the short is the premium received.

When the underlying security is priced above the strike price (X), the option is exercised. The payoff to the long is (S – X) and this reduces the short's profit. Note that until the payoff is large enough to wipe out the premium received, the short will still make an overall profit. This is reflected in the diagram where the profit line is downward sloping, but still above the horizontal $0 profit axis.

The line crosses the axis at the breakeven price. This is the price at which the short makes zero profit, i.e., breaks even. For the short call, this is the strike price (X) plus the premium. At this point the payoff is just enough to offset the premium received. Note that the breakeven price is identical for the short and the long call positions.

Maximum Gain

The maximum gain to a short option position is always equal to the premium. This is because the long will never exercise an option that would lead to a negative payoff. When the option is out-of-the-money, the long allows the option to lapse and the short simply pockets the premium.

Maximum Loss

Once the underlying security price moves above the strike price, the option is exercised by the long and the short makes a profit or loss of (P – (S – X)). As the underlying security price (S) can keep increasing without any upper limit, the maximum loss for the short call position is unlimited.

Example 15.4

Assume Carly sells a call option for a $10 premium with a strike price of $50. The best outcome for Carly is that the option is not exercised and she keeps the premium of $10. However, assume that the underlying stock increases to $90 and the buyer exercises. In this case, she makes $10 less the difference between the stock price and the exercise price, which equals $40 ($90 - $50). The difference equates to a loss of $30. Notice that this is the opposite result from a long call, as it is from the seller's perspective.

Long Put

A put is generally purchased in expectation of a downward move in the underlying price of the security. However, puts are also purchased to provide downside protection for long positions. Consider the following graph of the profit and loss for a long put option (the purchase of a put option).

Exhibit 15.6 | Long Put Option Profit and Loss

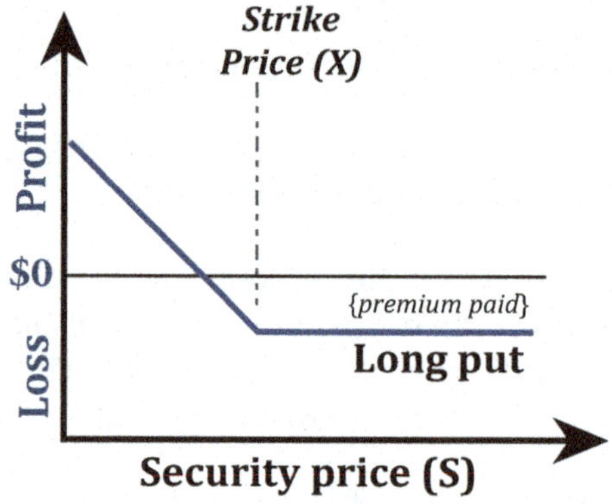

The profit or loss on a long put position is calculated using the payoff and the premium paid.

The payoff will be positive for the option holder if the option is exercised. This will occur for a put option when the price of the underlying security is lower than the strike price. In this case the holder has the right to sell the underlying security at the strike price which is higher than the market price. The payoff is therefore equal to the strike price (X) less the underlying price (S).

If the underlying security price is higher than the strike price, exercising a put option would result in a negative payoff. The holder will avoid this by simply allowing the option to lapse. In this case the payoff is zero.

The payoff on a put option is therefore the greater of zero or (X - S).

The profit or loss on a long put position is calculated by deducting the premium the long had to pay to purchase the option from the positive payoff.

Profit or Loss = Payoff – Premium

Exhibit 15.6 illustrates the profit or loss at various prices for the underlying security.

When the underlying security is priced above the strike price (X), the option is allowed to lapse. The payoff is zero, and the loss to the long is the premium paid.

When the underlying security is priced below the strike price (X), the option is exercised. The payoff to the long is (X - S) and the profit or loss is the payoff less the premium paid. Note that until the payoff is large enough to cover the premium paid, the long will still take an overall loss. This is reflected in the diagram where the profit line is upward sloping, but still below the horizontal $0 profit axis.

The line crosses the axis at the breakeven price. This is the price at which the long makes zero profit, i.e., breaks even. For the long put, this is the strike price (X) minus the premium. At this point the positive payoff is just enough to offset the premium paid.

Maximum Gain

Once the underlying security price moves below the strike price, the long put makes a profit or loss of (X - S – P). The maximum gain is limited by the fact that the underlying security has a minimum price of zero, at which point the gain is (X – P).

Maximum Loss

The maximum loss to a long option position is always equal to the premium. This is because the long will never exercise an option that would lead to a negative payoff. When the option is out-of-the-money, the long simply allows the option to lapse and loses the premium.

Example 15.5

Darby buys a put option with a strike price of $50 and a premium of $10. The chart below illustrates graphically and numerically the gain or loss based on purchasing the put option.

Put Options

Put options - Give the holder (buyer) the right (but not the obligation) to sell the underlying security for a specified price within a specified period of time.

Option cost per share	$10
Strike price	$50
Break even stock price	$60

Option Gain (Loss)

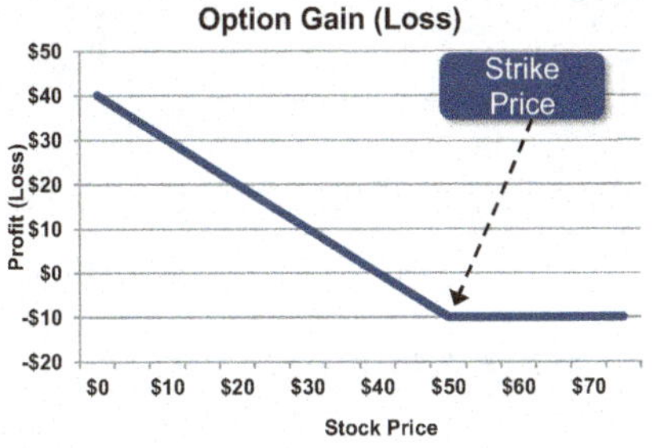

Stock Price	Intrinsic Value	Option Gain (Loss)
$0	$50	$40
$5	$45	$35
$10	$40	$30
$15	$35	$25
$20	$30	$20
$25	$25	$15
$30	$20	$10
$35	$15	$5
$40	$10	$0
$45	$5	-$5
$50	$0	-$10
$55	$0	-$10
$60	$0	-$10
$65	$0	-$10
$70	$0	-$10
$75	$0	-$10

If the stock remains above the strike price of $50, then Darby will not exercise the option and he will lose $10, which is the premium paid for the option. However, if the stock declines below $50, then he breaks even at $40 (X-S-P) and has a gain below $40. The breakeven point equals the exercise price minus the premium (X-P). At a stock price of $30, he will have a gain of $10. This is calculated as X-S-P, which equals $50-$30-$10. At a stock price of $0, Darby will have his maximum gain of $40.

Short Put

Puts are often written on stocks that have recently made new lows in price in an attempt to generate premium income. The investor hopes that the stock price will rise. However, if the stock declines, the stock may be "put" to the seller of the option. The seller will have to buy the stock at the exercise price, but will also receive the premium for writing the put option. Consider the following graph of the profit and loss for a short put option (the sale of a put option).

Exhibit 15.7 | Short Put Option Profit and Loss

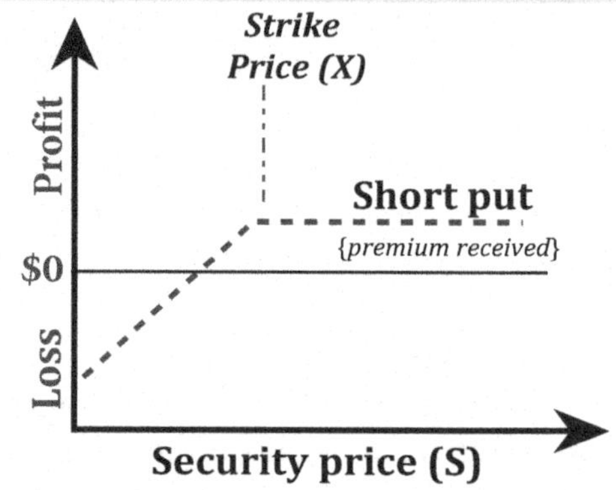

The profit or loss on a short put position is calculated by using the premium received and the payoff.

The payoff will be positive for the option holder if the option is exercised. This will occur for a put option when the price of the underlying security is lower than the strike price. In this case the holder has the right to sell the underlying security at the strike price which is higher than the market price. The payoff is therefore equal to the strike price (X) less the underlying price (S).

If the underlying security price is higher than the strike price, exercising a put option would result in a negative payoff. The holder will avoid this by simply allowing the option to lapse. In this case the payoff is zero.

The payoff on a call option is therefore the greater of zero or (S -X).

The profit or loss on a short put position is calculated by deducting the payoff from the premium the short received for writing the option.

Profit or Loss = Premium - Payoff

Exhibit 15.7 illustrates the profit or loss at various prices for the underlying security.

When the underlying security is priced above the strike price (X), the option is allowed to lapse. The payoff is zero, and the profit to the short is the premium received.

When the underlying security is priced below the strike price (X), the option is exercised. The payoff to the long is (X - S) and this reduces the short's profit. Note that until the payoff is large enough to wipe out the premium received, the short will still make an overall profit. This is reflected in the diagram where the profit line is downward sloping, but still above the horizontal $0 profit axis.

The line crosses the axis at the breakeven price. This is the price at which the short makes zero profit, i.e., breaks even. For the short put, this is the strike price (X) minus the premium. At this point the payoff is just enough to offset the premium received. Note that the breakeven price is identical for the short and the long put positions.

Maximum Gain

The maximum gain to a short option position is always equal to the premium. This is because the long will never exercise an option that would lead to a negative payoff. When the option is out-of-the-money, the long allows the option to lapse and the short simply pockets the premium.

Maximum Loss

Once the underlying security price moves below the strike price, the option is exercised by the long and the short makes a profit or loss of (P – (X - S)). The maximum loss is limited by the fact that the underlying security has a minimum price of zero, at which point the loss is (X – P).

Quick Quiz 15.3

1. The value of an American option should be less than that of an European option.
   a. True
   b. False
2. An investor who expects the price of IBM to increase might purchase a call option in lieu of buying the stock.
   a. True
   b. False
3. If Rob has 1,000 shares of Amazon and is concerned about the stock dropping in price, then he might try to protect his position by purchasing ten put option contracts.
   a. True
   b. False

False, True, True.

Example 15.6

Assume Fiona sells a put option for a $10 premium with a strike price of $50. The best outcome for Fiona is that the option is not exercised and she keeps the premium of $10. However, assume that the underlying stock decreases to $30 and the buyer exercises. In this case, she makes $10 less the difference between the exercise price and the stock price, which equals $20 ($50-$30). This difference equals a loss of $10. Notice that this is the opposite result from a long put as it is from the seller's perspective. Fiona will incur the maximum loss if the stock goes to zero.

Option Moneyness and Intrinsic Value

The term moneyness is a concept used to describe the relationship between the strike price of an option and the current trading price for the underlying security. The three terms associated with moneyness are in-the-money, at-the-money, and out-of-the-money.

In-the-money describes an option that has a positive intrinsic value. A call option that is in-the-money has an exercise price that is below the market price for the underlying security. A put option that is in-the-money has an exercise price that is above the market price for the underlying security. Note that this term is not referring to the buyer or seller, but rather to the option contract.

At-the-money describes an option with an exercise price equal to the market price. As a result, it has zero intrinsic value.

Out-of-the-money refers to a call option contract that has an exercise price that is above the market price for the underlying security. A put option that is out-of-the-money has an exercise price that is below the market price for the underlying security. In both cases the option has zero intrinsic value. Note that this term is not referring to the buyer or seller, but rather to the option contract.

Exhibit 15.8 | Moneyness of Call Options and Put Options

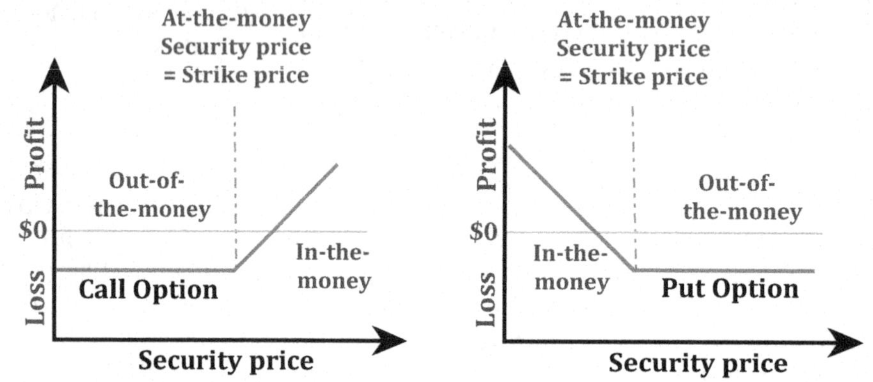

Exhibit 15.8 shows how the moneyness of call and put options changes with the underlying security price. Note that a call option moves from out-of-the-money to in-the-money as the underlying security price rises, whereas a put option moves from out-of-the-money to in-the-money as the underlying security price falls.

Intrinsic value - The intrinsic value of an option is the minimum price that an option will trade at. For a call option it is calculated as the greater of the underlying security price less the strike price, or zero. So intrinsic value will be positive when the call option is in-the-money, and zero otherwise.

For a put option the intrinsic value is calculated as the greater of the strike price less the underlying security price, or zero. Again, it is positive when the option is in-the-money and negative otherwise.

The total value of an option is made up of its intrinsic value and its time value. The time value results from the time the option has left to expiry. The longer the time until expiry, the longer the option has to move into the money, and the higher the time value.

Quick Quiz 15.4

1. If Sally owns 100 shares of Apple and believes that the stock is overvalued, then a good strategy to generate additional income would be to sell a put option on Apple.
   a. True
   b. False
2. Assume Seth buys a call option on Nike for $5, when the stock is trading at $55. The option has a strike price of $60. Based on this, the intrinsic value for the option equals $5.
   a. True
   b. False

False, False.

Example 15.7

Henrietta buys an ABC call option with a strike price of $20 when ABC stock is trading in the market at $17. She buys the option as an out-of-the-money option with an intrinsic value of zero. If the market price were to increase above $20, then the option would be in-the-money. At $23, the option is in-the-money with an intrinsic value of $3.

Example 15.8

Kareem buys an XYZ put option with a strike price of $50 when XYZ stock is trading in the market at $65. He buys the option as an out-of-the-money option with an intrinsic value of zero. If the market price were to decrease below the strike price of $50, then the option would be in-the-money. At $47, the option is in-the-money with an intrinsic value of $3.

TRADING OPTION CONTRACTS

Each option contract specifies the type of option (call or put), the strike price, the expiration date, as well as the underlying security. Option contracts are standardized, which has helped promote liquidity in the options market. Markets that are liquid allow for efficient trading.

A standard option contract represents 100 shares of an underlying stock and provides the buyer with the right to buy or sell the stock at the predetermined price within the contract.

Class of options - A group of option contracts with the same type (call or put), same style (American or European), that cover the same underlying security. For example, all American call options for Apple, Inc. are a class of options. All American put options for Apple, Inc. are another class of options.

Key Concepts

1. Know how many shares an option contract represents.
2. Differentiate between a class of options and an option series.
3. Recall the two types of opening orders and the two types of closing orders.
4. Compare market orders with limit orders.

Option series - A group of options that are part of the same option class and that have the same strike price and same expiration date. For example, all Apple, Inc. May 180 calls represent an option series. All Apple, Inc. May 200 calls represent another options series.

Option Orders

There are four types of option orders.

1. Buy to open
2. Sell to open
3. Buy to close
4. Sell to close

The first two are opening positions while the second two are closing positions. Options must be opened and either closed with a buy to close order or a sell to close order or they simply expire.

Opening Orders

Opening orders (buy to open or sell to open) are used when a trader wants to purchase (long) or sell (short) either a call option or a put option. These opening orders establish an initial position for the trader. Opening orders include buy to open or sell to open orders.

- **Buy to open** is used when a trader wants to buy (purchase) either a call option or a put option.
- **Sell to open** is used when a trader wants to sell (write) either a call option or a put option.

As discussed, the buyer maintains the rights, while the seller receives the premium. The buyer might exercise the option, but might also want to close their position.

Closing Orders

Closing orders are used to exit an option position and include buy to close or sell to close orders.

- **Buy to close** is used when a trader wants to close a previously opened short position. The trader is effectively buying back an option that was previously sold.
- **Sell to close** is used when a trader wants to close a previously opened long position. The trader is effectively selling an option that was previously bought.

Closing orders are simply the opposite of opening orders. For example, if the opening order were a long call option, then the closing position would be a short call option. This type of order is a sell to close order.

Quick Quiz 15.5

1. If Reese buys 25 call options on XYZ with a strike price of $45, then she has purchased the right to buy 2,500 shares of XYZ at $45.
   a. True
   b. False
2. All XYZ June 110 calls and all XYZ July 110 calls are part of the same option series.
   a. True
   b. False
3. If Jay sold a put option, then he could close the position by buying a call option.
   a. True
   b. False
4. Assume that ABC's stock price has been increasing this morning and that Andrew wants to place the fastest type of order to be filled. In this case, he should place a market order.
   a. True
   b. False

True, False, False, True.

Example 15.9

Jovi buys a 3-month call option on XYZ Company for a premium of $3.00. The option has a strike price of $20 and the underlying security is trading at $20. Since the security price and the strike price are equal, the option is at-the-money and the intrinsic value is zero. Since the premium is $3 and the intrinsic value is $0, the time value must equal $3. Assume the stock increases later that same day to $22. If Jovi were to exercise the option, he would only receive the intrinsic value, which would now equal $2 ($22 minus $20). Therefore, in this case, a better alternative is to enter a closing order by selling the option, which will allow him to recognize both the current intrinsic value and the current time value.

Exhibit 15.9 | Summary of Option Orders

Buy to Open A trader wants to buy (purchase) either a call option or a put option.	**Sell to Open** A trader wants to sell (write) either a call option or a put option.
Sell to Close A trader wants to close a previously opened long position. The trader is effectively selling an option that was previously bought.	**Buy to Close** A trader wants to close a previously opened short position. The trader is effectively buying back an option that was previously sold.

Market Orders and Limit Orders

Options can be traded using market orders or limit orders, which were discussed in Chapter 9. **Market orders** are filled by the broker at the next available price in the market. Market orders are almost always filled, but there is no control over the price at which the order is filled.

Limit orders indicate to the broker that the buy or sell order must be filled only at a specific price. Limit orders may or may not be filled, depending on the limit order price relative to the market price. In addition, the limit order must specify the time period over which the broker is instructed to fill the order. This time period might be a day, a week, a month, or the order might be placed as "good 'til cancel." A good 'till canceled order will remain open until it is filled or until the trader cancels the order.

Exhibit 15.10 | Option Quotes

Apple Option Quotes
(Quotes as of 08/26/21 - Market price of AAPL $148.50)

The cost of call options decreases as the strike price increases. This reflects the lower intrinsic value (S-X).

Type	Strike Price	Expiry	Last	Bid	Ask	Volume	Open Interest	Implied Volatility
Calls	140	Oct 1 2021	10.15	9.95	10.05	19	179	26.55%
Calls	145	Oct 1 2021	6.25	6.20	6.25	54	1779	23.87%
Calls	150	Oct 1 2021	3.35	3.25	3.30	776	4905	21.75%
Calls	140	Dec 17 2021	13.39	13.35	13.50	74	18451	27.25%
Calls	145	Dec 17 2021	10.35	10.20	10.30	158	11736	26.22%
Calls	150	Dec 17 2021	7.65	7.55	7.60	507	27827	25.39%
Puts	140	Oct 1 2021	1.56	1.46	1.49	42	1634	24.67%
Puts	145	Oct 1 2021	2.82	2.67	2.70	107	1104	22.60%
Puts	150	Oct 1 2021	5.00	4.80	4.85	29	776	21.31%
Puts	140	Dec 17 2021	4.98	4.95	5.05	1023	27392	27.88%
Puts	145	Dec 17 2021	6.79	6.75	6.85	6623	25429	25.67%
Puts	150	Dec 17 2021	9.06	9.05	9.15	96	10746	24.86%

The cost of an option expiring in December is greater than that for the same option expiring in October. This reflects the higher time value.

The cost of put options increases as the strike price increases. This reflects the higher intrinsic value (X-S).

Option Clearing Corporation (OCC)

The OCC, which was founded in 1973, is the world's largest equity derivatives clearing organization and is "dedicated to promoting stability and financial integrity in the marketplaces that it serves by focusing on sound risk management principles."

The OCC ensures that the obligations of the contracts it clears are fulfilled. It acts as the intermediary and the guarantor of the contracts, as the seller for options that are purchased, and as the buyer for options that are sold. Since it guarantees performance on option contracts, the OCC requires sellers of options to deposit funds to satisfy a margin requirement. This requirement helps ensure that sellers can fulfill their obligations under the contract.

Option Expiration[1]

Options have specific expiration dates, but most exchange-traded options have an expiration month in one of the three following formats:

- January Sequential Cycle: Expiration months are January, April, July, and October
- February Sequential Cycle: Expiration months are February, May, August, and November
- March Sequential Cycle: Expiration months are March, June, September, and December

The expiration date is the third Friday of the expiration month.[2]

Most option contracts are relatively short and expire in less than twelve months. However, there are longer-term options available. One such option is called a LEAPS, short for Long-Term Equity Anticipation Security. This type of option may have an expiration period of up to three years and allows investors to take longer-term positions. LEAPS are available on certain individual equity securities and certain indexes. They can be used to speculate on the direction of a specific equity security or index or alternatively to hedge a position that is currently held.

TYPES OF OPTIONS

Options are available on more than just equity securities. In addition to stock options, there are options written on indexes, on the value of foreign currencies, and on futures contracts.

1. **Stock options** - The underlying securities for stock options are shares in a publicly traded company.
2. **Index options** - The underlying security for index options is an index, such as the S&P 500 index. These options allow traders to obtain broad based market exposure with a relatively small investment. Investors also use these options to hedge long or short equity positions or to generate portfolio income. These options are settled in cash. Options are currently offered on the S&P 500, S&P 100, Dow Jones Industrial Average (DJIA), various Russell indexes (such as the Russell 1000 and 2000), as well as other indexes.
3. **Foreign currency options** - These options allow traders to take advantage of expected changes in currency prices or to hedge currency risk in a portfolio.

Key Concepts

1. Understand that options can be purchased on stocks as well as other securities.
2. Differentiate between index options, foreign currency options, and futures options.

1. https://www.cboe.com/tradtool/strikepricecode.aspx
2. Current as of 2022.

4. **Futures options** - These options use futures contracts as the underlying security and allow traders to enter into a specific futures contract. For example, the E-mini S&P 500 Weekly Option contract allows for delivery into one E-mini S&P 500 futures contract.

While there are other types of option contracts, the ones listed above are the most prevalent. These option choices are all standardized contracts or exchange-traded options. In addition to exchange-traded options, there are OTC (over-the-counter) option contracts, which tend to be customized contracts that may have more complexity than standard exchange-traded options.

OPTION STRATEGIES

Options are often used by investors create positions with payoff patterns that would not be available through the use of underlying securities alone. They can be used for speculation, but they can also be used to protect or hedge long or short positions in underlying securities. Options can be combined to take advantage of flat markets or volatile markets. While there are numerous combinations of options and securities, the most common are:

1. Protective puts
2. Covered calls
3. Protective calls
4. Collars
5. Straddles
6. Strangles
7. Strips
8. Straps

Key Concepts

1. Define each option strategy and understand the underlying reason for pursuing that strategy.
2. Diagram the profit and loss line for each option strategy.

Protective Put

Insurance provides loss protection in the event of some unfavorable event, such as fire, theft, death, etc. A protective put strategy, sometimes called portfolio insurance, is a form of insurance for a long position. A protective put is constructed by combining a long position in a security (or portfolio) and a long put option.

Exhibit 15.11 | Protective Put

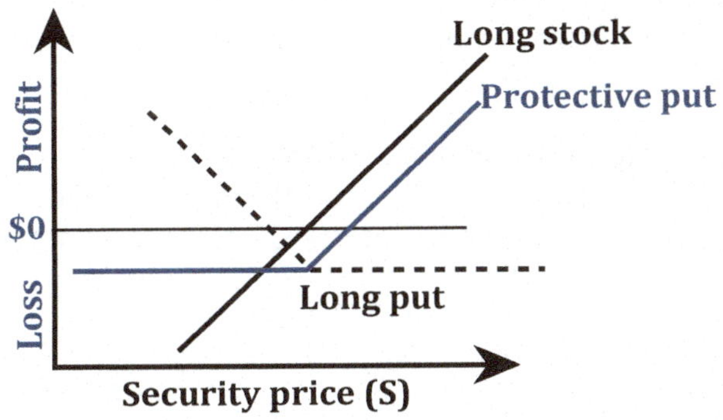

The long put provides downside protection for the long position in the underlying security. This technique is a hedging position, which can also be used with portfolios. Consider the following example.

Example 15.10

Byron owns a well-diversified portfolio valued at $800,000 that is highly correlated with a broad equity index. Byron is concerned about a substantial drop in equity prices over the next six months and does not want to sell any of the assets in his portfolio. He decides to hedge the downside risk by purchasing a six-month put option on the equity index. The details are shown below.

The index value is 10,000. There is a six-month put option on the index with an exercise price of 10,000 which makes this an at-the-money option. The put option's premium is $360 and Byron purchases 80 of these to fully hedge his portfolio. The total put option cost is $28,800.

The results of the protective put under two possible scenarios are shown below:

Scenario 1
• The index value is 15,000 (a 50% increase) when the option expires. • Bryon's portfolio will appreciate to $1,200,000 and he will allow the put to expire. • Bryon will lose the entire option cost. • The total value of his portfolio is now: $1,200,000 - $28,880 = 1,171,200.
Scenario 2
• The index value is 8,000 (a 20% decrease) when the option expires. • Bryon's portfolio will fall in value to $640,000 and he will exercise the put option. • Bryon's option finished in-the-money and he makes (10,000 - 8,000) × 80 = 160,000. • The total value of his portfolio is now: $640,000 + $160,000 - $28,800 = 771,200.

When the option finishes in-the-money, Bryon has placed a floor on the value of his portfolio. No matter how far the index value drops, Bryon's portfolio will be worth $800,000 (less the option premium). When the option finishes out-of-the-money, the portfolio value will rise linearly with the index value increase (less the option premium).

As illustrated in the above example, a protective put provides downside protection for a long position. **Portfolio insurance** buys a put option on an index (such as the S&P 500) to provide downside protection for a long portfolio.

It is important when implementing the portfolio insurance strategy to match the value of the assets controlled by the put option to the value of the long portfolio that will be insured. If these values do not match exactly, then there will not be a perfect hedge. In practice, perfect hedges are rare.

Covered Call and Naked Options

As discussed above, writing a call option has unlimited loss potential. The seller of the call option receives the premium, but is exposed to the increase in the value of the underlying security. An investor who writes an option without simultaneously taking an offsetting position is said to have a **naked option**. A naked call option is a particularly risky position to take as it has an unlimited amount of downside risk.

A covered call option involves the simultaneous sale of a call option combined with the purchase or ownership of the underlying stock. The term covered refers to the fact that the underlying stock can be used to satisfy the obligation of the call option in the event that the stock increases in price.

Exhibit 15.12 | Covered Call

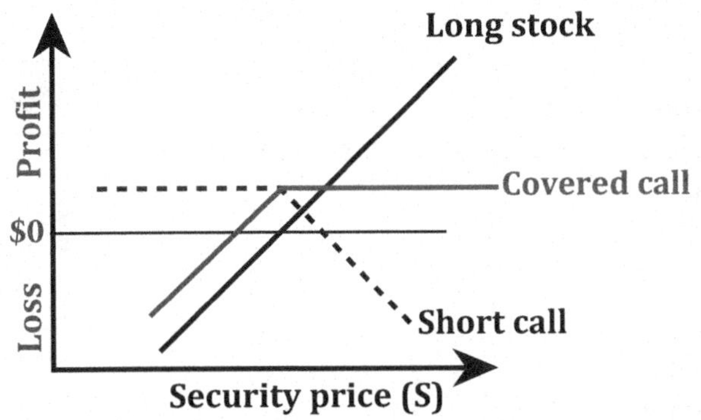

A trader who establishes a covered call position is often trying to generate premium income from the underlying equity position. This strategy is more likely to be successful when the expected volatility in the underlying security is fairly low. It should not be undertaken if there is a bullish outlook for the stock.

Protective Call

Although most unsophisticated investors attempt to grow the value of their equity portfolio by purchasing stocks, when markets display signs that they are overvalued, sophisticated investors may also try and profit from short selling. Short selling involves selling the stock without owning it. This technique is discussed in Chapter 9.

A protective call strategy involves buying a call option to protect a short position on the underlying security.

Exhibit 15.13 | Protective Call

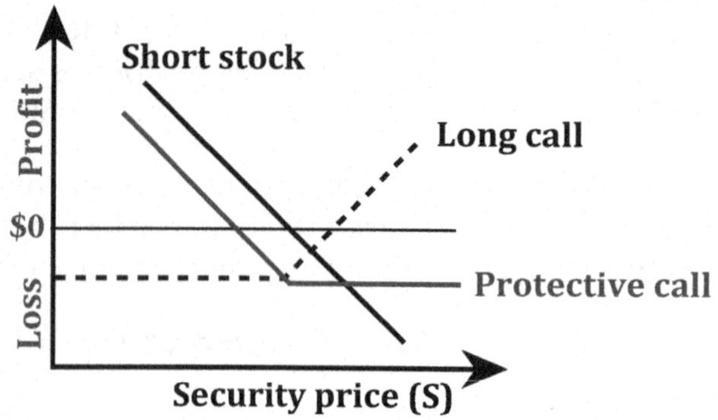

As the chart illustrates, as the underlying stock increases, the short position loses money, but the call offsets the losses. Thus, the protective call limits the loss potential of a short sale, while preserving the gain potential.

Collar

A collar limits the gains and losses on an underlying position in a security. A long put is purchased to give downside protection, but the cost of that option is offset by the premium received for selling a call option at a higher strike price. This short call position limits the upside potential of the position.

The position only has a variable gain or loss between the strike prices of the two options. Below the strike price of the put option, the loss is limited to the net of the premiums plus the difference between the stock purchase price and the put strike price. Above the strike price of the call, the gain is limited to the net of the premiums plus the difference between the call strike price and the stock purchase price.

Quick Quiz 15.6

1. Alexander owns a portfolio of stocks that is highly correlated with the S&P 500 index. Entering into a protective put option on the S&P 500 index to protect his portfolio would allow him to continue to participate in any gains in the market.
   a. True
   b. False
2. A covered call involves owning the underlying security while buying a call option.
   a. True
   b. False

True, False.

Exhibit 15.14 | Collar[3]

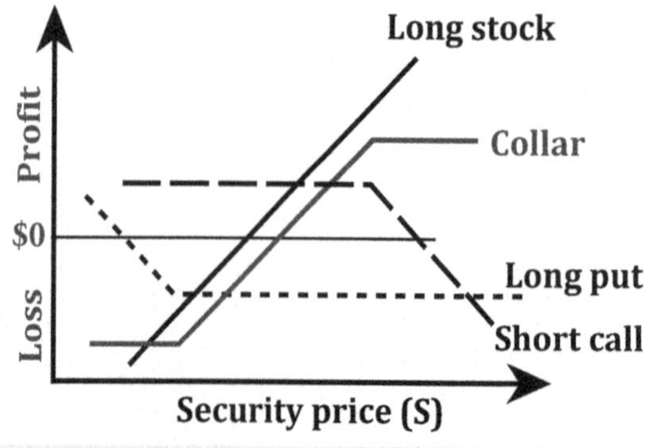

Example 15.11

Yvonne bought 100 shares of XYZ stock at $50 per share. The stock is currently trading at $49 per share. She decides to establish a collar around the stock position. Yvonne buys a MAR 45 put option on XYZ for $3 and sells a MAR 55 call option on XYZ for $2. Her investment totals $5,000 for the stock, $300 for the put, less the $200 received for the call for a net of $5,100. What will be her profit (loss) at various stock prices at expiration?

Stock Price at Expiration/Close	$40	$45	$50	$55	$60
Stock Profit/Loss	($1,000)	($500)	$0	$500	$1,000
Call premium received	$200	$200	$200	$200	$200
Put premium paid	($300)	($300)	($300)	($300)	($300)
Short call payoff ($55)	$0	$0	$0	$0	($500)
Long put payoff ($45)	$500	$0	$0	$0	$0
Profit (Loss)	($600)	($600)	($100)	$400	$400

As illustrated in the above example, the collar establishes a band around the value of the underlying security. The premium for the put option is partially offset by the premium for writing the call. The benefit of the collar is that it allows for downside protection at a lower cost due to writing the call option.

Zero Cost Collar

A zero cost collar is a specific type of collar which is structured to equalize the call premium to the put premium. This structure is designed to provide a band around the value of the underlying security at a zero cost to the investor.

Example 15.12

Assume Ben owns one million shares of Baily Company and currently has a substantial gain in his position. Ben might decide to enter into a zero cost collar to protect the value of the shares from downside risk. He could purchase a put option. However, put options are fairly expensive, especially for 1 million shares. With a zero cost collar, the premium for the call option will pay for the premium on the put option. It will, however, limit the upside potential of the stock position to the strike price of the call option.

It should be noted that the zero cost collar strategy is subject to complex tax rules and could also be subject to the constructive sale rules.

3. The actual collar profit (loss) line may be slightly different than what is depicted depending on the premiums for the put and the call options.

Straddles

There are two types of straddles, a long straddle and a short straddle, both of which require a put option and a call option. Long straddles consist of a combination of a long put option and a long call option, both with the same strike price and expiration period. Short straddles consist of a combination of a short put option and a short call option, both with the same strike price and same expiration period.

Long straddles are useful if the investor believes that the price of the underlying security is likely to move up or down significantly, but there is uncertainty about the direction. Effectively, the long straddle is a bet on the volatility of the underlying security. The investor can make profits if the stock goes either down or up. The largest loss the investor can sustain is the loss of both premiums, which could occur if the price of the stock remains constant.

Short straddles are the exact opposite of long straddles. The investor believes that the underlying security price is fairly stable. If correct, the investor keeps the premiums for both options. However, the investor has unlimited loss potential.

Quick Quiz 15.7

1. Assume Cooper owns 100 shares of XYZ stock, which is trading at $80 per share. If he buys a put option on XYZ with a strike price of $75 for a premium of $3 and XYZ's stock price plummets to $22 per share, he will lose $800.
   a. True
   b. False

2. A zero cost collar can provide downside protection at a cost of zero, while preserving the opportunity to participate in gains above the strike price for the call option.
   a. True
   b. False

True, False.

Exhibit 15.15 | Straddles

Straddle	Long Straddle	Short Straddle
How does the investor win?	Volatility of the underlying security	Lack of volatility of the underlying security
Max Profit	Unlimited	Call premium + Put premium
Max Loss	Call premium + Put premium	Unlimited

Consider the following exhibit that illustrates the long straddle and the short straddle.

Exhibit 15.16 | Long and Short Straddles

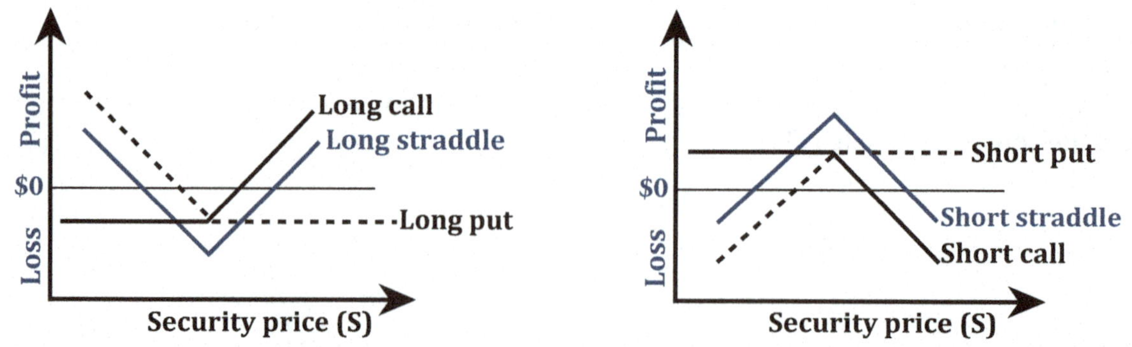

Example 15.13

Fly-Buy-Night Air Inc. (FBN) is an airline that focuses on night flights and "red-eye" flights. FBN has gained in popularity over the last ten years. However, the company is losing money and has entered into bankruptcy for reorganization. Despite the bankruptcy proceedings, the stock is remaining steady at $15 per share. The company has petitioned the bankruptcy court to eliminate its pension liability as part of a Chapter 11 restructuring. Investors know that the pension liability is enormous and relief from that obligation will cause the stock to soar. If instead, the bankruptcy court fails to provide relief, it will likely result in the stock crashing to zero. Based on that analysis, Kallen decides to purchase a long straddle.

Kallen's friend, Keira, decides that the court is almost assured of granting relief for the pension obligation and decides to enter into a short straddle. She believes that the market has already taken the bankruptcy proceedings into consideration and that the stock will not move much, if at all. Keira believes she will be able to generate investment income (premiums) from writing the options.

As illustrated in **Example 15.13**, straddles are a bet on volatility. Long straddles benefit from significant volatility, while short straddles benefit from the lack of volatility.

Strangles, Strips and Straps

Strangles, strips and straps are all variations of the straddle discussed above.

A strangle is effectively the same as a straddle, except that the strike price of the options is not the same. The long strangle consists of a long put option combined with a long call option that has a higher strike price than the put option. The combined premiums on a long strangle are less than the combined premiums on a similar straddle. However, the underlying security has to move more for a strangle than for a straddle to make the same profit.

A short strangle is just the opposite of a long strangle and consists of a short put and a short call. The short call will have a higher strike price than the short put. As with the short straddle, the potential profit is limited to the two premiums, while the loss is unlimited.

Exhibit 15.17 | Long Strangle and Short Strangle

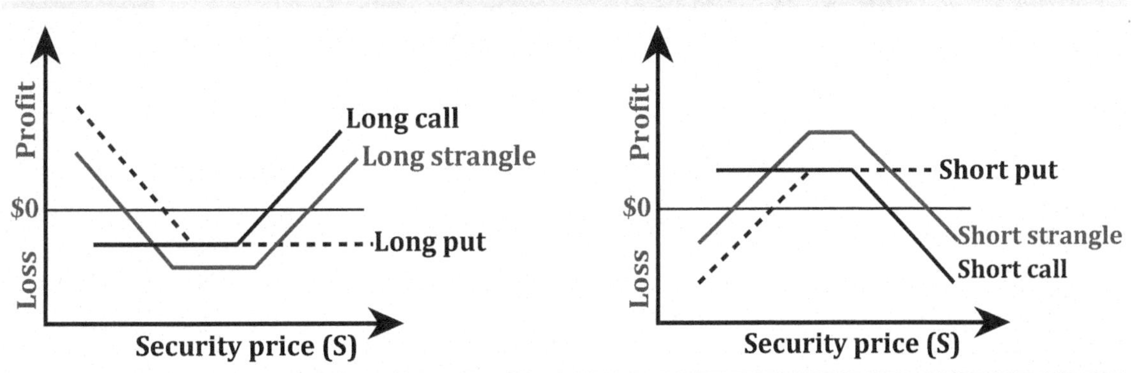

Strips and straps are also variations of the straddle, but involve three options. The strip consists of two long puts and one long call with the same strike price and expiration. The strap consists of one long put option and two long call options with the same strike price and exercise price.

These techniques are directional in nature. An investor who is more bearish than bullish might consider a strip, while an investor who is more bullish than bearish might consider a strap. For the strip, the investor believes the underlying security will change in price and thinks it will most likely move down. The profit potential for a strip is higher if the stock decreases rather than increases. For the strap, the investor believes the underlying security will change in price and thinks it will most likely move up. The profit potential for a strap is higher if the stock increases rather than decreases. If the investor believed that the underlying stock price would not fluctuate very much, then he or she might consider a short strangle or a collar, depending on the objective.

Quick Quiz 15.8

1. A long straddle involves the purchase of a long call and a long put with the same characteristics.
   a. True
   b. False
2. A short strangle involves the sale of a call option and a put option, with different strike prices.
   a. True
   b. False

True, True.

Exhibit 15.18 | Strip and Strap

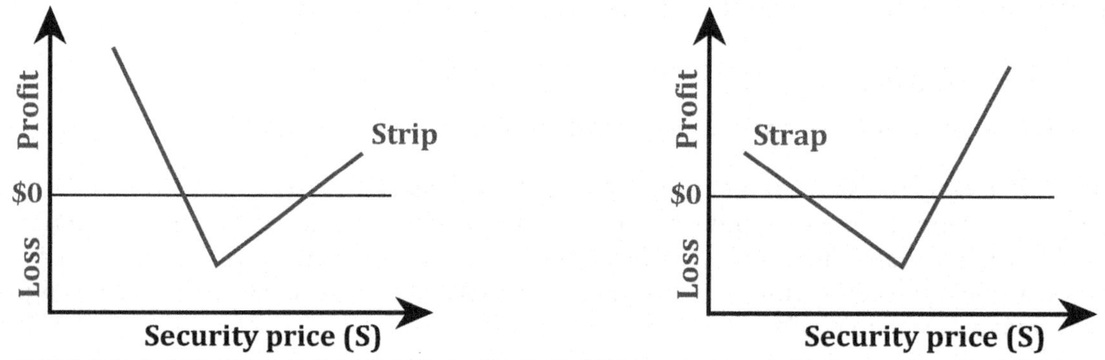

There are many more combinations of options that are beyond the scope of this text. However, the ones discussed above are the more common or relevant ones.

Exhibit 15.19 | Summary of Option Combinations & Strategies

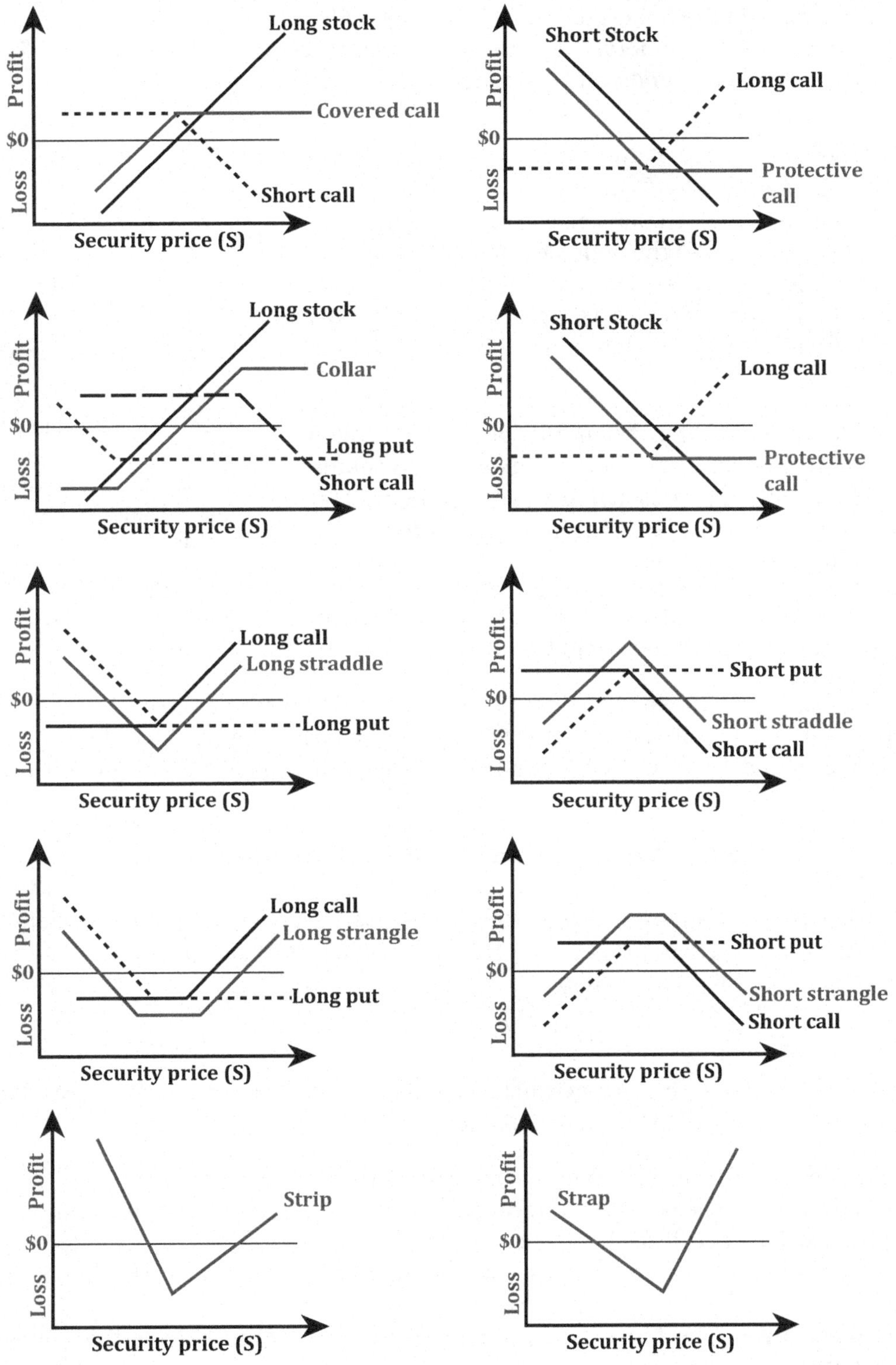

SECURITIES WITH EMBEDDED OPTIONS

Financial securities are often issued with an option embedded as part of the agreement. These embedded options change the value of the financial security. To fully understand the value of the financial security, the value of the option must be understood. Three examples of securities that contain embedded options are callable bonds, convertible bonds, and warrants.

Callable Bonds

Companies issue bonds as a way to raise money for capital projects or other needs. Callable bonds give issuers the right but not the obligation to repurchase the bonds before their maturity date. This will only happen when interest rates fall, as issuers hope to reduce their borrowing costs. Issuers will typically repurchase the bonds at par value plus the next coupon payment.

Callable bondholders will suffer when the bonds are called because they will be unable to sell their bonds at the premium which occurs when interest rates fall. To protect themselves against this extra risk, bondholders require higher returns and pay lower prices for callable bonds.

Consequently, callable bondholders are less concerned about yield to maturity than they are about yield to call.

Key Concepts

1. Explain how an embedded option changes the value of a security.
2. Describe the impact of a call option for a bond.
3. Identify the circumstances under which an investor with a convertible bond would want to take advantage of the conversion feature.
4. Compare warrants with call options.

The value of a callable bond has two components: the bond and the embedded option. The basic method of determining the value of the embedded option is to determine what the bond would be priced at without the embedded option and subtract that value from the current value of the bond with the embedded option.

Callable Bond Value = Option-Free Bond Value - Call Option Value

In addition to corporate bond issues, residential mortgages effectively have call provisions. Borrowers are almost uniformly permitted to prepay their mortgage balances, which permits them to refinance at a lower interest rate if such rates are available.

Convertible Bond

Bonds are sometimes issued with a conversion feature that permits the bondholder to exchange the bond for a stated number of shares of the issuing company's common stock.

There are several terms that are important to convertible bonds. These are:

- **Conversion ratio** - The conversion ratio equals the number of shares of common stock that the bondholder will receive if the bond is converted.
- **Conversion price** - The conversion price equals the par value of the bond divided by the conversion ratio.
- **Conversion value** - The conversion value is determined by multiplying the conversion ratio by the current value of the common stock.

The basic formula for the value of a convertible bond is as follows:

Convertible Bond Value = Option-Free Bond Value + Call Option Value

Clearly, the embedded call option, which is the conversion feature, is a benefit to the bondholder. It increases the price of the bond relative to similar bonds that do not contain a conversion feature.

Example 15.14

Lindsay buys a convertible bond with a conversion ratio of 10. The bond allows the holder to exchange the bond (which has a par value of $1,000) for ten shares of common stock. Since the $1,000 bond converts to 10 shares, the conversion price equals $100. If the common stock is trading at $75 per share, Lindsay is not going to convert. The value of her bond is $1,000 (assuming it is at par), while the value of the stock she would receive if she were to convert would be $750 (10 shares x $75 per share). If the stock were to increase to $150 per share, she could convert and have stock worth $1,500, which is significantly higher than the par value of the bond. In this example, $1,500 is the conversion value.

Preferred stock may also contain a conversion feature. Conceptually, convertible preferred stock functions very much like a convertible bond.

Exhibit 15.20 | Callable Bond and Convertible Bond

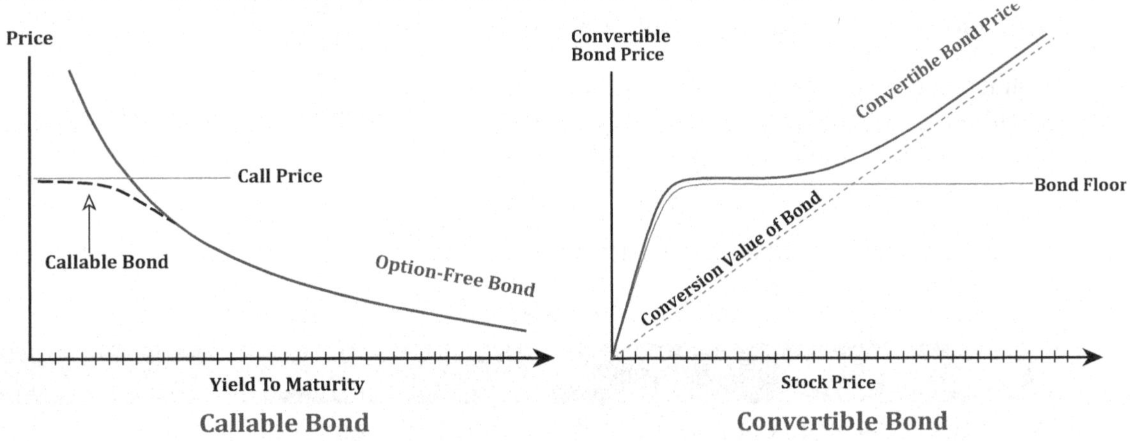

Exhibit 15.20 shows the prices of callable and convertible bonds and how those prices change when the price of the underlying asset changes. Callable bonds behave just like option-free bonds when interest rates are relatively high indicating that issuers are not likely to exercise their option to refinance. When rates fall, however, the option becomes valuable and the price of the bond has a ceiling equal to the call price which is likely to be the par value of the bond plus the next coupon payment. This is the maximum price the issuer will pay to call the bonds; therefore, the callable bondholders face an upper bound on the price they can sell their bonds. This is negative convexity at low interest rates, which is shown by the dotted line in the callable bond graph. Convertible bonds behave just like the underlying equity when stock prices are relatively high, indicating that bondholders are very likely to exercise their option and convert their bonds into shares of stock. At very low stock prices, convertible bond values drop at a faster

rate than the shares, indicating that the option is out-of-the-money. There is a minimum floor for the convertible bond, and that is the present value of the bond if it were option-free. At very low stock prices, both the convertible bond price and option free bond price drop towards zero due to the increasingly high risk of default.

Warrants

Companies sometimes issue bonds with warrants attached to the offerings. Warrants are essentially the same as call options to the holder, but issued by the offering company. Warrants give the holder the right, but not the obligation, to purchase shares of the company at a specific price within a specific period of time. Detachable warrants can be separated from a bond and traded separately.[4]

While warrants are effectively the same as call options to the holder, they do have differences. Warrants are issued by a company and, if exercised, can increase the outstanding number of shares for that company. This increase in the number of shares can dilute the ownership of the shares. Dilution simply means that the company's value is spread over more shares, which results in the per share value declining. In contrast to warrants, call options are written by other investors. Shares purchased as part of call options are already issued and outstanding. Call option exercises do not result in dilution.

Another difference between warrants and call options is the duration of the rights to the holder. Call options typically have an expiration of less than a year, while warrants might be exercisable from two to ten years.

Quick Quiz 15.9

1. The value of a callable bond equals the value of a non-callable bond plus the call option value.
   a. True
   b. False
2. The conversion value equals the conversion ratio multiplied by the current market value of the underlying security.
   a. True
   b. False
3. Warrants and call options are very similar. However, warrants generally have a longer maturity than call options.
   a. True
   b. False

False, True, True.

There are other securities with embedded, or attached, options. The ones discussed above are the more common types.

OPTION VALUATION

As discussed above, the value of an option is related to the intrinsic value and the time value of the option. Even if an option is out-of-the-money (intrinsic value is zero) the option has a value because the stock price could change such that the option could be exercised. As the expiration nears, the value of an option converges to the intrinsic value. On the day of expiration, the time value of an option is equal to zero, leaving only the intrinsic value. The basic formula for valuing options is:

Option Value = Intrinsic Value + Time Value

Most of the payoff charts in this chapter illustrate the payoff at expiration of the option contract. These charts reflect the intrinsic value of the option, as opposed to the intrinsic value plus the time value. The

4. Note: Some warrants are not detachable from a bond offering.

following chart is a more representative illustration of the value of an option, including both intrinsic value and time value, before and at expiration.

Exhibit 15.21 | Option Value

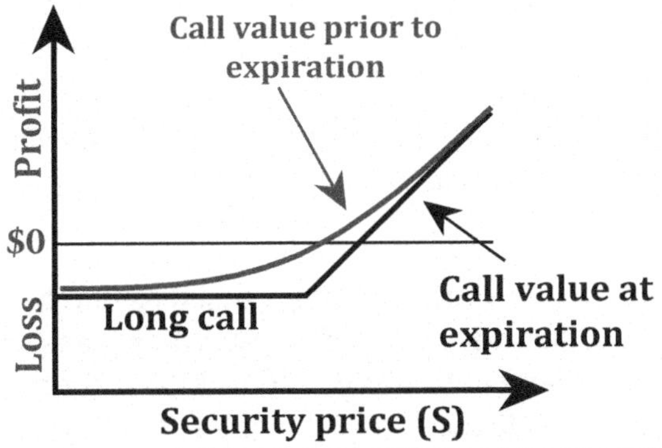

A range of factors affect the value of an option. The intrinsic value is simple to calculate using the strike price and the underlying security price, but the risk-free rate, the volatility of the underlying security, and the time to expiry of the option all affect its total value.

Several models have been developed that can be used to value options and the following section discusses three of the more popular ones; put-call parity, the binomial option pricing model, and the Black-Scholes option valuation model.

> ***Key Concepts***
>
> 1. Discuss the value of an option in terms of its time value and intrinsic value.
> 2. Recognize why the put-call parity model must be true.
> 3. Diagram a two-period binomial option lattice.
> 4. Assess the impact on the value of an option, based on changes in the factors that are part of the Black-Scholes Option Valuation Model.

Put-Call Parity Model

As discussed earlier in the chapter, options can be used to create outcomes that are not available with other securities. In addition, options can be used to create outcomes that are similar to those available from other securities. For example, consider the following exhibit.

Exhibit 15.22 | Long Stock vs. Long Call and Short Put

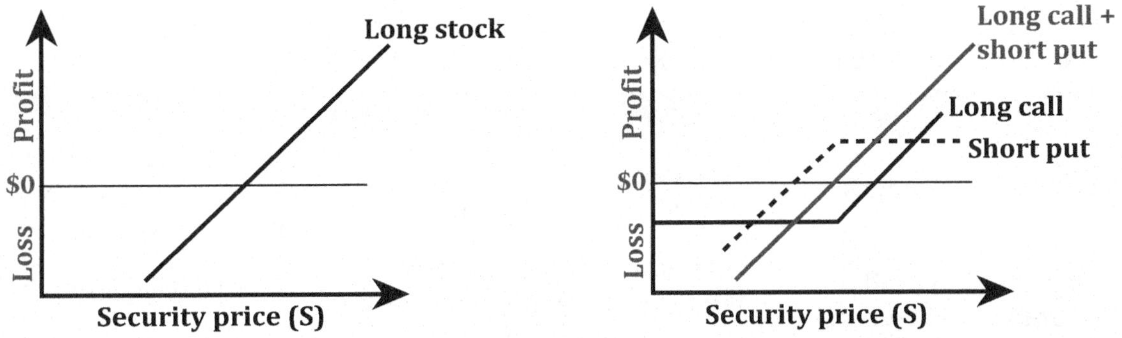

The chart on the left illustrates the payoff for a long position in a stock. The chart on the right illustrates the combination of a long call and a short put. It is obvious that the payoff of the two charts is very similar. However, one difference is that the long call short put combination has significantly greater leverage than the outright purchase of the stock. Another difference is that the payoff for the long call short put combination will always be slightly less than the long stock payoff, due to the difference between the premium on the long call and the short put. The put-call parity model can help explain why these two charts are so similar.

The put-call parity model defines the relationship between the price of a call option and a put option, both with the same expiration and strike price. The model is designed to determine the value of a put option from a corresponding call option.

The model starts with a protective put, an option strategy discussed in the previous section. The strategy is a combination of a long position in an underlying security, which gives an unlimited upside profit, and a long put, which establishes a floor that limits downside risk. A call option has a similar payoff with a limited loss potential and unlimited profit potential. Consider the following graphs of the protective put and the long call:

Exhibit 15.23 | Protective Put vs. Long Call

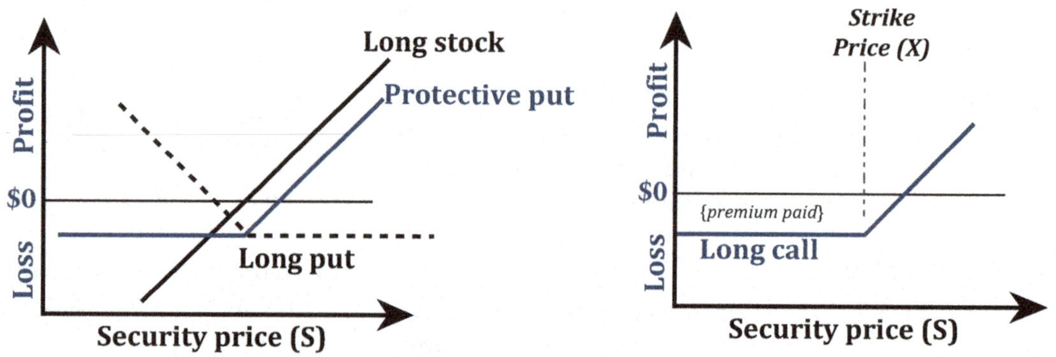

While the payoffs are graphically the same, they are not identical. To equate the two strategies, we need to add cash equal to the value of the exercise price (X) to the call option at the time of expiration. With that addition, the payoffs will be exactly equal.

Evaluating the payoffs at the point of expiration confirms the two are effectively the same. There are two possible scenarios:

- **Scenario 1:** the stock price is less than or equal to the exercise price
- **Scenario 2:** the stock price is greater than the exercise price

Strategy	Scenario 1	Scenario 2
Payoff of the protective put	Exercise price (stock can be sold for exercise price)	Stock price (the put option is out-of-the-money and will not be exercised)
Payoff of long call and cash equal to exercise price	Exercise price (the call option is out-of-the-money and will not be exercised)	Stock price (call option is exercised with cash)

Given that the payoffs are the same for each strategy under both possible scenarios, it follows that the two strategies must also cost the same to establish. If they did not, there would be an arbitrage opportunity.

The cost of the protective put is equal to the put premium (P) and the cost of the stock (S).

The cost of the other strategy, known as a fiduciary call, is the cost of the call option (C), and the cost of guaranteeing a cash payment equal to the exercise price of the options at expiry. The cost of that guarantee today is equal to the present value of the exercise price discounted at the risk-free rate.

Note that the model requires that the options are exercised at expiry, and hence is only suitable for European options. Therefore,

$$S_0 + P = C + \frac{X}{(1+i)^T}$$

S_0 - the stock price at time zero
P - premium on the long put
C - premium on the long call
X - exercise price for the put and the call
i - risk-free rate of interest
T - time

The part of the formula, $X \div (1+i)^T$, reflects the discounted value of the exercise price at the establishment of the two strategies.

The **put-call parity model** uses this equivalence to show the price of a put option must be equal to the cost of a call option with the same exercise price and expiry, less the cost of the underlying security, plus the present value of the exercise price:

$$P = C - S_0 + \frac{X}{(1+i)^T}$$

This formula can be rearranged to solve for any of the variables and thus create what is referred to as a synthetic security. A synthetic security is created out of other financial instruments.

Consider the example above comparing the long stock position with the long call short put. We noted the payoffs were very similar, and they are. Solving the above formula for S_0:

$$S_0 = C - P + \frac{X}{(1+i)^T}$$

Therefore, the value of stock today should equal the difference between the premiums for a long call and a short put plus the discounted exercise price.

The implication for the put-call parity model is that when there are imbalances in the prices of options or the underlying security, a trader can exploit these imbalances and earn a risk-free rate of return, which is known as an arbitrage opportunity.

Example 15.15

Assume the following for Acme, Inc.

P - premium on long put	$1.50
C - premium on long call	$3.00
X - exercise price for put and call	$50.00
i - risk-free rate of interest	3%
T - time (days)	30

The stock price today can be solved for using the put-call parity model:

$S_0 = C - P + X \div (1+i)^T$

$S_0 = \$3.00 - \$1.50 + \$50 \div (1.03)^{(30/365)} = \$51.38$

Therefore, based on above assumptions, the stock should be priced at $51.38.

Binomial Option Pricing Model (BOPM)

The binomial option pricing model is often used for its ability to incorporate a variety of conditions that other models cannot incorporate. The model traces the discrete movements in the underlying security over the period from valuation until expiration. This iterative process is completed using a binomial lattice. Each node on the lattice is representative of the price of the underlying security at a specific period in time.

Exhibit 15.24 | Binomial Lattice

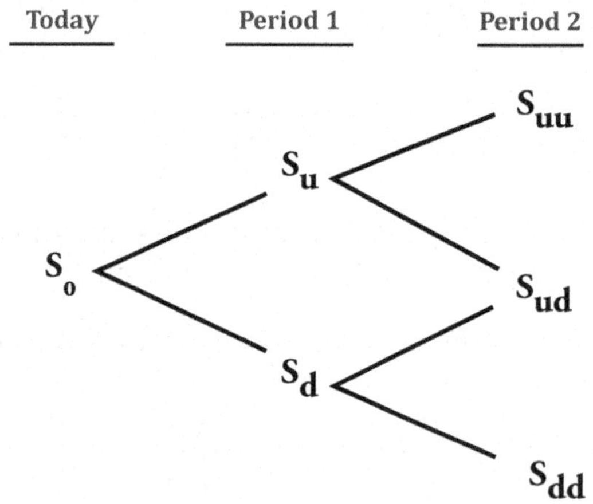

The BOPM attempts to estimate the price for a European call option by determining the value of a separate portfolio with the same payoffs as the call option being priced. If the payoffs of the portfolio and the call option are the same, then the value should be the same. Consider the following example.

Example 15.16

Assumptions:

- The price of ABC stock is currently at $100 and will either go up or down. It is assumed the stock price will be either $120 or $80 at the end of one year.
- The ABC call option being replicated has a strike price of $100.
- The replicating portfolio consists of the two following elements:
  1. A long position in ½ share of ABC stock, with a current market price of $50 ($100 share price times ½), and
  2. A short position in a risk-free bond that matures in one year with an initial price of $38.10 and maturing at $40.00. The short position is equivalent to borrowing the $38.10 for one year at 5%. Note, $38.10 times 1.05 = $40.00.

The replicating portfolio's value depends on whether the value of the stock is $120 or $80 at the end of one year. The one-half share will either be worth $60 or $40. Combined with the debt of $40, the outcome is either $20 or zero.

	High	Low
Value of ½ share of ABC stock	$60	$40
Repayment of debt	-40	-40
Net	**$20**	**$0**

The call option has a strike price of $100. Therefore, the option will be worth $20 if the stock is worth $120. This value is found by subtracting the strike price of $100 from the value of the stock of $120. Alternatively, the option will expire worthless if the value of the stock is $80 at expiration, as it will be out-of-the-money. Both the portfolio and the option have the same payoffs, whether the stock is at $120 or at $80.

Because the portfolio and the option have the same payoffs at all times, they must have the same initial value. Otherwise, there would be an arbitrage opportunity that could be exploited.

Why use ½ share of stock?

Creating a replicating portfolio that has the same payoff outcomes as the option contract is a way to determine the current value of the call option. To create the replicating portfolio, a certain amount of money will be borrowed at the risk-free rate and an unknown number of shares of ABC stock will be purchased at the current price of $100 per share. At the end of one year, the stock is sold for either $120 or $80 and the loan is paid off. The value of this replicating portfolio should be equal to the stock option under each scenario.

Scenario 1: ABC stock will equal $120 at the end of one year. If the stock equals $120, then the call option is worth $20 at expiration. This value equals the difference between the value of the stock at year-end of $120 minus the strike price of $100.

Scenario 2: ABC stock will equal \$80 at the end of one year. If the stock equals \$80, then the call option is worth \$0 at expiration because the stock price is less than the strike price of \$100.

Determining the number of shares to buy for the replicating portfolio:

- Define X as the number of shares of ABC stock that needs to be purchased.
- Define B as the value of the bond (loan) that must be paid back at expiration.

Two formulas have to be written to represent the outcome under each scenario. Each formula will have two variables, X and B. Solve for the two unknowns, as follows:

Two Formulas:

1. \$120X + B = \$20
2. \$80X + B = \$0

Subtracting the second formula from the first results in:
\$40X = \$20, therefore, X = ½ share of stock.

Now that the number of stock is determined, the value of the bond at expiration can be solved for in each of the formulas:

1. \$120(½ share) + B = \$20, therefore, B = \$40
2. \$80(½ share) + B = \$0, therefore, B = \$40

In summary, the replicating portfolio will consist of a long position of ½ share of ABC stock and a short position in a bond that will mature in one year at a value of \$40. If the future value of the bond equals \$40, then the present value, discounted at 5%, equals \$38.10. This result can be validated by multiplying \$38.10 by 1.05.

Since the replicating portfolio and the call option have the same payoffs, the value of both should be equal. The value of the replicating portfolio equals \$50 of stock minus the bond of \$38.10, or \$11.90. The value of the call option must therefore equal \$11.90 also.

BOPM Payoff Comparison

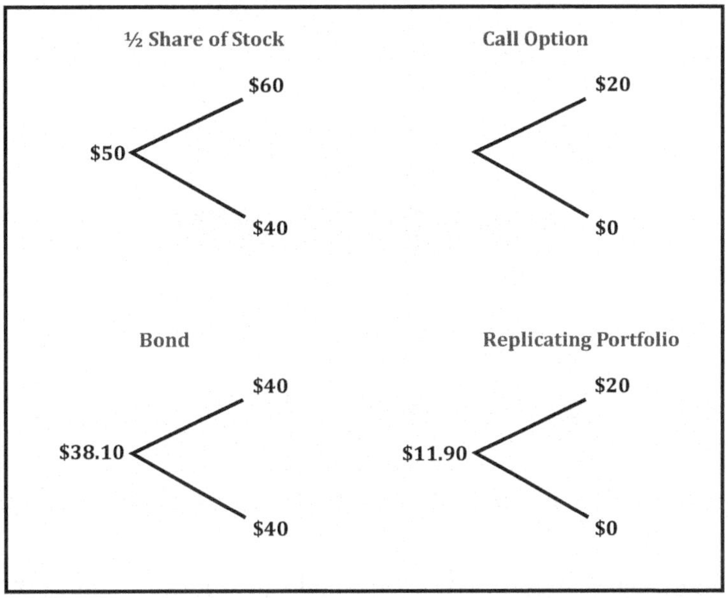

Therefore, the option must equal the difference between the value of ½ the share of stock and the current value of the short bond. This equals $11.90 ($50.00 - $38.10).

The binomial option pricing model can be further expanded for more than two possible outcomes and for multi-period analysis. For example, consider the above example, but assume that there is a value at the end of six months and at one year. In this case, the lattice looks like the following chart.

Exhibit 15.25 | Two-Period Binomial Model

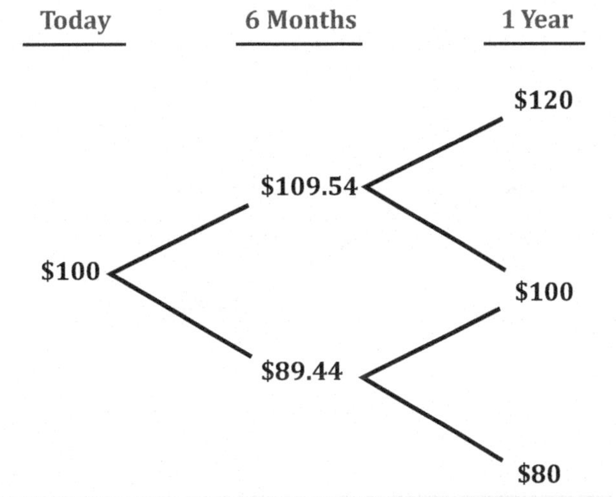

It should be noted that the values at each node are derived by determining the internal rate of return based on the number of periods.

For example, to determine the six-month value for the nodes above, the IRR is calculated as follows:

$$(\$120/\$100)^{1/2} = 1.0954 - 1 = 9.54\%,$$

and

$$(\$80/\$100)^{1/2} = 0.8944 - 1 = -10.56\%$$

TVM Method:

	High	Low
FV	120	80
N	2	2
PMT	$0	$0
PV	($100)	($100)
i	9.54	(10.56)

The reason the number is raised to 1/2 is that there are two periods in one year. With three periods, it would be raised to 1/3.

Taking it one step further, consider if there were values at four months, eight months and one year.

Exhibit 15.26 | Three-Period Binomial Model[5]

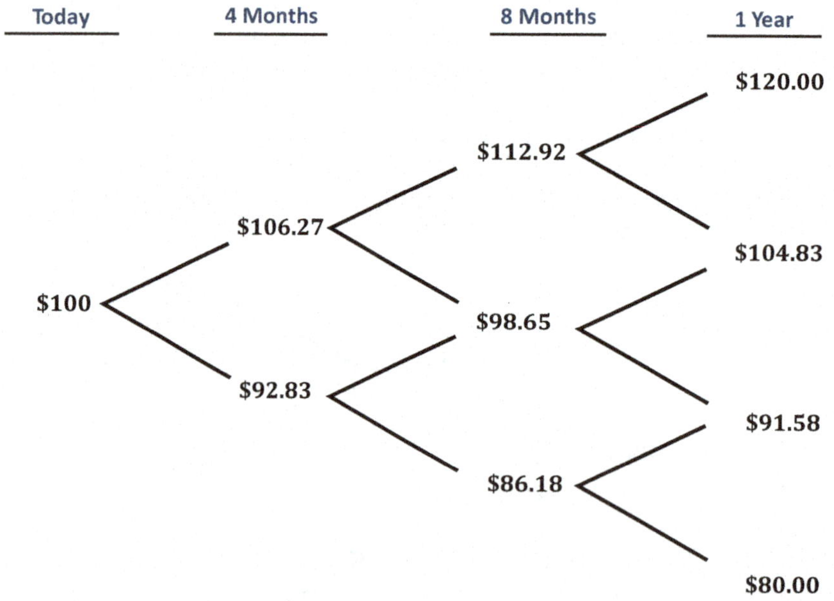

The same methodology can be used to value the option as in the previous example. The process begins at the end value and then works toward the starting point. As mentioned, the BOPM uses discrete time periods.

5. $(120/100)^{1/3} - 1$ = 6.27% | $100 x 1.0627 = $106.27 | $106.27 x 1.0627 = $112.92 | $112.92 x 1.0627 = $120
$(80/100)^{1/3} - 1$ = -7.168% | $100 x 0.9283 = $92.83 | $92.83 x 0.9283 = $86.18 | $86.18 x 0.9283 = $80

As more and more nodes or periods are added, this analysis leads to the Black-Scholes-Merton option pricing model, which is a continuous time model.

Black-Scholes-Merton Option Valuation Model

In 1973, the same year the Chicago Board of Options Exchange was established, Fischer Black and Myron Scholes developed the first option valuation model, which has since been referred to as the Black-Scholes-Merton Option Valuation Model. Robert C. Merton, an MIT professor, published a paper expanding the understanding of the model and coined the term, "Black-Scholes option pricing" model. Scholes and Merton received the Nobel Prize in Economics in 1997 for their work on option pricing. The Royal Swedish Academy of Sciences recognized Fischer Black and he would have been a part of the prize had he not passed away. Interestingly enough, the abstract of Merton's paper on option pricing discusses the history of option pricing and states that "the long history of the theory of option pricing began in 1900 when the French mathematician Louis Bachelier deduced an option pricing formula based on the assumption that stock prices follow a Brownian motion with zero drift."

Their model uses continuous time and was designed to determine the value of a call option based on certain variables. These variables include the following:

1. Current market price - The call premium is greater for higher priced stocks.
2. Exercise price - The call premium is greater for lower exercise prices.
3. Time to expiration - The premium increases as the time to expiration increases. More time is available for the stock price to trade above the exercise price.
4. Volatility (standard deviation) of returns - Stocks that are more volatile cause the premium to increase because there is more potential for the stock to trade above the exercise price.
5. Risk-free rate of return - The call premium increases as the risk-free rate increases.

All of the variables are positively related to the value of a call option except exercise price. The exercise price is inversely related to the value of a call option.

Quick Quiz 15.10

1. The value of an option equals the time value plus the intrinsic value.
   a. True
   b. False
2. As expiration nears, the value of an option approaches the intrinsic value.
   a. True
   b. False
3. According to the Black-Scholes model, the value of a call option increases as the volatility of the underlying security increases.
   a. True
   b. False
4. According to the Black-Scholes model, the value of a call option increases if the exercise price for the option increases.
   a. True
   b. False

True, True, True, False.

Exhibit 15.27 | Factors that Influence the Price of a Call Option

Variable	Call Option Price Increases if Variable	Relationship
Market Price	↑	Direct
Exercise Price	↓	Indirect
Time	↑	Direct
Volatility	↑	Direct
Risk-Free Rate	↑	Direct

The model is an enormous step towards accurately valuing options. However, the model is not perfect and relies on the following set of assumptions:

- The option is a European call option.
- There will be no cash dividends during the exercise period.
- The risk-free rate of interest and the volatility are constant.

It should be noted that the model can be modified to accommodate dividends.

American options are more complicated to value than European options since they can be exercised anytime prior to expiration. However, the variables used in valuing European options are the same as those for American options.

One of the important variables in option pricing is volatility, which is often assumed based on past volatility. The model requires volatility to be constant during the term of the option. In some cases, traders may use the current price of an option along with the Black-Scholes model to back into the assumed volatility priced into the option. Once the assumed volatility is calculated, traders can decide whether the option is fairly priced or not, and invest accordingly.

Example 15.17

Shepard is a research analyst using option pricing models to locate undervalued derivative securities. Shepard tracks Elite Technology's (ET) stock and option prices during a monthly period. He collects the following information:

ET's stock price	\$74
Exercise price on ET call option	\$70
Risk-Free rate of interest	8%
Expiration date of option	1 year
ET's volatility	20%

Shepard uses the Black-Scholes-Merton option pricing model to compute the price of the call option.[6]

$$\text{Call Premium} = \text{Stock Price} \times (P_1) + \text{Exercise Price} \times e^{-it}(P_2)$$

Where P_1 and P_2 are probabilities associated with the likelihood that the option will finish in the money and the discounted stock price at expiration exceeds the current stock price. These probabilities are computed assuming normal distributions and the Black Scholes Merton version of the z statistic.

According to the model, the probabilities can be computed as 0.7823 and 0.7190, so the call price is:[7]

$$\text{Call Premium} = 74 \times (0.7823) + 70 \times e^{-0.08\text{x}1}(0.7190) = 11.43$$

6. The original call pricing equation can be found at: Black, Fischer; Myron Scholes (1973). "The Pricing of Options and Corporate Liabilities." Journal of Political Economy. 81 (3): 637-654 and Merton, Robert C. (1973). "Theory of Rational Option Pricing". Bell Journal of Economics and Management Science.
7. The math involved in the calculation of P_1 and P_2 is far beyond the level of this text. However, there are many online resources that can calculate the call premium based on the five inputs in the problem.

Shepard should notice the following in his evaluation of the option:

- The option is currently in-the-money.
- The intrinsic value of the option is $4.00.
- The time value of the option is $7.43.
- If the price of the option is less than $11.43, then it is undervalued.

The call option's price is directly related to stock price, time, risk-free rates, and volatility, but inversely related to the exercise price.

Applications of Option Valuation

The valuation of options is not solely limited to that of exchange-traded options. There are many applications of valuing options. Corporations grant employees stock options, such as incentive stock options (ISOs) and non-qualified stock options (NQSOs). Real estate options are purchased and exchanged. These options must also be valued. Other applications of option pricing include professional athlete contracts in which either the player or the team has option to extend the contract for one year, options on movie scripts or novels, and options on real estate. These examples show that options and option pricing are not just for highly skilled traders or academics, but have real world applications.

During the late 1990s and into the early 2000s, many people argued about whether stock options should be expensed as part of financial accounting requirements. Warren Buffett was one of the outspoken few who advocated for reflecting options as an expense on the financial statements for publicly-traded companies. Buffett argued that not expensing compensatory employee stock options results in overstating income to the organization. The simplest example of the validity of expensing is that the options could have been sold for a certain amount of cash. In lieu of cash, employees are receiving stock options.

SUMMARY

Summary of key points:

- There are four option positions: long call (buy a call), short call (sell a call), long put (buy a put), and short put (sell a put). Options offer a cost-efficient way to hedge investments or speculate on price movements of underlying assets.
- A call option gives the buyer the right, but not the obligation, to purchase the underlying asset at the exercise price of the option. A put option gives the buyer the right, but not the obligation, to sell the underlying asset at the exercise price of the option.
- The value of an option, which can be found using the Black-Scholes-Merton model, equals its intrinsic value plus the time value. The intrinsic value of the option is the minimum price at which an option will trade and equals the difference between the stock price and the exercise price. The time value is the difference between the premium value and the intrinsic value.
- Long calls benefit when the stock price increases. Long puts benefit when the stock price decreases. Short calls benefit when the stock price decreases. Short puts benefit when the stock price increases.
- Various types of options can be combined for specific strategies, including protective puts, covered calls, protective calls, collars, straddles, strangles, strips, and straps.
- Bonds are often issued with embedded options, including callable bonds, warrants, and convertible bonds.
- The binomial option pricing model (BOPM) can be used to price a call option by determining the value of a separate portfolio with the same payoffs as the call option. As the number of periods within the BOPM increases, it leads to the Black-Scholes-Merton option pricing model, which is used to price call options. The put-call parity model is used to price put options based on the value of call options.

DISCUSSION QUESTIONS

***SOLUTIONS** to the discussion questions can be found exclusively within the chapter. Once you have completed an initial reading of the chapter, go back and highlight the answers to these questions.*

1. What are the two types of options?
2. Why do investors purchase or sell options?
3. What is the difference between an American option and a European option?
4. What does the term "at-the-money" mean?
5. What does the term "in-the-money" mean?
6. What is the intrinsic value?
7. What is an offsetting order?
8. What does the term "out-of-the-money" mean?
9. Why are options considered a "zero-sum game?"
10. Why would an investor buy a call on a stock he did not own?
11. Why would an investor sell a call on a security they own?
12. Why would an investor buy a put?
13. Why would an investor sell a put on a stock they own?
14. What is the difference between a market order and a limit order?
15. When was the OCC created, what does it do, and how does it do it?
16. What are the four most prevalent types of options?
17. What are the basic eight options strategies?
18. What are three examples of types of securities with embedded options?
19. What does the put-call parity model do?
20. What does the binomial option pricing model do and how?
21. What are the variables used in the Black-Scholes Model?

MULTIPLE-CHOICE PROBLEMS

A sample of multiple choice problems is provided below. Additional multiple choice problems are available at money-education.com by accessing the Student Practice Portal.

1. Nimoy buys 20 call options on XYZ March 60 for $5 when the price of XYZ is 61. XYZ falls to $40 and remains there through March. What is Nimoy's gain or loss?
   a. Gain 30,000.
   b. Gain 29,000.
   c. Loss 9,000.
   d. Loss 10,000.

2. Gerry expects the market to rise. Which of the following option strategies should he follow:
   1. Long call.
   2. Long put.
   3. Short call.
   4. Short put.

   a. 1 and 2.
   b. 1 and 4.
   c. 2 and 3.
   d. 3 and 4.

3. A put option is available on the stock of Rally Corporation. The exercise price is $65. The put option price is $1. Rally stock is currently selling for $70 per share. What is the "intrinsic value" of the put option?
   a. $0.
   b. $4.
   c. $5.
   d. $9.

4. Writing a call option on the S&P 500 Index results in:
   a. A gain if the S&P 500 Index falls.
   b. A loss if the S&P 500 Index falls.
   c. A gain if the S&P 500 Index rises.
   d. Neither a gain nor loss, no matter what happens to the S&P 500 Index.

5. When someone "writes" a call option, they have:
   a. Taken a "long" position in a futures contract.
   b. "Marked-to-market" a futures contract.
   c. Sold a call option.
   d. Bought a call option.

QUICK QUIZ EXPLANATIONS

Quick Quiz 15.1

1. False. She might exercise if the price drops below $100.
2. True

Quick Quiz 15.2

1. True.
2. True.
3. False. The value of the option equals the time value plus the intrinsic value. In this case, it equals $12 ($8 + $4).

Quick Quiz 15.3

1. False. The value of an American option should be greater than a European option due to the ability to exercise at any time.
2. True.
3. True.

Quick Quiz 15.4

1. False. She should write a call option. If the stock price of Apple increases above the strike price of the call option, then her stock might be called from her. If the stock price stays constant or decreases, then she will simply keep the premium that she generated by writing the option.
2. False. The intrinsic value equals $0 as the call option's strike price is above the underlying security price. The time value is $5.

Quick Quiz 15.5

1. True.
2. False. An option series represents all options of a given type (calls or puts) with the same strike price and expiration date.
3. False. She could close the position by buying a put option.
4. True.

Quick Quiz 15.6

1. True.
2. False. It involves owning the underlying security while selling a call option.

Quick Quiz 15.7

1. True.
2. False. A zero cost collar provides downside protection for a cost of zero, but the investor must give up potential gains above the top of the collar (strike price for the call option).

Quick Quiz 15.8

1. True.
2. True.

QUICK QUIZ EXPLANATIONS

Quick Quiz 15.9

1. False. The value of a callable bond equals the value of a non-callable bond MINUS the call option value.
2. True.
3. True.

Quick Quiz 15.10

1. True.
2. True.
3. True.
4. False. The exercise price is the only variable in the model that is inversely related to the value of the call option.

16
ALTERNATIVE INVESTMENTS

LEARNING OBJECTIVES

1. Define an alternative investment opportunity.*
2. Identify the different types of alternative investments.*
3. Compare the characteristics of alternative investments with more traditional asset classes.*
4. Discuss the benefits and risks of including alternative investments in a portfolio.*
5. Explain commodity markets and explain how investors can use those markets in managing portfolios.*
6. Describe the different types of commodities.*
7. Explain the specific risks associated with investing in commodities.*
8. Support the notion that commodities are used as an inflation hedge.*
9. Differentiate among the benefits of each type of commodity.*
10. Describe the role derivative securities play in portfolio management.*
11. Define a call option and a put option.*
12. Identify appropriate futures contracts as part of portfolio management.*
13. Explain venture capital as part of an alternative investment strategy.*
14. Identify the various stages of venture capital financing.*
15. Discuss art and collectibles as popular alternative investments.*
16. Recognize the importance of hedge funds in portfolio management.*
17. Discuss the use of leverage and derivatives in hedge fund management.*
18. Define private equity.*
19. Explain the risks and benefits of private equity.*
20. Describe real estate as part of portfolio management.*
21. Identify the various types of real estate investing.*
22. Describe cryptocurrency and its potential use as an alternative investment within a diversified portfolio.*

**Ties to CFP Certification Learning Objectives*

INTRODUCTION

Publicly-traded debt, equity, and cash holdings make up the universe of traditional investments. These securities are typically the most popular among investors as they attempt to achieve their risk and return objectives. An increasing number of investors, however, look outside this traditional universe to alternative investments as vehicles to potentially add significant value to their portfolios.

One reason that alternative investments gained popularity in the 1990's and 2000's is the fact that the number of equity securities available for trading significantly decreased. Many professionals cite increases in regulations and merger activity as the main reasons for the dramatic decline. For example, according to JP Morgan Asset Management, the number of U.S.-based corporations traded on the U.S. stock exchanges fell from approximately 8,000 in 1996 to about half that number by 2016. Additional data from the Wilshire Associates shows that its Wilshire 5000 Index shrunk from a high of about 7,500 companies in 1998 to about 3,500 companies as of the end of the first quarter of 2019. Since there were fewer companies from which to choose, it makes sense that more investors sought alternatives. In recent times the number of equities traded has recovered, and at the end of 2000 more than 6,000 companies traded on the NYSE and NASDAQ. The popularity of alternative investments has endured, however, partly due to the increasing ease with which retail investors can access these markets.

The alternative investment universe is one that can increase diversification benefits for investors, one that can offer superior returns, and one that might provide risk advantages that other securities do not. Alternative investments include:

- commodities
- derivative securities
- hedge funds
- private equity
- real estate
- collectibles
- venture capital
- cryptocurrencies

Each of these alternative investments has its own unique risk profile and return expectations. They are attractive to investors for at least two reasons: (1) for the low correlations with traditional asset classes and (2) for adding a risk premium not available from other asset classes. Consequently, portfolios that contain alternative investments often have higher expected returns and less volatility than portfolios that are constrained to the traditional asset universe.

CRITICAL ALTERNATIVE INVESTMENT FACTORS

Alternative investments provide a host of potential benefits but also expose the investor to different risks than traditional investments. The primary benefit of including alternatives in a portfolio is diversification, but there are other attractive features.

Benefits

Returns

A common motivation for investing in alternatives is the opportunity for generating higher returns than from traditional markets. Alternative investments are more likely than traditional asset classes to trade at inefficient prices because all relevant information is not always readily available. These inefficiencies create an opportunity to increase returns.

Diversification

The primary benefit of using alternative investments as part of an investor's asset allocation strategy is the pursuit of diversification benefits. A wide collection of academic and professional researchers have shown that a low correlation coefficient exists between individual alternative investments and traditional securities. Uncorrelated securities or those with very low correlations are especially helpful during down equity markets. By adding alternative investments to diversified traditional portfolios, investors can reasonably expect to offset losses in stocks and bonds with gains in alternatives.

Key Concepts

1. Discuss the significance of minimum investment requirements for many alternative investments.
2. Explain the diversification benefits of owning alternative investments.

Tax Benefits

Since alternatives are securities that are held for the long term, they might offer tax benefits by only being subject to the lower long-term capital gains (LTCG) tax rate. By holding investments long term, both managers and investors benefit from LTCG tax treatment. Hedge fund and private equity managers are typically compensated via **carried interest**, which is a distribution of profits designed to align the interests of the managers with the interests of the investors. For years after 2017, the carried interest in private equity and hedge funds has a three-year minimum holding period, which was outlined in the Tax Cuts and Jobs Act of 2017. In addition, real estate ownership allows for depreciation expense to lower annual tax liabilities. The TCJA also created a new 20 percent tax deduction for certain types of real estate investments, qualified REIT dividends, and master limited partnership (MLP) income.

Inflation Hedge

Some alternatives are viewed as an inflation hedge. Gold has always been thought of as an effective way to protect against the loss of purchasing power, but wine and stamps have been shown in recent years to be effective as well. Of course, the inflation hedge depends on correlations remaining stable during economic downturns.

Risks

Alternative investments expose investors to additional risks that must be carefully evaluated. In general, investors seeking to move outside the traditional investment framework should be aware of the following risks.

Poor Liquidity

Alternative investments are not traded exactly like traditional investments. Most have very thin if any secondary market trading which means alternative investors sacrifice liquidity over extended periods of time. If there is a secondary market available for alternatives it is generally not very liquid, at least when compared to trading on the floor of the NYSE. As such, investors who sell early can be expected to incur additional trading costs such as very wide bid ask spreads. In addition, hedge fund and private equity investors are generally subject to lock out periods under which they have little access to their capital.

High Research Costs

There is much less information available on alternative investment opportunities than traditional securities. Much more is known about large U.S. companies like Johnson and Johnson than on the ownership of a shopping center. To compensate for this lack of available information, investors incur additional research and due diligence costs. There is always the chance that information collected in this manner will be inaccurate, costly, and incomplete, leading to inefficient allocation.

Quick Quiz 16.1

1. The major risks of investing in alternative securities includes price risk and liquidity issues.
   a. True
   b. False
2. A significant benefit of alternative investment exposure is diversification.
   a. True
   b. False
3. Because many alternative investments are managed by experienced professional managers, there is little risk to principal.
   a. True
   b. False

True, True, False.

Performance Appraisal Issues

Traditional investors are accustomed to following their portfolios on a daily basis and making price-earnings comparisons on at least a quarterly basis, but this is virtually impossible to do with most alternative investments. Although spot prices are available for many derivative securities and most commodities, prices for many alternatives are not available on a daily or even monthly basis. In many cases, estimates of current market values are necessary to evaluate performance. These estimates, of course, are made with degrees of error that can be quite large. In addition, this lack of price transparency can lead to bubbles and crashes, as evidenced by the contribution of mortgage backed securities and credit default swaps to the 2008 financial crisis.

High Expenses, Fees, and Minimum Investment Requirements

Some hedge funds charge an expense ratio that is three times that of traditional mutual funds, and fees can be hidden inside operating expenses that make hedge funds among the most expensive investment vehicles. For example, hedge fund managers often charge a two percent fee plus 20 percent of any profits generated during the time period. In addition, minimum investments may range from $500,000 to $1,000,000 or more, with some funds requiring commitments that last five to ten years.

Principal Risk

The uncertainty surrounding future selling or exit prices is a major risk for investments in alternative assets, making them unsuitable for most small and unsophisticated investors. **Principal risk** can be particularly high because many alternatives require long-term horizons.

Lack of Expertise

Most traditional investors at least know something about mutual funds, or stock exchanges, or the companies included in their portfolios, but few of them know much about alternative investments. The novelty of alternatives is hampered by the odd result that naïve investors can be herded into investments that are inconsistent with their risk and return profiles.

Example 16.1

Long-Term Capital Management (LTCM) was founded by former Salomon Brothers vice-chairman, John Meriwether, back in the early 1990s. LTCM boasted two Nobel Prize winners in Economic Sciences as prominent board members. Myron Scholes and Robert Merton won the prize for their pioneering work in option pricing and derivative security research. In the early years of the fund, it generated significant returns that peaked in 1995 with an after-fee return of 43%. The 1997 and 1998 financial crises that hit Asia and Russia resulted in an approximate $5 billion loss for the fund, which was bailed out by a consortium of U.S. financial institutions at the request of the Federal Reserve Bank of New York. The major cause of the losses was a volatility bet that failed when Russia began a systematic devaluation of its currency. LTCM suffered losses because the Russian currency value changes exceeded the limits expected by the fund. Even a hedge fund that is operated by highly respected and well-known investment professionals is not a guarantee of success.

Volatility

One of the attractions of alternative investments is the expected low correlation with traditional securities, but alternatives can have high volatility and therefore more risk than equity securities. For example, the standard deviation of bitcoin exceeds almost any historical level recorded for traditional securities.

Scarcity of Regular Cash Flow Distributions

Investors in equity and fixed-income securities are used to receiving regular cash payments from the issuer, but alternative investments almost never offer them.

Example 16.2

Petra is a 50-year-old retired executive with a $50 million portfolio that is composed of fixed-income and equity securities. Petra hopes to add alternative investments and considers the following:

- A painting by the Spanish artist Joan Miro for $500,000.
- Minority ownership in a farm that raises cattle, goats, and camels for $1.5 million.
- A private equity investment of $750,000 in a firm that invests solely in energy companies.
- The long position in a gold futures contract in which the spot price of gold is $1,200 and the price of the six-month futures contract is $1,250. Standard contract size is 100 troy ounces of gold, and Petra considers the long position in 400 contracts.

Benefits:

Each is likely to have low or even negative correlation with Petra's current portfolio; each is expected to magnify the returns to Petra's portfolio:

- Miro's paintings have been soaring in value over the last decade.
- Petra is likely to receive cash flow from the farm operations.
- The price of gold tends to rise with inflation, so this position offers at least some protection in the coming year.
- The private equity investment is expected to provide income and capital gains over an extended period of time.

Risks:

- There is likely to be high volatility, especially with the farm investment and the futures position.
- Even though the futures position is highly liquid, the remaining investments are considerably less so.
- There will likely be high expenses paid to the private equity firm.
- Petra might suffer from over confidence as she probably does not possess complete information on gold, farming, energy, or artwork.

COMMODITIES

Commodity investing is the direct or indirect ownership in natural resources or agricultural output. Commodities are created by natural forces and include energy products such as natural gas and oil, precious metals such as silver and gold, and food output such as grains and sugar. **Commodities** are uniquely characterized by scarcity, delivery challenges, storage issues, and a variety of qualities and uses.

Physical commodities are either primary or secondary. Primary commodities originate from mines, farms, or wells. Gold has to be mined, corn has to be grown, and oil has to be extracted. Secondary commodities, however, are produced from primary sources for consumption by individuals or businesses. For example, oil must be refined to run machinery, and iron ore must be crushed, mixed and pelletized to make steel.

Historically, only farming and mining companies had exposure to commodities. Dating back to the creation of the CME Group in 1848, investors could use futures contracts to take positions in farming commodities, but the futures exchange was typically used as a hedge by farming companies and to speculate by financial institutions. The only chance individual investors had to gain exposure to physical commodities was through equity ownership in publicly held agricultural and mining firms. This was appropriate for some, but not all investors. It was not until the beginning of the 21st century when multiple mutual fund families opened commodity funds that individual investors could purchase.

Key Concepts

1. Explain how diversification benefits of investing in commodities might not be as significant as expected.
2. Compare the risks of owning different types of commodities.

There are several types or categories of commodities.

Agricultural

Agricultural commodities are a collection of farming grain and oilseed products, including wheat, corn, soybeans, canola, and sunflowers. Agricultural commodities are grown throughout the world and are priced mostly on supply and demand conditions. Agricultural co-ops and farming businesses generate cash flow by combining labor and capital resources to produce crops and then sell them in highly competitive markets.

The primary risk of all commodities is price risk, sometimes referred to as market risk. The spot price of commodities fluctuates, sometimes wildly.[1] Since agricultural commodities tend to perish over time, changes in spot price can lead to drastic effects on profitability for both farming producers and business and individual consumers. Investors must be aware of the standard deviation of each commodity so they can manage the price risk.

The use of leverage increases the total risk of commodities. When agricultural firms borrow to finance the purchase of farming equipment, machinery, and farming structures, their profitability often depends on the interest rate on the loan.

Operating risk to which farmers are exposed involves the uncertainty of producing an acceptable grade crop. In addition to the quality of the plants and seeds themselves, the final crop depends on weather, theft, disease, and destruction of crops by hungry animals.

Governments and regulatory bodies also contribute to the risk of agricultural products. Some products receive federal tax subsidies while others have unique tax circumstances. For example, the Energy Policy Act of 2005 was the first federal requirement that renewable fuels must be used as an energy source for automobiles. The price of a bushel of corn jumped from around $2.00 in 2005 to almost $8.00 seven years later. Although prices subsequently fell back towards $2.00 as production increased, prices in early 2021 reached $7.00 once again.

1. The spot price (the current price at which the physical commodity can be purchased or sold for immediate delivery) of commodities.

Example 16.3

Ethanol is a renewable, domestically produced transportation fuel that is derived from corn. Most gasoline today is really a blend of petroleum-based gasoline and ethanol. The most common blend is referred to as E10 (10% ethanol, 90% gasoline) or E85 (flex fuel). The benefits of using ethanol in gasoline include reduced emissions, less dependency on foreign oil (energy), and providing U.S. jobs. Considerable problems occur because a gallon of ethanol contains less energy than a gallon of gasoline, resulting in lower fuel economy when operating a vehicle. Automakers have sued the EPA over ethanol due to the increased risk of damage to gasoline engines from the use of ethanol blends.

Livestock

Livestock is mostly comprised of beef, pork, and chicken. Ranching companies typically manage the process from birth to slaughterhouse. Profitability depends on the health of the herd and the demand for the final food product. Additional operating risks stem from the variability in expenses. Ranches face uncertainty over the price of grains and corn used to feed the livestock as well as the cost of insurance against theft and disease. Severe weather conditions or events can wipe out a herd. Price risk for both inputs and outputs has driven innovation for many cattle farms. One interesting trend is the development of a process that converts manure into methane gas that can be used as an energy source for the ranch. Many ranches have installed anaerobic digesters in which cow manure is collected, transported, and then converted into methane gas which, in turn, is used to produce electricity that can power barns, farming equipment, and storage facilities. The profitability of installing the manure converting machines depends not only on the cost of the digesters, but the relative cost of other energy sources.

Dairy

Dairy commodities, which include products such as milk, butter, and cheese are used in a variety of production processes and therefore demanded by many different consumers and businesses. According to Statistica, the total 2020 U.S. milk market was about 101 million metric tons while the total cheese market was approximately six million metric tons. Dairy profits, like other commodities, are sensitive to price risk, which is one reason that state governments in the U.S. have significant influence over production, distribution, and pricing.

The U.S. federal government imposes rules and regulations in the corn and dairy markets as a means of helping farmers in an attempt to stabilize the agricultural markets. This tends to happen in two ways. The government can be the buyer of last resort by agreeing to purchase all unsold commodities or it can impose price controls. Both scenarios are designed to make farming profitable enough to avoid bankruptcies and a collapse in food markets. Dairy farm consumers have been subject to price controls for decades and within the last ten years, the government has mandated that corn be used as an input in the refinement of oil to gasoline, as discussed above.

Lumber

Lumber commodities are generally divided into two categories: hardwood and softwood. Hardwood is named because its seeds have a covering. Hardwood is used for the manufacturing of furniture, cabinets, flooring, and construction. Softwoods, on the other hand, are from trees that produce cones. The wood is soft and easily nailed or cut, so it is primarily used in construction. Lumber prices are sensitive to demand for lumber products, natural disasters, and also to U.S.-CAD exchange rates because there is so much production in both the United States and Canada.

Quick Quiz 16.2

1. The primary risk of investing in commodities is lack of liquidity.
   a. True
   b. False
2. Weather contributes greatly to the risks of investing in commodities.
   a. True
   b. False
3. Government actions can impact the supply and demand of commodities, thus impacting prices.
   a. True
   b. False

False, True, True.

Textiles

Textiles are flexible materials, such as cotton and wool, used to manufacture clothing and carpeting. Textiles have a unique structure because they are derived from agricultural and livestock commodities. Pricing of textiles is highly dependent on U.S. cotton subsidies, extreme weather events, and an increasing popularity in developing countries.

Softs

The **soft commodity** market consists of orange juice, sugar, coffee, and cocoa, although the term has been used to include almost any commodity that can be grown or planted, as opposed to mined. In recent years, however, the term has been limited to a handful of commodities that are traded on the futures exchange. Weather is especially important in the pricing of soft commodities because of the fragile nature of the plants.

One final concern for investing in commodities is the chance of convergence in spot returns during extreme events. Many investors experience diversification benefits from choosing a variety of commodities because they have low correlations with traditional securities and with each other. This relationship tends to hold over time with the possible exception of rising or falling oil prices, which tend to drag the rest of the commodities with them during both bull and bear oil markets. Thus, diversification benefits are reduced in times of stress.

Example 16.4

Stella is an experienced money manager with a successful history as an equity, fixed income, and hedge fund manager. Stella is hired as the first commodity fund manager for Atlantic Investments, which encourages her to invest in a wide range of commodities. The fund has a successful opening as several billion dollars flow into the fund during its initial months of operations. The investments Stella makes include the following:

- The purchase of a 100% ownership in a dairy farm that raises cows and goats, and produces milk and cheese. A farming management group supervises the daily operations over a ten-year period.
- The entry into an agricultural co-op in the U.S. Midwest and South that buys cotton, wool, silk, and linen. The co-op is a key member of the supply chain that provides multiple services to the textile industry.

- The opening of speculative long and short positions in coffee, orange juice, and lumber futures contracts.

The United States Congress considers the following changes to the laws associated with regulating the commodities industry:

- Place a cap on the number of cows allowed to graze on farming land per acre.
- Impose an import tariff or import quotas on various textiles from U.S. trading partners.
- Design new more stringent regulations on futures exchanges by limiting speculative positions.

Effect of the new laws on the performance of the fund:
The effect of a cap on the number of cows per acre would depend on the actual cap number as compared to the number of cows on the farm. If the farm exceeds the cap, this would obviously reduce the operating cash flows of the farm, but the larger political risk is that the lawmakers are increasing regulation in the industry. If Congress is willing to pass a cap on cow population, then the farm must predict future possible caps to other areas, such as the number of goats. Political risks can significantly reduce profitability.

There are two sides to the trade war. On one hand, the tariff might increase the demand for the co-op's textiles as it naturally raises the price of imported goods. On the other hand, the economy might suffer from an increase in textile products as suppliers may be tempted to raise their own prices of textiles.

Speculative positions are those that are not supported by ownership in the underlying asset, which reduces the ability of the fund to take significant positions in the orange juice, coffee, and lumber markets.

DERIVATIVE SECURITIES

Derivatives play a major role in portfolio management as they can be used to hedge and to speculate in an efficient manner. The derivatives market offers leveraged opportunities to reduce or to increase all sorts of risks.

Call options are used as substitutes for owning underlying assets, such as shares of stocks, indexes, currencies, commodities, and other derivatives. The owner of call options has the right but not the obligation to purchase the underlying asset at a specified price within a given time limit.

Put options are used as substitutes for shorting those same underlying assets. The owner of put options has the right but not the obligation to sell the underlying asset at a specified price within a given time limit.

Consider the following examples:

Option Type	Underlying Asset	Time Period	Spot Price	Strike Price of Option
Call	100 GHS Shares	Six Months	$50	$45
Put	Barrel of Oil	Three Months	$100	$90

The call gives the owner the right to buy 100 GHR shares, which currently trade at $50, at a strike (exercise) price of $45 in the next six months. Known as an in-the-money option, the call will likely sell for around $7 using the Black Scholes Merton option pricing model. The main advantage of using the option instead of buying the shares is to magnify returns because the option only costs $7 while the shares cost $50. The main disadvantage, of course, is realized if the option expires out-of-the-money and the owner of the option loses the entire investment.

The put gives the owner the right but not the obligation to sell a barrel of oil for $90 in the next three months, whilst oil is trading at a spot price of $100. Known as an out-of-the-money option, the put will likely sell for around $1.00 using the Black Scholes Merton option pricing model. The main advantage of using the put instead of shorting the barrel of oil is the ease with which it can be accomplished. Shorting oil is generally done by using futures contracts or shorting exchange traded funds, but the rules and margins associated with those types of positions can be onerous for many investors. Put options can be purchased by almost any investor. The main disadvantage with puts is identical to that of calls.

An important pricing concept in the option market is intrinsic value. At expiration, intrinsic value is either $0 or the difference between the price of the underlying asset and the exercise price of the option. For example, a call option with an exercise price of $20 and an underlying expiration date asset price of $25 has $5 in intrinsic value. On the other hand, given that same information, the intrinsic value of the put option is $0.

Example 16.5

Stefania purchases 100 call options on Peabody Inc (PI) common shares. PI has a market price of $43 and the call sells for $4.50 with an exercise price of $40. The option expires in six months.

Determine the profit or loss under two possible expiration date stock prices: $60 or $30.
The initial investment: $4.50 × 100 contracts × 100 shares = $45,000.

The payoff for a call option is Max (0, Intrinsic Value).[2]

If expiration date stock price is $60 (intrinsic value is 20):
Payoff = ($60 – $40) × 100 × 100 = $200,000
Profit = $200,000 – $45,000 = $155,000

If expiration date stock price is $30 (intrinsic value is 0):
Payoff = $0
Profit = $0 – $45,000 = -$45,000

If the stock price rises to $60, Stefania earns $155,000 and generates a return of 344%.

If the stock price falls to $60, Stefania loses $45,000 and generates a negative return of 100% (-100%).

2. This notation simply means that the payoff for the call option is the maximum of zero or the intrinsic value. In other words, the payoff cannot be negative.

FUTURES CONTRACTS

Futures contracts are standardized forward contracts that are traded on exchanges and characterized by daily settlement. Futures contracts are written on commodities and financial assets and are used in a similar fashion to options. The primary difference between options and futures is that futures contacts represent an obligation to trade, while options allow an investor to do nothing on the expiration date.

Key Concepts

1. Compare the futures contracts to forward contracts and options.
2. Explain the motivation for an investor who takes a long or short position in futures contracts.

Futures investors take either long or short positions depending on whether they believe prices will rise or fall.

Consider the following example:

Futures Position	Underlying Asset	Time Period	Spot Price of Asset	Standard Contract Size
Long	Corn	Three Months	$4.00 per bushel	5,000 bushels
Short	Lumber	Six Months	$6.00 per 1,000 board feet	110,000 board feet

The long position in the corn futures contract expects the price of corn to rise over the next three months. The short position in the lumber futures contract expects the price of lumber to fall over the next six months. Note there are different standard amounts for each contract, as determined by the exchange. As the spot price of each underlying asset changes, the futures price of the asset will also change causing the value of the futures position to change. Daily settlement requires that each position is cash-settled at the end of every trading day.

Quick Quiz 16.3

1. Both call and put options can be used to take advantage of asset price volatility.
   a. True
   b. False
2. The long position in a futures contract benefits when asset prices fall.
   a. True
   b. False

True, False.

There is little liquidity risk or third-party risk because these contacts are traded on reputable exchanges, but there is substantial price risk. For example, in 2007, the price of a barrel of oil dropped from $140 in July to $50 by the end of the year. Anyone who shorted the contract during the last half of the year made significant profits. There are many examples of wide price fluctuations in commodity prices that have offered great opportunities, but perhaps the most well-known example occurs in the fictional movie 'Trading Places' starring Eddie Murphy, Dan Aykroyd, and Jamie Lee Curtis. The three unlikely friends short orange juice futures contracts. They possess private information indicating the price of OJ will fall when the government releases the crop report, while everyone else expects the price to rise. Of course, their private information turns out to be accurate and the price of orange juice falls. They make enough money to buy a yacht and travel the globe.

Of course, someone had to take the opposite position in both the oil price and orange juice examples, which means someone suffered great losses.

Example 16.6

Pickett Financial Group (PFG) takes the short position in 500 oil futures contracts. The current spot price of oil is $60 per barrel, and the three-month futures price of oil is $61 per barrel. The standard contract is 1,000 barrels.

Determine the profit or loss on the maturity date of the contract under the following two possible future spot prices of oil: $45 per barrel or $72 per barrel.

Initial value of the contract: $61 × 1,000 barrels × 500 contracts = $30,500,000

If the spot and futures prices equal $45 on the maturity date (convergence in futures and spot markets will cause the two prices to be identical on the exact maturity date):

Profit = ($61 – $45) × 1,000 × 500 = $8,000,000

If the spot and futures prices equal $72 on the maturity date:

Profit = ($61 – $72) × 1,000 × 500 = -$5,500,000

The short position benefits when the price of oil falls and suffers when it rises.

VENTURE CAPITAL

Venture capital (VC) is a method of financing for startup companies or small businesses. The sources of venture capital are typically wealthy investors and financial institutions. The attraction of adding VC to an investor's portfolio is the ability to magnify returns by identifying new market growth areas.

The typical VC arrangement includes the development and review of a strategic business plan and a subsequent creation of a limited partnership in which the ownership shares are sold to investors. In most transactions, the venture capitalist receives minority ownership in the form of preferred equity shares. Funds are delivered to the business usually in stages.

Stage	Description
Seed	Begins with a small investment in which the business owner often has little more than an idea to develop a unique product or service. The seed stage is characterized by significant amounts of market research and product development ideas. Many times, the venture capitalist is an expert in the product area and offers advice and consulting.
Startup	The first significant investment that is used for marketing and production to begin attracting potential customers. Additional research is likely done to refine the product, its packaging, and distribution channels.
Emerging	The product is launched with advertising, sales, and distribution. Even more capital is required during this stage.
Expansion	This is the growth stage in which the product becomes successful. The capital provided in this stage is used to finance growth by entering new geographic markets, hiring more personnel, and expanding the product.
Bridge	A transition from being a relatively unknown business to a mature company that is ready to be acquired by another firm or ready for an initial public offering. The original venture capitalists frequently sell their ownership positions during this stage.

Risks

The risks associated with venture capital are similar to the risks facing all investors, but there are some unique factors that make venture capital more risky than traditional investments. There is significant start up risk because early stage failure is quite common. According to the Harvard Business Review, about 70 percent of all businesses that attract venture capital will fail. This can be attributed to poor market timing or failure to properly evaluate the competition, but most businesses fail because of a lack of a well-developed strategic plan. The venture capitalists can manage this risk by diversifying, but many new businesses collapse prior to a product launch.

> ***Key Concepts***
>
> 1. Explain the liquidity issues facing venture capitalists.
> 2. Describe the managerial role some venture capitalists serve.

Failure can occur at every stage, so underperformance is a significant concern. Success of the business depends mostly on the skill set of its management team. Venture capitalists invest resources to evaluate the team before making any commitments. Part of this due diligence includes a measure of market growth opportunities in the field.

There are also legal and regulatory risks facing venture capitalists. Finally, there are at least two substantial liquidity issues facing venture capitalists. First, there is virtually no secondary market for venture capital, at least until the IPO stage. The venture capitalist also faces the risk at exit if the company is unable to raise capital during the IPO. Second, investment horizons are quite long, which means venture capitalists must sacrifice liquidity over extended time periods, which can be five to ten years.

Angel Investing

During the period a company transforms from being an idea-based start-up to a scalable company, it regularly needs inflows of capital. Most entrepreneurs receive seed capital from institutions, but sometimes the capital is provided by wealthy individuals. These **angel investors** typically provide between $50,000 and $500,000 and often times have expertise in the field in which the business operates. Sometimes, they even are asked to serve on the board of directors, which gives them access to all the financial operations of the business and allows them to provide strategic input.

There are networks of angel investors throughout the United States. The combination of capital and advice offered by angel investors improves the chance of success of the business.

> ***Quick Quiz 16.4***
>
> 1. The emerging stage of venture capital financing includes an expansion into additional geographic markets.
>   a. True
>   b. False
> 2. Early stage failure is a rare occurrence in venture capital investments.
>   a. True
>   b. False
>
> False, False.

ART AND COLLECTIBLES

Collectibles as an asset class are fast growing for a variety of reasons, but mostly because of the classic motivations: the search for higher returns and diversification. The class includes any item expected to increase in value including artwork, sculptures, sports and entertainment memorabilia, wine, watches, and classic automobiles.

Decades ago, collectors of rare items traded in illiquid, unorganized markets with incomplete information. Today, however, with advances in technology, markets are highly visible, much more transparent, and can even enjoy high volume trading, at least as compared to historical collectible markets. The lack of liquidity is still a significant issue and investors should be aware that the collectibles market will likely never experience liquidity levels observed on the floor of the New York Stock Exchange.

Key Concepts

1. Explain the human element of investing in the collectible markets.
2. Describe the historical returns in the luxury item market.

Other collectible risks include the loss in value due to theft and destruction. One famous example is the 1633 painting by Rembrandt entitled, *The Storm on the Sea of Galilee*, which was stolen from a museum in Boston, and its current location remains unknown. Pablo Picasso's *Le Pigeon aux Petits-Pois*, valued at $28 million, was stolen from a Paris museum and was destroyed by the thief before he was captured. Apparently, the painting was thrown in a garbage can and has never been recovered.

Example 16.7

A Banksy painting was being auctioned at Sotheby's in October 2018 for $1.4 million. At the end of the bidding, the painting, titled *Girl with Balloon*, suddenly started to scroll down through the frame of the painting but was shredded into strips by a device installed in the frame by the artist. Normally, destruction of a work of art would decrease its value. Many are speculating that this shredding will actually increase the value of this work of art. Banksy is known for pulling pranks such as this one, but he may have even topped any previous stunts as the event has substantially increased interest in his work.

Collectibles are also subject to counterfeiting. Famous actor Steve Martin purchased a fake German expressionist painter Campendonk painting in 2004. Martin sold it at a loss two years later, and it was soon discovered that it was a forgery. One set of collectibles that have a reduced risk of forgery are non-fungible tokens (NFTs). NFTs are digital assets that use blockchain technology to verify their authenticity. An investor who purchases an NFT gains the official ownership of a digital file and possibly rights for displaying the associated image or video. In October 2020, for example, the National Basketball Association (NBA) launched an online NFT marketplace called 'NBA Top Shot' where investors (or fans) could purchase video clips of NBA highlights.

Anyone who invests receives a video highlight that has no doubt been viewed online before, possibly millions of times for more popular highlights, but the NFT's value is derived from the fact that the investor now has exclusive official owner of that version of the clip. As at September 2021, the most expensive clip (a LeBron James dunk) sold for $387,600.

Much like cryptocurrency, the NFT asset class is still in its infancy, and whether NFTs will deliver long-term gains is yet to be seen. However, short-term gains have been spectacular. An NFT by the artist known as Beeple purchased for $66,666, was sold for $6.6 million just four months later, and another of Beeple's NFTs sold at auction for $69 million.[3]

3. https://www.christies.com/features/Monumental-collage-by-Beeple-is-first-purely-digital-artwork-NFT-to-come-to-auction-11510-7.aspx

Collectibles can also incur substantial storage costs and sales commissions, plus there are no interest or dividend payments in the collectible market. There are tax consequences of buying and selling collectibles, as evidenced by former Tyco CEO Dennis Kozlowski, who was convicted of securities fraud, falsifying business records, and New York state sales tax evasion. The collectibles market is characterized by limited and incomplete information on price history, volatility, and quality. A final problem with owning collectibles is the fact that there are few reliable benchmarks.

Quick Quiz 16.5

1. Major risk factors in owning collectibles are counterfeiting and tax consequences.
   a. True
   b. False
2. Most artwork has highly liquid secondary markets.
   a. True
   b. False

True, False.

Investors become interested in collectibles based mostly on their consumption preferences. Individuals who like to drink wine will be highly likely to invest in vintage wine. Likewise, individuals who collected coins as a child will be very likely to begin more serious collection when they search for alternative investments. As such, there is an emotional attachment which can cause behavioral biases that may lead to substantial losses.

In conjunction with the risks created by the emotional attachment associated with collectibles, an emotional return is associated with these investments. Collectibles offer the pride of ownership that other asset classes do not. It is quite common for collectors to display their items in public and private showings. For example, when Harry Yeaggy purchased the Aston Martin that James Bond drove in the movie Goldfinger, he remarked that he was going to drive it around London and have some fun with it. Yeaggy paid GBP 2.6 million for the car in 2010.

The Knight Frank Luxury Investment Index tracks the performance of collectibles. A summary of ten-year annualized returns through 2020 are shown below:

Collectible	Ten-Year Annualized Return
KFLI Index	9.42%
Art	9.42%
Wine	9.24%
Watches	5.01%
Coins	11.35%
Jewelry	7.18%
Cars	11.23%
Stamps	5.07%
Diamonds	7.44%
Furniture	-3.50%

Investment advisers have become more willing to recommend collectibles as an asset class during the 21st century, but data on standard deviations and correlations remains limited. Since there is little active secondary market trading, the computed standard deviations of many collectibles may be understated.

One academic study by Dimspon and Spanjeurs published in *Risk and Uncertainty in the Art World*, the authors show that art, stamps, and musical instruments have appreciated in value by around 6.5 percent per year since 1900. Their more interesting findings suggests that the realized returns for artwork exceed those of bonds but are less than the returns to equities. In addition, the standard deviations of collectibles is between 10 percent and 13 percent, which is much less than the standard deviation of equities at 21 percent. Finally, the authors show low correlations between equity and collectibles with a correlation coefficient of approximately 0.20, illustrating that diversification with collectibles can be achieved. A partial summary correlation table from their research is shown below:

	Art	Stamps	Violins	Equities	Bonds
Art	1.00				
Stamps	0.14	1.00			
Violins	0.25	0.07	1.00		
Equities	0.22	0.00	0.02	1.00	
Bonds	0.08	0.24	0.03	0.51	1.00

HEDGE FUNDS

Hedge funds are investment companies that manage capital for their investors. The hedge fund manager acts as a **general partner** in managing capital for the fund's limited partners. Third-party investors such as financial institutions, pension funds, endowments, and wealthy individual investors provide capital to the general partner. Hedge fund managers invest the capital much like mutual fund managers, but they have far more leeway to pursue investment opportunities that are unavailable to mutual fund managers.

Key Concepts

1. Describe the hedge fund investment horizon.
2. Identify the similarities between hedge funds and equity mutual funds.

Hedge fund managers combine investments in traditional markets with strategies using unconventional markets and securities. To accomplish a policy that is often times expected to outperform traditional benchmarks, hedge fund managers use derivative securities, commodities, and other alternative investments. Hedge fund managers use **leverage** to magnify returns for the limited partners and can do it in ways prevented by significant regulation imposed on mutual fund managers. Because the hedge fund industry operates in a generally regulation-free environment, its general partners can pursue almost any investment strategy to boost returns. Of course, this means extra risk.

Important Risks of Hedge Fund Investing

Hedge funds are only available to investors who can afford minimum capital requirements of $250,000 or more. For individuals, the hedge fund market has minimum income and asset requirements and the hedge fund manager is not obligated to accept capital from any investor. In addition, many hedge funds limit the timing and amounts of redemptions. It is not unusual for a hedge fund to limit the number of redemptions to three of four times per year in addition to having periods under which there can be no redemptions. These are liquidity issues that make hedge fund investing a long-term prospect.

Leverage is used by many investors to magnify returns, but hedge fund managers appear to use leverage at its limits. The use of swap contracts is particularly risky because the manager chooses the notional principal of the swap, which exacerbates both gains and losses. For example, a five percent change in the yield on treasury securities would have a much greater impact on return for a hedge fund manager with a $100 million interest rate swap position than it would on one with a $10 million position.[4]

Quick Quiz 16.6

1. Hedge funds typically have minimal initial investment requirements.
   a. True
   b. False
2. Hedge funds are permitted to speculate in the derivative securities markets.
   a. True
   b. False

False, True.

The hedge fund fee structure is unique as well. There is a general management fee comparable to mutual fund expense ratios usually in the one percent to 2.5 percent range, but hedge fund managers also participate in the performance of the portfolio. Performance fees can be as high as 20 percent of the profits generated by the manager. In fact, most hedge fund managers charge a standard two percent plus 20 percent of profits. This fee means the hedge fund manager is paid two percent of invested assets plus 20 percent of profits for the fund.

The extra hedge fund risks must be added to systematic, interest rate, and default risks associated with traditional debt and equity securities.

Example 16.8

Martin Hedge Fund (MHF) uses derivative securities to increase its expected returns. MHF uses an equity swap to take advantage of relative market movements.

MHF agrees to enter into a swap as the fixed rate payer, paying a fixed annual rate of 12% (3% quarterly) in return for the quarterly return on the S&P 500 Index with a notional principal of $100 million. This is a pay fixed – receive floating rate swap.

Determine the cash flow at each quarterly settlement date if the returns on the S&P 500 Index for each quarter were:

Q1	Q2	Q3	Q4
4.8%	2.1%	-1.8%	5.2%

MHF receipt at Q1:
Profit = (0.048 – 0.03) × 100 million = 1,800,000

MHF payment at Q2:
Profit = (0.021 – 0.03) × 100 million = -900,000

MHF payment at Q3:
Profit = (-0.018 – 0.03) × 100 million = -4,800,000

MHF receipt at Q4:
Profit = (0.052 – 0.03) × 100 million = 2,200,000

4. Interest rate swaps do not involve a swap of financial products; instead, the institutional investors agree to swap the cash flows without changing their underlying investments. Similarly, an equity swap involves the exchange of cash flows from one investor with a fixed rate cash flow and another investor whose cash flows are determined by a particular equity index.

In an equity swap the pay fixed party will have to make a payment if the equity return is less than the fixed rate, in this case 3% quarterly. Higher equity returns benefit the pay fixed party. Note that it is possible to pay out on both legs in an equity swap. This occurs in Q3, when MHF must pay 3% and also pay out 1.8% as the index fell.

PRIVATE EQUITY

Ownership in businesses that are not traded on a public exchange is **private equity**. It consists of investors who own minority or majority positions by directly buying the equity in businesses.

Private equity firms are organizations that raise capital from wealthy individuals or institutional investors and use it to purchase equity positions in privately run businesses or sometimes to engage in a leveraged buyout of publicly traded firms.

Private equity firms operate by executing four functions, although not all private equity firms perform each one: they raise capital; they perform the duties of general business partners; they use their expertise to locate undervalued firms, and finally they attempt to transform those firms into successful businesses by using their extensive knowledge and expertise.

Key Concepts

1. Describe the risks specific to a private equity firm that maintains a supervisory position.
2. Compare private equity investment in construction firms to private equity investment in software providers.

Private equity firms raise capital usually from institutional investors who are offered limited partnership positions. The limited partners have a claim on the cash flows generated by the businesses.

The private equity firm acts as the general partner and can contribute as much as five percent of total capital. The limited partners are almost always asked to provide significant amounts of capital, sometimes as much as a few hundred million dollars. Institutions such as pension funds and endowments can easily handle investments like this as they pursue higher rates of return than are offered by traditional equity investments. High net worth individuals are frequently offered a discount on the required initial investment, but the amount can still be in the tens of millions of dollars.

The private equity firm searches for undervalued businesses. Sometimes these businesses are found through extensive research of specific industries, but often times the businesses approach the private equity firm in search of financing. Other times the private equity firm is approached by the investment banking community. Once businesses are discovered as potential targets, the private equity firm completes its due diligence by examining all the financial statements, interviewing the stakeholders of the business and surveying the industry landscape for the business.

Once the private equity firm infuses capital into the business, the general partner begins the process of improving the operations of the business. Private equity general partners usually agree to have board of director representation and they can restructure the leadership of the business, including firing under-performing managers, but they mostly provide consulting advice on a variety of issues. They mainly offer strategic and organizational visions concerning the future of the business. This process of management influence typically occurs over a three to eight year period, after which the private equity firm seeks an exit.

The final stage is exiting the business. The most common way this occurs is through an initial public offering or an outright acquisition by a larger more established firm. The private equity firm performs coordinating functions among the players but relies heavily on investment bankers to complete the transaction. For example, Door Dash made its first delivery in 2013, raised over $15 billion from private equity investments over the next seven years, then had its IPO in late 2020, pushing its market value to $60 billion. As of 2022, Door Dash remains an unprofitable company.

Risks

Traditional measures of risk are not very reliable when considering private equity, especially as there is significant positive skewness in private equity returns. For example, it is challenging to accurately estimate an equity beta for a privately held firm. Consequently, leverage and cash flow ratios are critical when estimating the likelihood of default. The traditional means of consulting one of the major ratings agencies or using the credit default swap market or spread analysis to gauge default risk are not available.

The major risks in private equity are:

- Funding risk
- Liquidity risk
- Market risk
- Exit risk

Quick Quiz 16.7

1. Successful private equity investments offer significant short-term returns.
   a. True
   b. False
2. Private equity investments reduce risk by guaranteeing exit strategies.
   a. True
   b. False

False, False.

Funding Risk

Private equity investors agree to make contractual payments to the fund, which in turn finds investments in businesses. Funding risk is the chance the investor is unable to make these payments, and the risk for the fund is the inability to make timely investments. The risk to the investor is the possibility of losing their entire capital, even capital that had been previously provided.

Liquidity Risk

Because private equity structures are structured to ensure the long-term commitment of each investor, a secondary market for limited partner commitments has evolved. This market has varying degrees of liquidity, and sometimes investors are forced to sell their shares at a steep discount to net asset value.

Market Risk

The value of the individual investments in the private equity fund fluctuates with economic conditions. In particular, private equity performance can be sensitive to changes in interest rates, foreign currency values, and commodity prices.

Exit Risk

The expected future value of private equity investments depends on factors specific to the portfolio. Fund manager experience and expertise, the ability to successfully manage multiple groups of business owners and coordinating visions and strategic plans greatly influence the performance of each business in the private equity fund.

Example 16.9

Knight Capital (KC) is a private equity firm created by four college friends who became highly successful entrepreneurs. The friends started their own businesses individually and sold them recently. Each remains involved in their firms as part-time consultants. They began KC a few months ago and have attracted significant interest from investors throughout the world. Although their businesses were mostly in the technology industry, they share a common interest in the technology of water treatment and electricity.

KC has raised enough capital to make the following investments:

- The purchase of a minority interest in a water bottling and distribution company.
- The purchase of a 100% ownership interest in a failing sewage treatment facility at a bargain.
- The purchase of a 60% ownership in an incinerator plant.

The four general partners in KC believe the water industry remains in its early growth stages. They believe they have the expertise to revitalize the failing sewage facility. They believe they can use the incinerator and sewage to convert waste into electricity to supply the U.S. electric grid.

Discuss the potential benefits and risks associated with these investments.

Clearly, the three investments offer diversification benefits to the private equity firm. Water, sewage, and incineration are generally considered to operate in unrelated industries, but the four entrepreneurs can leverage their technology expertise to magnify the firm's returns.

Risks include liquidity issues as the investments are most likely long-term ones. In addition, they need to make certain they have an exit strategy for each investment, especially the failing sewage plant.

Example 16.10

Pinnacle Equity Partners (PEP) is a private equity firm focused in the education sector. They purchase the following five companies for a total of $77.5 million in Year 1:

Company	Revenue	EBITDA	Price Paid	Price Multiple[1]	EBITDA Growth
Acme	$10.0 million	$3.0 million	$21.0 million	7x	15%
Baker	$5.0 million	$1.0 million	$7.0 million	7x	10%
Challenge	$12.0 million	$1.5 million	$7.5 million	5x	10%
Delta	$15.0 million	$3.0 million	$18.0 million	6x	12%
Echo	$8.0 million	$3.0 million	$24.0 million	8x	30%

1. The price multiple is the price paid for the business divided by EBITDA (earnings before interest, taxes, depreciation, and amortization). Effectively, this metric is the same type of metric as the PE ratio.

PEP is a great partner that helps drive strategic growth of the portfolio companies. PEP centralizes finance, accounting, HR, and operations, which helps with operational efficiency and reporting. It leaves each of the companies' leadership teams in place in a decentralized manner. For this analysis, assume the following:

- The companies' earnings grow as anticipated and generate about $26 million in EBITDA in Year 5.
- PEP financed 40% of the purchase price with debt at an interest rate of 6% structured to be paid off in 36 months.
- PEP is able to sell the five companies together at the end of Year 5 for 10 times EBITDA.

Below are the earnings and cash flows for each company by year:[5]

Company	EBITDA Growth	Initial EBITDA	Year 1 EBITDA	Year 2 EBITDA	Year 3 EBITDA	Year 4 EBITDA	Year 5 EBITDA
Acme	15%	3.00	3.45	3.97	4.57	5.26	6.05
Baker	10%	1.00	1.10	1.21	1.33	1.46	1.61
Challenge	10%	1.50	1.65	1.82	2.00	2.20	2.42
Delta	12%	3.00	3.36	3.76	4.21	4.72	5.29
Echo	30%	3.00	3.90	5.07	6.59	8.57	11.14
Total		11.50	13.46	15.83	18.70	22.21	26.51
Debt Payments*			(11.32)	(11.32)	(11.32)	-	-
Free CF			2.14	4.51	7.38	22.21	26.51

Based on the information above, the cash flows (in millions) for PEP are:[6]

CF_0 = -$46.50 ($77.5 x 60% equity) equity investment

CF_1 = $2.14

CF_2 = $4.51

CF_3 = $7.38

CF_4 = $22.21

CF_5 = $291.61 ($26.51 + $265.10 exit price at 10x)

These cash flows equate to an IRR of 51% and a return of 7 times invested capital. PEP is able to sell the combined companies for a higher multiple because the combined company is more diversified and operates as one organization. The rate of return and ROE are high due to the underlying growth of the combined companies as well as the leverage used in the purchase of the companies. If the exit multiple were 8 times instead of 10 times, then the IRR would drop to 46% and the return on invested capital would drop to 6 times.

Private equity companies are able to generate investment gains through leverage, improvement of portfolio company operations, and by increasing the exit multiple over the purchase multiple.

Return Multiple = (2.14 + 4.51 + 7.38 + 22.2 + 291.61) ÷ 46.5 = 7

5. Debt payment calculation: PV = 31(77.5 x 40%), N=36, i = 0.5(6/12), solve for PMT = 0.94308, 12 months of payments = 11.32
6. In reality, there are additional tax benefits that would accrue to PEP in this example. There are also other costs that would be incurred, including the cost of an audit. These factors have not been incorporated for purposes of simplicity.

REAL ESTATE

As a part of the alternative investment class, real estate is the most traditional in nature. Investments can be made directly or indirectly.

Key Concepts

1. Describe how Net Operating Income can be used to value real estate investments.
2. Explain the main risks associated with real estate investing, including political risk.

In ancient Egypt, land was considered to be owned by the gods but controlled by the pharaohs. For thousands of years, only kings and tribal leaders owned land, but that changed over time as the royal owners began trading land for goods and services. By the 1200s, there was a very sophisticated model of exchanging property for a pledge of service, either militarily or agriculturally. Historically, land ownership was the primary way to gain power, which of course was the reason for so many wars. In modern times, land is still equated with power, as evidenced by the global influence of large countries such as the United States and China.

Real estate investors seek income, appreciation, and diversification. Income typically is derived from the cash flows associated with ownership, such as rent, but can also be generated by commissions, fees, and ancillary assets such as vending machines located in popular locations. Appreciation occurs when buyers outnumber sellers, but can also occur because of government regulations, housing laws, and zoning restrictions. Diversification benefits are significant in that correlations between real estate and traditional asset classes is relatively low and sometimes even negative.

Real Estate Categories

Real estate investing can generally be divided into the following categories:

- Residential property
- Commercial property
- Industrial property
- Retail property
- Mixed-use property
- Lending-related ownership
- Secondary market investing

Residential Property

Most real estate investors get started by understanding the advantages of their own home ownership and extending that to the purchase of residential rental properties, including apartment buildings. Most of these rental or lease agreements extend for periods between six and eighteen months, making this type of real estate highly sensitive to market conditions. Income depends on vacancy rates, interest rates, and income levels.

Commercial Property

Office buildings can provide a steady stream of income because leases typically are signed for multiple years. Since most lease agreements involve fixed payments, the risk of owning commercial property is similar to that of a fixed rate bond. If lease rates increase, the property owner suffers because of being locked in to the lower income stream. On the other hand, if lease rates fall, the property owner benefits under the current leases. Once again, these dynamics are similar to owners of fixed-income securities.

Industrial Property

Property used by various industries includes warehouses, distribution facilities, storage centers, and auto washing buildings. These properties are frequently coupled with vending machines, which can add significant value.

Retail Property

Any property whose tenants market their goods or services to the consuming public are considered to be retail. This includes shopping centers and traditional and modern malls. Leases are typically renewed on an annual basis but can be for longer or shorter time periods. Many retail property owners agree to accept lower lease payments in return for a percentage of sales so there is tenant incentive to maintain the property as well as maximize value. Diversification among different locations and types is important, especially given the high bankruptcy rate for restaurants and retails chains like Toys 'R' Us and Radio Shack.

Mixed-Use Property

Any combination of the different types of properties into one project is known as a mixed-use property. Examples include office buildings that lease space on the ground floor to retail establishments. The mixed-use class is popular among very wealthy investors because of the built-in diversification benefits, but also because of the synergies available to each tenant. For example, office workers are more likely to stay close to work when deciding on a place to eat lunch.

Lending-Related Ownership

Investors can own minority percentages in smaller local banks and other financial institutions that underwrite mortgage and commercial real estate loans or become involved in sub leasing properties.

Secondary Market Investing

A significant issue with direct investment in real estate is the level of investment required. The cost of commercial properties, for example, is likely to be in the tens or hundreds of millions, making them accessible only to high or even ultra-high net worth investors.

Many investors choose an indirect route instead. One popular method is to invest in a Real Estate Investment Trust (REIT). A REIT is a company that earns income from real estate either by financing, operating or owning properties.

Investors can buy shares in publicly traded REITS or gain exposure through REIT ETFs or mutual funds. This makes exposure to real estate much more accessible to investors, and according to the National Association of REITs, 145 million Americans, or 44 percent of American households were invested in REIT stocks as at October 2020.

As well as the significantly lower investment required, indirect investment also avoids the need for the investor to actively manage a property, instead that burden falls on the REIT. Another advantage of REITS is that shareholders pay no income tax on dividends as long as the REIT pays out 90 percent of its taxable income to shareholders.

Risks

The major risks in real estate are:

- Market risk
- Liquidity risk
- Default risk
- Political risk
- Environmental risk
- Replacement cost risk

Market Risk

Like any other investment, real estate is subject to market risk. Changing economic conditions, including interest rates, income and employment levels, inflation, web-based competition, and productivity can have a substantial impact on the profitability of real estate investments. For example, many businesses have gone bankrupt because of the proliferation of ecommerce sites like Amazon and eBay. The real estate investors who own the land and buildings of competing businesses lose tenants regularly.

Liquidity Risk

Real estate, by its nature, is not very liquid and frequently is not marketable. Not only do investors have to concern themselves with the opportunity cost of having capital tied up in poorly performing properties, they suffer doubly when they cannot sell the property quickly or at a fair market value.

Default Risk

Real estate deals tend to be highly leveraged which makes default risk a major concern for investors, especially in down markets.

Example 16.11

The Mensa Group invested in Gulf Coast beach-front property for the purpose of developing condominiums for sale during 2005. The group paid $14 million for the property, but only put down $4 million and borrowed $10 million. One of the critical steps was to pre-sell enough units to obtain a construction loan. Unfortunately, due to a rash of hurricanes hitting the Gulf Coast, and the housing crisis occurring a few years later, the group ran out of money and was unable to pay the interest on the debt. The debt had to be refinanced several times during the time interest rates were increasing. The group attempted to sell the property, but there was no one who had an interest in buying the property at the time. The group finally let the bank foreclose on the property in 2010, and it was auctioned for $4 million. As a result, each of the members had to settle their personal guarantees with the bank and lost millions. In hindsight, the investors bought at the top of the market, leveraged the property too much, and did not have the key to making the project successful – buyers of the condos.

Political Risk

Government agencies and regulatory bodies place a significant burden on real estate owners to follow a wide variety of rules and laws. Zoning issues, property tax uncertainties, and fair housing policies influence the income stream and therefore the value of a property.

Environmental Risk

The global movement to green energy also impacts the value of properties as many businesses move to renewable energy sources. Air pollution and ground water and soil contamination can also reduce property values. Increasing average global temperatures and climate change over the last two decades have also increased the level of environmental risk.

Replacement Cost Risk

Owners of buildings will be forced to replace them eventually and face the risk of significantly higher construction costs. This also applies to the upgrade and maintenance of facilities.

> **Quick Quiz 16.8**
>
> 1. Real estate exposure can be obtained by investing directly in land and indirectly in equity markets.
>   a. True
>   b. False
> 2. Real estate investing necessarily requires expertise in understanding relevant tax laws.
>   a. True
>   b. False
> 3. Real estate investments tend to be highly liquid.
>   a. True
>   b. False
>
> True, True, False.

Net Operating Income

When evaluating real estate for investment purposes, a common method of valuation is to divide the net operating income (NOI) by an appropriate capitalization rate based on the investor's required rate of return for investing in the property, and the expected growth rate in NOI. Alternatively, a capitalization rate can be calculate d from comparable properties that have recently sold by dividing their sales value by their NOI. The NOI is typically averaged over several years to account for possible variations in occupancy (vacancy) or rents. NOI can be calculated as follows:

Gross potential rental receipts
+ Other income (such as vending machine, laundry, parking receipts)
= Gross potential income
- Vacancy and collection losses
= Gross income before expenses
- Operating expenses (excluding interest & depreciation)
= Net Operating Income

NOI is specific to the property and not the individual investor, hence any finance costs incurred by investors, such as mortgage interest, are not included in the property's NOI. Depreciation is also excluded as it is a tax adjustment and not a cash outflow.

Example 16.12

Carson is considering the purchase of a rental property. The property rents for $1,500 a month, and the fee for garage parking is $85 a month. The property and garage space are expected to be rented 90% of the year. Additional expenses associated with the property include real estate taxes of $1,800 a year, liability insurance of $1,200 a year, advertising expense of $200 a year, maintenance costs of $1,300 a year, depreciation of $3,800 a year, and interest expense on Carson's mortgage of $5,100 a year. If the appropriate capitalization rate on the property is 12%, what is the intrinsic value of the property?

$18,000	Gross potential rental receipts ($1,500 x 12)
+1,020	+ Other income (parking receipts) ($85 x 12)
$19,020	**= Gross potential income**
-1,902	- Vacancy losses (10% for both property and garage space) x $19,020
$17,118	**= Gross income before expenses**
-4,500	- Operating expenses (excluding interest & depreciation)
$12,618	**= Net Operating Income (NOI)**

$12,618 ÷ 0.12 capitalization rate = $105,150 intrinsic value

Note that the depreciation and Carson's mortgage interest expense is not included in the NOI calculation.

It is important to note that NOI ÷ capitalization rate does not give consideration to the cash flow or tax benefits provided to the investor. In other words, NOI should not be the sole determining factor for purchasing a real estate investment. The investor will also be very interested in the after-tax cash flows that the property provides. To determine the taxable income, interest expense and depreciation are subtracted from NOI. Taxes are then calculated based on the taxable income amount, and are, of course paid, leaving the investor with net after-tax earnings.

After-tax *cash flow* is equal to:

net after-tax earnings
+ depreciation
- principal repayment
= after-tax cash flow

Depreciation is added back in because it creates a tax deduction but does not require an annual cash out flow. The amount of principal repaid on a loan associated with the property is subtracted from the net after-tax earnings because it is a cash outflow but is not tax deductible.

CRYPTOCURRENCIES

In 2008 a whitepaper document was published outlining how a peer-to-peer electronic cash system called Bitcoin would operate. Bitcoin subsequently launched in 2009, and by September 2021 was trading at a price of over $47,000 per unit (coin) as part of a cryptocurrency market with a total capitalization of over $2 trillion.

Virtual Currency Basics

Unlike other currencies, such as U.S. dollars or euros, **virtual currencies** exist only in electronic form and are not associated with any particular country or central bank. These digital representations of value are controlled and managed by the developer, using blockchain technology to verify and record ownership units on a digital ledger. According to Coinbase (a cryptocurrency exchange), "At its most basic, a blockchain is a list of transactions that anyone can view and verify. This list of transactions is fundamental for most cryptocurrencies because it enables secure payments to be made between people who don't know each other without having to go through a third-party verifier like a bank."[7]

Units of **cryptocurrencies** are often referred to as tokens or coins, and can be used for investment purposes or can be used as a form of electronic payment.

Improved Access

Although investing directly in Bitcoin was not initially straightforward for most retail investors, its stunning growth created huge demand which in turn led to the development of a range of Bitcoin investment vehicles. Since 2012 investors have been able to buy and sell cryptocurrencies on exchanges such as Coinbase, a crypto exchange that boasts over 68 million users and a trading volume of over $460 billion in the first quarter of 2021. Payment platform Paypal also allows users to buy Bitcoin, and in September 2021 the SEC (Securities and Exchange Commission) indicated it may give approval for the creation of ETFs linked to the price of bitcoin futures contracts.

The ease with which investors can now purchase cryptocurrencies makes them a viable asset class to include as part of a diversified portfolio. However, the lack of regulation and lack of protection against fraudulent access to accounts must also be considered in determining whether, and how much, cryptocurrency is suitable for a particular investor.

Volatility

Despite the name 'cryptocurrency', the digital assets are not widely accepted as a form of payment in the real world. Although some high-profile businesses such as Tesla have at some stage accepted Bitcoin as a form of payment, its main function is certainly not as a medium of exchange. Its value is derived primarily from supply and demand, which has led to periods of high volatility. In May 2021, Bitcoin lost 50 percent of its value. By August 2021, it had recovered 40 percent of that loss. Cryptocurrencies are, therefore, only likely to be suitable for investors with a high risk tolerance.

Inflation Hedge

Many investors add a cryptocurrency to their portfolio in the belief that it will act as an inflation hedge. As with gold, the total amount in existence is limited. Bitcoin, for example, has a maximum of 21 million coins that will be 'minted'. As this limit is reached, the theory is that continued demand will lead to price increases. This distinguishes cryptocurrencies from real currencies which are controlled by central banks who can use monetary policy to increase the amount of currency in circulation.

7. https://www.coinbase.com/learn/crypto-basics/what-is-cryptocurrency.

SUMMARY

Summary of key points:

- The benefits of investing in alternative investments include the opportunity to generate higher returns than traditional investments, increased diversification, the potential to hedge against inflation, and tax benefits.
- Alternative investments expose the investor to the same types of risks as traditional investments, as well as additional risks including lack of both liquidity and marketability, high research costs, lack of appropriate benchmarks with which to evaluate performance, high volatility, and higher-than-usual fees/expenses and minimum investment requirements. Additional risks are associated with specific types of alternative investments.
- Many types of alternative investments may be unsuitable for small, unsophisticated, investors.
- Commodity investing involves direct or indirect investment in natural resources or agricultural output.
- The primary risk of all types of commodities is price risk.
- Commodities tend to have low correlations with traditional securities and with each other.
- Call options are used as substitutes for owning the underlying assets.
- Put options are used as substitutes for shorting the underlying assets.
- Options give the owner a right, but not an obligation. Futures contracts create an obligation.
- The intrinsic value of an option is either $0 or the difference between the price of the underlying asset and the exercise price of the option. The intrinsic value is not the profit because it does not account for the cost of the premium paid to purchase the option.
- An investor will take a long position in a futures contract if she believes prices will rise, and will take a short position in a futures contract if she believes prices will fall.
- Venture capital is a method of financing for start-up companies or small businesses.
- Venture capitalists face significant start-up risks because of the high rate of failure of new businesses.
- Investment in collectibles may yield higher returns than traditional assets, may provide a significant amount of diversification, and may provide the investor with an emotional return via the pride of ownership.
- Collectibles are sometimes referred to as emotional assets because investors often form an emotional attachment to the assets, which can lead to significant behavioral biases.
- In an effort to outperform traditional benchmarks, hedge fund managers combine investments in traditional markets with strategies using unconventional markets and securities. These strategies often include the use of leverage in an attempt to magnify returns.
- Hedge funds require high minimum investment amounts, charge substantial fees, and lack liquidity.

- Private equity firms (who serve as general partners) raise money from wealthy investors (who are limited partners) and use it to purchase equity positions in private businesses or engage in leveraged buyouts.
- Additional risks involved in private equity investments include funding risk, liquidity risk, market risk, and exit risk.
- Investments in real estate can provide the investor with income, appreciation, and diversification (correlations between real estate and traditional assets tend to be low).
- There are numerous types of real estate investments available, each with its own benefits and risks.
- Cryptocurrencies can be added to a portfolio but are only suitable for investors with a high risk tolerance.
- Some investors believe cryptocurrencies can act as an inflation hedge.

DISCUSSION QUESTIONS

SOLUTIONS to the discussion questions can be found exclusively within the chapter. Once you have completed an initial reading of the chapter, go back and highlight the answers to these questions.

1. Explain the diversification benefits of including alternative investments in traditional portfolios.
2. Discuss the relationship between the marginal benefits of alternative investments and their marginal costs.
3. Discuss the concepts of correlations and standard deviations as they relate to alternative investments.
4. Describe the lack of expertise in alternative investments as compared to traditional investments.
5. Explain the difference between direct and indirect commodity investing.
6. Discuss scarcity, delivery, storage, and multiple uses of commodities.
7. Explain the difference between primary and secondary commodities and provide two examples of each.
8. Define the primary risk in agricultural commodities and describe the manner in which it can be managed.
9. Explain corn and dairy government subsidies.
10. Discuss the risk of operating a livestock ranch and explain how some ranches use animal waste to increase profitability.
11. Explain the difference between hardwood and softwood lumber and explain why lumber prices are highly dependent on the exchange rate between the U.S. and Canadian dollars.
12. Explain the concept of rising agricultural commodity correlations during times of economic stress.
13. Explain how derivatives are used as alternative investments.
14. Explain the high frequency of start up risk in venture capital.
15. Discuss the various stages of venture capital financing.
16. Discuss the emotional attachment of collectible investing.
17. Compare the standard deviation and returns of collectibles to traditional securities.
18. Explain how hedge fund managers use leverage.
19. Describe the relationship between the general partner and the limited partners in private equity.
20. Discuss the importance of environmental risk in real estate investing.
21. Describe the differences between cryptocurrency and other types of currency (such as the U.S. dollar), and how cryptocurrency may benefit an investor when added to a diversified portfolio.

MULTIPLE-CHOICE PROBLEMS

A sample of multiple choice problems is provided below. Additional multiple choice problems are available at money-education.com by accessing the Student Practice Portal.

1. Primary commodities most likely include:
    a. Oil extracted from wells.
    b. Refined gasoline.
    c. Steel produced from iron ore.
    d. '2 by 4s' made in a lumber yard.

2. U.S. federal and state governments are most likely to impose regulatory price controls on:
    a. Dairy products.
    b. Lumber.
    c. Textiles.
    d. Orange juice.

3. A hedge fund manager believes the price of oil will fall over the next three months. The position most likely to result in a profit if the manager is accurate is:
    a. A long call option on a barrel of oil.
    b. A long put option on a barrel of oil.
    c. A long position in an oil futures contract.
    d. A short put option on a barrel of oil.

4. The net gain on buying a call option for $10 when the stock price is $28, the exercise price is $20, and the expiration date stock price is $40 is closest to:
    a. $0.
    b. $10.
    c. $20.
    d. $40.

5. Hedge funds are least likely known for:
    a. Complex fee structures.
    b. Unlimited redemptions.
    c. Heavy reliance on leverage.
    d. The use of short and long positions.

QUICK QUIZ EXPLANATIONS

Quick Quiz 16.1

1. True.
2. True.
3. False. There are plenty of examples of massive losses in alternative investments, including Long-Term Capital Management, which had two Nobel Prize winning economists as advisers.

Quick Quiz 16.2

1. False. The primary risk for commodities is price risk.
2. True.
3. True.

Quick Quiz 16.3

1. True.
2. False. The long position benefits when the asset price increases.

Quick Quiz 16.4

1. False. That describes the expansion phase. The emerging state is when the product is launched and marketed.
2. False. The failure rate for venture capital is significant.

Quick Quiz 16.5

1. True.
2. False. The market for artwork is very illiquid.

Quick Quiz 16.6

1. False. Hedge funds typically have large initial investment requirements, sometimes in the millions.
2. True.

Quick Quiz 16.7

1. False. The typical holding period for private equity is between five and seven years.
2. False. Once a private equity firm holds an investment, it looks to exit, which is typically uncertain. Often PE firms take companies public or sell to a strategic buyer or another PE firm.

Quick Quiz 16.8

1. True.
2. True.
3. False. Real estate is generally marketable, but not liquid, and in times of economic downturn, it may not even be marketable.

17
TAXATION OF INVESTMENT SECURITIES

LEARNING OBJECTIVES

1. Identify the three types of income.*
2. Determine the basis of an investment.*
3. Determine the basis for a stock inherited and for a stock received by gift.*
4. Apply the correct income tax rate to an investment transaction.*
5. Articulate long-term capital gain rates.*
6. Identify various types of portfolio income.*
7. Distinguish qualified dividends.*
8. Calculate a capital gain or loss.*
9. Determine the capital loss deduction limitation.*
10. Know that net capital losses may be carried forward indefinitely.*
11. Identify passive activities.*
12. Know that unused passive losses are suspended until disposition of the asset.*
13. Know that an exception from the passive activity rules exists for rental real estate by an individual taxpayer with adjusted gross income of no greater than $150,000.*
14. Identify the net investment income tax and its applicable rate.*
15. Determine the impact on basis and holding period of a stock split.*
16. Determine the three methods of determining basis of a stock (i.e., FIFO, specific identification, or average cost method).*
17. Describe the tax treatment of virtual currency transactions.*

**Ties to CFP Certification Learning Objectives*

INTRODUCTION

The taxation of investment opportunities might not be the most popular study topic, but the tax code has the ability to change investments that are profitable before tax into substantial after-tax losses. Understanding the basic tax rules that apply to various forms of investments is important from a practical perspective, and must be taken into account in the investment planning process. While total return on an investment may help distinguish between investment choices in a tax-free environment, after-tax return – what the investor keeps after paying taxes – is the real measure of financial well-being. This chapter introduces the basic tax aspects of investing, and is designed to provide an overview of the impact of the income and transfer tax systems on investment decisions.

In the United States, the federal government and many of the states levy a tax on income. The discussion here is limited to the federal tax treatment of various investments. To understand how investment gains (and losses) are treated in the income tax system, some basic tax concepts must first be understood.

The Three Types of Income

In the United States, there are three types of income: ordinary income, portfolio income, and passive income. The tax treatment that applies to a gain or loss on an investment depends on what type of income a particular investment generates. Classifying the income as ordinary, portfolio, or passive is the first step in ascertaining the tax attributes of a particular investment.

Ordinary income is income generated from active work at a trade or business. Ordinary income represents the fruits of labor. Employees are paid a salary, which is classified as ordinary income. Likewise, the author of a book or musical composition would receive ordinary income upon receipt of royalty payments, since the income is derived from the active conduct of a trade or business activity. Currently, ordinary income tax rates range from 10 percent to 37 percent.[1] Usually, gains from the sale of investment assets do not fall into the category of ordinary income. There are a few exceptions to that rule. Certain types of portfolio income (such as interest, nonqualified dividends, and short-term capital gains) are subject to ordinary income tax rates. Furthermore, returns on employment-related stock options, such as nonqualified stock options granted to a company executive, trigger ordinary income tax treatment upon exercise. Since ordinary income tax rates are much higher than the tax rates that apply to other types of portfolio income, it is important to understand the tax rules to maximize the after-tax benefit.

Portfolio income is income that is generated by capital. As Ben Franklin was reputed to say, "Money makes money, and the money money makes makes more money." In Ben's words, "the money money makes" is classic portfolio income. Examples of portfolio income include interest, dividends, and capital gains. As mentioned above, some types of portfolio income are taxed at ordinary income tax rates. Qualified dividends and long-term capital gains, however, receive special income tax treatment. The maximum tax rate that applies to qualified dividends and long-term capital gains under current law is 20 percent.

Key Concepts

1. Three types of income are ordinary, portfolio, and passive.
2. The income tax treatment of income depends on the type of income.
3. An asset's cost basis is generally the costs of acquiring the asset.
4. Generally, the basis of inherited investments is the FMV at the decedent/transferor's date of death.
5. Additions to, and depreciation on, the asset affect basis.

Passive income is income from a trade or business in which the taxpayer does not materially participate. Unlike portfolio income, passive income implies that the investor is receiving the fruits of labor – but in this case, an investor is receiving the fruits of someone else's labor. Classic examples of investments that generate passive income are limited partnerships, S corporations, limited liability companies, and real estate. Limited partnerships, limited liability companies, and S corporations allow a person to profit directly from the effort of others – the efforts of the employees of these entities (hopefully) result in a profit, which in turn is passed through to the investor. The business entity made the money through the efforts of its employees, and the investor receives the profit even if they may have done nothing to help the business make money except to provide capital. The investor passively receives the profits as opposed to actively creating the profits (in which case the income would be ordinary income). Note that the income of a C corporation (C corp) is treated differently because a C corp, unlike the other business entities listed, is treated as a separate person in the eyes of the tax law, and is subject to income tax on all of its income (it is not a pass-through entity for income tax purposes). Distributions of profits from a C corporation to its owners are dividends, which are classified as portfolio income but may be taxed at ordinary income tax rates or at the long-term capital gains rate, depending upon what type of dividend is distributed. Real estate investments were specifically defined as passive investments in the Tax Reform Act of 1986.

1. These rates are federal income tax rates. Income may be subject to additional tax by states or municipalities, and there is a 3.8% net investment income tax (NIIT, also referred to a Medicare surtax) for investment income in excess of a threshold amount that began in 2013, resulting from the Affordable Care Act legislation.

Basis Rules

Under the U.S. income tax system, income is subject to income tax only once. The purpose of the tax basis rules is to keep track of the amount of prior taxed income that is incorporated into a particular investment so that it is not taxed again when the investment is sold. This rule implies that an investor receives back their tax basis (or after-tax dollars invested in the asset) at the time the asset is sold or disposed of. Keeping track of tax basis is obviously important for the investor. As a taxpayer, the investor has the obligation of proving their basis in an investment. If the taxpayer cannot substantiate their basis in an asset, the Internal Revenue Service will often take the position that the investment had no tax basis and therefore the entire proceeds of the sale are subject to income tax.

The **tax basis** of most investments is equal to the cost of acquiring the investment, which is the sum of the actual cost plus any transaction fees necessary to purchase the asset. Basis is subtracted from the proceeds of a sale to determine the taxable gain or loss.

Example 17.1

Reilly purchases 1000 shares of Shamrock Industries, Inc. for $23 per share. The actual cost of the stock equals $23,000 ($23 x 1,000 shares), but in order to acquire the shares, Reilly incurs a brokerage fee of $29.95. Reilly's basis in the shares of Shamrock Industries is $23,029.95. Two years later, Reilly sells all of his shares at $30 per share and incurs a brokerage fee of $29.95. From the sale, Reilly receives $29,970.05 ($30,000 - $29.95). The taxable portion of the transaction is determined by subtracting Reilly's basis of $23,029.95 from his proceeds of $29,970.05, for a gain of $6,940.10. Since Reilly held the shares for more than one year, the gain is classified as a long-term capital gain.

However, the tax basis of an asset inherited from a decedent is the asset's fair market value on the date of the decedent's death, as reported on the federal estate tax return if filed. All assets inherited from a decedent that were included in the decedent's gross estate have a long-term holding period in the beneficiary's hands. However, assets that represent deferred income for the decedent, referred to as income in respect of a decedent assets, or IRD assets (such as IRAs, 401(k) and 403(b) plans, annuities, savings bonds, and accrued dividends), do not qualify for an adjusted basis equal to the fair market value of the asset as of the date of the decedent's death. Instead, the beneficiary will have a basis equal to the decedent's adjusted basis, if any, and will pay tax when the deferred income is distributed to the beneficiary. IRD is income a decedent was entitled to be paid but did not receive before their death. Denial of the step-to fair market value on the date of death assures the government that income taxes will eventually be paid on the potentially large amounts of deferred income in these accounts.

When property is received as a gift, the basis, and holding period, of the donor is usually transferred to the donee. However, if the value of the property on the date of the gift is lower than the donor's basis (loss property), the donee has a double basis, which limits the gain or loss when the donee subsequently sells the property.

- If the donee sells the property for less than the fair market value as of the date of the gift, the basis for purposes of calculating loss is the fair market value of the property as of the date of the gift. This is referred to as the "loss basis" in the property. When the loss basis is used to calculate loss, the holding period is deemed to begin at the date of the gift - the donor's holding period does not tack on to the donee's holding period to determine the nature of the loss.

- If, instead, the donee sells the property for a price that is higher than the donor's basis, the basis for purposes of calculating gain is the donor's carryover basis. In this case, the donor's holding period is also carried over to the donee.
- When a donor transfers property with a loss to the donee, and the donee sells the property for an amount between the donor's adjusted basis and the fair market value of the property on the date of the gift, no gain or loss is recognized.

Example 17.2

If Al has stock with a basis of $100,000 and gives it to his son Beau when the fair market value is $80,000, Beau will have a double basis in the stock. If Beau sells the stock for $50,000 he will use the FMV on the date of the gift, $80,000, as his basis and his loss will be $30,000. If Beau sells the stock for $120,000, he will use Al's carryover basis of $100,000 as his basis, and his gain will be $20,000. If Beau sells at a price between $80,000 and $100,000, his basis will be equal to the sale price and there will be no gain or loss.

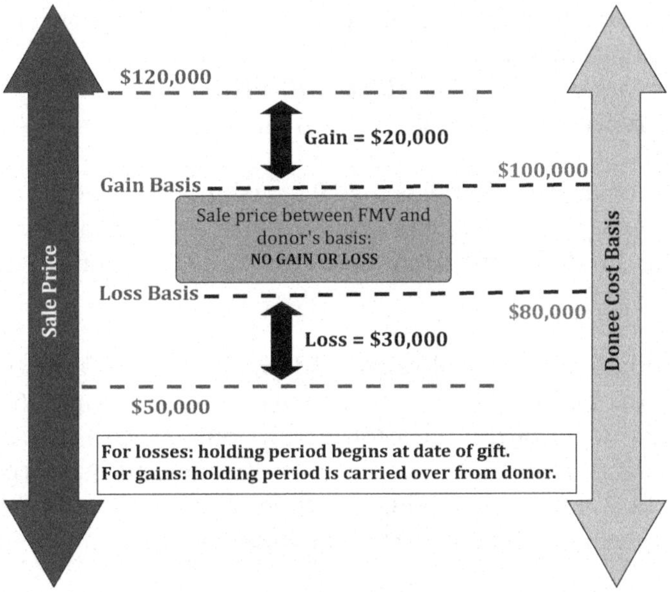

Notice that when loss basis property is given away and the asset is sold for less than the donor's cost basis, the difference between the donor's cost basis and the sales price represents a permanent loss of capital for the family. A better tax strategy is for the donor to sell the property and give the proceeds to the donee. By doing so, the donor is able to recognize a loss, recouping capital for tax purposes, while still giving the same benefit to the donee.

The basis of an investment in the stock of a company may change due to corporate actions, such as stock splits and spin-offs, or due to investor choices, such as electing average cost or specific identification of shares when computing gain or loss. These rules will be discussed later in the stock transactions section of this chapter.

When assets are purchased for active use in a trade or business or are purchased to rent to others, the income tax rules allow the investor to recoup their after-tax investment over the useful life of the asset through various cost-recovery methods (such as depreciation, depletion, and amortization). Since the asset is being used to generate current income that is subject to income tax, the tax rules allow periodic early recovery of basis so that the investor can reinvest that capital into other income-producing ventures and continue to create taxable income. Because the investor recoups after-tax dollars invested in the asset prior to its sale, an adjustment must be made to the cost basis of the asset to reflect the early recovery of the initial investment. As cost recovery deductions are taken, the basis of the asset is reduced on a dollar-for-dollar basis. The purpose of this rule is to prevent a double recovery of basis – once during the useful life of the asset, and again upon ultimate sale or disposition of the asset. When an asset is converted from a personal-use asset to a production-of-income-use asset, the basis for purposes of depreciation is the lower of the fair market value on the date of conversion or the taxpayer's adjusted basis in the asset.

Example 17.3

Nicco purchases a 10-unit apartment complex for $500,000. Of the purchase price, $50,000 is allocated to land (which is not depreciable) and the remaining $450,000 is allocated to the building. Each year, Nicco will claim a depreciation deduction of $16,364 ($450,000 / 27.5 years = $16,364), which will offset his ordinary income from the investment and will represent a partial return of his capital (basis).[2]

If Nicco operates the apartment complex for 10 years and then sells the asset, his basis in the asset for purposes of determining gain or loss will equal his initial cost basis ($500,000) less the total depreciation taken of $163,640 for an adjusted basis of $336,360.

Upon sale of the building, Nicco will recoup $336,360 of his after-tax investment, and during operation of the building as a rental activity he will recoup $163,640 of his after-tax investment in the form of depreciation deductions. Nicco receives his prior-taxed income, or capital, of $500,000 back tax-free, and any remaining gain from the sale will be subject to income tax. Note that in this example, it is assumed that Nicco made no additions or improvements to the property that would have had an effect on his tax basis.

In some cases, depreciation that is taken over the life of an asset is subject to recapture at ordinary income tax rates. This discussion is beyond the scope of this text, but is covered in-depth in courses on federal income taxation.

2. Under current law, all depreciation on real estate is taken on a straight-line basis. If the real estate is used for residential purposes, the recovery period is 27½ years, and if the real estate is used as commercial property, the recovery period is 39 years.

GENERAL RULES OF TAXATION

Ordinary Income

Ordinary income tax rates currently range from 10 percent to 37 percent. Ordinary income tax rates are the highest income tax rates that apply to individuals. The current ordinary income tax rates are relatively low in comparison to the rates that applied in the past, as illustrated in **Exhibit 17.1** below. An **investor's marginal tax rate** is the tax rate at which the next dollar of income will be taxed if the investment produces income that is taxed at ordinary income rates.

Exhibit 17.1 | Exhibit: Highest Marginal Income Tax Rates: 1950's - 2022

Year	*Highest Marginal Tax Rate*
1950's	92.0%
1960's	91.0%
1970's	72.0%
1980's	70.0%
1990's	39.6%
2005	35.0%
2013	39.6%
2022	37.0%

If a loss is incurred in the conduct of a trade or business, the loss is considered an ordinary loss and may offset, without limitation, ordinary income. Generally, when losses are incurred, it is better to try to classify the losses as ordinary losses as opposed to capital or passive losses because there is no limitation on the amount of an ordinary loss that can be used to offset other income.[3]

While ordinary income tax rates have declined over time, it is usually advantageous to avoid classifying income as ordinary income if possible, since other types of income receive more favorable tax treatment. For example, if an individual sells an asset that is held for a year or less, the tax rate that applies is that individual's marginal ordinary income tax rate. If the asset is held for a year and a day or longer, however, the maximum tax rate that applies to the gain (now characterized as a long-term capital gain) is 20 percent (for most taxpayers the long-term capital gains tax rate is 15 percent, and for those with lower income, there is a zero percent rate). For a taxpayer in the highest marginal income tax bracket, long-term capital gains treatment results in an approximate 46 percent reduction in tax liability (37% vs. 20%).

Key Concepts

1. Ordinary income tax rates vary.
2. There are five capital gain rates 0%, 15%, 20%, 25% and 28%.
3. There are three types of portfolio income.
4. Qualified dividends have a special income tax rate.
5. Passive activities include limited partnerships without material participation.

From a tax-rate perspective, classification of income as passive income instead of as ordinary income may also be advantageous. In addition to income tax, employment taxes are assessed on earned (or ordinary) income. The most significant of the employment taxes is Social Security and Medicare. The taxpayer and

3. TCJA 2017 introduced an 80% net operating loss limitation for years after 2017. While there are now limits to the deductibility of ordinary losses, they are minimal compared to the limits for capital losses.

the employer each pay 7.65 percent of earned income up to the Social Security wage base in taxes (for a total of 15.3%). In 2022, the Social Security wage base is $147,000. While earned income is subject to both income taxes and Social Security taxes, passive income is only subject to the income tax. The scenario becomes more complicated when losses result from passive investments. The passive loss rules are introduced below and are covered in much more depth in courses on federal income taxation.

Portfolio Income

Most income from investments is classified as portfolio income. The most common types of portfolio income are interest, dividends, and capital gains. As noted above, some types of portfolio income are taxed at ordinary rates, while other types of portfolio income receive more favorable tax treatment.

Interest

Interest is income earned on the use of money, and is perhaps one of the most frequently received types of portfolio income. Sources of interest income include earnings on demand deposits at depository institutions, interest on CDs, and, in some cases, imputed interest on wealth transfer techniques used to minimize exposure to estate and transfer taxes. As noted above, interest income is taxed at ordinary tax rates.

Dividends

Dividends are distributions of corporate earnings to the owners of a corporation. Both regular (C corporations) and small-business corporations (S corporations) can issue dividends. The dividends issued by an S corporation, however, are not taxable to the shareholder due to the pass-through nature of S corporation taxation. Each year as it earns money, the profits of an S corporation are passed through to the shareholders and subject to income tax, so a subsequent distribution of a dividend will not be taxable. Dividends of a C corporation, however, are taxable, but the tax rate that applies depends upon the type of dividend that is issued.

Prior to 2003, federal tax law subjected all taxable dividend distributions to the taxpayer's marginal ordinary income tax rate. Jobs and Growth Tax Relief and Reconciliation Act of 2003 (JGTRRA) created a special classification of dividends called "**qualified dividends**." Dividends issued by most U.S. domestic publicly-traded and closely-held corporations, as well as the dividends of certain foreign corporations issued on shares of publicly-traded stock listed on an established U.S. exchange meet the definition of qualified dividends. For a listing of dividends that are not classified as qualified dividends, see **Exhibit 17.2**. Qualifying dividends are taxed at the same rate as long-term capital gains. Therefore, the highest rate for these dividends is 20 percent, while the lowest is zero percent.

Any dividends that are not "qualified dividends" are taxed at the taxpayer's marginal income tax rate. The favorable tax rate that applies to qualified dividends applies to dividends received directly by an investor, or those that are passed through a mutual fund to the investor on an annual basis. As with long-term capital gains (which also qualify for a special reduced tax rate), a holding period requirement must be met to receive the reduced tax rate for qualified dividends. To receive the lower tax rate on a dividend distribution from an investment in corporate stock, the investor must own the stock for a minimum of 60 days during the 120-day period commencing on the date that is 60 days before the stock's ex-dividend date.

Exhibit 17.2 | Dividends Not Classified As "Qualified Dividends"

- Credit union dividends
- Certain mutual savings banks, domestic building and loan banks, savings and loan banks, or cooperative banks dividends
- Mutual insurance company dividends
- Farmer's cooperative dividends
- Dividends of tax-exempt cemetery companies
- Dividends from nonprofit voluntary employee benefit associations (VEBAs)
- Dividends of certain ESOPs
- Dividends of exempt organizations (organized under IRC Sections 501 or 521)
- Dividends from foreign corporations that are not qualified foreign corporations
- Dividends from hybrid preferred stock that issue interest that is deductible by the company
- Dividends paid on stock that was purchased with borrowed funds if the dividend was included in the net investment income of the taxpayer for purposes of claiming an investment interest expense deduction
- Dividends from money market mutual funds

Capital Gains

When an asset is sold, the difference between the amount received (referred to as the "amount realized") and the investor's adjusted basis in the asset is referred to as a **capital gain** or a capital loss. For income tax purposes, a realization event must occur in order to fix the gain on the asset. The most common type of realization event is a sale or exchange of the asset. Once realization of gain occurs, the gain may be subject to tax (for tax purposes, this is referred to as gain "recognition"), or it may be possible to defer payment of tax to a later time using special provisions contained in the Internal Revenue Code (IRC). There are a host of special tax rules that apply to capital gains and losses.

Assuming that the investor made money on the transaction, that a capital gain results from the transaction, and the gain must be recognized for tax purposes, the tax character will depend upon the investor's holding period. If the investor held the asset for more than one year before sale, the gain will be classified as a long-term capital gain, and long-term capital gains rates will apply. If the asset was held for one year or less before it was sold, the gain will be classified as a short-term capital gain and will be subject to tax at the taxpayer's ordinary marginal tax rate.

The tax rate that applies to long-term capital gains is 20 percent or less, which is significantly less than ordinary income tax rates. For some taxpayers with low income, the long-term capital gains tax rate is set at zero percent.

There are three exceptions to the long-term capital gains tax rates discussed above. The first exception deals with collectibles, which are taxed at a maximum rate of 28 percent. The second exception is IRC Section 1202 stock. The third exception deals with gains on real estate that has been depreciated using straight line depreciation. The portion of a gain that is equal to depreciation is taxed at 25 percent.

If an individual purchases a collectible (coin, stamp, antique furniture, oriental rugs, gems, gold bullion, etc.), holds the asset for a long-term holding period, and subsequently sells the asset, the gain that results will be taxed at the lower of their ordinary income rate or 28 percent.

Example 17.4

Patty, who is in the 37% marginal tax bracket, is a collector of Beleek China. She sometimes sells pieces in her collection to acquire better pieces. Recently, she sold a bowl that she purchased 10 years ago at a price of $120 for $350. Her gain on the bowl of $230 ($350 amount realized less $120 cost basis) will be subject to income tax at the 28% rate.

Section 1202 provides an incentive for individuals to invest in new start-up businesses by excluding from gross income up to 100 percent of the gain from the sale or exchange of qualified small business stock held for more than five years. Any taxable portion of gains on the sale of Section 1202 stock are also subject to tax at the 28 percent rate.

Real estate investors must make tax rate adjustments for their gains as well. If real estate is purchased, held for a long-term holding period, and depreciation deductions have been taken (implying that the real estate was used in a trade or business or production of income activity, or part of a home was used as a home office), the portion of the gain that represents straight line depreciation is subject to tax at a 25 percent rate.

Example 17.5

Jerome purchased a rental home for $150,000 several years ago. He took depreciation deductions of $30,000 over the term of the rental use, and recently sold the building for $250,000 (after fix-up expenses and real estate commissions were taken into account).

Jerome's gain in the property is the amount realized, $250,000 less his adjusted basis (cost basis of $150,000 less $30,000 of depreciation deductions, or $120,000) leaving him with a gain of $130,000. $30,000 of the gain will be subject to tax at the 25% rate, and the remaining $100,000 of the gain will be subject to tax at the 15% or 20% capital gains tax rate (depending on Jerome's total taxable income).

Up to this point, our discussion has been limited to the tax effects of a transaction that generates a gain. If an investor sells an investment and realizes a loss, the tax rules impose limitations on the deductibility of that loss. **Capital losses** may be used to offset any amount of capital gains, but if the losses exceed gains in a given tax year, the maximum capital loss that can be used to offset ordinary income is $3,000. If an investor incurs a net capital loss for the year in excess of $3,000, the excess amount can be carried forward to future tax years and used to offset capital gains in those years, or, alternatively, up to $3,000 of ordinary income in those years.

When a taxpayer has multiple capital transactions for the year, those transactions are first sorted as short-term or long-term. Short-term gains and losses are netted against each other, and long-term gains and losses are netted against each other. If the result is a net loss in either category, the two categories are then netted against each other. If the result is a net loss, a maximum of $3,000 can be applied against ordinary income. Any remaining loss will retain its character as short-term or long-term and will be carried forward as described previously.

Example 17.6

Wally bought 10,000 shares of BoomToBust, Inc. five years ago at a price of $30 per share. He paid a brokerage commission of $120 to purchase the shares. BoomToBust's stock price has been on a steady decline since then, and Wally finally got frustrated and sold the shares this year at $1 per share, paying a brokerage commission of $120 for the sale. He has no other capital transactions for the current tax year. Wally's loss on the stock is $290,240 (calculated as follows: amount realized of $9,880 [gross proceeds of $10,000 less brokerage commission of $120] less adjusted basis of $300,120 [cost basis of $300,000 plus brokerage commission to purchase the shares]). Wally will be able to offset $3,000 of his ordinary income this year with the loss, and carry the remaining loss of $287,240 forward indefinitely to future tax years.

Example 17.7

Assume the same facts as above, except that this year Wally also sold shares he owned in Heidi Enterprises, Inc. He purchased 10,000 shares 10 years ago for $10 per share, paying a $120 brokerage commission, and sold them this year for $14 per share, paying a $120 brokerage commission. Wally's gain on the sale of Heidi Enterprises, Inc. is $39,760 (calculated as follows: amount realized $139,880 [gross proceeds of $140,000 less brokerage commission of $120] less adjusted basis of $100,120 [cost basis of $100,000 plus brokerage commission of $120]). Wally could offset the entire gain on the sale of Heidi Enterprises, Inc. with part of his loss from BoomToBust, Inc. In addition, Wally could offset $3,000 of his ordinary income with part of his loss from BoomToBust, Inc. Wally's capital loss carryforward for the year would be $247,480 (calculated as follows: loss on BoomToBust of $290,240 less gain on Heidi Enterprises of $39,760 less $3,000 used to offset Wally's ordinary income).

While a net capital loss can be carried forward during the lifetime of the taxpayer, when the taxpayer dies, so does the ability to claim the carryforward losses. The decedent's executor will be able to claim the annual $3,000 loss deduction on the decedent's final return, but any remaining amount of the carryforward loss is lost. While most people do not know when they will die, planning to avoid loss of the carry-forward capital loss deduction can be an important issue. Investors with large carryforward losses who are close to death should consider recognizing capital gains to offset the carryforward loss deduction.

The special capital gains tax rates allow investors to lower their effective tax rate on investment income and must be taken into account when making investment decisions. A summary of current long-term capital gains rates may be found in **Exhibit 17.3**.

Quick Quiz 17.1

1. Generally, the adjusted tax basis equals the purchase price or cost of acquisition.
   a. True
   b. False
2. A taxpayer who pays at the highest marginal rate of income tax can save approximately 46% on a long-term capital gain transaction compared to ordinary income.
   a. True
   b. False

True, True.

Exhibit 17.3 | Long-Term Capital Gains Tax Rates 2022

Long-Term Capital Gains (more than one year holding period) Most Assets:				
	Taxable Income			
LTCG Tax Rate	Single	Married Filing Jointly	Head of Household	Married Filing Separately
0%	$0 - $41,675	$0 - $83,350	$0 - $55,800	$0 - $41,675
15%	$41,676 - $459,750	$83,351 - $517,200	$55,801 - $488,500	$41,676 - $258,600
20%	$459,751 or more	$517,201 or more	$488,501 or more	$258,601 or more
Gain on Depreciated Real Estate: Amount up to straight line depreciation taxed at 25%, remaining portion of gain taxed at regular long-term capital gains rate.				
Gain on Collectibles: Taxed at 28% or ordinary income tax rate, if lower.				
Qualified Sec. 1202 Gain: Taxed at 28% or ordinary income tax rate, if lower.				

Passive Income

Passive income is income a taxpayer receives from either a business activity in which they do not materially participate, or from rental real estate activities. Passive income is taxed at the same rates that apply to ordinary income.[4] One of the advantages of passive income, as mentioned above, is that passive income is not subject to employment taxes (such as Social Security and Medicare taxes). Passive losses, however, may not be used to offset other income except in a few rare circumstances.

Passive losses may be used to offset passive income. There is no limitation on this rule, with the exception of the amount of passive income.

Example 17.8

Kelly owns a 20% limited partnership interest in the Forsythe Partnership, a very successful and established business entity. This year, her share of the profits of the enterprise were $200,000. This year, Kelly also acquired an apartment house (real estate rental activity), that generated a tax loss (due to depreciation deductions) of $150,000. Since both the partnership and the rental real estate activities are considered passive activities, Kelly can offset her loss on the apartment building with the income from the partnership, leaving a net $50,000 of passive income.

Example 17.9

Assume the same facts as above, with the exception that the partnership gains were $150,000 and the real estate loss was $200,000. In this case, Kelly does not have enough gains to offset all of her passive losses. This year she will not receive any tax benefit from the extra $50,000 passive loss, but that loss can be carried forward to a future tax year when she has excess passive income, or to the year in which she disposes of the real estate activity.

4. For years 2013 and beyond, passive income may also be subject to the 3.8% net investment income tax (NIIT) to the extent that a taxpayer's income exceeds certain thresholds.

The passive loss rules were implemented to prevent high income taxpayers from offsetting their other sources of income with passive losses that can be generated on real estate and business enterprises in which they do not materially participate. By requiring that passive losses may only be written off against passive income, Congress has limited the taxpayer's ability to manipulate their income in any one year.

Passive losses that cannot be used in a tax year are suspended and can be used in future years to offset passive income. These suspended passive losses are fully released when the taxpayer disposes of an interest in a passive activity. These released passive losses can at that time be used to offset ordinary income.

There is one major exception to the passive loss rules that is important for individual investors. For individuals with adjusted gross income (AGI) of $100,000 or less (same threshold applies for single taxpayers and those who are married filing jointly), up to $25,000 of the losses on rental real estate may be deducted against other income if the following conditions are met:

- The taxpayer actively participates in the rental activity. To actively participate, the taxpayer must own a minimum of 10% of the activity, and must have substantial involvement in the management of the activity (such as approving all expenditures on the property and having the final say on leasing arrangements).
- The taxpayer is not a limited partner in the rental real estate activity.

Quick Quiz 17.2

1. The three types of portfolio income are interest, dividends, and wages.
   a. True
   b. False
2. The tax rate on qualified dividends is equal to the long-term capital gain rate.
   a. True
   b. False
3. The maximum net capital loss deduction against ordinary income is $3,000.
   a. True
   b. False

False, True, True.

Once a taxpayer's adjusted gross income exceeds $100,000, the special $25,000 loss allowance is phased out by 50 percent of AGI over the $100,000 threshold. When AGI reaches $150,000 the special loss allowance is completely phased out.

Example 17.10

This year, Skip's AGI is $120,000. Skip owns 50% of a rental real estate activity, and actively participates in its management. His loss associated with the rental real estate activity this year is $27,000. Because his income exceeds the $100,000 threshold by $20,000, Skip will lose $10,000 (50% of $20,000) of the special loss allowance. This year, Skip will be able to claim a loss of $15,000 against his other income from the rental real estate activity, and the remaining loss of $12,000 will be carried over to a future tax year.

This special loss allowance is important for many moderate income individuals who are seeking to grow their wealth through real estate investing. While the passive loss rules were designed to prevent high income taxpayers from manipulating their taxable income, Congress did not want to discourage individuals from engaging in activities that would increase their wealth, so this special exception was enacted for moderate income taxpayers.

OTHER TYPES OF TAXES

Net Investment Income (2013 and Beyond)

The **net investment income tax (NIIT)** is imposed by Section 1411 of the Internal Revenue Code. The NIIT applies at a rate of 3.8 percent to certain net investment income of individuals, estates and trusts that have income above the statutory threshold amounts. Individual taxpayers owe the tax if they have net investment income and also have modified adjusted gross income over the following thresholds, which are not indexed for inflation:

Filing Status	Threshold Amount
Married Filing Jointly	$250,000
Married Filing Separately	$125,000
Single	$200,000
Head of Household	$200,000

In general, investment income includes, but is not limited to: interest, dividends, capital gains, rental and royalty income, nonqualified annuities, income from businesses involved in trading of financial instruments or commodities, and businesses that are passive activities to the taxpayer (within the meaning of IRC Section 469). **Net investment income** is investment income less certain expenses properly allocable to the income.

Exhibit 17.4 | Net Investment Income

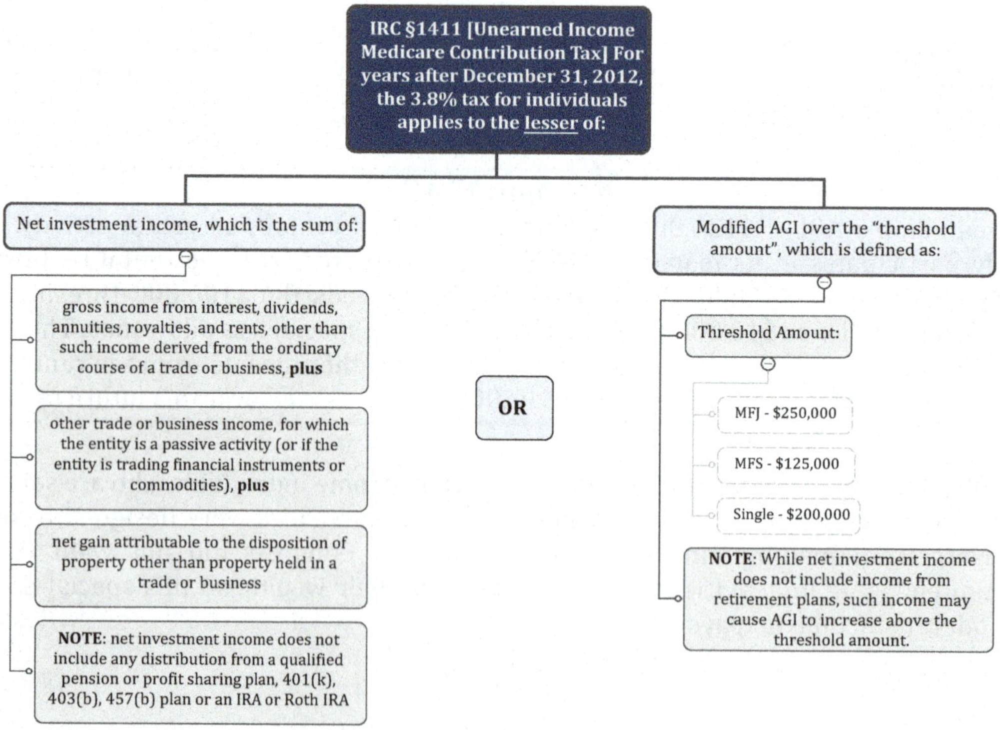

Example 17.11

Dan and Mary (MFJ) have $250,000 of dividend income, their only income for the year. In this case, they are not subject to the 3.8% NIIT.

Example 17.12

Same as **Example 17.11** , but Dan and Mary convert a traditional IRA to a Roth IRA. The taxable amount of the conversion is $100,000. Thus, they will have AGI of $350,000, and $100,000 (the amount of investment income over the $250,000 threshold) will be subject to the 3.8% NIIT.

Example 17.13

Same as **Example 17.11** , but Dan and Mary also take minimum distributions of $50,000 from their traditional IRA. They will be subject to the 3.8% tax on $50,000, which is the lesser of net investment income and the AGI above $250,000.

Example 17.14

Steve and Ashley (MFJ) have $100,000 of dividend income and $100,000 of wages. In this case, they are not subject to the 3.8% NIIT because they are not over the $250,000 threshold.

Example 17.15

Same as **Example 17.14** , but Steve and Ashley convert a traditional IRA to a Roth IRA. The taxable amount of the conversion is $100,000. Thus, they will have AGI of $300,000. The lesser of $50,000 (the income over the threshold) or $100,000 (the net investment income) will be subject to the 3.8% NIIT.

Example 17.16

Jack and Jill (MFJ) each earn wages of $250,000 and have interest income of $1,000 and $20,000 of passive income from an S corporation. The $1,000 would be subject to the 3.8% tax, as well as the $20,000 of passive income.

Alternative Minimum Tax (AMT)

The **alternative minimum tax** was devised to ensure that all individuals with a certain amount of income will pay some income tax on an annual basis. Before 1986, it was possible for those with very high income to avoid current income tax payments by taking advantage of passive losses (discussed above) and other special provisions of the IRC to wipe out their taxable income. The theory behind the AMT is that all individuals who have economic income during the year should be required to pay some amount of tax.

The mechanics of the AMT is discussed at length in income tax textbooks. For our purposes, a basic understanding is appropriate. The AMT begins with taxable income as calculated under the regular tax system, and then makes certain adjustments to that amount by altering deduction rules and adding back tax preference items. There is an exemption for AMT purposes that is available, with the amount determined by the filing status on the tax return (see **Exhibit 17.6**). High income taxpayers, however, begin to lose their exemption once their adjusted gross income exceeds certain thresholds.

For individuals, the AMT tax rates are 26 percent and 28 percent of alternative minimum taxable income, as outlined in the exhibit below.

Exhibit 17.5 | Exhibit: Alternative Minimum Tax Rates

Alternative Minimum Taxable Income	Taxed at a Rate of:
Up to $206,100 ($103,050 married filing separately)	26%
Over $206,100 ($103,050 married filing separately)	28%

Individuals who must pay the AMT receive an AMT credit equal to the alternative minimum tax that is imposed on deferral items (defined as items that do not cause a permanent reduction in taxable income) that may be used to offset regular tax liability in future years. For most purposes, therefore, the AMT affects the timing of the payment of tax (it makes taxpayers pay tax earlier than under the regular tax calculation); it does not increase the overall tax that a taxpayer must pay over the long run.

Exhibit 17.6 | AMT Exemption Amounts 2022

Filing Status	AMT Exemption	AGI Phaseout Begins	AGI Phaseout Ends
Single or Head of Household	$75,900	$539,900	$843,500
Married Filing Jointly or Qualifying Widow(er)	$118,100	$1,079,800	$1,552,200
Married Filing Separately	$59,050	$539,900	$776,100

From a simplistic perspective, if items of income taxed at a rate lower than the AMT tax rate (26% or 28%) exceed the AMT exemption amount, the taxpayer will suffer the imposition of the AMT. The alternative minimum tax may be imposed if a taxpayer has too much income that is taxed at a low rate, or if the taxpayer has special items that require adjustments for AMT purposes. The AMT impacts the taxation of investments in the following ways:

- **Qualified Small Business (Sec. 1202) Stock** allows taxpayers to exclude 100% of the gain on the sale of the stock, but if the taxpayer is subject to the AMT, the excluded gain on Sec. 1202 stock acquired prior to September 28, 2010 is subject to an AMT tax of 7%. Sec. 1202 stock acquired after September 27, 2010 that qualifies for the 100% exclusion is not subject to the AMT tax.

- **Incentive Stock Options (ISOs)** – The difference between the amount paid for the stock (the strike price of the option) and the fair market value of the stock on the date of exercise of the option, must be added to income and could be subject to AMT in the year of exercise (this issue is more fully described in texts dealing with retirement planning).
- **Private Activity Municipal Bonds (issued after August 7, 1986)** are tax-exempt under the regular income tax rules, but are subject to tax at the AMT tax rates if the taxpayer is subject to the AMT. A slight compensation for the taxation of these municipal bonds is that interest on loans used to acquire the tax-exempt bonds, which is usually not allowed as a deduction for normal tax purposes, may be deducted for AMT purposes.

It is important to keep the AMT in mind when developing an investment strategy, or when engaging in any of the above transactions, because the tax impact can be altered if the AMT is imposed.

SPECIAL TAXATION ISSUES WITH STOCK INVESTING

The tax attributes of equity securities go beyond dividend income and capital gains. There are several circumstances equity investors experience that could impact either the current taxation of the investment or the investor's basis in the security. In this section, we will review the tax consequences of various transactions concerning equity investments and close with a review of the methods of determining basis for calculating gain or loss.

Sale

When an equity security is sold, a realization event occurs, and, as a general rule, the gain or loss must be taxed (or recognized) at that time. The gain or loss is determined by subtracting the investor's adjusted basis in the security from the amount realized at the time of the sale. When making this calculation, remember that the costs to acquire an equity security (the brokerage commission) are added to the investor's basis, and the amount realized equals what the investor receives upon sale (the gross sales price less the brokerage commission). If the asset is held for more than a year, it has a long-term holding period and long-term capital gains tax rates will apply. If the asset was held for a year or less, the gain/loss will be subject to ordinary income tax rates.

Key Concepts

1. Stock splits have a direct impact on basis.
2. Splits and warrants are different in that warrants can change ownership percentage to an investor.
3. The wash sale rules are intended to prevent taking of losses while maintaining the investment.

Example 17.17

Gerald purchased 1,000 shares of Dunne's Stores, Inc. for $10 per share two years ago. He paid a $30 brokerage commission on the transaction. Today, he sold the shares at $20 per share, paying a $30 brokerage commission. Gerald's gain is $9,940 (calculated as follows: [amount realized = $20,000 gross proceeds - $30 commission] – [adjusted basis = $10,000 cost basis + $30 commission]).

Since Gerald held the shares for more than a year, the gain is classified as a long-term capital gain, and the long-term capital gains tax rates apply.

Splits

A stock **split** occurs when a corporation distributes shares of its own stock to its shareholders. Sometimes, this transaction is referred to as a stock dividend. Stock splits do not generally trigger recognition of income for tax purposes. The reason for no current taxation is simple: while each shareholder of the company owns more shares in that company, each shareholder owns exactly the same percentage of the company they owned before the split. There has not been a change in the taxpayer's economic position in that company, so there is no immediate tax result.

While there is usually no taxable income as a result of a stock split, there is an adjustment in the basis of each share owned by the taxpayer. The taxpayer's total basis, which remains the same, is spread among the old and new shares equally, and the holding period for the new shares is the same as the holding period for the old shares.

Example 17.18

Five years ago, Kaylie purchased 100 shares of SecureCo, Inc., a personal residence security firm. She paid $20 per share and a $30 commission to acquire the stock. Kaylie's original basis per share is $20.30 ($20 cost of stock plus $0.30 for commission). Due to the popularity of personal residence security systems, SecureCo's stock price has risen to over $400 per share. The company issued a stock dividend this year, which gave the owner of each share of stock three additional shares. After the stock dividend/split, Kaylie owned 400 shares of SecureCo, Inc. Kaylie's basis per share is now $5.075 per share ($2,030 / 400 shares).

Example 17.19

Assume the same facts as **Example 17.18** . Kaylie needs a little extra cash in anticipation of the arrival of her first child and decides to sell some of the stock two months after the stock split occurs. She sells 200 of the shares she received in the stock split for $105 per share plus a $30 brokerage commission. Kaylie's gain on the sale of stock is $19,955 (calculated as follows: [amount realized = ($105 x 200) - $30 = $20,970] – [adjusted basis = $5.075 x 200 shares = $1,015]). Kaylie's gain will be taxed as a long-term capital gain because the holding period of the new stock is the same as the holding period of the old stock, which she held for over one year, even though she received the shares she sold in the stock split only two months ago.

There are some exceptions to the general rule that stock splits do not trigger income tax. A taxable event occurs when any one of the following situations arise:

- The shareholders have the right to receive the corporate distribution in the form of cash or shares,
- The distribution results in a change in the shareholder's proportionate interest in the company, or
- The distribution is in the form of certain types of preferred stock.

Under the first exception, if a shareholder has the option to take cash or shares when the corporation is making a distribution, the shareholder is deemed to have constructive receipt of the value of the distribution, subjecting that amount to current taxation. This rule is consistent with the general income tax rules that apply when a taxpayer has the right to choose to receive or defer income, it is subject to tax.

Under the second exception, a stock dividend or stock split is taxable if, as a result of the split, the proportionate ownership of the company changes. For a stock dividend to be issued, all shareholders must receive the same number of shares for each share of stock currently owned. If, for example, the company gave some shareholders two shares of stock per share outstanding, while it gave other shareholders one share of stock per share outstanding, the company would not be issuing a stock dividend but would be recapitalizing the company. In this scenario, the stock dividend (or split) is taxable.

Finally, if common stockholders receive preferred stock as a stock dividend, this is a deemed recapitalization of the company and is subject to tax. While issuing preferred stock dividends on common stock may sometimes be wise from a planning standpoint (to deal with issues of control, for example), for federal income tax purposes the value of the distribution is subject to income tax.

Whenever one of the three exceptions to tax-free treatment of the stock dividend or split is met, the taxable distribution (fair market value of the stock distributed) is treated as a dividend for income tax purposes. As a result, the taxpayer has a basis in the stock received equal to the value included in income on their income tax return, and the holding period is deemed to begin on the date of the dividend distribution.

Companies often issue stock dividends or engage in stock splits to affect the per share market value of their stock. If the stock is trading at too high a price, the company may issue a stock dividend, or announce a 2:1 split, to reduce the per share price of the stock in the market. Presumably, this will allow more investors to purchase the stock and possibly increase the relative value by bringing new buyers into the market for the shares. If the price of the stock is too low, the company may effectuate a reverse split, for example, where one share of stock is issued for every five shares outstanding. A reverse split accomplishes two things: (1) it raises the per share price of the stock in the market; and (2) it often results in many small shareholders cashing out of their positions, which can save money for the company because issuing dividend checks to shareholders with only a few shares often incurs a greater expense than the dividends that are distributed to those shareholders.

Warrants and Rights

Sometimes companies issue stock rights or **warrants** to their shareholders. Warrants allow the shareholder to purchase new shares of stock in the company, usually at a discounted price. The tax rules that apply to the distribution of warrants and rights are the same as those that apply to stock splits. Generally, there is no current tax impact because at the time of the distribution, the economic position of the investor has not changed. If, however, the investor has a choice of taking cash or warrants, the issuance of the warrants could result in a change in the shareholder's proportionate interest in the corporation, and the fair market value of the warrants at the time of distribution will be currently taxed as a dividend.

Spin-offs

A **spin-off** occurs when a company decides, as part of a corporate reorganization, to split a portion of their business away from the parent company into a new company. When this occurs, a new company is formed, and the shareholders of the original company receive shares of stock in the new company so that their ownership percentage in both companies is the same.

Provided that the spin-off does not give the shareholders of the original company the option to take cash or shares, the spin-off of the shares is not a taxable event. Before the spin-off occurs, the shareholders own the same assets they own after the spin-off with one difference: two different companies own, together, what the original company owned initially. If the shareholders had no control over the spin-off, it would be unfair to tax them on their gains before they sell their interest in the companies. The tax law recognizes this situation, and generally treats spin-offs as nontaxable transactions.

Short Sales and Shorting Against the Box

When an investor expects the price of a stock to decline, they may wish to sell shares in the stock now, even if the stock is not included in the investor's portfolio. To accomplish this, the investor can borrow shares from their broker, and sell them in the market. After the stock declines in value (hopefully), the investor purchases the stock on the market, returns the borrowed shares to the broker, and closes out the short-sale position. This approach to investing is referred to as a **short sale**; the term "short" implies that the investor is selling something that the investor does not own yet. In most cases, the short-seller does not recognize gain or loss on the position until the short position is closed.

For income tax purposes, a taxable event occurs when the investor makes a purchase of stock to close out the short position by returning the shares to the broker. If the price of the stock declines over the open period, the investor has a gain on the position, and the gain is realized for income tax purposes on the date that the investor purchases the stock to close out the position. If, however, the value of the stock rises over the open period, the investor has a loss on the short position, and the loss is deemed to be realized on the settlement date that corresponds to the purchase of shares used to close out the short position. If an investor is planning to close out short positions by the end of the tax year, beware of these rules.

The characterization of the gain on a short sale is not determined by the length of time the short position is held open; it is generally calculated by looking at the holding period of the asset that the investor uses to close out the position.[5]

Example 17.20

Benjamin, a short-term employee of American Industries, Inc. decided to short sell shares in American Industries shortly after his departure from the company on July 10 of this year. Benjamin, having attended a financial planning seminar recently, decides he would like to characterize the gain on his position as a long-term capital gain. Consequently, he waits until July 15 of the next year to purchase shares of American Industries and close out his position. While the short position was open for more than one year, Benjamin's holding period is short term, since he held the securities used to close out the position for less than a year.

There are special holding period rules that apply to short sales as well. A gain on a short sale is considered short term if on the date of the original short sale, the taxpayer held replacement property for one year or less. A gain is also considered short term if the taxpayer acquires replacement property after the short-sale date but on or before the date that the short sale is closed. In these circumstances, if the investor purchases more shares than are necessary to close out the short position, the holding period on the additional shares begins on the later of the date that the short position is closed, or on the date that the additional shares are purchased.

5. IRC Section 1233(b).

A second special holding period rule applies when the investor holds, at the time of the sale, substantially identical property that has a holding period of more than one year. Regardless of whether the substantially identical property held at the time the short sale was made is used to close the position, the loss on the short sale will be treated as a long-term loss.

An investment technique that was once popular with investors due to its tax deferral benefits is "shorting against the box." When an investor holds a long position in a security and feels that the price of the security has hit its high and is headed back down, the investor should sell the stock and capture the gains. Selling the stock, however, is a realization event for income tax purposes that requires the investor to pay income tax on the gain in the year of the sale. To defer the gain on the sale one additional tax year, an investor could short sell the security instead of selling the long position. By holding a long position in the stock, and acquiring a short position in the same stock, the investor can lock in their gain in the security but avoid realization and recognition of income until the short position is closed by delivering the underlying stock to the broker. This transaction, popularly referred to as shorting against the box, was particularly useful if a stock was otherwise going to be sold close to the end of the tax year. To prevent this from occurring, Congress enacted IRC Section 1259 as part of the Taxpayer Relief Act of 1997. Under this IRC provision, all short-against-the-box transactions taking effect after June 8, 1997 are treated as constructive sales, requiring immediate recognition of gain (if any), but not losses. The constructive sale rules apply primarily to short-against-the-box transactions on publicly-traded securities.

Example 17.21

Edna purchased 1,000 shares of Chesapeake Yacht Builders, Inc., a publicly-traded company, several years ago upon the advice of her close friend, Garrette. Due to an increased interest in sailing, combined with a bull market, orders for Chesapeake Yachts have increased by over 1,500%, with profits rising at phenomenal rates over the last few years. Unfortunately, Edna sees some storm clouds and rough waters on the horizon for the company and the stock market, in her mind, is poised for a fall. Edna believes that the stock hit its height yesterday, December 13th, and decides to short sell 1,000 shares of Chesapeake Yacht Builders, Inc. Even though she did not sell her long position in the stock, and under normal rules the short position would not cause a realization event for tax purposes until it is closed, IRC Section 1259 will treat the short sale, in combination with the underlying long position, as a constructive sale, requiring realization and recognition of gain in the current tax year. Edna has frozen the gain in the investment but will not be able to defer the tax on the gain until another tax year.

There are several exceptions to the application of the constructive sale rules to short-against-the-box transactions. While a full discussion of these is beyond the scope of this text, the major exceptions include short positions that (1) are marked-to-market, (2) are straight debt, (3) involve positions in nonpublicly-traded property, and (4) are closed within 30 days after year end, provided that an unhedged appreciated position is held for at least an additional 60 days. The last exception was designed to provide a safe harbor for short-term hedges that are not tax-motivated.

When an investor engages in a short sale, there are transactions and carrying costs that must be considered when determining gain or loss for investment purposes, and gain or loss for tax purposes. These costs include the commissions paid to brokers for executing the transaction, as well as the dividends that the investor must pay to the lender of the security during the open short position. Since the dividends on the stock are paid to the purchaser of the stock in the short-sale transaction, the person who lent the stock to the investor to short sell must be reimbursed for the dividend payment. The tax treatment of these expenses depends upon the amount of time the short position is held open. For short positions that are open for at least 46 days, these expenses are treated as investment interest and are deductible on the investor's Schedule A (itemized deductions). If a short sale is closed by the 45th day, these expenses are added to the basis of the stock that is purchased to close out the short-sale position.[6]

Example 17.22

Diego is a research scientist who has been following the progress of PharmCo, Inc. PharmCo has recently had some FDA setbacks, and Diego thinks that it is time to harvest some profits. He sells 1,000 shares of PharmCo stock short for $80 per share on June 30th, incurring a brokerage fee of $120. While Diego's short position was open, PharmCo issued a dividend, payable on July 15th, to all holders of record on July 5th. Diego paid the lender of the security $250 to reimburse him for the lost dividend income. On August 1st, the FDA announced that it is revoking its approval of a major PharmCo drug, and the stock tumbled. On August 2nd, Diego purchased 1,000 shares of PharmCo stock for $35 per share and closed out his short position. Diego's basis, for purposes of calculating his taxable gain, is $35,490 (calculated as follows: $35,000 cost basis for 1,000 shares of PharmCo stock plus brokerage commissions totaling $240 plus the $250 reimbursed dividend Diego paid on July 15th). Diego's gain on the short position is $44,510 (calculated as follows: $80,000 received from sale of PharmCo Stock on June 30th less $35,490 basis). Since Diego purchased PharmCo stock and closed out his short position in the same day, his gain is characterized as a short-term capital gain.

Example 17.23

Assume the same facts as above, except that Diego purchases the PharmCo stock on October 10th. In this case, since Diego had a short position in PharmCo stock open for more than 45 days, he would be able to deduct the brokerage commissions and reimbursed dividend payment as investment interest expense on Schedule A, and his capital gain would increase by $490. Note that the $490 in expenses would only be deductible in the current year to the extent that Diego has investment income to offset the deemed investment interest expense created by the short sale.

An interesting variation on the short-against-the-box technique is the purchase of a put at the money instead of a short-sale of the stock. The long position in the stock would not cause a realization event to occur, because there has been no transfer of the stock, and no realization event would result for the put until it is exercised or it expires. While the economics of this transaction are similar to the short-against-the-box technique, there are differences, which means that the constructive sale rules would not apply to this transaction. Owning stock and purchasing a put option on the stock limits downside risk, but at the cost of purchasing the option. This type of transaction is different than shorting-against-the-box.

6. IRC Section 263(h).

Wash Sales

A **wash sale** is a technique that was used by investors to generate losses for income tax purposes without substantially changing the securities positions in their portfolios. Since the enactment of Section 1091 of the Internal Revenue Code, wash sales that result in losses do not provide immediate tax benefits for investors.

From an income tax perspective, a wash sale is a two-part transaction whereby an investor sells a security that generates a tax loss and repurchases the same (or a substantially similar) security within 30 days before or after the sale. Note that the rule has both a look-back and look-forward time frame. Obviously, purchasing the same security that was sold is substantially identical. In addition, buying a call option on the stock that was sold for a loss, or buying a convertible bond that can be converted to the stock sold for a loss, is also substantially identical. Fortunately, it's fairly easy to avoid a wash sale on a bond by purchasing a bond from a different issuer, or with a different coupon rate, or with a different maturity date. Selling a security at a loss in a taxable brokerage account and buying the same (or a substantially identical) security in an IRA is still a wash sale, as is selling in one spouse's account and buying in the other spouse's account.

When a wash sale occurs, gains are recognized for tax purposes, but losses are not deductible. If a wash-sale transaction results in a loss, the basis of the replacement property is increased by the amount of the disallowed loss. The holding period for the replacement property includes the holding period of the stock that was sold in the wash sale.

Example 17.24

Kendra owns 1,000 shares of XYZ company. She purchases the shares for $10 per share on July 1st and pays a brokerage commission of $30. The price of XYZ company declines to $5 per share on December 23rd, and Kendra decides to sell the shares to generate a tax loss of $5,060 (calculated as follows: [10,000 cost basis plus brokerage commission of $30] – [amount realized of $5,000 less brokerage commission of $30]). Over the holiday season, the shares continue to decline in value to $3 per share, and Kendra thinks the stock price has bottomed out. Kendra purchases 1,000 shares of XYZ company on January 15th for $3 per share, paying a brokerage commission of $30. Since Kendra purchased the same security that she sold within a 30 day period, she will not be able to claim the loss on her tax return. Her basis in the new shares, however will be $8,090 (which equals the $3,000 cost basis plus $30 brokerage commission plus disallowed loss of $5,060), and her holding period for the newly acquired shares is deemed to begin July 1st of last year.

Methods of Determining Basis on the Sale of Stock

When an equity investment is sold, gain cannot be determined on the sale until the basis of the security is determined. For investments that are unique, such as real estate, basis is always equal to the cost of acquiring the investment plus additional investments less cost recovery deductions. The basis of a stock or mutual fund that is sold is not always apparent, however, especially if the investor purchased the stock or mutual fund over time in several lots at different prices, or participated in a dividend reinvestment program that purchases additional shares of stock or units in a mutual fund each time the company issues a dividend.

The IRS default rule for determining basis on the sale of an equity investment purchased in multiple lots is to use the first-in first-out (FIFO) method. Using this approach, the cost of the first shares purchased will be used for calculating gain or loss. Since securities markets, and the stocks they list, tend to increase in value over time, using the cost basis of the first shares acquired when calculating the taxable gain/loss usually maximizes the taxpayer's taxable gain or minimizes the taxpayer's loss for the current tax period.

Instead of using the FIFO method that is preferred by the IRS, an investor could specifically identify the shares being sold from the portfolio, and use the actual cost of acquiring those shares in the calculation of gain or loss. To use this method, the shares sold have to be "adequately identified," which means that the investor must be able to specify the particular shares sold and receive a confirmation from their broker that those shares were sold. The specific identification method is usually the best approach for the investor who is selling securities that were acquired in multiple lots, since the investor can select the basis that will be used in calculating gain or loss taking into consideration the investor's overall individual tax situation. This approach can be difficult to use, however, unless the investor keeps good records of purchases and sales of the security, particularly if a dividend reinvestment plan or mutual fund reinvestment plan is being used. Most personal finance software packages, such as Quicken, provide tools for tracking individual shares of stock and specifically identifying the shares the investor would like to sell.

A third alternative to determining basis exists for those who do not wish to take the IRS approach and who have not kept records sufficient to specifically identify the shares that are sold. This alternative method, called the average cost method, is calculated by taking the investor's total cost of acquiring all of the shares divided by the number of shares actually owned. The average cost approach to determining basis tends to lower the taxable gain on securities sold if the cost of the security that was purchased increased over time. This method does not give the taxpayer the type of control that the specific identification method offers, but for taxpayers who have not kept good records, it provides an alternative to the IRS approach. Once the average cost method is elected, it must continue to be used for that security even if the security is held in different brokerage accounts. In determining the average basis of shares owned, all shares of the stock or fund are utilized without regard to short and long holding period classifications.

In practice, brokers are required to report stock sales on Form 1099-B. If the stock shares were purchased in 2011 or later (2012 for mutual funds), they also report the cost basis. For purchases prior to that date the investor will need to provide records to substantiate cost basis.

Quick Quiz 17.3

1. The basis of stock that has split is proportional to the stock split.
   a. True
   b. False
2. Stock splits change ownership percentages among investors.
   a. True
   b. False
3. Losses from wash sale treatment are added to basis.
   a. True
   b. False
4. The holding period for long-term treatment for stock that has split is from the split date.
   a. True
   b. False

True, False, True, False.

TAXATION OF BONDS

Bonds are long-term debt securities of governments and corporations, and receive different tax treatment than equity securities in some respects. This section reviews the common tax issues faced by the bond investor.

Interest (Coupon Payments)

For the bond investor, interest received on the bond is generally taxable. When a corporation pays bond coupons, it receives a tax deduction for the amount paid, so the general income tax principle that requires one taxpayer to report income if another taxpayer takes a deduction is met. An exception to this rule applies to bonds issued by states and local governments (municipal bonds) that may generate tax-free income for federal income tax purposes. Interest received by an investor on all corporate bonds, and most U.S. government bonds, is taxable. Coupon payments are taxed to the investor at the investor's marginal ordinary income tax rate.

If an investor purchases a bond at its par value, holds the bond to maturity, and collects all of the coupon payments, the only tax impact for the investor will be receipt of the interest payments that are taxed at ordinary income tax rates. If the investor purchases the bond for more or less than its par value, additional tax issues must be considered.

Original Issue Discount, Market Discount, and Market Premium Bonds

When a bond is purchased at a price other than its par value, the investor has to account for the premium or discount for income tax purposes in addition to paying tax on the bond coupon payments. The additional tax treatment that applies depends upon whether the bond was sold initially at a discount, or if the bond was purchased in the market at a discount or a premium.

Original Issue Discount

If a long-term bond is issued at a price lower than its par (or redemption) value, the difference between the par value and the issue price is referred to as **original issue discount (OID)**. The best example of an original issue discount bond is a zero-coupon bond. Zero-coupon bonds do not make coupon payments during their lifetimes, but rather pay the redemption value at maturity. An investor who purchases a newly issued zero-coupon bond has OID, and must make adjustments for this type of bond on their income tax return on an annual basis. The OID rules do not apply to short-term bonds, which are defined as bonds with a fixed maturity of one year or less from the original date of issue.

Key Concepts

1. OID rules require accrual of discount.
2. A market discount on a bond does not require an accrual.
3. Tax-free municipal bonds may be subject to capital gains tax.

If a long-term bond is issued at a discount, the OID rules require the accrued interest on the bond to be included in the investor's taxable income (subject to tax at the investor's marginal ordinary income tax rate) as it accrues each year, even though the investor does not receive the interest payment until the bond matures. The accrued interest is reported on Form 1099-OID. This rule applies to both cash-basis and accrual-basis taxpayers, and causes the investor to have phantom income until the year in which the bond matures.[7]

Example 17.25

On January 1, Elliott buys a newly issued $1,000 zero-coupon OID bond of 30 years for $57.31 to yield 10%. Elliott must recognize accrued interest of $5.73 as ordinary income. His total income in year 1 is $5.73. His basis going into year 2 will be $63.04 ($57.31 + $5.73).

The OID rules are a good example of the doctrine of constructive receipt. The constructive receipt doctrine requires cash basis taxpayers to recognize income in situations where the taxpayer has a choice to take or not take the income, and when income is permanently set aside in the account of the taxpayer. The choice to take or defer income is commonly associated with retirement planning, and is discussed at length in income tax and retirement planning texts. The second situation triggering constructive receipt – permanently setting aside income in the taxpayer's account, is what underlies the OID rules. As the bond approaches its maturity date, the value of the bond increases due to the accrued, but unpaid interest. While the investor will not receive the income until maturity, the coupon has been earned and is set aside for the taxpayer in the form of an increase in the value of the bond that the taxpayer owns, causing the doctrine of constructive receipt to apply. This example is similar to the situation an investor would face when purchasing a long-term certificate of deposit – while the interest is not received until maturity, it is taxed each year as it is set aside in the taxpayer's account.

Investors should be cautioned that the amount of income reported on Form 1099-OID may only be correct if the investor purchased the bond at issuance. For OID bonds purchased in the secondary markets, an adjustment to the interest reported on Form 1099-OID may be necessary. While this subject is beyond the scope of this text, investors should recognize the need to consult a tax expert when they have purchased OID bonds in the secondary markets.

Zero-coupon bonds offer many attractive investment features, such as the ability to match cash needs with the maturity proceeds of the bond, and the guarantee of a specified internal rate of return. While the tax impact of phantom income from zero coupon bonds does present some complications, it may not overshadow the use of these instruments in an overall financial plan. The negative annual tax implications can be overcome by holding OID bonds in tax qualified accounts, such as IRAs, where taxes are not paid until distributions are made from the account.

Market Discount Bonds

Market discount bonds are bonds that were initially issued at redemption value, but have declined in value due to changes in market conditions. As discussed in the bond analysis section of this textbook, the price of a bond is inversely related to a change in interest rates. Since an investor has no control over the coupon payment they receive, the only way to ensure that a market rate of return can be achieved on the bond is by adjusting the price of the bond up (in circumstances where interest rates have declined), or down (in circumstances where interest rates have increased). Purchase of a bond that carries a market discount gives the investor another source of investment return aside from the coupon payments that will be received on the instrument.

7. Phantom income is income that is subject to taxation that has no corresponding cash flow. For example, zero-coupon bonds generate income each year without any cash flow.

Example 17.26

Terra recently received a birthday present from her grandmother ($1,000 in cash), and decides (with the wise guidance of her parents) to save the money to pay for part of her college education. Long-term interest rates are currently 7%. Terra and her parents decide to invest the money in bonds, but there are no new bond issues coming to market currently. Terra decides to purchase a bond issued by HJK, Inc. that carries an interest rate of 5%. Terra can purchase each $1,000 par value bond for $925. In addition to receiving the annual coupon payments, when the bond matures, Terra will receive the redemption value of $1,000, which results in an additional $75 gain.

Unlike the situation with original issue discount bonds, a cash basis taxpayer who purchases a bond with a market discount does not generally have to include the discount in their taxable income before the sale or maturity of the bond. An investor could elect to report the market discount as it accrues on the bond as interest income each year (which results in phantom income similar to the situation with OID bonds). If the investor makes this election, the amount included in income each year is added to the investor's basis in the bond.

Example 17.27

Mike buys a 6% annual coupon, 30-year term bond one year after it is issued. He buys it for $935.46, priced to yield 6.5%. This price is Mike's original basis. He will have $60 of interest income every year. If he elects to accrue interest in the same manner as an OID, he will also have phantom income each year. This accrued (phantom) income is found by first determining the IRR attributable to the discount: PV = -935.46, N = 29, FV = 1000, solve for I = 0.2303%. The accrued interest for the first year equals 0.2303% x $935.46 = $2.15. Mike's new basis after year 1 equals $937.61 (original basis of $935.46 + $2.15 interest taxed in year 1). The second years accrued interest equals the IRR times the new basis. The basis again increases by the amount of interest recognized each year. This process is continued for the remaining term of the bond.

Assuming that no election is made to amortize the discount, the investor would recognize the market discount on the bond when the bond is sold or when it matures. The market discount is not taxed as capital gain, however. Instead, the gain is taxed as interest income (and subject to the taxpayer's marginal ordinary income tax rate) to the extent of the market discount that was accrued up to the date of the bond's disposition. Any gain in excess of the market discount is treated as capital gain. If a market discount bond is sold at a loss (due, possibly, to a further increase in interest rates), the loss would be classified as a capital loss. Recall that the reason for the market discount is to give the investor an interest rate on the bond comparable to current interest rates, and as a compensation for lost interest, the discount (to the extent it is received by the investor) is taxed as interest income.

Example 17.28

Maverick buys a 6% annual coupon, 30-year term bond one year after it is issued. He buys it for $935.46, priced to yield 6.5%. This price is Maverick's original basis. He will have $60 of interest income every year. If he elects to not accrue interest, then he will recognize the portion of the gain that is attributable to the market discount as interest upon sale or disposition of the bond. Assume Maverick sells the bond for $1,040 exactly

15 years after he bought it. The interest from the market discount can be found by first determining the IRR attributable to the discount:
PV = -935.46
N = 29
FV = 1000
Solve for i = 0.2303%

Use this interest rate to then find the FV:
PV = -935.46
N = 15
i = 0.2303%
Solve for FV = 968.31

Based on this calculation: $32.85 ($968.31 - $935.46) is treated as interest with $71.70 treated as a capital gain.

The interest income that results from either the amortization of the discount, or the recognition of the discount at the time of sale or maturity, is classified as investment income, and may be offset by investment interest expense.

This discussion of the tax impact of market discount bonds does not include municipal bonds purchased before May 1, 1993, U.S. Savings Bonds, or short-term (less than one year) obligations. The tax impact on these instruments varies from the discussion above.

Market Premium Bonds

Bonds trading at a premium, or at a price in excess of par value, are called **market premium bonds.** If interest rates decline over time, and an investor purchases a bond that was issued when interest rates were higher, the investor will likely pay a premium for that bond to compensate the seller for the higher-than-market coupon payments the seller of the bond was receiving. When an investor pays a premium for a bond, the amount of the purchase price that represents a premium is not returned to the investor.

Upon the purchase of a premium bond, the investor must elect the tax treatment that will apply to the bond premium. Two options are available: (1) amortizing the premium over the bond's remaining life or possibly to an earlier call date, or (2) not amortizing the premium and adding the premium to the bond's basis. If the amortization option is elected, the investor's basis in the bond will be reduced by the amount of premium amortization that occurs each year. The election, once made, is effective for all taxable bonds owned by the investor at the beginning of the tax year of the election and all bonds acquired thereafter. The election may only be revoked with consent of the IRS.

If the amortization method is not elected, and the bond is sold at a gain, the premium is returned tax free to the investor upon sale of the bond. If the amortization method is not elected and the bond is sold at a loss, the loss will be treated as a capital loss.

A special rule applies to tax-exempt bonds. No amortization of the premium on tax exempt bonds is permitted, but nevertheless, the bond's basis will be reduced by the bond premium. (IRC Section 1016(a)(5)).

Municipal Bonds

Generally, the interest or coupon payments received from municipal bonds are not subject to federal income tax. Congress exempted municipal bond interest income from tax to lower the cost of borrowing for states and municipalities, and to encourage investment in securities that provide support for public projects. High income investors also avoid the 3.8 percent net investment income tax on municipal bond income, which increases their taxable equivalent yield, making investment in municipal bonds an attractive addition to their portfolio from a tax standpoint. The tax exemption of municipal bond interest is not absolute, however. At the federal level, if an investor becomes an alternative minimum taxpayer, some or all of the municipal bond income may be subject to alternative minimum tax. The amount subject to the AMT is determined by the type of municipal bonds that the investor holds. Second, the states do impose an income tax on municipal bond interest if the bonds purchased by the investor are not bonds issued by the state of the investor's residence or a political subdivision of that state.[8]

As with all other bonds, the sale of municipal bonds could trigger a capital gain or loss, which would be subject to income tax even though the interest income from municipal bonds is generally exempt from federal income tax.

Types of Municipal Bonds and the AMT

Prior to the changes enacted by the Tax Reform Act of 1986, there were no distinctions between municipal bonds. All bonds issued by state and local governments received the same income tax treatment. Interest received on these bonds is tax-free, and the interest is not considered a preference item for the alternative minimum tax (AMT).

Municipal bonds issued after August 7, 1986 are categorized based on the projects they support. The two primary classifications of bonds issued after August 7, 1986 are public purpose municipal bonds and private activity bonds (sometimes referred to as non-governmental purpose bonds).

Public purpose municipal bonds are issued to support essential governmental functions. Some common projects that qualify a bond as a public purpose bond include building schools, police stations, fire stations, airports, docks, and roads. Public purpose municipal bonds generate tax-exempt income for regular federal income tax purposes that is not considered a preference item for the AMT.

> **Quick Quiz 17.4**
>
> 1. A 30-year zero-coupon corporate bond yielding 6% bought for 169.73 on January 1 at issuance will incur $10.18 of interest income in year 1.
>   a. True
>   b. False
> 2. A tax-free municipal bond yielding 10% sold at 90 is later resold for $950. There is no income tax.
>   a. True
>   b. False
>
> True, False.

Private activity bonds are used to finance certain private activities, subsidized housing, and student bonds. A relatively new category of private activity bond, called a qualified redevelopment bond, is used to finance land acquisition and redevelopment in blighted areas. These bonds also generate income that is exempt for regular tax purposes, but that is considered an AMT preference item. Once a taxpayer is subject to the AMT, which subjects private activity municipal bond income to taxation, the taxpayer may deduct investment interest expense incurred to acquire the municipal bonds, which is not deductible for regular income tax purposes.

8. Tax exempt income from municipal bonds may also increase the portion of Social Security payments that are subject to taxation.

In addition to public purpose municipal bonds and private activity bonds, some bonds issued by state and local governments after August 7, 1986 are referred to as taxable bonds. Taxable municipal bonds are used to finance projects such as the construction of sports, convention, and trade show facilities, air and water pollution control facilities, and may be used to promote private development, private activities, or used for arbitrage purposes. As their name implies, these bonds generate income that is taxable for regular income tax purposes, but are not considered preference items for AMT purposes.

U.S. Government Bonds

The U.S. government issues both marketable and non-marketable bonds, including EE bonds, Treasury Inflation Protection Securities (TIPs), Treasury Notes, Treasury Bonds, and inflation-indexed Series I bonds (the Treasury stopped issuing Series HH Bonds after August 31, 2004.) From an income tax standpoint, U.S. government bonds are the flip side of public purpose municipal bonds. The interest generated by U.S. government bonds is subject to federal income tax, but is not subject to state and local income tax.

One exception to this rule applies to the federal taxation of Series EE bonds. The income generated by Series EE bonds issued after December 31, 1989 is exempt from federal income tax if the bonds are redeemed to pay for qualified college education expenses of the bond owner, or the bond owner's spouse and dependents if all of the following requirements are met:

- The owner of the bond was at least 24 years old when the bond is issued.
- The bond is registered in the name of the bond owner.
- If married, the investor's filing status must be married filing jointly.
- The bond owner's modified adjusted gross income is not so high that the benefit is phased out. Individuals who are married filing separately are not eligible for the income exclusion.

If U.S. government bonds are sold at a gain or loss, the gain or loss is also subject to federal income taxation.

Bond Swaps

Bond swapping is the process of selling one debt instrument and replacing it with another. The goal of this technique is generally to increase the overall rate of return, but may occur in anticipation of changes in interest rates. As discussed in Chapter 8, there are many types of bond swaps. Unlike equities, bonds are usually not subject to the wash sale rules. It is relatively easy to exchange one bond for another bond with similar term, coupon rate, and yield to maturity, as well as maintaining the credit risk of the bond.

TAXATION OF MUTUAL FUNDS

Mutual funds are one of the most popular forms of investment vehicles for individuals. As discussed in other areas of this text, mutual funds allow small investors to diversify their portfolios by purchasing an interest in an underlying portfolio of diversified investments.

Open-End Mutual Funds

Open-end mutual funds stand ready to sell additional shares to investors, and to purchase back shares that investors wish to redeem. When an investor purchases an open-end mutual fund, there are two sources of investment return: (1) the increase [or decrease] in the value of the mutual fund shares over time, and (2) distributions of investment income from the mutual fund during the holding period.

The increase in value of the fund over the holding period is treated as a capital transaction, and the traditional rules that apply to calculation of gain or loss apply to mutual funds as well. The investor takes the amount realized from the transaction and subtracts their adjusted basis to determine the gain or loss, which is classified as a short-term or long-term capital gain based on the holding period of the investment.

A mutual fund investor's basis in the mutual fund is usually the actual cost of the mutual fund shares, if the shares that are sold can be specifically identified. If the shares that are sold are not specifically identified, the default rule for basis is the FIFO method, or, if appropriate, the investor can elect the average cost method. The general rules for determining basis when calculating gain or loss were reviewed earlier in this chapter. If a front-end load is paid to purchase the shares, that amount is added to the basis of the shares, and is prorated among the shares purchased in that transaction.

Key Concepts

1. There are three ways available for mutual fund owners to determine basis.
2. One method of determining basis for mutual funds is FIFO.

Calculating a mutual fund's actual basis may be difficult when distributions from the fund are reinvested in additional mutual fund shares. Each year as the distribution is made and reinvested, the investor includes the distribution in their income, and the investor's basis in the mutual fund shares increases by a like amount. To the extent that an investor wishes to use the specific identification method of determining basis when calculating gain or loss for tax purposes, careful records must be kept. Use of financial software packages may ease the record keeping burden and allow the investor to use the specific identification method of determining basis upon sale of the mutual fund shares.

As a general rule, mutual fund investors are subject to the same identification rules that apply to stock or bond investors. Three methods are available to mutual fund investors for calculating adjusted tax basis:

1. average cost method
2. first in, first out (FIFO)
3. specific identification

The averaging method must be elected, and if it is not elected, then shares sold are on a FIFO basis. For specific identification, each sale must be elected by instructions. Taxpayers may switch between specific identification and FIFO where no averaging election has been made.

1/1/01	100 shares	Mutual fund @ $12/share	$1,200
5/1/01	300 shares	Mutual fund @ $9.75/share	$2,925
2/1/02	250 shares	Mutual fund @ $14/share	$3,500
	650 shares		**$7,625**

1. *Average cost method*: (average share price = $7,625/650 shares = $11.7307692)

If 200 shares are sold on 4/1/03 for $16.00 =	$3,200.00
Basis 200 x $11.7307692 =	$2,346.15
Long-Term Capital Gain (LTCG) =	$853.85

2. *FIFO*:

Sales Price 200 x $16.00 =	$3,200.00
Cost Basis (100 x $12) + (100 x $9.75) =	$2,175.00
Long-Term Capital Gain (LTCG) =	$1,025.00

3. *Specific Identification*:

Sales Price 200 x $16.00 =	$3,200.00
Cost Basis 200 x $14.00 =	$2,800.00
Long-Term Capital Gain (LTCG) =	$400.00

The amount realized on the sale of mutual fund shares is reduced by the amount of the back-end load or sales charge.

In order to be exempt from federal income taxes, a mutual fund must pass through its interest, dividend, and capital gain income to its owners on an annual basis. Most mutual funds distribute all of these gains, less the costs that are incurred to operate the mutual fund. Each year, the investor must include the gains in their income, and must classify them in the same way that the income was earned by the mutual fund. Interest distributions are taxed as interest income and are subject to tax at the investor's marginal income tax rate. Dividends distributed by a mutual fund may be classified as either qualified or non-qualified dividends. A discussion of the income tax differences between qualified and non-qualified dividends was discussed earlier in this chapter. Long-term capital gains and losses are treated as capital transactions, so long-term capital gains tax rates apply. Short-term capital gains are subject to tax at the investor's marginal federal income tax rate. When a mutual fund or REIT declares a dividend or capital gain distribution in October, November, or December, that is payable to the shareholders of record on a date prior to the end of that year, even though it actually pays the dividend in January of the following year, it is treated as distributed on December 31 and taxed in the year of declaration. Distributions are reported to the shareholder on Form 1099-DIV.

If a mutual fund does not distribute capital gains to its shareholders, the investor is still required to include their share of any income or capital gain in taxable income. If the mutual fund pays a tax on the undistributed capital gain, the investor may claim a credit for the amount of tax paid by the mutual fund for the year. The difference between the investor's share of the undistributed capital gain and the tax on the gain paid by the mutual fund is treated as an increase in the investor's basis in the mutual fund shares.

In some cases, a mutual fund may make a distribution to shareholders that does not come from the earnings and profits of the fund. When this occurs, the distribution is treated as a return of capital, and the investor's basis is reduced by a like amount. Once the investor's basis has been reduced to zero, all additional distributions made by the fund are taxed as a capital gain.

Closed-End Funds

Closed-end mutual funds have a limited number of shares outstanding. Typically, an investor does not purchase or sell shares directly from the fund, but rather purchases and sells the shares in the secondary market. Gain or loss on the shares, therefore, is determined by market prices instead of by the redemption value of the shares calculated by the fund.

Similar to open-end mutual funds, closed-end funds generate their return from capital appreciation and investment income. If a closed-end fund elects to be taxed as a **regulated investment company (RIC)**, the taxation of gains and investment income in a closed-end mutual is identical to the taxation of gains and investment income in an open-end mutual fund.

Unit Investment Trusts

Unit investment trusts are similar to mutual funds in that they hold a portfolio of securities, and interests in that portfolio of securities are sold to investors. Unlike mutual funds, unit investment trusts are not actively managed. They usually hold securities that self-liquidate over time, such as tax-exempt bonds, mortgage-backed securities, or corporate bonds, and pass through all of the cashflow on those investments to the investor. Owners of unit investment trust interests receive a return on their investment through distributions of income from the trust and from realization of gains upon sale of their units.

The taxation of gains or losses on sale of unit investment trust interests follows the normal rules for calculating capital gains and losses. The taxation of the investment income of the fund depends upon how the fund is structured.

If the unit investment trust is set up as a grantor trust, all items of income, loss, deductions, and tax credits flow through to the investor in proportion to the investor's ownership interest. The items of income that are passed through to the owners retain their character for tax purposes.

If the unit investment trust elects to be taxed as a regulated investment company, the owners of interests in the unit investment trust are taxed in the same manner as the owners of mutual funds (discussed above).

Quick Quiz 17.5

1. A mutual fund investor must elect FIFO.
   a. True
   b. False
2. To use average cost, a mutual fund investor must elect average cost.
   a. True
   b. False

False, True.

TAXATION OF REAL ESTATE OWNED DIRECTLY BY AN INVESTOR

In General

The taxation of real estate held by an individual depends upon the purpose for which it is held. A dealer of real estate holds the property as inventory for sale to customers, and therefore the gains on the sale of real estate are treated as ordinary income. If the real estate is held in a trade or business, it is treated as an IRC Section 1231 asset and the depreciable portion of real estate (building and improvements) is generally taxable at capital gains rates, subject to adjustment for recapture of depreciation. If the land is held for personal use or for investment, it is classified as a capital asset and capital gains tax rates apply.

The gain or loss on the sale of real estate is calculated in the same manner as with other assets, and equals the amount realized from the sale reduced by the taxpayer's adjusted basis. If the buyer assumes debt associated with the real estate, the seller's amount realized is equal to the cash received plus the value of the liabilities from which the seller has been relieved. Costs associated with the purchase of the real estate, such as closing costs, brokerage fees, and attorneys fees are added to the taxpayer's cost basis.

These same amounts are subtracted from the amount realized upon sale. Gain on the sale of real estate held as a capital asset is taxable, with one major exception (IRC Section 121, discussed below). If an individual incurs a loss on the sale of real estate, it is deductible as a capital loss if the real estate was held for investment. If a taxpayer has a loss on real estate used for personal purposes (such as for a principal or secondary residence) no loss deduction is allowed.[9]

IRC Section 121 - Taxation of the Sale of a Principal Residence

IRC Section 121 allows for the exclusion of gain from the sale of a principal residence under certain conditions. If a taxpayer used a piece of real estate as a principal residence for two out of the five years prior to sale, up to $250,000 of the gain (for single taxpayers) and $500,000 of the gain (for married taxpayers filing jointly) is excluded from taxation. Any gain in excess of these amounts is taxable at capital gains rates.

A few special rules apply to the two-year use requirement. If a taxpayer has used property as a primary residence for at least one year and has been a resident of a nursing home within the five-year period prior to sale, up to one year of the stay in the nursing home counts towards the two-year requirement. Furthermore, if a taxpayer sells the principal residence due to a change in health, employment, or other unforeseen circumstance, a prorated exemption is allowed. To calculate the amount of the prorated exemption, take the number of months the residence was used as a principal residence divided by 24 and multiply by the applicable exemption amount.

Example 17.29

Raven, a recent single college graduate, bought a home in Connecticut nine months ago that she has used as her principal residence. Her basis in the home is $340,000. Raven has just been informed by her employer that she will be transferred to the San Diego office three months from now. Raven places her home on the market, and sells it the week before she leaves for San Diego (resulting in 12 months of use of the property as a principal residence) for $400,000. Because the sale of the residence was the result of a change in employment location, Raven is entitled to a partial exclusion on the sale of her home. She used the home for 12 out of 24 months, or one half of the normal use requirement.

Raven is therefore entitled to exclude up to $125,000 of the gain from income tax (12/24 x $250,000). Since Raven's gain is only $60,000 ($400,000 - $340,000), the gain will be tax-free.

The exclusion of gain on the sale of a residence only applies to the taxpayer's principal residence and may only be claimed once every two years.

IRC Section 1031

An important tax rule for real estate investors is found in IRC Section 1031. IRC Section 1031 allows investors to engage in like-kind exchanges to defer taxation of the gain on the sale or other disposition of a particular piece of property. Under general rules of income taxation, once the gain on a property has been realized as a result of the sale, transfer, or other disposition of the property, the gain must be

9. Keep in mind that gains on property held for personal use are taxable while losses on personal-use property are not deductible.

recognized. If, however, a taxpayer engages in a like-kind exchange, the realized gain is not recognized but rather deferred until the replacement property is sold.

In enacting this section of the IRC, Congress has recognized that if an investor exchanges properties but does not change their "investment solution," it would be unfair to require gain recognition at the time of transfer.

Key Concepts

1. Taxation of real estate depends on the purpose for which it is held.
2. IRC Section 121 allows the gain on the sale of a principal residence to be excluded from income if certain requirements are met.
3. IRC Section 1031 allows investors to engage in like-kind exchanges.
4. A REIT may be exempt from tax if certain requirements are met.

To qualify for like-kind exchange treatment, the property exchanged must be held for investment or for productive use in a trade or business, and must be exchanged solely for like-kind property. Non-like-kind property received in the exchange is called "boot;" if a taxpayer receives boot in a transaction, the gain on the property transferred is recognized to the extent of boot received.

Like-kind property is property of the same character as the property transferred. All domestic real estate is considered like-kind property provided that it is held for investment or for productive use in a trade or business.[10] For example, an investor who purchased raw land as an investment could exchange that land for an apartment building and defer recognition of gain under Section 1031. Exchanges of U.S. for foreign real estate, and foreign real estate for U.S. real estate do not qualify as a like-kind exchange and require gain recognition. Exchanges of foreign real estate for foreign real estate do qualify for like-kind exchange treatment.

The potential problem an investor may face when contemplating a like-kind exchange is finding another investor to trade the property with. Finding a person who has a property that you want, and who wants to receive your property in exchange, is a difficult task. Thankfully, the law does not require that a direct exchange be made, but rather allows an investor to sell their property and purchase a replacement property if additional requirements are met. The first requirement deals with the proceeds of the sale of the property. To effectuate a like-kind exchange, an investor must appoint a qualified intermediary to receive the proceeds from the sale. The qualified intermediary holds the proceeds in an escrow account, and brings those proceeds to closing on a new property. A replacement property must be identified by the investor within 45 days of closing the sale of the old property, and the new property must be received on or before the earlier of (1) 180 days after the closing of the property sold, or (2) the due date, including extensions, for the tax year that the original property is given up.

State and Local Taxation (Property Taxes)

In addition to the tax on gains in real estate, state and local governments often tax the value of real estate on an annual basis to fund their operations, often referred to as a property tax. Property taxes qualify as itemized deductions for the taxpayer (below-the-line deductions) for the year they are paid if a cash-basis method of accounting is used. TCJA 2017 limits the itemized deductions for state and local taxes to $10,000 for years after 2017. Since real estate taxes constitute a carrying cost for real estate, their impact must be factored into the investment decision, in addition to the calculation of the investment gain or loss that the investor realizes.

10.TCJA 2017 limited like-kind property to real estate for years after 2017.

Interest on Loans Used to Acquire Real Estate

The tax treatment of interest on loans used to purchase real estate depends upon the taxpayer's use of the real estate.

If a taxpayer obtains a mortgage to purchase a principal residence and up to one additional residence, the interest on the loan becomes an itemized deduction (the interest is deductible on Schedule A of Form 1040, and is a below-the-line deduction). There are limitations to the amount of mortgage interest that can be deducted for this purpose, however. For acquisition indebtedness (the debt incurred to acquire the property), a taxpayer may deduct the interest on a loan or loans of up to $750,000 for loans entered into after 2017. The $750,000 loan cap applies per taxpayer (or married couple if married filing jointly), not per home. Beginning in 2018, taxpayers are not permitted to deduct interest on home equity loans unless the money received from the loan is used to improve the property and the total indebtedness for which a tax deduction on the interest payment is taken does not exceed $750,000.

Real estate investors often borrow money to finance the acquisition of rental real estate. The interest on loans used to obtain rental real estate is deducted from the income generated by the real estate activity on Schedule E of Form 1040, resulting in an above-the-line deduction for interest expense since the interest directly reduces income that would otherwise be subject to tax. Rental real estate is, however, a passive activity for most investors, and if the activity generates a loss, the loss may not be deductible in the current tax year but can be carried forward until the property is disposed of or until passive income can be generated. The details of the passive loss rules are beyond the scope of this text but must be considered in assessing a real estate investment's performance, since the timing of the tax benefits generated on the real estate have an impact on the investment return.

Quick Quiz 17.6

1. IRC Section 121 exempts some gain from the sale of a principal residence if the taxpayer qualifies.
   a. True
   b. False
2. For IRC Section 121 to apply, the taxpayer must have used the property as their principal residence for 2 of the last 5 years.
   a. True
   b. False

True, True.

If real estate is purchased for investment but will not be rented, the taxpayer is not generally permitted to deduct the interest incurred on loans to acquire the real estate in the tax year the interest is paid. Instead, the investor capitalizes the interest (add the interest expense to their basis in the property) by making an election under Treas. Reg. Section 1266-1(b)(1). To make the election, the taxpayer must file a statement with their tax return for each year the election is made. The election is effective only for the year made, so the taxpayer must make annual elections if interest expense is incurred on an annual basis.

Taxation of Real Estate Investment Trusts (REITs)

From an investor perspective, a REIT is a mutual fund for real estate. REITs give investors the opportunity to own real estate indirectly through purchase of interests in a trust that owns and operates real property or owns mortgages on real property. Most REITs are publicly traded, closed-end investment companies.

One of the advantages of a REIT for an individual investor is diversification in real estate holdings. The price tag on most real estate is high, so if an investor wanted to create a diversified portfolio of real estate holdings, a large amount of capital would be required. By purchasing an interest in a REIT, the investor can achieve diversification while participating in the investment returns that real estate offers.

A REIT is exempt from tax at the entity level if it (1) derives a minimum of 75 percent of its income from real estate, and (2) distributes at least 90 percent of its income in the form of cash dividends to its owners on an annual basis. Provided that these requirements are met, the owners of interests in the REIT report their proportionate share of the REIT's income on their individual tax returns for the year in a manner similar to owners of mutual funds.

Cash dividends distributed from a REIT do not represent a distribution of earnings from a corporation that pays an entity-level tax, and therefore do not qualify as qualified dividends eligible for capital gains tax rates. To the extent that a REIT has invested in shares of a company that pays qualified dividends, those qualified dividends may be passed through to the shareholders of the REIT and reported accordingly on the tax return of the owner.

Beginning in 2018, the TCJA created a new tax deduction under IRC Section 199A that allows certain types of REIT dividends to qualify for a 20 percent tax deduction. The net result is to reduce the tax rate on qualifying REIT dividends by 20 percent. For example, a taxpayer in the 37 percent marginal tax bracket effectively pays tax at a rate of 29.6 percent on qualifying REIT dividends. The portion of the REIT dividends that qualify for the deduction is reported to the taxpayer on Form 1099-DIV beginning in 2018.

If an interest in a REIT is sold, the owner realizes a capital gain or loss that is calculated and reported in accordance with the general rules governing capital transactions.

Taxation of Rental Real Estate Income

Investment in real estate through direct ownership of residential rental properties is a popular source of income for many investors. An investor can buy an interest in a piece of real estate individually or as part of a group of individual investors.

Individual investors in rental real estate report rents as ordinary income, and deduct expenses for mortgage payments, taxes, insurance, maintenance, utilities, and depreciation, on Schedule E of Form 1040. Under current law, all depreciation on real estate is taken on a straight-line basis. If the real estate is used for residential purposes, the recovery period is 27½ years, and if the real estate is used as commercial property, the recovery period is 39 years. Deductions related to rental real estate occur above-the-line, reducing the taxpayer's adjusted gross income (AGI).

Taxpayers who itemize deductions are permitted to deduct the interest paid on up to $1 million (for mortgage debt incurred before Dec. 15, 2017; $750,000 for mortgage debt incurred after Dec. 14, 2017) of acquisition debt for a mortgage secured by their personal residence. This deduction limit applies to both first and second home acquisition indebtedness combined. Home equity loan interest is deductible only if the debt is used to improve the property and is included in the above limits. However, Interest actually paid or incurred during the year on mortgages taken out on investment property is generally deductible against the rental income generated from the property. This interest is not an itemized deduction but is subtracted from the investor's rental income and reduces adjusted gross income, as discussed above.

Passive Loss Limitations for Rental Real Estate

For investors who are not professional dealers in real estate, rental income is passive income and is subject to the passive loss rules discussed previously in this chapter. These passive losses may only be used to offset passive gains. Losses are further limited to the amount an investor has at risk (under the at-risk rules). If the property produces a loss, the loss generally cannot be used to offset earned income or investment income. The loss is suspended and carried forward to offset future passive gains or is used when the property is sold to decrease the realized gain on the property. A real estate professional must report any gain on the sale of rental property as ordinary income.

There is an exception for the small investor who actively participates in the management of the rental property. A small investor is a single or married individual with modified adjusted gross income (AGI) of $100,000 or less. Under the tax code, a small investor may use up to $25,000 of annual rental losses to offset active or portfolio income. The deduction is phased out at a rate of $1 for every $2 of modified AGI over $100,000 and is completely phased-out for modified AGI over $150,000.

Sec. 199A Qualified Business Income Deduction for Rental Real Estate

The Tax Cuts and Jobs Act of 2017 created a new deduction under Section 199A for "Qualified Business Income" of pass-through entities (sole proprietorships, partnerships, LLCs, and S corporations), for tax years 2018 - 2025. For purposes of Section 199A, some rental real estate investments reported on Schedule E of the investor's Form 1040 income tax return are included in the definition of pass-through entities. Business income from these entities flows through to the owners and is taxed at the owner's marginal rate.

The deduction is a below-the-line deduction on the investor's Form 1040, which reduces taxable income but does not reduce adjusted gross income. Taxpayers who qualify for the deduction are permitted to take the deduction, regardless of whether the standard deduction or itemized deductions are selected.

The deduction is generally 20 percent of the taxpayer's qualified business income (QBI). For rental real estate investors, the net result is to reduce the tax rate on the qualified rental income by 20 percent. For example, for a taxpayer in the highest marginal bracket (37% in 2022), the tax on the rental income is effectively reduced to 29.60 percent (37% x (1 - 0.20) = 29.60%)

The deduction is actually based on the taxpayer's "combined qualified business income", which can generally be described as a combination of the QBI from each flow-through business plus qualified REIT dividends and qualified publicly-traded partnership income. The deduction is also limited to 20 percent of the taxpayer's taxable income (after reducing by any capital gains) from all sources, including their spouse's income if married filing jointly. If the taxpayer's taxable income from all sources (without regard to the Sec. 199A deduction; and including the spouse's income if MFJ) is over $170,050 (single, $340,100 MFJ in 2022), additional restrictions apply.

Real Estate Safe Harbor

Rev. Proc. 2019-38 provides a safe harbor test for a rental real estate enterprise to qualify for the Section 199A deduction. A rental real estate enterprise that does not qualify under the safe harbor provision may still qualify for the deduction if it otherwise meets the definition of trade or business in Sec. 199A.

For purposes of the safe harbor, a rental real estate enterprise is an interest in real property held for the production of rents. A rental real estate enterprise may consist of an interest in multiple properties, although residential and commercial real estate may not be part of the same enterprise. The individual or relevant pass-through entity relying on the safe harbor must hold the interest directly or through a disregarded entity (e.g., real estate in a single-member LLC). If the taxpayer used the property as a vacation home, however, the safe harbor will not be available.

The following requirements must be met to qualify for the safe harbor:

1. Separate books and records must be maintained for each rental real estate enterprise.
2. a. For rental real estate enterprises that have been in existence less than four years: 250 or more hours of rental services (defined below) are performed per year with respect to the rental real estate enterprise.
   b. For rental real estate enterprises that have been in existence at least four years: in any three of the last five consecutive years, 250 or more hours of rental services are performed per year with respect to the rental real estate enterprise.
3. Contemporaneous records must be kept, including time logs regarding dates and hours or all services performed and who performed the services.
4. A statement must be attached to the taxpayer's timely filed tax return in each taxable year in which the taxpayer relies on the safe harbor. The statement must include a description of all properties held in the rental real estate enterprise, a description of properties acquired and disposed of during the year, and a representation that the requirements of Revenue Procedure 2019-38 have been satisfied.

For purposes of the above requirements, rental services include:
1. advertising to rent the real estate
2. negotiating and executing leases
3. verifying information in prospective tenant applications
4. collection of rent
5. daily operation, maintenance, and repair of the property, including purchase of materials and supplies
6. management of the real estate, and supervision of employees

Rental services do not have to be performed directly by the owners. Rental services also include the above services that are performed by employees, agents, or independent contractors of the owner.

TAXATION OF DERIVATIVES

The following section discusses the taxation of options and futures contracts.

Taxation of Options

Options Contracts

Options contracts allow investors to hedge their long positions in securities and markets, or speculate on the direction of a security price or the level of the market to leverage their gains (as well as their losses). Call options give the purchaser the right to purchase a specified stock at the strike price listed in the option during the option period. Put options give the purchaser the right to sell a specified stock at the strike price listed in the option during the option period. The investment uses of option contracts are covered in other sections of this textbook.

The taxation of option contracts depends on three separate issues: (1) whether the investor had a long or short position in the option contract, (2) the type of option held, and (3) the manner in which the investor disposed of the option. Our discussion of the taxation of option contracts in this chapter is limited to the purchase or sale of an option without a position in an option on the same security or the security itself. Advanced income tax concepts governing the use of combinations of options, or combinations of options and other securities, may change the tax results listed here and are beyond the scope of this text.

Traditional Exchange-Traded Options

Traditional exchange-traded (or listed) options are capital assets in the hands of the buyer. Upon purchase, an investor has a basis in the option equal to the cost of the option (called the option premium) plus the brokerage commissions paid to acquire the option. From the buyer's perspective, there is no taxable event upon purchase.

> **Key Concepts**
>
> 1. Taxation of options depends on three separate issues.
> 2. There are three ways a buyer can dispose of an option.
> 3. There are two primary types of options used for deferred compensation planning.

When the buyer of a put or call option disposes of the option, a taxable event will generally result. There are three ways the buyer can dispose of the option: (1) sell it before the expiration date, (2) exercise the option, or (3) let the option expire without exercise. The sale of an option contract prior to maturity, or the expiration of an option contract without exercise are realization events for income tax purposes, requiring calculation and recognition of gain.

If the purchaser of a call or put option sells the option in the market prior to its maturity, the taxable gain or loss on the position is calculated by subtracting the investor's basis in the option from the amount realized on the sale. Since most exchange-traded options are issued for maturities of nine months or less, the investor's holding period is less than one year, and therefore the gain or loss is treated as a short-term capital gain or loss. Some options, called LEAPs, have longer-term maturities, and if an investor holds a position in a LEAP long-term (> 1 year) prior to sale of the option, the gain or loss is classified as long-term capital gain or loss.

Instead of selling an option, a buyer of a put or call option could exercise the option (although, as explained in Chapter 15, this is usually not the optimal strategy for dealing with options). The exercise of a call option does not cause a realization event to occur for income tax purposes. Instead, the investor's basis in the stock purchased by exercising the option is increased by the investor's basis in the option contract. Recognition of gain or loss is deferred upon exercise of a call option until the stock purchased on exercise is sold.

The exercise of a put option by an investor is not treated as a taxable transaction. The sale of the underlying stock, however, to the writer of the put option is a taxable event. To determine the total gain or loss for income tax purposes, the investor's basis in the put option is subtracted from the amount realized on the sale of the stock. The result is treated as a capital gain. The character of the gain is determined by the holding period of the stock, not the put option. Usually, the capital gain or loss realized upon exercise of a put option is treated as a short-term capital gain or loss if the underlying stock was purchased at the same time or after the purchase of the put option, or if the underlying stock was held by the purchaser of the option for less than one year on the date the put option was acquired.

If the owner of a put or call option allows the option to expire without exercising it, a deemed sale of the security occurs and the option premium paid (including the brokerage commission paid on the transaction) is reported as a capital loss in the year that the put or call option expires. The nature of the capital loss is determined by the holding period of the option. Since most exchange-traded options are issued for periods of nine months, the expiration of one of these options would generate a short-term capital loss for the investor.

Quick Quiz 17.7

1. There is no gain or loss on the purchase of a call or put option.
   a. True
   b. False
2. Sale of a call option prior to maturity results in gain or loss equal to the difference between sales proceeds and basis.
   a. True
   b. False
3. Brianna has an unrealized gain of $10,000 in a Section 1256 contract at 12/31/2022. This gain is not taxable because she has not closed out the investment.
   a. True
   b. False

True, True, False.

Up to this point, the discussion has focused on the tax consequences to the buyer of a put or call option. Some investors take short positions in option contracts by selling put and call contracts, and while the tax consequences are similar in some respects to the long position in an option contract, there are some differences. A taxable event does not occur upon receipt of the option premium by the seller of the option. Rather, the sellers of put and call options will potentially be subject to tax when (1) the option is exercised by the buyer, (2) the option expires without being exercised, or (3) the option writer closes the position by repurchasing the option in the market or by making a closing purchase in the market.

If a call option is exercised by the buyer, the seller of the call option must add the option premium received upon sale of the call to the amount realized upon exercise when determining gain or loss of the stock. Remember that, since the writer of a call agrees to sell a particular stock at a set strike price, the amount realized equals the strike price of the option multiplied by the appropriate number of shares (generally one hundred shares). The seller of the call option would then subtract their adjusted basis from the amount realized upon exercise of the option to determine gain or loss. The characterization of the gain or loss as long-term or short-term depends upon the holding period of the stock in the hands of the option writer. The time period that the call is outstanding is not relevant.

When a put option is exercised by the buyer, the seller of the put option does not have any immediate income tax result. Recall that the owner of a put option has the right to sell a stock to the seller of the option at a specified price. With an exercise of the put option by the owner, the seller of the option purchases the stock at the strike price in the option, and does not recognize gain or loss until the stock is sold. In calculating gain or loss, the put option writer reduces their basis in the stock purchased upon exercise by the option premium received when the put option was sold. The holding period for determining whether or not the put writer's gain is long-term or short-term begins on the date that the option is exercised and the shares are purchased, not on the date that the put option was initially sold.

If a put or call option expires without being exercised, and the option writer had not previously closed the position, the premium that the seller received upon sale of the option is recognized as short-term capital gain. The gain is recognized in the tax year in which the option expires.

In some circumstances the writer of a put or call option may wish to close the option position. This can be accomplished in two ways: (1) the writer of the option can repurchase the option that was written in the market, thereby canceling the contract, or (2) the writer can purchase an option in the market that is identical to the option sold, creating both a long and short position in the same option and eliminating further price risk for the investor. In either case, the original seller of the option recognizes short-term capital gain or loss on the difference between the option premium received upon the initial sale and the option premium paid when closing out the position.

Exhibit 17.7 | Taxation of Options

	Buy Contract	Sell Contract
Call Option	• No gain or loss upon purchase of a call option. • Sale of a call option in the market prior to maturity results in gain or loss equal to difference between proceeds and basis. • No taxable event upon exercise of call option. Rather, the premium is added to the basis of the stock. • Expiration of a call option generally results in a short-term capital loss.	• No gain or loss upon sale of a call option. • If the call option is exercised, then the seller adds the premium received to the proceeds from the sale of the stock. • If the option expires without being exercised, then the premium is a short-term capital gain.
Put Option	• No gain or loss upon purchase of a put option. • Sale of a put option in the market prior to maturity results in gain or loss equal to difference between proceeds and basis. • The exercise of a put option is not taxable. The sale of the underlying stock is taxable, however. The premium for the put option is subtracted from the proceeds received on the sale. • Expiration of a put option generally results in a short-term capital loss.	• No gain or loss upon sale of a put option. • If the put option is exercised, then the seller reduces the basis of the stock purchased by the premium received. • If the option expires without being exercised, then the premium is a short-term capital gain.

Employment-Related Options (Retirement Planning Issues)

Stock options are often used by corporations in structuring deferred compensation plans for their key employees. By giving key employees the option to purchase stock of the company at its current price over a period that usually lasts for several years, the company is tying its interests to the interests of the corporate executives. The key employees and corporate executives have an incentive to increase the value of the company's stock, since doing so increases the value of their option positions. Unlike exchange-traded options, however, employment-related options are rarely transferable and are not traded on organized exchanges.

There are two primary types of options used for deferred compensation planning: (1) nonqualified stock options, and (2) incentive stock options (ISOs). Generally, the gains on employment-related options are subject to ordinary income tax and are included in the taxable income (and the employee's W-2) in the year the stock options are exercised. There are two exceptions to this rule. The first exception allows the employee to elect to include the current value of the option in their taxable income when the option is first granted, which will transform all future growth in option value into capital gain. This election is made under Section 83(b) of the Internal Revenue Code. The second exception applies to incentive stock options. If the grant of the stock options to employees meets the requirements for incentive stock options, and the employee holds the stock received upon exercise of an incentive stock option for two years from the date of the grant of the option and one year from the date of exercise of the option, the gain can be transformed from ordinary income to capital gain. The use of employment-related stock options, and the tax rules that govern the gains, are discussed at length in retirement planning textbooks.

Taxation of Futures and Other IRC Section 1256 Contracts

The income taxation of futures contracts depends upon the type of contract held by an investor. There are two general categories of futures contracts for income tax purposes: (1) securities futures, and (2) commodities futures.

Securities Futures

Gain or loss on "securities futures" contracts is covered by the same tax rules that apply to the sale of the underlying property. Securities futures contracts are defined in IRC Section 1234B(c), and include contracts for the sale or delivery of a single security or a narrow-based security index. The character of the gain or loss on the sale of a futures contract is determined by reference to the character of the property underlying the contract. If the underlying property is a capital asset, for example, the gain or loss would be treated as capital gain or loss in the hands of the investor. If the property underlying the futures contract is a capital asset in the hands of the taxpayer, the holding period for determining gain or loss includes the holding period of the futures contract.

Commodities Futures

Commodities futures are grouped together with other IRC Section 1256 contracts, and are subject to the mark-to-market provisions of the Internal Revenue Code. IRC Section 1256 contracts include commodities futures contracts, forward contracts, and regulated futures contracts (as defined in IRC Section 1256(g)). One of the most common types of Section 1256 contract is a contract for foreign currency. The tax law requires these contracts to be marked-to-market on the last day of the taxpayer's tax year. Marked-to-market means that the contract is treated as if it is disposed of at the current FMV. The gain or loss is treated as 60 percent long-term and 40 percent short-term each year the mark-to-market occurs, with an adjustment made upon ultimate disposition of the Section 1256 contract to reflect the true characterization of the loss. These transactions are usually entered into by sophisticated investors and financial institutions, and the mechanics of this process are beyond the scope of this text.

The tax treatment of futures contracts varies based on whether the contract was entered as a speculative position or as a hedging position. Speculative contracts are entered into by an investor whose motive is to make money on the price fluctuation of the commodity or on changes in interest rates or currency values. Hedging contracts are entered into in the normal course of the taxpayer's business with the primary purpose of providing price insurance on ordinary business property or protection against interest rate changes or currency fluctuations with respect to their ordinary borrowings or operations. For example, a farmer who grows corn might use a corn futures contract to protect against unfavorable price changes in the price of corn. Gains or losses from speculating are capital gains or losses (as described above) reported on Schedule D and netted against other capital gains and losses for the year, with a maximum net $3,000 loss permitted to offset ordinary income. Gains or losses on hedging positions, however, are business gains or losses, with gains taxed as ordinary income and losses offsetting ordinary income without limitation. To qualify for the exception to capital gain treatment, a hedging transaction must be clearly identified on the taxpayer's business books and records before the end of the day the taxpayer entered into the transaction.

TAXATION OF VIRTUAL CURRENCIES

Cryptocurrencies such as Bitcoin (discussed in Chapter 16) are a form of virtual currency, a type of property whose tax treatment is similar to other types of property in many ways. While a detailed discussion of the tax treatment of virtual currency is beyond the scope of this chapter, a few basic concepts are noteworthy.

Virtual Currency

While Bitcoin is one of the most well-known types of virtual currency, thousands of others also exist. Each virtual currency may be used in a variety of ways and/or for a variety of purposes. The IRS has broadly defined virtual currency as a digital representation of value that functions as a medium of exchange, a unit of account, or a store of value other than a representation of the United States dollar or a foreign currency, and defines **cryptocurrency** as a type of virtual currency that utilizes cryptography to secure transactions that are digitally recorded on a distributed ledger, such as a blockchain.[11]

> ***Key Concepts***
>
> 1. When virtual currency is sold or used as payment for goods or services, a capital gain or loss is recognized.
> 2. Virtual currency transactions are reported by the exchange to the IRS (beginning in 2023).

Virtual Currency Held as an Investment

As with other types of property transactions, when virtual currency is sold a capital gain or loss is recognized (subject to the $3,000 maximum loss against ordinary income as described previously). The holding period to determine short- or long-term capital gains begins on the day after the virtual currency is acquired and ends the day it is sold or exchanged.

The cost basis reported in the transaction can be determined via specific identification of units or via the FIFO method (as described previously in this chapter).

Virtual Currency Used to Make Payments

When virtual currency is held as a capital asset and used to make payment in exchange for goods or services, a capital gain or loss is realized (and must be recognized on the tax return for the year in which the exchange occurred). The realized gain or loss is the difference between the fair market value of the goods or services received and the taxpayer's adjusted basis in virtual currency.

Transfers of virtual currency from one digital wallet or account to another digital wallet or account owned by the same taxpayer are not taxable transactions.

Peer-to-Peer Transactions

When virtual currency is received as part of a peer-to-peer transaction (one that occurs outside of an exchange), the fair market value is determined at the date and time the transaction is, or would have been (if were an on-chain transaction), recorded on the distributed ledger. Substantiation of the reported value to the IRS can be accomplished through the use of a blockchain explorer (a form of software that can be used to analyze blockchain transactions to determine a value as of a particular date and time).

11.Rev. Rul. 2019-24.

Reporting Requirements

To ensure proper tax reporting, beginning in 2020, the Form 1040 individual tax return includes a question as to whether, during the tax year, the taxpayer received, sold, sent, exchanged, or otherwise acquired any financial interest in any virtual currency. Capital gains and losses are reported on Schedule D of Form 1040.

The Infrastructure Investment and Jobs Act (IIJA) of 2021 established rules requiring cryptocurrency exchanges to report digital asset transaction information to the IRS and to the taxpayer beginning in 2023. To accomplish this, IIJA expanded the definition of broker to include cryptocurrency exchanges. Therefore, reporting information will be similar to stock transaction reporting by brokers on Form 1099-B.[12 & 13]

For purposes of IRC Section 6050I, which requires any trade or business receiving more than $10,000 of cash in a trade or business transaction to provide certain information to the IRS (in an effort to identify money laundering activity), cryptocurrency is treated in the same manner as cash.[14]

INVESTMENT EXPENSES

Investment Interest Expense

While most forms of interest are not deductible, the IRC permits a deduction for interest incurred in activities intended to produce taxable income. Interest expense incurred on money borrowed to purchase investments is deductible, subject to a few limitations. One limitation has been covered previously – if interest is incurred to purchase securities that will generate tax exempt income, it is not deductible. The second limitation that applies to investment interest expense is that the deduction is limited to the investor's net investment income. In addition, interest expense related to the acquisition of passive activities, and interest expense that is capitalized, is not eligible for deduction.

In order to determine the deduction available for investment interest expense in a particular tax year, the taxpayer's net investment income must be calculated. Net investment income is gross investment income net of investment expenses.

Investment income includes interest and non-qualified dividends. In some cases, investment income may include distributions from annuity contracts or receipt of royalties if the assets generating these gains are held for investment. Qualified dividends (dividends that qualify to be taxed at the special 20 percent long-term capital gains tax rate) are not included in the definition of investment income. Long-term capital gains are also excluded from investment income, unless the taxpayer elects to include them on Form 4952. The cost of including long-term capital gains in investment income is the forbearance of the special 20 percent capital gains rate that normally applies to long-term capital gains.

12. The IIJA refers to "digital assets" in the reporting requirements, which may include some types of NFTs (discussed in Chapter 16), as well as cryptocurrencies, using blockchain technology. Under IIJA, the term 'digital asset' means "any digital representation of value which is recorded on a cryptographically secured distributed ledger or any similar technology as specified by the Secretary."
13. As of the time of printing, the IRS has not clarified whether digital asset transactions will be reported on Form 1099-B or whether a separate reporting form will be developed.
14. IIJA 2021, Sec. 80603.

Investment interest expense that may not be deducted in the year it is incurred due to the imposition of the investment income limitation rules are carried forward and may be deducted as investment interest paid or accrued in future years.

Investment-Related Expenses

Investment expenses incurred by a taxpayer for the production of income or for the conservation or maintenance of property held for the production of income were deductible on the taxpayer's tax return as a miscellaneous itemized deduction subject to the two percent floor. These expenses, which have to be ordinary and necessary to be deductible, include:

- Investment advisory fees
- Tax preparation fees and advice
- Custodial fees paid to asset managers and brokers
- Investment research costs
- Subscriptions to investment advisory services

All miscellaneous itemized deductions subject to the two percent floor were suspended by the TCJA 2017 for tax years 2018-2025.

Exhibit 17.8 | IRS Form 4952

Form **4952**
Department of the Treasury
Internal Revenue Service (99)

Investment Interest Expense Deduction

► Go to *www.irs.gov/Form4952* for the latest information.

► Attach to your tax return.

OMB No. 1545-0191
2021
Attachment Sequence No. **51**

Name(s) shown on return | **Identifying number**

Part I **Total Investment Interest Expense**

1	Investment interest expense paid or accrued in 2021 (see instructions)	1	
2	Disallowed investment interest expense from 2020 Form 4952, line 7	2	
3	**Total investment interest expense.** Add lines 1 and 2	3	

Part II **Net Investment Income**

4a	Gross income from property held for investment (excluding any net gain from the disposition of property held for investment)	4a			
b	Qualified dividends included on line 4a	4b			
c	Subtract line 4b from line 4a			4c	
d	Net gain from the disposition of property held for investment	4d			
e	Enter the **smaller** of line 4d or your net capital gain from the disposition of property held for investment. See instructions	4e			
f	Subtract line 4e from line 4d			4f	
g	Enter the amount from lines 4b and 4e that you elect to include in investment income. See instructions			4g	
h	Investment income. Add lines 4c, 4f, and 4g			4h	
5	Investment expenses (see instructions)			5	
6	**Net investment income.** Subtract line 5 from line 4h. If zero or less, enter -0-			6	

Part III **Investment Interest Expense Deduction**

7	Disallowed investment interest expense to be carried forward to 2022. Subtract line 6 from line 3. If zero or less, enter -0-	7	
8	**Investment interest expense deduction.** Enter the **smaller** of line 3 or line 6. See instructions	8	

For Paperwork Reduction Act Notice, see page 4. Cat. No. 13177Y Form **4952** (2021)

IRAs, 401(k)s, AND OTHER TAX-DEFERRED ACCOUNTS

Income earned within traditional IRAs, SEPs, 401(k)s, and other tax-deferred accounts is not recognized for income tax purposes until the income is distributed from the tax-deferred account. The earnings, as well as any pre-tax contributions, are taxed as ordinary income when they are distributed from the retirement account.

Traditional and Roth IRAs

Traditional IRA contributions may be tax deductible, and earnings grow tax-deferred. When a distribution is made from a traditional deductible IRA after the participant reaches age 59½, it is taxed as ordinary income, regardless of whether the earnings were from long-term capital gains, qualified dividends, or interest income. Traditional IRAs also require minimum distributions beginning at age 72, which will necessitate appropriate management of assets to ensure that sales of securities are not required at inopportune times in order to meet this liquidity need.

Roth IRA contributions are not tax deductible, and earnings in the account are tax-deferred and can be distributed tax-free if the distribution is at least five years after the first contribution and the participant is at least age 59½.

IRA assets can be invested in most types of securities (such as stocks, bonds, and mutual funds) and non-security bank products (such as certificates of deposit and money market accounts).

The following investments are prohibited:

- life insurance,
- collectibles (such as artwork or antiques); except gold, silver, and platinum coins issued in the U.S. (American Eagle coins), and gold, silver, platinum, and palladium bullion,
- margin accounts.

IRA funds invested in prohibited types of investments are treated as distributed and are subject to tax plus a ten percent penalty if the IRA owner is under age 59½.

To avoid violation of IRA rules prohibiting self-dealing, all investments must be at arm's length from the owner. The IRS reviews specific facts and circumstances to determine whether self-dealing has occurred, but the general rule is that investments directly benefiting the IRA owner or family members are self-dealing. For example, using the IRA funds to purchase a home for the IRA owner to live in, purchasing shares of a closely held corporation in which the IRA owner is the majority shareholder, or loaning IRA funds to the owner or a family member would generally be considered self-dealing. Self-dealing transactions can result in the loss of tax-deferred status for the entire IRA, causing the full balance to become subject to tax plus a ten percent penalty if the owner is under age 59½.

Additional rules that apply to traditional and Roth IRAs are beyond the scope of this textbook but are covered in-depth in courses on federal income taxation and retirement planning.

Appropriate Investments for Tax-Advantaged versus Taxable Accounts

An investor should generally avoid using tax-advantaged retirement accounts to buy investments that provide tax-exempt income, such as municipal bonds. The income is typically lower than on corporate or U.S. Treasury bonds, and retirement distributions of the tax-exempt income will be taxed as ordinary income, resulting in the loss of the tax-exempt advantage of the municipal bonds.

When an individual has investments both in tax-advantaged and taxable accounts, investments for growth and capital gains receive more favorable tax treatment when allocated to the taxable accounts, and investments that generate interest income should be allocated to the tax-advantaged accounts, where there will be no change in tax status upon distribution. Interest income will be taxable at ordinary income tax rates, and holding the interest-bearing investments in retirement accounts takes full advantage of the tax deferral offered by the retirement plans. The growth investments will take advantage of the lower long-term capital gain rates only if they are held outside retirement plans. Distributions of capital gains from retirement plans are taxed as ordinary income, so the benefit of lower capital gains rates is lost in the retirement plan.

Exhibit 17.9 depicts the ideal accounts for various investments from a tax perspective.

Exhibit 17.9 | Appropriate Assets for Tax-Advantage and Taxable Accounts (from a tax viewpoint)

Tax-Advantage Accounts	Taxable Accounts
• Should hold: - Corporate bonds - Zero-coupon bonds - TIPS	• Should hold: - Investments normally taxed at LTCG or qualified dividend rates - Municipal bonds
• Should not hold: - Municipal bonds - Investments that would be taxed at LTCG or qualified dividend rate if not held in a tax-advantaged account - Investments that violate rules against self-dealing in an IRA	• Should not hold: - Corporate bonds - Zero-coupon bonds - TIPS
• Exception: - Roth IRAs may hold growth securities (which would be taxed at LTCG rates in a taxable account) to take advantage of tax-free earnings potential over a long period of time.	

While the above chart reflects the ideal location for assets from a tax perspective, it does not take into consideration other factors. For example, much of the increase in value from equities is attributable to appreciation, which is taxed as a LTCG. The rate of tax for a LTCG is lower in a taxable account compared to a tax-advantaged account. However, an investor's asset allocation may not permit equities to be exclusively held in tax-advantaged accounts. Therefore, investors need to take the taxation of the various accounts and investments into consideration when allocating their funds.

SUMMARY

Summary of key points:

- There are three types of income: ordinary, portfolio, and passive.
  - Ordinary income is generated from active work or at a trade or business.
  - Portfolio income is generated by capital, such as dividends, interest, and capital gains.
  - Passive income is income from a trade or business in which the taxpayer does not materially participate.
- Tax basis is the cost of acquiring an asset and includes the actual cost of the asset plus any transaction costs. Assets acquired from a family member with a value less than the cost basis of the donor will be subject to the double-basis rule.
- Ordinary income tax rates range from 10% to 37% (in 2022).
- Qualified dividends and long-term capital gains are taxed at capital gains rates up to 20% (in 2022).
- IRC Section 1202 stock qualifies for an exclusion of up to 100% of the gain under certain conditions.
- Net investment income, introduced for years after 2013, is an additional tax of 3.8% that applies to income for taxpayers with income above certain thresholds.
- The alternative minimum tax was devised to ensure that all individuals with a certain amount of income will pay some income tax on an annual basis.
- A sale of stock requires the taxpayer to report the sale with the gain equal to the proceeds less the tax basis. A stock split will result in the taxpayer's tax basis being spread across additional shares of stock. Spin-offs result in a similar allocation of a taxpayer's tax basis.
- A short sale is a sale of borrowed stock. The sale does not trigger income tax recognition. Rather, it is when the transaction is closed that a gain or loss is realized.
- The wash sale rules prevent a taxpayer from recognizing a capital loss if they repurchase the shares within 30 days before or after the sale.
- Tax basis for shares of stock (and mutual funds) can be recognized on a FIFO basis, specific identification basis, or on an average basis.
- Coupon payments are generally subject to ordinary income tax. Original issue discount bonds must recognize income that accrues but that is not received over time. This tax treatment often occurs with zero-coupon bonds.
- Municipal bond coupon payments or interest is not taxable at the federal level and is generally not taxable if issued by the state in which the taxpayer is a resident.
- The interest from U.S. government debt instruments is not subject to tax at the state and local level.
- IRC Section 121 provides an exclusion on the gain from the sale of a principal residence of up to $500,000 for married couples filing a joint return and $250,000 for single taxpayers.
- IRC Section 1031 provides an exclusion for exchanges of like-kind real property.

- There is a federal income tax deduction for state income tax and property tax limited to $10,000 for years after 2017.
- Similar to a mutual fund, REITs pass income through to shareholders. There is also a deduction for years after 2017 under section 199A that allows certain types of REIT dividends to qualify for a 20% deduction.
- When the buyer of a put or call option disposes of the option, a taxable event generally results. There are three ways the buyer can dispose of the option: (1) sell it before maturity, (2) exercise the option, or (3) let the option expire without exercise. The first and third options are taxable transactions. The sellers of put and call options are potentially subject to tax when (1) the option is exercised by the buyer, (2) the option expires without being exercised, or (3) the option writer closes the position by repurchasing the option in the market or by making a closing purchase in the market.
- IRC Section 1256 contracts, including futures contracts, are required to recognize gains or losses at year-end: 60% long-term and 40% short-term.
- Cryptocurrencies such as Bitcoin (discussed in Chapter 16) are a form of virtual currency, a type of property whose tax treatment is similar to other types of property in many ways. When virtual currency is sold or is used to make payment a capital gain or loss is recognized (subject to the $3,000 maximum loss against ordinary income).

DISCUSSION QUESTIONS

SOLUTIONS to the discussion questions can be found exclusively within the chapter. Once you have completed an initial reading of the chapter, go back and highlight the answers to these questions.

1. Name the three types of income.
2. What is the basis of most investments?
3. What is the range for ordinary income tax rates?
4. What is portfolio income?
5. What are qualified dividends?
6. Are net capital losses fully deductible in a given year?
7. What is passive income?
8. What is net investment income (for purposes of determining deductible investment interest)?
9. When would an investor enter into a short sale?
10. Describe the tax treatment of virtual currency transactions.

MULTIPLE-CHOICE PROBLEMS

A sample of multiple choice problems is provided below. Additional multiple choice problems are available at money-education.com by accessing the Student Practice Portal.

1. Which of the following statements correctly identifies when income is subject to tax?
    a. Capital gains must be realized before they can be recognized on a tax return.
    b. Realization occurs when the gain on an asset is reflected on the taxpayer's return.
    c. As a general rule, realized gains are not recognized unless a provision in the IRC requires recognition.
    d. Recognition occurs when an asset has been sold or exchanged.

2. On September 20 of Year 1, Jorge purchased 1,000 shares of LMF, Inc. common stock for $25,000. He sold the shares for $35,000 on September 20 of Year 2. Which of the following statements correctly identifies the tax consequences of this transaction?
    a. Jorge will recognize a $10,000 ordinary gain on the sale.
    b. Jorge will recognize a $10,000 short-term capital gain on the sale.
    c. Jorge will recognize a $10,000 long-term capital gain on the sale.
    d. Jorge will not be required to recognize the gain on the transaction.

3. Three years ago, Iris purchased 1,000 shares of ABC, Inc. for $10 per share. She signed an agreement with the company that allowed the company to use her dividend payments to purchase additional shares for her. Over the last 5 years, Iris received a total of $1,200 in dividend payments, which purchased an additional 100 shares of stock. If Iris sells all of her shares for $24,000, what is her taxable gain?
    a. $0.
    b. $12,800.
    c. $14,000.
    d. $24,000.

4. Which of the following assets qualifies as a Section 1231 asset?
    a. Greeting cards held by the owner of a gift shop for sale to customers.
    b. A bicycle owned by a 12-year-old child.
    c. An apartment building held for rental to tenants.
    d. Artwork prominently displayed in a taxpayer's summer residence.

5. Which of the following is not portfolio income?
    a. Interest.
    b. Dividends.
    c. Capital gains.
    d. Limited partnership Income.

QUICK QUIZ EXPLANATIONS

Quick Quiz 17.1

1. True.
2. True.

Quick Quiz 17.2

1. False. Wages are not portfolio income but capital gains are.
2. True.
3. True.

Quick Quiz 17.3

1. True.
2. False. Warrants may cause changes in percentage ownership but stock splits do not.
3. True.
4. False. It is from original purchase date.

Quick Quiz 17.4

1. True.
2. False. There is capital gain of $50.

Quick Quiz 17.5

1. False. It is the default method of valuation of basis.
2. True.

Quick Quiz 17.6

1. True.
2. True.

Quick Quiz 17.7

1. True.
2. True.
3. False. Section 1256 Contracts must be marked-to-market at year-end with gains split 60% long-term and 40% short-term.

18

INVESTMENT POLICY STATEMENT

LEARNING OBJECTIVES

1. Understand the critical components of an investment policy statement.*
2. Differentiate between the investment objectives of various types of investors.*
3. Formulate a risk and return objective for an individual and an institutional investor.*
4. Demonstrate the construction of the investor constraints as part of portfolio management.
5. Identify investor constraints, including liquidity, tax, time, legal, and unique.
6. Understand the relationship between capital market expectations and investor preferences.
7. Craft a policy statement for individual investors.*
8. Craft a policy statement for pension funds and endowments.
9. Discuss the relationship between portfolio performance and asset allocation for investors.
10. Know that investment policy statements are a clear specific articulation of realistic and achievable long-term goals including investment objectives, constraints, and strategic asset allocation goals.*
11. Explain the difference between the planning, execution and feedback stages of the portfolio management process.
12. Identify the key components of an investment policy statement (IPS).*
13. Discuss the key types of constraints faced by individual investors.

**Ties to CFP Certification Learning Objectives*

INTRODUCTION

The portfolio management process involves three stages – planning, execution and feedback.

At the start of the **planning stage**, a financial adviser will first gather information from the client, determine appropriate risk and return objectives, analyze the current and expected economic and capital markets environment, establish the strategic asset allocation, and construct an investment policy statement (IPS).

It is crucial for the adviser to understand a client's investment objectives and the constraints they face in trying to achieve them. It is equally important for the client to understand the strategies the investment manager will employ in their effort to meet those objectives while operating within the given constraints.

Key Concepts

1. Explain the difference between the planning, execution and feedback stages of the portfolio management process.
2. Identify the key components of an investment policy statement (IPS).
3. Discuss the key types of constraints faced by individual investors.

Documenting these key processes in an IPS should minimize the likelihood of misunderstandings between the client and financial adviser and serve as an objective reference document when executing and monitoring the investment strategy.

During the **execution stage**, the financial adviser will implement an investment strategy that is consistent with the IPS. The IPS should direct the adviser as to the assets that are suitable to be purchased, and their weightings.

The **feedback stage** will include regular monitoring of the portfolio and a periodic performance evaluation against appropriate benchmarks as specified in the IPS. The IPS should also set out criteria for deciding when and how the portfolio should be rebalanced.

Exhibit 18.1 | Portfolio Management Process

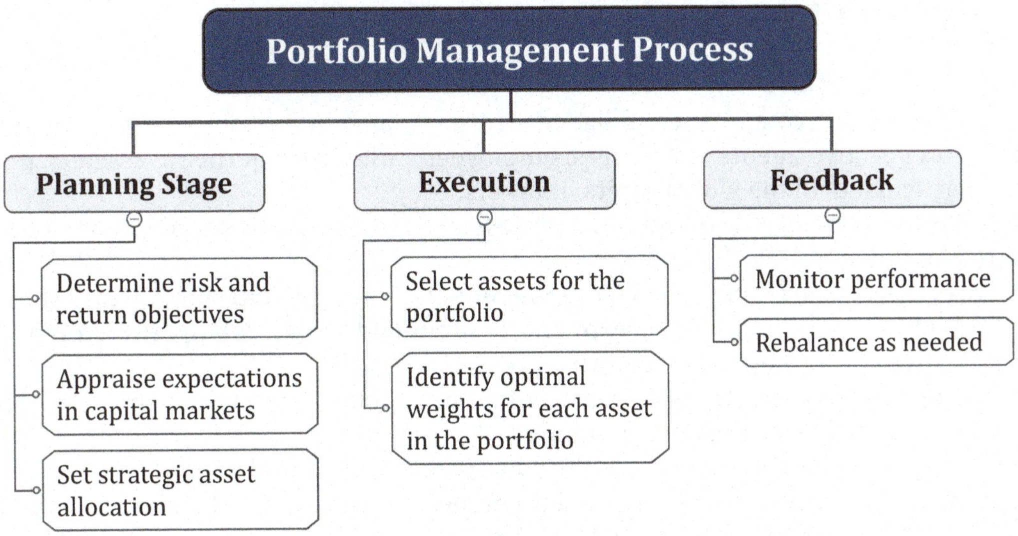

IPS FORMAT

The exact format and content of an IPS will vary from client to client depending on individual circumstances and the complexity of the investment plan. However, in their paper *Elements of an Investment Policy Statement for Individual Investors* the CFA Institute suggests the following sections as a useful template:[1]

- Scope and Purpose
- Governance
- Investment, Return, and Risk Objectives
- Risk Management

Quick Quiz 18.1

1. An individual's risk and return objectives are determined during the planning stage.
   a. True
   b. False
2. The feedback stage includes a determination of the strategic asset allocation weights of the portfolio.
   a. True
   b. False

True, False.

Scope and Purpose

The scope and purpose section should include a general description of the client(s), including relevant financial information. The individual client summary should include variables such as income, number of dependents, and asset base. An institutional client summary is likely to include details on the beneficiaries and liquidity requirements.

1. cfainstitute.org/-/media/documents/article/position-paper/investment-policy-statement-individual-investors.ashx

This section should also detail the responsibility of the financial adviser to act in the best interests of the client. The best way to ensure that duty is correctly executed is to follow a set of ethical standards, such as those outlined by the Chartered Financial Analyst Institute or the Certified Financial Planner Board of Standards, as described below.

The Chartered Financial Analyst (CFA) Institute is an organization that outlines a prescription for preferred behavior for its members. It defines its member responsibilities in its Code of Ethics and Standards of Professional Conduct which are summarized below:

CFA Institute Code of Ethics

- Act with integrity, competence, diligence, respect, and in an ethical manner with the public, clients, prospective clients, employers, employees, colleagues in the investment profession, and other participants in the global capital markets.
- Place the integrity of the investment profession and the interests of clients above their own personal interests.
- Use reasonable care and exercise independent professional judgment when conducting investment analysis, making investment recommendations, taking investment actions, and engaging in other professional activities.
- Practice and encourage others to practice in a professional and ethical manner that will reflect credit on themselves and the profession.
- Promote the integrity of, and uphold the rules governing, capital markets.
- Maintain and improve their professional competence and strive to maintain and improve the competence of other investment professionals.

CFA Institute Standards of Professional Conduct[2]

Professionalism

- **Knowledge of the Law:** Members and candidates must understand and comply with all applicable laws, rules, and regulations.
- **Independence and Objectivity:** Members and candidates must use reasonable care and judgment to achieve and maintain independence and objectivity in their professional activities.
- **Avoid Misrepresentation:** Members and candidates must not knowingly make any misrepresentations.
- **Avoid Misconduct:** Members and candidates must not engage in any professional conduct involving dishonesty, fraud, or deceit or commit any act that reflects adversely on their professional reputation, integrity, or competence.

Integrity of Capital Markets

- **Use of Material Nonpublic Information is Prohibited:** Members and candidates must not act or cause others to act on material nonpublic information.
- **Market Manipulation is Prohibited:** Members and candidates must not engage in practices that mislead market participants.

2. The details under each standard have in many cases been condensed for the sake of brevity. See the Standards of Professional Conduct on CFA Institute's website for the complete set of rules.

Duties to Clients

- **Loyalty, Prudence, and Care:** Members and candidates have a duty of loyalty to their clients and must act with reasonable care and exercise prudent judgment.
- **Fair Dealing:** Members and candidates must deal fairly and objectively with all clients.
- **Suitability:** Members and candidates must determine that an investment is suitable to the client's financial situation.
- **Performance Presentation:** Members and candidates must make reasonable efforts to ensure that performance presentation is fair, accurate, and complete.
- **Preservation of Confidentiality:** Members and candidates must keep information about current, former, and prospective clients confidential, except to the extent activities are illegal, disclosure is required by law, or disclosure is permitted by the client.

Duties to Employers

- **Loyalty:** Members and candidates must act for the benefit of their employer.
- **Additional Compensation Arrangements:** Members and candidates must not accept gifts, benefits, compensation, or consideration that competes with or might reasonably be expected to create a conflict of interest with their employer's interest unless they obtain written consent from all parties involved.
- **Responsibilities of Supervisors:** Members and candidates must make reasonable efforts to ensure that anyone subject to their supervision or authority complies with applicable laws and other rules.

Investment Analysis, Recommendations, and Actions

- **Diligence and Reasonable Basis:** Members and candidates must exercise diligence and must have a reasonable basis for recommendations or actions.
- **Communication with Clients and Prospective Clients:** Members and candidates must provide adequate disclosure to clients as well as use reasonable judgment as it relates to analysis and recommendations.
- **Record Retention:** Members and candidates must maintain appropriate records to support analysis, recommendations, and actions.

Conflicts of Interest

- **Disclosure of Conflicts:** Members and candidates must disclose conflicts of interest.
- **Priority of Transactions:** Investment transactions for clients and employers must have priority over investment transactions in which a member or candidate is the beneficial owner.
- **Referral Fees:** Members and candidates must disclose referral fees and other consideration paid for the recommendation of products or services.

Responsibilities as a CFA Institute Member or CFA Candidate

- **Conduct as Members and Candidates in the CFA Program:** Members and candidates must not engage in any conduct that compromises the reputation or integrity of CFA Institute or the CFA designation or the integrity, validity, or security of the CFA Institute programs.
- **Reference to CFA Institute, the CFA Designation, and the CFA Program:** When referring to CFA Institute, CFA Institute membership, the CFA designation, or candidacy in the CFA Program, members and candidates must not misrepresent or exaggerate the meaning or implication of membership in CFA Institute, holding the CFA designation, or candidacy in the CFA program.

CFP Board's Code of Ethics and Standards of Conduct[3]

The mission of Certified Financial Planner Board of Standards, Inc. (CFP Board) is to benefit the public by granting the CFP® certification and upholding it as the recognized standard of excellence for competent and ethical personal financial planning. As part of this mission, CFP Board requires all CFP® professionals to adhere to its ethical standards, which are discussed below.

CFP Board's Code of Ethics

A CFP® professional must:

1. Act with honesty, integrity, competence, and diligence
2. Act in the client's best interests
3. Exercise due care
4. Avoid or disclose and manage conflicts of interest
5. Maintain the confidentiality and protect the privacy of client information
6. Act in a manner that reflects positively on the financial planning profession and CFP® certification

CFP Board's Standards of Conduct

CFP Board's Standards of Conduct are designed to provide standards for delivering financial planning advice and include:

1. Duties owed to clients
2. Financial planning and application of the practice standards for the financial planning process
3. Practice standards for the financial planning process
4. Duties owed to firms and subordinates
5. Duties owed to CFP Board

Exhibit 18.2 | CFA Institute Recommended Sections of the Investment Policy Statement

IPS Section	Description
Scope and Purpose	• Provides a general description of the client(s), including relevant financial information. • Conveys the responsibility of the financial adviser to act in the best interests of the client.
Governance	• Outlines the responsibilities of the financial adviser. • Clarifies that the client is responsible for the approval of the investment plan and any subsequent changes to it.
Investment, Return, and Risk Objectives	• States the major investment objectives for the client. • States the return objective (in mathematical form). • States the risk objective (may be stated in mathematical terms or may reflect relative levels of acceptable risk). • Lists constraints (limiting factors that will affect portfolio performance). • Identifies a set of permissible asset classes, consistent with the client's risk and return objectives.
Risk Management	• Addresses the procedures that will be used to monitor portfolio performance, provide feedback to the client, and rebalance the portfolio to keep it consistent with the strategic asset allocation. • Details the frequency with which the portfolio is to be rebalanced. • Identifies the parties responsible for rebalancing.

3. The complete CFP Board Code of Ethics and Standards of Conduct can be found at: https://www.cfp.net/ethics/code-of-ethics-and-standards-of-conduct.

Governance

The governance section should give details of the responsibilities of the financial adviser, including the execution of the investment policy and the monitoring of its results. These responsibilities should include the determination of the asset allocation, and the process the financial adviser will use to arrive at an appropriate asset allocation and any subsequent required changes.

For most individual investors, the financial adviser will perform the duties of the investment manager, including identifying and purchasing securities. For institutional investors, the selection of money managers should be determined here.

The governance section should also make clear that the client is responsible for the approval of the investment plan and any subsequent changes to it.

Investment, Return, and Risk Objectives

This section should state the major investment objectives for the client, along with a risk objective, a return objective and a list of constraints the adviser will face when constructing the portfolio.

Return Objective

The investor's return objective is often stated in mathematical form, includes a measure of inflation, and reflects the investor's total return expectations. One simple approach to calculating the return objective is to use the following general equation:

$$\text{Return Objective} = \frac{\text{Portfolio Income Needs}}{\text{Investable Assets}} + \text{Inflation Expectations (\%)}$$

This objective should be adjusted annually as economic conditions and investor preferences change. In addition, the return objective should be clarified as to whether it is pre-tax or after-tax. Only relevant tax rates should be used.

Finally, the inflation rate should reflect the loss of purchasing power for each client. It is quite tempting to simply use the rate announced by the U.S. Bureau of Labor Statistics, but the CPI might not be reflective of the actual inflation facing each investor. Care should be taken by the financial advisor when assigning an inflation rate.

Risk Objective

The investor's **risk objective** is sometimes stated in mathematical terms but might reflect relative levels of acceptable risk. Either way, it must be measurable and reflective of the wealth level of the investor as well as spending needs and financial conditions. There are always two components of the risk objective: The willingness (propensity) and ability (capacity) to take risk.

Willingness is related to the client's personal attitudes toward risk while ability is more concrete. The ability to take risk is a function of wealth, income, age, and assets. Adjustments are necessary to account for any mismatch between willingness and ability to take risk, most likely a correction to both the risk and return objectives.

The challenge for every investor and their financial advisers is to link the risk and return objectives. For example, an investor with an average return objective and average risk tolerance has a natural match between the objectives and should be able to form a reasonable portfolio that can deliver a reasonable return for the risk taken. On the other hand, an investor with low risk tolerance but a high return objective finds it very difficult to find appropriate securities that will deliver. Educating the investor is always critical when there is a mismatch between the risk and return objectives.

Individual Investor Constraints

A major component of the objective portion of the policy statement is a description of the limiting factors that will affect portfolio performance. These are known as the investor's constraints and are discussed below.

Liquidity Constraint

The **liquidity constraint** includes any major one-time lump sum cash outflows that are expected to occur in the near future. Liquidity might also include repeatable cash outflows that can be easily predicted. Liquidity issues are not necessarily handled identically. For example, a known cash outflow occurring in six months for the purchase of an automobile might be set aside into a money market account until the time of purchase. It makes little sense to include this amount in the general portfolio as it may require transaction costs initially and at the sale. In addition, the assets could lose value during this time period. It makes more sense to protect the future purchase.

This model is also useful for education expenses, wedding costs, and down payments for home purchases. Sometimes, clients need regular cash distributions to help with the payment of daily living expenses. This occurrence is usually handled by an annual distribution at the beginning of the period, with the funds placed in a money market fund so the client has access to them.

> ### *Key Concepts*
>
> 1. Discuss different types of constraints facing individual investors.
> 2. Explain the need for a unique circumstance constraint as part of the policy statement.
> 3. Describe the tax constraint and identify the tax goals of individual investors.

Investment Horizon Constraint

The **time constraint** reflects the period over which the investments will be made. Most investors have a long-term investment horizon, typically divided into several stages. These stages include a 10-to 30-year period of continued employment, followed by a pre-retirement period, the retirement stage, and finally a stage that focuses on estate planning. Some of these stages can overlap. Long-term stages are usually defined as exposure to more than one economic cycle while short-term stages tend to occur during one economic cycle.

Tax Constraint

The **tax constraint** is significant mostly because the tax laws are created by governments and apply to all investors, plus tax rates are not low. Investors pay income taxes at the federal, state, and local levels, plus a variety of other taxes that are functions of ownership of real and financial assets. The goal is to avoid incurring any tax liability in excess of that required by law. In addition, there are limitations on the types of securities that can be held in certain types of accounts.

For example, life insurance and collectibles are not permitted to be held in IRAs (individual retirement accounts). Investments in partnerships, flow-through entities, and debt-financed investments, such as real estate, can create additional complications or problems with IRAs or qualified plans. This section of the policy statement provides this information to the investment adviser so that tax rules can be followed properly.

Legal and Regulatory Constraint

The secondary government constraint reflects any restricting factors that are contract related or imposed by any other regulatory body. Most regulators are government agencies but there are industry bodies that self-regulate. The investor must be aware of the spectrum of rules and regulations that will affect the performance of the portfolio.

Unique Constraint

The **unique constraint** typically includes any limiting factors that cannot be identified in the classic four constraints, namely health and currency issues, unresolved conflicts regarding portfolio performance, socially responsible investing, and client risk and security preferences.

At times a client may indicate a strong preference for security selection based on factors which are outside of the traditional analysis components of risk and return and which may conflict with the adviser's fiduciary duty, such as a preference for investments with a high ESG rating. In these circumstances, the ISP should specifically state the desired constraints and acknowledge that investment selection within these constraints may result in a portfolio with less-than-optimal risk and/or return metrics.

Behavioral Constraint

The **behavioral constraint** involves the client's inability to be a rational investor in the classic sense described by the founding fathers of modern portfolio theory. Some behavioral issues prevent the investor from identifying the best securities for the portfolio and limit the trading activity surrounding portfolio selection and asset allocation. Some wealth managers list a separate constraint for behavioral issues, but many simply add it as a unique constraint. See Chapter 6 for references on specific behavioral biases.

Identification of Asset Classes

A set of permissible asset classes, consistent with the client's risk and return objectives should be identified in this section. The IPS should provide a description of each class (and if required sub-class) of assets along with a suitable benchmark to be used for performance measurement.

> **Quick Quiz 18.2**
>
> 1. A parent of young children who was recently diagnosed with a terminal illness will have a short-term time horizon constraint.
>   a. True
>   b. False
> 2. An individual investor who wants to build a swimming pool in her back yard in one year will likely have a liquidity constraint.
>   a. True
>   b. False
>
> False, True.

The investment adviser will produce a strategic asset allocation using some or all of the permissible asset classes that is designed to achieve the client's objectives while adhering to the constraints.

The strategic asset allocation will typically specify a range of weightings for each class to both reduce the frequency with which the portfolio must be rebalanced and allow the financial adviser scope to adjust a class weighting to take advantage of perceived short-term value opportunities.

The strategic asset allocation may be included in the IPS as an appendix.

Example 18.1

Albert and Nancy Nichols meet with their new financial adviser, Trish. Trish takes the following notes during the meeting.

Summary Notes:

- Albert and Nancy Nichols are 45 years old with two college-age children. Albert is an FBI agent and Nancy is an accountant. Their combined income is $200,000.
- The couple has saved between $20,000 and $40,000 every year for ten years and expects to continue saving these amounts to accomplish three financial goals: to have their children graduate from college debt free, to purchase a cottage, and to have $1,500,000 in their retirement portfolio when they are 65 years old.
- Albert and Nancy have wisely planned for college expenses, and their children are expected to graduate without any student loans. The two children are excellent students who already have employment offers when they graduate.
- The couple's main remaining financial goal is to purchase a cottage in the Pennsylvania Pocono mountains without a mortgage. They intend to spend $250,000 and currently have $175,000 invested in a money market account paying 2%.
- Their final goal is to add to their retirement portfolio, which is currently valued at $300,000, all of which is invested in a stock market index fund. They have no savings other than these two accounts.
- Albert and Nancy have very different attitudes toward risk. Albert is a risk-taker while Nancy is much more conservative. They have continual discussions regarding their investments, with Albert hoping to add equities to their account.
- They are mortgage free and own two brand new cars. They like to travel and have generously included family members in their trips, including Nancy's mother, who is in declining health.

Using these notes, suggest appropriate Return and Risk Objectives for Albert and Nancy Nichols along with a suggested strategic asset allocation.

Suggested Solution:

Risk Objective

The couple has high ability to take risk because of their income level, their asset base, and seemingly financially secure dependents. Their willingness to take risk, however, is complicated by the different attitudes of the couple. Albert has high willingness, but Nancy has low willingness. The couple clearly has an aversion to debt being mortgage free and without automobile loans. This suggests a low willingness to take risk. Based on these combined factors, the couple has overall moderate risk tolerance.

Return Objective

Cottage: If the couple maintains its investment in the money market account, it will take approximately 18 years until they can purchase their cottage. Trish ought to recommend a change from the money market to a well-diversified equity portfolio with average risk earning 9% annually. They can expect to purchase their cottage in only 4 years.

Retirement Portfolio
With a current balance of $300,000 invested in an equity fund with a reasonable expected return of 9% annually, the couple will reach their goal (the future value is approximately $1.68 million:

PV = 300,000
i = 9
N = 20
PMT = 0
Solve for FV = 1,681,323

Their return objective is most likely moderate, which matches their risk objective.

The investment horizon for the couple is long term.

Asset Selection and Asset Allocation
Trish believes the couple should open a mutual fund account that will partially replace their current money market account. Trish also believes the couple should commit to annual savings of $30,000 split evenly between the retirement account and the cottage account. Adding $15,000 to the cottage fund reduces the four-year required rate of return from 9% to 2%. Based on the couple's risk and return objectives, Trish recommends the following portfolio:

Money Market Fund	10–15%
U.S. Well-Diversified Equity Fund	60–65%
Global Value Fund	25–30%

Risk Management

This section addresses the procedures that will be used to monitor portfolio performance, provide feedback to the client, and rebalance the portfolio to keep it consistent with the strategic asset allocation.

The metrics used to report performance should be specified in the IPS and applied consistently over time, and by asset class. Portfolio performance should be compared to the relevant benchmarks specified in the IPS.

The frequency with which the portfolio is to be rebalanced in order to stay within the specified strategic allocation range should also be detailed, along with the parties responsible for, and the process for undertaking the rebalancing.

Example 18.2

Pascal retired from his career as a welder after receiving an inheritance of $3 million. Pascal is 51 years old, has never married, has no children, and is very close with his cousins.

Pascal moved to Alaska 20 years ago for employment and wants to move back to Maine to be close to his mother, who is in poor health and requires in-home nursing care. Pascal's mother has depleted her lifetime savings to pay for her care, and Pascal agrees to assume her $40,000 per year expenses. Her pension benefits are sufficient to cover her other living expenses.

Pascal has a cousin who is a musician and has asked him for a $300,000 loan to start a recording studio business. Pascal is eager to help, and the cousin insists Pascal accept an equity position in the business. Pascal believes he will need $150,000 after taxes per year for living expenses, which includes health insurance premiums.

Pascal is in great health. He exercises and meditates daily, eats a healthy diet, and has no family history of cancer or heart issues. There is no history of cancer or heart issues with either parent or grandparents.

After selling his house in Alaska, he expects to have $250,000 in total savings invested solely in a money market mutual fund. Pascal has identified a piece of land that he will buy and on which he will build a house for $350,000. He intends to pay cash because of bad experiences he had in Alaska with a few creditors.

Pascal has no pension from his employer and will likely return to work at some time in the future, most likely to help his cousin. Pascal describes himself as conservative.

Inflation is expected to be 1.5%.

- Identify the constraints that should be taken into account when constructing Pascal's portfolio.
- Create Pascal's risk and return objectives.
- Discuss asset selection and asset allocation needs.

Constraints

Liquidity	$350,000 for the home; $300,000 for his cousin
Time Horizon	**Three stages:** Active retirement (age 51 to 60); Passive retirement (60 to 70); Estate planning focus (70 until death)
Legal or Regulatory	None
Tax	Property taxes on home; Income tax on portfolio income; Possible dividend income from recording studio investment; No mortgage interest deduction because he will pay cash for the home.
Unique	No pension; Excellent health; Private health insurance; Single; Equity owner in business; Mother in declining health

Objectives

Return Objective	**Portfolio Income Needs:** \$150,000 for living expenses; \$40,000 for his mother's care. **Investable Assets:** \$3 million from inheritance; \$250,000 in savings; \$350,000 for his house; \$300,000 for his cousin. $\text{Return objective} = \frac{\$150{,}000 + \$40{,}000}{\$3{,}250{,}000 - \$350{,}000 - \$300{,}000} = 0.0731$ **Add Inflation:** Return Objective = 0.0731 + 0.015 = 0.0881
Risk Objective	**Ability:** Age (moderate); Assets (moderate to high); Lack of Pension (low) **Willingness:** Self-described conservative (low); Preference to avoid mortgage loan (low); Equity position in business (high); Original move from Maine to Alaska (high) **Overall Risk Tolerance:** Moderate

Asset Selection and Allocation

Since Pascal will have no income, he will rely on his portfolio to generate the \$190,000 per year he needs for living expenses and to care for his mother. Pascal has a return objective of almost 9%.

One simple possibility for Pascal would be to find a bond that trades at par value with a 9% coupon rate. Such a bond, however, is not likely to be appropriate given Pascal's overall risk tolerance.

A more reasonable asset selection decision is to invest an equal portion of his wealth in fixed-income securities and equity securities. The bonds should have relatively high coupon rates and the stocks should pay dividends. The universe of securities appropriate for Pascal is most likely to include mutual funds that offer high dividend yields. Specific examples would include REITs and income-producing financial institutions.

THE ASSET ALLOCATION PROCESS

A well-constructed IPS should provide the universe of investable asset classes that an investment manager can use to construct the client's portfolio, along with the objectives that portfolio should meet, and the constraints within which the manager must work.

This framework should be used in conjunction with the investor's forecasted performance for each asset class to arrive at a strategic asset allocation.

Key Concepts

1. Discuss the use of capital market expectations when choosing asset classes.
2. Discuss the process of portfolio optimization.
3. Distinguish between active and passive portfolio management.

Market Expectations

The investment manager should perform a macroeconomic analysis in order to calculate the risk, return, and correlation between all of the investable asset classes identified in the IPS. These expectations can then be used in the application of modern portfolio theory to calculate the optimal portfolio weightings for each asset class.

To make the forecasts as accurate as possible, the macroeconomic analysis should cover the entire economy and its important components, such as inflation, interest rates, employment rates, expected changes in gross domestic product, and other macro variables.

Portfolio Optimization

Modern portfolio theory dictates that portfolio managers should consider the risk and return of assets collectively rather than individually. Since most asset classes display less than perfect positive correlation, combining classes together can result in a portfolio with a lower overall risk than the average risk of the two individual classes. The lower the correlation, the larger the risk reduction that is achievable.

As an extreme example, if two asset classes with a risk of 20 percent (as measured by their standard deviation) were perfectly negatively correlated, a portfolio equally weighted between the two would have zero risk. Although each class is volatile individually, the perfect negative correlation means that the risks offset, as one asset's return increases, the other decreases, and the resulting zero risk portfolio would deliver a return equal to the average return of the two classes.

Quick Quiz 18.3

1. The efficient frontier plays a critical role in portfolio analysis.
   a. True
   b. False
2. Passive managers spend a lot of time researching individual securities in an attempt to outperform the benchmark.
   a. True
   b. False

True, False.

In reality, most assets are positively correlated, but not perfectly. Although a zero-risk portfolio is difficult to construct, less than perfect positive correlation does allow for some risk reduction.

Most advisers input the applicable asset classes' risk, return and correlation expectations into an optimization program which will then use the inputs to identify the most efficient combinations of those asset classes. An efficient combination is one that provides the highest expected return for a given level of risk.

When plotted on a chart showing risk and expected return, efficient combinations of assets lie along an **efficient frontier**, and this frontier represents the set of portfolios that all risk averse investors will choose from (as discussed in Chapter 4). This is because a risk averse investor, i.e., one who demands an increase in return for taking on additional risk, will always choose an efficient portfolio over an inefficient one.

Which efficient combination an investor would prefer depends on their individual level of risk tolerance. A well-constructed IPS should provide the portfolio manager with this information.

As part of the ongoing monitoring of the portfolio, the **strategic asset allocation** that results from the optimization process should be regularly reviewed, along with the IPS, and updated in response to any major life events that may change the clients' objectives and constraints.

Example 18.3

When Mr. & Mrs. Cave were first married 25 years ago, they visited a financial adviser, who crafted an investment policy statement for their needs at the time. The same adviser has since updated the policy statement regularly. The most recent statement was changed a few years ago to reflect their children finishing high school and beginning their college education. The most recent policy statement states they have an average return objective and an average risk tolerance. Specifically, their portfolio has a return objective of 8.5% with a maximum standard deviation of 16.2%.

The couple's portfolio is summarized below:

Asset Class	Strategic Allocation	Current Allocation
Money Market Fund	2% - 5%	4%
Large Cap Stocks	35% - 45%	34%
Small Cap Stocks	15% - 25%	22%
Investment Grade Bonds	15% - 25%	28%
Global Equities	4% - 8%	12%

The Caves turned 55 in the past year and need to update their investment policy statement. Their children have graduated from college and are now beginning successful careers. They are now focused on their remaining work life and on retirement.

The Caves would like to take extended vacations annually and plan on making various upgrades to their home with the intention of selling it when they retire. The risk and return objectives for the Caves is likely to change from moderate to the range of low to moderate. A reasonable return objective might be 7.5% with a 13% standard deviation.

Identify a new strategic allocation for the Caves.

Suggested Allocation Rebalancing:

Asset Class	New Strategic Allocation	Current Allocation (prior to rebalancing)	Current Allocation (after rebalancing)	Change in Current Allocation
Money Market Fund	2% - 7%	4%	5%	1%
Large Cap Stocks	35% - 45%	34%	40%	6%
Small Cap Stocks	5% - 10%	22%	5%	(17%)
Investment Grade Bonds	30% - 50%	28%	40%	12%
Global Equities	0%	12%	0%	(12%)
BB-Rated Bonds	10% - 20%	0%	10%	10%

As the Caves' risk tolerance has changed from moderate to the range of low to moderate, it is appropriate to update the strategic asset allocation and reduce the overall level of risk in the portfolio.

Fixed income instruments on average have less risk than equities, so the reallocation has moved some of the Caves' investments from equities to fixed income. Originally equities made up 68% of the portfolio, that weighting is down to just 45% after reallocation.

There have also been changes in allocation within the equity and fixed income classes. Global equities have been removed entirely, removing exchange rate risk from the portfolio. Within fixed income, a new class of BB-rated bonds have been added. Although these are riskier than higher-rated investment grade bonds, they have replaced some of the equity allocation so still represent an overall reduction in risk. The allocation to lower risk investment grade bonds has also increased.

Note that although the new strategic allocation is likely to meet the aim of reducing the overall level of portfolio risk, the portfolio manager must still check that the new allocations meet the new risk (13%) and return (7.5%) objectives before submitting the allocation to the client for approval.

Security Selection

Once the portfolio optimization process is complete and the strategic asset allocation has been finalized, the strategy must be executed by choosing and purchasing the individual securities that make up each asset class.

A **passive manager** is likely to choose securities that closely match the selected benchmark for the asset class. For example, if the S&P 500 index has been identified as the appropriate benchmark for the portfolio's weighting in large-cap U.S. Equities, the manager is likely to purchase securities or funds that reflect the S&P 500's performance.

Active managers try and improve the performance of the portfolio through security selection. By conducting an extensive **industry and security analysis** process, the active manager hopes to identify industries and individual securities within that industry that will outperform the benchmark. A typical industry analysis would involve studying the key drivers of the industry growth rate such as expected trends in demand, energy cost inputs, technological advances within the industry, and government regulatory actions.

A manager may, for example, identify that the healthcare industry is likely to outperform its historic average over the coming period due to a relaxation in government regulation, and hence look to overweight that sector relative to the benchmark.

Quick Quiz 18.4

1. One reasonable conclusion a financial analyst could make after completing an industry analysis is that a specific industry is overvalued and therefore should be avoided in the security selection process.
   a. True
   b. False
2. Assets that have a perfect negative correlation can be used to produce a zero-risk portfolio.
   a. True
   b. False
3. Portfolio optimization guarantees the client will achieve the risk and return objectives outlined in the planning stage of the investment process.
   a. True
   b. False

True, True, False.

Having identified an opportunity to overweight an industry, an analysis of securities within that industry will then allow the portfolio manager to identify specific stocks to purchase. A thorough security analysis would include consideration of a firm's dividend policy, earnings estimates, merger activity, executive leadership skills, and any other relevant information that may impact the profitability of the firm.

At any given point in time, the portfolio manager may also identify value opportunities for an entire asset class and choose to increase the weighting of that class in the portfolio. The range of weightings specified in the strategic allocation provides guidance as to the extent to which these **tactical asset allocations** are permissible.

For example, after a macroeconomic shock and a period of falling stock prices, a manager may decide equities as an asset class are undervalued and look to increase their weighting in the portfolio in anticipation of a bounce back.

Example 18.4

Wilkes is a 50-year-old single man with a 25-year-old highly successful daughter. She does not depend on her father for any financial help, but Wilkes would like to provide her with a substantial gift on her 30th birthday. Wilkes has invested 60% of his portfolio in a mutual fund that is designed to track US large-cap equity performance and 40% in a mutual fund that tracks long-term investment grade corporate bond performance. He approaches an active portfolio manager for advice on how he might use security selection to increase the portfolio's overall performance.

The adviser determines Wilkes has high ability but low willingness to take risk, coupled with a 7% total return objective. She performs an evaluation of the macro economy and believes that mid cap equity securities are overvalued, large caps are undervalued, and BB-rated bonds offer a premium in yields because they are not investment grade. The adviser's research indicates the consumer products, home products, and residential construction industries have the highest growth potential. She also expects stability in pharmaceuticals because of improvements in industry regulations. The adviser is concerned about rising inflation because of a shift in Fed policy.

Following the adviser's evaluation, which securities might she suggest selecting to improve portfolio performance?

Possible Security Selections

The adviser may recommend the following securities be included in the portfolio:

- Bonds issued by the top two pharmaceutical firms. The durations of the bonds should be low to protect against rising yields.
- Bonds issued by large cap consumer product firms. The durations of these bonds can be slightly longer because they have higher coupon rates.
- Equity issued by large cap residential construction firms.
- Equity issued by large cap home products firms.
- Equity issued by large cap utility firms to protect against interest rate risk.

INSTITUTIONAL INVESTORS

The strategies for implementing policy statements for institutions that hold portfolios can be quite different than those for individuals. Institutions tend to have more specific goals than individuals and fewer tax concerns. Institutions do not have dependents but have beneficiaries, so the policy statement should be created to benefit that group. The beneficiaries can be employees (pension fund), shareholders (financial institutions), communities (foundations), or nonprofit organizations (endowments). Consequently, the risk and return objectives depend primarily on the needs of the beneficiaries but are influenced by the preferences of those who provide capital to the institution or by the preferences of the board of trustees who are responsible for decision making.

Key Concepts

1. Explain the return objective calculation for a defined benefit pension plan.
2. Discuss the important factors that determine the ability of a pension plan to take risk.
3. Define a pension plan's funded status.

These differences only solidify the fiduciary role of the investment adviser. Institutions almost always have significantly higher portfolio values than most individuals, which tends to make the role of the adviser even more critical to a wider audience of beneficiaries. Instead of writing a policy statement for a family of four to six individuals, the adviser for institutional investors must write a policy statement for hundreds, perhaps even thousands, of beneficiaries.

Policy statements for institutions are similar to those of individuals and contain the same components, with perhaps some slight differences.

Pension Funds

Pension funds provide retirement income for employees. There are two broad types of employer-sponsored pension funds: defined benefit (DB) plans and defined contribution (DC) plans. DC plans are typically directed by the employee who takes full responsibility for the investment performance of the portfolio and makes regular contributions to the fund. The employer is likely to make some contributions as well. Policy statements for DC plans typically are part of the individual investor's policy statement, created in conjunction with the individual's lifetime portfolio.

In a DB plan, the employer is obligated to provide retirement benefits for the employees based on a specific formula. This obligation means the employer is fully exposed to the investment risk. The benefits are usually based on a simple formula with years of service and salary as input variables. One simple formula is shown below:

Retirement Salary = Retirement Percentage × Years of Service × Average Final Salary

Example 18.5
Grey Brick Company
Pension Example 1

Jasmine is hired by Grey Brick at a salary of $50,000 per year and is expected to work for 35 years. Salary increases are expected to average 2% per year over Jasmine's life, which brings her average final salary to $98,046. Grey Brick uses a 7% discount rate to compute its pension liability and a 1.5% per year of service as the standard percentage benefit.

The following benefit formula has been approved by the pension plan sponsor:

Retirement Benefit = Standard % × Years of Service × Average Final Salary

Retirement Benefit for Jasmine = 0.015 × 35 years × $98,046 = $51,474

Grey Brick should invest the present value of the future liability today to ensure that it will have the cash to pay Jasmine during her first year of retirement. The present value (7%, 35 years) can be easily computed as $4,821.

Grey Brick must also show the entire pension obligation for Jasmine on its balance sheet. To accomplish this, Grey Brick must estimate Jasmine's life expectancy and compute the present value of the individual amounts of retirement income during that span. This will be the total pension obligation for Jasmine, and Grey Brick will do the same for every employee. If Grey Brick invests that amount today, the pension fund will be considered fully funded. Note this is a simple example and the actual pension obligation calculations are far more complex.

Example 18.6
Ridge Carpeting Industries
Pension Example 2

Ridge Carpeting is a national firm with 100 employees with an average age of 51 years and an average time to retirement of 15 years. The average expected salary at retirement is $75,000. Ridge uses the formula:

Retirement Benefit = 0.0225 × 15 × $75,000 = $25,312.50

This benefit translates into a total future pension obligation with 100 employees of $2,531,250, on average.

If every employee retires in 15 years and each employee lives to receive 20 years of retirement income (assuming no cost of living increase), Ridge will be have a pension obligation of $26,840,360 (should be calculated in BEGIN mode) in exactly 15 years at an 8% discount rate. Ridge will be required to report a current pension obligation on its balance sheet of $8,461,201.

Employers hire pension fund managers, either in-house or externally, to manage the portfolio of investments from which it is obligated to pay pension benefits when the employees retire.

Pension plans can be overfunded (surplus) or underfunded (deficit). The status is calculated by taking the difference between the current market value of plan assets and the present value of liabilities. Most defined benefit plans in operation today are underfunded. According to a study of 366 Fortune 100 companies carried out by Willis Towers Watson the aggregate pension funded status was 87 percent at the end of 2020. The aggregate pension deficit was $233 billion.[4] The statistics are even worse for government sponsored DB plans. The average statewide pension funded status was less than 75 percent at the end of 2019, with some states below 50 percent according to the Federal Reserve.

To compose the policy statement for a pension fund, the same model used for individuals can be applied.

The **return objective** is typically the discount rate used to compute the present value of the pension obligation plus a desired premium to reduce future contributions to the pension fund. The higher the discount rate and premium, the more pressure there is for the portfolio to perform over the working life of the employees.

Quick Quiz 18.5

1. An employer with a large portion of its workforce nearing retirement age with high salaries and an overall plan deficit will most likely have a low tolerance for risk.
   a. True
   b. False
2. The return objective is usually a simple calculation for a pension plan.
   a. True
   b. False
3. In a defined contribution plan, the risk exposure for the portfolio performance lies entirely with the employer.
   a. True
   b. False

True, True, False.

The risk objective depends on a few important factors:

The status of the fund: Plans that are not fully funded have a reduced ability to take risk. When a surplus exists, pension managers often take more risk with the surplus to generate higher returns.

Characteristics of the workforce: Age and salary and remaining work life affect the ability to take risk. A younger employee age increases the portfolio manager's ability to take risk.

Plan features: Some employers offer early retirement or the option to take pension assets in a lump sum. The existence of these options reduces the ability of the portfolio manager to take risk.

Financial performance of the employer: More profitable firms and those with stable cash flows have a higher ability to take risk.

Correlation between plan assets and the employer's cash flows: A high correlation (approaching 0.80) between the two reduces the ability to take risk because poor employer performance during periods of low or negative returns on plan assets increases the probability the firm will be unable to make contributions to the fund.

4. www.willistowerswatson.com/en-US/News/2021/01/health-of-largest-us-corporate-pension-plans-showed-no-improvement-in-2020

Example 18.7
Merritt Foods Example

Merritt Foods (MF) is a regional firm that manufactures crackers, bread, and cookies and sponsors a defined benefit pension plan. MF's chief financial officer terminates the current plan manager and hires French Investments (FI) as its sole money management firm. FI has three experienced portfolio managers, one specialist in equities, one in fixed income, and one who has experience running a hedge fund. Rocco French will supervise the three managers and serve on the Investments Committee. The Investments Committee will be comprised of French and representatives from MF. The Investments Committee acts as the fiduciary responsible for making decisions on behalf of MF and its beneficiaries. Extracts from a suitable IPS that French and his firm should create are shown below.

Scope and Purpose

MF is a well-known brand name with stable cash flows, 400 full-time employees and 28 currently retired employees.

The assets of the plan have a current market value of \$12.8 million, while the present value of the pension liabilities is \$12.7 million.

Workforce Characteristics

Average Age of Employee	46
Expected Average Retirement Salary	\$100,000
Average Remaining Work Life	17
Average Years of Service at Retirement	31

MF computes retirement income using the benefit formula:

$$\text{Retirement Benefit} = 0.011 \times \text{Total Service in Years} \times \text{Final Salary}$$

$$\text{Retirement Benefit} = 0.011 \times 31 \times \$100{,}000 = \$34{,}100$$

MF uses 8.5% as its discount rate.

MF offers no early retirement benefits, and employees must receive retirement benefits in the form of an annuity. MF expects to add 10% to its workforce over the next five years, with most of the new hires expected to be college graduates. The correlation coefficient between plan assets and the firm's performance is 0.38. The pension fund manager currently matches expected retirement dates for older employees to the duration of the fixed-income portfolio.

The investment options consist of four asset classes, including a short-term cash account. The primary asset classes are fixed income, equities, and a hedge fund exposure.

The purpose of the Merritt Foods policy statement is to provide assistance to the Investment Committee as a guideline for providing employees with retirement benefits.

Goals of the Policy Statement

- To provide a formal document that can be used as a summation of the Investment Committee's objectives, its strategy, and its expectations of all relevant variables that will influence the performance of the plan's assets.
- To establish a formal treatment regarding the management of the retirement plan's assets.
- To encourage communication between and among all significant parties involved in the retirement plan.
- To identify proper investment alternatives for plan assets.
- To establish risk and expected return guidelines for the plan assets in general and for each asset class.
- To control costs and expenses and to establish efficient procedures in the management of the plan's assets.
- To comply with ERISA requirements and all other laws, regulations, and requirements as a responsible and engaged investments professional.

Statement of Objectives

Constraints

Liquidity: The current cash amount represents approximately 5% of the plan assets, which covers the current pension obligations. All interest and dividend income should be placed in the cash account up to 5% annually.

Time: MF has a relatively young workforce with a high proportion of active workers to retired employees. The plan has a long-term investment horizon, so the manager should pursue strategies consistent with modern portfolio theory.

Tax: The plan has a tax-exempt status.

Legal and Regulatory: The fund should operate within the guidelines of the Employee Retirement Income Security Act (ERISA) of 1974.

Unique: No early retirement benefits are available.

Return Objective: The discount rate is 8.5% which is the return objective for the plan assets.

Risk Objective:

The plan is fully funded, with a small surplus of $100,000	Moderate to high
MF has brand name product lines and stable cash flows	High
Low correlation between plan assets and firm performance	High
Workforce characteristics include relatively low age of worker and moderate salary	Moderate to high
Plan features are largely standard	Moderate to high

Overall risk tolerance: Moderate to high.

Responsibilities:

The Investment Committee is responsible for the construction and maintenance of the policy statement. The Committee will provide sufficient asset class alternatives to provide diversification benefits for the plan participants and will select asset classes with prudence. The Committee will seek to minimize all expenses and will monitor the performance of the investment managers. The Committee is responsible for avoiding any conflicts of interest.

The three investment managers will manage the plan assets in accordance with the objectives outlined in this policy statement and specific to each of their agreements with the plan sponsor. The managers will buy, sell, and make investment decisions regarding the portfolios under their care. The managers will vote all proxies with the plan beneficiaries in mind and are responsible for communicating with all relevant parties. The managers will make all decisions with the skill and due diligence expected from investment professionals acting as fiduciaries.

The Investment Committee will be diligent in selecting and monitoring the investment managers according to the following:

- Each manager should fall under the authority of specific regulatory agencies as registered investment advisers or some other registered financial institution. The Investment Committee has a preference that each adviser has earned a globally recognized designation or certification.
- The assets under management by each adviser should have a high correlation to their general asset classes.
- The performance of the adviser will be compared against the return objective in the policy statement, against a peer group, and will be evaluated using well-established investment ratios, such as the Sharpe ratio.
- Acceptable fees and expenses for each asset class will place the asset class in the top 50% as measured against peer groups.
- Each adviser will present a comprehensive annual review of performance, which includes an evaluation of strengths and weaknesses. Quarterly reports can be electronically submitted to the Investment Committee. MF can also require the submission of other reports in response to significant market or firm events.

Asset Class Guidelines:

The Investments Committee (IC) believes the objectives of the retirement plan can be achieved through the use of three asset classes, with a separate class for short-term investments that meets the plan's liquidity requirements.

The asset classes are shown in ascending order of risk:

Asset Class	Characteristics of Securities in Class
Cash	Short-term money market securities with low risk and high liquidity.
Fixed Income	Investment grade bonds with sensitivity to interest rate risk. The IC has a preference for coupon-paying bonds issued by companies with a history of generating stable cash flows and government bonds in low income tax municipalities.
Equities	U.S. based corporations with a size mix and a preference against dividend paying firms.
Hedge Funds	Market neutral, capital structure, merger arbitrage, long-short, and event driven strategies. The IC is open to other strategies the manager might want to pursue, but requests prior approval.

The Investments Committee believes this asset mix will achieve the goals of the retirement plan and is consistent with the pursuit of diversification.

The Investment Committee allocates the plan assets as follows, with cash held being sufficient to cover current pension obligations:

Asset Class	Allocation	Expected Return
Cash	5.1%	0.8%
Fixed Income	21.6%	5.2%
U.S. Equities	63.4%	9.8%
Hedge Funds	9.9%	12.9%

The expected returns are provided by each manager and confirmed by surveying a wide range of financial professionals.

The expected return for the plan assets is calculated as 8.65%, which is 15 basis points above the discount rate used to compute the present value of the pension liabilities.

Monitoring and Rebalancing

The portfolio will be monitored continuously and rebalanced when asset prices move significantly from their beginning of the year values or when the plan's risk and return profile changes.

Endowment Funds

Endowments are institutions owned by nonprofit organizations such as hospitals and schools. They are almost always created with an original donation but can accept additional contributions. Endowments typically have stated purposes and are designed to be perpetual in nature. Some of the distinguishing characteristics include:

Key Concepts

1. Explain the return objective for a typical endowment fund.
2. Discuss the regulatory environment faced by endowment funds.

- The endowment's spending policy affects both the risk and return objectives.
- Spending is well planned with average spending rates between 3% and 7%.
- Most endowments are fully tax exempt in the United States.[5]
- The **Uniform Prudent Management of Institutional Funds Act (UPMIFA)** is a guide for endowments and other charitable funds for their money management strategies.
- Unique aspects of endowments include their size and social issues when investing.
- Spending rules are usually smoothed to remove the effect of market performance.
- Outperformance of endowment fund assets leads to an increase in risk tolerance.

Example 18.8
Atlantic Library Example

The Atlantic Library (AL) received a 2015 donation from Duane and Dawn Phelps of $10 million. The Phelpses are active art lovers and designed their donation to increase AL's presence in the national art scene. The donation has the following objectives:

- To build an art gallery wing on the east side of the current AL location.
- To hire an art professor to act as the art gallery director.
- To purchase modern day artists' paintings.
- To hold regular art exhibitions.

AL is to invest the funds in U.S. Treasury securities until these objectives are met and the art gallery is functional.

The Phelps family has purchased and donated a $1 million piece of work by Claude Monet that serves as the centerpiece of the gallery.

Five years later in 2020, the work is complete and AL hires Dirk Brennan as portfolio manager, who begins the process of forming an appropriate portfolio.

Brennan collects the following information:

- The Phelps family and AL's Board of Trustees agree on a 5% spending rate.
- Inflation is expected to be 1.3%.
- The new art director has begun programs to attract young artists, including offering formal classes and training sessions.
- The new art director has purchased supplies and arranged for travel to art museums for students during the coming year.
- Scholarships will be awarded for qualified students who plan on attending an art school or majoring in art at a university.

5. The majority of endowments are fully tax exempt, however, the Tax Cuts and Jobs Act (TCJA) of 2017 imposed a tax on a small number of extremely high value endowments of private nonprofit colleges and universities.

With some additional donations, the current market value of the U.S. Treasury portfolio is $15 million.

Constraints

Liquidity: The fund will need $945,000 or 6.3% of $15 million in cash to spend during the year. Brennan will likely invest in equity and fixed-income securities that pay interest and dividends. Brennan will also likely have to plan on selling some assets to meet the liquidity needs.

Time: The endowment fund is perpetual and will not spend the principal amount.

Tax: The endowment fund is U.S. tax-exempt.

Legal: Brennan will adhere to the terms of the UPMIFA.

Unique: Phelps is active in the art world and is likely to be involved in the gallery's activities. Phelps also donated a Monet painting, which is an additional indication of his love for art.

Return Objective: 5% plus 1.3% inflation. Total return objective of 6.3%.

Risk Objective: All indications are for a high ability to take risk.

Quick Quiz 18.6

1. Spending rates are very complex for endowment funds.
   a. True
   b. False
2. Endowment funds with socially aware limitations on security selection have unique constraint placed on the portfolio manager.
   a. True
   b. False
3. The average endowment fund has a high ability to take risk.
   a. True
   b. False

False, True, True.

SUMMARY

Summary of key points:

- Portfolio management for individuals as well as institutional investors is based on a total return approach in which invested assets are viewed collectively.
- The planning stage is one in which the individual client's risk and return objectives are determined, taking into account any constraints the investor faces.
- The execution stage is one in which the assets to be included in the portfolio are selected. This stage is followed by the use of an optimization model to identify the set of optimal weights for each of the assets in the portfolio.
- The feedback stage includes regular monitoring of the performance of the portfolio and a complete performance evaluation at the end of any relevant periods.
- An investment adviser should act as a fiduciary who is in a position of authority, who obligates himself or herself to act on behalf of another, and who assumes a duty to act in good faith and with care, candor, and loyalty in fulfilling that obligation. CFAs and CFP® certificants both have fiduciary responsibilities.
- The investment policy statement (IPS) for an individual should include the following sections: Scope and Purpose; Governance; Investment, Return and Risk Objectives; and Risk Management.
- Included in the objective portion of the IPS is a list of investor constraints. These might include liquidity issues, tax restrictions, time horizon constraints, legal constraints, or unique constraints.
- The return objective should be stated as a formula, include inflation, and specify whether it is pre-tax or after-tax.
- IPSs for institutions are very similar to those for individuals. These institutions include, among others, pension funds and endowment funds.

DISCUSSION QUESTIONS

***SOLUTIONS** to the discussion questions can be found exclusively within the chapter. Once you have completed an initial reading of the chapter, go back and highlight the answers to these questions.*

1. Describe the portfolio management process and identify the three stages critical for success.
2. Discuss in detail the planning stage and identify activities that commonly occur during this stage.
3. Discuss in detail the execution stage and identify activities that commonly occur during this stage.
4. Discuss in detail the feedback stage and identify activities that commonly occur during this stage.
5. Explain the importance of the investment policy statement to investors.
6. Categorize the constraints facing investors and discuss how each limits the investor in the portfolio management process.
7. Explain the manner in which a return objective is computed for individual investors and the importance of inflation as one of its components.
8. Explain the manner in which the risk objective is determined for an individual investor and differentiate between an investor's ability to take risk and the willingness to take risk.
9. Identify the appropriate course of action when an investor has risk and return objectives that do not match.
10. Explain the manner in which a financial analyst forms capital market expectations as part of the portfolio management process.
11. Discuss the details of a macroeconomic analysis.
12. Discuss the details of an industry analysis.
13. Discuss the details of a security analysis.
14. Explain how portfolio analysis fits into the portfolio management process and discuss how a portfolio can be optimized from a mean-variance standpoint.
15. Describe the risks associated with the two main types of pension plans and identify which party bears the risk in each type of plan.
16. Describe the constraints facing a pension fund manager.
17. Describe how the risk and return objectives are determined in a pension plan.
18. Describe the constraints facing the portfolio manager of an endowment fund.
19. Describe how the risk and return objectives are determined in an endowment fund.

MULTIPLE-CHOICE PROBLEMS

A sample of multiple choice problems is provided below. Additional multiple choice problems are available at money-education.com by accessing the Student Practice Portal.

1. Lavar is a financial adviser and interviews a new client. Lavar recommends an investment in longer-term bonds because of an expectation that interest rates will fall over the next five-year period. The recommendation is most likely a part of the:
    a. Planning stage.
    b. Execution stage.
    c. Feedback stage.
    d. Accumulation stage.

2. Annabelle is a first-time homeowner who purchases a home for $200,000 using a down payment of $20,000. The monthly mortgage payment is $1,079.19. The annual property tax bill of $6,321.82 is most likely a:
    a. Time constraint.
    b. Liquidity constraint.
    c. Legal constraint.
    d. Unique circumstance constraint.

3. Trina retires early and will have no income other than her portfolio income. She believes she will need $500,000 in before-tax income per year to cover her living expenses. Trina has $7 million in investable assets and inflation is expected to be 0.5%. She plans on donating $100,000 to the Atlas Foundation, $125,000 to the local hospital, and $33,000 her alma mater's endowment fund. Trina's return objective is closest to:
    a. 7.1%.
    b. 7.4%.
    c. 7.9%.
    d. 8.2%.

4. The execution stage of the investment management process most likely includes:
    a. Strategic asset allocation decisions.
    b. Purchase of individual securities.
    c. Analysis of capital market expectations.
    d. Interview with the client.

5. A financial adviser is crafting the policy statement for a client and investigates several key factors that will influence their allocation decision. The factors include commodity prices, rate of inflation, and exchange rates. The financial adviser is most likely performing:
    a. Economic analysis.
    b. Industry analysis.
    c. Security analysis.
    d. Portfolio analysis.

QUICK QUIZ EXPLANATIONS

Quick Quiz 18.1

1. True.
2. False. The feedback stage is the final stage in the process. The strategic allocation weights are determined in the planning stage.

Quick Quiz 18.2

1. False. It is tempting to identify her time constraint as short-term, but the portfolio must be managed for the benefit of any beneficiaries. The young children will have a long-term investment horizon.
2. True.

Quick Quiz 18.3

1. True.
2. False. Passive managers will choose investments that reflect the performance of the benchmark. Active managers try and outperform through security selection.

Quick Quiz 18.4

1. True.
2. True.
3. False. Portfolio optimization provides the foundation to determine the appropriate assets for the client but cannot in any way be interpreted as a guarantee of results.

Quick Quiz 18.5

1. True.
2. True.
3. False. In a defined contribution plan, the investment risk is born by the employee who makes all the investment decisions.

Quick Quiz 18.6

1. False. Spending rates for endowment funds are usually determined by a combination of the tax laws and the preferences of the board of trustees. They are not computed according to a complicated formula.
2. True.
3. True.

APPENDIX A
GLOSSARY

#

12b-1 Fee - A fee charged by a mutual fund company to pay for the services of brokers who sell the mutual funds and who maintain the client relationships. These fees include fees paid for marketing and selling fund shares, such as compensating brokers and others who sell fund shares, and paying for advertising, the printing and mailing of prospectuses to new investors, and the printing and mailing of sales literature. Under FINRA rules, 12b-1 fees that are used to pay marketing and distribution expenses (as opposed to shareholder service expenses) cannot exceed 0.75 percent of a fund's average net assets per year. 12b-1 fees can include other fees up to 0.25% for a total of 1.00%.

A

Accounting risk - The risk that financial statements do not accurately reflect the financial condition of a business due to fraud or error.

Accredited Investor - Someone who has earned income that exceeded $200,000 (or $300,000 together with a spouse) in each of the prior two years, and reasonably expects the same for the current year, OR has a net worth over $1 million, either alone or together with a spouse (excluding the value of the person's primary residence and any loans secured by the residence (up to the value of the residence)).

Active Funds - Funds in which the portfolio manager is actively engaged in selecting securities to be included in the fund.

Active Managers - Try to improve the performance of the portfolio through security selection.

Alpha - The difference between the actual return on a portfolio and its expected return as outlined by the capital asset pricing model.

Alternative Investments - An asset class that is expected to have low correlations with traditional securities and includes commodities, real estate, private equity, and other non-traditional investments.

Alternative Investment Market - A collection of opportunities that do not fit into one of the traditional financial markets.

Alternative Minimum Tax - Devised to ensure that all individuals with a certain amount of income will pay some income tax on an annual basis.

American Depositary Receipts (ADRs) - One of the easiest methods of acquiring individual foreign securities. They are certificates issued by U.S. banks representing ownership in shares of stock of a foreign company that are held on deposit in a bank in the firm's home country.

American Options - Options that can be exercised anytime up until the point of expiration.

Amos Tversky - A founding father of behavioral finance who developed prospect theory and the importance of loss aversion.

Analysis Effect - A component of fixed-income attribution analysis that measures the portfolio manager has the ability to invest in securities that are temporarily undervalued.

Anchoring - A cognitive error in which the investor uses the first available piece of information to make a decision, especially if the information is irrelevant or immaterial.

Angel Investing - Wealthy individuals who typically provide capital to entrepreneurs in the initial stages of their business. Angel investors frequently have expertise that they share with the business owner.

Appreciation - The change in the investment's value from the beginning of the year to the end of the year.

Arbitrage Pricing Theory (APT) - A multifactor model that estimates the expected return on an individual security using relevant economic factors as inputs.

Arithmetic Mean Return - A measure of the average of data points that is calculated by summing the annual holding period returns and dividing by the number of years in the holding period.

Ask Price - The price for which someone is willing to sell a security - the price an investor pays if they buy a security.

Asset Allocation - The investment decision that involves assigning portfolio weights to each asset. This can be achieved through software programs or through a portfolio manager's expertise.

Asset Bubble - A capital market mis-pricing in which asset prices rise far too quickly than would be expected based on fundamental or intrinsic values.

Asset Class - A group of financial securities that are similar in risk, liquidity, and cash flow expectations. Common asset classes include money market securities, fixed-income securities, and equity securities.

Asset Selection - The investment decision that involves buying securities that are appropriate for each client or each fund.

Asset-Backed Securities - Securities issued against some type of asset-linked debts bundled together, such as credit card receivables or mortgages.

At-the-Money - When the option exercise price equals the market price for the underlying security for both calls and puts. Note that this term is not referring to the buyer or seller, but rather the option contract.

Attribution Analysis - An evaluation tool that is used by investors to measure the ability of managers to outperform a benchmark portfolio. There are generally two components that can be attributed to managerial skill: asset selection and asset allocation.

B

Back-End Load - A sales charge that is applied to the ultimate sale or redemption of mutual fund shares rather than at the time of purchase.

Banker's Acceptance - A bank guarantee of an international payment that is sold in the secondary market. They typically sell at a discount and have credit risk according to the risk level of the guaranteeing bank.

Banking Act - Legislation passed in 1933 as a result of the stock market crash of 1929 that separates commercial from investment banking, also known as the Glass Steagall Act.

Basis - The relationship between the spot price and the future price (spot price less the futures price).

Behavioral Constraint - Involves the client's inability to be a rational investor in the classic sense described by the founding fathers of modern portfolio theory.

Behavioral Finance - A combination of economics, finance, and psychology disciplines that offers an explanation of human errors in financial decision making, particularly cognitive errors and emotional biases shown to be evident in capital markets.

Benchmark Portfolio - A portfolio that has similar securities, similar risk characteristics, and similar return expectations as an invested portfolio. It is used as a comparison performance metric. Also called normal portfolio.

Best Efforts - A method of raising capital in the primary market in which the underwriting firm attempts to sell all of the securities to the public but can return any unsold securities to the issuer.

Beta - A measure of the systematic risk of a portfolio or individual security and is commonly referred to as a benchmark for volatility.

Bid Price - The price a security dealer is willing to pay for a security - the price an investor gets if they sell.

Bid-Ask Spread - The difference between the price that a buyer is willing to pay and the price for which a seller is willing to sell an asset.

Blue-Chip Stock - A security issued by a well-known company with well-known brand name product lines that tends to perform well in all economies.

Bond Indenture Agreement - The legal document that sets forth the repayment schedules, restrictions, and promises between the issuer of a corporate bond and the purchaser.

Bond Market Line - An illustration of the relation between the expected rate of return on a bond portfolio and its duration.

Bond Swapping - The process of selling one debt instrument and replacing it with another.

Borrowing Portfolios - Portfolios on the capital market line where investors borrow funds at the risk-free rate to invest in the market portfolio.

Bottom-Up Analysis - A form of economic analysis in which the company is the primary focus of research. The firm is evaluated for its ability to generate cash flows, for its executive leadership, and for its market power, among other factors.

Bounded Rationality - A behavioral finance concept in which investors are bound by the amount of information they can locate and by their cognitive ability to process this information.

Breakeven Price - Where the line crosses the axis.

Breakpoints - The investments levels at which discounts for front-end sales charges become available.

Brinson, Hood, and Beebower - Three investment advisers who co-authored a seminal academic paper on attribution analysis.

Broker-Dealers - Individuals or firms that buy and sell securities, either for their clients or for themselves.

Business Cycle - Variations in business activity that includes periods of expansion, recession, peaks, and troughs.

Business Risk - The riskiness of a specific business, which includes the speculative nature of the business, the management of the business, and the philosophy of the business.

Buy and Hold Strategy - A simple investment strategy in which the investor forms a portfolio and holds onto the securities over the investment horizon. There is no rebalancing of security weights when investors pursue this strategy.

Buy to Close - A type of order used when a trader wants to close a previously opened short position. The trader is effectively buying back an option that was previously sold.

Buy to Open - A type of order used when a trader wants to buy (purchase) either a call option or a put option.

Buyer - The buyer of an option contract purchases the right to buy (call option) or sell (put option) the underlying security from or to the writer of the contract. The buyer pays the premium to the writer. The buyer is taking a long position in the option contract.

C

Call Options - Give the holder (buyer) the right (but not the obligation) to purchase the underlying security for a specified price within a specified period of time.

Call Provision - Permits the issuer to repurchase the bond from the investor prior to the stated maturity of the bond.

Call Risk - Related to interest rate risk in that the call feature on a bond will only be used when interest rates fall as issuers want to reduce their total interest payments by refinancing at lower rates.

Capital Asset Pricing Model - A theoretical model developed by William Sharpe that describes the relationship between individual stock returns and broad market returns.

Capital Gain - When an asset is sold, the difference between the amount received (referred to as the "amount realized") and the investor's adjusted basis in the asset.

Capital Losses - May be used to offset any amount of capital gains, but if the losses exceed gains in a given tax year, the maximum capital loss that can be used to offset ordinary income is $3,000.

Capital Market Expectations - The expected risk, return, and correlation between assets or asset classes that may be used in an investment portfolio.

Capital Market Line (CML) - When all investors have homogeneous expectations, the capital market line shows all efficient combinations of the risk-free asset and market portfolio.

Carried Interest - Distribution of profits designed to align the interests of the managers with the interests of the investors.

Certificate of Deposit - Short-term deposits with a financial institution that have stated maturity dates and interest rates. Most impose penalties if redeemed before their maturity dates.

Certified Financial Planner Board of Standards - The self-regulatory organization that grants the CFP® designation.

Charted Financial Analyst Institute - The self-regulatory organization that grants the CFA® designation.

Chartered Alternative Investments Analyst Association - The self-regulatory organization that grants the CAIA® designation.

Class A Shares - These shares charge a front-end load with a smaller 12b-1 fee.

Class B Shares - These shares charge a deferred redemption fee plus the maximum one percent 12b-1 fee. In addition, many of the class B shares have a conversion feature that automatically converts the class B shares to class A shares after a period of years.

Class C Shares - These shares often have a level deferred sales charge (often one percent), plus the maximum one percent 12b-1 fee. However, these shares do not convert to class A shares. Usually, class C shares are the most expensive if the fund is held for a long period of time.

Class I Shares - Institutional shares that have lower fees and expenses than other classes. Usually, the expense ratio is lower. These shares are offered to institutions, such as retirement funds, corporations, and investors with large account balances.

Class of Options - A group of option contracts with the same type (call or put), same style (American or European), that cover the same underlying security.

Clean Price - The price of a bond excluding any interest that has accrued since issue or the most recent coupon payment.

Closed-End Fund - A type of investment company whose shares trade in the same manner as publicly traded stocks in the secondary market.

Closing Orders - Used to exit an option position and are simply the opposite of the opening order.

Clustering Illusion - A cognitive error in which investors see patterns in small samples of data where none exist, especially over the long term.

Coefficient of Determination (R^2 or r^2) - A measure of the strength of the relationship between two variables.

Coefficient of Variation (CV) - A measure of the degree of risk per unit of return and computed as the ratio of standard deviation to expected return.

Cognitive Dissonance - An uncomfortable state of mind in which an investor is faced with mutually exclusive thoughts regarding a financial decision and resolves the conflict by eliminating one option through irrational short cuts.

Cognitive Errors - One of the two main behavioral mistakes made by investors, in which brain patterns distort information regarding an investment and leads investors to biased decisions.

Collateralized Mortgage Obligation (CMO) - A type of mortgage-backed security in which the interest and principal payments are divided into various tranches that have different levels of risk.

Collectibles - A component of alternative investments that includes coins, stamps, instruments, alcohol, and other collectible items that are expected to appreciate in value over time.

Commercial Paper - Short-term debt issued by corporations to finance working capital requirements.

Commodity - A primary agricultural product or raw material from natural resources that has value to consumers or industrial producers.

Common Stock - Represents an ownership interest in a company.

Complex Capital Structures - Companies that include potentially dilutive securities and are required to report EPS on a diluted basis.

Confirmation Bias - A cognitive error in which an investor searches for information that confirms earlier beliefs.

Constant Growth Dividend Model - A present value model in which the growth rate in the primary input variable is assumed to be constant. If the primary input is the dividend stream, then the assumption is that dividends will grow at a constant rate.

Consumer Price Index (CPI) - Measures the overall price levels for a basket of goods and services consumers purchase.

Contract Size - A specific standardized size represented in a futures contract, which does not change, and allows traders to easily determine how many contracts they may need for their trading objectives.

Contract Value - The value of a futures contract, also called the notional value, is determined by multiplying the size of the contract by the current price.

Conversion Price - Equals the par value of the bond divided by the conversion ratio.

Conversion Ratio - Equals the number of shares of common stock that the bondholder will receive if the bond is converted.

Conversion Value - Determined by multiplying the conversion ratio by the current value of the common stock.

Convertible Bonds - Bonds that permit the purchaser to convert the bond, which is a form of debt financing, into an equity position in the issuer.

Convertible Securities - Hybrid securities that permit the holder to acquire shares of common stock from the issuing company by exchanging the currently held debt security under a specific formula.

Convexity - The second derivative of the price of the bond in respect to interest rates. It measures the non linear relationship of bond prices to changes in interest rates.

Core-Satellite - A strategy that uses index funds to fulfill the "core" components of the desired asset allocation, such as large cap stocks, which tend to be extremely efficient, making it difficult to outperform the index.

Correlation Coefficient - A measure of the strength and direction of a relationship between two variables. CC ranges from -1.0 to +1.0 and can be easily computed by the ratio of covariance to the product of the standard deviation of the two variables. CC can be thought of as a standardized covariance.

Coupon Payments - Interest payments paid to the bondholder on a semiannual basis and based on a percentage of the face value, or par value, of the bond.

Coupon Rate - The rate of interest paid on the face value (par value) of the bond.

Covariance - A measure of the strength and direction of a relationship between two variables and is commonly thought of as a benchmark of how two variables move together. A covariance can take on almost any value.

Credit Risk - The risk that the financial well-being of the bond issuer will change over this long period of time. Also known as default risk.

Crowdfunding - Refers to a financing method in which money is raised through soliciting relatively small individual investments or contributions from a large number of people.

Cryptocurrency - A type of virtual currency that utilizes cryptography to secure transactions that are digitally recorded on a distributed ledger, such as a blockchain. Units of cryptocurrencies are often referred to as tokens or coins, and can be used for investment purposes or can be used as a form of electronic payment.

Cumulative - Preferred stock that is entitled to any unpaid preferred dividends from prior years before the issuing company pays a dividend to common stockholders.

Cumulative Voting - Allows one vote per share times the number of seats on the board of directors. Cumulative voting is used to protect minority shareholder interests. In addition, voting can be done in person or by proxy.

Current Yield - A bond's annual coupon divided by the current market price.

Cyclical Stock - An equity security that performs well during economic expansions and poorly during economic contractions.

D

Daniel Kahneman - A founding father of behavioral finance who developed prospect theory and the importance of loss aversion.

Date of Declaration - Date on which a corporation's board of directors declares a dividend payment which creates an obligation on the company to make a dividend payment to shareholders.

Date of Payment - The date that the dividend will actually be paid.

Date of Record - The date at which an owner of the common stock of a corporation is entitled to receive the dividend payment.

Debenture Bonds - Unsecured corporate bonds whose holders have no claim to specific assets of the issuing corporation.

Default Risk - The risk that the financial well-being of the bond issuer will change over this long period of time. Also known as credit risk.

Defensive Stock - An equity security that performs better during economic contractions than other stocks.

Derivative - A financial security whose value is derived from the value of an underlying security or asset (e.g., coffee, oil).

Derivative Security - A security whose value is derived from the value of another security and is used by hedge fund managers and investors who want exposure to the underlying assets of the derivative.

Direct Registration - The security is registered in the investor's name on the issuer's books, and either the company or its transfer agent holds the security in book-entry form.

Dirty Price - The price of a bond including any interest that has accrued since issue or the most recent coupon payment. Also known as full price or invoice price.

Discount - When a bond sells for a price less than its par value, which occurs when the coupon rate is less than the yield to maturity on the bond.

Discount Rate - The interest rate that the Federal Reserve charges financial institutions for short-term loans.

Diversification - The reduction in risk that arises from investments in securities that are less than perfectly correlated.

Dividend Aristocrats - There are a handful of S&P 500 companies (approximately 50) that have consistently increased their dividend over the last 25 years.

Dividend Discount Model - A model that uses the expected dividend stream to compute an estimate for a firm's stock price. The two other input variables are the investor's requited return and the growth rate in dividends.

Dividend Reinvestment Plans (DRIPs) - Plans offered by public companies that allow investors to purchase shares directly from the company, as opposed to through a broker.

Dividends - Positive net income that is paid to the shareholders of a corporation. Cash dividends, in some cases, may be paid that exceed net income. In addition, dividends may consist of stock, such as in a stock dividend or stock split.

Dodd Frank Act - Legislation passed in 2010 that established new government agencies to reduce volatility in financial markets in response to the Great Recession.

Dollar-Weighted Return - Measures the effect of all of the cash flows an investor controls. The objective is to determine the combined result of the timing and dollar volume of the transactions during the period, as well as the performance of the investment security. It would also be appropriate for gauging the performance of an investment manager with full discretion over an investor's account.

Downgrade Risk - The chance that a bond will be downgraded by one of the ratings agencies causing bond prices to fall.

Duration - The first derivative of the price of the bond in respect to interest rates. A concept developed by Fred Macaulay in 1938, that provides a time-weighted measure of a security's cash flows in terms of payback.

Dynamic Asset Allocation - An investment strategy in which the portfolio weights are constantly being adjusted to reflect changing market conditions and changing asset values.

E

Earnings Per Share (EPS) - Represent the profit of the company on a per share basis.

Effective Duration - A direct measure of the sensitivity of a bond to changes in interest rates.

Efficient Frontier - The locus of optimal portfolios that are defined as possessing the lowest risk for each level of expected return; first introduced by Harry Markowitz in 1952.

Efficient Markets Hypothesis - A modern portfolio theory developed by Eugene Fama that describes an efficient market as one in which prices reflect all relevant information.

Efficient Portfolio - A portfolio that has the highest return for a given level of risk.

Emotional Bias - One of the two main behavioral mistakes made by investors, in which emotions play a critical role in framing an investment and leads to biased decisions.

Endowment Fund - An institutional investor that is usually created by a nonprofit foundation and is used for the purpose of advancing the operations of the foundation. Common foundations include hospitals, universities, and museums. Endowments typically refrain from spending principal but use the cash flow from the investment portfolio to fund specific projects.

Enterprise Value Multiple - A relative valuation tool defined as the ratio of a firm's enterprise value over its earnings before interest, taxes, and depreciation.

Equity Dual-Purpose Fund - A fund that invests primarily in securities of U.S. companies but has two classes of shares: (1) shares that receive all of the dividend income but no capital appreciation and (2) shares that consist of capital shares that receive all capital appreciation but no dividend income.

Equity Market - A large market of ownership.

Equity Premium Puzzle - A mystery describing the difference between the returns on government bonds and the returns on equity securities that are much higher than the risk differential would predict.

ERISA - The Employment Retirement Income Security Act of 1974 is a law that established guidelines for voluntary private pension funds to protect employees. The law sets minimum standards for participation, funding, withdrawals, and vesting. It also establishes guidelines for acceptable behavior of pension fund managers.

Eugene Fama - A Nobel Prize winning economist who developed the efficient markets hypothesis and the Fama Decomposition.

European Options - Options can only be exercised at expiration.

Excess Reserves - Represents the amount of cash or deposits with the Federal Reserve in excess of the minimum amount required.

Exchange Rate Risk - The variability in asset returns due to the change in currency values.

Exchange-Traded Funds (ETFs) - An index-based equity instrument that represents ownership in either a fund or a unit investment trust and gives investors the opportunity to buy and sell shares of an entire stock portfolio as a single security.

Ex-Dividend Date - The date on which the market reflects the dividend payment.

Execution Stage - The second step in the portfolio management process, in which financial advisers execute trades that form portfolios for their clients. This stage is the portfolio construction stage and is characterized by asset selection and asset allocation that is consistent with the elements of the planning stage.

Exercise - Options provide the holder or buyer with the right to buy or sell the underlying security at the strike price. Exercising the option means forcing the seller of the contract to sell the underlying security for a call option and to buy the underlying security for a put option.

Expense Ratio - Stated as a percentage of total assets and includes the management fees, the 12b-1 fees, and other operating expenses related to running and operating the mutual fund, but it does not include sales charges.

Expiration - The point in time at which the buyer's rights under the call or put contract terminate.

Extraordinary Dividends - Dividend payments issued by a company that are outside of their normal dividend policy.

F

Fair Market Value - The market value of a firm's assets minus the market value of a firm's liabilities, with consideration for any preferred stock outstanding.

Fama Decomposition - An attribution analysis tool that identifies a portfolio manager's ability to use total risk and market timing to outperform a benchmark portfolio.

Federal Agency Securities - Public debt issued by agencies of the U.S. government as a means of raising funds for operations of the respective agency.

Federal Funds Rate - The bank-to-bank lending rate.

Feedback Stage - The third and final stage in the portfolio management process, in which financial advisers gather information from portfolio performance and client changes to rebalance the portfolio to reflect the new investment environment.

Financial Institutions - An intermediary that helps borrowers raise capital in financial markets and provides a wide range of financial services to all types of investors.

Financial Services Modernization Act - Legislation passed in 1999 that removes barriers among securities firms, financial institutions, and insurance companies.

Firm Commitment - A method of raising capital in the primary market in which the underwriting firm agrees to purchase the entire issue from the corporation and attempts to sell all of the securities to the public but can keep any number of securities as inventory.

Fiscal Policy - Represents the government's position on whether to expand or contract the economy. Congress uses taxes and government spending to implement its fiscal policy.

Fixed Income Market - A long-term debt market in which government and firms borrow large amounts of capital in return for promises to make interest and principal payments to lenders.

Fixed-Income Securities - Securities with specified payment dates and amounts, primarily bonds.

Foreign Currency Options -These options allow traders to take advantage of expected changes in currency prices or to hedge currency risk in a portfolio.

Foreign Securities - Securities issued by entities outside the United States.

Form 10-K - The annual report on Form 10-K provides a comprehensive overview of the company's business and financial condition and includes audited financial statements. Although similarly named, the annual report on Form 10-K is distinct from the "annual report to shareholders," which a company must send to its shareholders when it holds an annual meeting to elect directors.

Forward Contract - A legal agreement between two parties to buy or sell a specific asset at a specified future time, which is agreed to today.

Framing - A cognitive error in which investors are influenced in their financial decision making by the manner in which a decision is presented or framed.

Free Cash Flow to Equity - The amount of cash a firm has remaining after all expenses have been paid and all short and long-term investments have been made.

Front-End Load - A sales charge that is based on the value of the initial investment into the mutual fund. This load is incurred when an investor purchases shares of a mutual fund from a commission-based financial adviser.

Full Price - The price of a bond including any interest that has accrued since issue or the most recent coupon payment. Also known as dirty price or invoice.

Fully Diluted EPS - EPS taking into consideration the shares that could result from the exercise or conversion of dilutive securities.

Fundamental Analysis - A framework under which investors use basic investment tools to analyze the macro and micro economic environments to make financial decisions.

Funding Portal - An intermediary that allows the general public to participate in crowdfunding transactions.

Futures Contract - A financial agreement in which two parties agree to buy and sell an underlying asset at a predetermined price at some time in the future.

Futures Options - These options use futures contracts as the underlying security and allow traders to enter into a specific futures contract. For example, the E-mini S&P 500 Weekly Option contract allows for delivery into one E-mini S&P 500 futures contract.

Futures Price - The price of the commodity or asset at some time in the future.

G

Gambler's Fallacy - A cognitive error in which investors believe in a decreased probability of an event occurring in the future if the event has recently occurred more frequently than expected.

General Obligation Bond - A bond issued by a municipality for general financing purposes, such as building a school or financing the construction of buildings that improve the services provided by the municipality.

General Partner - The private equity fund that identifies and purchases businesses on behalf of the limited partners.

Geometric Mean - A rate of return that measures the average return over time under the assumption that any cash flows distributed are reinvested back into the security.

Global Association of Risk Professionals - The self-regulatory organization that grants the FRM® designation.

Going Concern - The assumption that firms will make decisions today based on the fact that they will exist over the long term.

Gross Domestic Product (GDP) - Represents the total final output of a country, by its citizens and foreigners in the country, over a period of time.

Growth Stock - An equity security that has above average expected growth rates in either earnings per share, operating cash flows, or dividends.

Guaranteed Income Contract (GIC) - A fixed-income security similar to a certificate of deposit that is sold primarily to large, institutional investors such as pension plan providers.

H

H Model - A model that estimates the price of a share of stock based on an assumption that dividends will gradually fall from a high growth period to a more normal growth period.

Harry Markowitz - A Nobel Prize winning economist who developed the efficient frontier and is credited with being the original developer of an optimal portfolio allocation model.

Hedge Fund - A type of financial institution that raises capital from shareholders and invests in a wide range of traditional and non-traditional securities.

Herd Mentality - An emotional bias in which investors are greatly influenced by the actions and decisions of their peers.

Heuristics - An approach to solving problems that is sufficient to satisfy short-term needs but is not likely to be optimal in the long term. It is a short cut method to solving problems when individuals do not have access to complete information sets or do not have the resources to process the complete information set.

Hindsight Bias - A cognitive error in which investors tend to forget the feelings of regret from poor investment outcomes but clearly remember the feelings of pride from successful outcomes. One consequence is that investors tend to believe that major financial events should have easily been predictable even in the absence of any prior evidence.

Holding Period Return (HPR) - Measures the total return over the entire period of investment. The Holding Period Return (HPR) is the ending value of the investment less the beginning value of the investment, plus or minus any cash flows, divided by the beginning value of the investment.

I

Illusion of Control - A cognitive error in which investors believe they have the ability to significantly influence or even control the outcome of a randomly occurring event.

Immunization - The concept of minimizing the impact of changes in interest rates on the value of investments.

In-the-Money - A call option that is in-the-money refers to a call option contract that has an exercise price that is below the market price for the underlying security. A put option that is in-the-money refers to a put option contract that has an exercise price that is above the market price for the underlying security. Note that this term is not referring to the buyer or seller, but rather the option contract.

Income Stock - An equity security that is expected to pay higher than average dividends.

indenture, which is the legal and binding document specifying the rights accorded to the bondholders and the duties of the issuing company.

Index Options - The underlying security for index options is an index, such as the S&P 500 index. These options allow traders to obtain broad based market exposure with a relatively small investment. Investors also use these options to hedge long or short equity positions or to generate portfolio income. These options are settled in cash. Options are currently offered on the S&P 500, S&P 100, Dow Jones Industrial Average (DJIA), various Russell indexes (such as the Russell 1000 and 2000), as well as other indexes.

Indexing - A passive investment strategy in which a portfolio is formed that mimics the performance of an index. Indexing is typically accomplished using mutual funds or exchange traded funds.

Indifference Curve - A curve connecting a set of portfolios that all give an investor the same level of utility. The investor is therefore indifferent between all portfolios on the curve.Industry Analysis - An analysis of specific industries, in which financial analysts estimate industry growth rates, evaluate the main competition, and form expectations about which industries are expected to outperform.

Industry Analysis - An analysis of specific industries, in which financial analysts estimate industry growth rates, evaluate the main competition, and form expectations about which industries are expected to outperform.

Industry Life Cycle - Industries go through five characteristic stages throughout their lives. The stages differ primarily by the patterns of growth and the measures of profitability that are exhibited.

Inflation - The rate of change in the price level for a specific economy. Inflation is an important component for the return objective for investors, as they require compensation against the risk of a decrease in their purchasing power.

Initial Margin - The amount of money that must be put up by the buyer and seller of a contract to initiate the trade (also known as a performance bond).

Initial Public Offering (IPO) - A private company's first offering of shares for sale to the public.

Interest Rate Risk - A systematic risk factor that describes the variability in asset returns due to changes in interest rates.

Interest Rate Sensitive Stock - An equity security that performs well during specific interest rate environments.

Internal Rate of Return (IRR) - A measure of the potential profitability of an investment in which all distributed cash flows are reinvested. The IRR is the discount rate that sets the net present value of an investment's cash flows to zero.

Intrinsic Value - The intrinsic value of an option is the minimum price that an option will trade. It equals the difference between the market price and the exercise price. The value of the option consists of two parts: the intrinsic value plus the time value of the option. The intrinsic value can never be less than zero. The intrinsic value of a call option equals the stock price minus the strike price, but no less than zero. The intrinsic value of a put option equals the strike price minus the stock price, but no less than zero.

Investment Advisers - Any person or firm that, for compensation, provides advice to others or issues reports or analyses regarding securities.

Investment Advisers Act - Legislation passed in 1940 that regulates investment advisers and requires registration with the SEC for firms or any individual advisers with assets under management exceeding $100 million.

Investment Company - A company that issues and invests in financial securities. It invests the money it receives from investors on a collective basis, and each investor shares in the profits and losses of the company in proportion to their interest in the investment company.

Investment Company Act - Legislation passed in 1940 that formed the backbone of financial regulation and established the foundation for mutual funds and hedge funds.

Investment Grade Bonds - The bond issued when a company has a high probability of making interest and principal payments.

Investment Policy Statement - A clear, specific articulation of realistic and achievable long-term financial goals of the investor, including a description of investment objectives, investment constraints, and strategic asset allocation goals (acceptable asset classes, relative weights, and acceptable ranges).

Investor's Marginal Tax Rate - The tax rate at which the next dollar of income will be taxed if the investment produces income that is taxed at ordinary income rates.

Invoice Price - The price of a bond including any interest that has accrued since issue or the most recent coupon payment. Also known as dirty price or full price.

Irrational Escalation - An emotional bias in which investors increase their commitment to an investment even when there are no rational reasons to do so.

Issuer Risks - Exposures that are unique to each firm or government entity issuing the bonds, such as default risk.

J

Jensen's Alpha - An absolute portfolio performance measure defined as the difference between the portfolio's actual return and its expected return.

K

Kurtosis - A measure of whether the data are heavy-tailed or light-tailed relative to a normal distribution.

L

Large-Cap Stocks - Companies with a market capitalization of at least $10 billion.

Leading PE Ratio - PE ratios based on expected 12 months of earnings. Also referred to as the forward PE ratio.

Legal and Regulatory Constraint - One of the main constraints facing investors when constructing their portfolios. Investors can be constrained through legal or regulatory restrictions that affect the performance of their portfolios.

Lending Portfolios - Portfolios on the capital market line that are weighted between the market portfolio and the risk-free asset.

Lending Securities - Securities in which an investor of bonds lends funds to the issuer in exchange for a promise to a stream of periodic interest payments and a repayment of the loaned principal at the maturity of the bond.

Leptokurtic - A distribution that is more peaked (more kurtosis) than a normal distribution.

Letter of Intent (LOI) - Outlines the terms of the investor's commitment and serves as an "agreement to agree" between two parties / if an investor commits to invest $1 million within a year, a fund may waive the sales charge. Usually, these commitments are in the form of a letter of intent and often extend for 13 months.

Leverage - The use of borrowing to magnify returns.

Limit Order - Acts as a ceiling for purchases and as a floor for sales, and the order will be held until filled or canceled.

Limited Partner - The institutions and individuals that provide the private equity manager with capital to invest in businesses.

Liquidity - The ability to sell an investment quickly at a competitive price without any price concessions.

Liquidity Constraint - One of the main constrains facing investors when constructing their portfolios. Investors can be constrained by one-time lump sum cash outflows expected to occur in the near future. These cash outflows reduce the investor's asset base.

Long Position - The purchase of a stock in hopes that it will appreciate over time.

Loss Aversion - The sense that investors are more averse to the pain of a loss than to the joy of a gain, which leads to biased financial decisions.

M

Macroeconomic Analysis - An analysis of an entire economy and its important components, such as inflation, interest rates, employment rates, expected changes in gross domestic product, and other macro variables. The analysis is performed during the planning stage of the portfolio management process to evaluate how macro variables will affect the performance of each asset class.

Maintenance Margin - The equity percentage that must be maintained in a margin account. It is typically 35 percent, which means that the equity in the account must equal or exceed 35 percent.

Management Fee - A fee charged by the investment adviser for the management of the fund assets.

Manager Tenure - The time period over which a manager (or team) has been directing the investment choices for a mutual fund.

Margin Accounts - Allow the investor to borrow funds from the broker to purchase additional securities without adding cash to the account.

Margin Call - A margin call requires a futures trader to increase the equity in their trading account due to the recognition of losses. This requirement generally occurs as part of the mark-to-market practice and helps to ensure that traders can meet their financial obligations for the contracts they have bought or sold.

Margin Requirements - Amount that both buyers and sellers must deposit with a broker when buying or selling futures contracts.

Marginal Income Tax Rate - Represents the percent of income earned that would be paid as income tax, whether at the federal or state level.

Market Anomalies - Situations in which predictable stock price reactions occur that are inconsistent with the efficient markets theory.

Market Capitalization - The outstanding shares for a company times the current share price.

Market Conversion Premium - Equals the difference between the market conversion price and the current market price.

Market Conversion Price - Represents the cost of each share of stock obtained through the conversion.

Market Discount Bonds - Bonds that were initially issued at redemption value but have declined in value due to changes in market conditions.

Market Orders – An order to buy or sell a security at the best current market price. Filled by the broker at the next available price in the market.

Market Premium Bonds - Bonds trading at a premium or at a price in excess of par value. If interest rates decline over time, and an investor purchases a bond that was issued when interest rates were higher, he or she will likely pay a premium for that bond to compensate the seller for the higher-than-market coupon payments the seller of the bond was receiving.

Market Risk - A systematic risk factor that describes the variability in asset returns to changes in market conditions.

Market Timing - An attempt to anticipate the movement of equities and earn returns in excess of the market through the use of technical analysis.

Marketability - The investor's ability to easily find a market to sell their investment.

Mark-to-Market - A practice that all futures contracts follow on a daily basis designed to allocate gains and losses occurring during the day to the accounts of buyers and sellers of futures contracts and to ensure that all traders can meet their financial obligations for the contracts they have bought or sold.

Maturity - The period of time through which the issuer has control over the bond proceeds and the period of time it must continue to pay coupon payments.

Mean-Variance Optimization (MVO) - An asset allocation technique in which securities in a portfolio are arranged according to their ability to contribute to the dual competing goals of maximizing expected return (mean) while minimizing risk (variance); the resulting portfolios are referred to as efficient portfolios.

Mean-Variance Optimization Model - Used to identify efficient portfolios, which have the highest level of return (based on combinations of asset classes and different weightings of asset classes) for a specified level of risk.

Mega Caps - Companies that have a market capitalization in excess of $200 billion.

Mental Accounting - A cognitive error in which investors tend to file their money into separate accounts, each used for a unique purpose instead of gathering all accounts into one diversified portfolio.

Micro-Cap Stocks - Stocks with a market capitalization of less than $300 million.

Mid-Cap Stocks - Companies with market capitalizations in excess of $2 billion, but less than $10 billion.

Minimum Initial Investment - Mutual funds often have a minimum amount that must be invested to set up an account. Some minimums are extremely high, while most are under $5,000, and some have minimums of zero.

Modern Portfolio Theory - A fundamental hypothesis in which security returns are functions of the level of relevant risk taken, in which investors form well-diversified and efficient portfolios, and in which investors maximize their expected utilities.

Monetary Policy - Represents the intended influence on the money supply and interest rates by the central bank of a country.

Money Market - Consists of debt securities that have the following characteristics: short-term maturity, low credit risk, and high liquidity.

Money Market Deposit Accounts (MMDAs) - Permit investors to earn interest on funds that are not currently deployed in other investment opportunities and are typically issued by banks or mutual fund companies.

Money Market Mutual Funds - Provide investors an easy and effective method of investing in money market instruments and provide a reasonable alternative to the returns that can be earned on bank certificates of deposit and bank savings accounts.

Moneyness - A concept that is used to describe the relationship between the strike price of an option and the current trading price for the underlying security. The three terms that are part of moneyness are in-the-money, at-the-money, and out-of-the-money.

Mortgage-Backed Security - A fixed-income security that acts like a bond but is supported by the underlying mortgage pool.

Municipal Bonds - Debt instruments issued by municipalities (states, counties, parishes, cities, towns) as general obligation bonds or revenue bonds.

Myopic Loss Aversion - A coupling of an investor's aversion to losses with frequent decisions regarding their investments, leading to short-term inefficiencies in portfolio management.

N

Naked Option - A trading position in which the seller of an option contract does not own any, or enough, of the underlying security to act as protection against adverse price movements.

Net Asset Value (NAV) - Price at which funds are sold. NAV is found by subtracting total liabilities from total assets of the fund and dividing the difference by the number of outstanding shares.

Net Investment Income - Investment income less certain expenses properly allocable to the income.

Net Investment Income Tax (NIIT) - A 3.8% rate applying to certain net investment income above a threshold amount.

Net Present Value (NPV) - TA measure of the potential profitability of an investment and is calculated by taking the difference between the initial cost of the investment and the present value of the expected future cash flows of the investment.

Net Selectivity - A product of the Fama Decomposition in which the ability of a manager to select mis-priced securities is identified.

No-Load Funds - Mutual funds that do not have sales charges. Generally used by investment professionals who charge asset-based fees or some other form of compensation other than commissions.

Non-Investment Grade Bonds - When a company issuing a bond has a high risk of default.

Normal Portfolio - A portfolio that has similar securities, similar risk characteristics, and similar return expectations as an invested portfolio. It is used as a comparison performance metric. Also called benchmark portfolio.

Notional Value - The value of a futures contract, also called the contract value, is determined by multiplying the size of the contract by the current price.

O

Odd Lott - A trade for fewer than 100 shares (a round lot).

Offsetting Order - An offsetting order is an order that closes an existing order. An offsetting order is the opposite of the initial order. Therefore, an offsetting order for a writer of an option is to buy an option contract. The offsetting order needs to consist of an option contract that is similar to the original contract.

Open Market Operations - The process by which the Federal Reserve will buy or sell U.S. Treasury securities such as T-bills, notes, and bonds.

Open-End Investment Company (Mutual Funds) - Investment companies that are not limited in the number of shares that can be sold. All shares are sold by the mutual fund family and redeemed by the mutual fund family.

Opening Orders - Used when a trader wants to purchase (long) or sell (short) either a call option or a put option.

Optimism Bias - An emotional bias in which investors believe they will be exposed to less risk when compared to others or experience greater gains.

Option - A financial contract in which one party purchases the right but not the obligation to trade an underlying security at a fixed price at some time in the future.

Option Premium - The cost of the option. The premium is the amount of money that must be paid by the buyer to the seller of the option contract for the right to buy or sell the underlying security. The premium consists of the intrinsic value plus the time value of the option.

Option Series - A group of options with the same strike price and expiration date for the same underlying security.

Options Contracts - An agreement that gives the buyer the right to buy (call option) or sell (put option) the underlying security (e.g., Apple Stock) for a specified price within a specified period of time.

Ordinary Income - Income produced from labor as distinguished from portfolio income and passive income.

Ordinary Income Tax Rates - Currently range from 10 percent to 37 percent. Ordinary income tax rates are the highest income tax rates that apply to individuals.

Original Issue Discount (OID) - If a long-term bond is issued at a price lower than its par (or redemption) value, the difference between the par value and the issue price.

Out-of-the-Money - A call option contract that has an exercise price that is above the market price for the underlying security. A put option that is out-of-the-money has an exercise price that is below the market price for the underlying security. Note that this term is not referring to the buyer or seller, but rather the option contract.

Outperformance - When portfolio managers generate returns that exceed the relevant benchmark portfolio.

Overconfidence - An emotional bias in which investors expect to outperform others because of their superior ability to predict future outcomes, and this overconfidence tends to increase with the amount of information processed by the investor.

P

Participating - The preferred shareholders share in the profits of the corporation.

Passive Mutual Funds - Funds that are generally thought of as index funds, which attempt to match the performance of an index, such as the S&P 500.

Passive Income - Income a taxpayer receives from either a business activity in which he or she does not materially participate, or from rental real estate activities.

Passive Manager - Likely to choose securities that closely match the selected benchmark for the asset class.

Payoff - The positive difference between the strike price and the underlying security price upon exercise of the option.

Payout Ratio - Equals a company's dividend payments divided by its earnings and provides information about the long-term sustainability of a company's dividend payments and policy.

PEG Ratio - Equals a company's PE ratio divided by the growth rate of its expected earnings.

Pension Fund - An institutional investor that provides income during retirement for its beneficiaries. The pension fund manager invests contributions from the employer and the employees according to the terms and characteristics of the pension plan so that enough capital is available to pay the benefits promised to employees during retirement.

Perfect Hedge - Occurs when all of the risk of buying or selling a commodity is fully offset by a futures contract.

Physical Certificate - Represents ownership of equity shares.

Piercing the Corporate Veil - Occurs in the context of a lawsuit in which the corporation does not act as a separate entity and acts more as an extension of the individual shareholders. When this happens, liability extends to the individual shareholders.

Planning Stage - The first stage of the portfolio management process in which financial advisers and clients meet to identify long-term risk and return objectives. This stage includes constructing and managing the constraints faced by the investor, setting strategic goals, and forming expectations from capital markets.

Platykurtic - A distribution that is less peaked (less kurtosis) than a normal distribution.

Policy Effect - A component of fixed-income attribution analysis that measures the return impact of the difference between the duration of the index and the duration of the invested portfolio.

Policy Statement - The contract between financial advisers and their clients that outlines investor goals, strategic plans, and the methods that advisers will pursue to achieve each objective. The policy statement serves as the point of reference for every decision made by advisers, which means that it should be thorough, complete, and easy to understand.

Porter's Five Forces Model - A strategic planning model designed to analyze how strong a company is in terms of competitive threats. It includes rivalry among present competitors, threat of new entrants, threat of substitute products, bargaining power of buyers, and bargaining power of suppliers.

Portfolio Analysis - The process of constructing optimal portfolios for investors. This includes the optimal asset allocation decision in which risk is minimized for the investor's level of required return.

Portfolio Income - Most income from investments. The most common types of portfolio income are interest, dividends, and capital gains. Some types of portfolio income are taxed at ordinary rates, while other types of portfolio income receive more favorable tax treatment.

Portfolio Insurance - The strategy of buying a put option on an index (such as the S&P 500) to provide downside protection for a long portfolio.

Portfolio Risk (Total Risk) - The combination of systematic and unsystematic risk, which can be reduced through diversification.

Portfolio Turnover - Typically defined as the ratio of the lesser of purchases or sales to average daily assets.

Preemptive Right – The right of shareholders to maintain their ownership percentage upon new stock offerings

Preferred Stock - Has characteristics of both fixed-income investments and of equity securities. Shareholders of preferred stock generally receive preferential dividends each year equal to a stated percentage of the par value of the stock if the corporation declares them.

Premium - When a bond sells for a price in excess of par value, which occurs when the coupon rate is greater than the yield to maturity on the bond.

Prepayment Risk - A special form of interest rate risk, and has to be considered by investors before purchasing a mortgage-backed security. It is the risk that homeowners will pay off their loans before the scheduled loan maturity date.

Present Value Model - A model that computes intrinsic value of a company as the present value of the expected cash from received from owning the security issued by the company.

Price Limit - Limits in daily price fluctuation imposed by some futures markets to help manage volatile price fluctuations.

Price-to-Book Ratio - A relative valuation tool defined as the ratio of stock price to the firm's equity book value per share.

Price-to-Cash Flow Ratio - A relative valuation tool defined as the ratio of stock price to the firm's cash flow per share.Price to Earnings Ratio - A relative measure of valuation that is defined as the stock price per share divided by the earnings per share.

Price-to-Earnings Ratio - A relative valuation tool defined as the ratio of stock price to the firm's earnings per share.

Price-to-Sales Ratio - A relative valuation tool defined as the ratio of stock price to the firm's total revenue per share.

Price Earnings to Growth Ratio (PEG) - A relative measure of valuation that is defined as the PE ratio divided by the growth rate.

Primary Market - The market for newly created financial securities.

Principal Risk - The risk of losing the initial investment, which is much greater in alternative investments than in traditional investments.

Private Activity (purpose) Municipal Bonds - Bonds issued by a state or local government to finance projects that have some component of private or business use.

Private Equity - The general partner who raises capital by selling partnership units to institutions and individuals, and who makes investments in privately-held businesses.

Private Placement - A securities offering exempt from registration with the Securities Exchange Commission (SEC).

Profit (or loss) - An investor's total gain or loss on their option position including the payoff and premium paid or received.

Prospect Theory - An investment choice theory in which individuals prefer certainty over risk, they make decisions to avoid losses, they evaluate outcomes based on relative performance, and they discount low probability events.

Prospectus - A document used to disclose information about a mutual fund to investors. The SEC requires mutual funds to include important information in the prospectus, including the fund's investment objectives or goals, its strategies for reaching those goals, the principal risks of investing in the fund, the fund's fees and expenses, and its past performance.

Proxy Voting - Involves sending a written authorization to an agent to cast the vote for the shareholder.

Public Purpose Municipal Bonds - Used to finance classic government projects, such as the construction of schools, police stations, fire stations, roads and bridges.

Purchasing Power Risk - The risk that inflation will erode the purchasing power of investor's assets. Because it is a systematic risk, purchasing power risk cannot be eliminated through diversification.

Put-Call Parity Model - Used to price a put option based on the price of a call option.

Put Options - Give the holder (buyer) the right (but not the obligation) to sell the underlying security for a specified price within a specified period of time.

Puttable Bond - A bond that contains a put option that allows the owner of the bond to sell the bond back to the issuer at a predetermined price prior to the stated maturity of the bond.

Q

Qualified Dividends - Dividends issued by most U.S. domestic publicly-traded and closely-held corporations, as well as the dividends of certain foreign corporations issued on shares of publicly-traded stock listed on an established U.S. exchange meet the definition of qualified dividends.

R

Rate Anticipation Effect - A component of fixed-income attribution analysis in which the portfolio manager is evaluated based on the ability to anticipate interest rate movements by changing the duration of the portfolio.

Ratings Agency - An independent financial organization that evaluates and publishes the level of credit risk for specific bond issues.

Real Rate of Return - Also called the inflation-adjusted return. Adjusts the nominal return to account for the loss of purchasing power due to inflation.

Realized Taxable Return - The return from the investment without considering income tax.

Recession - A significant decline in economic activity spread across the economy, lasting more than a few months, normally visible in real GDP, real income, employment, industrial production, and wholesale-retail sales. A recession begins just after the economy reaches a peak of activity and ends as the economy reaches its trough.

Regression Analysis - A statistical method for estimating the relationship among variables.

Regret Aversion - An emotional bias in which investors anticipate the feeling of regret and attempt to avoid this feeling when making financial decisions.

Regulated Investment Company (RIC) - An election by closed-end mutual funds to be taxed the same as open-end mutual funds regarding the taxation of gains and investment income.

Reinvestment Rate Risk - The risk that the investor is unable to reinvest cash flows at the required rate.

Relative Valuation Model - A valuation method that compares a firm's value to its industry competitors to make a determination on relative value. PE ratio is the primary relative valuation model.

Relative Value Analysis - A performance tool in which a security is compared to a peer group using multiples.

Representativeness - A cognitive error in which investors tend to believe that short-term performance represents the true long-term performance of a financial security, which means they tend to overweight recent news about a security while they discount historical information.

Repurchase Agreement - A contract between two parties in which one party agrees to sell a security to another party with an agreement to repurchase the same security after a short time, usually one day.

Reserve Requirement - The percent of deposits a bank must maintain on hand and not lend.

Retention Ratio - The percent of income retained by a company.

Return Objective - The compensation required by investors and defined in the policy statement. Mathematically, the return objective is the ratio of the investor's portfolio income needs over the total investable asset base, plus inflation.

Revenue Bond - A municipal bond that is issued to finance specific projects that will generate its own revenue stream, such as a toll road.

Reverse Stock Split - Occurs when a company wants to reduce the number of outstanding shares of corporate stock. A reverse stock split reduces the number of shares and increases the share price proportionately.

Richard Thaler - A founding father of behavioral finance who was a primary stock market anomaly researcher.

Risk - The uncertainty of future outcomes or the possibility of an adverse result.

Risk Indifference Curve - Indicates those portfolios an investor would be indifferent to holding.

Risk Objective - The level of risk that can be tolerated by investors and is defined in the policy statement. The objective has two components: the ability to take risk, which depends on wealth, age, and income and the willingness to take risk, which depends on the personality traits of the investor.

Risk Premium - The incremental return provided by a market portfolio over the risk-free rate of return.

Risk Tolerance - A measure of an investor's ability and willingness to expose themselves to risk (price fluctuation in investments) in order to seek higher investment returns.

Roaring 20s - The time period after WWI in which there was tremendous economic growth resulting in higher income levels for the middle class. The expansion was characterized by frequent borrowing for household items, automobiles, and eventually shares of stock.

Round Lot - 100 shares of a security.

S

Sarbanes Oxley Act - Legislation passed in 2002 that established expanded financial regulations in response to the major accounting scandals of late 1990s.

Secondary Market - The market for securities that have already passed through the primary market. The NYSE is the most famous example of a secondary market.

Sector Rotation - Another active management strategy in which economic data is analyzed in an attempt to predict where the economic cycle is headed in the future and, based on that information, position the portfolio in the most opportune industry sectors in an attempt to outperform the market.

Secured Bonds - Backed by some form of collateral, which gives the investor the ability to recover some or all of the invested capital in the event the bond issuer defaults.

Securities Act - Legislation passed in 1933 that regulates the offering and sale of securities to ensure more transparency in financial statements.

Securities Exchange Act - Legislation passed in 1934 that governs secondary market trading and established the Securities and Exchange Commission.

Securities Market Line (SML) - The security market line shows the expected return for an asset in equilibrium given its level of systematic risk as measured by its beta.

Securitization - The process of transforming mortgages into securities that can be sold to the public.

Security Analysis - The process of identifying which securities are appropriate for each investor.

Self-Control Bias - An emotional bias in which investors value short-term satisfaction at the expense of their long-term rational goals.

Self-Regulatory Organizations - Private non-governmental organizations that have limited authority to enforce ethical and fair standards among businesses operating in the financial services industry to protect investors, to promote trust among all market participants, and to improve the efficiency in the flow of capital and information.

Sell to Close - A type of order used when a trader wants to close a previously opened long position. The trader is effectively selling an option that was previously bought.

Sell to Open - A type of order used when a trader wants to sell (write) either a call option or a put option.

Semi-Strong Form Efficiency - A degree of market efficiency in which security prices reflect all relevant publicly available information.

Semivariance - Only takes into consideration volatility below the mean return.

Serial Bond - Has multiple maturity dates, and permits the issuer to partially retire the bond issue at dates specified in the bond.

Settlement Price - The settlement price is the average of the prices for which a futures contract trades immediately before the close of trading for a specific day. It is the price that is used to calculate gains and losses for the mark-to-market practice.

Sharpe Ratio - A relative measure of portfolio performance in which total risk as measured by standard deviation is used to estimate risk-adjusted performance.

Short Sale - When an investor expects the price of a stock to decline, they may wish to sell shares in the stock now, even if the stock is not included in the investor's portfolio.

Short-Term Debt Instruments - Issued in the public markets by corporations and referred to as commercial paper.

Simple Capital Structure - Companies that do not include any dilutive securities, which are securities that could convert into common shares and dilute the ownership of current common shareholders.

Skewness - A measure of the lack of symmetry for a data set.

Small-Cap Stocks - Companies with market capitalizations less than $2 billion.

Soft Commodity - Commodities that are grown and include coffee, cocoa, sugar, and wheat.

Soft Dollars - The payments for brokerage services in the form of commissions, instead of direct payments.

Special Purpose Acquisition Companies (SPACs) - A legal entity that is formed by one company to raise capital for the purpose of acquiring another company. The SPAC has no operations and uses an initial public offering for the exact purpose of taking over the assets or equity of a target firm.

Spending Rule - The percentage of the investable asset base that an endowment spends during a period.

Spin-Off - Occurs when a company decides, as part of a corporate reorganization, to split a portion of their business away from the parent company into a new company.

Split - Occurs when a corporation distributes shares of its own stock to its shareholders.

Split Rating - A difference of opinion between two of the independent ratings agencies.

Spot Price - The price of a commodity or asset to be delivered today (also called the cash price of the current price).

Spread - The relationship between two futures prices and the difference between the two futures prices.

Stages of Venture Capital - Seed, startup, emerging, expansion, and bridge stages that have specific capital requirement needs and business strategies in order to be successful.

Standard Deviation - A statistical measure of the variation of numbers or data around the mean of those numbers or data.

Statement of Additional Information (SAI) - Provides more detailed disclosures and generally includes information about: (1) the history and description of the fund; (2) fund officers and directors; and (3) other topics.

Stephen Ross - A founding father of finance who developed the arbitrage pricing model.

Stock Dividends - Shares or partial shares granted to shareholders based on ownership.

Stock Market Crash of 1929 - A series of consecutive daily stock market crashes that occurred at the end of October in 1929.

Stock Options - The underlying security for stock options is shares in a publicly traded company.

Stock Split - A stock split increases the number of issued and outstanding shares of stock and also decreases the par value of the stock, whereas stock dividends do not impact par value per share. A 2-for-1 stock split doubles the number of shares and reduces the par value per share in half.

Stop-Limit Order - An order to buy or sell a stock that combines the features of a stop order and a limit order.

Stop-Loss Orders - Used to protect investors from large losses.

Stop Yield - The highest yield accepted on a U.S. Treasury auction. It is the last bid accepted in a competitive auction process is and this is the yield that all purchasers of auctioned T-bills (through both the competitive and non-competitive bid process) will receive.

Straight Value - The value of the bond without the conversion feature and equals the discounted value of the bond's cash flows.

Straight Voting - Authorizes one vote per share of common stock and is the most common form of voting.

Strategic Asset Allocation - Diversification strategy across a broad set of asset classes in an effort to minimize the probability of substantial losses in one investment category significantly impacting the performance of the portfolio as a whole.

Street Name - When the security is registered in the name of the investor's brokerage firm on the issuer's books, and the brokerage firm holds the security for the investor in "book-entry" form.

Strike Price - Also known as the exercise price. The strike price is the price at which the option holder (buyer) can exercise the option. For a call option, the strike price represents the price at which the buyer can purchase the underlying security. For a put option, it represents the price at which the buyer can sell the underlying security.

STRIPS - Acronym for Separate Trading of Registered Interest and Principal of Securities. It is a program that permits investors to hold and trade the individual interest and principal components of eligible Treasury notes and bonds as separate securities.

Strong Form Efficiency - A degree of market efficiency in which security prices reflect all relevant information, including information that is publicly available and information that is considered to be private.

Style Drift - Refers to a change in investment style over time. Style shift might include changing from value to growth or changing from small-cap to mid-cap. These changes may be positive, but might also impact the overall asset allocation for an investor.

Superannuation - The risk of outliving one's assets

Sustainable Growth Rate - The maximum growth rate for a company, while maintaining its capital structure.

Swap - An over-the-counter agreement between two or more parties to exchange future sets of cash flows. Swaps include interest rate swaps and currency swaps.

Swap Contract - A financial agreement in which two parties agree to swap current positions.

SWOT Analysis - A strategic planning analysis of a firm's strengths, weaknesses, opportunities, and threats.

Systematic Risks - The variability of returns of an investment due to changes in macroeconomic factors, such as inflation, unemployment, and housing starts and commonly referred to as undiversifiable risks.

T

Tactical Asset Allocation - Attempts to outperform the market over shorter periods of time by placing investment dollars in those asset classes that the investor expects will outperform market returns over the period.

Tax Basis - Equal to the cost of acquiring the investment, which is the sum of the actual cost plus any transaction fees necessary to purchase the asset. Basis is subtracted from the proceeds of a sale to determine the taxable gain or loss.

Tax Constraint - One of the main constraints facing investors when constructing their portfolios. Investor wealth is reduced by tax liabilities at both the federal, state, and local levels, which makes it imperative for financial advisers to pursue strategies that minimize the tax liability.

Taxable Bond Market - One of two markets that make up the United States bond market, and that consists of U.S. Treasury bonds, U.S. government agency bonds, and corporate bonds.

Tax-Exempt Bond Market - One of the two markets that make up the United States bond market, and that consists of municipal bonds.

Technical Analysis - An asset selection tool that uses historical asset prices and volume to make portfolio selection decisions.

Terminal Value - The present value of all future cash flows discounted at a stable growth rate. It is used to account for cash flows occurring beyond the time period that can be realistically forecasted.

Tick Size - The smallest price change increment for a futures contract that is different for each type of futures contract.

Time Constraint - One of the main constraints facing investors when constructing their portfolios. Investor time periods are divided into life stages with each stage potentially having its own risk and return objectives.

Time Value - The time value equals the difference between the market value of the option contract and its intrinsic value.

Time-Weighted Return - Measures the effect of any cash flows associated with the investment security (such as a mutual fund or stock), but ignores the dollar volume and timing of investor-driven transactions during the period. This method is more appropriate for assessing the performance of a fund manager or a security because it includes the capital appreciation and dividends earned, but it is not affected by an investor's timing decisions.

Top-Down Analysis - A form of economic analysis in which the entire global economy is first evaluated, followed by an analysis of each industry, and then finally an evaluation of individual companies.

Total Risk (Portfolio Risk) - The total variability of returns of an investment that consists of both firm specific and economic factors.

Trading Effect - A component of fixed-income attribution analysis in which the efficiency of the portfolio manager in executing trades is evaluated.

Traditional Exchange Traded (or listed) Options - Capital assets in the hands of the buyer.

Trailing PE Ratio - PE ratios based on trailing 12 months of earnings or the most recent four quarters of earnings.

Trailing-Stop Orders - Allow an investor to place a stop order that trails the current stock price a specific dollar amount or a specific percentage of the market price.

Tranches - A portion or part of a debt obligation. Early tranches receive principal payments first, while later tranches receive principal in the future. As a result, later tranches will require higher rates of return.

Transfer Agents - Financial institutions that keep track of the ownership of the securities the investing public trades.

Treasury bills (T-bills) - Short-term securities issued by the U.S. Treasury Department to help finance the national budget deficit.

Treasury Direct - A web-based trading system for the purchase and sale of U.S. Treasury securities.

Treasury Inflation-Protected Securities (TIPS)- Pay interest at a fixed rate.

Treasury Security - A security issued by the United States Treasury Department for the purpose of financing the federal budget deficit.

Treasury Stock - Stock repurchased by a corporation from its shareholders and held in its treasury.

Treynor Ratio - A relative measure of portfolio performance in which systematic risk as measured by beta is used to estimate risk-adjusted performance.

Trust Indenture Act - Legislation passed in 1939 that requires the appointment of suitable trustee for security issues.

Turnover - The ratio of the lesser of purchases or sales to average daily assets.

Two-Stage Dividend Growth Model - A dividend discount t model in which a period of high dividend growth is followed by an infinite period of normal growth. This model is used to estimate the stock price.

U

Underperformance - When portfolio managers generate returns that are less than the relevant benchmark portfolio.

Unemployment Rate - Refers to the percentage of individuals 16 years of age and older who are not working and are making an effort to seek employment.

Uniform Prudent Management of Institutional Funds Act - A 2006 Act that established investment guidelines for institutional investors, particularly for charitable organizations. UPMIFA has been adopted by most states and offers standards for investment strategies and spending for these organizations.

Unique Constraint - One of the main constraints facing investors when constructing their portfolios.The unique constraint contains client investment restrictions that do not appear in any of the other four constraints. Example of unique constraints include medical conditions, insurance issues, and social investing preferences.

Unit Investment Trust (UIT) - A registered investment company that is passively managed and may invest in stocks, bonds, or other securities.

Unsecured Bonds - Sometimes referred to as debenture bonds, these bonds do not have any collateral backing up the issuer's promise to make interest and principal payments.

Unsystematic Risks - The variability of returns of an investment due to factors that are unique or specific to each security, such as dividend payments, mergers, board of director composition, and operating cash flows. It is commonly referred to as diversifiable risk.

Uptick Rule - Required that a short sale must occur on an uptick or zero plus tick. An uptick occurs when the price of a security. The uptick rule was repealed in 2007.

V

Value Stock - An equity security with relative valuation characteristics that suggest it is less expensive than other stocks.

Variance - Calculated by squaring the standard deviation. Investments with high variances tend to be riskier than those with low variances.

Venture Capital - Financing that investors provide to businesses for startup through expansion.

Virtual Currencies - Unlike other currencies, such as U.S. dollars or euros, virtual currencies exist only in electronic form and are not associated with any particular country or central bank.

W

Warrants - Allow the shareholder to purchase new shares of stock in the company, usually at a discounted price.

Wash Sale - A technique that was used by investors to generate losses for income tax purposes without substantially changing the securities positions in their portfolios.

Weak Form Efficiency - A degree of market efficiency in which security prices reflect historical price and volume information only.

William Sharpe - A founding father of finance who developed the capital asset pricing model and identified the importance of beta as a measure of the systematic risk of diversified portfolios.

Writer - The writer of an option contract is obligated to either sell (call option) the underlying security at the specified price in the contract or buy (put option) the underlying security at the specified price in the contract. The writer receives the premium for this obligation and has a short position in the contract.

Y

Yield - The amount of cash the investment generates and the amount the investor receives or reinvests in a year.

Yield Curves - Graphical representations that reflect current market interest rates for various bond maturities.

Yield to Call (YTC) - The expected return on a bond from the purchase date to the date that the bond may be called.

Yield to Maturity (YTM) - The compounded rate of return on a bond purchased at the current market price and held to maturity.

Z

Zero-Coupon Bond - A bond that does not pay periodic coupon or interest payments.

Zero-Sum Game - An economic situation in which the sum of the gains and losses from all contracts will total to zero.

Z-Scores - A measure of the distance of a data point from its data set's mean in terms of standard deviations.

APPENDIX

B

INDEX

C

D

E

F

G

H

I

Q

R

U

V

W

Y

Z